MARKETING IN CREATIVE INDUSTRIES

MARKETING IN CREATIVE INDUSTRIES

Value, Experience and Creativity

GABRIELE TROILO

First published 2015 by
PALGRAVE

Palgrave in the UK is an imprint of Macmillan Publishers Limited, registered in England, company number 785998, of 4 Crinan Street, London, N1 9XW.

Palgrave Macmillan in the US is a division of St Martin's Press LLC, 175 Fifth Avenue, New York, NY 10010.

Palgrave is a global imprint of the above companies and is represented throughout the world.

Palgrave® and Macmillan® are registered trademarks in the United States, the United Kingdom, Europe and other countries.

ISBN   978–0–230–38024–0

This book is printed on paper suitable for recycling and made from fully managed and sustained forest sources. Logging, pulping and manufacturing processes are expected to conform to the environmental regulations of the country of origin.

A catalogue record for this book is available from the British Library.

A catalog record for this book is available from the Library of Congress.

Typeset by MPS Limited, Chennai, India.

Printed in China

To my mother and my father,
the origins of my curiosity about the world,
and my inextinguishable desire to explore it.

The royalties of the book will be donated to La Gotita Onlus (www.lagotitaonlus.org),
a non-profit organization that supports projects for disadvantaged children in Bolivia.

CONTENTS

LIST OF FIGURES

LIST OF TABLES

PREFACE

Many scholars around the globe have been researching marketing in creative industries for years. Despite this, compared to research in other fields of the business world, these efforts are relatively limited. In particular, most are devoted to specific sectors within the broader set of creative industries (movies, music, performing arts, tourism, heritage, and the like), giving emphasis to the specificity of each one. However, far fewer studies consider the similarities across those industries and leverage these to identify and recommend appropriate managerial models. This is the main impulse that drove me to write this book.

I've been researching, teaching, and consulting in the field of marketing in creative industries for many years now. My aim here is to provide a marketing model that is effective given the specificities of the organizations that I've known throughout the years, operating in industries that can be defined as creative, whichever they may be.

The three key words of this model are: value, experience, and creativity. In fact, my point is that marketing in creative industries deals with creating customer value through the experience of creativity. In other words, the main objective of marketing in these industries is to transform the creativity of creative producers into an experience for customers, so that this experience is of some value for them. The link between creativity, customer experience, and customer value is what informs and distinguishes a marketing model that is effective for those industries from others for other industries.

Specifically, this book is divided into five parts. The first is devoted to delineating the borders of those industries that I consider creative and providing an overview of the marketing model detailed in the rest of the book. In drawing these borders my ambition is not to play an in-out game. On the contrary, what I wish to do is to provide a map of industry characteristics that are so peculiar as to require a specific marketing model, and then apply that map to suggest which industries share those characteristics: the final list is what I consider creative industries.

Then, I will describe what to me is a customer-centric model of marketing, that is to say, a managerial model that places at its center the customer and his or her satisfaction as the beacon for all organizational decisions. I will rely on a contemporary view of marketing that considers customer value management as the specific job of marketing people within an organization, and detail the four major processes that are their responsibility: customer value analysis, customer value creation, customer value delivery, and customer relationship management.

Customer value analysis will be the theme explored in the second part. In particular, I will separate the consumer side of the market of organizations operating in creative industries (the C-side) from the part made up of business customers (the B-side). In fact, producers create value propositions that are of value for both end consumers and corporate customers. The former get value from the consumption of these value propositions, the latter from their inclusion in productive and communicative processes. For this reason, I decided to distinguish the different stages of the consumer experience – through which end consumers extract value from creative value propositions – from the productive and communicative processes that are specific to how business customers use creative products.

The second part concludes with a description of the most typical marketing research methods and tools that creative organizations can use for their customer value analysis processes.

The third part is devoted to the customer value creation process. Basically, producers create value for their customers (end consumers or businesses) by realizing a value proposition that is aligned with the expectations of the segments of the market they decide to serve. In other words, an organization must first identify and select the portions of the market it wants to serve, then design a value proposition that is adequate to satisfy their needs and desires, and finally realize those propositions in such a way that customers will prefer them over alternative ones.

These processes are the realm of strategic marketing, which consists of market segmentation, targeting, designing propositions, and positioning them into the market. I will then focus on the three main determinants of customer value: the product, the brand, and the price, seeing that value also has a negative component and the price constitutes the most evident part of it.

Part four is about value delivery. Once the organization has created value propositions it has to make them available – in terms of knowledge and physical access – to target customers. For creative organizations today this means leveraging a multi-media and multi-channel environment, which requires new mindsets and new competences, in particular the capacity to share some control over owned processes and activities with other parties.

The digital world offers organizations many more opportunities than in the past. However, since that world is characterized by features that radically change the way people and organizations share information, communicate and socialize, a multi-media and multi-channel environment may also be rife with threats for organizations that try to operate using old paradigms. In this part I will give emphasis to both opportunities and threats.

Creating value propositions for different customer segments and making them available is not independent from the status of the relationship that the organization has with different customers. In every moment of its life, the organization will serve some customers for the first time, together with others who are frequent or loyal customers. This is what customer relationship management is all about: managing relations with customers while taking into account the different stages of these relations, which calls for different decisions. I will conclude part four of the book by highlighting the most important ones.

The final part is a chapter devoted to the relationship between Marketing and Creativity, terms that I use to name the unit/s responsible for marketing decisions and activities and unit/s responsible for creative – and often productive – ones. I think this topic is one of the most fascinating in the context of marketing in creative industries. In fact, in these industries creativity is the economic engine, and it lies in the domain of talented people who are very sensitive to their creativity, and the judgment and approval of people like them, sometimes more than that of customers.

For this reason the role of marketeers is a very difficult and peculiar one: always keeping the creative talent of those people aligned with the desires and wishes of customers. This requires not only a healthy dose of personal skills and capabilities, but also organizational structures and systems that make this task more efficient and effective.

To conclude, a couple of editorial choices. I strongly believe that research is only useful when combined with practice and vice versa (or, if you wish, it's not useful when one of the two is missing). For this reason, in writing the book I took both perspectives under proper consideration. The readers I had in mind were scholars, students, and managers: people who research, work in, or are interested in marketing in creative industries.

My main message to them is that managerial practice will be strengthened if it is anchored to solid theoretical learning. For this reason the book is crowded with mentions of solid research work (which also make a rich bibliography at the end) and interesting case histories. The former are dispersed throughout the chapters with systematic references, and snapshots of specific topics identified by what I called Research Focus (research boxes). The same is true for the second, with examples and real-life profiles that I called Case History (case boxes). Furthermore, all chapters (with the exception of the last one) conclude with a major case study, which represents an example of effective management of one of the topics covered in that chapter. I have included cases from different industries and different countries to illustrate the richness of best practices that can be found in those industries.

Finally, since creative industries host various kind of actors (be they for-profit or non-profit, individual or organizational, local and global, or other) I have decided to use the term 'organization' throughout the book to mean a generic actor operating in those industries. In fact, as I will point out very early in the book, in most cases I will take the perspective of an organizational actor (and its managers) rather than an individual one, although I will frequently mention the case of individual creative actors and their activities in the various chapters.

ACKNOWLEDGEMENTS

This book is a typical example of a creative product. As I will assert in the following chapters, the value of a creative product is the product of the effort of a network of actors. Therefore, although this book has one single author, the knowledge included in it is far from individual. Writing it has truly been a huge effort that could not have been undertaken without the help of many others whom I sincerely want to thank now that this effort has been concluded.

A generic but genuinely wholehearted thanks goes to my students in the 'Marketing in Creative Industries' course that I've taught at Università L. Bocconi over the last ten years. They have been – and still are! – a continual stimulus to deeper investigation, sharper clarification, and above all, systematic questioning of long-held conventional wisdom. This book includes reflections stimulated by many years of interactions with them.

To two of them I'm particularly grateful. Both have decided to proceed with an academic career, and now they are involved in a Ph.D. program. Maria Cristina Cito and Elena Fumagalli helped me a great deal with some of the case histories, with the bibliography, and above all with hours of discussions about interesting topics regarding creative industries and their actors. Some of the issues raised and covered in this book are products of challenging discussions with Cristina and Elena.

I also owe so much to Marilia Sciulli, Davide Neri and Elisa Moro. Marilia did research on tango dancers for her graduate dissertation, which we worked on together to write one of the major case studies reported in the book. The same is true for Davide, who helped me with the 'Magic: The Gathering' case study, which he initially investigated in his graduate dissertation. Finally, Elisa helped me with the data analysis of box office revenues used in some of the chapters, saving me a lot of time in finding the right sources and the most interesting data.

For some of the editorial work I could rely on the precious help of Chiara Solerio, a research assistant at my department. Without Chiara all the time needed to write the book would have been much longer. She made an invaluable contribution to the revision of some chapters, the bibliography, and many of the figures included in the book.

Throughout the years I had the chance to meet, work and share mutual knowledge with many brilliant managers in various organizations operating in creative industries. It would be too long a list to mention them all. Still, this book is rich with case studies, short and long. The majority of them could only have been written with the gracious collaboration of many managers working in interesting organizations in various industries and countries. I interviewed all of them, some of them wrote parts of the cases and all revised their own. Without their time, open-mindedness, and genuine appreciation for my research work these cases simply would not be such an interesting part of the book. Listing their names below, and thanking each of them for the great help they gave me, is my personal way of thanking all the managers from whom I learned so much over the years:

Andrea Beloni, Head of Digital Communication, Events & Sponsorship, Vodafone Italy; Almudena Bermejo Sánchez, Director of Espacio Fundación Telefónica, Madrid; Silvia Caselli, Ex Chief Marketing Officer, Feltrinelli Group; Monica da Cortà Fumei, Marketing and Communication Director, Fondazione Musei Civici Venezia; Antonella Di Lazzaro, Ex Head of Brand Management, MTV Italy; Andrea Duilio, Head of Marketing, Consumer Division, Vodafone Italy; Paola Giunti, Communication and Public Relations Director, Teatro Regio di Torino; Lidì Grimaldi, Head of Consulting, Interbrand Italy; Lanfranco Licauli, Marketing and Communication Director, Piccolo Teatro di Milano; Manuela Meunier, Head of Marketing Research, Musée du quai Branly, Paris; Pepa Octavio de Toledo, Marketing and Communication Director, Matadero Madrid; Pierluigi Parnofiello, Ex Brand Manager, Wizard of the Coast Europe; Manfredi Ricca, Managing Director, Interbrand Italy; Sue Wilkinson, Director of Supporter Development, National Trust, UK; Inna Khmyzova, Marketing Director, Shakhtar Donetsk, Ukraine.

I want to wholeheartedly thank the editorial team at Palgrave Macmillan with whom I have worked. All authors know how important the job of an editorial team is. I'm truly thankful to mine: Martin Drewe, Ceri Griffith, Rachel Bridgewater, Ursula Gavin, Jenny Hindley, Holly Rutter, for their patience, support, and advice along the very long process that gave life to this book. This is a team I'd like very much to work with again, although I'm not sure if they feel the same way!

There are three people who had a special role in this book. Imma Turbau opened the doors to me of the rich cultural world of Spain, with her broad knowledge and long contact list. Imma is a generous person who is able to combine her creative talent with a deep understanding of marketing, and her help was indispensible a great deal in identifying interesting case histories to share with the readers of this book. Next, Daniela Leone, who supported me in many ways. First, by providing me with a long list of contacts in various European creative organizations, only a few of which, unfortunately, have been used in the book; then, recommending interesting case histories identified on the basis of her innate curiosity, many of them, fortunately, included in this book; and most importantly, sharing tons of optimism and smiles, fantastic fuel for creativity! Last is Joanne Sykes. Jo is a brilliant manager with a deep knowledge of the marketing world, who helped me navigate the amazing and hyper-dynamic UK media and cultural system. Most of the UK data and cases come from her contacts and suggestions. To Imma, Daniela, and Jo lots of sincere thanks.

The last person that I want to thank is Jill Connelly, who translated the book into English. Jill is a perfect example of how a value relation functions. After years of joint work, Jill is much more than a translator. She is a personal trainer and a coach. She helped me not only in transforming the book in a different language, but in making my thoughts sharper, bolder, and clearer. I owe Jill not only days and days of patient Skype calls for the revisions of the chapters, but most importantly, her persistence in encouraging me to resist any temptation to bypass the difficulties of the task, her innate optimism, and many laughs about the cultural diversity of the US and Italy. I'm the author of the book, but without Jill the value of this book would have been much more limited.

Finally, the value of the network lies in its ties. And I'm lucky enough to rely on many very strong, very supportive, non-virtual ties. Writing this book has been a much longer task than I had planned and expected. Therefore, I'm aware I've been a taker much more than a giver with my beloved family and friends. To all of them I owe so much. But now I can reply to all their questions accumulated in the last 18 months about the end of the book, and I can finally say: it's over!

* * *

The author and publisher would like to thank the following for permission to reproduce material:

- Ipsos MediaCT for a figure from "The Pulse of the Affluent Market," *The Mendelsohn Affluent Barometer* (2013).
- John Wiley & Sons Ltd for a figure from Deeter-Schmelz and Sojka, "Wrestling with American Values: An Exploratory Investigation of World Wrestling Entertainment as a Product-Based Subculture," *Journal of Consumer Behavior*, 4.2 (2004): 132–43; and a figure from Leder, Belke, Oeberst and Augustin, "A Model of Aesthetic Appreciation and Aesthetic Judgments," *British Journal of Psychology*, 95 (2004): 489–508.
- Sports Business Group at Deloitte for a figure from Football Money League 2014 report.
- National Readership Survey and Newsworks for data and figures from NRS PADD January 13–December 13 / ComScore November 2013.
- Perseus Books Group for a figure from Csikszentmihalyi, *Finding Flow* (1997).
- Pion Ltd for a figure from Leyshon, "Time-Space and Digital Compression: Software Formats and the Geographical Reorganisation of the Music Industry," *Environment and Planning* 33.1 (2001): 49–77.
- The American Marketing Association for a figure from Plummer, J., "The Concept and Application of Lifestyle Segmentation," *Journal of Marketing*, 38 (1974): 33–7.
- University of Chicago Press for a figure from McCracken "Who Is the Celebrity Endorser? Cultural Foundations of the Endorsement Process," *Journal Consumer Research*, 16.3 (1989): 315.

Part I

THE ROLE OF MARKETING IN CREATIVE INDUSTRIES

Chapter 1

CREATIVE INDUSTRIES

LEARNING OBJECTIVES

After reading this chapter you should be able to:

- Map the landscape of the creative industries.
- Distinguish a creative industry from a non-creative one.
- Tap into the main characteristics of a creative industry.
- Understand their relevance in today's society.

1.1 A DEFINITION OF CREATIVE INDUSTRIES

Delineating the boundaries of an industry is an extremely complicated task. Essentially this process calls for the inclusion of some actors, relationships, and behaviors while at the same time excluding other actors, relationships and behaviors that fall within the confines of other industries. Today the undertaking is even more complex because in most of the world's economies even the borders of the most traditional industries are becoming blurred. (Can a clear line be drawn between the food and pharmaceutical industries, for example, when currently one of fastest growing markets is *nutriceuticals*, foods with high therapeutic value?)

A number of phenomena can explain this escalating ambiguity: the evolution of production and distribution technologies, business strategies that trigger cross-industry competitive dynamics, and changing consumer needs that prompt organizations to bundle together in single offerings benefits that in the past were provided by multiple products and services. (How many technological tools did we once have to have to get all the functionalities of today's smartphone?)

To compound the complexity even further, if our focus is a multi-sector context centered on an ambiguous and seemingly elusive concept like creativity, any attempt to make any sort of delimitation verges on the impossible. Can't the origins of all industries be traced back to a creative act that leads to the realization of products and services? So aren't all sectors essentially creative? Then how can we distinguish one from another on the basis of creativity?

Yet since the late 1990s, the term *creative industries* has been incorporated into the lexicon of politicians, public policy makers, entrepreneurs, managers, and experts in a variety of fields, probably thanks to a 1998 publication by the UK Creative Industries Taskforce, under the Department of Culture, Media and Sports (DCMS, 1998). This document provides a map of the creative industries, quantifying their size, measuring their performance, and identifying their distinctive characteristics.

With this seminal work, the British government began a systematic monitoring program, underscoring the critical role these industries play in the economic and industrial evolution of the UK. Here the terminology used in that report is worth mentioning: under the umbrella of creative industries come the more traditional *cultural industries*, a term which is a few decades older (as it was first coined in the 1960s). Beyond the conceptual and methodological repercussions, including traditional cultural industries in this way also carries symbolic weight and sends a clear signal: the time has come to recognize that traditional cultural industries are industries in every sense of the word. More importantly, some of them satisfy similar needs, though they've always been considered very different industries (compare fashion to video games or sport).

After the first British DCMS report was released, other countries followed suit and began studying and monitoring the impact of creative industries on their national economies (in many cases, adopting a nearly identical conceptual and methodological framework). These countries include South Africa (DACST, 1998), Hong Kong (CCPR, 2003), Australia (DCITA, 2004), the US (IIPA, 2006), the European Union (KEA, 2006), and Italy (Santagata, 2008), as well as the United Nations (UNCTAD, 2008).[1] This investment in developing a knowledge base on creative industries has on one hand

3

contributed to the dissemination of the term, and on the other has opened the debate on exactly which industries should be given the 'creative' label.

In light of the aims of this book, I don't see any point in scrutinizing the similarities and differences in the various definitions.[2] But I do believe it's worthwhile to keep in mind that every attempt to delineate creative industries is based on specific assumptions and objectives. To give an example, the goal of the British government in setting up the Creative Industries Taskforce, which authored the first report mentioned above, was to identify opportunities for economic growth in a nation emerging from two decades of deep de-industrialization. Consequently, the underlying aim was to glean some useful indications to apply in formulating national industrial policies in the years to follow. The end result was a definition of creative industries that clearly reflects an industrial view, focusing on variables such as the percentage and type of employment in these sectors, the value added of various phases of the production and distribution process, the technological level, and the potential impact on the economic and social development of Great Britain. The basic premise of the study was that industries labeled as 'creative' could and should contribute to the well-being of the country by generating and exploiting intellectual property. Accordingly, the broad definition of creative industries used in this report encompassed all sectors in which the original source of products and services lies in individual creativity and talent, and in which the protection of intellectual property is possible.

However, since this is a book on marketing, it takes a different perspective. The key concept that underpins this work is *value for the customer*. This leads to my initial premise: every economic phenomenon, and especially every market phenomenon, should be analyzed and interpreted from the viewpoint of the customer. By customer, I refer to the recipient of the value generated by the players who operate in the industry in question (in other words, the person who evaluates, appreciates, buys, and uses the product or service). My purpose in writing this book is to propose an effective marketing management model built on managing customer value, a model that is tailored to the specificities of creative industries.

This explains why I don't feel a pressing need to stake out the exact boundaries of creative industries. What I believe is essential, instead, is to pinpoint their distinctive features, which have a much greater impact on typical marketing decisions. So my aim in proposing a possible categorization is to formulate a working hypothesis that allows me to fashion a more effective ad hoc marketing management model.

That said, the first consideration that will help in defining creative industries is *the relevance that consumers associate with the creative content of the products and services offered in the industry*. In creative industries, the value offered to the customer depends mainly on the creative content of the offering, that is, products and services are compared, purchased, and evaluated primarily on their creative content. At the beginning of this chapter I presented two questions that commonly arise in attempting to pinpoint what makes creative industries unique: Aren't all industries essentially creative? How can we differentiate one from another based on creativity?

In my opinion, by adopting the perspective of value offered to the customer and recognizing the importance of the creative content of that offering, we can resolve these questions by shifting our focus. Instead of considering creativity as the *input* of production processes, we need to think of creativity as the *output*. (All sectors make products and services that spring from a creative idea, but only in certain sectors do customers associate the value of a product or service *primarily* with its creative content.)

Examples are products like washing machines, cars, body lotion, or laundry detergents on the one hand, and novels, video games, photography exhibits, or music on the other. Obviously, the starting point for the first set of products is one or more creative ideas (input) that have led to technical solutions, which in turn translate into specific performances. But what the customer buys is a set of performances in which the creative content isn't immediately perceptible or assessable. Of course, this doesn't mean that customers don't recognize or appreciate particularly innovative solutions. But even when there's nothing innovative about these products, they can still provide the performances customers want. In other words, limited creative content doesn't drastically lessen the value offered to customers.

The same is not true for products and services such as video games, photography exhibits, or novels for which the greatest share of value lies in the creative content, which customers can immediately perceive and evaluate. This doesn't mean that they completely disregard non-creative factors in the value offered (the bulk of a book, ease of access of exhibition space in a photography show, the memory needed to download and play a video game). But the value of the creative content outweighs all these considerations. As a result, for these categories of products and services, limited creative content means little or no customer value.

The second aspect we need to consider is the *relevance of creativity as a lever of competitive advantage, as seen by the players in the sector (firms and institutions that offer products and services)*. In creative industries, the basic ingredient in competitive advantage is the creativity incorporated in products and service through innovation. In fact, in these contexts, competition essentially orbits around innovation. This means that the firms and institutions that succeed in systematically feeding the flow of innovations to be launched in the market will survive and prosper, while the ones that fail to do so will disappear.

An obvious example is a publishing company, which won't last long by relying solely on backlist titles without regularly publishing frontlists. The same can be said for record or movie companies, as well as museums, theaters, and fashion companies. For all these firms and institutions, their competitive advantage – indeed their very survival – depends on their ability to systematically channel creativity into innovation to offer to their customers.

Clearly the two factors are interdependent (the relevance of creativity both for customers and for organizations), and there's no way to determine which one drives the other. As in every industry, supply stimulates demand, which in turn stimulates supply, and so on and so forth. Similarly, in creative industries, it is creativity in supply that spurs on the search for creativity in demand, and vice versa. Basically, creativity is the fuel that powers the economic engine connecting supply and demand. Creativity generates differential value in competitive dynamics, and use-value in consumption processes. In the words of Jeffcut and Pratt (2002: 228): 'Creativity is the enterprise.'

On the basis of these two defining features, industries classified as creative for the purposes of this book fall into four sub-groups:

- *Arts* – Production, conservation, and distribution of visual and performing arts, including museums, galleries, theaters, and festivals.
- *Media, information, and communication* – Production, conservation, reproduction, distribution, and transmission of contents (texts, sounds, images, ideas,

and messages), for example publishing, music, film, and communication.
- *Fashion, design, and architecture* – Production and distribution of goods with high symbolic content such as clothing, accessories, furniture, home accents, and architectural design.
- *Entertainment and leisure* – Production and distribution of recreational services, for example live shows, sports, natural parks and amusement parks, and tourism.

Like any classification, this one can't claim to be exhaustive, but simply effective in light of how I intend to apply it in the rest of this book. By the same token, as I mentioned before, I don't want to be too exact in distinguishing one area from another. So I don't see much use in debating whether or not live music should be considered art or live entertainment, or if live classical music should be classified as art while musicals or live rock should be labeled as entertainment.

What's more important, as I see it, is to include all these sectors under the umbrella of creative industries, because they share certain features that will shape the design and implementation of marketing strategies.

1.2 THE DISTINCTIVE FEATURES OF CREATIVE INDUSTRIES

The high creative content of the offerings of these industries, which generates customer value and a chance for competitive differentiation for firms and institutions, gives rise to certain distinctive traits of supply and demand. As far as demand goes, creative content affects consumer decision-making processes (choosing, buying, and consuming). For supply, this same content shapes how production and distribution processes are organized, and triggers unique competitive dynamics. Below is a list of the most significant specificities that impact the design and implementation of marketing strategies.

1.2.1 Non-objective preferences

Imagine we're listening in on two teens who are talking about two videogames and debating over which one is best. One teen says that the first game is better because it has cooler special effects and a more exciting, less repetitive storyline. The other teen prefers the second game because it's more challenging, and it allows for multiple players. Who is right about which game is best? It's hard to say – in fact, it's impossible.

Leaving price aside, in creative industries products are made up of *attributes for which consumer preferences are not based on objectively quantifiable parameters*. To give an example, when a consumer buys a car, there are parameters she can use to evaluate and compare different models objectively. For instance, she can look at engine power, fuel efficiency, and safety features, and she can measure these attributes objectively in terms of horsepower, miles per gallon, and number of airbags. In other words, for similar products consumers can base their preferences on objective parameters, so they tend to prefer the product that offers objectively better performance at the same price. This property is what economists call *vertical differentiation*.

But for products with high creative content, there are no such objective parameters; consumer preferences vary widely because they are based on extremely subjective criteria. Here's another example: if a consumer were choosing between two contemporary works of art that are different in sizes, she wouldn't necessarily prefer the larger one (if they both cost the same amount). Or when she is deciding between two photography exhibits to see, one with twice as many pieces on display as the other, she wouldn't necessarily decide to go to the larger exhibit.

The point is that preferences depend largely on a combination of personal experience, sensations, and inclinations which we refer to as taste (which I'll discuss further in Chapter 3). This property is what economists call *horizontal differentiation*. Consumers have subjective preferences based on their personal taste, which is why we are inclined to choose certain forms of creative expression over others, and certain combinations of product attributes over others. But none of this can be measured in any objective way.

1.2.2   Experience goods

Let's get back to our two teenagers, and imagine they're out buying a new game, trying to choose between two that they've never played before. How do they figure out which one is better? Which one is more challenging, more fun, more exciting? It's hard to say; in fact, in many ways it's impossible. Which leads me to my next point: *Creative products are experience products, not search products.*

With a *search product*, a consumer can get some idea of its quality before she uses it by simply searching for information on relative product features (hence the name). This process works because the quality of these goods is associated with attributes that can be objectively measured, so a consumer can find out about them before she actually uses the product (like with the washing machine or the laundry detergent).

For *experience products*, this mechanism doesn't apply because product attributes can't be objectively associated with product quality (like the artwork or the photography exhibit). So the only way a consumer can get an idea of this quality is through first-hand experience. Only after she's played the video game, or read the novel, or seen the exhibit, can she say whether she liked it or not; in other words, whether she valued its quality.

There are four consequences that arise from the 'experience' status of goods that are unique to creative industries. First, consumers can't resort to objective parameters to predict the quality of a product before they buy and use it; so to make their buying decisions, they rely on subjectively defined indicators, called *quality clues*. Examples might be comments on a gamers' blog for a video game, or the author's reputation for a novel, or the gallery's prestige for a photography exhibit. When consumers use quality clues, this further reinforces the chance for horizontal differentiation by producers, since various clues are subjectively defined, so they themselves can represent differentiation factors.

The second consequence of qualifying goods as 'experience' is that in creative industries, *consumers value product trials*. Listening to a song on the radio or during a concert, or reading a few pages of a book in a bookshop or on an online retailer's website, seeing a work of art on display in a gallery or using a demo of a video game: all these trials encourage (or discourage) us from buying the product in question, because these experiences constitute an anticipation of the product experience. By trying out the product consumers get a clue as to the quality they can expect from buying and consuming it.

The third effect of the 'experience' characteristic is that the *reputation of the players becomes a fundamental factor in market relations*. The fact is, consumers can't deduce the quality of experience products before they use them. So an alternative to actually trying out the product is to rely on the reputation of the players involved – the producer, the distributor, the brand, the critic. This becomes a very effective and powerful quality clue that consumers can instantaneously access at practically no cost.

Here are some examples: a consumer can make an educated guess as to the quality of an artist thanks to the reputation of the gallery hosting her exhibit, or anticipate the quality of a temporary exhibit based on the reputation of the museum that has organized it, or get an idea of the quality of a musical by reading a review from a reputable critic. As compared to non-creative industries, with search products and services as their output, reputation is extraordinarily important in creative sectors because it's a key quality clue.

The fourth consequence of being an 'experience' product is that consumers *need time to actually experience the product*. Attending a live concert, watching a volleyball game, reading a book, visiting a museum – these are all things that take time. Basically, the satisfaction people get from consuming a product with high creative content depends on the time they dedicate to consumption. There are two reasons for this, which I'll delve into further in Chapter 3. The first is that the time people spend consuming allows them to enhance their expertise and competence with regard to the product, refining their tastes and more clearly defining their preferences. The second is that it takes time to activate cognitive processes and elicit emotional states by which consumers can come to appreciate a creative product.

1.2.3　Infinite variety

In 2012 in India, 1,288 new films were produced (UNESCO, 2012a). In 2010 in the US, 328,259 new book titles were sold, of which only 53,139 were fiction (Bowker, 2012). In 2012, around 20 million songs were available for download from about 500 legal sites (IFPI, 2012). In 2012 in the modern art market, Edvard Munch's 'The Scream' fetched 192 million US dollars at auction, and at the same time millions of works by amateur artists were sold for a few dollars a piece at local art fairs.

To put it briefly, in creative industries, *product variety is practically infinite* (Caves, 2000, p. 6). But if you think about industries like cars, cell phones, detergents, or any mass market or durable goods, the number of new product launches in a single year is much lower than the same figure for any given creative sector.

Let's take a movie, for example. The same screenplay can generate countless end products, based on all the possible combinations of directors, actors, sound tracks, editing, and so on. This illustrates how creative industries are typically *hyper-fragmented, both in terms of supply and demand*, but with opposite effects on either side. For demand, hyper-fragmentation is the outcome of unlimited variety in the subjective tastes of consumers, which leads producers to launch new products continually. As a result of the massive number of products available on the market, consumer decision-making processes have become exponentially more complex. How can people navigate their way through the infinite variety of shows, books, exhibits, and sporting events?

In terms of supply, instead, producers have limitless possibilities for combining attributes to create products and services that offer a differential advantage over competitors. Yet all these possibilities generate tremendously intense competition, because every single product in any given sector competes with an enormous number of other products, first to capture consumer attention, and then consumer preference. How many local sporting events can a consumer go to in a week? How many weekend concerts can she actually find out about? How many TV programs can she watch on any given night?

1.2.4　Structural failure

Common wisdom among experts holds that 70 per cent of books can be considered flops (Thompson, 2010), and the same percentage of new CDs released on the market won't be able to cover their production costs (Wikström, 2009).

In creative industries, the *market failure of many products is inherent to the specificity of production and consumption processes*. This characteristic is rooted in the hyper-fragmentation mentioned above. What I mean by this is that with such extreme product proliferation, the fact that many products can't reach market success is intrinsic to the structure of creative industries. Put another way, in these industries, the failure of scores of products is offset by the market success of a few.

Hyper-fragmentation prompts consumers to notice only a tiny fraction of the products available on the market. Similarly, it's impossible for producers to pay the same attention to (read: invest the same financial and marketing resources in) all the products they sell. Clearly, the more products an organization has in its portfolio, the more significant this consideration is.

That's why in publishing, film, music, and fashion, structural failure is more obvious than in other sectors like natural parks and amusement parks, where normally every company or institution manages a limited number of 'products'.

What this means in financial terms is that producers realize that many of the products in their portfolio won't break even, so the ones that do will have to offset the losses of the ones that don't. One outcome of this is that many creative sectors are 'hit-driven' or 'chart-driven'. In other words, producers focus on making sure that a certain number of their products become hits, and break into the charts or bestseller lists, because these successes provide slack resources that serve to compensate for losses on less successful products. In commercial publishing, film, and music, as with modern art exhibits, tourist cities, fashion, and design, producers need to sell a certain number of products to millions of consumers in order to generate volumes and margins that can guarantee economic sustainability for the entire product portfolio.

1.2.5   Non-utilitarian consumption

If you were to ask someone why she's reading a mystery by Manuel Vasques Montalban, she'd answer: because it's exciting! If you ask a visitor at the entrance to a Damien Hirst exhibit why he's going, he'd probably answer: because I'm curious! Or, because I've heard so much about it I've got to go! And if you ask a heavy metal fan why she's going to see Metallica's next concert, she'd answer: because they're awesome!

Products in creative industries are consumed primarily for *their hedonic, experiential, and symbolic value.* The difference between hedonic and utilitarian consumption (and hedonic and utilitarian products) is by now consolidated in the marketing discipline. Consumption is utilitarian when a consumer buys and uses products to reach a goal. The product provides performance, and it's product performance that contributes to reaching the goal in question. (For example, a moisturizing lotion, thanks to its emollient ingredients, gives consumers softer skin.)

Conversely, hedonic consumption does not serve to attain a goal, it *is* the goal. Hedonic consumption engenders pleasure, aesthetic appreciation, and gratification. (For example, the value in listening to a classical music CD or reading a comic book lies in the aesthetic pleasure these activities provide.)

More broadly speaking, consumption in these industries is also *experiential* and *symbolic*. The first refers to the fact that it's not the product in itself that delivers value to the consumer, but the entire consumption experience (see Section 2.1.2). For instance, when a consumer goes to a stadium to watch a football match, the value of this experience doesn't depend exclusively on how well the two teams are performing. Other factors also come into play, like the atmosphere in the stadium before and during the match, the sociality of sharing her passion for football with other fans, the sense of growing anticipation in the days leading up to the match, and debates with other fans predicting the possible outcome. All these factors enhance or detract from the value of the consumption experience.

Finally, consumption in creative sectors has a high *symbolic* value. In other words, it bears the message that an individual belongs to certain social group and shares certain values, and conveys the image that she has of herself or that she wants to transmit to others. If a consumer reads a newspaper, for example, she can get up-to-date information on what's going on in her country and in the rest of the world. But she can also feel like an active participant in her country; she can share and compare her opinions with others; she feels like she belongs to a certain group.

In describing consumption in creative industries as hedonic, experiential, and symbolic, I don't mean that all consumption is all three things at the same time, or that there are no utilitarian factors involved whatsoever. (After all, listening to a talk show can satisfy the utilitarian need to learn more about an issue, as does reading in-depth coverage of a topic in a newspaper.) What I do mean is that consumption in these industries is *predominantly* characterized by hedonic, experiential, and symbolic elements, unlike non-creative sectors. What's more, the positioning of every product category and every single product or brand within a category centers more on hedonic or experiential or symbolic traits, or a combination of all three. We'll discuss this in the next section, and go on to explore it further in Chapter 3.

1.2.6   Aesthetic value

Why would a consumer buy an ugly shirt (if she could afford to buy a nice one at the same price)? Why would a family buy ugly furniture (again, instead of beautiful furniture at the same price)? And why would a teenager download a song she's already heard and doesn't like?

In creative industries, *the aesthetic value of a product is a fundamental component – if not the sum total – of the overall value of the offering as perceived by the consumer.* Granted, you might say, but people don't buy newspapers or geography books because they're pretty. In fact, thanks to our broad definition of creative industries, we can easily assert that in some sectors the aesthetic component isn't all that essential.

What's most important in a newspaper is accuracy and attention to detail, as well as up-to-date content. And a consumer would rate a geography book mainly on how thoroughly topics are covered and how clearly content is presented. Or take an advertising campaign, which more than anything else has to convey a message and resonate with a specific customer target. Therefore, it's reasonable to admit that readers appreciate the graphics in a newspaper, which make it easier to read; or the quality of the pictures in a geography book, which makes the content easier to understand; or aesthetic elements of an ad campaign that help capture the attention of the audience.

In sum, there is evidence that aesthetic appreciation applies to all the products of creative industries (as they are defined in this book). However, aesthetics do not have the same relevance for all products from the customer viewpoint. It is therefore useful to classify products on a continuum according to their aesthetic content (see Charters, 2006, for a similar classification).

At one endpoint there are products that are *primarily utilitarian*. For these goods, the aesthetic content is a secondary benefit within the broader customer value, without which the overall value would be compromised but not eliminated altogether. Examples of products on this end of the spectrum would include daily newspapers and professional publications or educational texts.

At the other end, there are *aesthetic* products (for example, paintings, live performances, musical compositions, novels). For these items aesthetic content represents an essential and even exclusive component of value perceived by the customer, without which the product loses its primary benefit. Aesthetic products have an intrinsic aesthetic value, which again may encompass the entire value perceived by the customer. Yet other factors can also come into play. For example, when buying a novel a consumer might also consider the size (easy to carry) or the font (easy to read). But

the bottom line – what delivers value for the customer, and determines (dis)satisfaction – is the aesthetic value of the content.

Two more categories fall in between these two extremes: products that are either *primarily experiential* or *primarily aesthetic*. In the first group are goods that provide value which is strongly associated with an experience. For these items the aesthetic element is one of the components of the experience itself; if it were lacking the value for the consumer would be diminished, but not cancelled out all together.

Going back to the football match, the atmosphere in the stadium is a fundamental aspect of the consumption experience, and certain elements of this atmosphere relate to aesthetics. Just think of the visual impact of a full stadium, with all the fans wearing their team colors, and the sound of music and chanting in the background. Without these sights and sounds, the whole experience would center on the quality of play alone, which for spectators would probably lessen the perceived value considerably.

Products which are primarily experiential are positioned closer to the utilitarian product endpoint of the continuum because aesthetics are important but not predominant in terms of the value sought after and supplied to customers.

Finally, there are products which are *primarily aesthetic*. The product categories positioned on this segment of the spectrum include clothing, jewelry, furnishings, home decor, and so forth. Here the aesthetic content is the main benefit, but utilitarian factors count too; in fact, without them overall product value would be drastically reduced, to the point of preventing customers from making the decision to buy.

When shopping for clothes, for instance, people make their choices mostly based on aesthetics, but also because the clothing breathes in the summer or protects from the cold in the winter. Or if they're in the market for a new home, they choose which house to buy and how to decorate it based on aesthetics, but faulty wiring or leaky faucets would reduce the perceived value appreciably.

1.2.7　Multiple product life cycles

How long is the lifecycle of a daily newspaper? A day. A movie at the cinema? A few weeks. A hit musical? A few months. A fashion collection? A season. After that, all of these products are replaced by new ones.

But they don't disappear, far from it. They simply reemerge, perhaps in some other form or on some other markets providing different benefits.

A single issue of a newspaper ends up in the archives where it can be recovered for research and reference. After a run at the theaters, a movie is released on DVD and then gets redistributed for pay TV and broadcast TV. Music from the hit musical is put into a compilation, or it becomes the soundtrack for a film or a television spot. The fashion collection is sold online or in factory outlets. In creative industries, *products have multiple life cycles*. The first is often short, sometimes extremely so, but later life cycles taken together can be very long indeed.

Just think of an opera, or classical music in general, or classics from literature. There are even some contemporary products that can be used as examples. Pink Floyd's album *The Dark Side of the Moon* stayed on the *Billboard 200* chart (the ranking of bestselling albums in the US, published weekly by Billboard magazine) for 815 weeks, and that's not even counting prior sales. (The album came out before Billboard 200 was first published.) And with every new LP the group released, fans kept going back to 'the Moon'. Other classic products are the *Keepall* and *Speedy* bags by Louis Vuitton, created in 1930, but continually updated over the years. In modern literature, Tolkien's *The Lord of the Rings* was first published in 1954, but much later it achieved worldwide success when it was made into a series of movies. The list goes on and on.

Some creative industries, it is true, have lifecycles that are anything but brief. Many European museums were founded in the eighteenth century, as were countless theaters. Also, since tourist destinations are on our list of creative industries, that means the lifecycles of many 'products' can be measured in centuries or even millennia.

But as I'll detail in Chapter 8, if we take the example of a museum, its 'product' isn't the museum itself, but the pieces on display at any given moment. Over time this body of art changes with new purchases added to the collection, or even when the same works of art are exhibited in new ways, conveying different themes. (The permanent collection is only one of a museum's products.) Consequently, museum products have multiple life cycles, albeit short ones, which taken together can span centuries.

Today, product life cycles in all sectors are shrinking, but in creative industries this time span is astonishingly short. Why is that? The answer lies in the role that creativity plays in these industries. As far as supply goes, since competitive advantage is built on innovation competitors are driven to launch new products on the market continuously. Moreover, since the failure of many products is structural, products that don't meet customer needs must quickly be replaced by others that have the potential to do so. This makes *planned obsolescence* a widespread product strategy in creative industries: life cycles are purposely designed to be short so as to ensure a systematic flow of new products on the market (Section 8.1.5.1).

In terms of demand, short life cycles are rooted in the *variety seeking* behaviors of customers (Section 4.5.5). In fact, to satisfy their hedonic needs, customers only rarely consume the same product more than once.[3] (That said, it's not unheard of for people to watch the same film or read the same book or visit the same collection in a museum several times.) But it's much more likely that people will buy and consume other products within the same category or related categories.

The fact that products in creative industries have multiple life cycles means *the brand is an essential and increasingly important resource*. For producers, in fact, growing the value of their brands is a way to capitalize on investments they've already made in individual products, in communication, in relationships with distributors, and of course with customers.

In creative contexts, hyper-fragmentation of the offering, combined with short, multiple life cycles, would make it financially unsustainable to support marketing activities for every single item. The chance to capitalize a portion of these efforts on a broader resource such as brand constitutes an investment in reputation that the organization can leverage to support new product launches. In fact, brand reputation is one of the typical quality clues that consumers use when they buy experience goods. So, as we'll see more clearly in Section 8.2, the brand serves for product endorsement, and brand management becomes a critical competence for success in creative industries.

1.2.8   Profit and non-profit coexistence

In Europe the vast majority of theaters, opera houses and museums are State-owned. In fact, in most countries of the world, the State (central or local government) intervenes directly in media sectors as owner of television and radio stations (UNESCO, 2012b).

Essentially, for organizations in creative industries, the priority goal is not always, or not only, profit. In fact, state-owned organizations that operate in these contexts are often non-profits. What's more, in other industries that are populated for the most part by privately-owned enterprises (for example, publishing, film, tourism, and sports), the state recognizes the cultural and social value of the products in question, and offers direct and indirect subsidies for relative suppliers. (For data on some major European countries, see the report by Nielsen and Linnebank, 2011.) This means profit is pertinent, but not a pressing priority.

Finally, in all creative industries, both public and private organizations, whether profit or non-profit, I believe that a fundamental aspect of their mission is to contribute to the civil, social, and cultural progress of their country and the world. Consequently, they give other organizational goals – like promoting new creative talent, raising the cultural level of the general public, and enhancing the image of their city or country – the same (or even higher) priority as profit (or financial sustainability, in the case of non-profits). If this weren't the case, there would be no explanation for the enormous number of market and financial failures in these industries.

Figure 1.1 sums up the distinctive features of creative industries. Their usage for the inclusion of an industry in the creative group is more effective – I believe – than any ex ante definition. The more of them an industry possesses, the more relevant is creativity in giving form to relative supply-demand dynamics. And the more necessary is a marketing management model that takes into account these features when providing recommendations on designing and implementing marketing strategies and tactics.

1.3   THE INCREASING ECONOMIC IMPACT OF CREATIVE INDUSTRIES

The world has always had creative industries. Any one of them included in the definition used here can trace its origins back several centuries, if not millennia. But never before have these industries captured so much attention from institutions and decision makers, both public and private.

The first indication that creative industries are taking the lead on the economic scene comes from economic data, which show that creative industry products (in other words, the so-called *creative economy*) account for a rising percentage of international commercial trade. In fact, the average annual rate of increase was 11.83 per cent from 2002 to 2008 (UNCTAD, 2010), surpassing growth in trade of other products by far.

Figure 1.1 – The distinguishing features of creative industries

What's more, today the creative economy contributes to the Gross Domestic Product of numerous developed or developing countries much more than traditional manufacturing output (UNCTAD, 2010). But what has triggered this boom?

I think the causes can be found by looking at the changes that have been driving the evolution of contemporary economies over the past two decades, changes that make creative industries well suited for satisfying specific needs of both organizations and individual consumers. In fact, for producers they make better growth opportunities compared to other industries, and individuals get a set of products that they can use to better express their identity and lifestyles.

Here are the most significant of these transformations.

1.3.1 The increasing value of intangibles

Expressions such as 'the information economy', 'the knowledge economy', or 'the service economy' have been incorporated into the lexicon of anyone who is interested in exploring the evolution of contemporary society (Castells, 1996, 1997, 1998; Powell and Snellman, 2004). The common root of these terms lies in the epic transformation that has dominated the twentieth century: *the primary source of value in contemporary economies has switched from tangibles to intangibles.*

In other words, knowledge content counts more than physical components in determining product value. For firms and institutions, this means that value doesn't lie in their tangible resources, so much as in the intellectual and relational capital they can leverage (know-how and reputation). Basically, in economies where tangible resources (capital, machinery, real estate, physical production input) are widely available to all competitors, organizations must build competitive advantage on mainly innovation capabilities, knowledge of the markets where these innovations are commercialized, reputation in markets providing factors of production (the financial market, the labor market, and so on), and reputation in markets where products are sold.

Consequently, products represent the materialization of knowledge. An iPhone, for instance, is a high-value product for consumers because it incorporates both scientific knowledge, and knowledge about the benefits consumers seek, making it possible to execute given functions and provide given performances. Naturally,

its physical components make an iPhone a quality product, but taken together they count much less than the know-how that went into creating it.

The terms 'information economy' and 'knowledge economy' are almost spontaneously associated with 'service economy'. As the importance of tangible product components decreases, the service component becomes more critical in providing value to customers. Going back to the iPhone, this product offers consumers an array of services that go far beyond basic communication, including entertainment, geo-localization, advising, and so forth. This exemplifies an ongoing trend: *products are materialized knowledge that supplies services for customers* (Vargo and Lusch, 2004).

These 'new economies' (information, knowledge, and service) are rooted in individual and collective creative talents. One of the most influential books in shaping the collective understanding of the economic and social role of creativity is indisputably *The Rise of the Creative Class* by Florida (2002). This author asserts that the transition to information, knowledge, and service economies is generating a new social class – a creative social class – made up of people who use their creative talent as a key factor of production in their economic activities.

Florida's work provides a solid argument underscoring the fact that the growing role of information, knowledge, and services in contemporary economies is also a driving force behind the increasing relevance of creative industries. In fact, these industries provide the most tangible evidence of the value generated via information, knowledge, and service.

In some of these sectors (for instance publishing, music, film, and entertainment) what customers value is content; the physical support that materializes this content is only a secondary component, serving mainly to facilitate access. In other sectors (art, fashion, design, architecture), the physical product is clearly a source of value in itself, but because it encapsulates a stock of knowledge that translates into a style, a form, an aesthetic project. In any case, the primary value that all these sectors provide to their customers is intangible. Consequently, creative industries enable companies to generate value for customers by opening up growth opportunities that other sectors can't guarantee.

Yet as I see it, labeling contemporary economies as intangible isn't simply a reference to production systems, but to consumption systems as well. Although products and services have always been consumed in part for their communicative value (Douglas and Isherwood, 1979), in contemporary societies where goods and services are widely available, more and more often products and brands are used to build self-image and convey this image to others.

To accomplish these complex communication tasks, individuals need competences and knowledge that are appropriate and updated. For consumers to understand the image of a product or a brand in order to use it to communicate their self-image or to show expertise in a social conversation, they must have knowledge, which they build by systematically gathering information and accurately interpreting it. Once again, it is intuitive to see how this aspect of contemporary 'intangible economies' drives creative industries to the fore. There are two reasons why. First, products in creative industries are highly 'positioning' (Caves, 2000: 180–3). In other words, people can get a much clearer idea of someone's attitudes and values by looking at the clothes and accessories she is wearing, or by listening to her talk about her favorite music or books, instead of finding out what brand of dishwasher she owns or what laundry detergent she uses. As we'll explore further in Chapter 3, *products from creative industries represent symbolic resources for consumers* (Bilton, 2007: 151–2), which are invaluable in information and knowledge societies.

The second reason why creative industries enjoy a higher profile in the context of intangible economies is that *many players in these industries take on the role of value agents* in the process of collecting information and assigning meaning by consumers. A fashionista who wants to discover the latest trends would read a fashion magazine. Teens who want to know what everyone's listening to would watch MTV. Someone with a passion for contemporary art who wants to find out about the season's most innovative exhibits would make it a habit to browse the websites of high profile art magazines. In contemporary societies, actors in creative industries play a central role in the process of assigning collective meaning to product categories, brands, and organizations.

1.3.2   The aestheticization of daily life

Another common connotation for today's society is 'post-modern'. In this book, I don't intend to get drawn into the far-reaching debate on the question of 'post-modern' or 'post-modernity', or to add my opinion to it.[4] But for the purposes of this particular section, I think it's interesting to focus on what many feel is a distinctive feature of post-modern societies.

The fact is that in the process of social sense-making, many institutions and major collective movements that influenced the nineteenth and much of the twentieth century no longer do so. States, religions, political parties, unions, workers' movements, students' movements, and so forth are losing (or have completely lost) their ability to provide individuals with a system of values, an identity, a cultural project to embrace in building individual identity. The 'post-modern condition' (Lyotard, 1984) is a more solitary one in which every individual builds his or her identity alone.

As a result, the opportunity, the risk, and the responsibility of this long, complex process rests entirely on the shoulders of each individual. A unique feature of individualization of identity-building is the *aestheticization of daily life*. Featherstone (1991: 66–7) isolates three dimensions of this process:

- The disappearance of the borders between art and daily life.
- Daily life as an aesthetic project.
- The role of images and signs in building meaning in daily life.

Beginning with the artistic works of the avant garde and surrealist movements in the early twentieth century, the barrier between art and daily life has become gradually more permeable. The use of everyday objects as works of art, or in works of art, is now common practice in artistic production. What's more, Pop Art has turned iconic twentieth-century products and brands into art. Today we also have video-art, which uses daily life as an artistic testing ground. All this reinforces the concept that our daily lives, what we do and the things we use, can take on an aesthetic value that precludes any prior separation between what is and is not art, leaving these questions open to answers both from producers and consumers of art.

At the same time, if daily life can have salient aesthetic content, individuals can become their very own aesthetic designers. The body becomes a canvas on which people can experiment by putting aesthetics into practice using physical manipulations (such as tattoos or piercing) or symbolic manipulations (clothing and accessories). Private spaces, where individuals live and work, also become aesthetic testing ground where they can choose, combine, and display objects that express their personal aesthetic project.

Finally, the media system regularly generates a myriad of images, transmitting them efficiently and rapidly to people, who can use these images as symbolic resources within our system of social and individual sense-making. Brands are an example of symbolic resources. The most famous and long-lasting brands are the ones that have become cultural icons; as such they contribute to sense making for social groups, communities, entire countries, or even lifestyles on a global level (Holt, 2004).

Due to the aestheticization of daily life, the output of creative industries has taken center stage.

On the one hand, thanks to its aesthetic value, this output makes creative industries particularly well-suited to the aesthetic connotation of daily life; on the other, its positioning value qualifies this output as a symbolic resource that serves to confer social value to individual aesthetic projects. Moreover, the production system of creative industries is a very powerful and efficient apparatus for generating and rapidly circulating flows of images and signs. So players in these industries have the competence and reputation that makes them extremely effective in the process of sense-making that underpins every individual and collective aesthetic project.

1.3.3   The digital revolution

It's no coincidence that in the conversation about the impact of digital technologies on the economy and on society at large we often hear the term *digital revolution*. These technologies have, in fact, totally transformed how products are made, distributed, and used in all economic sectors. And the revolution will continue in the years to come. Likewise, digital technologies have modified the way people communicate and interact, giving new forms to the way they relate to one another. This impact is particularly pronounced in creative industries, another reason why they have taken on greater relevance.

The most evident sign of this is online retailers, who have changed the way people buy and consume products in creative industries. In the US, for instance, the world's biggest publishing market, the market share for e-books was negligible until the introduction of the Kindle by Amazon in 2007, the Nook by Barnes and Nobles in 2009, and finally the iPad by Apple in 2010. These

e-readers boosted sales in some genres to 60–80 per cent of market share in 2011 (Thompson, 2012). That same year, the turnover from digital music sales accounted for 32 per cent of overall revenue in the global music market, but in some countries (the US, South Korea, and China) this figure exceeded 50 per cent (IFPI, 2012).

Although these data provide us with a telling image of the impact of the digital revolution, they only reveal the aspects that are more visible to the general public. Digital technologies have affected creative industries in all phases in the process of producing creative value. As far as generating creative ideas, there's no longer anything novel about video-artists who use the power of computers. But when David Hockney, one of England's leading painters of figurative art, presents his first exhibit of iPad artwork, this is tangible evidence of a radical change that is underway, even in the more traditional forms of artistic expression. Digital technologies broaden the spectrum of possible forms of creativity, from its very conception.

An equally revolutionary effect can be found on the production phase. Take the publishing sector, for example. Once upon a time writers would use typewriters; then the manuscript had to be transposed into a set of characters for the printing phase, the end result of which were the actual pages of the book. Think about how long this process used to be, and all the possible errors, corrections, and resulting delays, ending with the need to stock finished products. Today instead writers work on laptops, and send the finished files to their editors, who (after standardizing the format) send them to the printer or save them in a digital archive waiting for a request to print on demand.

How much time is saved? How many errors can be avoided? How many costs can be cut?

And what about other sectors like design, or home décor, or jewelry? Here objects are designed in 3D and actually molded with a 3D printer, rapidly creating a prototype that is nearly identical to the finished product in terms of quality.

So in creative industries, digital technologies have revolutionized the entire value chain because the different phases are compressed, and they interface much more efficiently because they share the same communication code. In the past, instead, every phase contained a different code, which had to be translated in order to move forward to the next phase.

In terms of product distribution, digital technologies allow producers to get a global reach for their products. Not long ago, it would have been practically impossible for a South Korean singer to become a global superstar and break the US Top 100 singles chart. Today, early 2015, with more than two billion hits on YouTube to his name, Park Jae-Sang (aka PSY) did just that with his 'Gangnam Style'. The same is true for Moroccan fashion designers, contemporary Indian artists, Nigerian film makers, Ghanian videogame creators. Any consumer in the world who has an internet connection can watch a Thai 'football tennis' match, or Pakistani cricket. Or if she wants to plan her next vacation, she can check out archeological sites in Cambodia or Mauritania; she doesn't need to go to any intermediary for information.

Access to products from creative industries is practically free, making them global by definition. There are two immediate – and opposite – effects of globalization. Today, for every producer of creative goods and services, the potential market is global. Digital technologies make it possible to overcome physical barriers that have always prevented consumers from purchasing or even finding out about certain products. But on the downside, globalization has drastically intensified competition in creative industries. As we saw in the previous section, the variety of creative products is practically infinite, and digital technologies make this infinite variety available to an unbelievable number of potential consumers. Because of this phenomenon, producers find their products competing against other products, but before now they didn't even realize these competitors existed.

If we wanted to sum up in a simple sentence the impact of the digital revolution on creative industries, we could say that for the first time *digitalization has made it possible to separate the content from the format*. While people used to go out and buy CDs, books, clothes, designer goods, or attend a live concert, today they can listen to songs on CDs, smartphones, PCs, or MP3 players. They can read a book in print format, or on an e-reader, or even listen to an audio book. A painter who creates a picture on a PC can print it on paper, canvas, or on fabric, or turn it into an object by using a 3D printer. People can listen to a live concert by going to the event, or by streaming it on one of their hi-tech devices. The content is no longer linked to the format. Different formats simply offer different ways to use a product, and at the origin of the entire process, greater creative freedom in generating new ideas.

1.3.4 Cross-industry dynamics

In 1988, Sony bought out Sony/CBS, a joint venture established in 1968 with CBS, that controlled approximately 20 per cent of the global market of recorded music at that time. Then in 1989 Sony acquired Columbia Pictures Entertainment. These were the first clear signs that two previously separate sectors – hardware and software (content) – were merging into one. In 1994 Sony launched the first *PlayStation*, which triggered the explosion of computer entertainment, reinforcing the conviction that the two sectors could no longer be thought of as distinct. The Sony example is only one of many that can be found in creative industries from the 1990s on.

One of the peculiarities of that decade was the emergence of competitive strategies that didn't apply solely within the confines of a specific industry; instead the aim was to identify growth opportunities that arise from the *blurring of boundaries between industries that were once considered separate*. This trend continued in the 2000s and is ongoing today. Diversification strategies resulting in indistinct industry boundaries is a phenomenon that is particularly apparent in creative industries.

Examples that spring to mind are in the media and entertainment industries, with big companies like Time Warner, Disney, or the News Corporation. However, the same is true for other sectors. The museum and exhibit industry has always been separate from the world of fashion. But now it has become a common occurrence for great contemporary art museums to host retrospectives of famous fashion designers, and companies like Gucci and Ferragamo have their own corporate museums. Or other fashion houses like Cartier and Prada have set up their own foundations to promote contemporary art. All these undertakings make it harder to raise barriers between the two industries. What's more, when the museum of FC Barcelona (the city's world class football team) draws more visitors than any other attraction in the city, it's clear that the line between sports, exhibits, and tourism is a tricky one to draw.

Creative industries represent contexts where blurry boundaries between different sectors can generate promising growth opportunities. There are two reasons for this, as we've discussed above. The first is the aestheticization process of daily life, which turns products from creative industries into invaluable symbolic resources for individuals. A firm or institution that can boast a portfolio covering various product categories in diverse creative contexts is an organization that can provide consumers a broad offering platform to support individual aesthetic projects. This capacity reinforces the organization's reputation as an important agent in the world of symbolic value production.

The second reason is the separation of content and format, made possible by digital technology. An organization that offers valuable creative content for consumers has the chance to increase the return on the investments it makes in creating content by using a variety of distribution channels. Therefore, controlling channels is a way to secure a significant competitive advantage, eroding the separations between different industries.

Summing up, then, the rise in the economic impact of creative industries, which can be seen from their growing weight in the global economy, essentially depends on the capacity of the creative economy to do two things: to provide organizations with better growth opportunities than other industries, and to supply individuals with a set of symbolic resources that is particularly suited to the needs of today's postmodern society.

1.4   CONCLUSIONS

My aims in this chapter were three. First, in order to propose a model for marketing management that works for creative industries I needed to provide a definition of those industries. But my point in doing so was not to come up with a rigid classification; instead my definition has a heuristic value. In other words, it serves to reach my second objective: to identify the specificities that distinguish creative industries from non-creative industries.

These specificities serve as a litmus test to determine whether or not the marketing management model I propose is effective for an organization that operates in a creative industry. This model will make it possible to design and implement marketing strategies that are suited to the unique characteristics of the market contexts that typify these industries.

My final aim was to highlight the reasons why creative industries are taking on greater economic relevance, because these reasons also represent vectors that impact the internal dynamics of the production and consumption systems that will characterize these industries in the years to come.

My focus in the next chapter is to describe the specificities of the process of value production in creative industries. These specificities will serve to delineate both the role of marketing in these contexts, and the features of the resulting marketing management model that is consistent with these processes.

REVIEW QUESTIONS

1. Which is the role of creativity in determining the main characteristics of a creative industry?
2. What are the characteristics distinguishing a creative industry from a non-creative one?
3. Creative industries produce experience goods. Which effects does the 'experience' quality of products have on the functioning of a creative industry?
4. Why are creative industries increasingly important in contemporary societies?
5. What are the impacts of the digital revolution on the production and consumption of creative products?

CASE STUDY

MATADERO MADRID: WHERE CREATIVITY CONNECTS PRODUCTION AND CONSUMPTION

Matadero Madrid was born in 2006 as a new metropolitan cultural center, a place for art, culture, and leisure. This structure is housed in what was formerly the city slaughterhouse (*matadero* in Spanish), located just south of the center in the Arganzuela quarter. Thanks to this location Matadero Madrid extends the center and fosters urban renewal in the southern part of the city, forging a fascinating inner-city space for abundant flows of residents and tourists who visit the center every day.

Since its foundation, Matadero Madrid has acted as an urban, social, and cultural catalyst for the city, an opportunity for Madrid to strengthen its cultural offering. The project has taken a multidisciplinary approach from the very start, overcoming the typical barriers erected around different art forms, including performing arts, cinema, music, design, architecture, urban and landscape planning.

In fact, the mission of Matadero Madrid centers on promoting all forms of artistic expression, with a distinct accent on the dialogue between different arts. To fulfill this mission, the institution focuses on three main areas of action:

1. *Artistic production,* by promoting interdisciplinary creation and experimentation through information, training, studio space, workshops, and laboratories.
2. *Dissemination, communication, and exhibits of the cultural offering* in an international circuit, by giving artists (especially emerging artists) an appropriate context for creating and presenting their work.
3. *Training and research*, by offering didactic activities and workshops open to all fields of culture.

The institution's mission entails the interrelation and reciprocal contamination of diverse art forms. There are two reasons behind this orientation. The first is that the culture of the management team that runs the institution is embedded in pluralism and diversity. The second is more practical: Matadero Madrid is enormous, covering nearly 200,000 square meters, so the institution needs to exploit a vast space.

The aspiration of Matadero Madrid is to constitute a true benchmark for contemporary art, at both a national and international level. In light of this ambition, the center takes on the role of guarantor of multiculturality and interculturality, reflecting the soul of Madrid, which is nourished by cultural diversity. The institution strives to serve as a permanent venue for creativity and diversity – social and cultural as well as artistic.

Matadero Madrid is developing groundbreaking initiatives in collaboration with other cultural institutions all over the globe. (The newly-opened space for artistic creation in Paris dubbed Le 104, the Delfina Foundation in London, the Lieu Unique in Nantes are only a few.) Some locations are part of a network of contemporary art centers which are all renovated slaughterhouses – including Macro-Mattatoio in Rome, Les Abattoirs in Toulouse, Arena Wein in Vienna, and MARTadero in Cochabamba, Bolivia.)

The building and its history

The old slaughterhouse is one of the most singular and fascinating industrial buildings of twentieth century Madrilenian architecture. It was built between 1910 and 1925, and used as a storehouse for food during the two world wars. In 1987, the building was converted into a space dedicated to socio-cultural activities; in 1990 the area became the Headquarters for the Ballet Nacional de España. Finally in 1996 the former slaughterhouse closed down entirely.

After it was abandoned, local associations stepped up and demanded they be allowed to use the rooms in the building for social and cultural activities. They protested against the reconversion project promoted by the city that would have granted rights to this public property to a private operator who planned to renovate the site. In 2003, a new municipal administration opted instead to reverse the strategy for the area and make the reconversion of the slaughterhouse a cornerstone in the program to recover the historical patrimony of Madrid, within the framework of a revitalization plan for the southern part of the city.

Madrid's City Council Department of Art decided that the conversion would center on a huge laboratory for creating and producing contemporary art. The official promoter of the project was the City of Madrid, flanked by a number of other public and private institutions. Matadero Madrid site was officially reborn in 2006, but reconversion activities are not yet finalized and the project is still in progress.

The recovery program for the space benefited from input from world-famous architects, designers, and artists from various disciplines. All of them are from Madrid, to strengthen once again the vital connection between Matadero Madrid and the city. The architect Arturo Franco took the lead in renovating the hall (sala Paseo de la Chopera) and the *Intermediae* (described below), restyled with the use of iron and glass. The theater director Mario Gas, in collaboration with the designer Jean Guy Lecat and other professionals (artists and architects) worked on the Naves del Español project. The guiding principles in this project were reversibility, flexibility, and versatility: new elements and materials were introduced (polycarbonate, for example) and combined with existing ones to spawn a polymorph and polyform space.

The Central de Diseño project, on the other hand, is the fruit of an initiative by José Antonio García Roldán, who united recycled and recyclable materials, using removable polycarbonate for the illuminated walls, secondhand industrial laminates for the flooring, and galvanized iron. I have mentioned only a few of the artists who have been involved in the recovery and renewal process over time. But my point is not to list them all, but rather to underscore the multidisciplinary approach along with an openness to plurality and contamination, values that are encoded in the institution's DNA and rooted in its modus operandi. Matadero Madrid pursues diversity and contamination not only through the activities it promotes, but also in the very spaces that host these activities.

Target audience

Matadero Madrid targets two main audiences: artists and consumers. Artists are quite a heterogeneous target, consisting of a high number of young emerging creative minds along with veterans who have worked at Matadero Madrid for years now. The aim is to provide structures and tools to encourage artistic production, and then to display this work to the public. 'Structure' refers to work space and work tools, venues and exhibition opportunities; 'tools' are all the different types of operational support (networks, professional services, and so forth) that allow artists to share their production with third parties (normally the public).

For example, the institution supplies training courses in art. Over time, Matadero Madrid has also established a management workshop to support artists, a place where they can learn useful financial notions such as how to write up an invoice and how to organize and develop a project.

Another key objective for Matadero Madrid is to export Madrilenean artists all over the world; at the same time the institution is committed to bringing foreign artists to Madrid, promoting integration and commingling with local artists. To achieve this objective the management team has set up accommodation inside Matadero Madrid that serves as living quarters for resident artists. In the spring of 2013, for example, Matadero Madrid hosted several Turkish artists who were invited to collaborate on an artistic project culminating in a show for the public based on their country. Finally, the institution has a tradition of offering scholarships for artists, to promote their professional growth and artistic production.

As for consumers, Matadero Madrid is meant to be seen as a cultural center oriented toward quite a heterogeneous public. The aim is to open up to the entire population (local and non-local), supplying spaces and activities that allow individuals complete freedom of experience. Matadero Madrid is planning to offer a varied series of cultural activities, from the late morning until the late evening, complemented by a set of accessory services, such as bars and restaurants. The idea is to motivate the local population to spend time at Matadero Madrid, even if they don't know what's on the daily schedule and or what specific activity they might be interested in. In this sense, Matadero Madrid becomes a gathering place where people can meet, offering things to do and a place to do them.

As we've said Matadero Madrid's public is quite heterogeneous and in fact the structure offers diversified products for children, young people, and adults. The audience can participate in the institution's activities somewhat passively, by simply looking at an exhibit or listening to a concert. But whoever feels the inclination to be more active can get involved in weekly workshops, special individual initiatives, laboratories, and collective activities.

CREATIVE CONTENTS IN CREATIVE CONTAINERS

The plan to reconvert the old slaughterhouse impacts an enormous area which is divided into sectors A, B, and C. Sector A isn't entirely renovated, but the remaining sectors (B and C, nearly 150,000 square meters) house spaces used for a wide range of purposes. As mentioned above, the activities offered are quite varied, to respond to the needs of myriad users. Here's a description of the different products and services that the institution offers, along with the intended audience for each one.

Casa del Lector. This is a specially designated reading area, where readers of all ages can mingle with professional writers. The *Casa del Lector* hosts numerous events: exhibitions, conferences, educational courses, workshops, music, film, and stage arts series, all responding to the objective of educating readers in focusing, understanding, interpreting, and sharing written texts.

Central de Diseño. Run by the Fundación Diseño Madrid, promoted by the Association of Madrid Designers (DIMAD) via the DIMAD Foundation, the aspiration of this center is to take the lead in promoting national and international design, including graphic design, product design, and spatial design. Since November 2007, the *Central de Diseño* has been located in Nave 17, renovated by the architect José Antonio Roldán. The center hosts national and international artists and seeks to satisfy the needs of the city and all its residents.

Cineteca. This cinema offers almost exclusively non-fiction film, in pursuit of its mission to become 'the Mecca of the documentary film genre in Madrid'. It's open to a wide audience, adults and young people alike.

Nave 16. With nearly 6000 square meters of floor space, Nave 16 is intended to be the largest, most exciting multi-purpose exhibition space in the city. Its versatility makes it home to various kinds of presentations, major events, concerts, workshops, live performances, and social activities. Artists from a variety of fields present one-shot works and/or temporary exhibitions. The offering of Nave 16 targets a vast audience, local and non-local.

Intermediae. This experimental program consists of a hands-on laboratory open to the public. The aim here is to get both artists and the public involved in a process of collaborative artistic experimentation based on dialogue and co-creation, all centering on proactive participation of the public (children, young people, and adults).

Naves del Español. This space, run by the Teatro Español through the public company Madrid Destino, was designed by the artist Jean Guy Lecat. It houses three highly flexible interconnected areas which can function independently. Nave 12 is the foyer or entrance to the building, and has a reception desk and a cafeteria; here small shows can be performed. Nave 11 was designed with an eye to flexibility, allowing the staging of multiple shows. And finally Nave 10 hosts Room 2, covering 2500 square meters, which opened its doors in September 2010 with the premier of 'El Proyecto Youkali' by Miguel del Arco.

Nave de Música. This space hosts the whole of the music offering of the center. It's a veritable musical village for artists, equipped with a radio station, a professional recording studio, nine practice rooms, and other features. The Nave de Música also hosts concerts in conjunction with some of the main music events in Spain. The Nave de Música guarantees facilities and instruments for young emerging artists with the aim of encouraging dialogue and facilitating the hybridization of various artistic disciplines.

Matadero Madrid also offers several social spaces (bars and restaurants), where people can sit down, eat, read, relax. There's a main street (calle Matadero) and a central square (Plaza Matadero), along with areas used for major events or simply as urban gathering places. The institution also makes research and reference areas available to the public (Archivo Documenta, Archivo Matadero), housing vast collections destined for both experts and the general public alike. The structure also offers natural spaces where people can admire the beauty of nature and develop a green culture by participating in a series of activities (Avant Garden and Deposito de Espices).

The organizational model

Diversity, the institution's distinguishing trait, also emerges in its governance model: Matadero Madrid is founded on intense cooperation between the public and private sectors. These dual sources of support guarantee a degree of independence in defining the business plan and making artistic decisions.

The heart of the institution is public, as it's sponsored and financed by the City of Madrid, but its soul is made up of a multitude of private entities (IFEMA, Fondazione Germàn Sànchez Ruipèrez, among others), which represent sources of third-party funding devoted to architectural renovation and cultural projects. Some joint ventures with third parties have become constants (Fundación Diseño Madrid, Fundación Germán Sánchez Ruipérez, Red Bull Spain, to name a few).

An example here is the *Casa del Lector*. The main room has 3,000 square meters of floor space, with other smaller exhibition areas, a number of classrooms set up as laboratories, and an enormous auditorium. The entire area is privately owned, sold to the Fundación Germán Sánchez Ruipérez, which enjoys total autonomy in managing its content. The foundation organizes courses, master classes, workshops, and events, supported by Matadero Madrid only in designing and delivering communication content.

Another impressive example is the *Red Bull Music Academy*. The partnership between *Red Bull* and Matadero Madrid began a few years ago almost by chance, when at the last minute the company needed to relocate the music event of the year, which was originally planned for Tokyo but then cancelled due to the 2011 earthquake. In light of the success of the event, *Red Bull* and Matadero Madrid began a permanent collaboration, managing the institution's musical offering, mostly hosted at Nave de Música. The joint venture between the two organizations satisfies the needs of emerging and established artists as well as audiences, providing the first with the spaces and instruments they need to work, and the second with concerts, laboratories, and countless music projects.

Another noteworthy example is the *Central de Diseño*, a space managed by the Fundación Diseño Madrid (DIMAD), thanks to an agreement with the city of Madrid. This collaboration between the two institutions tasks DIMAD with disseminating, promoting, and developing the culture of design and its myriad manifestations through exhibits and events, and training and services for designers and companies. With an average of around 20,000 visitors a month, a number that's constantly rising, the relationship is clearly effective and profitable.

In all the forms of collaboration described above, Matadero Madrid's partner companies and institutions generate and later manage activities with some level of autonomy. Matadero Madrid, with its official communication, takes on publicizing the programs and handling public relations with key stakeholders. The main communication tools it uses are online posts and banners, usually on small local sites; posters in key areas of the city (Callao, one of the most popular squares in the center); flyers distributed throughout the city; and the Matadero Madrid Web site.

Matadero Madrid's business plan calls for the City of Madrid to take on all the structural costs and to contribute to extraordinary expenses. All the activities proposed by Matadero Madrid are funded directly from operating income (coming from ticket sales, commercial activities, and so forth) and by the institution's patrons. Future orientation is leaning toward progressively growing the pool of private patrons. This would guarantee greater financial security in times of economic crisis. With increased private funding, Matadero Madrid could also continue to offer low-cost or even free activities, to ensure that people don't stop consuming culture.

REVIEW QUESTIONS

1. Matadero Madrid is an art center devoted to many art forms. What are the advantages of this multidisciplinarity? Any disadvantages?

2. Blurring the barriers between production and consumption is a distinctive trait of Matadero Madrid. What are the positive effects of this choice?

3. Matadero Madrid has very peculiar governance and organizational systems. What are the benefits they provide and what are the potential weaknesses?

Chapter 2

A CUSTOMER-CENTRIC MARKETING MODEL FOR CREATIVE INDUSTRIES

LEARNING OBJECTIVES

After reading this chapter you should be able to:

- Understand the network structure of value production in creative industries.
- Tap into the fundamental role of customer experience in value creation.
- Detail the role of marketing in creative industries.
- Identify the participative role of consumers in production processes.
- Identify the role of critics and experts in value creation.

OVERVIEW

Marketing deals with the relationships between an economic actor and the markets in which this actor operates. In its inception and early development, the focal point of this discipline was the firm. But gradually marketing knowledge expanded to encompass other entities as well, such as non-profits, individuals, and organizations that do not operate in competitive market contexts. So broadly speaking, we can define marketing as a set of knowledge regarding ways in which economic actors manage their relationships with their markets (mainly consisting of customers and competitors).

As this knowledge has evolved, both general and specific principles have taken form. The former hold true for any kind of organization; the latter are more applicable to specific market contexts (for example, services marketing or business to business marketing) or single sectors (marketing in health services, marketing of commodities, and so forth). What becomes apparent from this description is that the specificities of production processes and product usage call for an

adaptation of general marketing principles, or, in some cases, even ad hoc marketing concepts and models.

Following this line of reasoning, my aim in this book is to propose and describe a marketing model tailored to the specific features of production and consumption processes in creative industries. This chapter gives a general overview of the components of this model, which I'll detail in the chapters to follow.

In developing my model, the subject I have in mind is an organization (a firm or a non-profit), not an individual. Admittedly, individual creativity is the lifeblood of value creation in creative industries. But despite this, my attention focuses on the organizations that integrate various factors that generate creative value to be subsequently sold on the market. In other words, I'm not thinking of the painter, but the gallery or museum that exhibits her work; not the musician, but the record company that produces and distributes his songs, or the venue where he performs; not the individual basketball player but the company that manages her team; not the writers of a television series but the television company that slots that series into its primetime lineup. In this book, I often refer to creative individuals, but I always focus on the organization.

To begin this chapter, in my attempt to come up with an effective marketing model, I'll answer two questions. First: How is value generated in creative industries? According to the contemporary view of the discipline, marketing is about generating and distributing value to customers (Day, 1999; Kotler and Keller, 2011; Webster, 2002). In fact, many kinds of value can be generated in an industry beyond value for the customer: value for shareholders, value for the local or national community, and so on. After clarifying the specificities of the value generation processes in creative industries, I will formulate a marketing model that more effectively responds to the specific needs of organizations that do operate in these contexts.

Second question: Who decides what is and isn't valuable in creative industries? Whether it's a work of art, a television program, a volleyball team, a designer object, or any other creative product, we can consider at least four different perspectives when determining value: the creator of the product; other creators of similar products (peers); people with special experience or competence on the product (experts, critics, specialists); and customers who use the product, and who as a group represent the product's market.

Keeping in mind our answer to the first question, the marketing perspective (the one I've adopted in this book) is the customer's perspective. Put another way, in taking a marketing view, we're acknowledging that *the value of a creative product is determined by its customers*. Clearly, this doesn't mean that other perspectives (those of creators, peers, experts) carry no weight at all. In fact, they are essential to generating value for customers, in particular because of the constant, dynamic interaction among these different viewpoints. But following the tenets of marketing, to decide what is and isn't valuable in creative industries, the viewpoint we need to consider is (as in all industries) the customer's, with all the ambiguities, limitations, and preconceptions that go with it.

Summing up, the marketing model I propose here and describe in detail in later chapters will focus on the organization (whether a firm or non-profit) that produces or combines creative factors of production and sells them on the market. As far as determining what is and isn't valuable, I defer to the opinion of consumers of creative products.

2.1 VALUE PRODUCTION PROCESSES IN CREATIVE INDUSTRIES

Picture a girl walking down any street, in any country of the world, listening to Rihanna's latest hit on her mp3 player. Now I haven't given a definition of customer value yet, but whatever it may be, we can safely assume that if this girl is listening to this song, it must have some value for her. And since the song is a creative product, we can further assume that its value comes from its creative content. This brings us to our next question: What is the source of that creative content? Is it simply Rihanna singing that particular song?

It's true that Rihanna's voice is what resonates for listeners, and the lyrics are what inspire their imaginations. But if we rewind just a moment, and go back to the various creative phases involved in music making, we come to realize that Rihanna actually plays a very small part in the whole process. Seabrook (2012) gives a detailed description of the number and kind of creative actors who are engaged in making the song that will end up being performed by Rihanna. Key players in this process are *topliners* and *music producers*.

Music producers compose the backing track, set the beat, and arrange the instrumentals. Topliners create the song's more distinctive features: the melodies, and more importantly the *hooks* – riffs that hook listeners and become the song's identifiers. In fact, this is where the topliners' work begins. They first create the hooks, then try them out in the recording studio, and once they've found the right ones they move on to the rest of the song, with the hooks interspersed along the way. Working with the music producers, the topliners compose the remaining lyrics and then the instrumental tracks (taken from a enormous repertoire of samples). Next the backing track is added and the end result is the final demo. The whole process normally takes no more than a few hours. Once the music producers are convinced they've come up with an interesting demo, they pass it on to a singer who decides whether or not to buy the rights and record a definitive version.

So going back to the question about the source of creative content that represents value for the girl listening to the Rihanna song, clearly the reality of music making is much more complex than we might initially think. And the process doesn't end here. Let's fast forward to what happens after the final version of the song is cut.

This finished product debuts in the form of a videoclip on YouTube and on music television channels; the song circulates among radio stations, and DJs present it and critique it based on their musical taste and personal perceptions. Rihanna gives interviews on television, on the radio, and in magazines, talking about what the song means to her, why she chose to record it, how it makes her feel. People will dance to the song in discos and at parties. All the actors who make various contributions to this one song provide the girl who's listening with a series of stimuli, information, interpretations. All this taken together creates value, which is what prompted her to download the song onto her mp3 player in the first place.

My point in this brief description of the creative process of music making is to highlight two specificities of value production in creative industries, both of which impact marketing:

- Value in creative industries is the fruit of the creative contribution of a network of actors.
- From the customer's perspective, this value is experiential because it is always a fruit of the consumption experience.

2.1.1   The network of value, the value of the network

Normally the process of value production in an industry is represented by the value chain model (Porter, 1985), which illustrates the sequence of phases in the production process of goods or services, ending when they are utilized by the final consumer. Briefly, there are four value chains that together form the larger value chain of any given industry: the supplier value chain, the producer value chain, the distributor value chain, and the user value chain.

Every firm, in turn, has its own value chain, which is made up of the single phases in the production process that generates its product or service. Porter (1985) calls these phases *primary activities*: incoming logistics, production, outgoing logistics, marketing and sales, and post-sale services. These are combined with *support activities*, which supply resources for primary activities: infrastructure management (offices, facilities, factories); human resource management; technological development; purchasing management.

The traditional model of the value chain has three limitations that make it ineffectual in representing value production in creative industries (and today quite possibly in other industries as well):

- The sequence of the phases is linear.
- The roles of the actors are separate and distinct.
- The focus lies on transactions involving tangible items.

The reason behind these three limitations is one and the same. The model was created with physical production processes in mind, based on the industrial metaphor of the *supply chain*, by which a series of operators add components and services in sequence, and the finished product is the end result. Let's examine these three limitations individually.

2.1.1.1   *Non-linear value production processes*

In creative industries, value production processes can't be represented as linear. To illustrate this, let's take another

look at Rihanna's hit. Just who are the suppliers and who are the producers? From the value chain view, Rihanna (or better still her record company) appears to be the producer, seeing as she assembles various creative inputs; so the topliners and music producers must be suppliers. But we could also assert the exact opposite. In fact, since topliners and producers are the ones who are mainly responsible for creating the song, we can label them as the producers and Rihanna as the 'vocal' supplier.

What's more, can we distinguish between a 'before' and an 'after' in value production? Not very easily, it would seem. In creative industries, it would make more sense to interpret and illustrate value production processes as the simultaneous contributions of a *system* of actors in an organized network; it is the cooperation and integration of these actors that generates value for the customer (Becker, 1982). So, instead of a value chain, what we have is a *value network*. Figure 2.1 shows a possible representation of the value network of the music industry.

The value network model is a more accurate depiction of the interaction that takes place among various actors; it's the combination and integration of these actors which generate value for the final customer. In our musical example, the hooks created by the topliners, the backing tracks arranged by the music producers, and the performance by Rihanna – all these elements taken together bring the creative content to life. And it's this content which has value for the listener. Every actor in the network serves as an integrator of resources and a co-creator of the final value (Lusch et al., 2010). Put another way, all these people recombine their own talent and creative competences with the talents and creative competences of other actors to produce content that provides value to their customers.

At this point, we might wonder if there's any difference between Rihanna and her topliners, and the music producers who work with them. In terms of co-creating creative value, the answer is no, there's not, except for the specific contribution of each one (the hooks, the instrumentals, the voice). The real difference lies in their customers. The customers of topliners and music producers are singers like Rihanna (and the record companies who produce their songs). For Rihanna and other singers, customers are music consumers (like the girl who's listening on her mp3 player). So all these actors integrate their creative resources with an eye to the customers they want to serve, and, at the same time, they participate in the

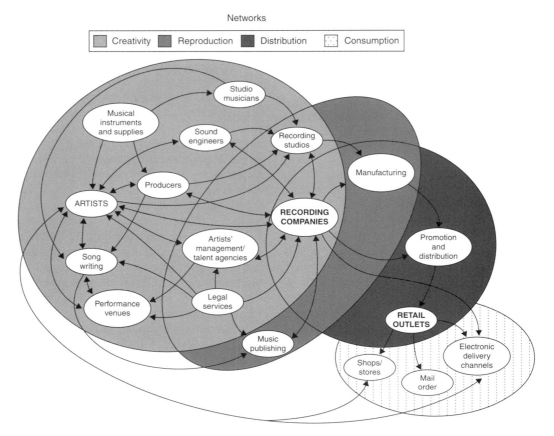

Figure 2.1 – The value network in the music industry
Source: Leyshon (2001: 61)

process of co-creating value for the customers of the other actors in the network.

Obviously, this is true not only for the music business, but for any creative industry. Here's another example: a personal exhibit of a young visual artist, organized by an art gallery with a reputation for spotlighting young up-and-coming talent; the exhibit is presented with a catalogue edited by an art critic who describes both the artistic development of the artist and the inspiration behind each individual piece. What is the source of value for the visitor? From our discussion above, it should be clear that value is co-created by the talent of the artist, expressed through his works; the expertise of the critic who helps the visitor appreciate these works thanks to her commentary in the catalogue; and the reputation of the gallery that has singled out the young artist a future success. In other words, it's the network that generates value.

2.1.1.2   Indistinguishable roles

The traditional value chain model assumes that the roles that various actors play in the value production process are essentially separate and distinct, and that the actors in one phase transfer the results of their activities to the actors in the next phase, and so on down the line. If we follow the chain, then, suppliers transfer factors of production to producers; producers provide finished products to distributors; and distributors make these products available to end users, in a given time and space. However, in creative industries, where value is co-created by myriad actors in a network, it's extremely difficult to distinguish between the separate roles of the actors who contribute to the value production process.

Taking more examples from the music industry, some famous producers of R&B and hip hop, like Dr Dree, Jay-Z, and Timbaland, have become singers in their own right, and they've opened their own recording companies. This means that depending on the project at hand, they play different roles in the different phases of recording and distributing a song or CD. As another example, Live Nation, a global leader in concert venue management, has recently become a recording company that produces and distributes music, tours, and merchandising for performers like Jay-Z (with the label RocNation, which the artist co-owns), Madonna, U2, and Shakira.

Moving beyond the music industry, it's become common practice for theaters and opera houses to produce their own shows and host shows by other companies, serving as both producers and distributors. Likewise, art museums curate exhibits and then send them 'on tour', to be displayed in other museums. From the perspective of a network of value, theaters, museums, and the like play different roles at different times, during various phases of value production, activating an array of relationships with the other actors in the network.

The real innovation in recent years is that users themselves are becoming more and more proactive as far as producing and distributing creative content. Consumers, who at one time simply used creative products and services, now actively co-produce content and co-create value. (This is a topic I'll explore further in Section 2.3.) So going back to the girl listening to Rihanna, she can share the music video with her friends via Youtube, actively distributing creative content. Or, she can comment on a Rihanna fan blog, actively communicating creative content – and creative value – for other potential consumers. Last, if she has the technical skills, she can remix the song and make a mashup with other tunes, producing completely new creative content.

To sum up, value in creative industries is co-created by all the different actors in the network, and the configuration of their roles can't be clearly compartmentalized. What's more, actors can play a number of roles at the same time in the process of value production for a creative product, or they can play different roles for different creative products.

2.1.1.3 *Integration of tangibles and intangibles*

In creative industries, the value generated within a network is the outcome of the exchange and integration of both tangible and intangible elements. The value chain model, instead, focuses exclusively on tangibles: factor of productions, finished products, and monetary payments.

In any firm, both primary and support activities produce goods or services that generate costs. By adding up all the costs of all these activities, the firm calculates the total product cost. This figure serves as an indicator for the final retail price, which must be higher than the total cost to generate margins and profits. But as we can see, the value chain model is incapable of factoring in transactions of intangible elements which take place among various actors in the sequence of phases, and among members of individual firms (Allee, 2008).

In any sector, the position of actors (producers, distributors, consumers) doesn't depend solely on their economic capital but also on their social and symbolic capital:

- *Economic capital* refers to available financial resources which allow a firm to invest in developing technology and market relationships and to hire highly skilled personnel who facilitate value production. Likewise, a consumer who has sizeable financial resources has access to higher-value goods and services.

- But there are other important kinds of capital to consider as well. *Social capital*, for instance, refers to the quantity and quality of an actor's formal and informal relationships with others. This kind of capital secures access to intangible resources for the firm, such as confidential information or quality knowledge. Both these resources facilitate the development of skills and know-how, and increase the organization's chances of capturing market opportunities. Likewise, consumers who have a wide array of social relationships will also have access to information and knowledge that facilitate the development of their own.

- The third kind of capital is *symbolic capital*, which encompasses aspects like the reputation and prestige an actor enjoys among his or her peers. This form of capital also provides ready access to intangible resources (again, like information and knowledge) that enable organizations to take on quality human resources and to capitalize on certain market opportunities. Here again we can draw parallels with consumers. In fact, a person with a good reputation among her peers has the chance to attract social relationships and build up her own competences and knowledge. And again, the value chain model is incapable of reflecting these flows of intangibles, because more often than not no monetary transaction is involved.

○ *The impact of social and symbolic capital in creative industries.* In creative industries, social and symbolic capital carry substantial weight. For example, in the book business, the top publishers with ample financial resources can afford to pay generous advances and attract high-caliber writers. At the other end of the market, however, small publishing houses may enjoy substantial social and symbolic capital that allow them to leverage what Thompson (2010) calls the 'economy of favors'. In other words, these publishers can take advantage of cost savings by cooperating with one another, sharing information (on individual authors or general market performance, for example) that they would otherwise have to purchase from market researchers. Also, small imprints can attract writers who are less interested in monetary compensation than the prestige that would come from being taken on by highly reputable publisher, however small. We can easily imagine similar scenarios in many other creative industries.

In light of the unique features of creative products, an essential element in creative industries is the exchange of intangible resources by actors with social and symbolic capital. In fact, as we saw in Chapter 1, creative products are *experience* products with *high horizontal differentiation* and which are *socially positioning*. Now let's look at each of these aspects individually.

First of all, because of their high horizontal differentiation, the value of these products can only be established subjectively, not objectively, based on the individual taste of the consumer. In any case, the value an organization offers depends on the creative competences it can tap. Here's where social and symbolic capital come into play: organizations with these assets are able to leverage the relationships they've established. In doing so, they can attract top quality creative resources, enter value networks with a higher chance of success, and enjoy a greater likelihood of achieving a horizontal differentiation that intersects with consumer preferences.

For example, let's imagine a publishing house that employs editors who have close relationships with prominent literary agents (social capital) and who enjoy respectable reputations (symbolic capital). These editors will most likely be the first people the agents approach when promoting promising new writers. This guarantees the publishing house the chance to replenish its catalogue and continually offer new products. The same thing can happen with a world-class football

team. Thanks to close ties with junior teams, this top team can spot rising stars among young up-and-coming players. Or if a tour operator has invested in stable relationships with local tour guides, it can get recommendations on new itineraries before its competitors.

As for the second aspect, creative products are experience products. Again, what this means is that consumers can't easily anticipate the quality of these products before they actually use them (Section 1.2.2). This characteristic has numerous repercussions, including the fact that consumers look for quality clues and rely on various sources of feedback (other consumers, experts, media).

The reputation of the actors involved in the value creation network is also highly influential because it becomes a substitute for product quality. Consequently, the actors who lay claim to greater social and symbolic capital have more valuable intangible resources to exchange. These exchanges, in turn, enhance the reputation of the actors themselves, with two beneficial effects. First, reputation turns into a quality clue that consumers associate with the products offered by these actors. Second, an enhanced reputation reinforces their role as *value agents* providing points of reference as consumers gather and interpret information. All this translates into an advantage over competing products and actors.

To illustrate this idea, let's take the example of a design magazine with strong relationships with the world's top designers and design firms. By leveraging its social capital, the magazine can publish articles that its readership will find insightful and informative. In addition, this magazine will become a source of 'insider' information for consumers looking for quality clues that help them when choosing which products to purchase.

Now we come to the third characteristic of creative products, the fact that they are socially positioning. Put another way, these products provide strong signals as to the tastes, opinions, and preferences of the people who own them or who can talk knowledgeably about them in a social setting. Obviously, the relative positioning value depends a great deal on the social and symbolic capital of the producer and the product itself.

With producers who have bad reputations (limited symbolic capital) their products won't offer much in the way of positioning value. On the contrary, by leveraging prestigious, reputable products, owners can establish their positions within their social networks. In this case, the product becomes a symbolic resource in every sense of the word for the consumer, who in turn will be more willing to provide information and knowledge to the producer, and give positive feedback on the product when chatting and socializing with friends.

All this sets in motion a flow of transactions of intangible resources between producer and consumer, and among consumers. This flow feeds and reinforces reciprocal social and symbolic capital, and is essential to generating value. But since these transactions are not economic ones, they aren't depicted by the value chain model. Consequently, a significant portion of value generation in creative industries is neglected.

In conclusion, value in creative industries is co-created by myriad actors in networks, actors whose roles to some extent overlap. What's more, the contribution of these actors, and their consequent power within the network, doesn't depend exclusively on the exchange of tangibles (products and services) that increase their economic capital, but also on the exchange of intangibles (information, knowledge, favors, opportunities) that enhance and reinforce their social and symbolic capital.

2.1.2 The experience of value, the value of experience

Let's go back once more to the girl listening to the Rihanna song. This time, though, let's imagine that she's not walking down the street. She's relaxing on the couch instead. Or she's studying, with the song playing in the background. Or she's dancing at the disco. It's the same song every time, but what value does it have for the girl? Leaving aside the definition of value for the customer a little while longer, let's imagine asking the girl what she thinks of the song in each of the scenarios above. Since it's always the same song, her answer should always be the same. But more than likely it won't be. In fact, the girl will probably have something different to say about the song in each of the different situations. In other words, it all depends on her user experience.

So basically, *the value of a creative product is experienced through the consumption of that product*. This means three things. First, without consumption there can be no value; second, different consumption experiences of the same product provide the consumer with different values; third, it is the consumer who decides whether or not a product has value.

I've dedicated most of Chapter 3 to analyzing the consumption experience, so here I'll only mention a few things that allow us to more accurately describe value production processes in creative industries. For many years, market transactions were based on the assumption that the value of a product is determined by the price a customer is willing to pay for it. It follows then that product value is equal to purchase value. Marketing, on the other hand, has always asserted that the economic value of a product is only one component of its overall value. In fact, the true value that a customer gets from a product is the value that derives from using the product, both in functional terms (performance) and symbolic terms (aesthetic, affective, and social value).

As I said, we'll explore all this more fully in Chapter 3, but for now what we need to remember is that *without product use, there is no product value*. So it's the consumption of the product that determines its value. This affirmation is particularly pertinent for creative products, given that they are experience products, as we know. Only if a consumer experiences the product by using it can she appreciate its quality and decide on its value. So once again, no product experience means no product value.

2.1.2.1 *The components of consumer experience*

But there are a variety of ways to consume a product, as we saw with the girl in the example above. Put another way, a product can be used in different situations and consumption contexts. For example, consumption can take place individually or collectively, in-home or out-of-home, in the one-shot or continuous, occasionally or repeatedly. These factors, among others, determine the context in which the consumer uses the product, and they impact product value. To sum up, a product experience always consists of a triad of components: the consumer, the product, and the context. Therefore, if the consumption context changes, so does the value of the product for the consumer.

From the consumer's point of view, as Schmitt (1999) suggests, experience always engages different spheres: sensorial (listening to a song), cognitive (understanding the lyrics and thinking about their meaning), emotional (feeling pleasure while listening), behavioral (dancing to the song), and relational (dancing with other people). Although not all of these spheres need to be stimulated at the same time, the more spheres that are engaged, the richer the experience will be.

As far as product, consumer experience doesn't depend exclusively on the product itself. Instead, in a broader sense, what comes into play are all the different components that are in any way related to the product, components that allow for consumer interaction. Going back to the Rihanna hit, beyond the song itself, consumers can read interviews with Rihanna describing the inspiration behind the song; they can listen to ads on the radio for Rihanna's new CD which features the song; and they can listen to other tracks while they download the song from an online store. If at this point we shift our focus to the firm or non-profit promoting the product, we can see an opportunity to build and enrich the consumption experience through a series of touchpoints with the consumer; the product represents only one component.[1]

Context is the combination of the environment (physical or virtual) and the relationships that provide the setting for the consumption experience. If we take a simplified view of the decision-making process that leads a consumer to buy and use a product, we can distinguish three major areas of context pertaining to product experience: the context in which she gathers information on the product; the context in which she buys the product; and the context in which she consumes the product. The first is a *communication experience*, the second a *purchase experience*, and the third a *consumption experience*.

Think of a recently published book. Reading a review of this book is a very different communication experience than going to a book signing and hearing the author talk about her work. Buying the book online is a very different purchase experience than buying it from a small bookshop run by an expert bookseller. Reading the book on the train on the way to work is a very different consumption experience than reading it while sitting in an armchair in the comfort of one's home. It's the same product every time, but for each experience the circumstance and configuration changes. Yet in every case, the value the consumer attains from the product comes from all these experiences combined.

2.1.2.2   *The customer is the center*

Context, then, is instrumental in determining value, which leads me to my final consideration on the value of experience. *The actor in the network who is most qualified to decide whether or not a product has value is the consumer.* In fact, since value is the fruit of experience, and consumers are the protagonists of that experience, they are the only ones who can determine if a product has value, and what that value is.

In the section above I described a process of value production in creative industries, emphasizing that this process is co-created by a network of value agents. We can reasonably assume that every one of these actors has an opinion on the relative value of a given product, and that this opinion is based on personal competences, beliefs, and inclinations. A writer has an opinion on the value of her book based on the effort she put into writing it; another writer has an opinion on his colleague's book based on his competence as an author and an expert on books; a book critic will have another opinion on the value of the book based on how it measures up to standard literary codes; a publisher's opinion of the value of the book takes into consideration both literary quality and commercial potential, and so on.

Many actors lend a hand in creating the value of that particular book, each playing a different role in the network and contributing with different competences to the creation process. And every one of them will probably have a different opinion on the value of the book, as we've said before. But that's not my point here. Shifting our focus from the presumed 'objective' value of the creative product to the value 'for the customer', obviously the only opinion that counts in determining that value is that of the customer, and of all customers taken together (the entire market).

This said, the actors in the network can contribute to the value that the customer (and the market) assigns to a product thanks to the role they play in the consumption experience (through product features, communication regarding the product, product reviews, the in-store atmosphere where the product is sold). But these actors cannot, and must not, substitute for the consumer in attributing product value.

This brings us to exactly what the Marketing Department in a organization must do: work to ensure that products are conceived, created, communicated, and sold in such a way that consumers associate them with a greater value than competitors' products. We'll explore this more fully in the following sections.

In conclusion, the value of a product in creative industries essentially corresponds to its unique creative content. This value is co-created by a system of actors who are connected in a network of relationships in which tangibles and intangibles are exchanged. Consumers are the ones who decide whether or not a product has value, and what that value is, based on their experience of the product and other relevant factors.

Briefly, creative industries can be represented as two systems that interact dynamically to create value. On one hand, there is a *production system* where a number of different actors work together, integrating their talents and creative competences to come up with a product with creative content.[2] On the other is the *consumption system*, where actors also interact and, after experiencing the product, form an opinion on its value. The production system generates symbolic resources which the consumption system acquires and incorporates into its sense-making processes.

The dividing line between the two systems is not an indelible one. More importantly, this line is continually and dynamically shifting, creating networks with different configurations depending on the product and the experience in question. Specifically, actors within the two systems can take on different roles, from product to product. And more notably, the actors in the consumption system are becoming more directly involved in the production of creative content.

2.2 THE ROLE OF MARKETING IN VALUE PRODUCTION PROCESSES

2.2.1 The concept of customer value

We've come to the point where we need a clearer idea of just what customer value means. Let's imagine asking an opera fan what prompts him to buy a season ticket to his local opera house. We can expect answers such as: 'Listening to live opera is a joyful experience!' 'Every time I hear opera music it takes me back to when I used to go to the opera with my parents as a child.' 'I like going to the opera and meeting the same people who share my love for classical music.' 'Every year the program is different.' But we'll probably also get answers like: 'I don't live far from the opera house so it's easy to get there.' 'They offer first dibs on tickets for season ticket holders from the previous year.' 'They always have delicious canapés at the bar!'

So we'll get a more or less detailed description of a variety of reasons why people choose to buy season tickets to that particular opera house year after year. The nature of these motivations varies: some are more emotional, others more aesthetic, and others still purely utilitarian. But the choice of these consumers is contingent on the fact that the theater offers a combination of things that allow them to satisfy their personal motivations, whatever they may be. And it is precisely this satisfaction that is the source of customer value. Therefore, the first component of this value is *the set of benefits that the organization's offering can provide.*

But as much as consumers might value certain benefits, they are also aware that these benefits don't come free; certain sacrifices must be made. The price of a season ticket is the most obvious one, but there are others that don't necessarily involve spending money, yet they counterbalance the value provided by the benefits in question. These sacrifices include the time it takes to buy a season ticket; the time it takes to get to the opera house for every show; the price of 'extras' (the coat check, the program, the canapés!); and the effort expended to verify whether or not other operas actually turn out to be better.

So basically the second component of customer value is the *set of sacrifices that the customer has to make in order to enjoy the benefits provided by the organization's offering.*

To highlight the dynamic relationship between benefits and sacrifices we can represent the value of the offering O for the customer c as a ratio between these two factors:

$$V_{Oc} = \frac{B_{Oc}}{S_{Oc}}$$

The ratio between benefits and sacrifices underscores a salient point: if sacrifices are excessive, even when benefits are considerable, the overall value of the offering for the customer is diminished. What's more, if benefits and sacrifices grow proportionally, the value offered to the customer over time doesn't change. In fact, the only way to enhance customer value is if there's a greater *increase* in the value of benefits than in the cost of sacrifices, or a greater *decrease* in the cost of sacrifices than the value of benefits. In Chapter 3 we'll detail the different types of sacrifices and benefits, and we'll also discuss how to measure value.

Defining the concept of customer value allows us to profile the role of Marketing in value production processes in creative industries. Broadly speaking, the Marketing Department of an organization is responsible for *representing the customer's viewpoint and ensuring that it is taken into account in value production processes.* Essentially, this means that it's Marketing's job to give direction to the value production processes of the organization (and its network) so that these processes are capable of generating value for the customer. Value takes the form of benefits that are aligned with the expectations customers have, and the sacrifices they are willing to sustain. To make this happen, Marketing has a cultural and managerial role to play within the organization.

2.2.2 Marketing and organizational culture

For a useful definition of organizational culture, we can turn to Deshpande and Webster (1989: 4): 'The pattern of shared values and beliefs that help individuals understand organizational functioning and thus provide them norms for behavior in the organization.' So essentially organizational culture is a set of values and beliefs that translate into management philosophies, which in turn give individuals a sense of membership in the organization and help guide their behaviors. To help clarify the cultural role of marketing, let's compare three management philosophies: market orientation, product orientation, and sales orientation.

2.2.2.1 Market orientation

Market orientation is a management philosophy based on the belief that the main goal of the organization must be *customer satisfaction*, with respect to the organization's performance targets. Essentially this means offering customers superior value to other organizations. Market orientation is anchored on the assumption that whatever the performance targets (for a firm, reaching acceptable profit levels; for a non-profit, realizing its mission), if an organization obtains resources from exchanges in a market context, it is fundamental for it to establish and reinforce relationships with the main actors in that market: customers. Satisfying their needs is the proper way to reinforce these relations.

The positive effect of this reinforcement is two-fold. First, the organization secures a continual and ever-increasing flow of revenues and intangible resources. The reason for this is that satisfied customers are more likely to make repeat purchases from the same organization, and over time they tend to buy more products, even at higher prices. (There is more on this in Chapters 4 and 10.)

Second, if the organization establishes long-term relationships with its customers, it can refine its knowledge of this customer base. This gradually translates into lower costs for serving customers. In fact, the highest costs and biggest investments in terms of customer relations come in the initial phase, learning about customers' needs and attempting to win their loyalty. In the end, having satisfied customers means being able to leverage tangible resources (financial, real estate, technology) and intangible resources (knowledge, reputation, reliability, prestige) more efficiently and effectively. Additionally, profit-oriented organizations can improve their capacity to generate revenues, and non-profits can more productively achieve their institutional goals.

2.2.2.2 Product orientation

Product orientation is the management philosophy that holds that the primary goal of the organization is to *make products and services with excellent intrinsic quality*, which can be measured against standards set by a community of experts (peers, critics, various kinds of specialists). This philosophy is not based on disinterest in the customer or the market; instead the underlying assumption is that a product with excellent intrinsic quality will always have a market, because the market is always capable of recognizing excellence, and consequently an excellent product is guaranteed to generate revenues.

Simply put, the fundamental belief here is that the value offered to customers is essentially equivalent to intrinsic product quality. Yet it is precisely this belief that also represents a major limitation of this orientation. Here is the reason why. When organizations focus primarily on intrinsic quality, consumers' expectations and perceptions move lower on the priority list in relation to production processes, and expert opinions move much higher.

But by ordering their priorities this way, organizations run a huge risk. First of all, as we'll see in the next sections (and in Chapter 3), it's not necessarily true that consumers have the same taste as experts, so they don't share the same experience (Holbrook, 2005). This means there's a chance that customers won't recognize the intrinsic quality of a creative product, so they won't buy it. Second, it isn't necessarily true that consumers buy creative products for their intrinsic quality; instead their motivation to buy might be more influenced by symbolic value (Section 3.1). Consequently, an organization that embraces the principle of qualitative excellence could find itself making excellent products, but finding no one interested in buying them.

It's fairly easy to see that product orientation is common among organizations in many creative industries. Consider artists, authors, stylists, designers, architects, directors, and coaches of sports teams. It's true that the vast majority are highly motivated by market success. But at the same time, they believe that they are the only ones who are capable of giving an accurate assessment of their own work, along with their peers and other experts. For most creative people, the underlying motivation for their creativity lies in the recognition of these experts (Hirschman, 1983). This belief finds an organizational equivalent in firms and institutions in creative sectors that operate under the conviction (and therefore the organizational culture) that the quality of their products can only be fully appreciated by peers and experts, and that the market will follow.

2.2.2.3 Sales orientation

Lastly, sales orientation is the management philosophy that holds that the primary goal of the organization is to *maximize sales*. This is based on the belief that whatever the performance targets, by selling as much as possible the organization can achieve them. With firms, maximizing sales means maximum profits; for non-profits, this approach makes it possible to secure financial resources, and to gain visibility in order to build consensus and attract public attention.

This management philosophy, like the previous one, is not completely disinterested in customers or the market. But the underlying assumption here is that customers don't generally have particular preferences, and that through intensive, insistent sales efforts and communication they can be prompted to purchase products, and purchase more of them. So basically the thinking is that since customers don't have a clear idea of what they want, these strategies can have an enormous impact on their expectations and preferences.

But the basic premises of this philosophy aren't failsafe. First of all, it isn't necessarily true that maximizing sales is a good way to maximize profits or attain institutional goals. To clarify, consider the fact that the most effective tool in maximizing sales is cutting prices. But this strategy would trigger a reduction in unitary margins, which in turn could translate into a decline in total profits.

What's more, maximizing sales in the short term can be detrimental to the perceived product quality.

This would lead to fewer repeat purchases, which again would result in an overall drop in sales, making it impossible to achieve whatever goals the organization may have set.

Another pitfall of this philosophy centers on the assumption that customers don't have clear-cut preferences. This may be true for some sets of customers in some markets, but the current market reality demonstrates the opposite. Today's customers usually have very clear expectations, and often they are not willing to settle for anything less.

Last, the notion that customers can be easily persuaded may have held water a few decades ago, when competition in many markets was limited and channels of communication were not yet over-crowded. But once again in today's markets, there is systematic innovation and a hyper-proliferation of means and messages of communication. This has dramatically reduced the capacity of organizations to influence customers, and what influence they may have depends less and less on sales efforts and communication.

Despite the fact that the management philosophy centered on sales is not very widespread in creative industries, what is prevalent is the belief that marketing people embrace the culture of sales. In other words, in organizations that do operate in creative industries, especially those with a product orientation, while the rest of the organization creates the products, the Marketing Department is often tasked with selling. This connotation can be traced back to the origins of the marketing domain, which initially encompassed sales activities, and in some cases advertising as well. Today, however, the notion that marketing equals sales demonstrates a lack of understanding among many organizations in creative industries. In fact, as we'll see in the rest of this book, marketing tasks and activities go far beyond simply selling.

2.2.2.4 The various roles of marketing

Organizational culture, as we've said, is a set of values and beliefs that serve as guidelines for management and behaviors of the organization's members. It follows, then, that the role of marketing is very different depending on which of the three orientations an organization adopts. In any case, and this bears repeating, the role of marketing is always to bring the perspective of the customers (the market) into the organization, and to ensure that this perspective is taken into consideration in decision-making processes.

Obviously, in an organization with a market orientation, the cultural role of marketing is greatly facilitated. Or better still, this role is already interiorized in the values and the profound beliefs of the organization. This is why all organizational functions, whatever their specific responsibilities, consider customer satisfaction their top priority, and the outcomes of all their decisions and activities have to move the organization closer to achieving this goal. As for the managerial role, instead, the people responsible for marketing decisions and activities in these organizations normally belong to a specific department.

In this case, the Marketing Department is tasked with handling the processes pertaining to the analysis, creation, and distribution of value for customers, as we'll explore in greater detail in the following section. Obviously, this responsibility is direct for marketing decisions, and indirect (in terms of advocating the perspective and interests of customers) for decisions that fall under the jurisdiction of other functions. For example, the Marketing Department in a publishing company with a market orientation is in charge of the market positioning of individual book series, but does not autonomously select new books. This job is taken on by an inter-functional committee (made up of editors and sales staff), which shares responsibility for book selection.

In organizations with a product or sales orientation, the cultural role of marketing is a more complicated one. As we've said, these organizations keep the customer and the market firmly in the background. This makes it far more complicated for marketing to do its job: to see that the expectations, perceptions, and behaviors of customers and competitors are given due consideration in organizational decision-making processes.

Clearly the first challenge in this job lies in the potential clash with the very identity of the organization. In fact, the identity of a more product-oriented organization revolves around the superior quality of its products. So any efforts that Marketing makes to bring the customer perspective center stage can trigger negative reactions from the rest of the organization, generating potential conflicts between various organizational units (Glynn, 2000).

Second, the cultural role of marketing becomes even more challenging when we consider that in all probability, organizations with a product or sales orientation don't even have a Marketing Department (perfectly reflecting the fact that they have less consideration for their customers/market). Instead, there are probably departments or offices within departments in these organizations that are charged with making typical marketing decisions.

The obvious result of all this is that in these organizations the managerial role of marketing is limited to certain specific decisions and activities. Examples might include communication management, media relations, sales promotions, market data analysis, and loyalty programs.

2.2.3   Marketing management: processes, decisions and activities

The managerial role of marketing consists in managing a series of processes, making a series of decisions, and executing a series of activities to implement these decisions. What materializes from all of this are offerings providing value to the market. In the section above, I highlighted the fact that the actual managerial role marketing plays in a given organization depends to a great extent on the prevalent management philosophy, which represents an attribute of the organizational culture. In this section, I'll describe the most complete form of marketing management, which we would typically find in market-oriented organizations. This is the marketing model for creative industries that I'll detail in the following chapters. As far as organizations with other management philosophies go, most likely the role of marketing is limited to a few decisions and activities that I'll describe below.

Keeping in mind that the goal is to create offerings that are more valuable for the customer (and for the market, as an aggregation of customers) than competitors' offerings, the four typical marketing management processes are as follows:

- Value analysis.
- Value creation.
- Value delivery.
- Customer relationship management.

2.2.3.1   *Value analysis*

Seeing that the specific role of marketing is to represent the customer's viewpoint and to keep it top of mind for the organization, the starting point in fulfilling this duty is to secure a solid foundation of customer knowledge. In fact, the goal of value analysis is to *build, feed, and modify the organization's repository of market knowledge*. It follows that the outcome of this process is a *set of knowledge* regarding market phenomena to be utilized in organizational decision making.

Marketing knowledge pertains to various actors whose behavior impacts customer value. For the consumer market, the key is to amass knowledge on factors that determine the various configurations of value that consumers develop when they choose, purchase, and use products or services. What's more, since the goal is to outperform competitors by creating superior value, it's equally essential to build a store of knowledge regarding the organizations that consumers perceive to be competitors, specifically pertaining to their strategies and behaviors.

Last, since value is co-created by a network, it's also imperative to generate knowledge on other actors who contribute to producing value for the market. This refers specifically to media, experts, critics, and more particularly the distributors who deliver products and services to consumers. Only by combining all these different sets of knowledge can the organization get a complete picture of consumer experiences with regard to communication, purchase, and consumption.

But we must remember that in creative industries, organizations don't compete exclusively in consumer markets, but also in contexts where an assortment of other actors operate who can furnish valuable resources. These actors might be donors, who in some creative sectors account for a sizeable share of revenues, or firms interested in making contact with customers/consumers of creative organizations (advertising investors, sponsors, and media). In these markets, many organizations in creative industries 'sell their markets'; in other words, they sell access to their customers.

Just think of the advertising spaces sold by various media, or product placement in countless television programs, films, or books. All these actors (advertising investors, sponsors, media) are also customers, and the organization has to offer them superior value than its competitors. These customers warrant specific market knowledge because their motivations and expectations are very different from those of final consumers, as are their processes for product purchase and use.

2.2.3.2   *Value creation*

The goal of the value creation process is *to develop offerings that more fully satisfy the expectations of customers, as compared to competitors, and to position these offerings on the market*. The end result of this process is a series

of *value propositions* designed to fulfill the expectations of various customer segments that the organization seeks to serve. Value creation involves a number of decisions: staking out the target market, identifying groups of homogeneous customers within this market who are looking for similar benefits (market segments), and pinpointing tangible and intangible features that value propositions have to provide to meet these expectations.

As I've mentioned before, Marketing has total autonomy and responsibility for some of these decisions. For others, it plays an advisory role, typically to the functions that manage product development (Chapter 11). A strategic aspect here is making recommendations, based on market knowledge, as to which actors in the network should be engaged in the process of value co-creation.

Running parallel to the process of delineating value propositions is identifying where on the market to position them, that is, examining customer perceptions and finding a space where the organization's offering will be seen as superior to its competitors'. The pertinent decisions in this process amount to building the *positioning of the value proposition*.

2.2.3.3   *Value delivery*

Identifying the right value proposition for meeting the expectations of specific market segments and building the right market positioning – these are the most strategic aspects of marketing decisions. The aim is to determine where and how to compete on the market. The next step is to make the target market aware of the value proposition that the organization has decided on; in other words, to align customer perceptions and organizational plans. So, the objective of the value delivery process is *to transfer to the market value propositions as designed by the organization, free of distortions or misinterpretations*. The outcome of this process is the offering's *market performance*, in terms of how the market perceives the product's positioning (product image), and how much of the market the product wins (sales and market share).

This process calls for meticulous management because once the value proposition has been designed, it must be made available and communicated to potential consumers. Distribution and communication processes involve a number of different activities, often performed by actors outside the organization (for example, logistic companies, retailers, advertising agencies). But if these activities aren't done properly, the risk is that the value proposition gets distorted along the way, and the offering delivered to the market differs from the original version.

Summing up, then, the process of delivering value to the market involves decisions regarding distribution and communication of the value proposition, so as to achieve the chosen market positioning. Distribution decisions pertain to designing and integrating the distribution channels the organization wants to use to deliver the product to the consumer, as well as managing relationships with various actors who operate in these channels. Communication decisions, instead, relate to formulating the communication strategy (i.e. selecting the most effective set of communication tools for positioning the offering on target markets), composing communication messages, and choosing communication channels.

2.2.3.4   Customer relationship management

The underlying assumption of market orientation is that a superior value proposition leads to satisfied customers, and satisfied customers make repeat purchases from the organization. This means that managing customer value doesn't end with the sale, but instead continues over time in the form of managing customer relationships. During the different phases of these relationships between customers and firms or non-profits, changes take place as customers' expectations, attitudes, and behaviors evolve.

Here are some examples that readily come to mind. A long-time season ticket holder for the opera would expect special services that aren't available to someone who buys a ticket for a single performance. The same goes for a sports fan with a season pass with respect to someone who only goes to the stadium to watch the season final, or a member of an association of museum supporters and a tourist whose visit to that same museum is a once-in-a-lifetime event. These are all cases of customers in different phases of their relationship with an organization who modify their attitudes – and consequently their behaviors – toward that organization.

Managing customer value during various phases of the customer–organization relationship is commonly referred to as *customer relationship management* or CRM. The aim of CRM is to build, nurture, and cultivate long-term relationships with customers, in the belief that the duration of these relationships is directly proportional to benefits they can provide, both financial (profitability) and institutional (realization of institutional goals). With decisions and activities normally associated with CRM, the description of the managerial role of marketing in organizations that operate in creative industries is complete.

2.2.4   The organizational role of marketing: aligning the organization with the market

The value proposition that the organization offers to its customers is the outcome of a joint effort by various personnel from the Marketing Department and other units. In the section above, I explained that the managerial role of marketing consists in managing value analysis, creation, and delivery processes over time with regard to the customers that the organization wants to serve. This is a role that marketing plays both directly, by making decisions and undertaking activities autonomously, and indirectly, by orientating the decisions and activities tasked to other organizational units. Simply put, *the managerial role of marketing calls for decisions and actions that aim to align the organization with the market.*

The customer-centric marketing model I've outlined in this chapter helps highlight the causes of potential misalignment between the value of an offering, from the viewpoint of the organization that proposes it, and the value of that offering perceived by the customers it targets. Preventing this misalignment is Marketing's top priority.

A number of valid management models suggest that misalignment between the quality offered by a firm and quality recognized by the market is the result of a gap that can be traced back to specific processes inside and outside the organization (Golder et al., 2012; Parasuraman et al., 1985). With the help of these models, potential causes of the misalignment can be highlighted and the organizational role of marketing clarified.

A classification can simplify this task, with five separate but interrelated concepts of value (Figure 2.2):
- *Value offered* by the organization to its customers, who experience this value through their consumption processes.
- *Value expected* by customers before buying and consuming the organization's offering.
- *Value perceived* by customers following their communication, purchase and consumption experience.

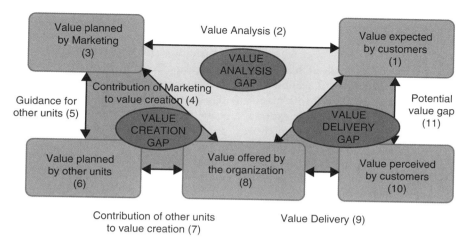

Figure 2.2 – Potential causes of misalignment between organization and market

- *Value planned by Marketing*, that is, the value proposition designed according to customer expectations.
- *Value planned by other organizational units*, or value that these other units think customers expect.

Let's look at the relationships in the figure above sequentially, beginning with Expected Value (1). Through the Value Analysis Process (2), Marketing garners knowledge of these expectations, and designs a Value Proposition (3). To realize this value proposition, Marketing makes certain decisions and performs certain activities, which constitute Marketing's contribution to the Offered Value (4). At the same time, Marketing gives direction to the decisions and activities of other organizational units (5). These units, in turn, plan their contribution to the Offered Value (6) and then actually make that contribution (7). The joint efforts of Marketing and the other units result in the value offered to the market by the organization (8). At this point, the value in question is delivered to customers via distribution and communication processes (9). After experiencing the offering, customers form their opinion of its value based on their perceptions (10).

2.2.4.1   *Value gap analysis*

When the organization and the market are aligned, the value customers expect should coincide with the value they actually perceive. In this case, we can say that Marketing has done a good job managing value analysis, creation, and delivery processes through the decisions and activities it undertakes autonomously and

those of other organizational units which it guides. If, on the contrary, there's a *value gap* between expectations and perceptions, the value-based marketing model underscores the possible causes and indicates the appropriate corrective measures.

The most common cause of the gap between expectations and perceptions is ineffective value analysis. In this case it's incomplete or inappropriate market knowledge that can lead Marketing to make the wrong decisions when designing a value proposition, and to steer other units in the wrong direction. The resulting value proposition won't satisfy customer expectations. What's more, even if it's properly delivered, when customers experience this value proposition, what they perceive is far from what they expected. Here, a *value analysis gap* has caused a misalignment between market and organization that has repercussions on value creation and delivery processes.

Now let's consider a value analysis process that does generate adequate market knowledge, so Marketing can appropriately plan the value proposition. In this situation too gaps can emerge, this time in the transition from design to realization. The reasons behind this might be an ineffective implementation of marketing decisions in subsequent activities, or unproductive orientation provided by Marketing to other organizational units, either due to lack of influence or communication glitches within the organization. The end result: the organization won't create a suitable value proposition, not because market knowledge is lacking, but due to internal misalignment. In this case, a *value creation gap* translates once again into a divergence between the value customers expect and the value they perceive.

Last of all, let's say that value analysis has generated adequate knowledge, and that this knowledge translates into a value proposition aligned with market knowledge and consequently with customer expectations. If the value delivery process isn't effectively implemented, due to inadequate distribution or communication processes, we would find a *value delivery gap*. Although the value proposition is aligned with customer expectations, their communication and purchase experiences lead customers to perceive a very different value offered by the organization with respect to what they expected. Here, too, the value delivery gap translates into a divergence between customer expectations and perceptions.

When describing the potential causes for organization–market misalignment, which makes consumers perceive a value gap, for simplicity's sake I've assumed that the different actors involved in value creation all work in the organization, either in Marketing or some other department. But since value in creative industries is produced through the cooperative efforts of a network of actors, I've also emphasized that one of the tasks of Marketing is to identify and recommend the actors who should lend a hand in this cooperation.

It follows, then, that when value creation gaps arise, the cause might be either failing to identify the right actors outside the organization who should be involved in designing or realizing the value proposition, or failing to build a constructive relationship with these actors. Clearly, diverse contributions are needed for different industries and products, depending on their specificities (sound engineers are needed for music tracks, curators for art exhibits, and so forth). But for all creative industries there are two main categories of actors: consumers and experts. So we must understand the contribution each of them makes to value creation processes.

2.3   THE ROLE OF CONSUMERS IN VALUE CREATION

It might seem contradictory to talk about the role consumers play in creating value for themselves. How can they produce something that they also consume? But there is only contradiction if we take a traditional view of value production via the value chain, with its distinctly separate and sequential roles and activities. If instead we represent value creation as a network of cooperating and co-creating actors, the contradiction disappears. Consumers can be seen as both final users of value propositions, and as the ultimate authorities on this value. And above all, they actively create value for themselves and, more importantly, for other consumers.

As we now know, for consumers value is experiential, that is, it is the fruit of their consumption experience. So logically the protagonists in the process of value creation can be none other than consumers through their experience of the product. Consumers' sensorial, emotional, cognitive, and behavioral reponses to the product are where value resides (Hirschman and Holbrook, 1982): in the joy of listening to a symphony, in the wonder of traveling to new places and experiencing different cultures, in the thrill of roller coaster rides in an amusement park.

So the creative inspiration of a product designer, encapsulated in a producer's offering, has no value until – and only if – it is encompassed in consumption processes and elicits a response from consumers. In the words of Barthes (1977: 148), referring to literary products: 'A text's unity lies not in its origin but in its destination.'

Summing up, then, product consumption is a necessary ingredient in value creation. But consumers aren't simply product users. More and more often *they actively participate in the production phase*, and in doing so they generate value for themselves and for other consumers. Basically, the value that every consumer obtains is what she has created herself, along with the organization and other consumers.

Traditionally in creative industries, consumer participation has always been concentrated in the downstream stages of value creation processes. To illustrate what I mean, let's look to the theater for a literal and symbolic example. In order for 'the show to go on' there have to be people in the audience. But being in the audience involves passive participation in the production process, so much so that the physical space is visibly divided – the production space (the stage) from the consumption space (the seating area) – symbolically underscoring the separation of roles. Consumers watch but only actually participate by showing their appreciation, for example by applauding. The actors are the ones who put on the performance. But even in the world of theater things are changing.

Case in point: the Gob Squad, a company of English and German artists established in 1994. Here is how they describe themselves: 'We make performances and videos which search for beauty in the everyday, and look for words of wisdom from a passing stranger. [...] We try and explore the point where theatre meets art, media and real life. As well as theatres and galleries, we place our work at the heart of urban life – in houses, shops, underground stations, car parks, hotels or directly on the street. Everyday life and magic, banality and utopia, reality and entertainment are all set on a collision course and the audience are often asked to step beyond their traditional role as passive spectators and bear witness to the results.' (www.gobsquad.com).

The Gob Squad invite spectators to become active participants in their shows and to play parts in the plot, essentially – and deliberately – attenuating the aura of sacredness that surrounds theater actors and performances. As described by Charles Isherwood in his *New York Times* review (2012): 'That the group manages to do so with such guileless amiability is a testament to the appeal of the performers and the cleverness of the show's execution. [...] It is liberating for observers too to see how easily and how intimately the creation of theater and the experience of watching it can be integrated.'[3]

Another interesting case is *Sleep No More*, a show by the English company Punchdrink, which debuted in 2003 and is still touring today. Loosely based on Shakespeare's *Macbeth*, all performances are site-specific and interactive, which means they're slightly different every time. Essentially, this play disavows yet another canon of classical theater which holds that all spectators watch the play at the same time. Instead, *Sleep No More* is executed in multi-storey buildings or in several nearby buildings. (The current version of the play is being performed in a number of old warehouses that have been refurbished to resemble a hotel.) Spectators are given masks to wear (the only thing distinguishing them from the actors) and are invited to move freely among the buildings and watch silently as the actors perform.

Hilton Als (2011) reviews the play in *The New Yorker*: 'Because language is abandoned outside the lounge, we're forced to imagine it, or to make narrative cohesion of events that are unfolding right before our eyes. We can only watch as the performers reduce theatre to its rudiments: bodies moving in space. Stripped of what we usually expect of a theatrical performance,

we're drawn more and more to the panic the piece incites, and the anxiety that keeps us moving from floor to floor.'

Beyond these examples from the world of theater, there are myriad others from all creative industries. Just think of television series like *Star Trek* (Kozinets, 2001) or *Xena: Warrior Princess* (Schau et al., 2009). Their fans are enthusiastic members of active communities who even write their own episodes, reproduce the costumes of their favorite characters, and attend meetings where they share their passion with thousands of other fans. In the comic book sector, manga fans do *scanlations* (Lee, 2010): they scan their favorite comics, translate them from Japanese into other languages, and circulate them in other markets.

In architectural design, there is a group of architects who call themselves *ContRoprogetto* (*Counter Project*) (Calcagno, 2012). They design street furniture and home accents using recyclables, and get their clients involved in designing, recovering, and assembling materials. (Clients are normally the residents of the urban areas that will host their projects.)

2.3.1 The different forms of consumer participation

The list of examples is endless, which shows that the culture of direct consumer participation in production processes is becoming more common, creating major challenges to the traditional management approach to value creation processes. But looking more closely, the same examples also suggest that consumers can participate in value creation in a variety of ways, as we can see in a comparison of the Gob Squad and Punchdrunk. This makes it crucial for Marketing to distinguish between the different ways consumers participate in order to recommend how to design and realize forms of participation that contribute to value creation for the customer, to the advantage of the organization.

An effective way to categorize the forms of consumer participation in co-production processes for creative products is according to how much control there is over the production activity, and how much the participation is shared.

The *degree of control* indicates the ways in which the consumer is involved in the production process (measured along a continuum). The endpoints are minimal participation (limited to the consumption experience alone), and maximum control. This latter extreme involves autonomous production, with the consumer taking the lead in making choices, while the organization may (or may not) provide support through knowledge and competences. The midpoint on the continuum is more evenly distributed participation and contribution of both the organization and the consumer. The *degree of sharing*, instead, indicates whether participation in production is individual or shared with other consumers. The matrix in Figure 2.3 illustrates six different typical forms of participation in co-production processes for creative products.

The traditional way that consumers experience a creative product is passive participation. Reading a book, watching a TV show, visiting an art exhibit, traveling alone to a new place – these are all forms of *individual consumption*. Friends going to a concert or an amusement park, travel with a tour group, a couple giving an architect ideas on how to design their new house are all ways to share the buying or consumption experience; in other words, examples of *collective consumption*.

In both consumption categories, production control is entirely in the hands of the producer, while the consumer obviously takes over in the consumption phase, 'receiving' the product that the producer has created (possibly, but not necessarily, on the basis of indications provided by the consumer).

On the opposite end of the spectrum we find forms of participation in which consumers have complete control of the production process, where traditional producers (firms and institutions) are completely absent, or simply support consumer activities. In *individual self-production*, the consumer autonomously produces a creative product. Today's digital technologies, which we discussed in Chapter 1, allow consumers to bypass traditional producers and directly access the market. A recent study conducted by the Bowker Research Institute (www.bowker.com) reveals that in 2011 in the US, 43 per cent of all printed books and 37 per cent of all e-books were self-published, and that the total number of these works grew by 287 per cent from 2006 to 2011. Another example of the individual self-production category is manga scanlation mentioned previously.

Collective self-production, on the other hand, involves a group production project, which means that several users get together and cooperate to reach a common goal. Wikipedia is the most famous case, with content created, maintained, and expanded by groups of users who cooperate together. Additional examples include all communities linked to a brand, but not managed by the owner of that brand (see Star Trek and Xena). An even older example of collective self-production is the board game Monopoly. Before it was patented in 1933 by Parker Brothers, a very similar version of the current game had been created in the early 1900s by a group of Americans who called it *The Landlord's Game*. Curiously, the aim of this group was solely educational, quite the opposite of the actual objective of the game: to promote the idea that private property has negative repercussions on the social progress of a community (Ketcham, 2012).

Forms of co-production involve a greater balance of control between the organization and consumers. The organization can activate either *individual contributions to co-production*, enlisting the cooperation of each consumer to produce the creative product in question,

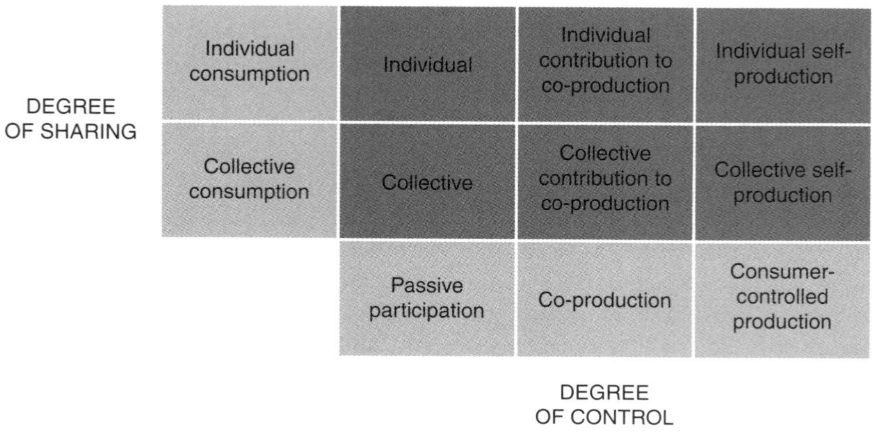

Individual consumption	Individual	Individual contribution to co-production	Individual self-production
Collective consumption	Collective	Collective contribution to co-production	Collective self-production
	Passive participation	Co-production	Consumer-controlled production

DEGREE OF SHARING (vertical axis label)

DEGREE OF CONTROL (horizontal axis label)

Figure 2.3 – Forms of consumer participation in co-production processes

or *collective contributions to co-production*, establishing a cooperative relationship with a network of interconnected consumers.

An example of the first type is Threadless, a US company founded in 2000 that produces consumer-designed T-shirts (Lakhani and Kanji, 2008). Leveraging its community, today nearly 500,000 strong, Threadless invites its members to send in their design proposals which are then put to the vote of the entire community. The winning designs are produced and the winning designers get a share of the profits. In this case, there is an individual contribution to the product design phase, and a collective contribution to production decisions. Another relevant case in point is CNN's i-Report. The television news station asks its viewers to send in reports (text or video) on interesting facts and events. These are published after being vetted by CNN producers, with the aim of providing a broader 'bottom up' view of the news.

An example of collective contribution to co-production is Fantasy Football. Here consumers create a simulated football championship, forming teams, organizing entire tournaments, buying and selling players, playing matches, and basically putting their skills and their passion into play. More examples of this form of participation are all the brand communities created and nurtured by firms. Just look at the community created by Propellerhead Software, developers of computer-controlled musical instruments. This company has succeeded in generating a constant flow of successful innovations by cooperating with its community of users (Jeppesen and Frederiksen, 2006).

2.4 THE ROLE OF EXPERTS AND CRITICS IN VALUE CREATION

In any given sector we can find people recognized by consumers for their expertise, competence, or access to useful information that can be applied when selecting among different market offerings. For example, if a consumer's cat was overweight, she'd ask a vet about what to feed her; or if she were in the market for a new car, she'd read a specialized magazine to decide which one was right for her.

The vet and the magazine are examples of 'experts' in their fields (knowledgable about the needs that different offerings must satisfy, the various products on the market, the activities associated with buying or using a given product, and so on). These experts can

provide information and help consumers minimize the uncertainties associated with product choices. In creative industries, experts take on an even more decisive role, one that in many cases is institutionalized. In other words, it's not only consumers who recognize the expertise and competence of experts, but the entire social system.

In fact, given the unique features of creative products, as far as consumers are concerned, experts play two fundamental roles in value creation (Lampel and Shamsie, 2000). The first has to do with the experiential nature of creative products, which makes it difficult for consumers to anticipate satisfaction before actually experiencing them. For this reason, consumers look for information from experts – the quality clues we discussed in Chapter 1 – to help them choose between the different options that are available.

Second, in creative industries new products are being launched continuously. This means consumers are constantly trying to understand and interpret new offerings in order to incorporate them into their consumption processes. To do all this, expert knowledge is extremely useful (specialized media, critics, bloggers, editors, curators).

To sum up, in creative industries there are actors who are assigned the institutionalized role of value agents. This institutionalization takes the specific form of the function of critics or experts whose job is to give their opinion via reviews on the quality of creative products. This also positions experts in an additional system that *crosses production and consumption* (Botti, 2000; Caves, 2000; Hirsch, 1972). Individual experts can contribute to value creation for specific consumers who tap into their expertise, but it's the *system of experts* as a whole that contributes to value creation for the entire market.

2.4.1 Experts and critics as market makers

There is a long tradition of research on the role of experts and critics as market makers. Their impact on the market success of creative products has been studied for some time, in particular in mass-market industries such as motion pictures, live theater, and publishing.[4] In this last field, for instance, programs like the Oprah Book Club in the US or the Richard and Judy Book Club in the UK (Case History 2.1) have the power to create bestsellers, so much so that in America people talk about the 'Oprah Effect':

skyrocketing sales guaranteed after a book is presented on the *Oprah Winfrey Show*. In the theater world, instead, Reddy et al. (1998) calculated that a high opinion from the *New York Times* critic can extend the run of a Broadway production by 76 performances.

These examples, and relative research, pertain to the value of expert reviews for producers in terms of sales or value for shareholders (Research Focus 2.1). But within their networks, experts in creative industries contribute to generating value for consumers as well.

Case History 2.1

The market-making effect of television book clubs: The Oprah Book Club in the US and the Richard and Judy Book Club in the UK

Book clubs (or reading groups) are becoming increasingly popular in most Western markets, a phenomenon that has prompted some television stations to launch talk shows dedicated to books. The two most famous and influential programs are The Oprah Book Club in the US and the Richard and Judy Book Club in the UK.

The original television book club was created in 1996 by the famous television hostess Oprah Winfrey during her talk show (probably the most successful television show of its kind in US history), which averages 40 million viewers. Oprah stopped televising her book club in mid-2011, and reactivated it online a year later, calling it The Oprah Book Club 2.0, with a format similar to the original, but utilizing various technological platforms.

According to the club's original format, Oprah selected a book that had a transformational effect on her life (either a classic or a new publication), and presented and discussed it during her show, often interviewing the author as well. The program's vast public, along with the highly respectable reputation of this TV personality, her casual style (positive and upbeat, addressing topics of interest to her audience, not literary experts), and links to countless book clubs throughout the country all added up to immediate fame and an extended stay on US bestseller lists for all the books presented on the program.

To illustrate this phonomenon, Thompson (2010) cites the example of *Night* by Nobel Peace Prize winner Eli Weisel, published in English for the first time in 1960, and for years garnering weekly sales of 2,000–3,000 copies in the US. When Oprah selected it to present on her show, weekly sales soared to nearly 140,000 copies, gradually leveling out at 17,000 three months after the show aired.

The Richard and Judy Book Club in Great Britain is very similar to Oprah's. The hosts of this British program, a real life husband and wife team, conducted their afternoon talk show from 2001 to 2009, with viewership peaking at two and a half million. The bookclub was created in 2004 and continued for the rest of the show's run; in 2010 an online version was relaunched in partnership with the bookstore chain WHSmith.

Every month Richard and Judy presented a book and discussed it with their guests or with the author.[5] Every year the public would vote for the Richard and Judy Book of the Year Award, presented during the British Book Awards. Unlike Oprah's Book Club, Richard and Judy asked publishers to recommend the books that would appeal to their viewers: middle class people (Sedo, 2008) who were not terribly sophisticated yet not lacking in taste. In other words, they were looking for the typical 'book club book'.

The same skyrocketing sales occurred with books presented by Richard and Judy. In fact, the 82 books presented in the televised version of the Club sold 26.6 million copies, for an overall sales value of £159.2 million, according to Stone (2008). Although this same author recommends caution in interpreting these remarkable numbers (since there may be other factors at play as well), comparing total sales of the authors in question before and after appearing on the show, an increase of 490.5% is an impressive figure by any standard.

Research Focus 2.1

The impact of reviews on the financial value of a firm

As we've seen, the impact of reviews on sales of creative products has been indisputably demonstrated in various studies. Adopting a new perspective, recent research by Chen et al. (2012) explores the effect that reviews have on the financial value of firms in the movie industry. The basic premise here is that investors, like consumers, try to reduce the risk inherent to the choices they make by acquiring as much information as possible on any relevant phenomenon that may have any impact. The choices in question relate to buying shares in companies, after evaluating their future financial returns. Simply put, a company that does business in an area where high returns are guaranteed will attract investors, and as a result will see an increase in share prices.

In the movie industry, launching a new film is what typically generates financial returns. Investors are likely to buy shares in a film studio that launches new movies that are sure-fire box office hits. But since the success of a picture is hard to predict before it's released, according to the researchers, investors turn to expert reviews (film critics from major newspapers and specialized magazines) to predict the success of a movie and decide whether or not to invest in the studio.

Their research shows that it's not the final judgement of critics (positive or negative) that sways investors, so much as the relative judgement, in other words, a given opinion as compared to previous reviews. Basically, if in the days leading up to a film's premiere the critics give increasingly positive (or negative) reviews (in other words, more recent reviews are more positive (or negative) than initial reviews), investors will buy more (or fewer) shares, driving the share price up (or down). What's more, the researchers show that negative opinions decrease share prices to a greater extent than positive reviews increase share prices.

2.4.2   Experts and critics as sense makers

So if for producers experts can play the role of market makers, for consumers they serve primarily as sense makers in value creation processes (Griswold, 1987). What does this mean? Some examples will help clarify this concept. Here's how Dave Simpson (2012) presents the latest album from Soundgarden in the *Guardian*: 'Soundgarden are indeed back. Still, their first new album since 1996 makes a surprisingly good fist of plugging back into the sound that made them the moodiest and heaviest of the Seattle grunge bands: anvil-heavy riffs, crunching collisions of punk and hard rock, and psychedelic explorations. With storming opener Been Away Too Long sounding like a manifesto, 52-year-old guitarist Kim Thayil reels off blistering solos with a juvenile's glee. Grunge-era nostalgia mixes with classic rock and, on the eerie Rowing, experimental mantras. Cornell's reference to being "born again" on Black Saturday may raise more than an eyebrow, but the rocker-father has powerfully traded twentysomething darkness for middle-aged uncertainty and fear.'

And here's Cathy Horyn, writing for the *International Herald Tribune* (2012), reviewing the latest Narciso Rodriguez collection presented at the New York Fashion Week: 'As a minimalist, Mr. Rodriguez has to constantly deal with technique-mad editors who want more, more, more – without thinking that technique is largely to blame for turning clothes into costly wrecks, and turning smart shoppers off. Besides, the best technicians at the moment (and Mr. Rodriguez is certainly among the very best, with Azzedine Alaïa) will tell you

that technique is essentially the mastery of cloth on the body. The rest, like Oscar de la Renta's ruffled latex tops in Easter-egg colors, is just for show.'

From these two brief examples we can identify three main activities carried out by experts that constitute value creation for consumers of creative products (Caves, 2000; Shrum, 1991). These are discussed in the following sections.

2.4.2.1   Pre-selection

Experts create value by paring down the infinite variety of creative products and focusing consumer attention only on the items that they believe are worthy of note (in a positive or negative way). So essentially, experts *pre-select the options available to consumers*. The *Guardian* critic picked the Soundgarden album out of myriad new releases. The *International Herald Tribune* spotlighted the Narciso Rodriguez collection among the countless collections presented during the New York Fashion Week. Oprah Winfrey, in fifteen years since her first Book Club, has presented 70 books; Richard and Judy, 82.

Pre-selection produces value for the customer in that it *contributes to reducing the sacrifices associated with the offering*. In Section 2.1 we looked at the value components for customers that have a negative impact on overall value: the set of sacrifices that the customer has to make to enjoy the benefits of the offering in question. A number of these sacrifices are connected to gathering information on all the options. The bigger the number of options, the greater the sacrifice, if consumers want to make a broad comparison. So pre-selection by experts allows consumers to expend less effort on gathering information, which means making fewer sacrifices, which in the end enhances the value of the offering in question.

But we shouldn't mistakenly think that pre-selection goes only in one direction, or that experts select products to review for consumers, who are passive recipients of this information. What Griswold (1987: 1082) has to say about book reviews is applicable to any creative product: 'Meaning in book reviews is a two-stage fabrication: part comes from what reviewers find significant, part from what they think their readers will find significant.'

Pre-selection is fruit of the reciprocal influence between the system of experts and the system of consumption, reinforcing the premise that value in creative sectors is co-created by the numerous actors involved in the process. Consumers focus on the products pre-selected by experts, but by the same token experts pre-select products that they think will elicit consumer interest.

Research into the effects of film reviews (Basuroy et al., 2003; Eliashberg and Shugan, 1997) proves the existence of a correlation between these critiques and cumulative box office revenue, and not only in the first few weeks following a film's release. This means that critics are able to interpret spectators' taste, and incorporate that taste into their opinions. Put another way, critics are influenced by viewers.

2.4.2.2   *Framing*
Experts also produce value by providing consumers with a product ranking system that makes it possible to distinguish between the different offerings available on the market. Specifically, by framing a product, *experts give consumers a tool for comparing and evaluating creative products*. Look back at Simpson's description of the Soundgarden album: 'Grunge-era nostalgia mixes with classic rock and [...] experimental mantras.' Or in Horyn's review, the use of the term 'minimalist' as a label for the Narciso Rodriguez style.

In both cases, experts associate the product in question with a category that consumers can easily identify. In every creative industry, products can be slotted into different categories, which often take the name of 'genre', 'movement', or 'style'. In the movie industry, for example, we can differentiate between romantic comedies and dramas, between horror movies and action flicks. In publishing we have non-fiction and

fiction, the latter including murder mysteries, romance, historical fiction, and so on. Similarly, modern and contemporary art have seen Surrealism, Dadaism, Abstract Expressionism, Pop Art, and Arte Povera.

Even in sectors where categories are less 'canonized', it's common practice to draw distinctions on the basis of similarities and differences. In the tourism industry, art cities are different from mountain towns or seaside resorts; regions that offer natural beauty differ from those with casinos or amusement parks. In the world of sports, teams are often classified on the basis of their playing style (offensive or defensive, for example).

Product categorization corresponds to one of the basic cognitive processes that individuals use to attribute meaning to reality through their perceptions (Howard and Sheth, 1969). When people receive a stimulus from their environment, the first step they take in making sense of that stimulus is to asssociate it with one of their cognitive categories. So people realize that a vehicle with four wheels is a car and not a truck because it's relatively smaller, it doesn't have a trailer, and it has room for five passengers.

Categorization is a cognitive process that helps people make sense of reality by providing parameters of similarity and distinction, and by enabling them to make judgements. If an individual wants to evaluate a vehicle based on how easy it is to park, she'd say that a car is easier to park than a truck, but even within the truck category, some are easier to park then others. For these two evaluations (between categories and within a category) people would apply different parameters.

So basically, the process of categorization produces value for customers in two ways. On the one hand, categorization makes it possible *to effectively predict the benefits a product offers*, because it provides parameters for assessing distinctive product features. On the other, this process allows consumers to *make fewer sacrifices*, rendering the evaluation and selection processes more efficient.

By categorizing an album as 'grunge', consumers who don't like that type of music would stay away, while grunge fans would take note, and depending on the album's distinctive features, may decide to buy it. Likewise, when consumers hear about a fashion collection labeled as 'minimalist' they don't associate it with loud 'baroque' styles, colors, or accessories. As the review suggests, this type of collection should be appreciated and evaluated in light of the 'mastery of cloth on the body.'

Because of the systematic innovation in creative industries, there are two specific phases that typify the process of categorization by the system of experts: the creation of new categories (genres, movements, styles, and so forth) and differentiation within existing categories.

- *Creation of new categories*. In the evolutionary process of a creative industry, the inspiration and skill of product designers are incorporated in innovative offerings from producers and driven by consumer appreciation for creative content. All this can lead to the creation of a product (or more often a set of similar products) that can't be readily slotted into the established system of shared categories. This kind of product has the potential to generate an entirely new category (a new movie genre, a new artistic movement, a new style of design).

Cirque du Soleil, for example, has crafted a new product category by blurring the boundaries between circus and musical; the contemporary dance troupe Momix is unanimously recognized for fostering a product category that combines dance and gymnastics. Before a potential category actually comes into use in a sector, *the system of experts must recognize and qualify it as a new category*. Interestingly, experts don't always do so before consumers. In fact, some highly competent and keenly insightful consumers may recognize the emergence of a new product category, and be willing to buy it as such. Still, until the new category is acknowledged at a sector level (that is, until it's socially constructed) the system of experts makes a fundamental contribution, providing the category with *social legitimacy*.

For an exemplary case of the creation of a new category we can look to the emergence and success of the Impressionists in the art world in the second half of the nineteeth century (Research Focus 2.2).[6] Similar examples can be found in any sector that can be called creative. Just think of 'voluntourism'; the 'new' sports which are now included in the Olympic Games (snowboarding, beach volley, badminton); 'biker style' clothing and footwear.

Research Focus 2.2

A new category in the world visual art of the nineteenth century: The Impressionists

Wijnberg and Gemser (2000) have explored the origins of the Impressionists' success in the late nineteenth century in France. This success can be traced back to changes in how artists were selected and evaluated, following a radical shift in power relationships in the art world.

Before the Impressionists came on the scene, the artistic value of any work was established by the artists themselves, who gathered in the Academies (established during the Renaissance). It was the Academies that deemed an artist worthy to be admitted and promoted by means of exhibits in the Salons, which were regularly organized by the Academies themselves.

The Academies and their Salons served as selection and categorization systems. In fact, if an artist did not gain admission, his work was not categorized as 'art' but as a form of artisanship. Works of art were not evaluated in light of their innovation, but based on their respect for classical canons dictating what could be represented (typically historical events). At that time, museums were institutions that preserved the works of dead artists and exhibited them with the aim of training young artists. There were no professional art critics, although some journalists would occasionally present the Salons and art work exhibited there.

The company of artists known as the Impressionists was regularly excluded from the Salons, as they represented innovation both in style (the representation of 'impressions' that a given scene would elicit) and in subject (scenes from daily life, not historical events). For this reason, after countless rejections, some of these artists decided to organize their own exhibits, both as solo and collective shows, with the help of enlightened art dealers. At the same time, some Parisian art museums decided to begin exhibiting living artists, with the intention of presenting innovations in contemporary visual art, and some critic-journalists began to play their role professionally, having more opportunities to review artistic activities.

The Impressionists, representing true innovation in the art world of the time, were the focal point of the exhibition activities of the galleries, the first art museums, and the first art critics; this gradually shifted the center of power outside the halls of the Academies into this widespread network of experts. A new artistic trend (a new category) was recognized and socially constructed by this network. The innovative scope of the Impressionists' work prompted the establishment of innovation as a primary parameter for evaluating artwork, one that retains its validity even today.

○ *Differentiation within existing categories*. Clearly new categories are not created at the same rate as innovation within an existing category. When a category becomes established in a market, both the inventors and producers of creative products are prompted to exploit it by launching offerings that correspond to the canons of this category. Moreover, the very fact that a category becomes established means that there are consumers who value and are willing to buy the offerings that are consistent with the canons of that category.

Cognitive and social categories that exist at a given time in history also engrain certain conventions that individual creators or producers would find hard to change (Becker, 1982: chapter 2). In fact, the system of production and consumption as well as the system of experts (which generates social legitimization) all adapt to current categories and function efficiently by applying them. Imagine how complicated decision making would be for producers and consumers alike (regarding production for one, and purchase and consumption for the other) if creative product designers systematically came up with ideas that were so innovative they could not readily be classified according to existing categories.

Becker (1982: 32–3) describes the case of the composer Harry Partch, who used a musical scale with 43 tones per octave, as compared to the 12-tone scale normally used in Western music. The consequences of such an innovative creative choice was that normal musical instruments from the Western world could not reproduce these tones, nor could any musicians play them, nor would there be many consumers capable of appreciating the musical result. Consequently, the dominant system of categories for a creative sector serves as an efficient structure providing the framework for realizing and consuming products.

For existing categories, experts contribute to value creation for consumers by providing *parameters for distinguishing between various offerings within a category*. Going back for a moment to the review of the Soundgarden album, we have a clear example of an expert making this kind of distinction: 'Grunge-era nostalgia mixes with classic rock and [...] experimental mantras. Cornell's[7] reference to being "born again" on Black Saturday may raise more than an eyebrow, but the rocker-father has powerfully traded twentysomething darkness for middle-aged uncertainty and fear.'

This review gives some indication of the differences between the new album and other grunge music, and previous Soundgarden releases. In fact, this album is described as a mix between grunge and other genres (classic rock and experimental music), with mature style and content, thanks to the professional (and biological!) maturity of the singer.

These indications give readers a set of qualitative parameters which help them make a choice: the grunge purist will probably steer clear of the album, but classic rock fans might be tempted to listen for themselves. Summing up, experts support consumers in their cognitive categorization processes by promoting *grouping* and *distinguishing*. The first process is done by classing a product in an existing category, or suggesting the creation of a completely new one; the second process involves highlighting the differences within a category (Arnould et al., 2002: 311–16). Categorization is the first step in assigning meaning to the countless creative products on the market.

2.4.2.3 Interpretation

This is the third way that experts contribute to value creation for consumers. Through interpretation experts give consumers a *'preview' of the experience they can expect from a creative product*. As a result, interpretation generates value for customers because *it makes their selection process more effective and efficient* – effective because they can better qualify their expectations of individual offerings, efficient because they can save time and cognitive effort in searching and interpreting information. Lampel and Shamsie (2000: 251), in their study of the movie industry, underscore this activity, pointing out that 'Critics act as commentators that provide viewers with vital information that can allow them to appreciate its more subtle qualities, which usually deal with the film's content and meaning.' Interpretation can be broken down into five components, according to Shrum (1991).

The first is *descriptive*. As the term suggests, the expert provides information on product features based on first-hand experience. Generally the description refers to the product category as well. For a novel reviewed by a literary critic, for instance, the descriptive component might include a brief overview of the plot, the main characters, or the setting, which identify the work with a specific genre. If we consider a review of a tourist destination in a specialized travel magazine, the description would include the main attractions, where to stay, where to eat, and average prices, all of which would identify the type of destination in question. A description of a building would detail the location, the date of construction, the materials used.

Next comes the *analytical* component. Here the critic offers a personal interpretation of the content in question, positioning it within a context of meaning, using references, metaphors, and associations. Going back to the novel above, a critic might put forward a social interpretation, placing the content within the debate on current social issues; or she may take a psychological view, underscoring the functional and dysfunctional relationships among the story's main characters. For the tourist destination, the magazine might recommend it for people who are looking for a quiet place to relax, or who want contact with the local culture.

Then there is an *entertainment* component, which would have the reviewer adding a few humorous comments, flaunting his expertise, adding an anecdote here and there. For the book, this might mean offering an opinion on the characters, highlighting their negative or positive qualities, or recounting a personal experience in the places where the story is set. For the tourist destination, the magazine could include feedback from former visitors, or the personal experiences there of the journalist who wrote the review.

In the review there may also be an *instruction* component, that is, an opinion expressed by the reviewer on how the product creator could or should have carried out a certain activity. For a book, the critic could say, for example, that the author should have described one of the characters in more detail, or clarified the relationship between characters to make the plot easier to follow. The reviewer of a tourist destination, instead, could suggest that local hotels collaborate to offer collective tourist services.

The final component is *evaluative*. Here the reviewer gives a positive or negative assessment of the product, and recommends whether or not the consumer should buy it. The reviewer's opinion might be implicitly understood from the other components, or summed up in an explicit statement which, in some sectors, is expressed in conventional codes (for example stars to indicate the quality of a film).

Obviously, since the review itself is a creative product, each expert has her own style and her own way of utilizing and combining the components described above. And each reviewer will use her specific competence, her preferences, and her cognitive maps to formulate her interpretations, which means that different experts will offer different interpretations of the same product (Griswold, 1987). In any case, a review that contains all five elements (descriptive, analytical, entertainment, instruction, and evaluative) gives consumers useful information for interpreting the product in question, grasping the benefits that they can expect and foretelling the associated sacrifices.

Consumers who are in the habit of consulting experts are not simply passive receptors. Instead, these consumers offer their own opinions on a given expert review based on whether they agree, whether their experience validates the review, and whether or not they found it useful. Consumers tend to select an expert who they think is capable of generating greater value for themselves; they stand by the opinion of this person, and ultimately shore up his or her reputation, thereby contributing to the institutionalization of the entire system of experts.

Interpretation and framing are interrelated activities, and are often presented together in the same review by an expert, critic, or commentator. This is why reviews highlight the evolution of categorization systems. For a good example, we can take the reviews of performances by the Atlanta Symphony Orchestra, studied by Glynn and Lounsbury (2005). In the 1990s, the board of this orchestra decided to cut costs and to open up the repertoire to music that was more contemporary, more 'simple', and more in tune with the tastes of the general public; in other words, compositions that the musicians considered more 'commercial'.

These decisions led to a conflict with orchestra members that deteriorated into a ten-week strike in 1996. The protest ended when a compromise was reached, with cost cutting measures having less impact on the musicians, who in turn agreed to broaden their repertoire to include more contemporary commercial works. An analysis of the reviews of the orchestra's performance, after revising its program, shows a gradual modification of the category 'symphonic concert', in which the more commercial elements become part of the qualitative parameters. In fact, the critics gradually began to take into consideration not merely the technical aspects of the performance, but the public response and commercial success as well.

2.5 CONCLUSIONS

In this chapter my aim was to outline the constituent components of a marketing model for creative industries. The focal point of this model is customer value, and its fundamental processes are four: value analysis, value creation, value delivery, and customer relationship management. The effective and efficient management of these processes has to be consistent with the culture of the organization and the value production processes in the industry.

To gain a better understanding of the role of marketing in an organization that operates in a creative industry, I dedicated most of this chapter to exploring the management philosophies that possibly determine the different roles that marketing can take on. Most importantly, I detailed the specificities of the value production processes in these sectors, pointing out that value is produced by a network of actors who cooperate and integrate their competences and creative resources, and that consumers and experts are key actors in this production.

The conclusion to be drawn from all this is that beyond a managerial role, marketing has a cultural and strategic role in its organization: to represent the viewpoint of the customer, and consequently to keep the organization aligned with the market, in the belief that this is the only way to create and deliver value to customers, to satisfy their expectations, and to establish lasting relationships.

In the next chapter, I'll start by describing the value analysis process; in other words, the series of activities dedicated to building, enhancing, and modifying the repository of market knowledge that is available to an organization. Specifically, I'll detail the various components of consumption experiences to bring to light the key factors which must be thoroughly understood by the organization.

REVIEW QUESTIONS

1. Why isn't the traditional value chain model able to capture value production in creative industries? Why are value networks more effective in representing value production?
2. Why is customer value in creative industries experiential? What are the components of this experience?
3. What are the processes identifying the managerial role of marketing in creative organizations? What can be considered the main organizational role of marketing?
4. What are the different ways consumers can participate in value production processes?
5. What roles do experts and critics play in these processes?

CASE STUDY

TECNOBREGA DO PARÁ: AN INNOVATIVE VALUE NETWORK AND 'DISTRIBUTED' MARKETING MODEL IN THE MUSIC INDUSTRY

Tecnobrega is a musical genre that emerged in the early 2000s in Belém, Brazil, in the northern state of Pará. This genre became the focus of international attention following the release of *Good Copy Bad Copy*, a documentary on copyright in the music industry. Aside from its economic impact (Duffy, 2009; Lester, 2012), tecnobrega represents true innovation on the global music scene thanks to its unique value creation model (Lemos, Castro, 2006; Bowe, 2010; Domb Krauskopf, 2010) and associated marketing model.

Brega debuted on the Brazilian music scene in the 1960s and peaked in popularity in the 1980s. This genre featured romantic melodies and very simple, almost cheesy lyrics that were easy to memorize. (In fact, the word *brega* actually means 'cheesy' or 'tacky'.) Brega slowly evolved into tecnobrega as the original version was fused with electronic music. So beyond giving birth to a new genre, easy to listen to and dance to, electronic technology has given rise to a revolutionary value creation model. Here's why: essentially, the actors involved in value creation play a variety of roles simultaneously, interacting dynamically and together inventing a music business that's vastly different from the traditional music industry, which is made up of artists, record labels, distributors, and above all copyright.

But first, what is tecnobrega? The typical music content is a remix of old tunes (many from the 1980s) or new ones, which might be regional, national, or international hits. These remixes are created by DJs in 'garage' recording studies, thanks to low-cost digital technologies. However, the basic products in the tecnobrega sector aren't albums, but parties where the DJs perform. These parties can attract anywhere from a few hundred to a few thousand people. So to get an idea of the size of this sector, simply consider that in the city of Belém alone, with a population of around one and a half million, in any given month more than 4,000 parties and 2,000 concerts are organized (Lemos, Castro, 2006).

A wide range of different actors cooperate in the process of value creation.

DJs

These are the primary players in content production. Normally they get new songs from artists and then create mashups with old tunes to come up with the final product to play at the parties. The DJs produce the music in home recording studios using a computer and sampling software. The standard procedure is for a DJ to create a compilation, which is then burned onto a CD in the same recording studio, and sold through a network of street sellers, who are described below.

The heart of any party is the sound system (*apparerlhagems* in Brazilian Portuguese), a movable apparatus made up of a somewhat theatrical 'command post' that normally hosts two DJs with their musical paraphernalia, two or three speaker towers, a video system that films the audience and projects the footage onto a maxi-screen, stage lighting, and platforms for fireworks. The quality of the party depends on the size of the sound system and the DJ's technological arsenal (Domb Krauskopf, 2010).

DJs are recruited and paid by the owners of the sound systems. Usually every sound system has its 'resident' DJs, so their reputations are indelibly linked. DJs and sound systems are so important that many artists create exclusive songs for a specific DJ-sound system.

Sound system owners

DJs are key players in the value network, and although they are normally paired up with a specific sound system, the sound system owners play no part in producing musical content. Instead they are actually investors, since the sound system is the only real capital investment in the sector. Often sound system owners and DJs are members of the same family (Lemos, Castro, 2006).

Party organizers

These play a more traditional entrepreneurial role. They arrange to rent locations, sound systems, and DJs for parties or hire artists and bands to play; they handle permits and authorizations; they conduct promotional activities and sell tickets; and organize the bar, the security, and all the other services that ensure the party will be a success.

Promotional activity is done mainly with traditional tools, such as posters and radio ads on local and community stations. (The latter typically broadcast from speakers positioned on the street corners of various neighborhoods.) Other forms of advertising are *stereo cars* and *stereo bikes*, which are private vehicles whose owners are paid to cruise the streets of the city with loudspeakers announcing the day, time, and sound system of a party.

Artists

Composers, singers, and bands – the artists – were once the primary producers of creative content. Today this is rarely the case, although some enjoy national fame (Gaby Amaranto, for example). With the rise in popularity of mega-parties as the way to experience tecnobrega, to the detriment of live performances by singers or bands, most artists produce songs directly for DJs, hoping to get play time on their sound systems.

The more people who hear a song, the more famous it will be, and the more likely the artist will get invited to perform live. To 'grease the wheels' of this mechanism, artists often include their own names and the names of DJs in the lyrics of the song to attract their attention (Domb Krauskopf, 2010). In the end, artists get paid when they give live concerts, seeing as DJs handle the production of CDs and DVDs for the most part. But it's not uncommon for singers and bands to produce their own CDs and DVDs to sell during their concerts.

CD and DVD Reproducers (or 'Pirates')

Here is the real difference between tecnobrega and the traditional music business. The role of pirates in reproducing music is accepted and even institutionalized within the network; in fact, the concept of 'piracy' is only valid from the perspective of a traditional system. The bottom line is that in the tecnobrega sector there is no copyright, and the role of the recording houses and labels is a peripheral one.

Compilations created by DJs and self-produced CDs are handed over to the reproducers who make copies and sell them on the street, as we'll see below. So CDs and DVDs are not seen as the main source of revenue (which instead comes from mega-parties with sound systems), but rather a promotional tool for the whole system. Artists and DJs give their CDs to reproducers to get into the market and to build a reputation, which leads to invitations to perform live concerts. The reproducers earn their money from selling CDs and DVDs on the 'unofficial' market.

Street vendors

These are the key distribution channel for tecnobrega. Hundreds of sellers on the streets of Belem and all over Pará buy CDs and DVDs from reproducers, and sell them in the markets and on the streets. Some sellers also reproduce music, but most don't since this requires equipment, and buying equipment involves risks. The research conducted by Lemos and Castro (2006) shows that the system of street vendors accounts for around 300,000 CDs and 180,000 DVDs a month, providing a primary income for many of them.

Consumers

Consumers are an essential component of value creation in the tecnobrega sector. Although there are countless opportunities to hear tecnobrega (listening to the radio, or downloading tracks from dedicated blogs), the key role of consumers comes during the parties. As with any party where music is playing, the mega-parties with their sound systems are experiential events; the enjoyment of the experience depends on both the quality of the sound system, the size of the party, and the kind of people who go.

But it's when the people in the audience interact with the DJs that they truly participate in value creation. The DJ–audience relationship is a close one, and it's highly interactive. During their performances, DJs create ample opportunities to spotlight members of the public thanks to the rich instrumentation of the sound system, and the fact that they know many regulars personally. In fact, DJs often do 'shout outs', calling their biggest fans by name, showing them on the maxi-screens, inviting them up on the stage and giving them closeups for everyone to see.

DJs also make up new dance moves and have the audience try them out, and they invite individual spectators (or the entire audience) to sing along to songs. During parties people who work for the organization take instant photos of the crowd, which are printed up with the DJ's logo. Then spectators collect these photos in albums, or post them on their profiles on different social networks. Super Pop, one of the most famous sound systems, runs an online radio station where consumers can upload their pictures, which are shown along with songs (Domb Krauskopf, 2010).

So essentially an experiential dynamic is created between the audience and the DJ, which is what gives the party its true value. As a result, it is the consumers who continually build up the cultural capital of individual DJs. Beyond buying the compilations by their favorite DJs and sound systems, consumers also call radio stations to request their favorite songs, or talk about them on their blogs, creating actual fan clubs or *crews*, who play a totally unique role in the world of tecnobrega.

Crews

These are groups of consumers who have become an institution in the world of tecnobrega. They form associations (albeit informal ones), they give themselves a name, they chose their trademarks (logos, t-shirts, or items that display their logos), and they go to every party where their DJs play. Often they have stereo systems in their cars and they start up spontaneous mini-parties, or they can create their own performance spaces during mega-parties.

The biggest crews become integral value components at the parties they go to. DJs know their crews well, and interact with them even outside of the parties (for instance, by having them try out new dance moves). DJs always get their crews involved during performances, greeting them when they arrive and spotlighting them during the party. The biggest crews, the ones with financial resources, may even go so far as to pay artists to write songs for them, including the team name in the lyrics and then performing these songs during parties. This enhances the social and symbolic capital of the crews themselves and of their DJs (Domb Krauskopf, 2010).

The relationships among the different actors involved in value creation appear intricate and complex. In fact, the same actors can play a variety of roles: DJs produce compilations, they perform with sound systems, and they sell to street vendors, who in turn sell music and also make copies of CDs and DVDs; artists create new songs which they perform and sell directly during concerts. So several actors compete and cooperate at the same time in the value network. Figure 2.4 illustrates this network, distinguishing between different relationships depending on whether they involve exchanging tangibles or intangibles.

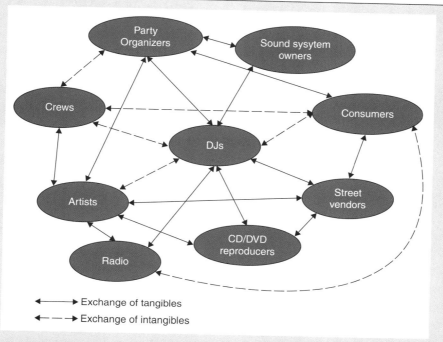

Figure 2.4 – The value network in the tecnobrega sector
Source: Adapted from Domb Krauskopf (2010)

The marketing model in the tecnobrega sector is a unique one, with marketing activity distributed among the actors in the network. Since many of them are individuals, these activities are not performed by specialists in an organization; instead, marketing is part of personal competence sets. The individual who most closely resembles a producer in more structured sectors is the party organizer, who has the typical role of integrator of creative competences, which when combined create a value proposition for end users (party goers). The organizer rents the location and the sound system with DJs, promotes the event, and organizes any additional services that are needed.

Essentially the party organizer creates the conditions that enable effective interaction to take place: between the audience and the DJ, between the audience and the crew, and between the crew and the DJ. Whatever perspective is adopted as far as the different actors who participate in the network, a series of marketing activities are clearly being carried out. For example, by interacting with the audience and the crews, DJs have to figure out which songs will be most popular, and make their shows enjoyable and memorable for the public. DJs also need to keep up relations with their fan base even outside of the parties, and distribute their compilations to radio stations and CD/DVD reproducers to enhance their own reputation and that of their products. This generates an audience for their sound system.

Artists have to write songs that appeal to DJs to ensure play time during parties. When a song gets popular the artist who wrote it becomes famous, and this creates demand for live concerts. Crews have to create an image, establish relationships with DJs and party organizers, and finance musicians to write songs for them. By doing so they'll get asked to attend parties, they attract the public's attention, and they actively contribute to the entire experience.

To sum up, every actor carries out a series of marketing activities that serve to create value for themselves and for their customers, while generating value for the entire sector at the same time.

REVIEW QUESTIONS

1. What is the intricate network of relations that ties together tecnobrega producers and consumers?
2. How different are the exchange relations among various actors?
3. Marketing activities in the network are dispersed across many actors. Who are the main ones and which specific activities do they do?

CUSTOMER VALUE ANALYSIS

Chapter 3

THE CONSUMER SIDE OF THE MARKET: THE CONSUMPTION EXPERIENCE

LEARNING OBJECTIVES

After reading this chapter you should be able to:

- Identify the different types of value that creative products can provide.
- Detail positive and negative components of customer value.
- Understand the dynamic of value that leads to customer satisfaction.
- Identify the practices that consumers use to get value from creative products.
- Tap into the most typical consumption experiences of creative products.

OVERVIEW

For an organization in a creative industry that wants to carry out effective, systematic value analysis it's important to possess solid knowledge regarding the types of value that creative products can provide. In the previous chapter, we discussed the fact that customer value has a positive component (product benefits) and a negative one (the sacrifices needed to get these benefits).

Creative products provide consumers with different types of benefits and require different sacrifices. So, the first question I'll look into in this chapter is: What are the types of value associated with the benefits offered by creative products, and what kinds of possible sacrifices do consumers have to make so they can enjoy these benefits?

As we'll see, benefits can be classified according to four different types of value, depending on whether this value lies in the consumption experience itself or in other goals this experience enables consumers to achieve, and whether the consumption experience can generate value for the consumers themselves or for other people they are interested in.

Then we'll explore how sacrifices are related to the activities along the various stages of consumer experience with a creative product. During each stage, consumers use their personal set of resources (economic, cognitive, emotional, and temporal) to get product benefits. This is where sacrifices come into play. As the negative side of value, sacrifices actually diminish value itself; and if sacrifices outweigh benefits, consumers might decide not to purchase the product in question after all.

In Chapter 2, we discussed the concept of value from the consumer's standpoint, and saw how it takes various forms depending on pre-purchase expectations and post-consumption perceptions. In order to effectively manage the processes that engender customer satisfaction, an organization must meticulously analyze both these aspects. In other words, it's crucial for organizations to develop knowledge on the determinants of both expected value and perceived value.

Another point made in the previous chapter is that the value consumers get from a creative product is a fruit of their experience of that product. For this reason I decided to start exploring the topic of value analysis by dedicating the current chapter to perceived value, which is the immediate outcome of the consumption experience. Specifically, I'll try to answer the question: How can consumers extract the potential value of a creative product?

The answer lies in how consumers experience the product, in particular in the set of processes that this experience entails, which are called consumption practices. In this chapter I'll describe typical consumption practices for any type of creative product: attributing meaning to the product, and then integrating it into daily life and social relationships.

In discussing creative products in the last chapter, I highlighted their specificities, which provoke a level of intensity in the consumption experience that is rarely found with non-creative products. With this in mind, in the following sections, I'll detail the consumption practices for creative products that constitute the overall consumption experience, which in turn generates perceived value for consumers.

3.1   A CLASSIFICATION OF THE VALUE OF CREATIVE PRODUCTS

To clarify how creative products provide value to consumers, the assumption I'll rely on is that in their daily lives people strive to achieve, maintain, and preserve their own personal concept of 'well-being', both at an individual and social level. *Individual well-being* centers on good health and psychological equilibrium. However, *social well-being* has to do with feeling at ease within one's network of social relationships (as part of a couple or a member of a family, a circle of friends, a community, a sports club or cultural association and ties with relevant others). The concept of well-being is inherently an individual one. But the distinction between individual and social well-being is an expedient that enables the organization to identify the underlying value sources and understand value generation processes more clearly.

One way people can achieve a fulfilling level of well-being is by consuming various kinds of products, including creative ones. As a consequence, and in light of what we've discussed in the previous chapter about marketing, the ultimate role of this discipline in a society is to provide/promote products and services that can contribute to the individual and social well-being of its members.

Based on this premise, the different types of value can be distinguished according to two dimensions: purpose and direction.[1] In terms of *purpose*, it's possible to differentiate between intrinsic and extrinsic value. Value is *intrinsic* when the consumption experience itself provides it, with no ulterior goal beyond the experience per se. One the other hand, value is *extrinsic* when consumption of a product is instrumental to reaching other goals beyond consumption.

As for *direction*, *self-oriented* value is different from *other-oriented* value. With the first, consumers appreciate value for how it affects them personally; with the second, they appreciate it for how it affects relevant others. Put another way, self-oriented value impacts individual well-being, and other-oriented, social well-being.

Let's go in depth now on the four different types of value.

Hedonic value (as already mentioned in Chapter 1) derives from the consumption experience per se, with consumers mainly appreciating its effects on themselves. The value of taking a solitary walk in a nature reserve, for instance, comes from the benefits of escaping from the daily routine, and perhaps even gaining a sense of spirituality through close contact with the natural world.

When the benefits a consumer gets from a product are functional to the achievement of ulterior goals beyond the experience itself, and when the consumer appreciates these benefits for their effects on herself, the value is *utilitarian*. For example, for a commuter who rides a motorcycle to work, the ultimate goal might be to shorten travel time from home to work, thanks to the greater maneuverability in city traffic and easier parking compared to a car.

Communicative value is when consumers use a given product to impact some relevant others. For example, buying a special bottle of wine to take to a dinner with friends is a way to give the impression of being an expert sommelier.

Finally, consumers obtain *ethical value* from a consumption experience when this experience provides value per se and positively affects some relevant other. To illustrate, buying a brand of sweets from a company that donates a portion of its profits to support an environmental project is a way to make a contribution to the well-being of the planet as a whole.

All this refers to generic products. Now let's look at the types of value that creative products specifically generate, beginning with the most typical.

3.1.1   The hedonic value of creative products

As I mentioned in Chapter 1, people consume creative products mainly for their hedonic value, (that's *mainly*, not exclusively). There's no denying that for most products in creative industries, it's the consumption experience itself that provides value to consumers. Reading a book, visiting an archeological site, owning a work of art, going to see a sporting event or a concert, listening to a radio program, or watching a TV show: these are behaviors that have value in and of themselves. But what kind of value? What do we mean by hedonic value?

Traditionally, marketing studies contrast hedonic consumption with utilitarian consumption, placing them on opposite ends of the spectrum in terms of reaching practical goals (Hirschman and Holbrook, 1982; Holbrook and Hirschman, 1982). But beyond this general distinction, hedonic value can relate to a vast range of consumption scenarios.

3.1.1.1 The emotional value of creative products

First of all, creative products provide hedonic value because they *elicit emotional reactions*, which in turn give a sense of pleasure. Actually, it's possible to go so far as to say that creative products that don't trigger emotions don't provide consumers with any value at all. Consumers buy and use creative products because they're fun and entertaining; they can feed their fantasies, awaken memories, and inspire daydreams. Marketing studies normally classify the emotions that these products bring out as positive (joy, serenity, optimism, surprise, love) or negative (anger, fear, sadness, worry) (Richins, 1977).

People consume creative products mainly (but again not exclusively) for the positive emotions they elicit. Yet studies on the theater (Walmsley, 2011) the cinema (Andrade and Cohen, 2007) and extreme sports (Arnould and Price, 1993; Celsi et al., 1993) show that some consumers of creative products actually seek negative emotions. Their aim is to learn to deal with these emotional states, which are all part of the human experience.

3.1.1.2 The identity value of creative products

Beyond the emotional reactions that creative products trigger, they also supply hedonic value because they *contribute to defining consumer identity* due to their high *symbolic* content. Integral to the concept of self that each individual has is also the *extended self* (Ahuvia, 2005; Belk, 1988), that is, the set of objects, relationships, and places that each individual believes to *represent* her, which she thinks of as 'her own'. What this means is that the self is not only defined by what I can call 'me' but also by what I can call 'mine', as well as activities I would describe using the verb 'to love' ('I love skiing' or 'I love Caribbean literature'). Since creative products can serve as a mark of distinction in today's society (Chapter 1), they play a key role in building self-identity.

Just think of how loyal people can be when it comes to their favorite vacation spot or sports team. Or how strongly people might identify with a character in a book or a film, or on TV, or even with a sports personality. Or how the clothes a person wears or the way she decorates her home are seen as manifestations of her deepest inner self. Likewise, by consuming certain creative products, people can reaffirm their regional identity (Barcelona football fans who show they're proudly Catalan by buying a season pass), their ethnic identity (Cuban immigrants in Florida who always listen to salsa), or religious identity (Catholics who wear cross-shaped pendants).

What's more, the concept of self (if it's a positive one) generates *self-esteem*, which the consumption of creative products can help create and reinforce. Reading a serious-minded newspaper every day, or regularly visiting contemporary art exhibits, or going on vacation far from the international tourism circuit, or following a little-known sport: these are all consumption behaviors that contribute to creating the self-image of an intellectual, an independent thinker, a non-conformist.

3.1.1.3 The sacred and spiritual value of creative products

Last of all, many creative products provide a *bridge to the sacred and spiritual sphere*, which also comes under the umbrella of hedonic value. Here the 'sacred and spiritual' can be thought of by looking upward or inward, as a connection with either a higher power or the deepest and most intimate part of ourselves.

Religious tourism is an obvious example. According to World Tourism Organization estimates, every year anywhere from 300 to 330 million people travel to holy sites the world over, with Mecca attracting the highest number of pilgrims. Now add the number of people who travel to spiritual retreats, conferences, and workshops, or take part in 'voluntourism' sponsored by religious organizations. These statistics clearly show why some cities or even entire countries are striving to establish a market position through well-designed tourist offerings (see the Web site for Spain's board of tourism: http://www.spain.info/en/reportajes/turismo religioso_en_espana.html). In addition to tourism, entire sectors in several creative industries revolve around religion and spirituality: publishing, radio, television, and visual arts.

Naturally, the sacred and spiritual is not limited to religion. In fact, getting in touch with one's most intimate inner self may well have nothing to do with religious faith. But here too there are places, books, music, and objects that serve as a bridge to help make this connection. Belk et al. (1989: 2) underscored how the process of secularization in Western society has led to anointing some consumption phenomena as sacred: 'Consumption can become a vehicle of transcendent experience'. In other words, some actions that were once expressions of religious faith are associated with consumption phenomena in today's society. (Examples include the use of rituals, the mythification of objects or places, or a pilgrimage as a journey to draw physically closer to the sacred, as we'll see in Section 3.3.4.)

It is in this transcendence – the extraordinary nature of the experience linked to certain moments of consumption – that 'sacralization' emerges. Although this is a highly subjective phenomenon that can center on any kind of product, there's no doubt that creative products are a particularly precious source of sacred and spiritual value as vectors of powerful symbolic content.[2]

3.1.2　The utilitarian value of creative products

Creative products are often represented as lacking functionality, but this doesn't mean that they can't provide utilitarian value. This kind of value comes from product benefits that are instrumental to achieving other goals consumers aspire to. So value doesn't lie in the consumption experience per se, but in the ulterior goal that can be achieved through consumption.

The utilitarian value of most consumer goods might be obvious, but it isn't immediately so for creative products. However, for some creative products the primary value is actually utilitarian. For others utilitarian value is vital for certain market segments. And for still others, this value might not be a top priority, but it certainly carries weight.

Examples of the first type of creative product (offering mainly utilitarian value) are professional or educational publications. When workers use technical manuals or students use textbooks, the aim is to acquire or expand their knowledge. Although it's true that such books can also be judged by aesthetic parameters, the central value they offer depends on how effectively they convey their contents. The same can be said for guidebooks. Newspapers or news TV programs can

also be considered primarily utilitarian, since consumers access them for the latest news or commentaries on current events; likewise for specialized magazines (dedicated to gardening, DIY, fitness, and so on), which provide value thanks to their 'how-to' advice.

Other creative product categories offer utilitarian value to specific market segments. An example might be museum visits for students who want to gain first-hand experience of the art or collections that represent the specific historical period they're currently studying.

Even purely hedonic product categories such as the performing arts always have a fundamental utilitarian component linked to purchase and use. Several studies on this sector (Hume, 2008; Hume et al., 2007) show that the value perceived by spectators depends largely on purely functional benefits, like easy access to the theater, the courtesy of the personnel, and whether seats are comfortable. Likewise, a recent study by Ipsos Mori (2012) shows that breakfast radio may satisfy benefits like giving consumers a lift, giving them a kick, and preparing them for the day.

So basically, although the main distinction between creative products and other categories lies in their hedonic connotations, such products also offer a utilitarian component (which is primary for some, secondary for others), that is, value that serves to reach ulterior goals beyond consumption experience per se.

3.1.3　The communicative value of creative products

As repeatedly mentioned in the first two chapters, creative products have a positioning value within the framework of interpersonal relationships: to figure out who someone is, what she's all about, it's much more telling to consider her taste in books or her favorite vacation spot, rather than the brand of vacuum cleaner she uses.

Put another way, it's the creative products people consume, more than other goods or services, that allow them to communicate to others something about themselves. This means that thanks to creative products individuals can create an image of themselves and project it to others, generate esteem and build reputation, and indicate which social groups they are (and are not) affiliated with.

As DiMaggio (1987) pointed out, the basic ingredient in every social relationship is *conversation*. This is a ritual in which all the people involved use the choice of topics and the tone of the discussion to reveal something about themselves; in doing so they establish a level of intimacy with their interlocutors. Creative product consumption is a common topic because it can facilitate conversation and smooth the transition from minimal contact to close intimacy in interpersonal relationships.

In addition, consuming creative products is a very effective way for individuals to show their *status*. Beyond socio-economical standing, status also refers to a person's position within her network of interpersonal relationships. Being able to speak knowledgably about certain products enhances a person's reputation within her social circle, and secures a more central role. Essentially, social and symbolic capital are becoming more influential status-builders than economic capital (Section 2.1.1.3). This is where the value of creative products lies: it is generated by the impact that a consumer's personal choices have on what other relevant people think of her.

Some time ago, Bourdieu (1984) showed how consumption of different categories of cultural products served to shore up the boundaries that differentiated one social class from another. But as Western society has evolved toward post-modernism (Section 1.3.2), it's becoming increasingly clear that consumers of creative products are much more omnivorous than

ever before (Peterson, 1982). This enables them to choose from a vast selection of similar products to create their basket of consumption, subjectively setting its value. These consumers, thanks to new social relationships, can actually transition from one social class to another. Basically, *creative product consumption serves as a symbolic resource* within the framework of the social relationships people take part in, and this resource can be utilized for a variety of purposes (Research Focus 3.1).

3.1.3.1 The value of creative products in social relationships

Consuming creative products people can *reinforce existing social relationships*. A vivid illustration of this comes in an interview in *La Vanguardia* (Chavarrìa, 2012) with Joan Francesc Marco, Managing Director of the Gran Teatre del Liceu in Barcelona, one of Europe's premier opera houses. Marco talks about one aspect of the Liceu offering that is highly prized by season ticket holders: each patron is always assigned the same seat every year. This means opera-goers meet the same people on a regular basis, creating a familiar atmosphere where they can consolidate their friendships.

Therefore, people reinforce their social relations thanks to creative products, both by simply attending social events and by systematically striking up relationship-building conversations. Obviously this holds true in interpersonal relationships at various levels.

Research Focus 3.1

The symbolic value of music

Music is one of the creative products that, beyond pure listening pleasure, people consume to communicate their social identity and to show that they belong to certain social groups (and have nothing to do with others). Most people develop their musical tastes, along with their self-identity, when they're young.

Larsen et al. (2010) analyzed the symbolic value of music consumption by studying a group of 18- to 24-year-olds in New Zealand. Their main finding was that the decision to listen to a certain kind of music in a specific situation depends on the congruence of that music with the self-image of the individuals (identity value) and the image they want to convey to the other people in that same situation (communicative value).

So basically, when deciding what kind of music to listen to, consumers factor in the situation, their musical taste, and the image they want to convey to others. In other words, consumers consider their own taste in light of whether or not it's congruent with the image they want to present to others in a given situation (the so-called 'presentational self'). If consumers don't perceive this congruence, they can either decide not to listen to that type of music, or to listen to other music that they believe is more congruent with the self-image they want to project.

For example, let's say a group of young punk rockers are about to meet up with kids they don't know very well. They might decide not to listen to punk in this situation because they don't want to scare off the new kids or risk making a bad impression. Or maybe another group of kids want to show what a good dance crew they are. They might play music that fits their dance style, so they feel more confident in their abilities.

The North American tradition of going to see the Nutcracker during the holidays is a way to strengthen family ties through an annual ritual. Another example emerges in a study by Thyne (2001), which shows that the primary motivation in visiting a museum, according to the visitors surveyed, is to pass time with family and friends.

But when people consume creative products they can also *create new social relationships* while varying and expanding current ones. Different kinds of creative products allow consumers to participate in diverse relational networks, activating new social relationships (DiMaggio, 1987). Boorsma (2006) reports a number of studies on spectators of performing arts, underscoring that one of their underlying motivations is to establish social contacts and to initiate social interaction.

3.1.3.2 Creative products and sub-cultures of consumption

A fascinating phenomenon that marks the post-modern evolution of Western societies, combining the two motivations described above, is the *emergence of sub-cultures based on creative product consumption*. Schouten and McAlexander (1995: 43) define a sub-culture of consumption as follows: 'A distinctive subgroup of society that self-selects on the basis of a shared commitment to a particular product class, brand, or consumption activity.'

Simply put, a group of individuals with a shared interest or passion spawns the creation of a community, which might be physical or virtual. This community can be structured on values, rules of participation and membership, informal hierarchies, rituals, or idiosyncratic language – all factors that constitute culture. Through the interaction of its members, the community creates culture and, as we'll see in Section 3.3.5.1, value.

When people participate in a sub-culture of consumption, they can establish new social relationships by making initial contact and gradually taking part in the community; they can also consolidate existing relationships when they become engaged, active community members. Examples in creative sectors are countless, and include communities that spring up among followers of television series like *Star Trek* or *Lost*, bestselling books like the *Harry Potter* series, films such as *The Rocky Horror Picture Show*, and the fan clubs of sports teams the world over.

The music industry might well be where the clearest cases of sub-cultures of consumption can be found, mainly because so much media attention is focused here. A variety of music cultures are also the topic of research, such as punk (Fox, 1987), heavy metal (Arnett, 1993), rave (Goulding et al., 2002), and hip-hop (Arthur and Sherman, 2010). Findings highlight that for members, participating in community life is a fundamental part of social life and social identity.

People display their membership in a music community with their clothing and body art, with the idiosyncratic language they use, and with the rituals they perform during concerts. Being initiated into the community also involves rituals, and climbing the informal hierarchical ladder means acquiring cultural capital (expertise on the genre, its history, its stars) and social capital (interaction with the community).

3.1.4 The ethical value of creative products

When the consumption process has value in and of itself for the consumer, and the effects of this consumption impact relevant others, creative products generate *ethical value*. Many creative industries are highly respected as vectors of civil, social, and cultural progress in a community. It follows, then, that people are driven to consume these creative products by a desire to make a personal contribution to this progress. To cite Chen's study (2009) on collectors of contemporary art and visitors to contemporary art exhibitions, several interviewees gave philanthropic reasons for their purchase and consumption choices.

A case in point here would be buying the work of a young artist as a way to contribute to her career and give her work visibility, to the benefit of the entire art world. Likewise, many visitors to contemporary art exhibitions also say they want to support artistic creation and evolution, and in doing so contribute to collective well-being.

3.1.4.1 Creative products and cultural legacy

The perception of ethical value can also be expressed through people's desire to *pass on a cultural legacy* to their younger family members or their social network, to make their 'heirs' better people. This can be done by handing down creative products with high cultural value to young people, or by exposing them to similar products. Research on theatergoers by Walmsley (2011) reveals that one of the motivations cited by the interviewees is that they want to leave their children or grandchildren a legacy.

3.1.4.2 *The ethical value of donations*

In addition to consumption, one of the most common behaviors associated with the ethical value of creative products is *making donations* to organizations and institutions in creative industries. We'll discuss the topic of individual donations more fully in Section 3.4, but here it's worth mentioning that behind many donations made to artistic institutions lies the desire to 'do a good deed'. In other words, donations are seen as a way for people who've gotten a lot from society to give something back, to help people in need (for instance by offering scholarships to talented young artists), because giving is simply a part of life (Barnes, 2011).

3.1.5 An overview of benefits for consumers

The classification outlined in the previous sections suggests that a creative product can offer benefits to consumers that tie into four different areas of value, stemming from a combination of two dimensions. The first identifies the extent to which value depends on the actual consumption experience as opposed to the goals that this experience serves to achieve; the second indicates the extent to which the value depends on the effects that the experience has on the consumer or on relevant others. Here I want to emphasize once more that, when consuming goods, the benefits people look for ultimately serve to attain individual and social well-being, and this well-being represents the final parameter by which the value in question can and should be measured.

So the source of a creative product's value depends on the *meaning* that that product has for the individual (Richins, 1994). If the product has a purely *private* meaning (that is, one subjectively defined by the individual) and consuming the product is what generates value, this is hedonic value. If the product has a private meaning and its value derives from the goals that consumption makes it possible to achieve, this is utilitarian value. If instead the product has a *public* meaning (defined by others, not by the individual) and consumption generates value, this value is ethical. Lastly, if the meaning is public and consumption serves to reach ulterior goals, then the value in question is communicative.

At this point, though, it's important to remember that every consumer expects to attain product benefits that relate to every kind of value; likewise, every product category is generally able to provide all types of value. What makes individual consumers unique is the varying degree of importance they attribute to the benefits associated with the different components of value. A basketball fan who goes to the arena to watch her favorite team can get all sorts of value: hedonic if she feels emotions such as excitement during the game, or if she identifies with a team member; ethical if she brings her kids along to share her healthy passion for sports; communicative if she belongs to the team's fan club; utilitarian if she wants to learn more about the game. Then, depending on her unique personal traits (as we'll see later on), our basketball fan will assign more or less importance to the different components listed above.

This holds true for all creative industries. In a study on people who buy artwork, collector's items and antiques, for example, Zolfagharian and Cortes (2011) demonstrate that the benefits these buyers seek from their purchases can be utilitarian (increasing or maintaining the economic value of the item over time, or acquiring knowledge about a specific historical period), communicative (being accepted in or identifying with a certain social group), ethical (contributing to the success of an artist or to the exposure of an artistic movement), or hedonic (aesthetic pleasure, self-expression). On the same theme, Slater (2007) showed how the motivation for visiting an art gallery can be linked to three broad areas of value: escapism from the daily routine, social interaction with family or friends, and learning more about an art form or art in general, or discovering something new.

By the same token, if every creative product category can provide all types of benefits, consumers will perceive a single product within a category as more or less capable of providing specific benefits. Take apparel, for example. Buying a Prada or Gucci dress might be all about communicative value; shopping at a fair trade store is most likely motivated by ethical value; bargain hunting at a local market has the utilitarian value connotation of savings; and lastly purchasing clothing from an up-and-coming young designer is prompted by the hedonic value that comes from the satisfaction of being a 'talent scout' of sorts.

Up until now we've talked about one aspect of value, that is, benefits for consumers. In the next section we'll look more closely at the negative component of value.

3.1.6   The negative component of value: sacrifices

In Section 2.2.1, we saw that value for a consumer can be represented as the relationship between the benefits that a product offers and the sacrifices the consumer has to make to enjoy those benefits. In the previous section, I described four types of value that any creative product can provide. So from the standpoint of consumers, a product (or a brand, as we'll see in Chapter 8) generates value if the related benefits offer the types of value that they want most, and the perceived sacrifices they associate with the entire experience don't outweigh these benefits.

As I've already explained (Section 2.2.1), price isn't the only sacrifice pertaining to a product. More broadly speaking, sacrifices have to do with *all resources available to the consumer that can be invested in* that specific product rather than in alternative products/activities. Here's an example of a rock music fan. If she wants to go to a free three-day festival out of town she wouldn't have to pay for a ticket. But because of other sacrifices, she may still decide it's not worthwhile to go. First, there are additional costs like transportation to the festival and room and board. Then, if there's limited space available, our fan would have to arrive hours or even days early to be sure to get in and stake out a spot, which might mean using vacation days from work. And if she plans to go with friends, and they don't like some of the groups that are playing at the festival, she'll have to listen to them criticize and complain. And she could go on and on. When she tallies up all the pros and cons regarding the festival, our fan might end up deciding that the sacrifices outweigh the benefits, however badly she might want to go.

So the question is, for any given experience, what kinds of sacrifices do consumers have to make? And what resources do they use to deal with these sacrifices?

3.1.6.1   Sacrifices and stages of the consumer experience

Sacrifices can be classified according to the stage in the consumer experience they're connected with, or the kinds of resources consumers use to contend with them. The model I'll refer to in the following sections considers four different stages in consumer experience: pre-consumption experience, purchase experience, consumption experience, and post-consumption experience (Arnould et al., 2002).

In the *pre-consumption stage*, consumers gather the information they need to guide their purchase and consumption choices; they imagine what consumption will be like, and anticipate some of the emotions they'll experience; and they work out how much they'll have to spend and evaluate other risks associated with purchasing and using the product. This stage may or may not be followed up by a purchase and subsequent consumption. In fact, if consumers realize that the price is over budget, they might opt not to buy after all. Or they may pursue other routes to obtaining the product, like putting it on their birthday wish list, or chipping in with friends to make a collective purchase.

The next step, if the consumer decides to take it, is the *purchase stage*, which completes (and is still a part of) the pre-consumption experience. Since in most industries consumers make their purchases via specialized operators, be they physical or virtual (a Web site, an event, a shop, and so on), the purchase experience itself takes on value too. That makes it worthwhile to draw a distinction between the purchase stage and the pre-consumption stage. In any case, in the purchase stage consumers choose which product/brand to buy, normally paying some monetary amount, and they interact with the seller and the context where the products are being sold (physical or virtual).

The *consumption stage*, obviously, is when consumers actually use the product in a given context, and through this experience they co-create value. Consumption can be one-shot (watching *La Traviata* at Teatro alla Scala in Milan) or repeated (listening repeatedly to a recorded version of *La Traviata* at home). The second type of consumption sometimes calls for additional costs over time (with clothing, for instance, a leather coat occasionally needs special cleaning treatment).

Last comes the *post-consumption stage*, which generates additional sacrifices, such as disposing of a product that the consumer no longer wants. Another example of a sacrifice in this stage would be an art collector who decides to sell a favorite piece from her collection at a loss, and feels regret from losing an object that was deeply meaningful for her.

3.1.6.2   Consumer resources

The resources consumers use throughout all the stages of their experience can be classified as economic, temporal, cognitive, and emotional.[3] *Economic* resources obviously include money that the consumer has on hand, or has access to thanks to gifts, loans, or credit. *Temporal* resources refer to the time spent by consumers during all the different stages. *Cognitive* resources are the consumer's knowledge, expertise, and cognitive capabilities. And lastly *emotional* resources are the unique set of emotional states and sensations that an individual consumer is capable of feeling, both with respect to the product category and the specific stages in the consumption experience.

It is reasonable to assume that every consumer has a finite set of these resources, which implies that when she uses some of them for a given consumption experience, she has fewer to use for other experiences. This is what gives rise to perceived sacrifices. Table 3.1 illustrates the different types of sacrifices that a consumer can make, divided according to the stages of the experience and the relative class of resources.

3.1.6.3   *Types of sacrifices*

Let's say there's a couple that is trying to decide where to spend their summer vacation; both are interested in going somewhere off the beaten track. In the pre-consumption stage, the couple uses all types of resources to gather information on different destinations and travel options, on the best way to purchase their tickets (online or from a travel agent), and on how much the trip should cost. These activities call for investments in time, and in understanding and processing information.

What also happens in this stage is that the couple starts to imagine how various trips would turn out, anticipating the emotions they'll feel, both positive

Table 3.1 – Types of consumer sacrifices

Stage of the experience	Resources utilized	Type	Description
Pre-consumption	*Temporal, cognitive and emotional*	*Information*	Time and effort spent on gathering information
	Temporal, cognitive and emotional	*Search*	Time and effort spent on product search
	Economic, cognitive and emotional	*Opportunity costs*	Value lost by not buying and/or using an alternative product
	Cognitive and emotional	*Risks*	Risks associated with buying and using the product
	Economic, temporal, cognitive and emotional	*Switching costs*	Time, effort, and costs associated with converting other products or activities to use the purchased product
Purchase	*Economic*	*Monetary*	Purchase price
	Temporal, cognitive and emotional	*Shopping*	Time and effort spent on buying the product
Consumption	*Economic*	*Monetary*	Costs associated with using the product
	Temporal, cognitive and emotional	*Learning*	Time, effort spent on learning how to extract value from the product
	Economic, temporal, cognitive and emotional	*Maintenance*	Time, effort and costs spent in order to enjoy the value of the product over time
Post-consumption	*Economic, temporal, cognitive and emotional*	*Disposal*	Time, effort and cost of disposing of the product

and negative (the feeling of discovery they'll enjoy, but also the sense of risk if they're considering travelling to dangerous areas) (Kwortnik and Ross, 2007).

At the same time, the couple is calculating their available economic resources. Here we're not referring to the actual amount of money they'll need to budget but the perception of the value of other purchases they'll have to sacrifice, in other words, *opportunity costs*. At this point, they become aware that paying for their vacation means not having enough left over for a new television, a realization that triggers a negative emotional response.

What also happens during pre-consumption is that the couple perceives risks, which are predictors of possible sacrifices. First, *financial risks* entail wasting money on a product, in this case a trip, which might turn out to be disappointing. Then we have *performance risk*, which ties into the experiential nature of the product, making it impossible to anticipate relative quality before actual consumption. Next comes *psychological risk*, which arises if the vacation proves to be inconsistent with self-image. Our couple would be exposed to this risk if, for example, they see themselves as very sensitive to cultural integration, but some of the activities on their itinerary seem too intrusive with respect to the local populations. Last is *social risk*, that is, the couple's final travel plans might not meet with the approval of the social network they belong to (for instance, their very conformist friends would think their choice of destination is too eccentric).

As a final example, let's say the couple has always booked their holidays through a trusted travel agent, but this time she quotes a price for their trip that's much higher than what they found online. This triggers an unpleasant feeling due to having to change their habitual service provider, also known as *switching costs*.

During the purchase stage, the couple makes their decision, a process that entails comparing available options, weighing the pros and cons, and gathering additional information to iron out the details of their choice. These activities also call for investments in time, thought, and emotions. And since our couple has opted to go to their regular travel agent after all, this is when they need to spend money and time to actually finalize their purchase.

The consumption stage is when *monetary costs* are incurred that might go over budget (expenses that come up during the trip, for instance). There are possible *learning costs* here too, which relate to specific vacation activities (setting up the tent if they go camping). Finally, there may be sacrifices in the post-consumption stage, for example if a few years down the line the couple decides they want to get rid of some of the souvenirs they bought on vacation.

From this example, it should appear evident that the purchase price of a product is only one of the myriad components of the sacrifices that our couple has to make to go on vacation. At this point it's possible to draw a generalization by saying that if consumers perceive sacrifices as excessive, in the first stage they may decide not to go through with the purchase in question; on the other hand, if they've gone ahead with the experiential process they may feel unsatisfied by the product they've consumed. It's easy to imagine that the concept of value that the consumer uses takes various forms during different stages, and this is the topic of the next section.

3.2 THE DYNAMIC OF VALUE: FROM EXPECTED VALUE TO PERCEIVED VALUE TO CUSTOMER SATISFACTION

In Section 2.2.4, I introduced the different concepts of customer value that an organization has to manage to guarantee alignment with the market. Two of these are customer-centric: expected value and perceived value. The first is the relationship between benefits and sacrifices that the consumer expects from the product she's considering buying. The second comes from the benefit/sacrifice relationship that the consumer perceives after she's consumed the product. Referring back to the stages of the consumption experience, we can see that *expected value is associated with pre-consumption, while perceived value is the result of the consumption experience.* Value is the outcome of an assessment that the consumer makes of the product before (expected value) and after (perceived value) consuming it. By comparing these two forms of value, the consumer ends up feeling satisfaction or dissatisfaction. So, *satisfaction and dissatisfaction are cognitive and emotional responses to a consumption experience.*

As for the cognitive component, the consumer evaluates whether there is alignment or misalignment between her expectations and the actual end result of consuming the product. The emotional response, instead, is the type (positive or negative) and level (high or low) of emotions associated with this evaluation.

Both satisfaction and dissatisfaction derive from a disconfirmation of consumer expectations. Satisfaction comes from a positive disconfirmation (perceived value is superior to expected value), which in turn triggers positive emotions to varying degrees (pleasure, surprise, joy). Dissatisfaction, instead, is the result of a negative disconfirmation (perceived value is lower than expected value), which as we'd expect brings about a negative emotional reaction (disappointment, sadness, anger). When expectations are confirmed (perceived value matches expected value), consumers feel contentment, which is certainly positive both cognitively and emotionally, but not particularly intense. Figure 3.1 illustrates the relationships between the stages of experience, the concepts of value, and satisfaction/dissatisfaction.

Customer satisfaction is the primary goal of any market-oriented organization (Section 2.2.2); understanding and managing the relationships between expected and perceived value throughout the stages of consumer experience are the keys to attaining this goal. That's why in the value analysis process an organization needs to focus on the determinants of expected and perceived value; thorough knowledge on this score is what enables the organization to stay aligned with the market. And since the consumption experience lies at the heart of consumer activity, this is what we'll focus on first. We'll then go back and explore the other stages in the experiential process in the following chapter.

3.3 AT THE ROOT OF PERCEIVED VALUE: CONSUMPTION PRACTICES

Perceived value is a fruit of the consumption experience. Consumption is usually conceived as an activity entirely determined by the product being consumed: a book is read, a radio program is listened to, an art exhibit is visited, a sports event is followed on TV. But a consumption experience is much more complex than that, and organizations have to come up with far more sophisticated analytical and interpretative models to gain deep knowledge of market phenomena.

Every consumption experience engages the consumer on a sensorial, cognitive, emotional, and behavioral level, translating into a series of interactions with the product and the consumption context, in which various competences come into play (Carù and Cova, 2011). Basically, when people consume products, they adopt *consumption practices*, which are behaviors used to extract value from the product. This is how consumers co-create value. Although these practices are

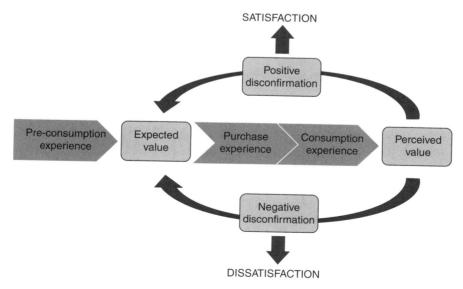

Figure 3.1 – Experience–value–satisfaction relationships

product-specific (consuming a book is different from consuming a holiday resort), by applying a higher level of abstraction it's possible to come up with a useful classification.[4]

3.3.1   Sense making practices

First of all, consumers use sense making to attempt to assign meaning to a product. This process, which can be found in all consumption experiences, includes categorizing and associating,[5] evaluating, and appreciating.

Every experience starts with an inclination to consume a product. (How long this stage lasts is totally subjective.) Preparing for consumption involves placing the product in a category (*categorizing*), which brings up a number of cognitive and emotional associations (*associating*).

For example, if a consumer is about to read a Wild West comic book, she'll be ready for a story with a specific setting and a somewhat predictable plot. She makes these assumptions based on the comic books she's already read that belong to the same category. Then while she's reading, she'll be *evaluating*, or judging the experience by comparing the content with certain norms and conventions that apply to Western comics

(how the characters are portrayed, the art style of the comic book, and so on), and with her previous experience (with similar stories, characters, and the like). Last comes *appreciating*, both in terms of type and intensity of her emotional response (Research Focus 3.2).

Clearly sense making activities are often done subconsciously; the consumer doesn't realize what she's doing unless she stops and thinks about it. And just as often, these activities are automatic, thanks to prior experience. In fact, novice consumers (people who've never read a Western comic book before) spend greater cognitive and emotional effort in these cases, since they lack the models that help them frame, perceive, and assess the experience they're having. Likewise, when a product doesn't readily fall into any category (because it's innovative enough to actually warrant a new one, or because it's a hybrid of several categories) consumers are thrown off balance because they don't have consolidated sense making practices to rely on.

3.3.2   Integration practices

Integration here refers to making the product a part of one's consumption system and lifestyle. Clearly integration practices are vital for any product that provides

Research Focus 3.2

Emotions and sense making practices in reading

Reading a fictional narrative elicits very particular emotions (Corna and Troilo, 2005). Generally speaking, there are two components of a text that affect emotions: style and subject matter (Cupchik et al., 1998). The distinction between stylistic and semantic factors leads to the classification of F-emotions and A-emotions (Dijkstra et al., 1994; Kneepkens and Zwaan, 1994). *F-emotions* (*fiction-based emotions*) encompass all the emotional states that readers experience in response to the characters and to the story as the plot unfolds. On the contrary, *A-emotions* (*artifact-based emotions*) are aroused by the aesthetic components of the text.

The emotions that reading can elicit are linked primarily to sense making practices, and can be classified as *emotions of the mind* and *emotions of participation* (apart from the difference between stylistic and semantic elements). The first are what individuals feel as simple spectators of everything that happens; the second arise when they actually enter into the story (Oatley, 1994). Key processes in sense making that trigger participation emotions are empathy and identification, which lead readers to an appreciation of the narrative. For both of these processes, readers have to create a mental model. In other words, they build a mental representation of the story based on their knowledge and on both the inductive and deductive processes they enact.

So when people are reading, they're not only seeing the book in front of them, but also in their minds they're creating an image that reflects the world in the story. The mental model that emerges while reading, the mental picture of the setting, the characters, and the plot, is what lets readers escape to a sort of parallel universe, where they connect with the characters themselves. This enables readers both to identify and empathize with them. When they become so engrossed in their reading that they're 'seeing' the story, and not just reading it, readers can immerse themselves in the setting and interact with the characters as if they were real people – that's when they're experiencing the story from the inside, not watching from the outside.

value through its contribution to consumer identity, in which case it is integrated into *the very concept of self*.

Let's look at an example. Say a consumer buys a dress that's a complete break from her usual style as a way to demonstrate she's making a change in her life. We can easily imagine a series of activities that she carries out, such as trying her new dress on again and again in front of the mirror at home before wearing it out, matching it up with different shoes and accessories, or even trying new hair styles. Eventually, she realizes that some of the clothing in her wardrobe doesn't 'fit' with her new look, and she starts thinking that it doesn't fit the new lifestyle she wants to adopt either. Then she might remember that she saw a photo feature in a fashion magazine with clothes in the same style as her dress. And so on.

By activating these processes, an activity known as *assimilating*, consumers lessen the cognitive and emotional distance between themselves and the product, and gradually make the product part of their consumption systems (and in some cases, their extended selves), where eventually it becomes an integral component. Naturally, once a given product has been integrated, assimilation activities become more routine.

The integration process also has a more operative component called *producing*, which refers to actual product use. This is when the consumer tries out her competences in using the item. In the previous example, the consumer puts on the dress and starts to think about and appreciate how she feels when she's wearing it on different occasions and in relation to the reactions of the people who see her.

During this stage, cognitive and social resources along with consumer competences are all critical. In fact, when competences are lacking, producing may prove unsatisfactory. Not because the product isn't capable of providing the expected value, but because the consumer doesn't get optimal use out of the product due to her limited competence. This would be the case if the woman with the new dress didn't have the good taste to choose the right accessories, and ended up looking mismatched and gaudy. (Of course, if that was her intention, it's a whole different story!)

As with assimilating, for producing consumers have to pay closer attention the first few times they experience a product, although it later becomes automatic. Individuals can standardize producing by applying conventions shared in their consumption systems, or between the consumption and production system

(accessorizing the dress the way the shop assistant suggests, or the way it's illustrated in a fashion magazine), or through *personalizing* processes.

By personalizing a product, the consumer ignores standard product use, and gives the item in question a unique, distinctive, and idiosyncratic meaning. This activity represents value co-creation in its truest sense, since the consumer isn't passively adopting the value the company or institution proposes, but adding her own touch of distinction instead. Going back once again to our consumer and her dress, she can personalize it by what she wears it with (a completely different style of accessories or shoes), or when she wears it (to the pub, where everyone else is wearing jeans, for example).

The meaning behind personalization can be private or public, as subjectively defined by the consumer, depending on whether consumption is totally private or if there is a public dimension as well. For example, if a couple celebrates their anniversary every year by visiting the city where they first met, the meaning is clearly private, even though the consumption experience is public.

3.3.3   Sharing practices

Many consumption experiences, rather than taking place individually, happen through interactions with social contexts of consumption, and involve *sharing practices regarding the product*.[6] To illustrate, reading a book is something individuals can do alone in private, but it can also be a collective activity that happens in a public place.

One such practice, *communing*, takes place when consumption is part of an interaction with a social context, but here the product isn't central to the social experience. (A woman reads a book on the subway, but it's not the book that motivates her to take the subway.) Another practice is *socializing*, when the consumption experience is deliberately done in conjunction with others, the social aspect being essential to the experience. (The same woman belongs to a book club that meets regularly to read together.)

Last there are practices involving *communicating through the product*, when the item in question is intentionally used because of its communicative function within social relationships, becoming an expression of social identity. This is a way for consumers to show that they belong to this social group, but not that one.

On an evening out with her friends, our reader might strike up a conversation about the erotic romance novel she's reading as a way to reinforce her image as a woman who's free of inhibitions or social constraints.

Summing up, the consumption experience translates into a series of practices that consumers activate to get value from the product, participating in co-creating this value. Specifically, the hedonic, ethical, and communicative value of creative products generates particular consumption experiences and practices which we'll explore in the following sections.

3.3.4 Consumption rituals

Consumption practices are often behaviors that follow pre-set, institutionalized patterns that are sometimes collectively shared. In these cases, experience takes the form of a consumption ritual. Since creative products provide hedonic value also through their sacredness/spirituality and by contributing to identity, they are particularly well-suited to becoming objects of ritual. Rook (1985: 252) defines a ritual as: 'A type of expressive, symbolic activity constructed of multiple behaviors that occur in a fixed, episodic sequence, and that tend to be repeated over time. Ritual behavior is dramatically scripted and acted out and is performed with formality, seriousness, and inner intensity.'

Consumption rituals can be meaningful for the individual alone, or may have shared value. In the study on the reading experience presented in Research Focus 3.2 (Corna and Troilo, 2005), we discovered that many consumers activate precise individual rituals when they read, depending on the book. For example, with books that are loaded with symbolic value, people create a very specific setting for reading, perhaps making a cup of tea, getting comfortable on the couch or in an armchair, taking the phone off the hook, and so on. In other cases, instead, getting in touch with nature is what enhances appreciation of certain content, so for some books the more appropriate reading setting is out in the open, sitting on a park bench, for instance.

Other consumption experiences for creative products involve collective rituals. On this topic, Walmsley (2011) researched theatergoers and found that some consumers enact an individual ritual that revolves around dressing to go to the theater. Others use collective rituals focused on appropriating physical and social space in the theater (meeting people before the show, looking for their seat, and so on).

In the world of music, different genres call for different collective rituals that are played out during concerts. Some typical rituals found at heavy metal concerts, for example, are headbanging, slam dancing, or moshing (jumping up and down and bumping into other spectators) (Arnett, 1993), but completely different rituals would be enacted at a pop or hip-hop concert.

Through individual and collective consumption rituals, symbolic connotations take on a sacred and spiritual tone. It's possible to go so far as to say that without ritualistic behaviors, consumers aren't able to make sacred connotations with an experience or a product (Belk et al., 1989). Interesting examples are provided by art cities, archeological sites, monuments, and even temporary exhibits in museums and exhibition spaces. Visiting these places is becoming more and more like a (post-)modern *pilgrimage*. In other words, these experiences are spiritual journeys to 'sacred' places, laden with the revered value of culture. Individuals go to these 'places of worship' with groups of other 'devotees', often interacting with them respectfully and silently, and taking home (post-)modern relics in the form of souvenirs (Troilo, 2002).

3.3.5 Collective consumption

In Section 3.3.3 we saw that many consumption experiences of creative products revolve around sharing practices. Some of these involve socializing, when consumers deliberately decide to live the experience with others, which is what generates value. In this case, value co-creation is collective (Section 2.3), and the entire set of practices takes on a different connotation beyond simply sharing.

Sense making practices, for example, are carried out collectively, generating processes of categorization, association, evaluation, and appreciation on a group level. It's easy to see how this happens, for example, when a group of friends goes to the movies together, or to a concert, or to watch a football match, or on holiday. These are all examples of sense making deriving from mutual influence.

To illustrate, we can look again to the increasingly popular trend in the book world: *book clubs* or *reading groups*. Childress and Friedkin (2012) show that in discussions among group members after reading a given book, individual interpretations make way for a collective one. This is the outcome of the set of resources and competences of single members and the mutual influence they have on one another. Consequently, the result of the experience (that is, the value extracted by each person) is the fruit of the collective co-creation of meaning, a process that would have a different outcome if the book in question were read individually.

3.3.5.1 Brand communities

Brand communities represent a collective consumption phenomenon that's on the rise in many creative industries. In these communities, value-generating consumption practices are unique.

In Section 3.1.3 we already came across the concept of sub-cultures of consumption. This is exactly what brand communities are: a group of people who share a passion for a brand and create a community that becomes institutionalized through rituals, shared rules, an informal (and sometimes even formal) hierarchy, and, above all, regular meetings. At the center of all these activities is the brand.

Brand communities can be established and run by brand owner, or independently created by brand fans. Such communities might revolve around a current brand (like the *Magic: The Gathering* game described at the end of Chapter 4) or a historic brand (the *Star Trek* saga). In any case, community participation facilitates collective consumption experiences that generate value for individual consumers.

Every community sets up consumption practices that are specific to the brand in question. However, certain value co-creation processes are common to all communities. Schau et al. (2009) suggest that there are four types of value-generating consumption practices in brand communities:

- *Social networking* practices seek to create and reinforce social connections within the community, for example, welcoming new members, offering support to other members, or establishing procedures for conflict resolution.
- *Impression management* practices target people outside the community with the aim of attracting new members and creating a positive impression of the community itself. Some examples include addressing non-members with personal communication activities, or demonstrating the hedonic and ethical values of pleasure, fun, and a sense of belonging that come from the time dedicated to the community.
- *Community engagement* practices aim to solidify membership in the community. This is done by sharing memorable anecdotes about personal brand experience, or using distinctive signs linked to the brand or highlighting and appreciating all the diversity among members who have the same passion.
- *Brand use* practices have to do with specific behaviors such as grooming or personalizing the products related to the brand.

Schau et al. (2009) studied a number of different communities, some centering on creative products. Here's a fascinating example of an American community dedicated to *Xena: The Warrior Princess* (Case History 3.1).

As compared to individual practices, collective consumption differs because of joint participation in production processes, which arises from the shared passion for a given brand. Collective production is what generates all the different kinds of value we've talked about: hedonic value through pleasure and fun,

---

Case History 3.1

The brand community of *Xena: The Warrior Princess*

Xena: The Warrior Princess is a TV series that ran from the mid-1990s until 2001 in the US. This program's fan community regularly organizes conventions where new members are inducted and 'veterans' get the chance to shore up their relationships, exchange information on brand-related activities, or resolve doctrinal debates on how episodes or characters in the series should be interpreted (*social networking*).

At the conventions, community members show their devotion by dressing up like their favorite characters; there's even a competition for best costume (which fans often make themselves) (*community engagement* and *brand use*). Another popular activity is based on *fan fiction*, when members write stories involving characters from the series, circulating them throughout the community to get feedback and recognition (*community engagement*) and to attract new members (*impression management*).

building self-esteem and identity; communicative value, creating and reinforcing social relationships and defining social identity; ethical value, with community members helping one another become happier people; and utilitarian value, because members can buy new and used products and services associated with the brand, enjoying the economic advantages of belonging to the community.

3.3.6   Collecting

Countless creative products are collectors' items. From priceless art to baseball cards, collecting is a popular hobby that for some is a passing interest and for others a life-long endeavor. Collecting represents a unique form of consumption because here value lies in the set of items that make up the collection, the end result of activities aimed at creating and expanding the collection itself.

A collection consists of items that are similar in some way, with this similarity subjectively defined by the collector. Whether *Spider-Man* comic books, Ming vases, Louis Vuitton bags, or art deco lamps, for a series of objects to actually be a collection, owning them has to be contingent on the fact that they belong to a pre-defined category. This category is perceived as a collection to complete, and each constituent item has a precise cognitive and affective position and value.

But this doesn't mean that the value of a collection derives from its completion – quite the contrary. Often collections are impossible to complete (as with all the Ming vases in the world, or all the shells on the planet), and value for the collector comes from the feeling that she's moving forward toward a conclusion, even though she'll never be able to reach it. The value of every single item comes from the meaning it takes on within the collection. A single issue of *Spider-Man* is worth an hour of light reading, but as one of hundreds of issues, its value lies in the fact that it completes the collection. And this value can be considered incalculable.

Collecting can provide all the different types of value we discussed in Section 3.1. First, hedonic value comes from the intellectual stimulation of becoming an expert in whatever is collected, the pleasure of acquiring a new item in the collection, the aesthetic enjoyment elicited by the beauty of the objects. All these factors are what motivate the majority of collectors, along with the

capacity to contribute to self-identity and to nourish self-esteem (Guerzoni and Troilo, 1998).

In addition, as a collection grows, its contents become sacred, and the collector gains a sense of spirituality (Belk et al., 1989). The ethical value of a collection, instead, comes from the chance to help the producers of collector items by providing financial support and encouraging them to develop their competences. A collection can also promote civil progress in a community, as is the case with an art collection that is open to the public (Chen, 2009). Contributing to creating social identity, and establishing and reinforcing social relationships are ways that collections produce communicative value (Guerzoni and Troilo, 1998). And finally, a collection can also offer utilitarian value, for example if its economic value increases over time (Zolfagharian and Cortes, 2011).

3.4   EXPERIENCE WITHOUT CONSUMPTION: DONATIONS

One way for individuals to get value out of their relationships with providers of creative products is to donate to these organizations. Generally speaking, the majority of non-profits benefit greatly from donations (which obviously is not the case for most for-profit ventures). With respect to traditional consumption a donation is a different kind of experience that doesn't revolve around product use, but centers on a value relationship with the producer. So rather than a consumption experience of creative products, donations are a *consumer's experience with creative products*.

Since the act of donating is a value-generating experience for the donor and for the receiving organization, it must be given the same consideration as other consumption experiences. By making a donation, people offer their money, time, goods, or services to an organization to help it reach its goals. Most of the world's non-profits depend on donations of money, goods, services, or volunteer work to support their activities. Common examples are volunteers who act as guides or provide information or security services for museums and theaters in the cities where they live. But what's in it for donors? What value do they get from the experience?

Donating is a behavior primarily associated with ethical value (Section 3.1.4), since the beneficiaries

Table 3.2 – Some examples of the different types of value generated by individual donations

	EXTRINSIC	INTRINSIC
SELF-ORIENTED	Tax benefits	Identification
	Cost savings	Sense of belonging to the community
OTHER-ORIENTED	Social relations	Giving back to society
	Public recognition	Support of societal progress

of donations are people other than the donors themselves. Yet beyond ethical value, different people can associate donating with different benefits, as illustrated in Table 3.2 (Barnes, 2011; Johnson and Ellis, 2011; Ko et al., 2011). Hedonic value emerges, for example, if people identify with the institution as a symbol of the local community, or its basic values. Social value might derive from the chance to build relationships with other donors or gain public recognition, so as to expand and reinforce social capital. Finally, donating can also generate utilitarian value, considering that in many countries donations are tax deductible. Also, a number of institutions offer exclusive services to their donors that are not available to ordinary consumers.

To sum up, the act of donating constitutes a value-generating experience, one that can enrich consumers' relationships with suppliers of creative products. I'll come back to the topic of donations in Chapter 5.

3.5 THE INTENSITY OF THE CONSUMPTION EXPERIENCE

Up to this point we've categorized consumption experiences on the basis of specific practices activated to extract value from creative products. Another possible classification takes into account the intensity of these experiences. The most enthusiastic supporters of the experience economy (Pine and Gilmore, 1999; Schmitt, 1999) underscore that intensity is a fundamental feature, and recommend that companies create extraordinary, memorable, transformative experiences.

Yet empirical evidence suggests taking a less emphatic approach, since not every experience can be extraordinary and transformative. Logically, an experience that happens frequently can no longer be considered exceptional. So organizations have to be aware that every experience can be placed somewhere along a continuum of intensity, which certainly impacts customer satisfaction.

On the positive side, creative products by nature are well-suited to generating memorable and transformative experiences. (Everyone can clearly remember a life-changing book, or film, or football match, or vacation spot, or work of art.)

But the flipside is that this very nature is what raises consumer expectations. In other words, compared to products with less creative content, people tend to be immediately dissatisfied if the consumption experience of a creative product is lacking in intensity. (Everyone has read books, watched films, seen football matches, visited vacation spots, and looked at works of art that have left no impression at all, because they were uninteresting or insignificant.)

So what is it that gives an experience high intensity? To answer this question a helpful classification is the one proposed by Csikszentmihaly (1997) based on two dimensions: how challenging the experience is, and what skills the experience calls into play (Figure 3.2).

As these two factors increase, so does the intensity of the experience (and consequently the consumption experience). So a very challenging experience that calls for a high level of skill is extremely intense; the experience gradually loses intensity as the challenge and the required skill level diminishes. Csikszentmihaly calls the highest level of intensity *flow*. This is when an experience elicits the utmost attention and absorption. When people are in a state of flow, they lose all sense of time, of the surrounding environment, and of anything that takes place at the fringes of their experience.

How often have we found ourselves so absorbed in a reading a book or gazing at a work of art that we don't even hear someone nearby talking to us, trying to get our attention? In the lexicon used by experts on consumption behavior, the concept of flow often translates to *immersion*. This term refers to the consumer being one with the experience; when the cognitive, emotional, and often physical distance between the consumer and the situation diminishes to the point of disappearing altogether. An aesthetic experience often elicits this reaction (Research Focus 3.3).

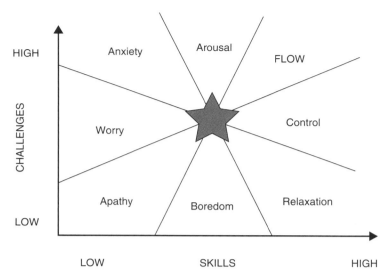

Figure 3.2 – A classification of experiences
Source: Csikszentmihalyi (1997)

Research Focus 3.3

A particular type of experience: the aesthetic experience

One of the distinctive characteristics of most creative products is their aesthetic content (Chapter 1). In fact, with aesthetic products, this is one – and often the only – component of value perceived by the customer. The consumption experience of these products (that is to say, the aesthetic experience) is a unique one, and has long attracted the attention of experts in a variety of fields. Whatever perspective is adopted to interpret this singular phenomenon, there is a common starting point linking aesthetic experience to the concept of *beauty*, to the different ways beauty manifests itself and the myriad forms it can take. Summing up, then, beauty is the true protagonist of the aesthetic experience.

Like all experiences, the aesthetic experience engages the senses, cognition, emotions, and behavior of consumers. Wagner (1999) suggests that there are four components to an aesthetic experience. *Contemplation*, the fruit of interaction with the aesthetic product, is when individuals concentrate on certain characteristics that capture their attention and gradually immerse them in the experience. Aesthetic contemplation is 'disinterested', with no ulterior motives (as would be the case, on the contrary, if an individual were appraising an aesthetic object to estimate its economic value or to determine whether it's an appropriate gift). The experience is an end in itself; the aim is to feel aesthetic pleasure from interacting with the product.

Contemplation is followed by the *apprehension* of beauty: recognizing the product's stylistic elements and contents that give it aesthetic value, and then recomposing these qualities to get a holistic view. In recognizing beauty, the focus might lie on the content (flowers in a vase in a still life, for example) or stylistic elements (a decomposed vase in a cubist style), depending on the tastes and other characteristics of each consumer, as we'll see in Section 4.3.4.1. It follows, then, that an aesthetic experience is valuable only if the consumer perceives it as such.

After apprehension comes *appreciation*, which is the end result of a process of evaluation in which consumers compare the product to similar ones they're familiar with, or to their ideal of beauty. Comparing activates the processes of categorization and association we talked about in Section 3.3.1.

Appreciation can lead to *aesthetic pleasure*, the positive reaction that the experience of beauty triggers, which is the basis of satisfaction (if enjoyment is greater than anticipated). This form of pleasure engages various spheres of the individual: cognitive, by activating previous knowledge and providing intellectual stimulation; emotional, because it elicits an emotional response, either negative or positive (recalling Section 3.1, even negative emotions can provide aesthetic pleasure); sensorial, engaging all the senses; and physical, because people can have intense physical reactions, for example when pleasure brings tears to their eyes or makes their heart race.

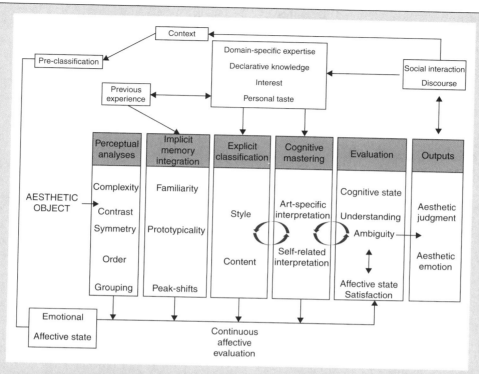

Figure 3.3 – An interpretative model of aesthetic experience
Source: Adapted from Leder et al. (2004)

So when an aesthetic experience is effective and satisfying, it consists in a gradual immersion in the interaction with the aesthetic product to the point of creating a state of flow.

But it would be wrong to think that this aesthetic experience is a passive one. In fact, in their study on museum visitors, Joy and Sherry (2003) demonstrated that aesthetic experience is the outcome of behaviors and practices that engage all the senses, leading to an experience that is perceived and physically absorbed as *embodied imagination*.

For instance, when visiting a museum, people have to walk around to see the works on display. They also move close to certain items, to catch the scent of the colors and materials; they touch things if it's allowed (and even if it isn't!); they try to step back from certain pieces to get a different perspective. So immersion means progressively reducing the physical and cognitive distance between themselves and the aesthetic product, which can set off an intensely emotional reaction.

From a distinctly psychological standpoint, Leder et al. (2004) propose a more detailed model of aesthetic experience than the one described above. Their model identifies the different cognitive and emotional components that characterize this kind of experience, and the contextual elements that impact various phases of aesthetic appreciation. Figure 3.3 illustrates the model.

The experience of consuming creative products can create total immersion for consumers. But it's important not to forget that this kind of experience can also trigger responses all over the map in Figure 3.2. Watching a TV show can elicit apathy; seeing a theatrical production that breaks all the rules can generate anxiety; seeing a documentary can cause boredom. So basically, the intensity of the consumption experience is always subjective: a product might provoke total immersion in some consumers, yet leave others utterly indifferent.

Since satisfaction is the result of a positive disconfirmation of expectations, organizations shouldn't make the mistake of thinking that they should always aim to provide high-intensity experiences. The truth is that if consumers expect low intensity from a given experience, they may not be satisfied by something that is extremely challenging or that requires great skill. If a consumer buys a book to read on a plane, for instance, her aim is relaxation. So she might be disappointed if that book takes more concentration than she is willing to invest.

3.6 EXPERIENCE WITHOUT POSSESSION: ACCESS

Consumption experiences can also be categorized according to whether or not the consumer actually owns the product in question. In fact, countless consumer experiences in creative industries don't require possession. Visiting an art museum, reading a book in the library, watching a sports competition, or attending a live show or concert: all these activities can provide consumers with value, but without the need for ownership. In these cases, a consumption experience is the result of product *access*.

The big difference between ownership and access is that the first allows consumers to *repeat the consumption experience* over time more easily and frequently, and affords them complete control. If a consumer buys herself a book, she can read it and reread it as often as she likes. If she buys a work of art, she can enjoy it any time she wants. If she fancies watching all the seasons of her favorite TV series again, she has to buy it on DVD. If she feels like re-experiencing the emotions of a live concert, she has to buy the CD. In other words, she has to transform access into ownership.

Ownership represents a basic premise of traditional marketing. But one of the current trends in the capitalistic world is to substitute possession with access (Rifkin, 2000), often shared access. This phenomenon is consistent with the philosophy of curbing the consumption of the planet's natural and economic resources. An excellent example is co-housing, which began in the 1970s in Scandinavian countries and gradually spread to several European countries. This style of architectural design allows a number of residents in the same community to share space. Munksögård in Denmark (www.munksoegaard.dk) or Wandelmeent in Holland (www.wandelmeent.nl) represent standards of excellence for residential communities designed according to a philosophy of minimal environmental impact and shared community space. This shows that access is

becoming a means of experience in various sectors, and is no doubt commonplace in creative industries.

Owning a product allows for repeated use, so owners have a *degree of control* or *power* that is partially or totally lacking for people who only have access. Moreover, the desire to control a product is a sign of its role within the extended self of the consumer (Belk, 1988): the more important the product is to a consumer's identity, the more the consumer will be prompted to possess it.

Simply consider when someone borrows a book from a friend or sees a film at the cinema, and she's so taken with it that she wants to have it for herself. Even though she's already experienced the product, she's impelled to buy a copy so she can use it whenever she wishes. Chen (2009) shows how art collectors and visitors to art exhibits have several shared motivations underlying their experiences of possession and access. Yet the difference lies in the role the artwork plays in the process of self-identification and the construction of social identity.

Another difference between ownership and access is that the two *lead to different consumption practices*. Specifically, ownership calls for activities like caring and grooming, which are an essential part of the value that the product can provide. Possession also allows owners to have a sense of nostalgia; they can rediscover past emotions, and relive particularly significant moments in their lives. Access, on the other hand, often comes with collective consumption practices, such as visiting a museum, going to a live concert, or making a pilgrimage, which involve less control but offer other types of value.

3.7 CONCLUSIONS

My aim in this chapter was to provide a compass that allows an organization to find its way amidst the various forms of value that creative products can offer, and the different practices that consumers can use to get that value. Since value for consumers is a combination of benefits and sacrifices, first I summarized the areas of value associated with benefits, and the different kinds of sacrifices that arise along the stages of the consumer experience. Companies or institutions offering creative products need to effectively manage the value analysis process; to do so they should have a clear idea of the areas of value that relate to the benefits offered by their products, and the sacrifices these products require to ensure a satisfying consumer experience.

I also concentrated on the concept of perceived value, since this form of value is the immediate outcome of consumer experience. In particular, I detailed the practices that constitute the experience, highlighting both the general and specific forms that it can take, depending on the unique features of creative products.

Organizations that operate in creative industries must accumulate knowledge of relevant consumption practices in order to understand the source of the perceptions of value that consumers associate with their products. Without this knowledge, these organizations will be missing a piece of the puzzle explaining consumer satisfaction or dissatisfaction, since this, as we now know, depends on how expected value and perceived value compare.

To complete the picture, in the next chapter I'll discuss the concept of expected value, its causes, and the stages in the consumer experience that anticipate and directly result from this value. With the right knowledge of perceived value, expected value, and their respective determinants, an organization will have the upper hand in managing value creation and dissemination processes for the consumer, processes that form the basis for long-term relationships and market success.

REVIEW QUESTIONS

1. What are the different types of value a creative product can provide to consumers? Why can they be considered resources for consumers?
2. What are the typical sacrifices that are related to creative products?
3. What are the processes that drive customer satisfaction and dissatisfaction?
4. What are the different consumption practices by which consumers can get value from creative products?
5. How can consumers get value from creative products without possessing them? Which kind of value can they get without possession?

CASE STUDY

ARGENTINE TANGO: CONSUMPTION PRACTICES FOR A TRANSFORMING EXPERIENCE

This case was co-authored with Marilia Sciulli[7]

Born in the brothels on the outskirts of Buenos Aires, today Argentine tango – the dance and the musical genre – are famous the world over. In 2009 tango even earned a place on UNESCO's World Heritage list (www.unesco.org). Thanks to its wealth of cultural connotations, rituals, and codes, Argentine tango is unique among Latin dances. And thanks to its hedonic and communicative value, the consumption practices of tango are, in some ways, remarkably original.

The allure of tango is rooted primarily in its history, its fame as a forbidden dance. Its origins date back to the second half of the 1800s, when middle-class men and European immigrants first danced tango in the brothels of Buenos Aires. From there, despite its being taboo, tango gradually caught on in the night spots and dance halls in the city center, enjoying a positive reception among the higher classes. In the 1920s came the golden age of tango, when the dance appeared in the cabarets of far-away Paris.

In the decades since, Argentine tango has experienced alternating periods of decline and renewal, but it is forever present in the history of the Argentinean people. In fact, even when it was banned by the authorities from 1955 to 1983, tango went underground but never disappeared entirely (Denniston, 2003). Today tango has become an international phenomenon involving more than 3.5 million people in Buenos Aires alone, 70 per cent of whom are tourists, and generating business volumes worth 130 million dollars (MercoPress, 2007).

The tradition

Tango is an elegant, passionate dance based on improvisation. The fundamental principle is 'the man is the conductor, the woman the seducer'. Various styles of tango differ with regard to music and movements. Here are a few: the milonguero style, with partners dancing very close together, making precise, measured movements; the salón style, with a more open embrace; and the tango show, used in competitions and exhibitions, which is actually choreographed with exceptionally dramatic, sweeping movements.

The *milonga* is the place where people dance tango. Tradition dictates precise standards of behavior (although these rules are gradually falling into disuse in Argentina, even more so in the rest of the world). In any case, the custom is for men and women to sit on opposite sides of the milonga. The man looks at the woman from across the room (*mirada*) and if she meets his gaze, he invites her to dance with a discreet nod of the head (*cebeceo*) and accompanies her onto the dance floor. To refuse a man's initiative, the woman simply looks away. The invitation to dance is a ritual meant to preserve the man's honor on the one hand (especially if he gets turned down), and the freedom of the woman on the other, who doesn't feel obliged to accept an explicit invitation.

In the milonga, all the couples move counter-clockwise around the dance floor, and it's the man's job to protect the woman from running into other dancers. The music generally consists of *tanda* and *cortinas*. A *tanda* is a sequence of four or five songs with a similar style and rhythm. A *cortina* is a song played in between two tandas, which serves to create a change of rhythm and to give the dancers the chance to change partners or have a chat.

Since tango is so intimately embedded in the history and culture of its country of origin, the experience of people who dance and listen to tango music outside of Argentina takes place through special consumption practices. These are a mix of the original codes, together with the value systems, lifestyles, and cultures of the countries where the dance is 'consumed'. The example we'll explore here is Italy.

Argentine tango in Italy

The widespread popularity of Argentine tango in Italy is remarkable, as reflected in the following figures. As of 2013, there are 147 Argentine Tango Associations, members of a Federation (Faitango), which organize courses, regularly scheduled dance nights, and festivals lasting several days; the same year counted 23 such festivals (Manetti, 2013). What's more, there are thousands of dance schools that offer tango classes and tango nights on a fairly regular basis in most of the large and medium-sized cities in the country. In fact, milongas have become so common that almost every night people can find a place to go to dance tango.

Sense making practices

The motivations that spark people's interest in tango are typically hedonic (a fascination with the stereotype of tango, and an interest in the music and/or dance) and communicative (a desire to socialize). Because of the technical intricacies of tango, people normally take classes offered at various levels through dance schools, where they can learn the basics and build on them. Here dancers acquire not only technique, but notions about tango culture as well: the different types of tango, the names of the top artists and classic dances, and places made famous by tango. Beyond lessons, students can also attend *práctica* sessions, which give them the chance to practice what they've learned in class and to perfect their technique. Additional opportunities to learn and practice come at national or international festivals, where people dance all day long, and there are often performances by professional dancers and special guests.

Creating competences through this system of schools and festivals renders sense making practices fairly structured and codified. At school people learn to *categorize* not only the steps but also the different types of tango, the tradition, and the evolution of the dance. This also enables them to develop a capacity for *evaluation* and *appreciation*, which is useful both for actually dancing, and for refining their personal taste over time.

Integration practices

It's in integration practices that the most patent peculiarities of the tango experience outside its homeland can be found. In Argentina, people easily integrate the dance into their self-identity, but elsewhere this process is more complex, and calls for negotiation between the different selves. There's no doubt that for those who have a true passion for tango, dancing at every opportunity, this becomes a distinctive component of their self-identity.

The first factor that has a major impact on integration practices is accepting/negotiating the *system of roles in the couple*. According to Argentinean tradition, the basic principle is 'the man is the leader, the woman the seducer'. But this concept clashes with the norms of contemporary Western society (Italy included), where there is a more balanced relationship between men and women. Consequently, the widespread popularity of a dance that masks underlying male chauvinism appears contradictory. This contradiction is typically reconciled (in a very postmodern fashion) in two converse ways:

a. Emphasizing the active role in the couple of the woman, who doesn't have a sense of inferiority, because she feels that the man takes the lead, but only in a formal way. Actually, women are the ones who add color, expressing their freedom by embellishing their movements. The men, for their part, have taken the principle 'the man is the leader, the woman the seducer', and updated it to 'the man proposes, the woman accepts'. In doing so they've re-envisioned the role of the autocratic male.

b. Accepting traditional roles as a way to accomplish an old-fashioned social order. For many women tango represents a chance to escape, a moment to set aside their strength and their sense of responsibility that comes with everyday life, and abandon themselves to their partner, allowing him to take the lead. For men, tango is a way to regain the determination of the past, and to become the decision maker in the couple once again.

The second feature that impacts integration practices is *accepting close physical contact*. Unlike the choreographed version of tango that is typically seen in so many television shows and dance competitions, when a couple dances tango in a milonga the two partners share an intimate embrace. This means that from the very first tango lesson, what takes center stage is the dancer's relationship with his or her own body and with physical contact.

When the two partners embrace, each invades the other's space to no small degree: often they dance cheek to cheek, sharing one another's sweat and smells. How dancers react to physical contact depends not only on personal preference but on their cultural background and environmental factors as well. Despite the challenges involved in the initial contact, the philosophy of the tango embrace satisfies an implicit need for physical proximity and connection with other people, a need that isn't very easily filled in everyday social relationships in contemporary societies.

Tango not only compels dancers to explore themselves, but also makes them feel free to reveal themselves to their partners. Physical contact is elevated into a language that transcends words; it's honest and open, devoid of intentionally erotic messages. Tango becomes a silent dialogue in which dancers learn the vocabulary of gestures and acquire greater sensitivity to touch. This allows male dancers to exert the slightest pressure with their bodies (*marca*), which is perceived and codified by their partners and translated into combinations of dance steps.

The dialogue that emerges between the partners is essential in a dance that is completely improvised. The responsibility for improvisation, and it's a heavy one, rests with the male dancer, who has to imagine the steps and then adeptly communicate them to his partner, who in turn executes them and enriches them with embellishments. So the skill of a male dancer lies in his ability to improvise and communicate with his partner; the skill of the female partner, however, centers on codifying her partner's messages and embellishing them (in which case, she's called a good '*seguidora*').

The third significant factor pertaining to integration practices is *accepting traditional rituals*. Some dancers believe that the codes of conduct engrained in Argentinean tradition are a 'sacred' element of the entire tango experience and should be respected and faithfully replicated. Others instead think that the rules should be adapted to the local context, to prevent them from becoming constraints which might negatively influence the overall dancing experience.

The invitation is a case in point. In Italy this ritual is one of the basics, taught in the first few tango lessons, but it's not common practice in the milonga. One of the rare scenarios in which people resort to the *mirada* and *cebeceo* is when they go dancing in a place where they don't know anyone. But as soon as the utilitarian function of the invitation has served its purpose, this ritual is immediately replaced by a more common method: simply asking a person to dance.

Within the framework of integration practices we also find *production* and *personalization* practices. An example is dressing, specifically choosing shoes and clothes. Shoes are almost an object of worship, a means for expressing personality and identity. There are a variety of styles and colors of shoes, which reveal something about dancers in the milonga beyond their skill on the dance floor. The same can be said of clothes, which can represent either a form self-expression or disguise. In the first case, the lack of a dress code gives people a sense of freedom that they would be hard pressed to find in more ordinary situations. And in the second case, choosing dance apparel is a way to put on a disguise, and go on stage to play a role that's a complete break from everyday life.

Sharing practices

Tango is often compared to an experience that involves every aspect of people's lives; it's a world in itself. Once people enter this microcosm, they have a hard time leaving. And it's this self-perception that marks the distance between who's in and who's out. The 'outs' are often people who don't enjoy the music because to their ears it's too old-fashioned. Or it might be the intimacy of the embrace that makes them uneasy. Often tango informs friendships and social relationships, demanding effort and sacrifice from dancers to strike a balance between partaking in the tango community and preserving their relationships outside this community.

The tango microcosm is founded on social dynamics that differ from what we normally find in the rest of society. First, tango prompts people to socialize thanks to the rules of the dance. Specifically, the dance brings people together who share the same passion, regardless of age, profession, or social class. So what emerges is a powerful sense of freedom as far as what and how much to share with others, with no social pressure whatsoever, because what matters above all else is tango.

Another essential feature of the tango microcosm is *social networking*, especially with regard to the process of joining or being initiated into the community. First, people have to acquire cultural capital through lessons, at the milonga, via online sites and forums, and in virtual spaces and real places where they can share their tango experience. Over time, dancers learn the tango terminology (tanda, cebeceo, ronda, and so on), the codes of conduct, the stars (from Gardel to Piazzolla), and the styles of tango.

Sharing the culture is a vital part of the tango community. Individual members tend to take on more or less active roles in promoting and disseminating this culture. Some are disciples, others simple spectators; still others take part in festivals, write blogs, and join discussions on forums or promote events dedicated to dance.

Among all the different members, dance instructors are beyond a doubt the most influential in the community. Some of them have Argentinean roots, so teaching tango for them is a mission to spread authentic Argentine culture. Others are driven by a powerful passion. Many take frequent trips to Argentina to immerse themselves in the original tango culture; for them tango becomes their purpose in life as well as the source of their livelihood. This is a typical *community engagement* practice: Buenos Aires is revered as a sacred place that pilgrims flock to, both teachers and dancers, almost like prophets who then return to their home countries with stories and images to share with other devotees.

Another important social aspect has to do with *status* within the community. Status depends mainly on the technical ability and empathy of the dancer. The better men are at dancing, or women are as seguidoras, the more respect they'll win within the group; the level of involvement or culture alone isn't enough to guarantee a high status within the community. So it could be said that tango is a meritocratic dance: the quality of the dancers is measured by their sense of rhythm and ability to improvise and interpret the music, and their openness to the flow of emotions. When the quality of dancing is high, couples can more easily reach a state of flow, and the public is treated to a captivating, emotionally charged performance. There's no doubt, then, that the status of 'good dancer' is highly prized, and earning this status means having no shortage of partners.

Also with regard to sharing practices, the *venue* where people dance tango is key. On this point too there are differences with respect to Argentina. 'The' place to dance tango, according to tradition, is of course the milonga. Normally this is a modest locale, with lights, tables, and chairs placed around the dance floor, a bar, and a spot for the *musicalizador* (DJ). The dance area is made of hardwood or some other material that makes it easy for dancers to glide along the floor. The image of the milonga is a temple or an oasis, a safe haven where dancers can escape from the stress of everyday life.

As for atmosphere, this varies from milonga to milonga. Some are more rigid, with rules as to what people wear and who is allowed to dance. Others have a more informal feel, where everybody's welcome. Milongas are often run by people who manage bars or dance halls and organize tango nights a few times a week. In other cases, dance teachers open milongas as a side business to supplement their schools. But some people look down on this kind of initiative, seeing it as a way to make money, instead of a reflection of a pure passion for the tango. As a contrasting trend, milongas organized by the dancers themselves are becoming more and more common and garnering the most success. Here a group of tango lovers would rent a venue to organize a milonga, or to obviate the problem of space entirely they might decide to take the milonga to the streets.

In fact, a recent phenomenon is for people to gather to dance the tango in unconventional places: streets, train stations, piazzas, parking lots, and other public places that host flashmobs or 'illegal tangos'. *Flashmobs* are organized via social networks some time in advance so participants can find out the details of the event and the choreography to perform. *Illegals*, using the English term, involve occupying public spaces without a permit (hence the name) to improvise open-air milongas. The dancers who participate preserve an air of secrecy by communicating via closed mailing lists. At an illegal more modern music genres would more likely be played (for example electronic tango), so normally younger dancers who are less traditional-minded take part.

The reasons for the rise in the illegal tango are very practical. In the beginning, around the 1990s when tango became popular in Italy, there weren't many milongas, so the only way to get together and dance tango was to make do with open-air milongas. What's more, it was (and still is) an extremely economical and entertaining way to spend an evening out: at an illegal everyone brings something (music, food, drinks) but the most important ingredient is the joy of sharing the tango experience. Over time, the illegal tango has taken on deeper shades of meaning: for some it's a way to refuse to give in to the commercialization of tango, but it's also an opportunity to feel free to choose the place, time, and music to dance to, and an occasion for people to (re)discover their city or culture through the culture of Argentina.

REVIEW QUESTIONS

1. The tango experience outside of Argentina is characterized by a combination of elements that are typical of the original culture, and adaptations to the culture of the country where it is imported. What are the components of consumer experience that reflect these adaptations?

2. What are the practices implemented by dancers in the various stages of their experience? Which ones are typical of the apprentice stage and which ones of single dance sessions?

3. The dance floor is a fundamental component of the tango experience. How do traditional and innovative dance floors affect the overall experience?

Chapter

4

THE CONSUMER SIDE OF THE MARKET: THE OTHER STAGES OF THE EXPERIENCE

LEARNING OBJECTIVES

After reading this chapter you should be able to:

- Identify the determinants of a consumer's expected value for a creative product.
- Distinguish consumers according to their individual characteristics.
- Understand the differences among various consumer choice processes.
- Understand the role of online and offline shopping experiences.
- Detail post-consumption consumer experiences.

OVERVIEW

Now that we've analyzed how the consumption experience determines the *perceived* value of a product, in this chapter we'll focus on *expected* value. As we learned in the last chapter, consumer satisfaction (or dissatisfaction) derives from perceived versus expected value. Consequently, for an organization that offers creative products, recognizing which factors engender these two forms of value is the key to market alignment.

The first question I'll address in this chapter is: What is the source of the value that consumers expect to obtain when they're about to purchase a certain creative product? Why do they expect what they do when they decide to buy a book or a trip, or tickets to a musical or a rugby match? The answer to this question is more complex than it may initially appear, especially if we rephrase it in a way that's more salient for the decision makers in an organization's marketing department: Why do different consumers expect to get different benefits?

As we'll see, expected value is the outcome of an intricate web of interacting factors that fall into two broad thematic areas: what consumers *want* (motivations) and what they *know* (knowledge). When they go to buy a product, they expect to get a series of benefits depending on what prompts them to make that particular purchase, and what they know about similar products available on the market.

But underpinning their motivation and their knowledge are a number of variables. Some directly relate to consumers themselves and are dependent on the personal characteristics that make each of them unique. Others, instead, are independent of consumers. In other words, these variables are contingent on the actions of organizations operating on the market, as well as the features of the macro-context in which they live and act, and the micro-context in which they make decisions. We need to consider all these factors to answer the question of why different consumers have different value expectations.

Expected value emerges within consumer experience, which is made up of several stages (outlined in the previous chapter). So the second question I'll answer in this chapter is: Where does the formation of expected value fit into consumer experience? Specifically, which stages of the experience contribute to creating expected value, and which take consumers from expected to perceived value, giving rise to satisfaction or dissatisfaction?

As I just said, one of the determinants of expected value is consumer knowledge of the products available in the market. But to gain this knowledge, consumers have to gather information on the products and suppliers. The related activities constitute the pre-consumption experience, which entails accessing a variety of information sources, making sense of content, and then using the resulting information in the successive stages of the product experience.

Let's picture a consumer in a situation where she has clear expectations and information about a range of product alternatives. What happens now? How does she get from this stage to actual consumption? Clearly she has to make a choice and then buy the product she's decided on. These two activities constitute the purchase experience, at which point the consumer has the product in hand that she's about to consume. The purchase experience is complex too, engaging consumers both on a cognitive level and an emotional and social one as well. As we'll see, inherent to this experience are relationships with multiple products, actors, and physical and virtual environments.

Consumers don't live their lives or have experiences in a vacuum. Instead their experiences are all interconnected in a given context over time. So at the conclusion of this chapter, we'll discuss the post-consumption experience that activates a series of possible behaviors that link one consumption experience to others. This will complete the picture of the consumer experience, and enable us to identify all the areas of knowledge that an organization in a creative industry should have to design and realize value propositions that win consumer appreciation.

4.1   EXPECTED VALUE

Expected value is the set of benefits that consumers anticipate that a product will provide, along with the corresponding sacrifices. This expectation constitutes one of the determinants of satisfaction or dissatisfaction (Section 3.2), depending on how it measures up with the perceived value of the product after the consumption experience. But what are the determinants of expected value?

Again, there are two: the motivations that prompt consumers to act and the knowledge they possess. These components are shaped in turn by a series of variables that are intricately interconnected. Figure 4.1 shows a map of these relationships, which we'll explore in the following sections.

4.2   MOTIVATIONS

Motivation is the inner drive to achieve an objective, a state of arousal that prompts individuals to act. This drive arises from the perception or the sensation that there is a discrepancy between their desired state and their actual state. The greater the perceived discrepancy, the stronger the inner

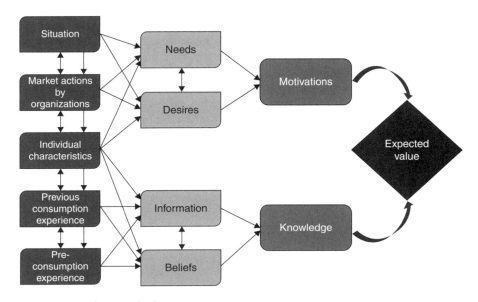

Figure 4.1 – The determinants of expected value

drive, the more urgent the need to respond to the stimulus.

Motivation underpins the array of behaviors consumers adopt, from searching information on how to remedy this discrepancy, to acting on this information by purchasing and consuming products. Inner drive can be physical (the feeling of hunger), emotional (the desire to have fun), or cognitive (the aspiration to enrich one's knowledge). Reaching a new state (eating, having fun, learning more) is the underlying goal of these behaviors.

The causes behind motivations can be grouped together into two broad areas: needs and desires. *Needs* are the discrepancies between a consumer's current state and her desired state, which are rationally perceived and dealt with as problems to solve. For example, if someone is planning a vacation but she doesn't have a specific destination in mind, she'd read travel magazines to get some ideas. As Holbrook and Hirschman (1982) suggest, needs are associated with *secondary process thinking*: a structured mental activity, a product of the socialization processes all people experience, which leads to making an evaluation and judgment before making a choice.

Desires, on the contrary, are associated with *primary process thinking*. These mechanisms, closer to instinctive impulses, center on the search for pleasure and immediate satisfaction. Mental activity in this case is less structured or deliberate, more dictated by imagination and expressed physically (Belk et al., 2003). For example, the desire to go see a show at the theater can lead a consumer to make a choice without spending much time evaluating or pondering many options, simply because of the promise of intense emotions conveyed by the show's marketing campaign.

Obviously, needs and desires interact. So as far as it's possible to identify their source as purely rational or manifestly impulsive, most consumer motivations are a mix of primary and secondary process thinking. Last of all, because of their specific configuration, motivations determine expected value for consumers, spurring them to search for satisfaction through a specific set of benefits, and to accept the related sacrifices.

Now the question is: What gives rise to the motivations that are unique to a specific consumer, singling her out among all the others? There are three main sources: the individual characteristics of the consumer, the situation in which she finds herself, and the market strategies implemented by the companies and non-profits vying to win her as a customer.

4.2.1   Individual characteristics

Individual characteristics that differentiate one consumer from another, shaping needs and desires, can be classified as follows.

4.2.1.1   *Demographics*

These factors characterize a consumer in a specific stage of her life, and basically coincide with all the information included on an identification card: age, gender, physical traits, address, and marital status. Some of these variables change over time and others don't, but all of them play a role in generating needs and desires.

A child's needs are very different from an adult's, for example, in terms of reading material: children love colorful illustrations, while as people grow older and their vision gets weaker, they might look for more functional benefits in a book like large print. For teens, the communicative value of products such as clothing or accessories is critical, during a stage in their lives when they're building their social identity. One more example: when a couple decides to live together, for instance, they might buy a pay TV package that offers a wide range of programs to satisfy both of their tastes.

4.2.1.2   *Resources*

In Section 3.1.6.2 we identified some of these resources consumers tap into during the different stages of their experience. Here we'll examine them in more detail, and link them to various forms of consumer capital: economic, social, cultural, and symbolic.

Obviously *economic capital* (the set of economic resources that consumers can access during the different stages of their experience) shapes consumer expectations. Logically, the more economic capital consumers have, the more access to a variety of sources information on market offerings, the greater the opportunity to purchase products and to enjoy certain types of consumption experiences or post-consumption experiences. For an art lover with a passion for nineteenth-century English landscapes, the availability of economic resources will dictate whether this person can own these kinds of paintings or simply access them by visiting a museum. This in turn determines the expectation of certain benefits/sacrifices as opposed to others.

Social capital consists of the consumer's social relationships, in terms of number, type and intensity. All people take part in a number of primary social groups that they normally belong to through no choice of their own (families, school mates), and secondary social groups, which instead they more or less consciously choose (friends, sports teams, clubs, brand communities) or which they can modify depending on some of the choices they make (social class).

Here's a simple illustration of two women who are the same age, but have very different social capital: one is an amateur volleyball player, the treasurer of a local non-profit animal adoption association, and a union representative in the company where she works; the other is self-employed and works from home, she doesn't play any sports and she spends her free time gardening.

Social capital generates expectations because people's affiliation and degree of engagement with certain social groups (and not others) shape the benefits they look for and the sacrifices they're willing and able to make. So back to the example above, for the first woman the communicative value of creative products will be essential, along with the symbolic value correlated with her self-image as an active person who's open to social contacts. What's more, she'll be able to leverage a wide array of social relationships, which can help to alleviate sacrifices.

Symbolic capital equates to the prestige, reputation, and respect the consumer enjoys in her social network. Basically, beyond the characteristics listed above, every individual has a more or less central position within the sphere of her social relationships, which translates into more or less status. For instance, the studies on subcultures of consumption cited in Section 3.1.3.2 report that in every brand community there are members who play a more central role and in doing so enjoy more status. This is contingent on their knowledge of the product the community is built around, their ability to create a sense of belonging, and their desire to perpetuate the fundamental values of the community.

The symbolic capital consumers have also impacts the value they expect. It's easy to see that an individual with high symbolic capital will prize the communicative value a product has within her social group, which serves to reaffirm her status. On the other hand, people with less symbolic capital who want to garner more might value products that show they espouse the values and norms shared by the social group they aspire to.

Cultural capital identifies the stock of knowledge, competences, and cultural sensitivity that characterizes every individual. Consumers acquire and evolve this kind of capital through formal instruction as well as informal processes, which unfold within the networks that make up their social capital (Bourdieu, 1984), and through the experience of consuming creative products.

Knowledge and competences in languages, technology, and art also inform the benefits individuals expect and the sacrifices they're willing to face. A lack of cultural competences, on the other hand, prevents them from gaining certain benefits, for example those associated with digitalized content in industries such as publishing or music.

Research on aesthetic products (Becker, 1982; Hoyer and Stokburger-Sauer, 2012) provides additional examples that demonstrate that the higher a consumer's artistic competences, the more the aesthetic value of a product will be linked to formal aspects rather than content. For instance, less competent consumers would judge a painting of a landscape with an eye to how the setting is represented (content), while a more expert consumer would consider the stylistic choices of the artist (the form, which might mean that the landscape isn't even distinguishable!). This discussion of aesthetic products ties into a key component of cultural capital – *aesthetic taste* – which is fundamental in creating value expectations and later evaluating the consumption experience (Research Focus 4.1).

Research Focus 4.1

Aesthetic taste

Several disciplines – primarily aesthetics, but also sociology, psychology, and marketing – study aesthetic taste.[1] In everyday usage, and very often in market analysis, the word 'taste' (read: aesthetic taste) has two different meanings. The first refers to a 'preference' for a given product category; taste is what people like or don't like. For example, a consumer might say that a certain literary genre or theatrical production is more or less to her taste. The second meaning, instead, is 'aesthetic sensitivity', or as Wagner (1999: 130) puts it: 'The ability to recognize or discern beauty.'

These two meanings of the same word embody very different phenomena, and in discussing the determinants of consumers' expected value, it's important to keep these two definitions separate. The reason for this is that although both phenomena contribute to expected consumer value, they do so by acting on different elements: one on motivation and the other on knowledge. In fact, taste as aesthetic sensitivity constitutes a component of consumers' cultural capital, shaping their expectations of value and influencing their motivations. Taste as preference, instead, is the result of expertise, which comes from repeated consumption experiences of certain categories of goods. This repetition can generate greater satisfaction with respect to some products rather than others. So to be more precise, this second phenomenon contributes to determining expected value because it's a component of consumers' accumulated knowledge.

For numerous marketing studies that analyze whether or not 'ordinary' consumers have 'good taste', 'bad taste' or 'little taste', the very concept of good taste refers to the ability to discern what is aesthetically valuable according to expert opinion in the specific cultural field in question (Holbrook, 2005; Holbrook and Addis, 2007). The research on this topic, conducted mainly in the movie and music industries, shows a positive correlation between the opinions of experts and of ordinary consumers, verifying that these consumers (taken together at a market level) actually have 'good' taste.

On the other hand, these same studies reveal that for many individual consumers, good taste (read: the ability to recognize what experts consider beautiful) doesn't necessarily translate into taste as preference. In other words, while consumers often recognize what's aesthetically beautiful, they prefer creative products that are less pleasing by expert standards, but more satisfying thanks to other benefits they can offer.

Case History 4.1

Micro Teatro por Dinero

Micro teatro por Dinero (www.teatropordinero.com) is an innovative theatrical format launched in 2009 by a cultural association in Madrid. The initial project was scheduled to run for just ten days, but thanks to its overwhelming success, the temporary initiative has become a permanent one.

The basic formula consists of short sketches, no more than 15 minutes long, in performance spaces with a maximum seating capacity of 15. Performances are repeated several times every evening (like movie times at the cinema) in the same multi-purpose venue in the center of Madrid. Spectators can decide how many shows to see, what time to go, and what price to pay (seeing as the price varies by number of shows).

In the end, consumers enjoy the greatest possible flexibility in how they spend their temporal resources and as a result their economic, cultural, and social capital as well. The success in Madrid of Micro Teatro por Dinero led the association to expand to other Spanish cities, and to travel as far as Miami, Florida in late 2012.

Temporal resources are unique because they intersect various forms of capital: consumers spend time during pre-consumption, purchase, consumption, and post-consumption phases. But how can the time consumers dedicate to a product determine their value expectations? To answer this question, it's worth remembering that experiencing creative products takes time, which in turn has a powerful influence on consumer satisfaction (Section 1.2). What's more, using temporal resources is one of the sacrifices associated with the various stages of the consumption experience (Section 3.1.6).

Consequently, time primarily represents a component of economic capital. What I mean by this is that time has economic value because the more time a consumer dedicates to working and earning money, the less free time she'll have to spend consuming creative products, in all the different stages of the experience. By the same token, the more time consumers spent on revenue-generating activities, the more economic resources they'll be able to invest in the different stages of consumption. So essentially, time has a dual and opposite effect on consumer experiences of creative products.

A creative product designed with an eye to the time consumers need to invest would provide value while diminishing the opportunity cost of temporal resources (Case History 4.1). Generally speaking, the availability of temporal resources impacts the needs and desires of consumers by determining their opportunity cost for the use of these resources. But time also represents a component of consumers' social and cultural capital, because developing these kinds of capital takes time. The more time spent, the greater the capital. Consequently, by impacting consumers' cultural and social capital, the availability of temporal resources further shapes the motivations underpinning expected value.

4.2.1.3 Values

The consumer's value system is a powerful force in molding the motivations that give rise to expected value. A long-established approach in marketing studies holds that an individual's value system is the enduring belief that certain *end-states* and *modes of conduct* should be pursued because they are preferable to other end-states or modes of conduct (Rokeach, 1973). End-states are terminal values that involve no ulterior motives; examples are peace, freedom, beauty, love, and happiness. Modes of conduct are instrumental values that characterize behaviors that enable individuals to reach desirable end-states: capability, imagination, broad-mindedness, or responsibility toward others.

An individual's value system impacts her needs and desires and her value expectations, because this system leads her to consider certain benefits as more important than others. For example, when planning a vacation and considering travel options, a person whose terminal values include freedom will probably look for benefits like flexibility and time to dedicate to herself, and overall will want a less structured trip. On the other hand, someone who prizes security will probably organize her trip down to the last detail, planning everything minute-by-minute and leaving nothing to chance.

4.2.1.4 Lifestyles

Since a consumer's value system seems too abstract with respect to her purchase and consumption choices, the concept of lifestyle makes its impact on motivation more readily apparent. Lifestyle refers to a patterned way of life: how people live, carry out activities, and use their time and resources. Lifestyle reflects activities, interests, and opinions; these, combined with certain demographic variables, are the basis for the AIO model used in marketing studies (Table 4.1).

Affirming the value of creative products in building a consumer's identity and social positioning, what emerges from the table is that many different creative products connote various possible lifestyles.

Compared to value systems, which tend to be relatively stable throughout a person's life, lifestyles are more changeable because they're affected both by the evolution of the relevant demographics and the sociocultural context. As a result, lifestyles have a more immediate connection to motivation. Put another way, the same values can correspond to different motivations throughout our lives, because these values connote different lifestyles which evolve as our life cycle progresses.

Table 4.1 – The AIO Model

ACTIVITIES	INTERESTS	OPINIONS	DEMOGRAPHICS
Work	Family	Themselves	Age
Hobbies	Home	Social issues	Education
Social events	Job	Politics	Income
Vacation	Community	Business	Occupation
Entertainment	Recreation	Economics	Family size
Club membership	Fashion	Education	Dwelling
Community	Food	Products	Geography
Shopping	Media	Future	City size
Sports	Achievements	Culture	Stage in life cycle

Source: Plummer (1974: 34)

4.2.1.5   Involvement

A key variable in differentiating the personal traits of consumers is their level of involvement in the various product categories. Involvement here is defined as 'a person's perceived relevance of the object based on inherent needs, values, and interests' (Zaichkowsky, 1985: 342). There are both cognitive and affective aspects to involvement, corresponding to the time consumers spend thinking about a product category and the emotional connection they have to it. Yet I think it's useful to position this variable within the system of values because the level of consumer involvement reflects their activities, interests, and opinions about the category in question.

Involvement can be *enduring* or *situational*, that is, abating as soon as the situation in question has ended. For example, if a consumer wants to find a gift for a friend who loves to read, her involvement in books increases. But when the situation resolves (she's found the book and presented the gift) her involvement dissipates (unless there are other factors at play). Enduring involvement, on the other hand, depends on a number of more stable personal factors. For instance, if a consumer has always listened to classical music since she was young, she'll have high, long-term involvement. The same is true when a consumer's passion for classical music contributes to her self-identity.

Even though the effects are slightly different, both types of involvement play a motivational role and impact value expectations. As we can easily imagine, a highly involved consumer will have more sophisticated expectations of product benefits with respect to someone with less involvement. (People who are very involved in classical music will be more sensitive to a performance of a rare symphony; those with less involvement will be more moved by a very famous symphony.) This same consumer will also be willing to make bigger sacrifices. (The music enthusiasts above will spend hours and hours searching for that rare recording, reading reviews on it, and talking to other music fans about it.)

4.2.1.6   Psychological factors

The first item in this category is *self-concept*, in other words, the perception that all individuals have of themselves and their uniqueness. Self-concept shapes both their interior and interpersonal processes according to the principle of consistency, which holds that individuals perceive, feel, and act in such a way as to preserve their self-concept (unless they consciously decide to change it).

Self-concept gives rise to *life projects*: the set of roles and identities that individuals take on during their lifetimes, which they more or less freely choose (depending on whether or not peer pressure comes into play). Examples: a model student, a responsible parent, a successful entrepreneur, a faithful companion. The roles and identities that constitute individual life projects can be consistent or conflicting. Whatever the case, they are enacted with a set of behaviors.

Also in the sphere of psychological variables, and closely linked to self-concept, is individual *personality*: the set of enduring characteristics or *traits* that identify the way a person faces and adapts to life events. Personality traits are codified in various ways in psychological studies so they can be identified and measured.

Some of these traits are vital to consumption and purchase experiences: dogmatism, the inclination to resist new ideas and change in general; conformism, the tendency to follow the generally accepted way of thinking or behaving; introversion or extroversion, a preference for living a solitary life and avoiding social relationships, or the opposite; the need for cognition, a desire to dedicate oneself to intellectually stimulating activities; self-esteem, an appreciation for oneself 'as is'.

Naturally, all these psychological variables shape needs, desires, and value expectations. By the same token, personality traits influence the types of choices and the choice processes regarding creative products. For example, a dogmatic person will likely be more motivated to consume creative products that respect traditional canons, not ones that break with these canons. An introvert will prefer forms of entertainment that allow for individual space, while an extrovert will look for the chance for intense social interaction.

4.2.2   Situations

Situations can relate either to the environment where consumers live, or the micro-context in which purchase and consumption experiences take place. The first tend to last over time, while the second are normally temporary, in some cases extremely so.

4.2.2.1   The macro-context

A vital factor here is the *general economic situation* of the country or the area where the consumer lives. When there is a recession, needs and desires are influenced not only by a possible reduction in available economic capital, but also by the general climate, which leads people to rethink their personal basket of consumption. Logically, consumer behavior is the opposite in times of economic expansion.

The *level of technological development of a country* or area also impacts motivation. To illustrate this, just think of how the diffusion of broadband can facilitate the use of digital content, and shape expected benefits and sacrifices.

In addition, the *social structure* and *dominant cultural system* can also be influential. Purchasing and consuming certain products might be stigmatized or considered inappropriate in the dominant system of social relations and values of the community in question. As a result, individuals who don't share the same values or don't identify with the consolidated culture or social system may find it difficult to access certain products. In such a case, they would be forced to modify their value expectations.

In many countries, for instance, when sensitive topics like religion or local traditions are addressed in theatrical productions (like *Burqavaganza* from the Pakistani company Ajoka, or *Corpus Christi* by McNally) or books (the classic *Satanic Verses* by Rushdie), hostile reactions are unleashed that may even lead the product in question be censured or banned.

Lastly, the *system of laws and norms* of the country or area can encourage or discourage the manifestation of certain motivations and the search for certain benefits. Some countries, for example, offer free admission to public museums, or free tickets to the theater for students, or free newspapers to high schools to get students to read up on the news. On the other end of the spectrum, some laws prohibit or limit the use of certain product categories. An example is erotic literature, which is censored in many countries, creating a major impediment to circulation.

4.2.2.2   The micro-context

Beyond the variables that constitute a consumer's macro-context, there are also situations that characterize the micro-context where she makes her purchase and consumption choices.

Even the weather and the seasons trigger motivations to consume creative products. In fact, for industries like fashion, the seasons mark the transition from one clothing type to another, informing the kind of benefits consumers look for. In other industries, people are motivated to consume some products and not others. For instance, in Mediterranean countries, consumers aren't in the habit of going to the cinema during the summer; instead they prefer to attend live outdoor events. Specific occasions can also lead to the purchase of certain creative products. Beyond anniversaries, birthdays, and commemorations that are meaningful for individual consumers, there are also celebrations that encompass entire communities (Case History 4.2).

Some situations relating to purchase and consumption experiences are even more temporary. For example, a consumer on a business trip might decide to spend a few hours of her free time visiting a museum or art gallery. Another who's driving to a meeting might make a stop along the highway at a gas station with a convenience store and decide to buy a book or CD. Another traveler who finds herself with a layover in an airport might buy a magazine. In these cases, motivations are mainly linked to passing the time, alleviating the stress of traveling. These motivations lead consumers to search for entirely different benefits than they might want from the same product categories in different situations.

4.2.3   Market actions of companies and institutions

In an attempt to win customers, organizations that operate in creative industries implement market actions (such as launching new products, creating communication

Case History 4.2

El Día del Libro

In Cataluña on April 23, the feast day of Saint George (Día de San Jordi), the tradition is to gift a book. The origins of this tradition can supposedly be traced back to the commemoration of the deaths of Cervantes, Shakespeare, and Inca Garcilazo de la Vega, all of which occurred on April 23, 1616 (though this date isn't official). Over time this day has become known as Book Day (Día del Libro). The celebration has won recognition by UNESCO, which has promoted the annual initiative World Book Capitals since 2001, with a different city hosting initiatives linked to the world of books and reading each year.

campaigns, staging events) with the aim of shaping consumer needs and desires. This in turn gives rise to motivations and value expectations. However, since these activities relate to value creation and value delivery processes, we'll discuss them in detail in later chapters.

Summing up, consumer needs and desires are a product of the unique combination of demographics and psychological variables, along with available resources, value systems, lifestyles, and involvement. This combination evolves along with the single variables that make up the different categories, shaping the set of motivations and value expectations that characterize consumers at specific moments in their lives.

In addition, personal traits interact with the three factors described above: the macro-context, specific purchase and consumption situations, and the actions of companies and institutions that offer various products. Clearly, interaction means reciprocal influence, so consumers can actually drive the evolution of all three. For the first, for example, people can petition for a change in legislation or campaign for social reform in their country; for the second, they can create new purchase and consumption occasions. As for the third, consumer demand is what prompts companies and institutions to modify their market strategies.

4.3   KNOWLEDGE

The value that consumers expect to get from a product derives not only from their motivations, but also from their knowledge. In other words, what consumers expect depends on what they want, but also on what they know. Picture an individual with vast consumption experience of a specific product category, who's an expert on all the alternatives available on the market. The benefits this consumer expects and the sacrifices she's willing to make are very different to those of a novice consumer who is only familiar with a few products. A consumer's knowledge consists of the set of information she has and the beliefs she applies when interpreting this information and making her consumption choices.

4.3.1   Information

The relevant information for creating value expectations concerns product categories and the single products and brands that fall within those categories. Consumers build *categorization systems* based on stimuli from the environment to which they assign meaning (Section 2.6). They use subjective and flexible hierarchies to do so: subjective because consumers decide for themselves what criteria to use to create these categories and related sub-categories; flexible because they can reorganize their information in whatever way best suits their needs.

If a consumer wants to have a night out with friends, she can access the information she retains in her memory pertaining to all potential alternatives, and group them together according to product similarity (distinguishing the restaurants from the cinemas and from music clubs). But she could also group together alternatives by how far they are from home; in this case a cinema and a restaurant in her neighborhood would belong to the same category (close entertainment opportunities), while a music club or a cinema on the other side of town would be in a different one (distant opportunities).

4.3.2   Beliefs

In addition to information, a consumer's knowledge also includes her beliefs: the associations linking this information together, and the associations connecting information to attitudes or judgments. If a consumer is convinced that the best hip-hop music is American, or the greatest opera is Italian, she's associating information related to a product category (hip-hop or opera) to information on the geographical origins of the product/producer, and this association forms the basis for her judgment.

What can often be found in creative product categories are 'canons' or 'standards of quality', which distinguish one from the other as far as genre, trend, movement, or style (Section 2.4). If these canons are absorbed into consumer categorization systems, they become norms that contribute to informing expectations. For example, when choosing a cinema, consumers expect all cinemas to meet certain basic criteria, and every sub-class to respect specific ones. So a multiplex has to have several screens, spacious seating, and offer multiple showings of the same film on any given day. But an art house cinema would probably only have a few screens, perhaps less comfortable seats, and limited show times. These norms contribute to creating consumer expectations of the 'cinema' product category and relative sub-classes.

4.3.3   Attitudes

A key concept in analyzing consumer knowledge is attitude, which refers to a positive or negative disposition toward an object (in our case a product, brand, store, or Web site) or a subject (an organization, a seller, an information source). Consumer attitudes arise from their prior experience of an object or a subject (Section 4.3.5), and consist in a combination of cognitive elements (beliefs) and affective elements (emotions).

Aesthetic taste as preference, which we talked about earlier, is a form of attitude. If a consumer says that she likes 'chick lit' but she doesn't like noir fiction, that means she has a positive attitude toward the first and a negative attitude toward the second, which in turn leads her to search for a certain set of benefits and accept certain sacrifices, but not others. The information consumers have and the beliefs and attitudes they hold are contingent on their individual characteristics, their previous product experience, and the information sources they access.

4.3.4   Individual characteristics

Some of the individual characteristics that we've already discussed as determinants of motivations are also applicable to knowledge. Various forms of capital that consumers have impact the amount and type of information that they can access. Abundant social capital allows them to access more information from a variety of sources, and to discuss their beliefs with others. The same is true for economic and cultural capital, as well as temporal resources.

What's more, social and cultural capital also inform consumer attitudes and aesthetic taste (Bourdieu, 1984). Peterson and Kern (1996) demonstrated that individuals who have more socio-cultural capital are also bigger 'omnivores' in terms of tastes, consuming creative products that belong to various categories. On the other hand, individuals with less capital focus their preferences on a limited number of categories. Likewise, some lifestyles and personality types favor exposure to a wider range of information and to more flexible beliefs, while others do the opposite. Moreover, a consumer who's very engaged in a product category generally has more information on that category and a more sophisticated categorization system in general.

4.3.4.1   Expertise

Expertise is a highly distinctive factor that characterizes a consumer's knowledge with regard to a given product category. Here it's essential to draw a distinction between two concepts. The first is product *familiarity*, which relates to the number of interactions that a consumer has with a product, either consuming it personally or hearing about it. Product *expertise*, on the other hand, centers on the breadth and depth of product knowledge available to the consumer.

It's important to differentiate between the two because while it's true that a consumer has to be familiar with a product before becoming an expert, there's no guarantee that familiarity always leads to expertise. We can take an example of a consumer who often goes to the cinema (familiarity) because she has friends who are movie buffs, but she doesn't have broad or deep knowledge of genres, writers, or actors (expertise). Clearly a consumer's degree of familiarity and expertise shape how much information and what kind of beliefs she has.

In the world of creative products, it's useful to class consumers into three categories according to their degree of product expertise: ordinary consumers, connoisseurs, and consumer-producers. Each class differs widely in terms of information, attitudes and expectations of value with respect to the product in question.

○ *Ordinary consumers*. What little expertise these consumers have comes mainly from a certain degree of product familiarity. Generally their level of involvement is more situational than enduring, and their attitudes are positive toward a limited number of products/brands. The knowledge of ordinary consumers is sometimes minimal, and never excessively wide or deep. They aren't very aware of the canons that pertain to different product sub-classes. Instead they apply subjective norms that they acquire either through direct product experience or by a modicum of cultural socialization, through formal instruction or by sharing with other consumers.

Let's take someone who occasionally watches rugby, either live or on TV. She's learned the rules by watching matches, by playing at school, or by asking friends. She only watches big matches, and doesn't fully understand all the tactics and playing styles. This is an example of an ordinary consumer.

○ *Connoisseurs*. These consumers have a high degree of expertise both through familiarity and enduring involvement; this leads them to dedicate a great deal of time learning all they can about the product category in question. Connoisseurs have deep knowledge of canons of quality for various sub-classes, and can tap varied and continuous cultural socialization. Fans can be classed as connoisseurs. Continuing with the sports example, connoisseurs are people who pore over the rugby news, rankings, and team stats; they go to the stadium regularly, and follow matches in other countries on TV; they're enthusiastic bloggers, and they participate in fan forums.

- ○ *Consumer-producers.* With respect to the previous categories, consumer-producers have not only theoretical experience of a product, but applied experience as well. These amateur producers are highly engaged and have specialized training. Back to the sports example, these would be trained athletes who probably play in a recreational league. So they invest time not only in theoretical knowledge by following the sport, but in practicing it as well.

For some product categories, these individuals represent a sizeable segment of consumption. As Becker points out (1982), in myriad areas of the art world (dance, classical music, theater, and visual arts) a considerable portion of the public is made up of students or people who have had formal training and who practice the art form, although not in a professional capacity. These consumers are also keenly aware of any alterations in the canons of the category, and more readily accept innovations. In this sense, they serve to convey transformations in the product category to other groups of consumers (as we'll see in Section 8.1.2.2).

4.3.5   Personal experience

The source of much of what consumers know and believe comes from their previous consumption experiences. Consumption practices involve a series of activities aimed at extracting value from the product (Section 3.3). Through these practices, consumers acquire broader and deeper knowledge through sense making, before integrating the product in question into their lifestyles and social processes. So basically by using a product, consumers generate new information and slot it into their previous knowledge. This is a way to enrich their knowledge, both in terms of variety (breadth) and detail (depth).

Furthermore, the contrast between perceived value after consumption and expected value gives rise to satisfaction or dissatisfaction (Section 3.2). These have an emotional and a cognitive component, which is how the consumer judges the experience. This judgment then becomes a part of the consumer's knowledge in the form of her attitude toward the product or brand. Obviously, a satisfying experience will reinforce a positive attitude toward the product/brand in question, while dissatisfaction will have the opposite effect.

All this is even more pertinent for creative products, seeing as they are experience products. As I've often reiterated, for products with value that is hard to predict before consumption takes place, first-hand experience is the most effective way to judge whether they can provide satisfaction and generate expected value for subsequent purchase and consumption. Summing up, the consumption experience broadens and deepens consumer knowledge, in such a way that every new experience can leverage on the learning accumulated through prior experience.

This means that value expectations change according to how much prior experience the consumer has. Here's an example. A consumer who has never been to an amusement park can only have very generic expectations (to have fun, to spend some quality time with friends). But someone who's been to several different parks on a number of occasions will expect much more detailed benefits (to avoid wasting time waiting in line, to go on the most exciting rides) and will make smaller sacrifices, having accumulated knowledge about how to 'do' the park, what rides to go on first, which ones to leave for later, and how to get the most out of the experience.

4.3.6   Pre-consumption experience

Previous experience isn't the only source consumers can tap to accumulate information and develop beliefs and attitudes about products. If it were, people with no product experience would have only their needs and desires as the basis for their value expectations, which might be completely unrealistic and easily lead to dissatisfaction.

Every consumer, beyond recalling information from personal memory, can also activate a process involving *information search from external sources.* This process constitutes the pre-consumption experience, which calls for investments in temporal, cognitive, and emotional resources, and represents an abundant source of sacrifices (Section 3.1.6). So what is it that prompts consumers to invest their resources in this stage? And above all, how can consumers effectively spend their time, seeing that information gathered before actually experiencing a product can't provide fully reliable feedback on product value?

At first, one might think that the initial impulse to activate external sources of information springs from a lack of prior experience. Or, at the other extreme, having vast experience can lead the consumer to trust only her own memory and rich stock of knowledge, to avoid having to make sacrifices that could diminish the final value of the product. Although the first affirmation is obviously true, the second, though plausible, isn't necessarily so, especially with regard to creative products.

In fact, with creative products consumers look for quality clues (Section 1.2.2) that can help them predict what kind of value (and satisfaction) they can expect from the product. So consumers who have no prior experience can only turn to external sources to pick up the quality clues they need. In these cases, the information that they get and the beliefs they cultivate depend a great deal on the sources they access.

But even expert consumers are likely to search for additional information. This happens when they are highly involved; they think that the product category is important for them on a personal level, so they continually dedicate time and attention to finding relevant information. If a consumer is passionate about the theater, for example, she doesn't search for information about a show only when she's decided to see it. Instead she'll be on the lookout for news, debates, and discussions on the theater, actors, and directors, because she finds all this enjoyable and satisfying.

The difference between an expert and a novice consumer lies in the breadth and depth of their knowledge, and their competence in exploiting that knowledge. Expert consumers probably have a clearer idea of which external sources provide authoritative, useful information. Novices, instead, are less adept at discerning which sources are valid, so they'll rely either on whatever sources they happen to come across or on expert consumers.

4.3.6.1   Information sources

External sources can be classified according to their *origin* and *intent*. As far as origin, sources are *personal*, when the supply of information is via direct contact, or *impersonal*, when it is via an intermediary. Based on intent, there are *commercial* and *non-commercial* sources. The first offer information with the aim of convincing recipients to modify their attitudes or behaviors to prefer the product or brand referenced in the communication. The second provide information with no ulterior motives beyond interacting with recipients (Table 4.2).

Commercial sources are typically firms and nonprofits that provide information on their offerings to inform consumers and shape their preferences. In turn, these sources can be personal (salespeople from a company) or impersonal (advertising, events, package and other communication tools). The relationship between non-commercial sources and consumers is either direct (friends, family members, brand communities) or indirect (media, third party information providers). Of the latter, for creative products experts and critics play a vital role as value agents in pre-selecting, framing, and interpreting processes (Section 2.4).

Broadly speaking, non-commercial sources enjoy greater *credibility* in providing information because consumers don't associate them with ulterior (commercial) motives. Likewise, credibility depends on how experienced and competent consumers believe a source is: the higher these two factors, the greater the credibility in the eyes of consumers. In fact, thanks to the competence attributed to critics and experts, consumers rely on them to obtain the quality clues they need to predict the benefits of creative products.

4.3.6.2   *The experiential components of information search*

By accessing information sources, consumers can build and enrich their knowledge, which they can tap into every time they need to evaluate and choose which product to consume. But information search can also play a fully experiential role, contributing to consumers' overall product experience.

Table 4.2 – Types of external information sources

		ORIGIN	
		Personal	**Impersonal**
INTENT	**Commercial**	Sales staff of organizations	Advertising Events Packages Stores
	Non-commercial	Friends Family Other consumers Consumption communities	Experts, and critics Mass media Specialized media Consumer forums Public bodies Third parties

Let's try to imagine two very different situations. First, let's say a consumer is looking for a cinema. She searches for information on the features of various products available on the market in a very rational, structured way on the basis of her personal motivations (the film she wants to see, how far the cinema is from home, and so forth). She investigates the benefits she can expect to gain and the sacrifices she'll have to make. In this case, information search plays a utilitarian role, which serves in decision making: choosing the best product given the consumer's expectations. In short, it's goal-oriented.

Now let's imagine a couple who have to choose where to spend their vacation, or a rock fan who needs to decide whether to go and see a concert. During their respective information searches, these consumers will begin to fantasize about their future vacation or concert; in their daydreams their excitement will start to rise in anticipation of the upcoming event. These situations illustrate the fact that during information search, *people anticipate the consumption experience* and the emotions that they expect to feel. This anticipation is an experience in itself, and serves as a component of the overall experience that consumption provides. Creative products elicit powerful emotions, contribute to self-identity, and have spiritual content, so it's easy to imagine that anticipation of the consumption experience during information search is a key ingredient in the overall experience.

Summing up, *information search plays two complementary roles*: to build a set of information and knowledge that serves in decision making, and to prefigure the value that the consumption experience will provide. The first role emerges primarily from the search for utilitarian value; the second in the search for hedonic, ethical, and communicative value.

When consumers choose a vacation spot, for instance, they not only need detailed information on possible travel dates, itineraries, and prices; they also need to fantasize about the places they'll see. It's no coincidence, then, that the bulk of creative content for many products in the media industry (magazines, television, and radio programs) provides information along with previews of the experience in question.

Thanks to the World Wide Web, information search has exploded in the last few years. This exceptional phenomenon deserves a closer look (Research Focus 4.2).

Research Focus 4.2

Web-based information search for experiential products

Can the availability of endless, easy-access information on the Web make experience products less experiential, and more similar to search products? Never before have consumers been able to access this quantity and quality of information with a single means of communication. Nowadays before making a purchase, people can find myriad quality clues with little effort – even with experience products. So does this make them more similar to search products?

To answer this question, Huang et al. (2009) conducted research on a sample of North American consumers comparing online information search processes for experience products and search products. Their basic hypothesis was that in online contexts, the difference between experience and search products diminishes. In fact, because information search in traditional offline contexts is more labor-intensive, consumers focus more effort on search products than experience products. Huang et al.'s reasoning is that for search products, information search helps consumers envision product quality, but for experience products search efforts aren't as useful in this sense. With online searches, on the other hand, information is available not only in far greater quantities, but also in forms that can enable consumers to anticipate product quality. For example, people can find out about the experiences of other consumers, or get a better grasp of product quality thanks to different formats (videos and product presentations, virtual tours, or interactive tools that illustrate product features).

Research findings show no difference between the amount of information consumers search for relative to the two product categories (confirming that because information search calls for fewer sacrifices, consumers gather more information on experience products as well). But differences do remain for the type of information and the search methods. In fact, for experience products (unlike search products), consumers look for deeper, but not broader information. In other words, they might check out fewer Web pages, but they spend more time on each page.

In addition, for experience products consumers do less free-riding (searching for information from one seller but purchasing the product in question from another). Consumers strongly and subjectively associate the information they collect on experience products with the seller who provided the information, making it less transferable to other sellers. So essentially, although Huang et al. confirm that Internet information search makes experience products more similar to search products, due to the specificities of the first kind there is still a significant different in search methods.

One outcome of the complementarity of the two roles is that consumer knowledge isn't just a collection of information, but also an inventory of emotions, fantasies, sensations, and intuitions linked to that information. Every time individuals recall information, all these other aspects come to mind as well.

4.3.6.3   From information to knowledge

This complementarity also helps the organization understand the complexity involved in transforming the information consumers collect into knowledge that they can utilize in the subsequent stages of the experience. This process consists of subjectively appropriating informational content provided by various sources.

- *Exposure*. Representing this process as a series of sequential stages, every consumer comes in contact with informational stimuli, either deliberately or incidentally: driving by a billboard, listening to a friend talk about her consumption experience, reading a review on a blog. All these are examples of exposure.
- *Attention*. But not all the stimuli consumers are exposed to end up in their memory enriching their knowledge. Why? First of all, obviously, not all stimuli capture their attention. Attention is the process of allocating cognitive resources to stimuli (thoughts, interpretative models, and so on). But why do consumers pay attention to some stimuli and not others?

It depends on certain characteristics, both of the stimulus and the individual. For example, there may be pre-existing motivations: if an individual has already decided to buy a book she'll pay closer attention to book reviews. Or a consumer may have a positive attitude toward the object of the information: if she likes chick lit, she'll be more alert to information on this genre than people who prefer other kinds of books. But whatever the motivations or interests, she won't pay much attention if she's overwhelmed by stimuli: if she's already read ten reviews, she won't be able to focus on the eleventh. And finally, when people don't have much time, they usually don't pay much attention.

There are characteristics of stimuli that also draw more attention. Examples are size, color, contrast, position, movement, novelty. Picture a billboard: if it's big and bright, with lots of colors and contrast, if it has moving parts and eye-catching innovation, it's more likely to capture consumers' attention.

- *Comprehension*. Once consumers pay attention to a certain stimulus, the next step is to comprehend it. Comprehension calls for interpretation, which means applying interpretative models developed from previous knowledge, and making sense of the stimulus.
- *Acceptance*. The fact that consumers understand the content of a given stimulus doesn't necessarily mean they accept it. Acceptance is when they consider this content credible and they're persuaded by it. This isn't just a cognitive process; in fact, a stimulus can also elicit an emotional response. Normally people more readily accept stimuli that trigger a positive emotional response; a negative one would drive them away.
- *Retention*. Even once consumers have accepted the content of the stimulus in question, there's still no guarantee that it will become a part of their knowledge. But if it does, that's retention: when content gets stored in long-term memory where it can be accessed whenever needed. All the stimuli that pass through the previous stages have reached short-term memory, but here there is limited storage space, and more importantly nothing remains for more than 30 seconds or so.

Short-term memory is a cognitive space needed for carrying out the previous phases. But in order for the content of a stimulus to be incorporated into a person's knowledge, it first has to be stored in her long-term memory, which is practically unlimited in size and much more stable. This is where knowledge lies.

In all these phases consumers make *selections*. Of the countless stimuli they're exposed to, only a very small number capture their attention. And of these, which they comprehend and accept on a subjective basis, they retain only a few in their long-term memory.

In conclusion, consumers' knowledge and motivation contribute to determining their expected value. Level of expertise, prior consumption experiences, access to certain external sources – all these things enable consumers to develop a set of information and a series of beliefs that shape their value expectations. If consumers have similar motivations but knowledge sets that differ in scope or depth, they'll have diverse expectations of value.

4.3.6.4   Online flow experience

Experience in computer-mediated environments warrants special attention. Since the World Wide Web has become a familiar place for countless people the world over, interaction with virtual environments has changed the way people search for information and experience the different stages of consumption for many products. What's more, with digitalization having transformed so many creative industries (Section 1.3.3), the Web plays a vital role: it's where consumers search for information and where they have consumption experiences. In fact the Web itself is such an experience.

The Web is a creative product that has spawned innumerable categories of additional creative products: Web sites, search engines, online stores, virtual worlds, and more. On the Web, consumers can access impersonal commercial sources (Web sites of companies and institutions), as well as personal non-commercial sources (expert blogs), which like the other external sources enjoy different reputations and credibility. On the Web consumers can search information that has intrinsic experiential value, which gives rise to the two complementary roles that are entirely intertwined (described in the previous section).

This is why for years now the Web experience has inspired an endless series of studies that reveal how the process of surfing the Web can produce a particular kind of experience: online flow. Tying into the general concept of flow (Section 3.5), this is when individuals are so completely absorbed by an experience that they lose all sense of time, of their surroundings and of anything happening on the fringes of their experience. Hoffman and Novak (1996: 57) describe online flow as: 'The state occurring during network navigation, which is (1) characterized by a seamless sequence of responses facilitated by machine interactivity, (2) intrinsically enjoyable, (3) accompanied by a loss of self-consciousness, and (4) self-reinforcing.'

Online flow can be experienced when consumers are highly focused on the interaction at hand, when the skills that the interaction demands give them a sense of challenge, and when both these factors are more intense than typical daily activities. Online flow is activated by the sensorial richness or *vividness* of the stimuli, in terms of quantity and quality, as well as the level of *interactivity* that the environment allows. Thanks to the Web, information search naturally becomes an experiential process because it entails systematic decision making (which pages to see, how long to look at each one, what tasks to carry out, what information to request and provide) facilitated by both vividness and interactivity. Reaching a state of flow also has noticeable effects on process effectiveness, enhancing the stages of attention, comprehension, acceptance, and retention (Hoffman and Novak, 1996; Van Noort et al., 2012). The state of flow is achieved by definition when consumers focus intently on stimuli and immerse themselves in navigation.

In addition, with the Internet consumers can get more detailed information while accessing several sources simultaneously; this augments comprehension and acceptance (seeing as the arguments put forward by various sources can be verified and confronted with counter-arguments). Lastly, immersion allows for greater capacity for memorization, seeing that flow increases the motivation to interpret information. The Web also favors 'external' memorization mechanisms, through bookmark files generated by other subjects.

Specifically, online flow prompts *exploratory search behavior*, which is less goal-directed, and more prompted by curiosity and the pleasure of discovering something new (Hoffman and Novak, 1996, 2009; Noort et al., 2012). This type of search leads consumers to broaden the number and type of external informational sources and acquire deeper information, enriching the entire process experientially.

Exploratory search is typical of a consumption experience with high hedonic and symbolic value, in which consumer expectations center on intrinsic value (Section 3.1); this behavior is closely linked to consumption processes for creative products. In fact, when consumers search for information on these products, it's very likely that their search process is exploratory rather than goal-directed. Consequently, reaching a state of online flow favors the effectiveness of the search while enhancing the pleasure derived from the pre-consumption experience. In addition, since creative products often elicit intense involvement in consumers, Internet navigation is more like an ongoing search process, and less like ad hoc goal-directed search. This circularly reinforces the experiential content and the possibility for online flow experiences.

4.4 FROM EXPECTED VALUE TO PERCEIVED VALUE: THE PURCHASE EXPERIENCE

As we've said before, consumer satisfaction derives from expected value (before consumption) versus perceived value (after consumption). But prior to the consumption experience comes the purchase experience (Figure 3.1). In this stage consumers choose the specific product they want to experience and eventually buy it. To come to their final decision, they consider various options. Along with choosing what to buy, they also decide where, when, and how to make the purchase, how much time they want to spend, and how much they want to buy.

As we'll see shortly, these specific decisions can be made simultaneously (in a retail store or on a Web site) or sequentially (first choosing what to buy and then where to buy it). So the purchase experience can be broken down into the choice experience and the shopping experience.

4.4.1 Choice experience

Evaluating product options equates to comparing various alternatives on the basis of certain criteria. But how is this done? And which products are compared? And what about products or brands that differ widely? The comparison process consists of three components: establishing the evaluation criteria, defining the evoked set, and judging the individual options, which ultimately leads to the final choice.

4.4.1.1 Establishing evaluation criteria

Consumers approach the purchase experience with a number of motivations that drive them forward, along with knowledge regarding products, brands, and stores. They have a more or less clear and conscious idea of the benefits and sacrifices they expect, and they also have information on specific features of the product options on the table. So how do consumers

take into account benefits, sacrifices, and features at the same time, to come up with a choice?

The answer to this question lies in *means-end theory*, by now consolidated in marketing studies, which asserts that in their memories consumers associate attributes with benefits and sacrifices, and in turn connote all these with values in a map of hierarchical means-end connections. Such connections can be represented on what's called a *hierarchical value map*. Product attributes are the means to gaining benefits and limiting sacrifices (which are called 'consequences' in the original model). Benefits and sacrifices, in turn, are the means for attaining certain values.

Referring back to our discussion of consumer knowledge above, clearly information has to do with product attributes, while beliefs relate to associations between certain attributes and given benefits and sacrifices, which in turn are linked to specific values. Figure 4.2 shows the means-end chains identified in a study on American television viewers who watch professional wrestling. Various levels are represented by different colored circles: light grey for product attributes, grey for benefits/sacrifices (labeled consequences), and dark grey for values.

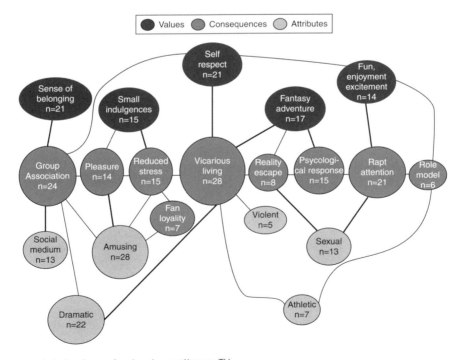

Figure 4.2 – The means-end chains for professional wrestling on TV
Source: Deeter-Schmelz and Sojka (2004: 137). The number of consumers who cited the specific attribute/benefit/value is indicated in the corresponding circle

This map doesn't represent the means-end chains of individuals, but instead the compilations of chains of all the consumers in the study. The thicker the lines that connect the different levels, the more frequently the connection is mentioned by respondents.

With wrestling, the two most often cited benefits (so presumably the most important) relate to vicarious learning and group association. As far as the value categorization detailed in Section 3.1, hedonic value comes first, communicative value second. So what attributes of the TV show are associated with these benefits? Vicarious learning ties into the drama of the match, the soap-opera-like story and the background music, but also the violent action and the athletic skill of the wrestlers. This benefit is also linked to the values of self-respect and living a fantasy. Group association arises from the fact that television gives an opportunity to get together with friends, wrestling offers entertainment, and the match again provides drama. The benefit of group association is strongly associated with the value of belonging to a community.

Maps of means-end relationships among product, benefits/sacrifices, and value represent the associations among these variables, and constitute a part of the knowledge of each individual consumer. All consumers have different motivations and knowledge sets (Section 4.2), which means that different consumers with different motivations will consider certain benefits and attributes more important than others. This is what generates the criteria for comparing and judging various alternatives.

Let's consider a consumer who wants to pick out a movie to watch at home tonight. She has high involvement with avant-garde cinema, a genre she associates with a certain type of plot, or a certain director, or prizes from various film festivals. When she browses through the films available on demand through her cable TV provider, she uses these attributes to evaluate the available options. Now let's say our consumer is feeling a bit down (a typical situational variable), so she doesn't feel like watching a dramatic film. Instead she wants to relax, or maybe have a laugh; she'll probably associate these benefits with different attributes, with a comedy or with certain actors, with the country of origin or with a film she's heard a lot about. So different expected benefits entail different evaluation criteria.

4.4.1.1.1 *Explicit and implicit benefits*   One final note pertains to the capacity of consumers to explain benefits, in other words, to express them and discuss them as the basis of their choices. To do so people need to be conscious of these benefits and have the competence to converse about them. In this case benefits are *explicit*. An example might be a consumer who says she's buying a dress because it suits her aesthetic taste and it flatters her figure; in this case, explicit benefits correspond to product attributes such as size, bright colors, and design.

But sometimes consumers aren't actually conscious of the benefits they're looking for, or they don't have the competence to link certain benefits to the attributes of various value propositions on the market. As we know now, motivations are also based on individual characteristics such as personality traits, social and cultural influences of peer groups, and consumption situations, but often consumers aren't aware of the effects of these factors. And we've also seen that just as often motivations are triggered more by desires than by needs, so they are the outcome of primary process thinking that by definition is difficult to structure or verbalize. The benefits that are linked to these factors are *implicit* or *latent*. As a result consumers have a hard time justifying their preference for certain product attributes or more in general a given value proposition.

The consumer in the example above who's choosing a dress might focus on famous brands, not because they actually provide products that match her taste, or because the individual garments are flattering, but because she's implicitly seeking social approval and she wants to convey her affiliation with a certain social group. These implicit benefits, combined with a somewhat conformist personality, will prompt her to prefer certain brands.

4.4.1.2   *Defining an evoked set*

Once consumers have established their evaluation criteria, they apply these criteria to products to come up with a final choice. But what alternatives do they consider? Those that make up their *evoked set*, that is, the group of products, brands, and points of sale (physical or virtual) that they consider capable of satisfying their needs or desires.

In the previous section we delved into the topic of consumer knowledge, pointing out that this is structured into categorization systems that are hierarchically interconnected. Every consumer has information stored in her long-term memory about a number of products based on prior pre-consumption and consumption experience.

But we can't assume that she evaluates all of these products. In fact, from all her consumption experiences, she has probably developed a positive attitude toward some products but not others, (which she most likely no longer takes into account). For still other products, she may not have much information so she might exclude them simply because she doesn't want to make additional informational sacrifices. In a consumer's evoked set there is information related to a very limited number of products, brands, and stores that she has pre-selected based on her prior pre-consumption and consumption experiences. She applies evaluation criteria to these products to come up with a final choice.

4.4.1.3 Judging alternatives, forming preferences, and making choices

Again, once consumers identify evaluation criteria for product options in their evoked set, they apply these criteria, and make a judgment about each alternative. Consumers are aware of certain attributes, but not others (which of course they don't take into account when making their judgments).

Attributes can be classified as *tangible* (objectively measurable) or *intangible* (the product of subjective judgment). For the first, the most obvious is price, but there are also specific product attributes: the size and weight of a magazine; the date of execution of a sculpture; the running time of a show; the distance from home of a theater; the duration of a trip. Intangible attributes include the style of a dress or home décor; the plot or the cast of characters in a film or a book; the words and the rhythm of a song.

As often stated in Chapter 1, the value of creative products primarily lies in their creative content and their experiential nature. So the intangible attributes and the unique features of creative products tend to weigh more heavily on consumer choice. When consumers form an opinion on the individual attributes of a creative product, four factors come into play: prior product experience, the opinion of others, additional information gathered during pre-consumption, and the norms relating to the product category in question that are recognized by the consumer.

Since creative products are experience products, consumers can express a personal opinion on their quality only after consumption. As a result, previous experience

is the most reliable source for judging product attributes, both tangible and intangible. When consumers don't have prior experience to refer to they can resort to other people's opinions, for example, experts, critics, or other consumers. In judging product attributes, how much trust consumers place in external sources depends on their credibility (Section 4.3.6.1).

The opinion of others is especially important with regard to intangible attributes, which, due to a lack of standard parameters, call for subjective evaluation. What's more, we've seen that consumers tap a variety of sources when gathering information on attributes, and interpret this information in light of their knowledge to come up with an opinion of their own. Lastly, consumers often know the norms that apply to a given category (for instance, the aesthetic canons of an art form or a literary genre) and use them as a benchmark for judging different product options.

The choice process involves taking into account the assessments of every single attribute to come to a preference for one product option, which is the basis for choice. This process combines both cognitive and affective aspects. The first serve to assess tangible attributes, and lead to the application of decision-making rules that utilize detailed information. The second apply to intangibles, and, being more holistic, lead to more immediate overviews of product value. While cognitive aspects are activated primarily when motivations are driven by needs, affective aspects are more evident when desires underpin motivations.

4.4.1.3.1 Cognitive assessment processes   Beginning with assessments that are more distinctly cognitive, compensatory processes can be differentiated from non-compensatory one. For the first, negative opinions on certain product attributes are compensated by positive opinions on others, resulting in a final judgment that puts them all in the balance. The second type of process places more importance on extremely negative or positive attributes, and no compensation comes into play.

4.4.1.3.1.1 Compensatory processes
These are normally illustrated with *multi-attribute models*, which assume that consumers base their judgments on several attributes of available alternatives. The most widely recognized model used in marketing studies measures the expected value of every alternative being assessed as the weighted average of the

evaluation of the single product attributes, according to the following formula:[2]

$$V_p = \sum_{i=1}^{n} A_{ip} \times I_i$$

where
V_p = expected value of product p,
A_{ip} = subjective assessment of attribute i for product p,
I_i = the importance of attribute i,
n = the number of attributes taken into consideration in the judgment.

Here's an example. Imagine two girlfriends who want to spend a weekend in a European art city, something they've never done before; they're considering four possible destinations. The benefits they expect from this trip are hedonic, centering on the aesthetic experience of the cultural attractions of the city (museums, theaters, galleries), and the local cuisine; the sacrifices center on the cost and the travel time. To find out more about the cities on their list, they've searched the Web for information on how much vacation packages cost, and how long the journey would last. They've also read guidebooks to get an idea of the reputation of both the cultural attractions of the cities and the food they offer. After spending hours discussing the various options, the two friends come to the conclusion that since they're not experienced flyers, the number one benefit they're looking for is a short plane trip, followed by low cost. Next comes the reputation of the cultural attractions, and lastly the local cuisine. (They're not taking a vacation just to eat, though!)

Now as an example, let's represent their judgments on individual attributes of the four destinations, rating them on a scale of one to nine, with one being very negative and nine very positive. Next, taking overall importance as 100 per cent, let's assume they allocate relative importance among the four attributes they've discussed. Table 4.3 accurately summarizes the opinions of the two friends.

Applying the formula above to the data in the table, it appears that the best option is Destination D because it costs less (9 presumably corresponds to the lowest-priced destination), but also in light of the attractions, the famous cuisine, and the fact that the journey is not too long or too short.

Destination A would be the worst option, because even though it's the shortest, it's also the most expensive; what's more, reviews are quite critical of the quality of both the cultural attractions and the cuisine. Destinations B and C seem very similar, but for opposite reasons. While C offers comparable attractions, cuisine, and price, it involves the longest flight. Instead B has a good, but not exceptional, score on all the attributes. So unless some other problem comes up, the two friends will probably choose Destination D.

To clearly describe the compensatory decision-making model, however, it's important to add more details. In fact, it's very unlikely (except in certain cases or for people with highly structured thought processes) that consumers would make a quantitative assessment of each product, weighting the importance of each attribute quantitatively.

The formula above and its application in the example are one means for *representing* consumer assessment processes. In other words, marketing researchers can utilize this when they ask consumers to *make their judgments explicit using quantitative language*. For the

Table 4.3 – An example of the compensatory selection process

Attributes	Destination A	Destination B	Destination C	Destination D	Importance
Travel time	9	6	3	6	40%
Expected cost of the week end	3	7	9	9	30%
Reputation of cultural attractions	4	6	8	8	20%
Reputation of local cuisine	4	6	8	8	10%
Expected value (weighted rate)	5.7	6.3	6.3	7.5	100%

choices consumers systematically make every day, they often apply the same compensatory process, but most of their judgments on individual attributes are qualitative. So they're content to make a more or less positive judgment on the single attributes of each alternative ('super', 'very good', 'alright', 'not bad'), and to say that one option is better or worse than another in terms of the attribute in question ('they're pretty much the same', 'there's no comparison'). Consumers can then come up with a concise judgment that encompasses the varying degrees of importance that they allocate to different attributes, without expressing their opinions in quantitative terms.

4.4.1.3.1.2 Non-compensatory processes   Here consumer focus is concentrated on attributes at opposite ends of the spectrum, in other words, either very positive or very negative ones. Let's go back to the two girlfriends planning a trip. Since they're not experienced travelers, they're hesitant to take a long flight, so for them 'flight time' is the attribute they won't compromise on. Here's how they would probably express this condition: 'The destination has to be as close as possible to home', or 'We want to spend as little time as possible on the plane.'

So according to this line of reasoning, the destination these two women would prefer is most likely A, which during the compensatory process was the worst. This type of decision-making process is called *lexicographic*. Here consumers compare different options in light of the most important attribute: if one option emerges as the best, they chose it and the process ends; if products are equal on the first attribute, consumers consider the second most important attribute. The lexicographic process is typical of situations in which consumers are subject to restrictions on their resources (time, money, emotional states). As a result, they opt for alternatives that maximize the efficient and effective use of those resources.

Another typical way in which consumers adopt non-compensatory processes is when they establish minimum or maximum *cutoffs*, which some or all of the attributes in question must (or must not) exceed.

In this case our two friends might decide that they don't want to spend more than a certain amount of money, which means they'll discard all the options that exceed that threshold. But they may also decide not to consider options that cost too little, thinking that if the price is too low the quality of the package might be disappointing. This would constitute a minimum cutoff. Additional examples might involve travel time (four hours at the most, including layovers), or the quality of the attractions (at least one world-famous museum), or local cuisine (at least one Michelin-starred restaurant).

The use of cutoffs can generate two different selection processes. The first, *elimination by aspects*, is similar to the lexicographic process. Here the consumer sets a minimum (or maximum) cutoff for the top attribute, and only considers the options that exceed (or don't exceed) that limit. If there are several options with respect to the top attribute, consumers continue with the second most important attribute and relative cutoffs, until there is only one option remaining (as with the lexicographical process).

Going back to our previous example, let's imagine that the different destinations are characterized by the values for the attributes 'travel time' and 'total cost' reported in Table 4.4.

Now let's say that the two friends have set maximum cutoffs of four hours of travel including layovers, and 800 euro as far as cost. Beginning with the most important attribute, travel time, they would first eliminate Destination C, which lasts five hours. Next they'd look at the second most important attribute, total cost, and they would discard Destinations A and B, ultimately choosing Destination D.

The second process that uses cutoffs is called *conjunctive*. In this case, cutoffs are set for every attribute; alternatives that don't meet these requisites for every attribute are eliminated, and the remaining ones are considered. The conjunctive process is more similar to the compensatory process because all the options are taken into account. But rather than having the positive and negative aspects compensate one another, more

Table 4.4 – An example of consumer assessment through cutoffs

Attributes	Destination A	Destination B	Destination C	Destination D	Importance
Travel time (hours)	1	3	5	3	40%
Expected cost of weekend(€)	1000	850	500	500	30%

emphasis is placed on the negative ones, which are used to eliminate the alternatives that don't reach pre-set minimum thresholds. In the previous example, the destinations that would be eliminated are all those that are more than four hours away, or that cost more than 800 euro, or that don't have at least one world-famous museum, or that don't have at least one Michelin-starred restaurant.

Clearly the different evaluation processes can be used simultaneously or in sequence. What very often happens is that consumers have several alternatives on the table, so they apply cutoffs to pare down the number of options, and then they apply the compensatory process to choose among the few that remain.

4.4.1.3.1.3 Attitude-based processes

One final aspect that deserves mention is that the judgments consumers make about products form the basis of their attitude, or positive or negative disposition, toward those products (Section 4.3). Attitude becomes part of consumer knowledge, regardless of whether the product was actually chosen or not. In other words, *preferences are different from attitudes*, even though they derive from the same evaluation process. Preference has to do with the product alternative that the consumer believes is best, based on pre-established selection criteria; attitude is the result of the judgment given to individual alternatives after applying those criteria.

So let's say the two friends decide to spend the weekend at Destination D; they still would have given Destinations B and C a positive rating, but a lower one for Destination A. That means Destinations B, C, and D will be included in their evoked set, and may be re-evaluated if a reason to do so should arise. Let's imagine that over time the two friends gradually overcome their anxiety about flying, so travel time becomes less important. This might mean that Destination C would move up to become the top pick. Destination A, which was judged quite negatively (the only real plus being its vicinity to home) probably wouldn't be considered during subsequent evaluations, unless the travelers' motivations or the destination's attributes change substantially.

When consumers have strong attitudes, they use simplified assessment and selection processes that are called *attitude-based*. What this essentially means is that if consumers have a very positive attitude toward a given product, the next time the need or desire comes up, they'll skip right to the purchase stage. This

is a common occurrence in creative industries. Simply think of all the times a new film comes out by a consumer's favorite director, or starring her favorite actor, or a new book is published by an author she loves, or when she's deciding where to go on vacation and she immediately thinks of a place she's always enjoyed: in these cases to make a choice a consumer doesn't have to think twice! So having a strong attitude qualifies the set of consumer knowledge, and allows consumers to minimize the sacrifices associated with information search, evaluation, and choice.

4.4.1.3.2 *Affective evaluation processes*

The processes we've examined so far are markedly cognitive, and call for complex mental activities: using information, making comparisons, forming preferences, and finally choosing. We've seen that these processes are activated primarily when motivations are rooted in needs, and when the available options either have tangible attributes, or attributes that are rendered tangible through the judgments of consumers or other parties.

But what happens when motivations reflect desires instead of needs? When the value expected from a creative product is intrinsic, given by the pleasure that people want to experience, or the effect on their self-identity, or the sense of sacrality or spirituality that emerges? When consumers have to choose a show to see at the theater, or a work of art to buy, or a comic book to read, or a television series to watch, do they scrutinize all the relevant information? Do they compare in detail all the available options? Do they establish cutoffs that products have to respect?

Not exactly, and not always. Consumers probably do a bit of all these things, because in the end they do have to come up with a choice. They make some sort of comparison; they use some information. But what comes more naturally is to let their feelings be their guide, the emotions that they expect to experience. In other words, consumers enact evaluation processes that are more patently affective.

Generally speaking, affective decision-making processes work in much the same way that attitude-based processes do, in the sense that they tend to be more immediate. This doesn't mean that they take less time than cognitive processes; far from it. In fact, often the emotional scope of the decision makes these processes far more protracted. So the anticipation of the emotions that a consumer expects to feel during the consumption experience leads more directly to a preference and a choice, without activating many thought processes or complex mental activities.

As I said at the beginning of this section, cognitive and emotional levels interact, so choosing doesn't simply mean activating one or the other, but rather that one may be predominant over the other. Sensations and emotions come into play to varying degrees in various experiences, to the point where they have a major impact on emotional processes.

The compass that guides an organization in understanding the role of emotions in consumer choice processes is a general rule stating that *human beings tend to approach activities, events, people, and products that elicit positive emotions, and avoid those that do the opposite*. Consequently, every activity in the various stages of consumer experience can trigger approach or avoidance. So if a consumer is searching for information, and she comes across something that she associates with a negative emotion (she's reading a review by a movie critic whose description of a film brings repellent images to mind), she'll store the memory of the emotion along with the information. This will affect how a consumer builds her evoked set (she won't include the film described above). The same thing can happen during the comparison and judgment stages.

For products with expected value that's tied to pleasure or identity, sacrality or ethics in particular, consumers are continuously stimulated by sensations triggered by the selection process. What happens is a consumer focuses a great deal on how she feels when searching for information, evaluating and comparing alternatives, and finally choosing. In fact some alternatives resonate (or fail to resonate) so completely with a consumer's sensations and emotional states that they elicit a positive (or negative) judgment and lead her directly to preference and choice (or exclusion), reducing (or amplifying) the impact of the negative attributes or sacrifices. For instance, if a consumer is browsing through an art magazine and the photograph of a painting leaves her breathless, she immediately feels the need to go see the exhibit being advertised, even if it's in another city.

Kwortnik and Ross (2007) draw a distinction between the positive emotions consumers feel during the evaluation process, labeling them fantasy feelings or facilitative feelings. *Fantasy feelings* are emotions that consumers consciously experience during the process. In a sense, they foreshadow the emotions they can expect during the actual consumption experience, and make

certain information very vivid regarding the available options. This information, as a result, will carry more weight in the evaluation itself.

In their research, Kwortnik and Ross studied the choice of vacation, and showed participants a picture of a posh resort that would anticipate the aesthetic and sensorial pleasure that such an elegant environment might provide. This photo would enhance the importance of the attributes 'design' and 'resort atmosphere' in the assessment of the single vacation packages. Fantasy feelings can have a direct impact on preferences, triggering an immediate connection between the emotion elicited and the product to purchase.

Facilitative feelings, instead, are emotions experienced at a sub-conscious level that are hard to describe ('it's like a feeling of...' 'I don't exactly know, it's sort of...'). These are instinctively positive reactions that don't necessarily have a direct effect on preferences; instead they augment the importance of certain attributes that are under evaluation. In other words, consumers give greater weight to some characteristics of the offerings but they don't really know why. They simply recognize at a gut level that these characteristics 'feel' right, useful, or appropriate.

Affective evaluation processes, like their cognitive counterparts, prompt positive and negative attitudes about the various alternatives in question. Consumers store these attitudes in their memories, with all the varying shades of emotions that will come to mind whenever the same motivations arise.

4.4.2 *The shopping experience*

The shopping experience consists of consumer interaction with the physical context (stores) in the case of offline shopping, or virtual environments (Web sites, virtual worlds) for online shopping, with the aim of purchasing a preferred product. Very much like the pre-consumption stage, when consumers search for useful information to develop their expectations of value and then go on to choose a product, for the purchase experience two different roles can also be identified.

The first is goal-directed and *utilitarian*, that is, instrumental in making the purchase in question. In this case the store or virtual environment (as we'll see in Chapter 9) is nothing more than a window display where consumers can choose their preferred products. The second is *experiential*, providing hedonic, symbolic, and communicative value beyond what the product in question offers, so this role is not goal-directed. In this second case, both online and offline stores are interaction environments that can supply additional value, beyond the assortment of products and brands.

4.4.2.1 The offline shopping experience

The impact of the physical atmosphere on consumer experience is analyzed in marketing studies primarily through the use of environmental psychology. This discipline studies the influence of environmental stimuli on individuals' inner processes (cognitive and affective). Specifically, the most popular of these environmental psychology models represents the effects of store atmosphere as a set of stimuli capable of triggering emotional responses in consumers, which in turn lead to certain behaviors (Donovan and Rossiter, 1982).[3]

Store atmosphere consists of the set of tangible and intangible elements that activate sensorial stimuli in consumers (Zaghi, 2008). Specifically, as we'll discuss in more detail in Chapter 9, stimuli can be induced by the external or internal store design, by the layout of interior spaces (position, size, sequence), and the displays inside the store (techniques and methods for displaying products, in-store communication), in addition to product assortment, complementary services, and interaction with sales staff.

The impact on consumers arises from the capacity of the atmosphere to trigger emotional states. This in turn depends on the *novelty* and *complexity* of the stimuli. Novel stimuli are unexpected and surprising; complexity instead relates to the number of stimuli, the relationship among them, and whether or not they are static or dynamic. The more novel and complex the stimuli, the greater the capacity of store atmosphere to stimulate customers.

As for *emotional responses*, consumers can feel *pleasure* (joy, contentment, a sense of well-being) or *arousal* (feeling alert and stimulated, like an active participant). Their *behavioral responses*, on the other hand, include *approach* or *avoidance*, in terms of wanting (or being willing) to:

- Enter or remain in the store, as opposed to not entering at all or leaving.
- Explore and interact with the environment (assortment, in-store communication, displays), rather than avoiding interaction.
- Mingle and communicate with other people in the store (other customers or sales staff), instead of refraining from this kind of contact.

- Carry out activities (visiting the store more frequently, or staying longer during each visit) and feeling satisfied, rather than remaining inactive and dissatisfied.

The offline shopping experience is more intense when the store atmosphere can provide consumers with novel, complex stimuli that trigger emotional responses of pleasure and excitement. These emotions, in turn, translate into both cognitive processes involving greater attention, comprehension, acceptance, and retention of product-related stimuli, and the intrinsic pleasure of shopping (Section 9.7.2).

4.4.2.2 The online shopping experience

This experience is also made up of a series of cognitive, emotional, and behavioral responses activated by stimuli, but this time they're found in the virtual environment. The online experience is normally associated with the concept of online flow (Section 4.3.6.4). In fact, the specific dimensions of flow impact the cognitive processes of utilizing information to make comparisons and choices.

The state of flow gives consumers *greater perceived behavioral control*, which equates to more confidence in their ability to carry out the tasks at hand (for example finding and adequately understanding useful information) (Hoffman and Novak, 1996). What's more, flow allows consumers to retain more information in their memory than would otherwise be possible, which makes learning more effective.

In terms of emotional responses, online flow positively impacts *the pleasure of the navigation experience*, eliciting an approach response instead of avoidance. Actually, flow enhances the sense of enjoyment associated with the experience, increasing its hedonic value as well. As a result of these cognitive and emotional responses, consumers tend to spend more time online interacting with the virtual environment, and they're more inclined to purchase the products they've been researching.

4.4.2.3 The complexity of the purchase experience

The purchase experience can be broken down into a series of interconnected decisions. First, consumers decide what product category to purchase. For example, choosing how to spend the evening means deciding between going to the cinema or the theater, going out to dinner with friends, staying at home to read a book, or staying at home and doing nothing at all. Then consumers decide on a specific product or brand within this category: if they opt for a movie, which one? Then they decide where and how to buy whatever they've decided on, and where and when to consume it: should they go to the cinema, or rent a DVD or download it from an online store and watch it at home? Then they decide how to pay: cash, credit card, or debit card?

Many of these decisions are linked to other less important decisions. Should they go to the cinema by car, or on foot, or by bus? Alone or with friends? All these choices taken together can generate an incredible number of purchase experiences reflecting the specificities of the consumer, the situation, and the offerings available. In fact, it would be impossible to come up with a comprehensive classification.

However, keeping in mind that the *complexity of the experience* consists of the number of activities the consumer performs, along with the temporal, cognitive, and emotional resources invested in these activities, and the number of parties involved, an organization should identify the factors that can influence this complexity so as to make effective decisions. The following are the most typical factors.

4.4.2.3.1 The degree of planning
Based on this variable, purchases can be classified as fully planned, partially planned, unplanned, or impulse, in order of decreasing complexity (all other conditions being equal).

Fully planned purchases

In this case the choice experience is separate and comes before the purchase experience. Consumers invest time and other resources in information search, and then choose both the product category and the specific product/brand before going to the online or offline store. So with planned purchases the shopping experience tends to be very goal-directed, for example, if a consumer has to buy new clothes and she already knows what style and brand she wants, and what store to go to.

Partially planned purchases

In these cases normally consumers decide ahead of time on the product category but not the specific product or brand. That choice is put off until the actual shopping experience. So in the clothing example, the consumer might decide she wants to buy a sweater, but she has no idea which style or brand; she'll decide that once she gets to the store.

Unplanned purchases

In these situations, consumers haven't even made a decision about the product category (much less the specific product) before going shopping. They decide what they want to buy while they're shopping. What happens here is that they have a generic list of needs and desires in mind, and they use the store as a sort of surrogate shopping list.

Unplanned purchases are very common when it comes to products people use every day and buy frequently; for example, things they buy at the supermarket. Consumers know that they need to buy certain items repeatedly, and they go to the store convinced that while walking from aisle to aisle they'll remember what they need. Unplanned purchases are also very common with creative products. In fact, here shopping itself plays an experiential role, and the actual purchase of a specific product or brand is only one component of the experience (as we saw in the previous section).

Impulse purchases

Although impulse purchases are also unplanned, they differ from this last purchase type for other reasons. Rook (1987: 191) defines an impulse purchase as: 'A sudden, often powerful and persistent urge to buy something immediately. The impulse to buy is hedonically complex and may stimulate emotional conflict. Also, impulse buying is prone to occur with diminished regard for its consequences.'

People sometimes express this sensation by saying that the product or brand was 'calling out' to them, and that they 'couldn't resist'. Essentially, it's as if their need or desire was provoked by the product and not the other way around. They see something and they 'have to have it'. In this sense, impulse purchases clearly entail a minimal level of complexity, seeing as they typically involve very few activities, temporal/cognitive resources, or even other subjects. The impulse purchase is typically individual; in fact, if other people are nearby the impulse buyer might think they're passing judgment, which inhibits this behavior.

Summing up, for any purchase, made in response to a specific need or desire, there is some degree of planning, depending on factors underpinning motivations and knowledge. To get an idea of the breakdown of different types of purchases for a specific creative product category, let's take a look at offline book sales (excluding technical manuals or textbooks). Data reported by Thomson (2012) relative to the US market in 2007 show that 53 per cent of people who bought a specific book had made their purchase decision before entering the store (fully planned purchase); 28 per cent went to the store with the intention of buying a book, but hadn't decided on a specific title (partially planned); and 29 per cent purchased a book without having planned to do so before entering the store (unplanned or impulse).[4]

In conclusion, the intrinsic value of the shopping experience depends on the type of the broader purchase experience: this value increases as the amount of planning decreases. With fully planned purchases, in fact, the shopping experience is extremely goal-directed, and serves solely the actual purchase of the product the consumer has already decided on. For unplanned purchases, instead, the shopping experience fully supplies its hedonic and symbolic value, and the actual product purchase is simply one component of this value. Finally in extreme cases, the shopping experience actually becomes more important than the choice experience.

4.4.2.3.2 Degree of newness
Generally speaking, the newer the purchase is for the consumer, the more complex the purchase experience will be, all other conditions being equal. The first time a consumer seeks to satisfy a specific desire or need, she doesn't have the experience or the knowledge about the different products categories that can help her make a decision. So she'll have to search information and interact with a variety of external sources; her emotional resources will often be called into play, on occasion intensely so. All this adds to the level of complexity. On the other hand, habitual consumers of a certain product category have a rich set of knowledge, the product of prior personal experience. For them there is no need to activate additional sources to decide which products to purchase.

4.4.2.3.3 Strength of attitudes
When a consumer has developed strong attitudes toward certain product categories, products, or brands, external sources, or online/offline stores, both the experience of choosing and shopping are impacted (Section 4.4.1.3.1.3). Very likely the effect is an overall simplification of the purchase experience. However, when consumers don't have strong attitudes, they'll probably invest time and cognitive and emotional effort in building more contemplated or more emotionally satisfying choices.

4.4.2.3.4 Level of involvement
As the level of involvement in the purchase experience increases, so does the level of complexity, which is why more involved consumers will invest more in the experience of choosing and shopping. The level of involvement relates to the expertise of consumers, even more so with creative products, so the two variables interact in influencing the complexity of the experience (Section 4.3.4.1).

Yet the type of involvement can have different effects on the way in which complexity emerges. In fact, situational involvement leads consumers to concentrate the resources they invest in the experience in the time frame of the specific situation. For instance, if a consumer wants to give herself a gift to celebrate her birthday, the emotional and cognitive resources she invests will be high but temporary, centered exclusively on that event.

Enduring involvement, on the contrary, pushes consumers to more steadily dedicate resources to the category or product in question. For this reason, complexity mainly characterizes the pre-consumption stage. Consequently, the purchase experience could be greatly simplified, because when consumers are ready to choose and purchase a product, they have very clear ideas on the one that would best suit their needs.

4.4.2.3.5 Perceived risks
In Section 3.1.6.3 we highlighted how some sacrifices that consumers expect are not actual but potential; in other words, they are risks associated with the purchase and consumption of a given product. The higher the perceived risks, the higher the complexity of the purchase experience. The most effective way for consumers to reduce these risks is for them to increase their knowledge by tapping external information sources, exchanging opinions and insight within their social network, comparing product alternatives, visiting online and offline retailers, and so on.

By doing all this, consumers can develop product competence and reduce performance risk. Also, they can understand whether there are ways to reduce the financial risk, and intuit whether the product is acceptable to peer groups and consistent with self-image. Basically, consumers can make sacrifices today to reduce expected risks tomorrow, up to an appropriate threshold, or give up the purchase in question. And this increases the complexity of the experience.

4.4.2.3.6 Purchase roles In discussing the purchase experience, up to this point I've made an implicit assumption: consumers are autonomous decision makers. Although this is the case for many motivations and consequent purchase and consumption decisions, it's also true that there are many other motivations and decisions that have to do with groups, giving rise to collective purchase experiences.

Just think of groups of friends who decide where to go on vacation, what show to see, or what birthday gift to buy for a member of the group. Or family purchases, when family members have a say in some decisions. There are even groups bonded by shared passions, like book clubs.

Although these are examples of very diverse groups in terms of stability, formality, and internal relationships, the specificity of group purchase experiences is that selection and purchase processes involve people who play various *purchase roles*.

Six such roles can be identified:

- The *Initiator* is the person who identifies the need or expresses a desire underlying the motivation.
- The *Gatekeeper* is the person who controls information that serves to make a choice.
- The *Influencer* has the knowledge and competence to guide the product selection.
- The *Decider* has the last word on the various options.
- The *Shopper* makes the purchase in a store or through some other channel.
- The *User/Consumer* experiences actual product consumption.

The individual consumer, instead, would play all these roles at once, even though she may be swayed by external influencers (information sources, critics, experts, other consumers). In group choices, however, the people involved play different roles. An example is a family with kids buying a children's book. Here most likely the Initiator will be a parent, the Influencers are other parents or the children's schoolmates. The Gatekeeper is the teacher, the Decider one of the parents, the Shopper one of the older children, and the User the younger child.

A crucial distinction in analyzing the purchase experience is between the shopper and the consumer. When these roles are separate, it means that one person does the choosing and another the buying, but these two people are subject to different factors of influence. Obviously, the shopper is the protagonist of the shopping experience and the consumer of the consumption experience. As we'll see in Chapter 9, the separation of these two roles has implications for both communication and distribution strategies, and may also give rise to a particular purchase process – gift-giving – which is detailed in Research Focus 4.3.

Research Focus 4.3

Purchase without consumption: gift-giving

Thanks to their high symbolic content, creative products are commonly used as gifts. Gift-giving is an ancient tradition, and has long been a topic of study for a variety of disciplines, from anthropology to sociology, from economics to psychology, and naturally, marketing. Gift-giving is always a sign of an interpersonal connection, and a gift can signify the desire to establish or strengthen a relationship. Arnould et al. (2002: 690–4) propose a classification of gifts based on the aim of the giver and the degree of obligation surrounding the gesture.

As far as the *aim* is concerned, some gifts are given simply for altruistic pleasure, with no ulterior motives. In this case, the giver has no thought of getting anything in return, and the gift is justified by an affective attachment between the giver and the recipient. With other gifts, however, the aim is to get a certain response or provoke certain behavior in the recipient, so there is an expectation of some form of reciprocity. The *level of obligation* differentiates gifts that are given for special occasions, with some degree of social obligation (a wedding or birthday gift), and those that aren't a response to shared social norms.

If a parent gives her daughter a honeymoon trip, she's giving an altruistic gift that also has some strings of social obligation attached. If instead she gives the same trip to her boss's daughter, she probably wants to get something in return. Or if a grandfather gives his granddaughter a ticket to see her favorite volleyball team, he's acting on an altruistic and voluntary impulse. However, giving tickets to the same match to the managers of a client company isn't obligatory, but it is instrumental, and serves to build business relations.

So the thoughts and emotions involved in the different gift categories vary widely depending on the type of relationship that exists between the giver and the recipient (Joy, 2001). In a strong affective relationship (between partners, family members, close friends), when a person gives an altruistic gift (either voluntarily or out of respect for social norms) there is hedonic value, because this gesture gives pleasure and expresses the identity of the gift giver. In a more distant relationship (between acquaintances), or a more formal one (between professional colleagues or extended family members), an instrumental or obligatory gift has more communicative value.

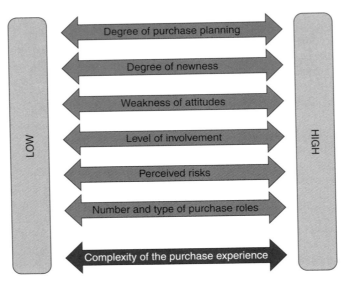

Figure 4.3 – Determinants of the complexity of the purchase experience

Figure 4.3 summarizes the main factors that impact the complexity of the purchase experience.

4.5   THE POST-CONSUMPTION EXPERIENCE

The set of activities that are done after the consumption experience along with the comparison between expected and perceived value constitute the post-consumption experience. The variable that has the most impact on this stage is the degree of satisfaction measured after the consumption takes place. Depending on whether this is positive or negative, the consumer is more or less likely to adopt certain behaviors.

4.5.1   Word of mouth

First, of course, consumers can share their satisfaction or dissatisfaction about an experience via word of mouth, an informal communication of information from consumer to consumer about a product. Word of mouth often centers on telling a story about a product experience, leading up to a recommendation or a complaint. Obviously word of mouth is positive when customers are satisfied and negative when they're not. Research (Anderson, 1998, for example) shows that consumers at either end of the spectrum (very satisfied or very dissatisfied) activate word of mouth, while it's less likely that consumers in the middle who are fairly neutral will do the same. What's more, dissatisfied consumers tend to enact negative word of mouth far more often than satisfied customers do positive.

Thanks to the Internet, it's common practice for today's consumers to engage in digital word of mouth (usually called *eWOM*), which often takes the form of reviews. These are collected by online retailers (like Amazon) or by other sites that actually specialize in reviews (like Tripadvisor) (Case History 4.3).

Case History 4.3

The impact of consumer reviews on book sales: Amazon vs Barnes & Noble

Chevalier and Mayzlin (2006) analyzed consumer reviews on amazon.com and barnesandnoble.com and their impact on sales of reviewed books. First, these researchers report that on both sites, positive reviews far outnumber negative ones, demonstrating that satisfied consumers are more likely to write reviews, as opposed to dissatisfied customers. Second, on amazon.com reviews are more numerous and on average longer than on the competitor site, suggesting that Amazon customers are more inclined to write reviews than Barnes and Noble users.

What's more, positive reviews boost sales of the books reviewed on respective sites, while negative reviews do the opposite, but the impact of negative reviews is greater than that of positive ones for both sites. Interesting to note is that visitors don't simply take into account the number of stars given to a book; instead they read the entire review. This substantiates the informational value attributed to the experience of other consumers, as underscored in Research Focus 4.2.

Research Focus 4.4

The impact of word of mouth on box-office revenues

In numerous creative industries, word of mouth is activated even with products that are about to be released. In this case word of mouth isn't based on consumer experience, but on expectations of the possible experience. But what type of word of mouth is that? And how can its impact be explained?

Liu (2006) studied the effects of word of mouth on box office revenues for films in the first week of their debut. This research focused specifically on the impact of reviews posted on Yahoo Movies with regard to ticket sales for 40 films released in the US. The theory was that this impact can be linked to two factors: the number of comments by consumers (*volume*) and the opinions expressed in the comments (*valence*). Volume generates knowledge of the film among consumers, and valence (a positive, negative, or neutral judgment) could shape the preferences of the people who read the comments.

The results of the study show that word of mouth has positive impact on box office sales, but this effect can be attributed to volume much more than valence. Basically, this means that sales are influenced to a greater degree by the awareness of the film, generated by the number of posted comments, rather than the opinions expressed by consumers.

As compared to commercial sources, the information transmitted via word of mouth is considered more credible (Section 4.3.6.1), which means it has a stronger impact on the knowledge of the consumers on the receiving end, and on their choice and purchase behaviors (Research Focus 4.4).

4.5.2   Product sharing

Sharing can happen through loaning, gifting, or permitting collective use of a product (Belk, 2009): lending a friend an engrossing book, or buying someone tickets to a hit show, or sending a fellow rock fan a YouTube link to a music video. The reason behind product sharing is similar to gift-giving, as described in Research Focus 4.3. In other words, it's based on generosity, often with an expectation of reciprocity, with the aim of strengthening social ties.

For many creative products, contents are digital and can be transferred via electronic files. The filesharing trend has led to widespread behaviors that are considered illegal because they infringe on copyright law. In some creative industries like music and cinema, peer-to-peer filesharing is cited as one of the chief culprits of plummeting sales volumes, though research findings are inconclusive (see research by Oberholzer-Gee and Strumpf, 2007, on music sales).

Analyzing the post-consumption experience, it's interesting to explore the motivations behind filesharing, to see if they constitute a different consumer experience, and not simply a way to avoid paying for a product. This topic is addressed in Research Focus 4.5.

Research Focus 4.5

Illegal file-sharing

People share files containing creative content for different reasons. Of course, filesharing minimizes the sacrifices associated with pre-consumption and purchase, because consumers can save economic, temporal, and cognitive resources. But at the same time, sharing is also a key component of the post-consumption experience, falling under the sphere of altruism, giving something away for free. If a consumer likes a song, a video, a film or simply information, she's eager to share it with other people in her social network.

Two recent studies offer interesting insight on this topic. The first was conducted by Huang (2005) on the motivations underlying illegal filesharing of music among a sample of students in Taiwan. The second is by Hennig-Thurau et al. (2007) on illegal filesharing of films by a sample of German consumers. The studies suggest that this practice can be motivated by all four types of value associated with the consumption of creative products.

In fact, within the framework of reciprocity, sharing files provides hedonic value (as with gift-giving (Research Focus 4.3)). But there are also utilitarian benefits such as the enormous quantity of files that can be stored on portable flash drives; the minimal storage space needed; and the vast number of products that can be collected regardless of available economic resources.

Filesharing also provides communicative value, because it shows technological expertise, which enhances the status of the consumer in her social network, where she can create new relationships or shore up existing ones. Lastly, at the root of illegal filesharing, ironically, is ethical value, which springs from the belief that sharing is both a way to counteract the excessive market power of multinationals in creative industries, and a means for empowering art forms to revert back to their purest state, beyond commercial or profit motives.

4.5.3   Complaining

Consumers express dissatisfaction for a consumption (or purchase) experience by complaining directly to the producer or to various subjects involved in the experience (offline or online stores that sold the product, or the magazine that published a product review).

There are various reasons why people complain; some might be utilitarian, others more affective. Utilitarian motivations include the expectation of a partial or total reimbursement of the price of the product, or compensation for temporal, emotional, or cognitive sacrifices. Consequently, complaints are more common for expensive products than for less expensive ones.

An affective motivation for complaining, however, is that it lessens the negative emotions connected to the unsatisfactory experience with a sort of cathartic effect. If consumers don't 'get it off their chests', so to speak, they feel more and more dissatisfied by the experience in question, because they keep going over it in their minds, which only adds to their negative feelings.

Certain individual characteristics are also related to complaints. For example, consumers who are more involved and have greater expertise are more likely to complain compared to less expert consumers (who might attribute their unsatisfactory experience to their

lack of expertise) or less involved consumers (who believe that complaining wouldn't serve any purpose).

Often people are disinclined to complain because they find it hard to express their negative emotions publicly, or because they don't want to tarnish their public image by openly admitting that they've failed at a consumption experience. What's more, in the past there were limited means of direct communication with the producer. Today, however, with digital communication, the proliferation of touchpoints connecting consumers with producers (Chapter 9), and the emergence of Web sites run by consumers themselves to provide a forum for airing complaints, it's much easier for customers to express dissatisfaction, and the number of complaints has risen noticeably as a result (Ward and Ostrom, 2006).

4.5.4   Repeat purchases

Repeat purchases are the building blocks of a long-term relationship between a consumer and a product (Chapter 10). Consumers who are satisfied with their experience with a product/brand will probably buy it again if the need or desire arises, so they can replicate the same experience. Obviously dissatisfied consumers probably won't make repeat purchases because they don't want to risk experiencing the same disappointment. Yet it's important to point out that this purchase behavior can disguise a wide variety of post-consumption experiences.

Certainly a repeat purchase is one component of *product or brand loyalty*, since consumers engage in this behavior when they believe that the specific product/brand satisfies her needs or desires better than others. This normally happens when consumers have tried out different products or brands, so they can actually compare how well each of them meets their expectations.

But a repeat purchase can be prompted by other factors too. It may simply be a *habitual purchase* that has nothing to do with product/brand loyalty. Consumers who make habitual purchases are not terribly involved in the category in question; they've found a product or brand that meets their minimum requirements for satisfaction, so they keep on buying it. These consumers are more concerned with sacrifices than benefits, so their aim is to minimize the effort required in choosing and shopping, seeing as the product has little importance in their value system. For example, if a consumer isn't very involved with the product 'radio station', she tends to consider them all pretty much the same. Once she's found one she likes, she probably won't look for others on the radio or on the Web, because for her it's simply not worth the effort.

Obviously, for the two situations described above, we assume that consumers have options to choose from. If this isn't the case, a repeat purchase may happen simply because it's the only available alternative. If a consumer lives in a small town that only has one cinema, she either goes there when she wants to see a movie or she doesn't go at all.

4.5.5   Variety seeking

One specificity worth mentioning for experiential products – like creative ones – is that there may be no link between satisfaction and repeat purchases if consumers adopt variety-seeking behaviors. When consumers associate creative products with hedonic benefits, the search for pleasure and positive emotions may not center on a single product/brand, but on the variety of available options instead.

In other words, even if a consumer is a big fan of a certain writer, director, sports team, vacation spot, or historical monument, she won't completely satisfy her needs and desires linked to the related categories only through these specific products. Instead, she'll probably enjoy reading different authors, seeing different films, and so on, because it's the variety that gives her the greatest pleasure. Essentially, for creative products the relationship between satisfaction and repurchase is valid (if a new movie by a consumer's favorite director comes out, she'll go see it), but it isn't universal.

4.5.6   Product/brand attachment

It's intuitive that repeating a satisfying consumption experience creates and reinforces the relationship between the consumer and the product or brand. The greatest impact on this relationship emerges when there is *identification* between the consumer and product/brand or producer. Identification is the perception of similarity/overlap that an individual has with something or someone else in terms of values, aims, or characteristics. This phenomenon gives rise to a strong cognitive and affective bond, to the point where the individual considers this connection as something that defines her self-identity. The other subject might be a product, brand, or a component of one or the other, or a producer.

There are countless examples of this in creative industries. Consumers can identify with a cultural institution they belong to (Bhattacharya et al., 1995), or with the characters in their favorite book series (Corna and Troilo, 2005), or with movie stars they love (Addis and Holbrook, 2010). But it's also easy to imagine people identifying with a sports team or a world-class athlete, a place or a monument, a designer or a clothing brand. Identification serves as a reinforcing mechanism for the relationship with the product/brand, prompting repeat purchases, brand loyalty, positive word-of-mouth and a desire to extend the relationship over time (Chapter 10).

4.5.7   Product disposal

Following a consumption experience, consumers can also decide to dispose of the product (if of course they own it). There are many ways to do this. The product can be sold, traded, gifted, donated, discarded, or recycled. Like in the other stages of consumer experience, there are various benefits and sacrifices involved, so there can be many different motivations for disposing of a product.

The consumer can expect to get utilitarian value by selling the product to other consumers or intermediaries, or trading it for other products. She can sell her comic book collection at a flea market, or sell a work of art to a gallery, or trade clothes with a friend. There is also hedonic value if she gifts something to someone for the pleasure of giving, or to strengthen interpersonal connections, or to pass on a cultural legacy. But she can also throw the product out if she associates it with a part of her self-concept that she wants to eliminate or change.

Other disposal options are donating or recycling the product for ethical reasons (works of art donated to museums, old clothes given to charity shops, books donated to libraries). Recycling can also be motivated by the desire to cut down on waste of the planet's physical resources. Lastly communicative value may also be the reason for disposing of a product. This is the case when someone gives an item to a social group she belongs to (a brand community, or cultural association, or sports team) so it can be used collectively.

Disposal processes also call for sacrifices linked to the use of temporal, cognitive, and emotional resources. So it's likely that the decision to get rid of a product is the outcome of an assessment (rational or emotional) of the related benefits and sacrifices. It's only when the first outweigh the second that a consumer will opt to dispose of a product.

4.6 CONCLUSIONS

Now the picture is complete. With our analysis of the determinants of expected value, and the stages of the experience that lead up to and follow consumption, we've covered the processes, the activities, and the resources that consumers activate to get satisfaction from the creative products they consume. We've talked about how the different stages of the experience engage consumers on a cognitive, emotional, and social level, calling into play all types of resources. We've also highlighted that during these stages, consumers activate relationships with several other subjects and contexts, both physical and virtual. Figure 4.4 illustrates the complex web of relationships among all the variables we've analyzed here and in the previous chapter, in an attempt to represent the determinants of consumer satisfaction.

We've seen how the comparison between perceived value (a product of the consumption experience) and expected value (the product of the interaction between consumer motivation and knowledge, and pre-consumption experience) generates satisfaction or dissatisfaction with regard to the product in question. We've also discussed the fact that satisfaction and dissatisfaction trigger the next stage in the

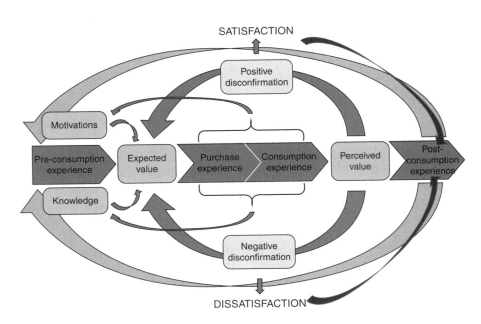

Figure 4.4 – A summary of the different stages of consumer experience

experience: post-consumption. This stage contributes in turn to shaping future expectations of consumers by informing their motivations and their knowledge.

Together with the retroactive effects of the post-consumption experience, in this chapter we've also focused on how both the purchase and consumption experiences can create consumer expectations of value, and shape behavior toward the products offered on the market. The next chapter centers on a different vision of the market and the customers of creative products. In fact, instead of consumers we'll focus on the companies or other institutions that use creative products as factors to incorporate into their production or communication processes, or as vehicles for indirectly accessing their customers: the B(usiness) side of the market for creative products.

REVIEW QUESTIONS

1. What are the determinants of consumer motivations? What are the main characteristics that differentiate consumers?

2. What role does consumer knowledge play? What are the main sources of information and beliefs?

3. Which are the steps in choice processes? What are the different processes leading to consumer judgments and preferences?

4. What are the components of the offline shopping experience? Are they different from the ones characterizing the online experience?

5. Consumer experience continues after the consumption itself. What are the typical behaviors that give rise to post-consumption experience?

Return to Ravnica (October 2012–May 2013)
[https://www.wizards.com/magic/magazine/article.aspx?x=mtg/daily/feature/209]

Ravnica is a sprawling cityscape so vast that it covers the entire world. This mosaic of Gothic spires, cobblestone plazas, dangerous slums, and ancient ruins is home to races and cultures of incredible diversity. [...] Back-alley deals, crime syndicates, and the black market thrive on Ravnica, but the true power resides with the guilds.

The ten guilds are the foundation of power on Ravnica, each with its own identity and civic function. The guilds have existed for centuries. Their history is a web of wars, intrigue, and political machinations as they have vied for control of the plane. As the wild places of the world vanished under layers of stonework and resources grew scarce, each guild carved out its own sphere of influence. For millennia, the Guildpact, a magical accord, helped maintain a relative peace on the plane. The Guildpact has been dispelled, and for a time the guilds fell into chaos. But the ten-thousand-year-old guild culture and division of duties has reasserted itself, and the ten guilds are once again dominant. However, tensions between them are building and rumours of trouble can be heard in both the hallowed guildhalls and rustic taverns of the unguilded citizens.

The planeswalker Jace Beleren has made Ravnica his adoptive home. But he's not the only planeswalker drawn to this diverse and complex plane. Tezzeret, Garruk Wildspeaker, Liliana Vess, Gideon Jura, and Chandra Nalaar have all visited here, drawn by its secrets and possibilities, and the plane boasts more than one planeswalker native as well. [...] After a years-long absence, the ancient dragon has returned to his aerie and has recently sent his guild into a frenzy of research and projects, which no one seems to understand but him. The League's activities haven't gone unnoticed – that many explosions are hard to miss – and the other guilds are beginning to worry if there is a method behind the Firemind's madness.

CASE STUDY

MAGIC: THE GATHERING: AN ALL-ROUND EXPERIENCE

This case was co-authored with Davide Neri, Community Manager Italy at Wizards of the Coast[5]

Magic: The Gathering (simply Magic in the rest of this case study), the first trading card game to appear on the global market, was launched by Wizards of the Coast (hereafter Wizards), a publisher of board games and role playing games (including the world-famous Dungeons & Dragons). The man behind Magic is Richard Garfield, a math professor with a passion for games, who designed a game that was meant to be economical, portable, and easy to play.

The idea was to come up with a card game for breaks between long role-playing sessions, for instance at gaming conventions. In the early 1990s these events were very popular, especially in the United States, where people would spend the whole day participating in role playing games like Dungeons & Dragons. So Garfield designed Magic, taking his inspiration from baseball cards and turning them into a game: no characters to create, no castles to build, just two supra-natural characters who had to fight to the death armed with various kinds of magic.

Wizards gave the green light with the 1993 Magic launch, actually inventing a new product category in the game market. Initially intended as just a way to kill time, 20 years on Magic has developed a cult following, counting more than 12 million fans and players the world over. Digital versions of the game are also available for a variety of platforms (Xbox, PlayStation, PC, iPad, and Android tablet).

Briefly, two or more players impersonate characters with special powers who can travel through various planes of existence: hence the name *Planeswalkers*. Each Planeswalker can cast powerful spells and summon various creatures for help, creatures that are represented by cards. The object of the game is to take life-points away from adversaries until they run out and die.

So each Planeswalker has a deck of cards to play with, either real or virtual (thanks to Magic Online). Buying cards, either singles or packs of 15, is actually part of the gaming experience because building the deck means searching for and selecting cards depending on the power of each one and the possible synergies between various card combinations. Currently more than 12,000 different cards are available and each year Wizards launches hundreds more.

Specific sets of cards correspond to certain stories describing different worlds populated by Planeswalkers. Each year, Wizards creates a story (called a 'block') that's played with three sets of cards published at regular intervals (fall, winter, and spring), called 'expansions sets'. Every one of these can be interpreted as a standalone chapter in a single story. In the box below is an excerpt from a story (*Return to Ravnica*).

Magic cards are sold in 70 different countries and translated into 11 different languages, Mandarin Chinese included. 2012 was the fourth year in a row to see double-digit growth in the European market. The biggest market is the US with around 250,000 players; Europe comes next with just over 80,000. In a breakdown of the European market, Italy takes the lead, followed by the UK, Spain, and France.

But Magic isn't simply a card game: it's a social phenomenon that brings together people of all ages and lifestyles. Nearly 3.5 million players all over the world meet in shops that belong to the network set up by Wizards (Wizards Play Network – WPN) to play and share experiences and knowledge. But success didn't come right away; in fact, it took a radical change in the company's original strategy.

The initial marketing strategy

Magic was born in a context of hardcore, semi-professional players. As mentioned before, Garfield designed the game as a pastime for people who would meet to participate in day-long role-playing games. Over the years, international tournaments were set up with substantial cash prizes.

The strategy of Wizards was to create an aura of exclusivity around a small circle of professional players, who would in turn enhance product awareness, attract amateur players, and increase card sales. Magic was commercialized through mass distribution channels such as newspaper stands, supermarkets, and specialized toy stores to guarantee easy access to potential beginners. Consistent with this strategic model, communication was based on mass market tools: intense advertising campaigns and public relations.

But this strategy didn't seem to work; card sales simply weren't taking off. Since the aspirational model created by the company centered on professional players, new players were not drawn in, they were turned off. In fact, around people who were already familiar with the game, new players (and non-players) felt intimidated. Magic looked too complicated, a perception that was reinforced by the intensely competitive atmosphere at gaming sessions in the hobby and games stores (the very gaming centers that Magic was actually created for). This represented a major barrier for potential new players.

The new strategy: from selling a product to creating an all-round experience

All this is what prompted the company's decision to implement a strategic turnover in the late 2000s: no longer a niche market served through a mass channel, but a mass market served through niche channels; no longer selling a product but offering a *full branded play entertainment experience*. The new strategy called for redefining the market, as well as creating new models for consumer relations.

As for the market, the strategic focus shifted from professional to amateur players. Wizards took the product off super-market shelves and newspaper stands and embarked on a campaign to simplify the product image. To achieve this goal, in addition to international tournaments the company organized more activities in shops, focusing exclusively on the ones that were members of the Wizards Play Network.

Regarding customer relations, *shops would become the center of the entire gaming experience*. But this meant the company needed greater control over the activities hosted by WPN stores. Since Wizards didn't own any stores or franchises, management opted to increase the resources dedicated to two internal teams – Trade Marketing and Retail Support – tasked with providing stores with professional and promotional support for organizing in-store events and tournaments.

Specifically, Trade Marketing handled creating and delivering promotional and communication materials to stores, while Retail Support offered coaching. In addition to sharing best practices and providing consulting services, this team also dealt with communication and promotion for in-store activities.

Wizard's ultimate goal was to enhance the appeal of the network for potential member stores by guaranteeing higher sales not only on cards but on the entire product assortment. The new strategy was a huge success. Referring to 2012 data alone, 1,575 new stores joined the European network, while worldwide the increase was 36% compared to 2011.

The cycle of consumer experience: the role of events

Events lie at the heart of the consumer experience because they encompass pre-consumption, purchase, and consumption experiences. A vast range of events are held in stores, primarily targeting amateur players. In 2012, in Europe alone there were 175,734 events, and 72,024 new players signed up to participate.

Events include pre-releases when new 'expansions' are presented. Here players can not only get information on the plotline and characters of a story, but also a taste of the emotions they'll experience in playing the game. Other events are for buying sets of cards and playing ongoing stories; still others are just for playing.

Here are the most common event formats, ranked in order of target participants, from real beginners to professionals (www.wizards.com/wpn):

- *Friday Night Magic*: Friday Night Magic (FNM) is Magic's recurring weekly program that brings players together on Friday nights to play. FNM is the event where new players can approach the game, and start building their community.
- *Pre-release events*: Pre-releases happen all around the world on the Saturday or Sunday before a new Expansion Set is available for retail sale. It gives players their first chance to see and play with the new cards. Plus, a special-edition foil promo card is given out to participants just for signing up to play at the pre-release.
- *League*: This is a great way to kick off the release of a new Magic Expansion Set. Beginning on the day it goes on sale, players will have an exciting, ongoing event to participate in until the next Expansion Set is released. A League Kit, including different prizes, is sent out to every participating store.
- *Game Day*: Magic Game Day gives players their first glimpse of the setting of the newest 'expansion. And the structure of each Game Day changes for each set, giving players a unique experience every time. These events are run in local game and hobby stores all around the world three weeks after a new card set is available in stores.
- *Gran Prix Trial*: Grand Prix Trials are regional Magic Tournaments that award one two-round bye to the appropriate Grand Prix to the winner. Players with a two-round bye at a Grand Prix get a 'leg up' in the event – they don't have to play in the first two rounds of the tournament; it's as if they'd automatically won those rounds. Grand Prix Trials are run in eight- to ten-week rounds that open up periodically during the year. Normally each of these events attracts between ten and 60 new players.
- *Grand Prix*: Grand Prix events are large, regional Magic tournaments open to all players. Grand Prix awards include invitations to upcoming Pro Tours and cash prizes. Other activities offered at Grand Prix include Magic artist signings and dozens of other public tournaments.
- *Pro Tour Qualifier*: These are regional Magic Tournaments that attract from 200 to 300 participants. Unlike Gran Prix Trials, which retailers can request, PTQs are assigned by local Wizards to stores that are leading members of the WPN. The prize awarded to the winner of each qualifier is an invitation to participate in the next Pro Tour, travel expenses included.
- *Pro Tour*: This is where legends are born. Three annual worldwide stops make up the Tour, with each event showcasing a prize pool of $250,000. Unlike the Grand Prix, the Pro Tours are invitation-only, reserved exclusively for winners of the Pro Tour Qualifiers.

The in-store experiences of players center on entertainment and socialization, so stores become places for meeting and sharing as well as having fun. In a broad sense, the experience naturally revolves around playing Magic, but events also offer the chance to create social relationships, to build a personal identity, and to try it out when interacting with other people who share the same passion.

As proof of this, it's not unusual for players to turn up in costume (this is called 'cosplaying'), or to participate directly in the plot (in a completely spontaneous and autonomous way), contributing to co-creating the experience. Players do this either by reading the story and acting out some scenes, or more often by performing certain actions designed and directed by Wizards' artistic team.

The post-consumption experience

Playing Magic isn't an activity that begins and ends in stores. Players and fans regularly meet in forums and on blogs where they can show their passion. In Italy (the biggest European market), today the main Magic communities interface on three internet sites: MetaGame.it, MagicFriends.net, and MTGSalvation.com. The first two are entirely Italian, and the third is the number one Magic site in the world that isn't directly owned and operated by Wizards. The company collaborates with these sites by sending products, requesting reviews, and even offering exclusive spoiler cards to give a sneak peak of upcoming releases.

But the real reason behind these sites is to provide the chance for *various actors in the community to interact*. Players can share their opinions, mainly on new strategies, new cards, and deck building; all this elicits emotions beyond what they experience during games. As with any forum worthy of its name, there are community opinion leaders who might be professional players, judges, or performers.

The average player would approach these people depending on what he or she is looking for in any given moment. Professionals are usually known for their skill at deck building and discovering synergies between new and existing cards. Judges moderate major competitions, so they are experts in the rules of the game. Players contact them when they have questions or need clarification on how the game works. Performers are people who believe that the main purpose of Magic is fun.

Community activities can also lead to the creation of new playing methods. An example is Commander, developed around 2004 in a community of the same name (with considerable input from the community of judges). This new format is a different way to play Magic with special rules.

REVIEW QUESTIONS

1. At the end of the 2000s, Wizards decided to change its marketing strategy. What were the motivations behind the change? What did not work with the original strategy?

2. Building the card deck is a fundamental part of the consumer experience. How did Wizards make this activity the core of the different stages of the experience?

3. Today events play a major role in Wizards' marketing strategy. How can they affect the experience of different targets of players?

Chapter 5

THE BUSINESS SIDE OF THE MARKET

LEARNING OBJECTIVES

After reading this chapter you should be able to:

- Understand how corporate clients differ from consumers in their experience of creative products.
- Distinguish the value of creative products as components of production and communication processes.
- Detail the typical benefits corporate clients get and the sacrifices they bear.
- Tap into the typical tools used by business customers to leverage the value of creative products.
- Understand the specific choice processes of corporate clients.

OVERVIEW

Creative products not only have value for final consumers who experience them, but also for organizations (companies and non-profits alike), which utilize them in a variety of ways. These organizations constitute the business side of the market, that is, the market of subjects whose aim in purchasing creative products is not to consume them, but rather to incorporate them into production and communication processes.

In the business market, creative products are considered *properties*, the term most often used in managerial jargon to underscore the role they play in this context. On one side is the seller, an individual or organization, who holds the *property rights* to a given product; on the other the buyer, normally a company, who isn't interested in acquiring the product itself so much as the right to use it in some way.

Value expectations, choice processes, and the exploitation of property rights on creative products by corporate clients differs in essential ways from final consumers, which means all these factors merit specific study. The theme of this chapter, in fact, is the value analysis of creative products for corporate clients. Building on

what we've already discussed in Chapters 3 and 4, now I'll move on to detail the specificities of these clients and how they differ from final consumers in light of various processes involved in their choice of creative products. Specifically, I'll answer two questions.

First, what kind of value can a creative product provide to a business client? In Chapter 3 we saw that value for the final consumer can be broken down into a combination of benefits that fall into four categories. Do the same categories of value apply for corporate clients as well?

The answer is no, and the reasons will soon be clear. Creative products provide mainly extrinsic value for corporate clients, which serves to reach other objectives beyond consumption. So by examining what these objectives are and consequently what forms this value takes, we'll see that for a corporate client a creative product can serve a number of purposes. It can be utilized as a component of the products and services that this client makes and sells, or as a vehicle for reaching a certain target audience, or finally as an element of the image the client wants to build in the mind of a specific group of subjects (customers, investors, and other stakeholders).

By following this line of analysis, we'll come to understand that a creative product can be both a consumer and a business product depending on the buyer. If final consumers use it within their consumption experience, then it's a consumer product, and they'll evaluate, choose, and consume following specific processes. If instead organizations use the product in their production and communication processes, then this same item is a business product, which calls for entirely different processes for evaluation, choice, and use.

The second question pertains to the ways in which corporate clients can utilize a creative product. Specifically, are there specially designed tools that enable these clients to reach different objectives through creative products? We'll see that depending on whether the objective is to create products and services, to communicate with specific targets, or to build a particular reputation or image, corporate clients can implement various tools that leverage creative products as primary or secondary components.

We'll investigate the most common tools found in managerial practice today, exploring what characteristics they have, how they are used, and what makes them most effective. By the end of the chapter, we'll have completed the picture of the markets for creative products, and the different areas of market knowledge that companies or non-profits operating in creative industries need to effectively and efficiently handle customer value management processes.

5.1   THE SPECIFICITIES OF THE VALUE OF CREATIVE PRODUCTS FOR CORPORATE CLIENTS

Imagine someone playing *Guitar Hero III: Legends of Rock*. She'd expect to hear a classic from the 1980s by Foreigner, and she wouldn't be surprised if the musicians in the game were all playing Gibson guitars. But why Gibsons and not Fenders? On the stage there's the Red Bull logo on trash cans and posters for Axe deodorant on the walls. But she may or may not notice these details, because it all looks so realistic, and nothing seems out of place from what she'd find in a real rock venue. But if she stops to think about it, why Red Bull and Axe?

Now imagine a shopper at a supermarket. While she goes up and down the aisles with her cart, she hears soothing background music that makes the experience more pleasant. After a few minutes, she realizes that the music is an in-store broadcast, with ads for the products and brands on offer after every few songs. Now she picks up some candy from the shelf and reads the label saying that the producer will donate ten cents on every packet sold, with the proceeds financing the restoration of a famous national monument.

Later at home, she turns on the television, waiting for the football match to start, and watches an ad featuring a Formula One racecar driver who's promoting a watch brand. Later, during the match, she notices ads for insurance companies and car manufacturers running along the sidelines, and the two teams on the field are wearing jerseys with the names of airlines or consumer electronics.

There are several considerations to make from all these examples. First, consumers often experience many creative products within other products that may or may not be creative (listening to music while playing a videogame or doing the grocery shopping). Second, during an experience (communicative or consumption) of a creative product, someone else is sending other messages (Gibson, Red Bull, and Axe in the videogame; radio ads in the supermarket; perimeter boards around the football field and the names of team sponsors on the players' shirts). The third is that often actors in creative industries speak to consumers about or through other subjects (the Formula One champion in the watch ad, the monument under restoration mentioned on the package of candy).

In each of these examples, there's a third party (generally a company) that interacts with consumers together with a creative product or the organization that produces it. Clearly this company finds value in the creative product, and it's willing to pay a price for that value. This price can also make the product cheaper (or even free) to consumers.

But value creation of creative products for business clients is the result of processes that have different characteristics as compared to the processes used by final consumers.

- *The value of a creative product for a corporate client is not result of the consumption experience.* Unlike final consumers, who enact consumption practices to extract value from the creative product, the business client acquires the *rights to use the creative product* (property rights) in order to incorporate it into organizational production or communication processes for its own offering, as it does with other production or communication factors.
So the rationale of the corporate client centers on production, not consumption: it's not the experience of the creative product that generates value in this case, but how it is utilized in organizational processes aimed at attaining certain results in terms of production or communication. As a result, value analysis for organizations that produce creative products doesn't center on understanding consumption practices, but on decision-making processes that constitute purchase practices.
- *The value of a creative product for a corporate client is linked to this client's relationships with its customers.* Corporate clients produce and communicate in order

to establish and reinforce relationships with their customers (who in turn are final consumers or other corporate clients), and include creative products in production and communication processes to achieve this aim. Basically, creative products are valuable for a corporate client if they are valuable for its customers: the value of a creative product derives from the value attributed to it by current and potential customers.

This is why demand for creative products in business markets is normally said to be *derived* from demand in consumer markets. An organization that produces creative products and wants to get an idea of their value for business clients has to find out the value these products can provide to the clients of its clients. So value analysis must be integrated at two levels: the first is value for the organization's corporate client; the second, which is less immediate, is value for the clients of this client. If one of these two levels is lacking, market knowledge will be incomplete and will not be constructive in making decisions relating to the value proposition to offer business clients.

◉ *The value of a creative product for a corporate client is primarily communicative.* In describing the different types of value that a creative product can provide to the final consumer (Section 3.1), I said that one way to distinguish between them is to ask whether or not the consumer extracts value from the consumption experience itself (intrinsic value) or if instead this experience serves to reach other objectives (extrinsic value), and whether the final outcome is measured on the consumer level (self-oriented value) or on others (other-oriented value). As mentioned above, business clients buy creative products to reach ulterior aims, so the value they attain is always *extrinsic*, and these aims have to do with their customers, so the relative value is *other-oriented*. Considering these two dimensions, we can say that *the value of a creative product for a business client is essentially communicative.*

As we'll see, some purchases may be driven by philanthropic motivations connected to ethical value. But this value applies more to individual decision makers within organizations rather than the organizations as a whole (see Research Focus 5.1). Companies buy the property rights on creative products as production factors to incorporate into their production processes (for example, music purchased to be used as the soundtrack for a videogame) or to gain access to a certain audience (sponsoring a cultural event to enhance the company's reputation with a certain target).

5.2 THE VALUE OF A CREATIVE PRODUCT AS A COMPONENT OF PRODUCTION PROCESSES

Let's consider a television company that manages several different channels. Each channel broadcasts a number of programs following a specific schedule, with weekly programming that dedicates a few hours to sports coverage, including some live sporting events. For this company, live events (such as football matches, cycling races, or tennis tournaments) are nothing more than production factors, just like sportscasters, television studios, and interviews with sports stars. Production for a television company (a single program and more broadly speaking the entire lineup) is the combination of all the necessary production factors. Consequently, a live sports event is treated just like all the others in producing the final product.

For the owners of sports teams, competitions are products to sell not only to spectators who go to watch the event in the stadium, but also to television channels that want broadcasting rights. To illustrate how important the business market is in the sports world, Figure 5.1 shows the revenues from the top European football clubs, broken down by stream: ticket sales in stadiums, television rights, sponsorship fees, and merchandising.

As the figure clearly shows, for the majority of clubs the revenues from business markets (referred to as commercial revenues, primarily from television broadcasting and sponsorships) are higher than receipts from ticket sales. From this we might conclude that football – and by extension sport in general – is a typical corporate creative product. But this would be stretching the point because the value of sport on the business market (as with any creative product) is totally contingent on the consumer market: no television station would broadcast sport competitions or team events unless they drew a large enough audience to make it worthwhile.

As with sports, *all products in creative industries have the potential to become production factors for other industries.* An archeological site, for instance, can serve as

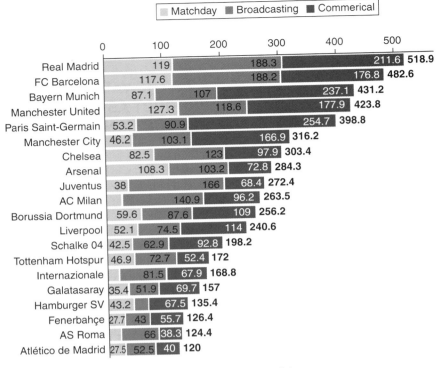

Figure 5.1 – Revenues of the top 20 European football clubs (2012/2013, ml/€)
Source: Deloitte (2014)

a fantastic movie set; a museum or a theater can host high society events, both public or private; a dance troupe can perform during a corporate convention. Many creative industries rely on the value that their products can provide for the business market to secure revenue streams that are vital to their survival and success (Case History 5.1). In fact, recently in industries such as music (Case History 5.2) and cinema growth in the business market is what has offset the shrinking consumer market.

Case History 5.1

Marvel: a library of superheroes

Marvel was founded in 1939 as a publisher of comic books. Throughout its history the company has compiled an exceptionally rich collection of characters, known and loved by millions of people all around the world. Spider-Man, the Fantastic Four, Iron Man, the Incredible Hulk, X-Men: all these creative products have won the hearts of children and adults alike from a variety of cultures, religions, and political backgrounds. Yet in the late 1990s the once-listed company was on the brink of bankruptcy mainly due to its plummeting core business of publishing. Then in 1998 Toy Biz Inc stepped in, acquired Marvel, turned it around and made it the success story it still is today.

The strategy of the new ownership was founded on two pillars (Elberse, 2011): concentrating on three businesses (traditional publishing, toys, and licensing), and leveraging the vast library of characters (around 4,700), which was the company's core resource. This library represented not only the content of the stories to offer consumers of comic books, but even more importantly property rights to offer companies in the entertainment industry, who could then incorporate Marvel characters into their production processes.

It's the Licensing Division that handles property rights for comic book characters, and buyers include a wide range of different companies. First in line are related sectors such as cinema (with films and sequels, many of which are global box-office smash hits), television (the Spider-Man series, broadcast on MTV in the US), DVDs, videogames (the Spider-Man game by Activision, with sales in the millions of copies), and amusement parks. But following close behind come apparel, accessories, shoes, and even food products. All these contracts earn Marvel either a percentage on sales or profits (as with the movie industry) or a minimum guaranteed payment plus a percentage on sales beyond this threshold.

A special case for Marvel is the toy industry, with a product assortment including action figures and accessories (mitts shaped like Hulk's huge hands, or Spider-Man's gloves) and role-playing games. Here the company has retained greater control. Thanks to the original business of Toy Biz, Marvel has opted to keep design, marketing, and commercialization in-house, while outsourcing production through a long-term partnership.

The outcome of this strategy is that the Licensing Division generates far more revenues for the company than any other: more than double the income from toys and nearly triple that of publishing. The bottom line? Marvel is once again a highly lucrative business, proof positive of the success of this strategy.

Case History 5.2

The business-to-business market in the music industry: music publishing

Although it's only natural to think of the music market as the CDs consumers buy and the songs they download from online stores, this is only the consumer side of the market: the purchase of recorded music. On further reflection, it's clear that music arrives on the market through other channels as well. Music production that moves through other operators without going directly to the final consumer is referred to as *music publishing*, and represents the business market of the music industry.

This market generates revenues for artists and record labels through *royalties*, a special form of compensation paid to holders of property rights (copyright) on musical works (composers, lyricists, singers, and so on) in exchange for the liberty to use these works in various ways. *Mechanical royalties*, from the consumer music market (recorded music and sheet music), are a percentage of the purchase price of the song or the sheet music paid to copyright holders (either artists or record labels).

Performance royalties and synchronization royalties come from the business market. Whoever wants to reproduce a given song, in whatever the context, would pay *performance royalties*: a singer or an orchestra during a concert, a DJ during a live show, a radio station during a transmission, a ringtone store that includes the song on its playlist, a retailer that wants to create a certain atmosphere, and so on. However, when the song is used with images, for example in a film, television spot or videogame, *synchronization royalties* are due.

As the sale of recorded music has declined over the past decade, so have mechanical royalties; but royalties from music publishing are on the rise. These trends can be explained by the fact that music has become a key factor of production in a variety of different industries, beyond the ones traditionally associated with music (radio, discos, and so on): advertising, mobile communications, videogames, and even retail stores that play background music (Wikström, 2009: 93–100).

In addition to royalties, which can be earned directly from the sale of the right to use songs in these industries, not to be overlooked are the indirect promotional benefits that can be gained. For example, a song that's background music in a television ad or the soundtrack of a movie or video game has the potential to reach far more final consumers than it would through CD sales or downloads alone. So the business market of the music industry generates positive returns on the traditional consumer market.

5.3 THE VALUE OF A CREATIVE PRODUCT AS A COMPONENT OF COMMUNICATION PROCESSES

Some creative products, besides serving as production factors, can also be key components in the communication processes of companies and other institutions. The sub-area of creative industries labeled 'media, information and communication' (Section 1.1) is made up mostly of sectors offering products that are exceptional vehicles for promotional communication. In fact, television, newspapers, magazines, and radio still garner the greatest share of advertising investments on a global level, and forecasts show that this situation is not likely to change in the near future.

Consequently, a key component of products in these sectors is the advertising space made available to interested for-profit or non-profit organizations. So creative

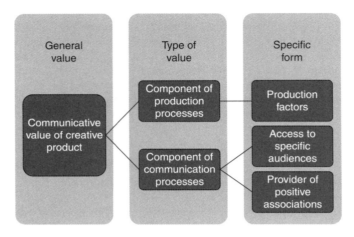

Figure 5.2 – The types of value of creative products for corporate clients

products supply communicative value to corporate clients by *allowing access to specific audiences* who may be targeted by other organizations. But that's not all.

As I've frequently reiterated, creative products are socially positioning and contribute to identity building for final consumers, providing them with communicative and symbolic value. So these products are also vehicles of public and private meaning, depending on how consumers perceive and assess them. The Teatro alla Scala in Milan, for example, isn't simply one of the most famous opera houses in the world; it's also a symbol of tradition, culture, and the history of the city, representing music, elegance, virtuosity and more.

In addition, creative products, the organizations that produce them, and the individual actors in the production network (artists, athletes, authors, experts, and so on) enjoy *positive associations that can be transferred to other subjects* (businesses, for example), if an effective connection is established between one and the other. So the communicative value of creative products for business clients can be found here too.

An extensive set of tools can be used to create this connection, and we'll explore them in the following sections. At this point we simply need to remember the example above, that a solid percentage of revenues from the top European football clubs comes from sponsors (refer back to Figure 5.1). Why would a company sponsor a football team, beyond the aim of establishing a connection with its fans and the spectators at its matches? For no other reason than to promote

the transfer of the positive associations that fans and spectators attribute to that team (values of fair play, athletic skill, victory, and national identity, among others). Before taking a closer look at the benefits that corporate clients can expect from creative products, Figure 5.2 summarizes the different types of communicative value that they can provide.

5.4   THE BENEFITS OF CREATIVE PRODUCTS FOR CORPORATE CLIENTS

Like final consumers, corporate clients expect to gain specific benefits from creative products, and to sustain the corresponding sacrifices. And when they compare their expectations to the perceived value they obtain after purchasing the property rights for these products and incorporating them into their production and communication processes, this comparison will determine their satisfaction or dissatisfaction.

Before discussing benefits, it's worth mentioning that sacrifices for business clients, have to do with investments in economic, temporal, cognitive, and emotional resources used in the different stages of product selection, just as they do for final consumers (Section 3.1.6). But one thing to keep in mind is that even though the classification of sacrifices works well for corporate clients too, consumers and organizations utilize different resources to extract value from products.

Benefits, instead, warrant closer investigation because, compared to final consumers, corporate clients associate different value with creative products, and expect to attain different benefits. We'll focus primarily on benefits corresponding to the value of these products as communication factors, but first a word about their value as production factors, value that depends on the specific product said factors contribute to. A song can be part of a soundtrack of a film; a concert may appear on the programming schedule of a television channel; a new series of objects might be featured in a specialized design magazine. All these are valuable production factors if they are properly integrated with other factors in order to produce value jointly for the final consumers.

Now, let's take a closer look at the benefits of products as components of communication processes. Consider the question (which we'll discuss further in Chapter 9): Why does an organization communicate with its consumers? The answer that immediately springs to mind is: To convince them to buy its products! And no doubt this is true. But when we analyzed the consumer choice process (Chapter 4) we came to realize that it encompasses various stages of experience. Specifically, consumers choose to purchase a product if they've developed a preference for that product over competing offerings. There are two prerequisites to preference: first consumers must be aware of the product, and second they must have a positive attitude toward it.

Consequently, a company that wants to use specific creative products as communication vehicles expects to gain the three following types of benefits.

5.4.1 Reaching a target audience

The precondition for this first benefit is that the producer of a creative product (or the owner of relative property rights) must know which audiences its product can access, and be able to demonstrate this to potential advertising investors. Let's say that a men's clothing company is planning a communication campaign and wants to reach a target of potential male consumers. Clearly a women's magazine, a televisions series with a female fan base, or sponsorship of a women's field hockey team are not attractive vehicles for this company. What would be interesting, instead, is a radio program with a predominantly male listenership, a financial newspaper whose readers are mostly men, or sponsorship of a football team. A variable used to measure the capacity for a medium to communicate with a target audience is *reach*, which indicates the percentage of a pre-defined audience that the medium in question actually accesses. Figure 5.3 reports the capacity of main UK newspapers to reach different audience demographics, whereas Figure 5.4 represents their overall reach.

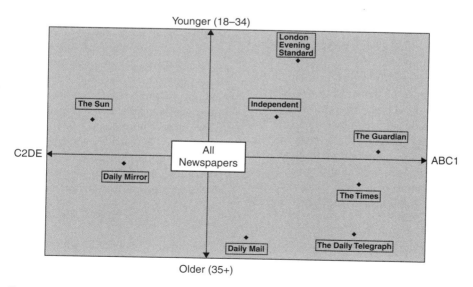

Figure 5.3 – Audiences of main UK newspapers
Source: NRS PADD: NRS Jan12-Dec12 / comScore Nov 12 *NRS print only figures (NRS PADD data not available pre 2012)

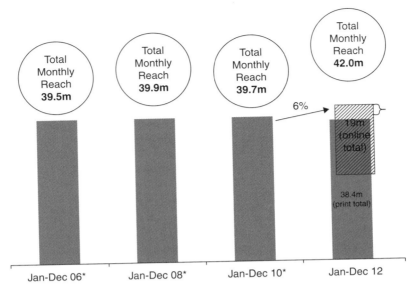

Figure 5.4 – Total monthly reach of main UK newspapers (2006–2012)
Source: NRS PADD Jan 13 – Dec 13 / comScore November 2013

5.4.2   Enhancing the audience's product knowledge

Once the target audience is accessed, the next step is awareness. Creating or enhancing product knowledge happens when the consumer pays attention to the message, understands it and stores it in her memory (Section 4.3.6.3). The message is a key trigger activating this process (as we'll see in Chapter 9). But the medium also has a part to play. In fact, memorization depends on both repetition of the message as well as credibility of the medium.

A television spot that's aired during a single day won't have much chance of penetrating the selective attention of consumers, whereas the same spot shown over several days would be more likely to do so. This *frequency* is an indicator reflecting the number of times a medium can reach an audience over a given time period. Taking a week as the basic unit of time, a daily newspaper has a frequency of seven; a weekly has one; a monthly magazine, 0.25; a daily radio or television program, seven; and so on.

Moreover, as we've said before, certain media vehicles represent value agents for many consumers. That means certain radio programs, magazines, or newspaper columns can be considered by consumers as reliable information sources which they then use to categorize and interpret products. Going back

to the previous example, the clothing company can expect a varying degree of effectiveness from an ad in a national newspaper as opposed to a fashion magazine, or an editorial in a men's magazine compared to a short spot played on a few radio stations. *Impact* indicates the degree to which the channel adds qualitative value to the message thanks to its credibility and image.

Reach, frequency, and impact measure different dimensions of the capacity of a medium to provide access to a target audience and to create or increase product knowledge among that audience. To get a comprehensive view of the effectiveness of a given medium, in the business world companies often use indicators that express all three aspects simultaneously.

The most common one is the *Gross Rating Point* (*GRP*), which is reach (*R*) multiplied by frequency (*F*). The resulting number reflects the capacity of a communication medium to maximize the total number of audience exposures to a certain message:

$$GRP = R \times F.$$

Let's compare a daily radio program and a daily newspaper. Say the reach for the first is 20 per cent of the target audience, and 50 per cent for the second; both have a frequency of 7 (based on a week). The resulting GRP for the radio program would be 140 (20 x 7), and for the newspaper 350 (50 x 7). So the newspaper would have a greater capacity to create exposures to the marketing message among the target audience. The GRP can also be multiplied by *impact* to obtain the number of qualified exposures. Clearly, since impact isn't an objective datum like reach or frequency, it is estimated with relation to single vehicles.

In practice, when corporate clients acquire a creative product (ad space in a newspaper or on a radio program) with the aim of reaching a certain audience and enhancing awareness of their brand, they're actually buying GRPs, or exposures of the target audience to their message. The benefit of a communication medium for business clients is expressed in GRP points, a number that they can use to compare various media and gauge expectations (Section 9.6.4).

5.4.3 Creating or improving the product or company image

Creating or improving the image of a product, brand or company means generating or consolidating positive associations that consumers attribute to it, which in turn can lead to consumer preference. As I emphasized in the previous section, since certain groups of consumers make positive associations with a number of creative products (or subjects that operate in creative industries), companies can impact their image and the image of their products by means of a transfer mechanism.

So a company seeking an 'image upgrade' could attempt to make some kind of a connection with the creative product that enjoys positive associations in the mind of the audience that the company needs to win over. An alternative tactic would be to use other communication tools (such as advertising) to convey a message addressed directly to that audience. In opting for one or the other, business clients take a number of factors into consideration, as we'll see in Chapter 9. Some of the assessment criteria will logically center on the type and strength of the associations with the creative product, and capacity of these factors to modify consumer behavior. Clearly, to convince a corporate client to buy a specific creative product, the producer has to know which associations various groups of consumers make with that product, and pass the information along to the potential client.

The description above details the main benefits that corporate clients can obtain by purchasing creative products or relative property rights. Through the years in the business market for creative products certain tools have come into common use for acquiring these benefits. These tools are corporate support, product placement, and celebrity endorsement, which are the focus of the following sections.

5.5   CORPORATE SUPPORT

Most non-profits operating in creative industries manage to maintain their financial sustainability thanks to support from companies that do business in other sectors. By the same token, many for-profit organizations that work in creative industries can find revenue sources in corporate support that provide a critical contribution to their financial equilibrium. The three most common forms of corporate support in creative industries are: sponsorships, cause-related marketing, and donations.

5.5.1   Sponsorship

This involves an agreement between two organizations that gives one (the sponsor) the right to publicly associate its name and its logo with the other (the sponsee) in exchange for some form of payment, either monetary or in-kind (Cornwell and Maignan, 1998). This association can relate to the name as well as an activity, event, or product of the sponsee (which is the property). Here's an example with sports: a sponsor can associate its name with a sports team (a name), with a tournament (an activity), a specific event (a match), or a product (the arena or stadium where the team plays).

Sponsorship, obviously, must be explicitly communicated to the public. This means that sponsorship doesn't end with the association between the sponsor and the sponsee (or an activity, event, or product of the sponsee). Instead it involves the integration of the sponsorship in communication activities of the sponsor.

5.5.2   Cause-related marketing

Like sponsorship, this involves an agreement between two organizations for the public association of respective names and logos, but the mechanism used here is very different. In this case, a company's support for a cause (or the organization that promotes the cause) derives from the purchase of its products. Specifically, the company donates a certain portion of the revenues generated from product sales to the chosen cause. So consumers in this case are called to play an active part, because they must first buy the product in order for the company to make the donation (Case History 5.3).

The term *cause-related marketing* originated in 1983 to describe the initiative by the American Express credit card company to support the restoration of the Statue of Liberty in New York. The company pledged to donate one cent for every credit card transaction, and one dollar for every new card activated in a three-month period. The project ultimately raised 1.7 million dollars.

5.5.3   Donations

With donations, instead, a company offers money, goods, or time to a non-profit. Often the term *unconditional donation* (Dean, 2003) is used to differentiate this from cause-related marketing. (Although donations can come from individuals (Section 3.4), this section focuses on corporate donors.) Here is a statistic that gives an idea of just how vital donations are for artistic and cultural institutions: in the US in 2011 these institutions received 13.12 billion dollars in donations. This figure has remained relatively stable in recent years and represents 4 per cent of all the donations made in the country (Giving USA, 2012).

Once the difference between donations and sponsorship centered on the expectation of returns: since the first springs from philanthropy, there were none; the latter, on the other hand, is part of a communication strategy that serves the precise purpose (to generate returns). But today the borders between the two forms of corporate support have blurred, and the

real difference lies in which objectives are a priority for the donor (see also Research Focus 5.1). In fact, with a few rare exceptions (when donors remain anonymous), simply making a donation public impacts consumers and generates returns (positive or even negative) for the company.

5.5.4   The objectives of corporate support activities

To understand the value that companies can expect to obtain when they support organizations and activities in creative industries, a salient question is: What objectives can they reach through sponsorships, cause-related marketing, and donations? One of most significant is *to improve or reinforce the company's reputation, or the image of its products and brands*.[1]

There are two reasons why this objective is attainable. First, creative industries are seen as key actors in the civil and social progress of a community; second, individual creative products have precise associations and value for certain targets. This means that linking a company name to a specific creative product (or to the organization that holds the respective property rights), paves the way for transferring positive associations from the product/organization to that company. And this, in turn, reinforces the relationships of the company with its current customers (shoring up brand loyalty) and establishes ties with new customers.

Let's say that a contemporary art festival has a reputation for presenting avant garde works. A company could take advantage of this sponsorship opportunity if it's seeking to build or reinforce an image as an innovator on the cutting edge of technological trends. Another

Case History 5.3

The World Wildlife Fund: an example of virtuous management of cause-related marketing

The World Wildlife Foundation (WWF) is a non-profit that has made cause-related marketing a consistent source of funding for its projects all over the world by setting up long-term partnerships with a number of global companies.

For instance, since 2008 WWF has partnered with Gap, becoming one of the charities benefiting from the retailer's 'Give & Get' shopping events. During these weekend-long sales promotions, which are held several times a year, customers who shop at Gap, Banana Republic, Old Navy, or Piper Lime stores get a 30 per cent discount, and then they can pick one of six charities (including WWF) to be the recipient of a percentage of the total value of their purchase, donated by Gap. Also, WWF's partnership with CVS/Pharmacy, which ran from 2010 to 2013, brought in a five-cent donation on every Green Bag Tag fidelity card issued by the store. With this card, customers could accumulate points and get money back every time they took a plastic bag back to the store.

example might be a theater that's the symbol of a city; sponsoring a season of performances would be a rewarding option for a company that wants to be associated with the traditions and the identity of that city.

Transferring positive associations from a creative product/organization to a company that supports it isn't easy or automatic, but this process can be facilitated by the perception of *compatibility* between the two (Trimble and Rifon, 2006). Gwinner (1997) suggests that this compatibility can be function-based or image-based.

Function-based refers to the products offered by the sponsor and the organization, activity, event, or cause of the sponsee. Here are some examples: a musical instrument producer that sponsors a concert series, a sportswear manufacturer that donates a euro for every garment sold to a charity that promotes sports in low-income neighborhoods, a manufacturer of plumbing supplies that helps fund a sea life sanctuary.

Image-based compatibility, instead, is when some elements of the image of the company or its products correspond to certain aspects of the sponsee's activity, event or organization. Let's take a national company that implements traditional techniques or high quality materials sourced domestically. For this organization, supporting the restoration of an iconic national

monument (through sponsorship, cause-related marketing, or a donation) would have image-based compatibility because both are connected with the history of the country (albeit in different ways).

Although it's true that perceived compatibility smoothes to way for the transfer of positive associations, this transfer doesn't happen automatically. Compatibility must be communicated to ensure that consumers remember it. If, on the other hand, there is no perceived compatibility, that doesn't make this transfer impossible. Here too communicating compatibility is essential, but in this case to justify it to consumers (Case History 5.4).

The second objective of corporate support is to *enhance awareness* of the company or its products and brands; underpinning this aim is the broader awareness of organizations, activities, and events in creative industries that afford access to the target audience. Let's take a company that wants to break into a new foreign market where it's practically unknown. One quick way to increase awareness is to sponsor a sports team from that country, or a cultural event, or the restoration of a monument that's a symbol of national pride. These are all ways to convey the name of the sponsor company rapidly to a wide audience, thanks to the visibility of the cause or the subject benefiting from the sponsorship (Case History 5.5).

Case History 5.4

Rolex: a long-standing tradition of corporate support

Throughout its history, Rolex has developed strong ties with the world of sports and art. Initial sponsorships centered on sports competitions in which speed – hence time – was critical; gradually the company expanded its sponsorship activities to include other sports associated to the idea of elegance, technology, and excellence in performance: racing, equitation, sailing, tennis, and golf. Rolex has sponsored both individual athletes who become Rolex Ambassadors, and events (the US Open for golf, Wimbledon for tennis, the Sidney Hobart Yacht Race, Formula 1 racing, and the Chio Aachen World Equestrian Festival).

In the art world, Rolex supports leading institutions and artists in classical music, such as Teatro alla Scala, the Royal Opera House, and the Vienna Philharmonic. In 2000, the company launched one of its most innovative projects, *Mentor & Protegé*, offering financial support in pairing promising young artists with seven experts (selected each year) from as many artistic disciplines (music, literature, dance, visual arts, architecture, theater, and cinema). The aim of this year-long shadowing program is to transfer competences and best practices.

Case History 5.5

Unicredit: sponsorship of the UEFA Champions League

Unicredit is a leading European banking group founded in 1998 following the merger of numerous Italian banks and the subsequent acquisition of several additional European banks, in particular in Austria, Germany, and a number of Eastern European countries. By 2007 Unicredit's portfolio boasted around 400 local brands in 22 European countries, many of which did not visibly display any link with the Group, its name or its brand signs.

The Group decided to consolidate its branding strategy by substituting all the local brands with the Unicredit brand, where possible, or highlighting the local bank's membership in the Group by associating its name with Unicredit. The ultimate aims of this strategy were to enhance Unicredit brand awareness in various markets served by the Group, to improve brand image, and to create a single, unequivocal image shared by all local branches.

To achieve these objectives as quickly as possible, Unicredit designed an integrated communication strategy centering on a major sponsorship initiative. The property in question was the UEFA Champions League, and the reasons for this choice were numerous (Penna and Guenzi, 2014). First, the UEFA Champions League is the most prestigious football tournament in Europe. Also, its reputation and distinct associations are excellence, leadership, Europeanness, and professionalism, which Unicredit sought to connote with their corporate brand. Moreover, the audience of the tournament is transversal in terms of age and income, coinciding with the Group's target.

The Champions League provides extensive reach (in particular thanks to television broadcasts: one billion exposures per season!) and extremely high impact, both of which guarantee an increase in awareness among the Group's target audience. Finally, this sponsorship gives Unicredit the chance to organize other customer relations activities with different stakeholders such as business partners, personnel, and key clients.

The sponsorship agreement stipulated that from 2009 UniCredit would become the official sponsor of the UEFA Champions League, giving the Group the right: to display the UniCredit logo (on backdrops for interviews, the UEFA.com site, perimeter boards, and so forth); to run the exclusive Trophy Tour throughout Europe; to use the UEFA Champions League logo in communication campaigns; and to supply hospitality services in football stadiums and free match tickets for select clientele.

The effects of the sponsorship are measured every year in all the countries where UniCredit offers banking services, and results have been impressive. From 2009 to 2011 brand awareness nearly doubled from 14 per cent to 21 per cent (Penna and Guenzi, 2014) and at the same time the image of the Group improved on all the associations linked to excellence, Europeanness, and customer service.

With regard to the third objective, *attaining economic benefits*, these can be direct (increasing product sales) or indirect (tax breaks). With cause-related marketing the impact on sales is clearly demonstrated by the sale of the products linked to the initiative, but sponsorship can also boost sales by enhancing awareness and image. As for tax breaks, donations are more effective since fiscal regulations in many countries make allowances for fiscal reductions/deductions.

5.5.5   The audiences of corporate support activities

As we can easily imagine, the preferred audience of sponsorship, cause-related marketing, or donations are current or potential customers. But it's essential to realize that they are not the only target, or in some cases even the most important one.

In fact, countless corporate support activities center on a *community* (a city, country, or even a group of countries), to include residents, public and private stakeholders, and other institutions. When community is the audience for corporate support activities, the underlying motivation is to win or reinforce the company's reputation as a 'model citizen'. Many of these activities fall under the category of actions inherent to *corporate social responsibility*, driven by the realization that no organization (be it a company or non-profit) exists in isolation from the surrounding community. Instead, companies reap the direct and indirect benefits of belonging to that community (in terms of the availability of qualified personnel, an efficient infrastructure, and so on). Consequently, supporting initiatives or organizations in local creative industries is one way that companies can demonstrate their willingness to become integral and active members, to give something back to the community.

Another audience is made up of the company's *business partners*: suppliers, investors, distributors, and key clients. Links with organizations or activities can enable the company to build or strengthen its relationship with its business partners. In fact, in contracts for sponsoring certain subjects and events, as with donations to certain organizations, there are often provisions for services that the company can access and share with its partners.

For instance, with a sports competition or a musical or cultural event, a special seating area is often reserved for sponsors that they can use to organize hospitality activities for their partners. Donations to a museum, an environmental protection agency, or a historical society usually grant access to special services such as ad hoc guided tours, exclusive opening times, or specially designed itineraries. Since these services are built in to the agreement between the donor company and the recipient, they are exclusive, and as such have high economic and symbolic value, which can be constructive in forming relations with the company's partners.

Finally, there is *company personnel*, an audience not to be overlooked, considering that companies don't compete solely for corporate clients or for consumers, but also for qualified staff. Beyond monetary compensation, the ties that link employees with their company, and ensure their willingness to invest their intelligence in their work, are also based on symbolic considerations. An example is when the company makes contributions to organizations and activities connected to creative industries that employees take an interest in. To do so, the company can ask them to indicate the cause of their choice, or allow them to dedicate some of their working hours to doing volunteer work for their favorite charity. In these cases, the company leverages its support for a cause to enhance its image with its employees, reinforcing the employer–employee relationship and moving beyond the basic work-for-pay transaction.

5.6   PRODUCT PLACEMENT

The definition of product placement is 'the purposeful incorporation of a brand into an entertainment vehicle' (Russell and Belch, 2005: 74). The basic assumption here is that many brands have editorial value, in other words, since they have an image, they are vehicles of meaning for consumers. This value can also be exploited by painters, authors, screenplay writers, or lyricists, or leveraged in any artistic production to create more believable works and to more clearly delineate the traits of a character, the events in a story, the details of a setting, and so forth.

For instance, crime novels are brimming with detectives who drink whisky, action movies spotlight heroes who drive sports cars, and television shows feature desperate housewives who use dozens of consumer products. But it makes a difference if the detective drinks Chivas or Lagavullin, if the action hero drives a Mazda or a Ferrari, if the housewife drinks Coca Cola or Innocent. And the difference lies in the meanings that each brand can contribute to the creative content of the product.

Behind the decision to include a certain brand within a creative product, there are two possible scenarios that diverge in a fundamental way: either the artist makes a purely creative choice, or the product placement is stipulated (and compensated)[2] in a business agreement between the brand owner and the creative producer, within the framework of a precise communication strategy to support the brand.

Paid product placement dates back many years. In the early 1900s, American radio programs were actually created by consumer goods manufacturers as a channel for product promotion. Later, with the advent of television this practice became even more ingrained, and in the 1960s some television series were created by manufacturers, with the help of their advertising agencies, for patently promotional purposes (for example, Kraft Television Theater).

Still today television is the industry that attracts the most investments on a global scale for obvious reasons: the vast number of programs and variety of formats make it possible to reach myriad targets; investments are lower and the time needed to go from production to broadcast is far shorter than with cinema (Russell, 2002). But beyond radio and television, over the years, product placement has become common practice in many other creative industries as well.

The cinema is the sector where it's easiest to find different brands, some actually woven into the plot of the film itself (Karniouchina et al., 2011 Nelson and Davanathan, 2006; Sung et al., 2008). No coincidence, then, that it's a movie that marks the starting point of the proliferation of product placement in today's entertainment industry: Spielberg's 1982 film *E.T.* showed a scene with Reese's Pieces, and sales of the candy skyrocketed as a result.

For some time now product placement has also been popular in videogames, such as with Mazda's RX-8, which appeared in Gran Turismo 3, two years before debuting at the Detroit Auto Show in 2002 (Lee and Faber 2007; Nelson, 2002). The practice has also permeated music lyrics and videoclips, especially those of hip-hop and rap (de Gregorio and Sung, 2009; Delattre and Colovic, 2009); and even literature (Brennan, 2008; Friedman, 1985), where product placement is often referred to as a *fictomercial* or a *literatisement*. The 2001 book *The Bulgari Connection* by Fay Weldon became the first novel ever commissioned by a company to promote its brand (Nelson, 2004).

The major reason for the propagation of product placement over the last 20 years is that traditional advertising media have become so overcrowded that consumers have become inured. This makes it far more challenging to capture consumer attention and to find effective vehicles for product promotion. Yet the characteristics of product placement allow it to circumvent some of the obstacles that traditional advertising faces, because (if properly done) this tool can capture consumer attention and do so far more persuasively. For this reason, placement is often called *hybrid advertising*. Corroboration of this can be found in US market data, which shows that the total value of placement investments (both paid and unpaid) reached 7.35 billion dollars in 2009, with average growth rate from 2004–2009 of just over 27 per cent for paid placement alone (PQ Media, 2010).

5.6.1   The outcomes of product placement

To understand the value that a creative product can provide to companies that want to use product placement in their communication strategies, it's important to clarify what effects this tool has on consumers. Then, moving upstream, the next step is to explore their antecedents, or what determines these effects: the characteristics of both the placement execution, and of the consumers who are exposed to it. Balasubramanian et al. (1996) proposed a model that sums up relevant cause–effect relationships. As far as effects on consumers, these can be linked to three components of the stages of experience: cognitive, affective, and behavioral.

Cognitive outcomes that companies want to realize from a product placement are normally increased brand visibility, in terms of the public perception of the brand's market penetration and power. But more importantly, the idea is to insert and consolidate the brand in consumers' evoked set, increasing brand recognition and recall.

Affective outcomes have more to do with developing a positive attitude toward the brand by identifying it with a celebrity who uses it or a context of use. The process of identifying a brand with a celebrity could prompt consumers to include the brand in question into their extended selves, enhancing the brand's symbolic value.

Finally, *behavioral outcomes* relate to consumers' intention to purchase or use the brand. As Balasubramanian et al. (1996) point out, *while positive cognitive outcomes are corroborated by the majority of studies on product placement, emotional and behavioral outcomes are much less apparent.* Contrary to a common assumption in managerial practice, product placement doesn't appear to be particularly effective if the company's aim is to improve consumer attitudes toward the brand or to prompt consumers to purchase it. What's more, research also shows that it's extremely complicated to pursue different objectives simultaneously (cognitive, affective, and behavioral); in fact, there's very likely a tradeoff whereby attaining one puts the others further out of reach.

5.6.2   The antecedents of effective product placement

Whether or not an organization succeeds in achieving some or all of these objectives depends both on how it executes the placement, and the individual characteristics of the target consumers.

5.6.2.1   Placement execution

Positive cognitive effects are generated by brand prominence within the creative product (TV program, book, and so on), that is, how evident the brand is. The exposure duration also matters (for instance, how long the brand is shown in the film, or the number of times it's mentioned in a song or book), but only in terms of its impact on cognitive outcomes; affective or behavioral spheres are not affected.

Likewise, the placement modality, or how the brand is displayed, can give rise to positive cognitive outcomes, but again not affective or behavioral ones. If the brand is presented in various ways (both verbally and visually, for example) the cognitive outcomes are more powerful. This explains in part why the preferred contexts for product placements are television, movies and videogames instead of books or music. Also, cognitive outcomes are more likely to occur with placement priming, or additional communication regarding the placement. For example, the effect of product placement will be stronger if it's the focus of media attention, or the feature of an ad campaign.

Last, the amount of information provided on the brand has positive cognitive outcomes but negative affective ones. There's no doubt that more information increases recall, but at the same time it negatively impacts attitudes toward the brand because consumers become annoyed by too much information that distracts them from the film, book, or song. This dual effect also depends on the strength of the association between the brand and the story, the character, and the creative product itself. If the association is strong (the brand makes sense in the story, or fits the personality of the character) this can trigger both positive cognitive and affective outcomes.

5.6.2.2 Consumer's individual characteristics

These include their relationships with the brand, with corporate communication in general, or with the specific creative product. First of all, brand familiarity attenuates cognitive outcomes. Taking the opposite tack, this means that the less familiar the consumer is with the brand in question, the greater the cognitive outcomes from the placement because an unknown and unexpected stimulus attracts more attention than a familiar one. Second, the congruence of the brand with the plot, the text, or the character can have varying effects: incongruence does attract attention that translates into positive cognitive outcomes, but it's congruence that generates positive affective outcomes.

Consumer skepticism toward advertising and commercial communication in general minimizes the affective outcomes of product placement. By the same token, the growing use of this tool has increased both awareness and acceptance by consumers. So a positive attitude toward product placement has a positive impact on placement outcomes with regard to the affective sphere. The same is true for involvement in the creative product that the consumer is experiencing (the videogame she's playing, the book she's reading).

5.7   CELEBRITY ENDORSEMENT

Some people who work in creative industries become so popular, and earn such a distinctive public image, that they become celebrities. This is true of countless movie stars, singers, television personalities, actors, directors, and athletes: their creative skills are conveyed through their creative products. Celebrities can generate value by playing the role of endorser for products, or spokesperson for organizations that use testimonials in communication campaigns.

Endorsements can take a variety of forms: direct use of a product (Madonna wearing Dolce & Gabbana), recommendations (Valentino Rossi's testimonial for Ford), simply appearing with the product, or attending events organized by the producer (Scarlett Johansson at parties organized by Moet & Chandon). But aside from all this, to understand the value of the endorsement for the organization, the question to ask is: Why should consumers value the endorsement? There are two determinants of this value (McCracken, 1989): effectiveness as an information source, and the capacity to transfer meaning.

5.7.1   Effectiveness as an information source

In Chapter 4, I underscored that the information gathering that happens during the pre-consumption experience (Section 4.3.6), which then becomes an ongoing search if there is enduring involvement in the product category (Section 4.2.1.5), brings up a problem for consumers: the quality of information sources. This quality derives mainly from *credibility*, which in turn depends on the expertness and trustworthiness of the source. Now, celebrities' expertness and behaviors in their specific creative spheres make them by definition credible information sources in those contexts. An athlete who endorses a brand of sports equipment, a rock singer who promotes a brand of musical instruments, or a writer who recommends a book by another author: all these are examples of expert, trustworthy sources.

But how can the association be explained between celebrities and products that are completely outside their fields of expertise? George Clooney endorses Nespresso coffee, just like Cecilia Bartoli with Rolex watches and Sting with the region of Tuscany. Beyond credibility, the quality of the source – and the effectiveness of the endorsement – also depends on the *attractiveness*, how familiar consumers are with the celebrity, how pleasant they find her as far as physical appearance and behavior, and how similar they believe she is to themselves (in whatever way they might define 'similar'). The more attractive the celebrity the more effective she is as endorser of a product or brand. In other words, consumers are more willing to be persuaded and more accepting of the messages conveyed by an attractive source as compared to an unattractive one.

5.7.2   The capacity to transfer meaning

Celebrities are effective as information sources within the framework of promotional messages, which is why they can provide value to consumers, but this only explains part of the value of endorsements. As McCracken (1989) points out, if it were simply a question of a spokesperson's credibility and attractiveness, any celebrity with these qualities could be a valuable endorser for any product. But the fact of the matter is that endorsements don't always work, and often an individual celebrity successfully endorses certain products/brands but not others. This underscores that in some cases consumers recognize the value of an endorsement, but in other cases they don't.

McCracken suggests that whether or not endorsements by celebrities can provide value may also depend on something else: their ability to transfer meaning. And this factor is perfectly consistent with the value of creative products (and the actors in the system that produces them), which we've discussed frequently in the previous chapters. In fact, in today's society creative products have high social and cultural value, because for the community they are considered both drivers of progress and signs of identity.

Consequently, some of the actors in the production system (having won enough public recognition to be elevated to the status of celebrity) have earned positive associations with regard to values, lifestyles, behaviors, that go far beyond their specific competences or trustworthiness. This makes them vehicles of meaning that can be associated with other products, with the right communication campaigns, via the multi-phase mechanism illustrated in Figure 5.5.

In the *first stage*, the celebrity conveys distinctive meanings that are recognized and recognizable within the cultural system in question. Just think of the difference between a celebrity and any anonymous person in a television spot. This person is placed in a communicative context, so meanings are attributed to her by consumers based on their perceptions of her demographics, personality, and lifestyle. But these meanings are simple and fairly ambiguous, precisely because the person is anonymous.

With a celebrity, demographics aside, people recognize her personality and lifestyle; they know how she behaves in public (and are probably well-informed about her private life as well). So the meanings that she can communicate are much more precise; more importantly they tie into a system of values, ideals, norms, and convictions that characterize the cultural system in question. This makes her a much more powerful vehicle of meaning as compared to an anonymous person in an ad (Case History 5.6).

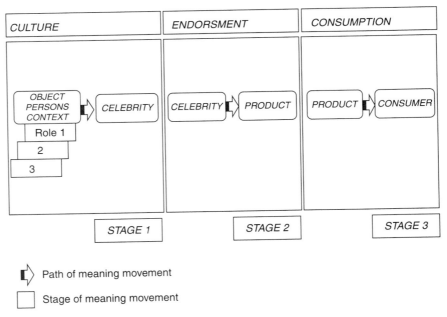

Figure 5.5 – The transfer of meaning in the endorsement process
Source: McCracken (1989: 315)

Case History 5.6

Maria Sharapova: a brand with a wealth of positive meanings

Maria Sharapova became a household name for sports fans when she won Wimbledon in 2004 at the age of 17. Since then, this young Russian tennis phenomenon has ascended the rankings of the world's top players, and in just a few short years become the highest paid athlete in the history of professional women's tennis.

But most of the star's income comes from activities off the court, with endorsements accounting for the largest share by far. The reasons for her success lie in a number of positive associations that Sharapova, the athlete and the person, successfully evokes in the public's mind, along with astute brand management by the company who represents her, IMG.

According to her managers at IMG, Sharapova's image, deriving from her sports accomplishments and her persona, can be summed up in two concepts: power and pretty (Elberse and Golod, 2011). The first refers to her athletic prowess, and associations such as strength, intelligence, skill, which in turn evoke images such as dreams, determination, desire, vision, and focus. The second represents her story and her personal qualities, which call to mind images like family, modesty, grace, and youth.

Thanks to Sharapova's success on the court, numerous companies courted her as endorser in their communication campaigns. Beyond the major sportswear manufacturers, which could readily count on a reciprocal transfer of positive associations, other endorsement contracts were selected with extreme care. The tennis star was at the very beginning of what would hopefully be a long career; other talented, up-and-coming tennis players like her were associated more with the jet set than the sports world. For these reasons, the initial strategy was to opt for companies, products, and brands that reinforced the associations of 'power' and 'pretty', where pretty never detracts from power.

One of these companies was Canon. Doug Fidoten, President of Dentsu America, Canon's communication agency, which handled the endorsement contract, explained the reasons behind selecting Sharapova as endorser: 'We chose her because she already possessed a number of qualities that fit with the Canon PowerShot digital camera brand which we wanted to promote – she plays aggressively but with precision, and she has a sense of style. We felt Maria Sharapova was a good fit with Canon' (Elberse and Golod, 2011: 3).

By carefully managing Sharapova's image in the early years of her success as a world-class tennis player, her portfolio of endorsements was consolidated on initial meanings. This later enabled the athlete to expand her portfolio systematically over the years.

In the *second stage*, meaning moves from the celebrity to the product being endorsed. This happens by building a communicative message in such a way that some of the meanings associated with the celebrity are transferred to the product (as we'll see in Chapter 9). This stage isn't a simple one, because a celebrity can convey multiple meanings, and not all of them are necessarily consistent with the message the organization wants to send. The solution is to create a communication context. This ensures that the only meanings associated with the celebrity that emerge are the ones that the company wants to transfer to the product. If this stage is effective, consumers recognize the rationale behind the celebrity/product association and develop a favorable disposition toward the meanings that are conveyed.

In the *third stage* the final vital transition happens: from the product to the consumer. If this transfer is successful (obviously from the consumer's perspective) then the endorsement has generated value for the consumer. According to McCracken, if consumers can appropriate the meaning being communicated and

make it their own, integrating it into their self-concept, then this final transition has been realized. It's as if consumers in the third stage accomplish what the celebrity already enacted in the first: absorbing the meanings that the cultural system makes available through the celebrity, who absorbed these meanings previously.

The celebrity has already shown that she has absorbed certain meanings, which she conveys through her professional and private life. This makes her a 'super-consumer', that is, an example of an individual who has built her self-concept in a certain way, which consumers might want to develop for themselves. So the consumption experience of the celebrity-endorsed product gives the consumer the chance to acquire meanings to integrate into her self-concept, which she shapes as she so desires. If the process of meaning transfer is successful (that is, consumers are satisfied by the consumption experience), the celebrity has contributed through her endorsement to creating value for consumers, and as a result for the organization she represents.

5.8 THE CHOICE PROCESS FOR CREATIVE PRODUCTS: SPECIFICITIES OF CORPORATE CLIENTS

Choice processes for businesses differ with respect to final consumers, as can be easily imagined. But these differences have more to do with how the process is organized, rather than with its structure. As we've said, corporate clients extract value from creative products not by experiencing them directly, but rather by inserting them in their production and communication processes. Beyond this, corporate clients naturally have expectations based on their motivations and their knowledge, which they've accumulated from direct experience and gleaned by tapping information sources. What's more, they establish choice criteria with which to compare various alternatives before finally making a purchase. This entire process can be represented in the exact same way as for final consumers (Chapter 4).

What changes is that a corporate client is an organization that employs a number of people who cover different roles in various departments. This means that, aside from a few rare exceptions (which we'll discuss shortly), the purchase of creative products as factors of production or communication isn't a decision made by individuals, but by groups of decision makers who constitute so-called *buying centers* (Webster and Wind, 1972). A buying center is the organizational unit made up of all the individuals or groups that have a voice in an organization's purchase decisions.

However, a buying center is not necessarily formal or stable over time or for a range of decisions. In fact, it isn't actually a formal organizational unit responsible for purchases; it won't be found on the organizational chart. Generally, any organization with a minimal structure would assign formal responsibility for purchases to a Purchasing Department. But depending on the type of purchase, this department (or the director or an employee) has to call in other units/members of the organization to make decisions, and this is where the buying center comes into play. So if a company decides to sponsor a football club, the Purchasing Department would no doubt be involved, but so would Marketing, to evaluate the repercussions on awareness and image; Finance to assess the financial impact; Legal to set down contractual stipulations; and probably other departments as well.

Secondly, a buying center is activated to deal with a specific purchase decision; different decisions may call for different buying centers. So with the previous example, if the decision involves buying property rights for songs to be used in the soundtrack of the company's official video, there's no need to call on some of the roles listed above (Finance, for example, since the expense is relatively small). But others might be added to the list, such as the Public Relations Office, which could organize collateral events to accompany the video's premiere.

Why do buying centers exist? Because whether a creative product is purchased as a factor of production or communication, it can provide benefits and require sacrifices that fall under the domain of various organizational departments. In the sponsorship example above, it's the Finance Department that's responsible for investment decisions, while the final price for agreement may be set by the Purchasing Department; Marketing deals with the impact on image, and risk mitigation is taken on by the Legal Office. So all these subjects have to be involved, but clearly not everyone does the same thing. Typically *in buying centers there are different roles* (Webster and Wind, 1972), which resemble the ones that emerge in purchasing scenarios with final consumers (Section 4.4.2.3.6):

- The *Initiator* is the person or unit who requests the purchase, demonstrating the need. (For instance, the Brand Manager proposes a new brand strategy, and suggests sponsoring a football team.)
- The *User* is the person or unit who uses/manages the product in question; the User and the Initiator are often one and the same. (The Brand Manager would handle the new brand strategy that includes the sponsorship.)
- The *Influencer* is the person/unit who has the knowledge and the competence to guide the choice, often determining the specific features of the product or the purchase criteria. (The Legal Office would recommend which items to stipulate in the sponsorship contract; a football expert would consult on which team would be the best pick.)
- The *Gatekeeper* controls the information that serves to make the purchase, and can facilitate or prevent the circulation of this information in the buying center. (The Finance Department knows what budget constraints the company has to face.)
- The *Decider* has the formal or informal power to choose the spokesperson for the sponsorship. (This

would be CEO if large investments are required, or the Marketing Director for less costly initiatives.)

- The *Buyer* has the authority and responsibility to negotiate the terms of the contract, and to sign it. (Generally this role is taken on by the Purchasing Department.)

Obviously the same person or unit can play more than one of the roles listed above; whether or not this happens depends mainly on the degree of newness of the purchase. With a repeat purchase or *straight rebuy* the specifics of the product and the choice criteria are already set, and the organization will probably choose the same supplier it used in the past, without having to make any ulterior considerations. In the opposite case, with a *new buy*, the organization has no prior experience so the various roles that will potentially enjoy the benefits of the purchase or bear the sacrifices have to be called in to verify reciprocal expectations and consequent demands. Last, with what's known as a *modified rebuy*, some departments want different product features than the previous purchase. In this scenario other units need to be involved, but now the organization can rely on prior knowledge so fewer roles are activated.

The existence of a buying center and different buying roles complicates value analysis as well as the consequent value creation by the producer of the creative product. In fact, this organization first needs to identify the different subjects involved in the choice process and the roles they play; understand the specific expectations of each, and whether these expectations are complementary or divergent; and be aware of the power relationships between the subjects (collaboration or conflict) (Research Focus 5.1).

The complexity of the market structure where creative products are bought and sold also augments the complexity of value analysis and management for corporate clients. Seeing as the evaluation of these products requires specific competences, which most corporate clients don't have, the business market for creative products is replete with specialized operators who liaise between producers and clients as qualified agents of value. This gives rise to a dense network both in terms of relationships and contributions to the choice process.

5.9   THE NETWORK OF ACTORS INVOLVED IN THE CHOICE PROCESS

Let's imagine how the purchase of a creative product by a corporate client comes about. The most straightforward way would be for the client to turn to various producers who sell the product in question and purchase the one that's most suited to the organization's needs. But the process is rarely this simple, and there are a number of reasons why.

Research Focus 5.1

Decision-making processes in arts sponsorship investments

In corporate support choices, whether referring to sponsorships, donations, or other activities, the personal preferences of individual managers often carry substantial weight, aside from the organization's objectives. In fact, if the CEO or Marketing Director of a company is an opera lover, or a fan of a local basketball team, or has a passion for sailing, their personal interests will come to bear on the choice to support certain causes or institutions.

Daellenbach (2012) analyzed a number of case studies of corporate support for artistic institutions, examining how the orientation of the company toward this support (tending toward philanthropic or commercial) and the artistic preferences of the senior managers interact. Specifically, she investigated how this interaction impacts the decision-making path that leads to the choice to support a specific institution, and later how this relationship is managed.

The author's findings highlight the fact that when the company's orientation is more philanthropic (the support choices are justified to a greater degree by a desire to contribute to the progress of the community) and the CEO is an art lover with decisive tastes, this executive plays a central role in the decision-making process by helping set down assessment criteria for decision making, and speeding up the entire process, which becomes more intuitive than rational.

However, if the company's orientation toward corporate support is more commercial (with the aim of impacting the image of the company and its products) and the senior manager has no specific preferences or competences, relevant decisions are made by the Marketing Director. A more rational choice process ensues, involving a precise assessment of the compatibility between the company and the institution to sponsor. In these cases, senior managers simply sign off on the final decision.

First, creative products are practically infinite (Section 1.2.3). To illustrate, think of the owner of a chain of cocktail lounges who wants to compile a soundtrack to create a certain sort of atmosphere: How many songs are there to choose from? Or another company that's looking to sponsor a sports team, or make a donation to a cultural institution: How many options are out there? The sheer number is what prompts corporate clients to rely on other organizations that are familiar with all the available alternatives and have the expertness to choose the most appropriate one.

Second, if the value of creative products as factors in communication processes is considered, it's also important to keep in mind that the aim of communication strategies is to reach a target audience and shape the awareness and image of a brand or a company by using a combination of media vehicles (various creative products). It takes specialized competences to determine the optimum combination of media that will maximize audience exposure to the messages the company wants to send; generally speaking these competences can't be entirely sourced from inside the sender company or institution. Consequently, relationships between business clients and the owners of creative products are mediated by a number of subjects who have the competences to bring together the demands of business clients to the offerings of the creative product owners.

The subject who serves as liaison between clients and producers is the *communication agency*: a company specialized in creating communication messages and choosing the best combination of media to convey them. So a business client who wants to set up a communication strategy (Chapter 9) normally turns to a communication agency to help create messages and interface with owners of the communication media to be used.

Communication agencies can be *full service*, supplying all the communication tools and media their clients need. Others are *specialized* in specific stages of the process (creative strategy, media planning, and so on) or in certain tools (advertising, sponsorships, product placement, and more). With a variety of agencies competing on the communication market, each with specific competences and specializations, corporate clients are likely to have relationships with several, which results in a complex relational network (Collett, 2009; Russell and Belch, 2005).

5.10   CONCLUSIONS

This chapter completes our description of the markets in which creative products are bought and sold. The two previous chapters focused on consumer markets. Here we've explored the specificities of business markets for creative products, noting that the two are closely related because there would be no business market for these products if it were not for the consumer market downstream.

Corporate clients use creative products very differently than consumers do. The latter incorporate these products into their experiential processes, while the former leverage them as factors within their production and communication processes. This means that the value they extract is essentially other-oriented, or communicative, and serves to generate additional value for customers.

We've seen that managerial practice has led to the creation of specially designed tools for achieving specific objectives. Today sponsorship, cause-related marketing, and donations are forms of corporate support that many non-profits in creative industries rely on to expand their revenue sources and solidify their financial equilibrium. Similarly, in more industrialized sectors, with a broader audience, product placement and celebrity endorsement are additional tools that allow organizations to furnish value to corporate clients.

In order to effectively manage the value analysis processes, organizations that do operate in creative industries mustn't stop at the consumer market, but extend their assessment to potential business markets, so they can offer interesting value propositions to potential clients. In fact, the ability to develop knowledge of consumer markets is the prerequisite to creating value for corporate clients. As we've seen, these clients can use creative products as vehicles to access specific targets and to build awareness and image. The broader and deeper an organization's knowledge, the greater the value that it can potentially create for its business clientele.

But to know the market, organizations need not only analytical models to apply to the choice, purchase, and use processes activated by their consumer and business clients, which we've discussed extensively in this chapter and the previous two. In fact, these models are no more than the content of the knowledge relating to market phenomena. But developing this content requires data in hand that represent these phenomena, and techniques for analyzing these data.

To generate market knowledge organizations need to have methods and techniques for collecting and analyzing data that satisfy their knowledge needs. This is what we'll address in the next chapter. After introducing the macro-topic of managing marketing information, the chapter will focus primarily on presenting the main methods and techniques used in marketing research, that is, the specific set of tools used in marketing to develop knowledge of the market.

REVIEW QUESTIONS

1. What are the main differences between corporate clients and end consumers in terms of extracting value from creative products?

2. What are the main benefits and sacrifices of creative products that provide value to business customers?

3. Which are typical forms of corporate support? Which are the main objectives of this activity?

4. How does product placement work? What are its main effects on the consumer decision-making process?

5. How do celebrity endorsements function? What conditions can ensure that endorsement is effective?

6. Which are the steps in corporate clients' choice processes? What are the factors that affect its complexity?

CASE STUDY

VODAFONE: A MULTI-LEVEL SPONSORSHIP STRATEGY

Founded in Great Britain in 1985, today Vodafone is one of the world's telecommunications giants, counting 434 million customers, 43.6 billion pounds in turnover, and around 93,000 employees as of 2014. The Group operates directly in 30 countries, and has network partnerships in 50 more. Vodafone's major markets are Germany and India, the first in revenues (8.3 billion pounds, market leader with a share of 34%) and the second for sheer number of consumers (166.6 million).

The Group is a major player in other big European markets as well, such as Italy (Vodafone's number two European market for number of consumers; here the Group is market leader in revenues with a 33% share) and Great Britain (25% market share). Outside of Europe, the Group plays a major role in Africa, with ownership of 65% of Vodacom, operating in rapidly expanding markets such as South Africa.

As far as number of customers, the consumer market overwhelmingly predominates (92%); for services, the biggest income sources come from voice (55%), data (16% and growing fast), text messaging (12%), and landlines (11%). Beyond running telecommunications networks and providing services, the Vodafone Group is also the biggest mobile telephone retailer in the world with around 15,000 branded stores.

'To give people the power to connect with each other – and to learn, work, play, be entertained and broaden their horizons – wherever and however they choose': this is Vodafone's mission. And in keeping with this mission, Vodafone has always sought to build relationships with its customers is based on trust. This pillar of corporate strategy underpins two critical assets: technological infrastructures and brand image.

With regard to infrastructures, Vodafone consistently strives to be the first-mover in launching and propagating new technologies, and in doing so invests enormous sums in its network. At present the Group is focusing on disseminating 3G technology and developing 4G that can more effectively support data services, which have the biggest potential for future growth.

Brand image is another asset of the Group and a major purchase driver for consumer and corporate customers. This explains why Vodafone constantly invests in building brand awareness in developing markets, and in reinforcing brand image in developed markets. The brand image evokes powerful associations with innovativeness, internationalism, dynamism, and the like. To build brand awareness and reinforce image, Vodafone invests heavily in communication through a vast range of tools and activities, a vital one being sponsorships.

Choosing which properties to sponsor

Sponsorships by the Vodafone Group break down into three levels (Figure 5.6):

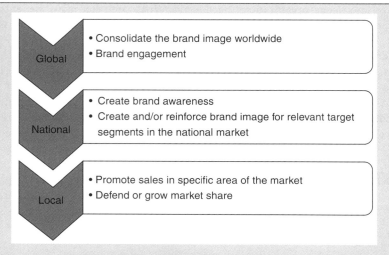

Figure 5.6 - Levels and goals of Vodafone Group's sponsorship strategy

○ *Global*: The goal of initiatives at this level is to *consolidate the brand image worldwide*. At the end of 2013 the Vodafone Group announced a shift in its global sponsorship philosophy: from a traditional brand 'badging' strategy to a new brand-engagement oriented one, to be deployed over the next few years in different markets. This basically means that Vodafone will not only 'sign' sponsored properties with its brand as it has done in the past (for example, by sponsoring Formula 1 racing teams like Ferrari and McLaren or the UEFA Champions League), but also design and run a set of highly engaging consumer events and activities directly, under the label *Vodafone Firsts*. The original 'First' event was the 2013 New Year's Eve fireworks display in London, the world's first multi-sensory fireworks display, where attendees were able to taste and smell as well as see the show.

○ *National*: These sponsorships are set up with the goal of *creating awareness and/or reinforcing brand image for target segments* in individual countries. National operating companies handle these initiatives, and earmark a portion of their communication budget to fund them. Here the properties are selected from events and activities which are relevant and impactful in the country for the targeted audiences.

○ *Local*: Here the goal is to consolidate, defend, or reinforce the Group's competitive position in a smaller geographical area within a country. Specifically, Vodafone seeks to *promote sales and defend or grow market share.* The properties selected in this context are high-visibility events in local communities; the bottom line is to maximize return on investments. Local marketing departments run these initiatives.

Sponsorships targeting young consumers

Young people have always been the favored target of the Vodafone Group, given their high propensity to use mobile communications and new technologies in general. In fact, the more developed the market, the bigger the part young people play as consumers. A case in point is Europe, where the penetration of mobile phones is near the saturation point and telephone companies fight hard to win competitive positions on specific targets.

Music is a vital part of everyday life and a crucial element in identity building for young people. In light of this, many Vodafone national operating companies have decided to channel their investments into sponsoring properties chosen from the world of music or, in some cases, organizing music events directly. What's more, music brings people together and gives them something to share. These values, both function-based and image-based, are a perfect fit with the image of a mobile phone company, and especially so for Vodafone's specific brand associations.

In every country, each national company singles out the properties that best serve to achieve the goals of brand awareness and image, depending on the visibility and impact of the properties in question. Below are three examples of sponsorship activities in three different European countries.

Vodafone Italy

Vodafone Italy's value proposition targeting young people is *unlimited*, an offering that allows younger customers to use their cell phones with no restrictions, consistent with their lifestyle. To do so the company has styled the concept of unlimited as 'unique, unrepeatable experiences' (which are in effect 'unlimited'), using this as a criterion both for selecting properties and for creating events spotlighting these properties.

Vodafone Italy has sponsored tours of popular Italian artists such as Jovanotti, Negramaro, and Modà, and organized music shows with international stars like Steve Aoki. Basically the tactic is to focus investments on a few events that enjoy high visibility with the target audience. There are two ways in which Vodafone implements the concept of a 'unique, unrepeatable experience', one that will create a lifelong memory:

- Bringing events and artists to areas of the country that don't pull in enough profits to host many major tours. For example, the 'Vodafone Unlimited Hip Hop Tour' went to Southern Italy, where groups like Club Dogo and Marracash (artists with a substantial fan base among young Italians) performed.
- Creating pre-concert contests, where participants don't simply get the chance to win a ticket (not a unique experience since anyone can buy a ticket) but they can do something that wouldn't otherwise be possible thanks to *VIP Day*, an entire day with artists and their entourages; meet and greets before the concert; backstage passes and so on.

To accentuate the emotional content and maximize effectiveness from a communications standpoint, each event is slotted into a *system of communication activities* aimed at dilating the effects over a longer time horizon, beyond the duration of the event itself. This happens mainly through relationship building by leveraging social networks, using them in different ways during various stages:

- *Before the event*, by setting up contests both online (Facebook) and offline (in stores), with the aim of reinforcing brand image and attracting new customers.
- *During concerts*, by distributing coupons that spectators can use in stores, and encouraging them to produce creative content (photos, videos, interviews, etc.).
- *After the event*, encouraging consumers to share content on social networks, and prompting them to go into stores to redeem the coupons distributed during the event to get a discount.

In this sense, contests multiply the experiential nature of sponsored events, because consumers share their stories, their dreams, and their experiences on social media, piquing the interest of other consumers and enhancing positive brand associations.

Vodafone Spain

In Spain, Vodafone has set up a sponsorship system centered on music, consistent with the value proposition for young people: *yu*. The system is made up of a live component (concerts, tours, or meet and greets with artists) and a radio program on *Radio Los 40 Principales*. This station, owned by the Grupo Prisa, is market leader in the music radio format with around four million listeners in 2012, and as far as radio in general is second only to *Cadena Ser*, owned by the same group.

The program, called *yu: no te pierdas nada*, uses radio in an innovative way. Through active involvement via social networks, listeners become co-authors of the program, deciding what artists to interview, the topics to address, the songs to play, and so on. The daily program is a huge hit. What's more, it also serves to multiply contacts for live events, thanks to interviews with artists on the program and videos and live streaming of events posted on the website.

Vodafone also set up a contest on Facebook for young up-and-coming bands called *yu*: *MusicTalent*, where users can vote for their favorite bands. After several elimination rounds, four finalists have the chance to perform (one for each geographic area: North, South, East, and Central Spain) at the opening of the following *yu* events.

Vodafone Hungary

For another initiative targeting young people, Hungary is an interesting case since for several years Vodafone has been the main sponsor of Sziget. This is one of the biggest music festivals in the world, attracting around 400,000 people from 70 countries every year, and four million virtual visitors who stream the event live. Multiple initiatives are connected to this festival.

For example, in 2010, festival ticket-buyers could get a special-edition mobile phone launched specifically for the event (the Szigetfone), with discounted rates for participants, especially people from countries outside Hungary. Vodafone also created an augmented reality app that can provide information on the events through a smartphone camera. In 2011, 30-meter high Vodafone towers were built offering aerial views of the festival; there were also special DJ sets, video games, and high-speed Wi-Fi.

A contest was organized involving the other European branches of Vodafone as well, offering customers the chance to be Sziget reporters for their home countries. The event was also used to test out a NFC payment platform, which allows consumers to use their mobiles in place of cash.

REVIEW QUESTIONS

1. How is the multi-level Vodafone sponsorship strategy is designed? What are the specific objectives for each level?

2. What are the criteria Vodafone adopts to select the properties at the three levels?

3. How do the sponsored properties fit the specific objectives in the different countries, when referring to the young target?

Chapter 6

METHODS FOR DEVELOPING MARKET KNOWLEDGE

LEARNING OBJECTIVES

After reading this chapter you should be able to:

- Understand the components of a marketing information system and the specific role of each one.
- Identify the steps of a marketing research process.
- Design a marketing research project.
- Choose the most appropriate approaches, methods and techniques for the marketing informative problem to be solved.
- Distinguish the various quantitative and qualitative marketing research methods and their potential applications.

OVERVIEW

The aim of value analysis is to develop market knowledge that is both broad and deep. On this foundation organizations can build better value propositions than the competition and transfer them to the market effectively. In Chapters 3, 4, and 5, I gave an overview of the *content of market knowledge* that organizations need to have: the variables that denote the concept of value from the customer's perspective (whether a consumer or a business), the different forms this value can take, the components of value and value generating processes, and the complex web of variables that impact these processes.

Market knowledge provides an extensive, detailed map. But knowing a given market isn't a binary state (an organization either does or doesn't). Instead, the amount of market knowledge should be taken as an indicator of how much of a given market is represented on the map, and in how much detail. If an organization only has a little knowledge, sizeable portions of the map will be fuzzy or even completely empty, and the parts that are filled in won't be very precise. The greater the knowledge, the more detailed and complete the map. By representing knowledge in this way, we can come to a clearer understanding of the meaning of market alignment, whether referring to a business or a non-profit institution.

If an organization has limited market knowledge, this translates into fewer opportunities to be aligned with its market, because descriptive and interpretative models are lacking that represent relevant market phenomena. The managers of this organization make decisions guided by intuition or 'gut feelings', but they run a high risk that these decisions will turn out to be ineffectual and inefficient. At the other end of the spectrum, an organization with thorough market knowledge has a better chance of identifying the most lucrative opportunities for investing resources and competences. As a result, managers in this organization will be more likely to make effective and efficient decisions.

Moreover, by representing market knowledge as a map, we come to realize that there is no difference between the map and reality, so from the organization's perspective *the map is reality*. Whatever isn't on the map, the organization has no knowledge of, and therefore doesn't exist. We can compare this to when we visit a city for the first time and we rely on a guidebook. What we know about this new place is what's written in the book. All the places that aren't included don't exist for us because we don't have any information about them, and they'll only become real if we stumble across them by chance.

Following this line of reasoning, something else may become clear. The better the map (that is, the deeper and broader the market knowledge), the more vast and detailed the portion of the market that emerges. What's more, by systematically updating its map the organization can accurately illustrate the evolution of the market. On the other hand, if an organization continues to act on the basis of an approximate, out-of-date map, it's quite likely that this action will exacerbate a misalignment with the market, and may even cause the organization to lose its market position altogether.

One final consideration follows from the others discussed above: the more that the competitors in a given industry share their knowledge (that is, their maps), the more they'll rely on the same information and enact similar market behaviors. The end result of this is that the market will move toward stability and maturity, as we'll see in Chapter 7 (at least until these competitors decide to modify the map or redraw it completely) (Research Focus 6.1).

This introduction to the essential role of knowledge in aligning the organization with the market underscores the relevance of *tools for building market knowledge*, which we'll discuss in this chapter. Since market knowledge is the outcome of a process of interpreting data on market phenomena, the first question I'll address is: What system can organizations use to build knowledge? The answer lies in a complex set of activities, technologies, methodologies, and people, which together make up the *marketing information system*. As

we'll see, knowledge can be developed starting with a range of data and by tapping various data sources. What's more, in order to transform data into knowledge organizations need to take a series of steps that call into play different functions.

An organization's market knowledge differs from the other kinds of knowledge, such as that pertaining to production, human resource management, or finance. This leads us to the second question I'll discuss in this chapter: What are the specific tools that a company or institution can leverage to gather market data? We can find the answer in marketing research, a set of methods and techniques that are specially designed to collect market data. So most of this chapter centers on describing how to design a marketing research project, what approaches to use and what information an organization can expect to gain from each, and how to calibrate efforts and investments to the expectations of market knowledge that the organization wants to develop.

Research Focus 6.1

When the map is the reality: the case of the US recording industry

One of the most highly respected data sources in the US recording industry is *Billboard Magazine*. In fact, recording companies regularly look to Billboard's rankings to monitor the effectiveness of the marketing strategies they implement to promote their artists and products.

Founded in the late 1800s, the monthly magazine originally reported on the entertainment offerings in Cincinnati, Ohio. Over time, Billboard evolved and eventually launched the *Hot 100* in 1958, a ranking of the best-selling singles in the US. When CDs came to the fore as the new standard music format, the Hot 100 became the Billboard 200, a ranking of the nation's top albums.

This is how Billboard compiled its ranking. First the magazine selected a representative sample of US record stores. (Actually this sample was a panel, which we'll talk about in Section 6.5.5.) Then the staff of the market research department faxed these stores a list of hundreds of albums, the week's potential top sellers, asking retailers to indicate their weekly sales for each one. These data were utilized to estimate weekly sales for the entire domestic market. The resulting ranking listed the top 200 in order and specified all the albums that had moved up from the previous week. So Billboard's ranking represented the industry's standard for evaluating market performance of every single album, and reflected the competition among the record labels.

Then a new information and sales tracking system was introduced called *SoundScan*; Anand and Peterson (2000) analyzed its impact on how competitors represent the market. This system was made possible thanks to bar codes on retail products, implemented in the mid-1980s, which allow stores to accurately record daily sales of all the products in their inventory. With respect to Billboard's method, SoundScan was much more exact and, more importantly, it enabled companies to keep tabs on all product sales. After some initial opposition, the management at Billboard decided to convert to the SoundScan system in 1991. This transition had tremendous repercussions on three levels.

The first thing that became clear was the different weights of various musical genres on the market. Specifically, country music turned out to be more popular than pop. Before SoundScan, on average 17 country albums made the weekly ranking, but this figure nearly doubled to 32 with SoundScan. What's more, while before only two country albums hit the top 50, after SoundScan there were six. In most cases these albums substituted pop albums. The second surprise was the greater volatility of the positions in the ranking. There were far more albums vying for the top, and it took them far less time to get there. The year before SoundScan, five albums reached the number one position, after an average of 13.6 weeks. The year after SoundScan, 16 albums made it to number one, after just 2.9 weeks. The third revelation was that independent labels had a smaller market share than previously believed. The number of independent albums in the weekly ranking after the new system was introduced dropped from 30.9 to 23.7.

Basically, the introduction of a new sales tracking system changed the market map. First, it revealed that musical genres once considered niche actually had a relatively substantial market share; this highlighted market opportunities that hadn't previously been considered. Second, SoundScan showed that the actual situation did not corroborate the traditional strategy of investing gradually over time (based on the erroneous assumption that it took several weeks to climb to the top of the ranking); the more effective approach was to concentrate investments on the launch. Third, the new system underscored the fact that independents were more highly valued by the experts on the Billboard staff than by consumers, as reflected by actual purchases; this recalibrated the perception of the weight of indie labels on the market.

6.1   THE MARKETING INFORMATION SYSTEM

Let's imagine that the curator of an archeological museum wants to modify the exhibition layout of the permanent collection to enhance the visitor experience. Where would she begin such a project? She'll probably want to have data in hand that tell her what current visitors think of their museum experience, along with information on what other innovative museums do as far as exhibitions. She'll also be looking for input on the potential of new interactive technologies which she's considering buying to give visitors a fuller experience.

At this point, we can picture our curator calling a meeting with the museum's Director of Marketing (if there is one) or Visitor Relations (again, if) and requesting the relevant information. This person, in turn, might use the museum's intranet to access the data, say, from a survey conducted the year before on visitor satisfaction. The next step could be to search the website of the Ministry for Cultural Heritage to find the results of the annual survey on visitors to the country's museums. Then the curator may remember having read an article on a contemporary art museum in another country that adopted particularly sophisticated interactive technology, and she'll try to find it. At the same time, she'll ask the head of the museum's budget committee if there are still funds available to run a study on visitors to fill in the information gaps. Once this is confirmed, she'll contact a number of marketing research agencies and ask them to propose research projects that can provide the missing information. In the end, when all of these activities are complete, the curator will have the information she needs to make her decisions.

The brief description above shows how a marketing information system works. It's a set of activities, technologies, procedures, methodologies, and people working together to *gather*, *process*, *store*, *distribute*, and *interpret* market data. Essentially, the marketing information system collects relevant market data, and empowers the organization to transform these data (which are snapshots of market phenomena) into information, or interpretations of phenomena. Then the system integrates this information into the organization's knowledge repository so that decision makers can anchor their actions on solid market knowledge. These decisions, in turn, will impact the market, activating new phenomena that will potentially set in motion the knowledge production cycle all over again (Figure 6.1).

Figure 6.1 – The circular process of market knowledge generation

Here are the specific components of the marketing information system:

- *Activities* constitute the various phases of the process of transforming data into information, information into knowledge. Examples include defining the information problem to solve, identifying potential information sources, choosing the most effective/efficient data collection technique, and so on.
- *Technologies* make the system work effectively and efficiently. For example, referring to the data/information distribution phase, intranet or web systems internal to the organization allow data access for any number of people, which means faster data distribution with minimal distortion.
- *Organizational procedures* consist in guidelines on how each activity should be performed. Often these guidelines are described in formal documents, and any deviations have to be justified and approved by a supervisory body. For example, the procedure for acquiring marketing research from a research institute might call for a written request from the Head of Marketing (in the example above) signed off by a direct superior (the museum Curator).
- *Methods and techniques* make it possible to collect, process, and interpret data so as to transform them

effectively into useful information (as we'll discuss in the following sections of this chapter).
- *People* are the true drivers of the marketing information system because they represent the generators and the users of market knowledge.

6.1.1   Types of data and data gathering activities

The data produced by a marketing information system can be classified by the *purpose* they serve and the *sources* that can be tapped to obtain these data. Typically data are primary or secondary, and information sources are internal or external.

Primary data are gathered to conduct specific analyses or to make specific decisions. *Secondary* data, on the other hand, are produced for other reasons, although they can also be useful for additional analysis or decision making. Sources, instead, are classed as *internal* when they come from departments or personnel within the organization, or *external* if they refer to institutions or people outside the organization. This distinction is useful for categorizing different types of data that make up the information repository represented by the marketing information system, and determining the data gathering activities that are best suited to each data type (Figure 6.2).

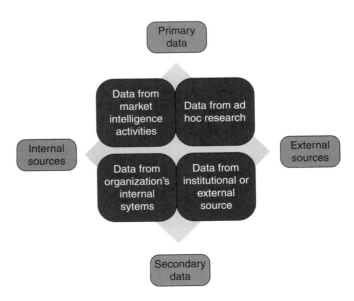

Figure 6.2 – Different data types in a marketing information system

6.1.1.1   *Primary data from internal sources*

The organization can activate internal sources to collect primary data, an activity that is called *market intelligence*. First the specific information needed to conduct an analysis or make a decision is identified, and then some of the organization's personnel begin to gather relevant data. Referring back to the museum example above, the curator might ask some of her staff to visit avant-garde museums to verify the visitor experience and write up a report on what they see.

6.1.1.2   *Secondary data from internal sources*

These data are normally generated by other units in the organization for their own purposes, but the same data can serve as useful input for marketing decisions. In fact, myriad data are systematically produced by a variety of organizational systems in the accounting, sales, and production departments. Data from ticket sales, for example, tell the curator which exhibits draw the biggest crowds; starting from these figures she can deduce the reasons why.

6.1.1.3   *Secondary data from external sources*

Organizations use data sourced from other institutions, companies, or individuals who, for their own goals, collect, process, and interpret these data. There are a number of abundant data sources that can be tapped to build and consolidate market knowledge in all creative industries. Here are just a few: national and supranational organizations that compile both general statistics (Eurostat, United Nations, OECD and others) and sector-specific statistics (*Media Sales* for European cinema); ministries of national governments (various reports on creative industries cited in Chapter 1); trade associations (IFPI for music, EURMPA for cinema, and so forth); market research agencies that publish public reports or specialized journals and magazines (*Billboard* for the US music industry).

6.1.1.4   *Primary data from external sources*

The external sources referred to here are generally companies specialized in marketing research that design and implement ad hoc processes for collecting and interpreting data. Based on input from the organization that commissions the research, these processes are customized to enable this customer to conduct specific analysis or make particular marketing decisions. In the example above, the person in charge of

marketing for the museum might outsource marketing research to a specialized research institute. Since marketing research is a typical tool used by organizations to gather market information, we'll discuss this topic further in the following sections.

6.2   THE MARKETING RESEARCH PROCESS

Marketing research involves a set of activities aimed at collecting, analyzing, interpreting, and distributing data on market phenomena in an organization. The kind of research I'll describe in this chapter is ad hoc; that is, designed and realized to produce information that serves for specific analysis or decision making by the organization. The underlying aim might be to understand common consumption practices, to measure consumer satisfaction, to comprehend the motivations behind corporate donations, to launch a new product, to gauge the market potential of a product, to change the price of a product, and so on.

Marketing research can be designed and realized directly by an organization or commissioned to a marketing research agency. On occasion some stages of the research process are done internally (such as research design), while others are outsourced to specialized companies (often data collection). Whatever the case, the research process consists of the following stages (see Figure 6.3):

1. *Defining the marketing problem*. Here the organization clarifies the problem that it's looking for information to solve. This may be an analytical issue (revealing the motivations that generate different expectations from different consumers) or a decision-making problem (choosing which kind of company is best suited for product placement).

2. *Turning the marketing problem into research questions*. Marketing research doesn't aim to solve marketing problems; instead it serves to provide information that's essential to finding a solution. So at this point the marketing problem is transformed into a series of research questions, which in turn will guide the choice of research method and techniques. For instance, if the problem is to figure out the motivations of different consumers, the research questions could be: Do consumers have utilitarian motivations? If so, what are they? Are there hedonic motivations? And if so, what are

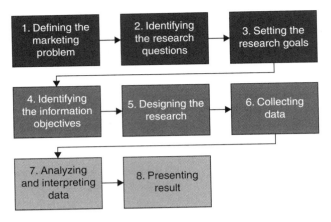

Figure 6.3 – Stages of the marketing research process

they? What individual characteristics can explain these different motivations? And so forth.

3. *Setting research goals.* After formulating research questions, the next stage is goal setting. Organizations need to ask: Why should we do this research? Obviously the answer is: To get information! But the question should dig deeper: What's our ultimate goal? Research goals fall into three categories:

   a. *Explorative*: This type of research aims to build a knowledge base regarding a phenomenon when there is no prior knowledge. For example, if a fashion company wants to enter an unfamiliar foreign market, the first step it would take is to develop basic knowledge on the key market characteristics, consumer expectations and habits, competitor brands, and so on.

   b. *Descriptive:* With this type of research a company or institution wants to obtain a description of a market phenomenon in terms of its basic variables. Descriptive research assumes basic knowledge, and strives to extend that knowledge. Once the fashion house has secured its knowledge base, it would want to get a grasp of the individual characteristics of consumers who make up the different segments of the foreign market, or the image of the various competitor brands on that market.

   c. *Causal:* The aim of this research is to investigate the cause–effect relationships between two or more variables. Basically the question here is: What happens to a variable (effect) if

the state of a second variable changes (cause)? For example, how do product sales change in the face of a 10 per cent price rise? Or how do testimonials by Brad Pitt or George Clooney change the company's image?

4. *Identifying information objectives.* In this phase the organization specifies the information it expects to get from the study (basically what it wants to find in the final report). For the clothing company of the previous example: How many consumers belong to segments X, Y, or Z? What are their demographics and psychographics? If this stage is conducted effectively, the organization will be able to draw up a *research brief* summing up the previous points. The aim here is to facilitate the creation of an effective research project. If the organization opts to hire a research institute, this brief provides all the necessary information for realizing a specific research project.

5. *Designing the research.* In this stage the fundamental components of the research project are established: the approach (qualitative, quantitative, or integrated), the sample, and the methods and techniques for collecting and analyzing data. In the following sections we'll look more closely at research design; suffice to say here that it equates to the project content. So, a specialized company commissioned to take on the task must identify the best possible design, propose it, and implement it (once approved by the organization). However, if research is to be carried out internally, staff members would be responsible for all these steps.

6. *Collecting data.* Now it's time to implement the data collection methods as specified in the project. As we'll see shortly, this stage is the most intensive in terms of time, human resources, and finances. Very often the data collection stage is outsourced to specialized *field companies*, even if the organization intends to realize the research project with internal resources.

7. *Analyzing and interpreting data.* The data are now analyzed using techniques for qualitative or quantitative data, depending on the research goals, which in turn are contingent on the topic of study.

8. *Presenting results.* Following data analysis and interpretation, a report is drawn up containing the results and the information that address the underlying research goal. The report is normally presented at meetings and circulated throughout the organization to the marketing analysts and decision makers who need these findings to do their jobs.

6.3   THE MARKETING RESEARCH DESIGN

The key decision in designing the marketing research project is determining the most suitable approach to use. Depending on their goals, researchers may opt for a qualitative, quantitative, or integrated approach (using one and then the other in different stages). The choice of research approach is essential because it will determine the sample and method to use. (Qualitative and quantitative research call for different methods and samples.) There are three main differences that distinguish qualitative and quantitative research: the size of the sample, the freedom accorded to respondents, and the type of information generated.

We'll explore these characteristics further in the following sections, but here it's worth making a few introductory comments. First, the *research sample* refers to the type and number of subjects that are analyzed to obtain relevant research data. Regarding sample size, qualitative research calls for a very small sample of no more than a few dozen subjects, depending on the research method. Quantitative research, on the other hand, can involve hundreds or even thousands of cases, depending on the number of subjects that make up the market phenomenon being investigated (the *universe* or *population*).

So comparing one study aimed at describing the motivations that differentiate football fans of each individual team in Europe, and another that seeks to depict the consumption practices of loyal consumers of a designer clothing brand, the two are clearly very different. For the first the universe is made up of millions of people; the second may only encompass a few hundred.

Second, the *freedom accorded to respondents* refers to how much leeway they are given to express their opinions, sensations, emotions, and desires. Qualitative research allows for broad freedom, while quantitative research is far more restrictive, utilizing tools that offer only a limited set of possible responses.

Finally, regarding *type of information*, qualitative research obviously produces qualitative information expressed in the form of written content, images, and sounds. Quantitative research, however, generates numbers and measurements. When designing a research project it's essential to keep in mind the different nature of these two types of information.

Qualitative information has no quantitative value. In other words, no generalizations can be made on a larger number of subjects than the ones in the sample, because data haven't been collected according to a sampling procedure that ensures statistical significance and representivity (typical of quantitative research). So clearly there are tradeoffs between acquiring deep knowledge and obtaining generalizable results: the first is the prerogative of qualitative research, the second falls in the domain of quantitative research.

This tradeoff has two major consequences. The first is that *qualitative and quantitative research are not interchangeable.* In other words, the results generated by one will never be obtained from the other. The second, closely related to the first, is that there is a *significant complementarity between qualitative and quantitative research.* Since relative research goals and resulting information are inherently different, by combining the two types of research an organization can gain a broader view and deeper understanding of the market phenomenon under investigation.

Generally speaking, when an organization knows little or nothing about a given phenomenon and wants to learn more, research begins with a qualitative stage. The aim here is to clarify the confines of the phenomenon and come up with research hypotheses. The next step is to verify these hypotheses through quantitative study. In other cases, the research path can lead in the opposite direction, beginning with a quantitative phase and then moving on to qualitative. This is often what happens when the organization systematically collects quantitative data, and at some point needs to gain a deeper understanding of the meaning behind the numbers, or the possible causes, explanations, factors that potentially provoke or influence certain findings.

6.4 QUALITATIVE MARKETING RESEARCH

6.4.1 Research objectives

Qualitative research is the best – and in fact the only – solution when an organization wants to have a *deeper understanding* of market phenomena. Acquiring this understanding means having the ability to grasp the underlying complexity of these phenomena, in other words the dense web of their constituent components and how they all interrelate. For instance, just think of the interplay of emotions, memories, and enthusiasm when a ballet devotee finds out that her favorite dancer is coming to town to perform a much-loved ballet.

Managers might be tempted to think that it's easy for consumers to communicate their interior world and explain their decision-making processes; it's just a matter of asking. But in Chapters 3 and 4 we saw that a multitude of interrelated variables come into play, which often consumers aren't even aware of. So in the end, it's not enough to ask. If an organization wants to take an in-depth look at a phenomenon, it needs to use specific tools, methods, and techniques that fall under qualitative marketing research. Quantitative research instead uses different methods and techniques that do not allow the organization to reach the same depth.

The generic aim of acquiring deep knowledge can be broken down into a number of more specific objectives. The first is to *explore a phenomenon that is entirely new to the organization*, one that the organization knows little or nothing about. Here the goal of marketing research is exploratory, and the only effective research design would involve a qualitative approach. Without prior knowledge, the organization or the manager has to understand the possible variables that comprise the phenomenon using tools that reveal its fundamental characteristics.

A second objective of qualitative research is to *emerge latent variables* that constitute the market phenomenon in question. Often knowledge is limited to the more obvious or superficial aspects of an occurrence or trend. But as we've said before, in the vast majority of cases the constituent variables of any given market phenomenon are closely interrelated, so variables must come to the surface that are less overt but that still contribute to determining other variables. To illustrate, let's try asking a consumer why she purchases a certain accessory brand. The first answer we'll get is: 'Because I like it.' But aesthetic appreciation, as we discussed in Chapter 2, is the outcome of an array of different determinants. So in order to understand it, an organization needs to delve into the personal history, the emotional baggage, and the social relationships of the consumer.

A third objective is to acquire *consumer knowledge and competences*. As we saw in Chapter 2, in creative industries consumers have become more and more proactive in generating value through various forms of participation. If the organization wants to acquire consumer knowledge and competences to create winning value propositions, qualitative research alone offers the toolkit that makes it possible to achieve this goal. Let's say, for instance, an organization wants to understand the integrating practices a consumer uses as she mixes and matches different items of clothing. Instead of asking what she's doing, it's more effective to observe her while she's doing it. In fact, consumers are completely unaware of many of the behaviors that make up consumption practices. The only way to gather data without necessarily asking questions is through observation, one method of qualitative research.

6.4.2 Data collection methods

With regard to the characteristic aim of qualitative research – in-depth investigation – it's common to find three types of barriers that individuals put up when asked to communicate their opinions, values, beliefs, or behaviors. These barriers pertain to the following:

- *Communicability*: Individuals are hesitant to reveal personal information to a stranger. Also, they might not be able to articulate the motivations and factors that shape the beliefs, attitudes, and judgments that they consciously constructed in the past, but which are now engrained and have become a matter of habit or routine.

• *Context dependency*: Individuals often find it hard to separate certain knowledge from the context in which it is created or used. (As an example, imagine asking a consumer to describe how she uses a product without actually having it at hand to demonstrate.)

• *Consciousness*: It's not uncommon for individuals to acquire information and insert it into their system of knowledge and behaviors through a process that occurs at a subconscious or unconscious level.

With qualitative research, data gathering methods aim to overcome these barriers and make deeper knowledge emerge. This is possible thanks to a number of tools that relate to the researcher–respondent relationship and to techniques for asking questions. The most common data collection methods in qualitative research are individual interviews, focus groups, and observation.

6.4.3 Individual interviews

In qualitative research, interviews are normally in-depth, and have the following characteristics.

• Interviews are *personal*. In fact, only through direct contact between the interviewer and the interviewee, with no intermediary, is it possible to grasp deeper meaning and gain a holistic view of the phenomena in question.

• Interviews are *semi-structured* (a few questions are set down before the interview begins, but most come up as the interview progresses) or, for some research objectives, even completely unstructured. The degree of structure is contingent on the relative informational objectives.

• Interviews favor a process of *reciprocal influence between interviewer and interviewee*, which can either help or hinder an effective interview. The process of reciprocal influence is triggered by certain factors such as the different expectations of the interviewer and interviewee, or the emergence of positive or negative emotional states linked to the issues being discussed, or the recognition by both parties of the difference in the two roles, in other words, one is interested in obtaining information from the other.

6.4.3.1 *Research data*

The data generated by an in-depth interview are represented by the *content*, in other words, all the information verbalized by the interviewee. But another equally significant source of data, and a unique feature of qualitative research, is *non-verbal communication*. This provides clues as to the emotional and affective states that emerge during the interview. While it's true that verbal communication is an excellent source of data on an individual's explicit cognitive and behavioral sphere, non-verbal communication is similarly relevant with regard to the emotional sphere.

Typical components of non-verbal communication are the *exterior appearance* (clothing, accessories, makeup, tattoos, piercing); *posture* (standing or sitting position); *head movements* (nodding or shaking one's head, voluntary and involuntary movements); *gestures* (hands, arms and legs, again voluntary and involuntary); *facial expressions*; *eye contact* (direction of gaze, fixed, unfocused); *paralinguistic aspects* (tone of voice, non-lexical fillers, rhythm, hesitations, silences).

Another key consideration is the *context* or setting of the interview, which should be chosen by the interviewee and not the interviewer. The more familiar the setting is to the respondent (in an affective and emotional sense), the easier it is for the interaction to take place in a relaxed, comfortable fashion. Moreover, if the interview is done in a personal space (whether that be the home or workplace) this allows for an insider's view of the objects that the interviewee lives with and how she relates to them, in other words, the interviewee's extended self. To capture this wealth of data, in-depth interviews are normally recorded, even videotaped if possible, so non-verbal communication can be studied in more detail.

6.4.3.2 *The role of the interviewer*

The interviewer is the key to a successful in-depth interview. Expert interviewers leverage highly complex competences developed through systematic firsthand experience. They must be able to observe others (to pick up on non-verbal communication and aspects of context as well as content), to observe themselves (to be aware of their own non-verbal communication) and to observe themselves observing (grasping the influence of their own verbal and non-verbal communication on the emotional states of respondents).

To satisfy the expectations of the interviewee, and to be consistent with the perceptions linked to their role, interviewers must also:

• Show interest in the respondent (*active listening*, to dig beneath the surface of the words and bring out the underlying ideas, emotions, and beliefs).

- Avoid any prejudice toward the respondent (*non-judgmental listening*, without any predisposition toward the interviewee, favorable or unfavorable, which might influence his or her emotional states and impact the transmission of information).
- Explain the content of the questions as clearly as possible, matching the style of the respondent to facilitate a positive relational dynamic.

6.4.3.3   *Interview guide*

This in-depth interviewing tool consists in a list of points that the interviewer will touch on to get information from the respondent, and only a few actual questions. The essential feature of the interview guide is its *flexibility*. Usually the interviewer uses it as a reminder of the concepts to pick up on, but the actual sequence of the questions is often determined by the flow of responses from the interviewee. (This means that the interviewer can modify the type and the order of the questions as the interview is taking place.)

There are three different types of questions (Daymon and Holloway, 2002: 173–7; Sayre, 2001: 136–9; Spradley, 1979: 78–91):

- *Descriptive questions* ask respondents to express their representations of reality with regard to the topic of research. Some examples: 'Can you tell me what happens leading up to your decision to visit an exhibit in an art gallery? Where do you get your information? Do you read reviews?' Or, 'Can you give me an example of an exciting television program? How about a boring one?'
- *Structural questions* serve to gain an understanding of the way respondents cognitively organize their ideas, their knowledge, and their emotions. Examples: 'If you were to draw a map of the main clothing brands you know, which ones would you group together, and which would you place far apart?' Or, 'If you were to describe the different motivations that prompt you to listen to the radio when you wake up in the morning, which ones would you mention?'
- *Compare/contrast questions* are used in an attempt to emerge the perceived similarities or differences between situations, events, products, and online/offline stores. Example: 'What do you think are the main differences between football fans and basketball fans?' 'What European city do you think is most like Paris?'

As far as the *sequence of the questions*, the general rule follows the typical aim of an in-depth interview

(to obtain deep knowledge), so questions run from general to specific. In terms of *how questions are framed*, they can be direct or indirect.

- *Direct questions* are usually open-ended, and ask for a personal perspective, opinion, judgment, behavior, and so on.
- *Indirect questions* instead attempt to shift respondents' focus from themselves to other contexts, aspects, or topics (to overcome the barriers of communicability, contextualization, and consciousness). A very particular type of indirect questioning are *projective tests* (fairly ambiguous verbal, graphic, or symbolic stimuli that prompt respondents to project their thoughts and feelings onto other people, situations, or objects). Here are the most common ones:
- *Association tests* call on respondents to associate themselves or third persons or products, brands, or companies to other elements. By decoding relevant responses, researchers can infer the thoughts and emotions of the respondents (example: 'If brand X were a person, what kind of a person would it be?')
- *Completion tests (sentences, cartoons, stories, drawings, illustrations)* involve giving respondents incomplete sentences, or cartoons showing people in typical consumption situations with empty speech balloons, or the first few lines of a story, a fragment of an illustration, or an incomplete drawing; respondents then need to complete these sentences, stories, or pictures either with verbal descriptions or by drawing or writing.
- *Third person tests* are when the interviewee is asked to describe the characteristics, opinions, attitudes, behaviors, and so on of a hypothetical individual who is facing a typical decision-making scenario regarding the purchase or use of a product.
- *Interpretation of figures or drawings* uses illustrations that usually depict product purchase or use, or interactions among customers, or between customers and stores, and so forth. The aim is to draw out the set of opinions and emotions that these situations elicit in the interviewee.

6.4.3.4   *Some structured interviewing methods*

Certain interviewing methods have been codified in practice and have proven their functionality over years of application. Some of these methods are particularly useful in building market knowledge in creative industries, as they are well-suited to investigating the hedonic, symbolic, and communicative value of products and services. Here I'll summarize the ones that are most effective in this application.

○ *Storytelling*. The storytelling method is based on the premise that people's perceptions take a narrative form. Compared to a simple, linear description of a phenomenon, a story is a far richer and more complex means of sense making. So how does storytelling actually work in the context of an interview? The interviewer simply asks the respondent to narrate a series of events or situations that are relevant to the research at hand. The idea is to try to draw out key content or themes, using the story as the general outline to be filled in with the intricate flow of events.

Two additional methods can also be grouped under the heading of storytelling: first, the *self-narrative* or *life history*, and second the *critical incident technique* (CIT). An in-depth interview that uses the self-narrative method focuses on the respondent's account of her own experiences and those of people she's close to. With CIT, the stories only pertain to incidents or events that clash with the narrator's expectations or the normal sequence of events.

○ *Zaltman Metaphor Elicitation Technique (ZMET)*. Zaltman's work (Zaltman, 1997; Zaltman and Coulter, 1995) is based on the assumption that individuals think with images, and that the metaphor is the most effective means for expressing these images. The rationale is that metaphors make it possible to overcome the barriers of communicability and of consciousness. What's more, by expressing images respondents reveal what they may not even be aware of as far as their moods, sensations, and thoughts.

The ZMET serves to make metaphors emerge which enable researchers to analyze the cognitive and emotional structures underpinning respondents' behaviors. Here's how it works. A week or so before the interview, respondents are asked to collect images (from magazines, books, websites, photos, or any other iconographic material) and use them to compose collages. These collages should express feelings, emotions, and thoughts on the topics under investigation, and each one should be given to a title. After this preparatory stage, the interview is conducted following ten predefined steps (Research Focus 6.2).

Research Focus 6.2

A metaphor-based research on the experience of live theater

That theater is a creative product with high hedonic value leaves little room for doubt. But studies that seek to identify the emotions that theatrical productions can elicit in spectators are very few. This is what prompted me, along with a colleague, to conduct research into the topic using ZMET (Cito and Troilo, 2013).

The aim of our research was to identify the emotions spectators feel when experiencing a theatrical production; to do so we elicited metaphors associated with the experience. In our study, we ran in-depth interviews with 20 individuals, from 19 to 63 years old, who came from two different Italian cities. We selected the participants from among theatergoers who had been to the theater at least once in the previous 12 months. The interviews, which we recorded, lasted between 45 and 90 minutes.

Ten days prior to the appointment, we sent participants a letter inviting them to create their own personal collage and providing instructions on how to do so. In the letter we explained that they should pick out photographs and images from magazines and newspapers, and/or make their own drawings to express how they felt about their theater experience. To complete their collage, we asked participants to come up with a title for it.

We processed the data from the interviews and collages by identifying the metaphors that the spectators used to depict their experience at the theater.

The *metaphors* that spectators used to describe their experience at the theater emerged both from what they had to say in their interviews and in the images they included in their collages. Some metaphors are hidden in verbal expressions. 'Today I feel emptied out', for example, alludes to the metaphor of a container. 'It's all uphill lately', instead, refers to the metaphor of a journey. Other metaphors are revealed directly through the images. Zaltman and Coulter (1995) lists seven deep metaphors: balance, transformation, journey, container, connection, resource, and control. We revealed four of these in our study:

1. *The theater as transformation*. Transformation appears as a growth process that allows spectators to evolve. In the minds of participants, it's not only the actors who undergo a transformation on the stage, but through their experience of the show spectators are also transformed into something else.

2. *The theater as a journey*. The journey used to describe the experience at the theater is a path toward the unknown; whoever takes this path doesn't know what the final destination is. The respondents who referred to the theater as a journey asserted that the fascinating thing about the experience is this element of surprise. What's more, the theater experience is often a path to be taken with other people, not alone.

3. *The theater as a container*. The fact that this metaphor emerged comes as no surprise if we consider the central role of the theater itself in the experience (the building, that is). In fact, the theater building is a perfect container designed to enclose, separate, and protect; yet it can be thought of as having a dual function. The walls of the theater protect whoever is physically present inside, so all the spectators have a shared experience. But these same walls open onto an unknown world.

4. *The theater as a resource*. Just as many different resources enable individuals to attain their objectives, the theater is also considered a valid means to attain something else. For instance, an experience at the theater is described as a facilitator of social relationships, or a way to enrich personal knowledge. This experience is also seen as a resource for achieving a greater sense of inner peace.

○ *The ethnographic method*. The aim of ethnographic marketing research is to investigate ways in which the culture of a social group informs and is informed by the behaviors and consumption experiences of its members (Arnould and Wallendorf, 1994). The basic assumption here is that some consumer behavior patterns are not solely the outcome of conscious cognitive processes, but rather arise from complex webs of cultural and social factors that characterize the specific group in question (family, community, immigrants living in a certain country, and so on).

The ethnographic method normally involves extended interaction with the phenomenon under investigation (anywhere from a few days to several months). As a result, data collection always takes place in the context that is relevant for the subjects being studied (where consumers live or gather, or where they purchase or consume products, and so on). In addition, this method uses a combination of in-depth interviews and participant observation (see Section 6.4.5). Documentary analysis is another useful tool, seeing as traces of the culture of a group or an individual can also be detected in the context where they live and on occasion in the documents they produce and utilize.

A unique feature of the ethnographic method consists in interviews with subjects who are seen as key to the cultural dynamic that comes into play. For example, with a heavy metal community this person might be the president of a fan club, or the editor of a specialized magazine, or certain artists who are seen as trendsetters. These people shape the dynamics in question.

As mentioned above, the ethnographic method always involves participant observation, which we'll discuss further in Section 6.4.5 (Research Focus 6.3).

Research Focus 6.3

The impact of sports event sponsorship: an example of ethnographic research

One of the goals of sponsorship is to enhance the awareness of a company or brand (Section 5.5). The usual strategy implemented to achieve this goal is to ensure high visibility of the distinctive elements of the firm/brand (logo, colors, symbols), during a sponsorship event for instance. To ascertain the effectiveness of a specific sponsorship, Choi et al. (2006) carried out a study using the ethnographic method on the *LG Action Sports Championship*. During this event, LG was visible everywhere with banners flying the LG logo, inflatables with LG colors and logo, a marquee for product demonstrations, and so on.

The research objective was to verify whether or not the extensive on-site sponsorship activities were interesting for consumers. Specifically: Was the massive on-site communication by the sponsor effective in capturing visitors' attention? What tools were most effective? What were the emotional reactions of the visitors to the sponsor's activities?

To reach this objective, researchers selected a sample of 17 visitors, gave each of them a mobile phone with a camera, and asked them to attend the event for a few hours (just like they planned to do before being asked to participate in the study) and use the phone to take pictures of the things that struck them most. Two hours later, the 17 participants were interviewed to gather their interpretations of the reasons that prompted them to select the subjects they photographed and to understand the cognitive and emotional factors underlying their motivations.

Laddering. This is an interview technique used to reveal the means–end chains that consumers apply to represent attribute-benefit-value connections (Section 4.4.1.1) by encouraging the interviewee to come up with the reasons behind the way she thinks and behaves. Here's an example describing a laddering interview with a person who loves to travel; with the aim of understanding her preference for travelling alone. The questions would go something like this: 'Why do you like to travel alone?' 'Because I can meet new people, I don't have to negotiate every little daily decision with any other travelers, and I can decide for myself where to go and when.' 'And why is it important to you not to have to negotiate?' 'Well, I don't know, I guess it's because if I had to negotiate all the time I'd feel less free, and I think it's a crime if you don't feel free when you're on vacation!' 'But don't you think there are any advantages to traveling with other people?' 'Well, I suppose you wouldn't feel lonely, but feeling lonely is what spurs me to meet other people.'

Unlike storytelling or ZMET, laddering is a more structured interview technique that presumes that the interviewee is capable of consciously communicating the connections among the different concepts. The typical output of the laddering technique is a hierarchical value map (Section 4.4.1.1), which is drawn up by analyzing the frequency of the connections among concepts expressed by the respondents, and highlighting distinctive patterns on the basis of the strength of these connections. Generally, as we can see in Figure 4.2, the stronger the connection, the thicker the line linking the concepts.

6.4.4 Focus groups

Data collection with this technique involves a small group of people who are asked to discuss topics relevant to the research in question. The basic assumption with a focus group is that many of the variables that constitute market phenomena (motivations, judgments, attitudes, preferences, for example) take shape through social interactions among customers, and between customers and product suppliers.

There are two key characteristics of the focus group method:

- *The unit of analysis is the group*. This means the resulting data does not come from individual group members, but from the group as a whole. It's the entire group that is asked to give answers, and these answers might differ among individual members, so the group response represents the complexity of positions on a specific topic.
- *The main focus of analysis is participant interaction*. More accurately, the focus centers on the influence of the interaction on the 'state' of individual participants: their cognitions, their emotions, and their behaviors. To be even more categorical, we can say that without effective interaction, there is no focus group. The degree of interaction that the group moderator elicits is a good indicator of the success of the focus group.

6.4.4.1   Pros and cons of focus groups

Thanks to the structure of the focus group, it offers incontrovertible advantages as compared to in-depth individual interviews.

- Focus groups *encourage social interaction*. By doing so researchers can reconstruct a situation that is relatively homologous, however circumscribed, to what actually happens in the market. This makes it possible to investigate mechanisms that influence the perception of reality and its social construction.
- Focus groups are more *flexible*. Since the group dynamic triggers reciprocal influence among participants, the moderator can leverage this effect to cover all the topics she wants to investigate, exploiting the unique traits of the individuals in the group and bringing them to the table to encourage discussion and debate.
- Focus groups require *relatively limited time and expense*. In fact, researchers can run several groups simultaneously to reduce data collection time and overall research time. Individual interviews within the same time frame, on the other hand, would call for many more interviewers, which would clearly raise costs.

Nonetheless, there are also disadvantages to focus groups with respect to individual interviews:

- Focus groups can provoke *group inhibition*. There are some topics that certain people would have a very hard time discussing with strangers. This would result in an immediate communicability barrier, which would be difficult for the moderator to circumvent.
- Focus groups are *less effective on certain research targets*. If group members are competitors, for example,

it would be extremely problematic to have a fruitful discussion that would serve research objectives (for example managers from competing companies who are asked to discuss which film they would choose for product placement). With children and adolescents too discussion would not flow because they would have a hard time behaving normally in a focus group setting.

- Researchers have *less control* with focus groups. Although flexibility is a clear advantage, the downside is the risk inherent to interaction. Depending on the topics and the type of participants, this interaction can be very difficult to control (for example, if one group member is verbally aggressive, or another is inept at discussing or debating issues with other people).
- There are *complex logistics* involved in running focus groups. Unlike interviews, which are often conducted in the respondent's home or workplace, putting together a focus group means finding a meeting room equipped with audio and visual equipment, which allows researchers to record all the subtleties of verbal and non-verbal communication. Also, focus groups are often held in rooms with two-way mirrors or closed circuit television to allow the managers of the firm that commissioned the study to follow the discussion.

6.4.4.2   Designing research using focus groups

There are four key decisions to make when carrying out research with focus groups:

a) The number of participants in each group.
b) The number of groups.
c) The characteristics of the participants.
d) The type of group to set up, and more specifically, the style to be used by the moderator in running the group.

- *The number of participants in each group.* Since the effectiveness of the focus group depends on the quality of participant interaction, the number of group members must optimize this interaction. *Group size* is normally from five to ten participants. Any smaller and members would be more likely to take turns expressing their opinions in an orderly fashion, limiting true interaction; any bigger and not all participants would be able to voice their opinions and interaction would become chaotic and unmanageable.

- *The number of groups.* Since research with focus groups is qualitative, there's no need for a numerous sample. The number of groups has to represent the variety of subjects involved in the phenomenon being investigated. This said, however, above a certain number the differential information that can be obtained by adding additional groups isn't worth the cost or the effort. So normally this kind of research uses from four to six groups, for a maximum of around 60 participants in all.
- *The characteristics of the participants.* Focus group participants obviously have to be interesting in light of the research objectives. Consequently, in some cases groups aren't made up of real consumers of the product in question, but opinion leaders or experts. While quantitative research requires representative samples, qualitative research calls for interesting subjects, even if they don't represent the population being investigated.

    Keeping in mind that group discussion should encourage interaction, it's important to remember that this is facilitated if the group is homogenous in terms of age, social class, and product competence. In fact, if group members don't share these characteristics, their interaction be conflictual and ultimately fail to serve the research objectives.
- *The type of group.* There are three different types of focus groups: exploratory, phenomenological, and clinical. Each addresses different topic categories, and moderators adopt different styles as a result.

    Exploratory focus groups investigate phenomena 'from square one' without any prior knowledge. The aim here is to emerge relevant constituent variables, often with the intent of following up with a quantitative phase to verify whether or not these variables and the relationships between them can be generalized. For example, a television production company looking for a new sports show may want to explore the characteristics of different sports that make them fun and exciting for a generic audience (in other words, for people who aren't fans).

    Phenomenological focus groups are useful for fully exploring the characteristics of a familiar phenomenon and related causal factors. These groups require basic knowledge of the phenomenon the organization wants to learn more about, and the moderator acts more like a discussion leader, keeping group members on task. For example, think of a theater specialized in modern dance that wants to find out why customers were satisfied (or dissatisfied) with the previous season's shows, to discover how next year's program can be improved.

Clinical focus groups are appropriate when the research objective is to ascertain whether motivations, preferences of behaviors of consumers are driven by unconscious or implicit factors that are difficult to verbalize. An example here would be a publishing house that wants to explore profound emotional reactions elicited when consumers choose a book to give as a gift.

It's worth pointing out that the three types of focus groups can overlap to some extent, and this may become apparent at different times within the same group. At one extreme it's possible to picture a single group that transitions from exploratory to clinical to phenomenological. Although theoretically this is possible, in practice it would extremely time consuming, and require continual shifts in the moderator's style to accompany the relational dynamics among the participants.

6.4.4.3 Running a focus group

The *type of data* generated via focus groups is comparable to the output from individual interviews, with the exception of context-based data. By running a focus group, data on content can be obtained, verbally expressed by participants, as well as data on process, conveyed through non-verbal communication. But because the setting isn't chosen by the respondents, it can't be taken as a vector of meaning.

The choice of location for a focus group requires careful thought. Beyond the need for technical support, the features of the meeting room can impact relational dynamics. This is why focus groups are usually set up with people sitting at a round table (so everyone can see each other and interact more easily among themselves and with the group moderator). Food and beverages are also offered, and an appropriate atmosphere is created with the right lighting, room temperature, and so on. Imagine bringing people together for a group discussion lasting the standard three hours in a room that's too hot or too cold, without any refreshments. It would be difficult for any favorable dynamics to emerge that would lead to achieving informational goals.

With focus groups the moderator also uses a guide that's compiled in exactly the same way as for an individual interview, keeping in mind the same principles as far as type of question, the sequence and the way they should be presented. (Case History 6.1 provides an excerpt of a focus group guide used in a marketing research project exploring the process of adopting textbooks for science subjects in Italian middle schools.) Also, there is usually an assistant or *recorder* who helps handle any operative problems that might arise, and who takes notes on any relevant non-verbal communication that occurs. As with the in-depth interview, focus groups are usually recorded and videotaped.

The most unique feature of a focus group is the moderator, who is responsible for facilitating interaction and encouraging discussion so as to obtain the information pertinent to the study. The moderator should be able to adapt her style to the type of group she's conducting. In phenomenological groups this style would be quite direct, because the discussion has to stay on track, centering on the distinctive traits that typify the phenomenon in question. In exploratory groups, and even more in clinical groups, the moderator's style is far less intrusive, to leave ample room for open discussion, and allow unexpected and insightful observations to come out.

Case History 6.1

An example of a focus group guide (except)

1. Warm up
   Thank participants, explain professional ethics and privacy norms.
   Present the research project (in general terms), go around the table and have participants introduce themselves.

2. Evolution of the role of science teachers in middle school (time: one hour)
2.1 'Comparing your own teaching methods with those of your colleagues in other disciplines, what are the specific characteristics that are unique to science subjects?'
   Encourage participants to discuss the specificities of:

○ Content.
○ Instructor competences.

- Learning goals.
- Student attitudes.

2.2 'Looking back on the past five years, has anything changed with regard to the things we've discussed up till now?'
   Encourage participants to discuss changes in the following:

- Extra-scholastic context (general attitudes toward school and science subjects, attitudes of families).
- Scholastic context (school autonomy, new subjects, new learning goals).
- The student body.

2.3 'Today it's becoming more and more common to find science-based television programs, specialized magazines, exhibitions, websites, and other forms of communication dedicated to science. In what way do all these represent educational tools for your subjects?'
   Encourage participants to discuss:

- Reputation and image of the media listed above.
- Perceived positive and negative effects.
- Possible complementarity with science teaching.

2.4 Personification test: 'Describe the typical science teacher, and how s/he differs from other teachers.'
   Encourage participants to discuss various characteristics:

- Demographic.
- Cultural.
- Motivational.

2.5 'Till now we've talked about changes in the way you teach, and in the attitudes toward scientific subjects. Now let's focus on the didactic tools that are available to science teachers. What do you think of them?'
   Encourage participants to discuss the role of:

- The textbook.
- The laboratory.
- Technology in general and new technologies specifically.

3. The decision to adopt a textbook (time: 30 minutes)
3.1 'Now let's talk about adopting a textbook: What are the things you consider when deciding which textbook to choose?'
   Encourage participants to discuss:

- Characteristics of the ideal textbook and didactic materials.
- Characteristics of the ideal publishing house.
- Motivations behind using the same text or adopting a new one.
- The role of the sales rep from the publishing house.

6.4.5   Observation

This method involves direct interaction with the phenomenon under investigation, overcoming contextualization and consciousness barriers. As an example, think of a visitor to an amusement park who's asked to describe the rides she went on and the time she spent on each one. If we ask her directly for this information (in an interview, for instance) we'd probably get superficial or simplified information, or a summary of an ideal situation that doesn't correspond to the actual experience. The reason for this is that people find it very hard to remember in detail how they behaved in a specific situation or how they normally behave when interacting with a product, a place, or a service for a given period of time.

Observation solves the problem of having to recall data from memory, because data is collected directly by observing the phenomenon while it's happening. In the example above, the researcher would observe the consumer as she goes through the amusement park, enjoying various rides and interacting with other people.

6.4.5.1   Types of observation

A number of different types of observation can be used when conducting qualitative marketing research (Daymon and Holloway, 2002, Chapter 14; Sayre, 2001,

Chapter 10), depending on the role of the person collecting the data (the observer):

- *Complete participant*. In this case, the observer becomes entirely immersed in the phenomenon under investigation, without revealing her identity but rather acting like everyone else. This type of observation is extremely time-consuming, because the observer has to become part of the group, and adopt norms of behavior, acquire competences, learn to carry out certain tasks, and so forth.

By not revealing his or her identity, the researcher can observe the phenomenon in its purest state and collect data in real time. But there are some limitations. The first is ethical, since the people being studied are unaware of this fact so they don't give (or deny) their consent. This is the main reason why complete observation is not a very common practice in marketing research. The second is methodological: the risk is that the observer becomes so wrapped up in the phenomenon that she loses the necessary cognitive and emotional detachment. The third limitation is more operational, having to do with the cost and the time needed to carry out this type of investigation. An example of complete participant observation is when a researcher studying a brand community becomes an active member.

- *Participant as observer*. In this case, the observer reveals her identity and her aims, and asks the other subjects to consent to her participation. This form of observation also involves high interaction between the researcher, the subjects, and the context in question. The advantage here is that the risks listed above for complete participant observation are minimized; the corresponding disadvantage ties into barriers the subjects might erect when they find out who the observer is and what she's trying to do.

An example of this type of observation is an *accompanied visit* to a store or any place where the consumer experiences the product, for example a museum, art gallery, or cinema. In this case the consumer agrees to being accompanied during her experience by the researcher who observes, asks questions, and seeks an explanation for behaviors or attitudes that emerge.

- *Observer as participant*. Here social interaction with the subjects involved in the phenomenon under investigation is reduced to a minimum, if not eliminated entirely. An example in this case would be a researcher who observes the behavior of visitors in a museum, without interacting with them at all. This option is useful when the sole aim of the research is analyzing behaviors and not the motivations behind them or people's interpretations of their behaviors.

6.4.5.2   *Carrying out observation*

Once the organization has decided on the most appropriate type of observation, the next step is to identify the specific dimensions of the phenomenon to be observed. These dimensions are typically (Daymon and Holloway, 2002: 210–11; Spradley, 1980):

- *Space*, or the place where the phenomenon occurs.
- *Actors*, whether they play a primary or secondary role.
- *Activities*, or behaviors adopted by the actors in reciprocal interactions.
- *Objects*, all the things that are in the place in question, and the interactions that the actors have with these things.
- *Actions*, or individual behaviors.
- *Events*, everything that happens during the period of observation.
- *Time*, duration, timing and sequence of events.
- *Objectives*, the aims that the actors intend to achieve through their actions.
- *Emotions*, associated with the activities and events.

All observations are recorded as they happen and compiled in reports at the end of every temporal unit of observation (a portion of a day, an entire day, a week, and so on). In this case researchers also use technical tools such as video cameras; notes taken during observation make a crucial contribution to successive analysis. If observation is done in a structured way, an observation sheet can be used listing all the factors to be monitored (Research Focus 6.4).

Research Focus 6.4

A museum visit experience: an observation-based research project

In Chapters 3 and 4 we highlighted the role of the context in which a product is purchased or consumed, and how that can affect the perceived value of the consumer experience. With a museum, for example, it's interesting to reflect on whether or not the atmosphere impacts the value visitors perceive, and how.

To find an answer to this question, Goulding (2000) conducted research at the Birmingham Museum and Art Gallery, using pure observation as her data collection method. First the researcher played the role of a visitor, observing her own interaction with the environment. The aim of this phase was to familiarize herself with the context, and to get ideas from her experience for the observation sheet. Next she observed 112 visitors as they explored the museum, focusing on two visit itineraries: the permanent collection and the temporary exhibit. The latter was remarkably innovative with regard to the level of interactivity and the pieces on display.

Here are some interesting findings from Golding's study:

- When new visitors enter the museum for the first time, they're struck by a sense of physical and psychological disorientation, due to the vast size, the numerous paths they can follow, and the lack of information on how to proceed. As a result, many visitors wander around with no sense of direction, and this generates anxiety.
- The sense of disorientation is increased by signs inside the museum that are complex, difficult to decipher, and concentrated in a few points. This creates congestion and prevents people from retaining information while visiting individual rooms in the museum.
- Crowded rooms have different effects on different visitors. Generally, too many people (and the resulting noise and jostling) provokes irritation and discomfort. Instead, visitors who are more deeply immersed in the experience show more tolerance, as if they were less aware of the presence of so many other people and the negative sensations associated with being in the midst of a crowd.

6.4.5.3 *Some structured observation methods*

As with in-depth interviews and focus groups, for observation too we can identify some methods that have become consolidated and structured after years of implementation.

- *Protocol analysis.* Here individuals are asked to perform an activity while applying a specific technique, either *talking aloud* or *thinking aloud*, referring to verbalizing either all the *actions* they *perform*, or all the *thoughts* that come to mind while carrying out the activity in question. Protocol analysis is particularly effective when analyzing the difficulty that consumers might have in interacting with the product or with the place where the consumption experience occurs. Example: a chain of bookstores could use this technique to understand the difficulty consumers might have in reaching books on shelves.
- *The diary.* This form of self-observation calls for the individual subjects (or groups) to write down all the activities, sensations and related emotions, and opinions they associate with certain tasks they're asked to carry out in a given period of time. This type of observation is particularly suited to studying consumption experiences with a longer duration; this would be the case with reading a book, visiting a tourist destination, or spending a month-long vacation in a foreign country.
- *Netnography.* Netnography consists in the adaptation of the ethnographic method to the study of computer-mediated environments: newsgroups, chat rooms, communities (Kozinets, 2002). Similar to more traditional ethnography, the aim of netnography is to explore the impact that cultural and social variables have on consumption behaviors. What makes this method unique is that it does not necessitate physical participation in the contexts where the phenomena under investigation occur; instead data collection is done by observing discussions that take place in virtual environments.

This can take the form of either participant observation or pure observation. The greatest advantage in netnography as compared to ethnography is clearly the possibility to collect an astounding quantity of data with far less effort or cost.

6.5   QUANTITATIVE RESEARCH

6.5.1   Research objectives

While qualitative research seeks to acquire deep knowledge of a phenomenon, the main goal of quantitative research is to *measure* a given phenomenon. Normally the aim is either to come up with a *description* of the phenomenon in question with reference to its constituent variables, or to reveal its underlying *causes* by appraising causal connections among these variables.

So an organization needs to design research with a quantitative approach when it wants the answers to questions such as: How big is the market for this product? How much weight do different motivations have on creating value expectations for a certain group of consumers? How common is a given consumption practice? How much customer satisfaction am I winning as compared to my competitors? The generic goal of measuring a phenomenon can be broken down into more specific objectives, which in turn will dictate the final research design.

First a typical objective of quantitative marketing research is to *generalize results*. Many phenomena studied in marketing research encompass universes made up of tens of thousands, hundreds of thousands, or even millions of people. (Just consider the reputation of institutions, companies, and sites such as the Teatro alla Scala in Milan, the Louvre in Paris, the city of Rio de Janeiro, or the Great Wall of China.)

To study these phenomena efficiently and without excessive cost to the organization, research must focus on a portion (or sample) of the subjects that make up the universe, based on the premise that the information obtained from these people applies to the entire universe. This is the basic concept of generalizability. And as far as the quality of quantitative research, this also gives an idea of the critical nature of sampling, or the procedures used to build a sample.

The second aim of quantitative research is discovering *the relationship among variables* that constitute a phenomenon. For instance, let's take an organization that manages a number of historical monuments in a city and say that this organization wants to establish new policies to facilitate combined visits to various sites. The managers might want to know if it's better to invest in a comprehensive ticket that allows people to visit multiple sites at a discounted price, or a free shuttle service from one monument to another. How can they decide which option would have the biggest impact on visits to the monuments in question?

To make many marketing decisions, managers need to know whether or not there are relationships among certain variables relating to market phenomena, and if so what kind of relationships they are and how strong. The only way to come up with these measurements is to design marketing research with a quantitative approach. In conclusion, it's essential emphasize that while the exploratory goals of research can be pursued with a qualitative approach, descriptive and causal goals require a quantitative approach.

6.5.2 Designing the sample

The most effective strategy for obtaining reliable measurements is to collect data on all the subjects that constitute a given phenomenon; in other words, to run a *census*. This means analyzing every member of the target population. So to measure customer satisfaction for an architectural studio, or to gauge customer expectations prior to their visit to a small museum, or to calculate the propensity of visitors to a minor archeological site to purchase merchandising products: in all these cases a census would be appropriate because customers would only number a few dozen (or a few hundred at most).

But similar situations are quite rare. In nearly all circumstances, as I mentioned before, the target of marketing research consists of thousands or even millions of subjects. This means that the only viable option is to collect data on a portion – or sample – of the universe in question.

The reliability of data from quantitative research depends on the *size* and the *representativeness* of the sample: the first indicates the capacity of the sample to provide statistically significant results; the second its capacity to encompass the variety of characteristics of individual subjects that make up the population. A series of statistical procedures has been developed that allow researchers to come up with significant and representative samples; these procedures constitute the sampling process.

6.5.2.1 *The size of the research sample*

To ensure that results are significant and the sample is representative, the sample size has to be sufficiently large in comparison with the size of the population being studied and the variety of characteristics of its members. As we can easily imagine, a more varied population calls for a bigger sample size.

Although in theory the bigger the sample the better, in practice this rule doesn't apply because as the sample size increases so do research costs. As a result, an organization needs to identify the optimal sample size, one that strikes a perfect balance between significant results and acceptable costs.

Marketing research practices recommend samples of around 1,000 to 1,500 subjects for statistically

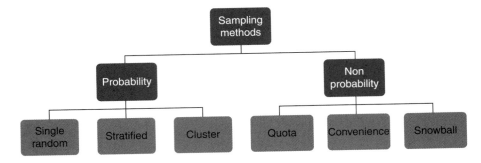

Figure 6.4 – Primary sampling methods

significant results with reference, for example, to the population of a large European country (France, Germany, Italy, or Poland), on research regarding phenomena without much in-depth information (motivations and knowledge regarding a specific product category or brand, or purchase and consumption practices, to name a few).

But it's important to point out that if an organization wants to analyze data broken down into sub-samples (product/brand knowledge among various consumer groups categorized by a series of demographic variables), then as a rule the individual sub-samples (*sample cells*) have to include at least 100–120 subjects. So if there are several levels of sub-sampling, the overall sample size can run into the thousands.

6.5.2.2   Sampling methods

To increase the probability that the research sample is representative and provides statistically significant results, various sampling methods can be used. First, sampling can be *probability* or *nonprobability* (Figure 6.4). A probability sample is when every member of the target population is given the same chance to be a part of the research sample. If instead some subjects do not have this possibility the resulting sample is defined as nonprobability. The probability that the sample is representative increases with the first method, and decreases with the second.

Let's say that the city of Dresden wants to commission a market research company to study how 15- to 21-year-old residents spend their weekends, looking specifically at their cultural consumption habits. The company selects a probability sample, giving all the young people of the appropriate age who live in Dresden the chance to participate. To do so, the company could

randomly select 15- to 21-year-olds from city records (see *single random sampling* below). Another option would be to send out researchers to interview young people who happen to pass through the Neustadt station, for instance, in the morning of any given weekend. In this case, the resulting sample would be a nonprobability sample. In fact, this approach would exclude out of hand all the young people who don't use the train or who don't stop in that station or who take the train in the afternoon or the evening or during the week. If the young people who are excluded from the study have different characteristics (social, cultural, economic) and different cultural preferences with respect to the ones who are included, the sample won't be representative of the population targeted in the research.

Here are common types of probability sampling:

- *Single random sampling.* With this method the sample is extracted from a complete list of members of the population, following any given random procedure. Above I mentioned an example of single random sampling, with the research firm randomly selecting subjects from a list of all the Dresden residents between the ages of 15 and 21. Clearly one obstacle in single random sampling is that it necessitates a complete list of the population, which is often impossible to obtain in marketing research.

- *Stratified sampling* This is a two-stage procedure. First the population is divided into strata, and then a single random sampling is run on each one. The prerequisite for utilizing this method is that the population must possess certain characteristics (known to researchers) that impact the phenomenon under investigation. With the Dresden example, let's say that family income impacts consumption habits of under-21s. In other words, young people have similar habits if their families have similar incomes. So a population (families with children who live in Dresden) can be broken down into a finite number of strata (different income levels) and the number of subjects that we need in our sample selected by randomly extracting them from various strata.

- *Cluster sampling*. This method follows the same rationale as the previous one. Here sub-groups are also indentified within the population that are significant in light of research objectives, and that allow the researchers to sample individual groups. The basic difference here with respect to stratified sampling is that the individual cluster, unlike the stratum, is made up of subjects who are highly heterogeneous as far as the characteristic that impacts the phenomenon under investigation. Continuing with the Dresden example, different areas of the city could be used; in each neighborhood there would be young people who differ widely in their cultural consumption habits. At this point the sample is built by grouping clusters together until the proper sample size is reached, assembling all the subjects belonging to the selected clusters. So, all the age-appropriate young people would be analyzed who live in certain neighborhoods of the city until the proper sample size is obtained.

Common types of nonprobability sampling include:

- *Quota sampling*. This method is identical to stratified sampling, except instead of randomly selecting subjects, convenience criteria are used; this means there is no equal probability of being included in the sample. So going back to Dresden, once family income is set as the variable, families and young family members are selected for study because they're acquaintances of the researchers or because they're easy to contact.
- *Convenience sampling*. In this case subject selection is based on convenience as far as time (the first people who accept the request to participate), space (the easiest people to reach), cost (the people who volunteer), and so on.
- *Snowball sampling*. Here the sample is built by asking the first subjects in the study to suggest the names of other subjects, until the target sample size is reached.

Summing up, because it guarantees more reliable data, probability sampling is preferable to nonprobability. In fact, nonprobability samples are not built according to a pre-defined probability rule, so subject selection is based on particular knowledge needs, subjective criteria, or special characteristics. This said, it's worth noting that a great deal of quantitative marketing research conducted with nonprobability sampling turns out very reliable analysis and outcomes, because the subject selection process follows logical criteria.

6.5.3 Data collection methods

In Section 6.3 we saw that in quantitative research large samples are used, quantitative information is generated, and respondents are given a limited number of possible responses. At this point we can say that the first two characteristics of this type of research lead to the third by creating the conditions that restrict interviewee responses.

If the aim is to measure phenomena through data collected on samples that can be generalized in the form of information applicable to the entire population, then the corresponding sacrifice is an in-depth understanding of these phenomena. In other words, researchers can't expect to grasp the cognitive, emotional and behavioral richness of the subjects under investigation. Let's say there is a sample of 3,000 consumers, each of whom is free to express her ideas and emotions and describe in detail her behaviors. Aside from the cost of collecting this vast quantity of data, their richness would make it practically impossible to aggregate them in any meaningful way. This means that the resulting information would not be generalizable.

As a result the data collection methods in quantitative research allow the organization to grasp only the surface of phenomena by using highly structured techniques that limit respondents' freedom of expression. The four most common methods in quantitative marketing research are surveys, panels, experiments, and structured observation.

6.5.4 Surveys

The survey method consists in controlled individual interviews, which use structured questionnaires (with all questions set beforehand) on a sample of subjects selected according to appropriate criteria. In a structured interview, there is little or no room for flexibility, and the interviewer must simply read the questions and record the answers. So every interviewee is asked exactly the same questions.

A key consideration here is that this type of individual interview is entirely different from the semi-structured (or unstructured) format used in qualitative research, in which the interviewer is free to add any questions she deems necessary to delve into the various topics of discussion. As a result, in these circumstances every interviewee may be asked a different set of questions.

6.5.4.1   Designing a questionnaire

Here are the steps that are generally followed in designing a questionnaire (Malhotra, 2005).

- *Specify information objectives*. Information objectives obviously derive from the research aims, as we said in Section 6.2. The questionnaire contains a battery of questions to elicit data that serve to achieve these aims.
- *Choose how to administer the questionnaire*. A variety of tools can be used here: surveys in the form of personal interviews, or via telephone, mail, email, or the web.

Personal interviews: This involves face-to-face contact between the interviewer and interviewee. The interviewer reads the questions and records the answers, either on paper or electronically (also known as computer aided personal interview or CAPI). The advantage of the personal interview is that the interviewer can clarify any doubts that the interviewee may have on the meaning of the questions. What's more, visual aids can also be used (also from multimedia sources with a CAPI), which are essential in researching things like advertising material, logos, or packages. Finally, personal interviews also afford more control over the sample, because researchers can verify the identity of respondents and confirm that they meet the sampling criteria. The biggest disadvantage of personal interviews is the time it takes to conduct them, and the relative cost of employing several interviewers.

Telephone surveys: This type of research involves selecting a sample from the telephone directory and conducting interviews by phone. The interviewer can record responses on paper or by using a CATI system (Computer Aided Telephone Interview). As far as the advantages of telephone interviews, the time and cost involved are relatively limited; targets can be reached over a vast geographical area; the makeup of the sample can be progressively monitored and corrected it in a timely fashion if need be. What's more, experienced interviewers can collect sensitive and complex information without having interviewees put a stop to the interview before it's finished. On the negative side, it's impossible to use visual aids; the interview can't take too long, which means limiting the number of open questions; the interviewer's approach may give rise to distortions; and in some cases there is no way to verify the identity of the respondent.

Mail surveys: In this case, subjects receive a package at their homes or workplaces in the mail that contains the questionnaire, instructions for filling it in, a return envelope, and normally an incentive for responding. The interviewee is asked to fill out the questionnaire and send it back, generally without any direct interaction with the researcher. It's also fairly common practice to combine both a telephone and mail survey, first mailing the questionnaire to the subjects and then contacting them by phone to solicit their responses or assist them in answering the questions (or actually gathering data directly).

The main advantage of mail surveys is the cost, which is quite a bit lower than the other two options above; visual aids can also be included in the packet that help respondents complete the questionnaires. But there are two limitations to be aware of. First, the response rate is normally very low (which makes it hard to use this approach to obtain high quality research). Second, the responses to mail surveys tend to come from people who are highly motivated with regard to the topic in question (either in a positive or negative sense), so the risk is a resulting sample that is not representative. Surveys via traditional mail and e-mail are similar in many ways, with the same pros and cons; the only difference is the delivery channel.

Web-based surveys: Web-based surveys are done with questionnaires, like those used with CAPI systems, which make it possible to skip questions, check for logical consistency, add multimedia stimuli, offer links to other web pages. Data are also immediately available and usable for analysis. Traditional methods are used to recruit respondents (mailing lists, customer databases, telephone). Interviewees are provided with indications on the site where the questionnaire is posted, and if they agree to participate they're given a login and password to access the questionnaire (in the case of controlled-access research, which would be preferred).

The biggest advantage of web-based methods is the minimal time and cost involved; also any type of visual aid can be used. Limitations are the response rate, which is usually quite low, and the low complexity of the survey that can be used with this approach. (Many interviewees, in fact, only spend a few minutes answering a questionnaire, and then quit without completing it.) What's more, given that Internet use is still far from universal, in particular for certain targets (seniors in many countries, for example), the risk is still high that the resulting sample would not adequately represent the entire population.

- *Formulate the questions*. Here are some good general rules for choosing the right questions:
  - *There must be a real need*. The first thing to consider is whether the question is absolutely necessary. A simple way to determine this is to reflect on how the resulting information will be used. If there is no satisfactory answer, the question can be deleted.
  - *The question has to provide the information the organization needs*. It's crucial to understand whether or not the question can lead to the information objective. If it doesn't, it must be reformulated or broken down into two or more parts.
  - *The wording of the question must be clear*. Questions should be as simple as possible, leaving no room for misinterpretation. It's also critical to avoid leading questions.
- *Format the questions*. The format of the questions can be *open-ended* or *closed-ended* (or *open/closed*). The first gives respondents greater freedom of expression, and allows researchers to grasp subtleties that would not otherwise come to the surface. But normally with quantitative research, questionnaires have only a few open questions. In fact, closed questions are far more common in quantitative investigations for several reasons. First, researchers need to aggregate data quickly and easily. What's more, questionnaires with closed questions are simpler to administer, responses are more reliable, and analyzing and interpreting information is facilitated, all reasons why this type of question is most common.

  One kind of closed question is *dichotomic*, which has only two possible answers: yes/no, satisfied/dissatisfied, purchase/don't purchase, for example. These questions don't provide terribly rich data from an informational standpoint, and are used mainly in questionnaires built on multiple response paths. For example, if the answer is 'satisfied', one set of questions follows; a 'dissatisfied' response will be followed by different questions.

  With *multiple choice*, interviewees are given a list of possible answers to choose from. This type of question is a way to classify respondents on the basis of

certain variables. For example, let's imagine asking a visitor to an archeological site if she went there alone, with another person, with her family, or with a tour group. Depending on her answer, she can be classified in terms of her 'visit type'. Or if she's asked about her reasons for visiting (to learn more about the relevant historical period, to pass the time, to accompany her children, and so on) the classification would be 'visit motivation'.

Other questions can be answered on *scale*, which is a way to measure the intensity of the respondent's perception of the variable in question. Here's an example measuring visitor satisfaction on a scale from 1 to 9, with 1 meaning 'extremely dissatisfied' and 9 'extremely satisfied': 'How satisfied are you with your recent visit?' The scale format is extremely popular because it enables researchers to measure all the categories of variables that we described in Chapters 3 and 4 (cognitive, affective, behavioral), meaning that this type of question can reveal interrelations among variables.

- *Sequence the questions*. The sequence that questions follow has a notable impact on the effectiveness and the efficiency of the response process, keeping in mind the fundamental objective: to keep respondents focused all the way to the end of the questionnaire. So a good idea is to start with simple, interesting questions to capture respondents' attention and prompt them to continue. The more complicated questions should come during the main part of the survey, when cognitive energy is still high. It's also advisable to build the questionnaire in thematic blocks of questions, such as product benefits, perceived sacrifices, emotions, and behaviors. That way, the respondent will find it easier to recall data from memory to answer the question.
- *Run a pre-test*. To ensure that the questionnaire is effective (that is, it will provide data that serve to obtain quantitative information), it's always advisable to run a pre-test before administering the questionnaire to the entire sample. The pre-test is normally given to a group of subjects who share the same characteristics as the research sample. These initial respondents, once they've taken the pre-test, are asked to comment on whether the questions and answers are clear and understandable, whether they can actually answer the questions, how long the questionnaire takes to fill out, and so forth. If the pre-test brings out any anomalies in these areas, the questionnaire is modified accordingly.

6.5.5 Panels

It wouldn't be accurate to define a panel as a data collection method; instead it's a sampling method. But the fact is that some research companies are specialized in using panels, and they sell panel-based studies as specific, distinctive forms of research. What's more, panels are one of the most commonly used types of research in both creative and non-creative industries. So we've come to consider the panel as a research method in its own right.

Panels are actually *fixed-sample surveys*, with data always collected on the same sample. Beyond this, the panel is no different to a traditional survey. But why would an organization want to conduct research with a panel? The typical motivation is to monitor changes in a phenomenon over time. Panels can be assembled with samples of consumers, corporate clients, or retail stores. In some creative industries such as publishing or recording, panels run by multinational research institutes provide monthly or bi-monthly sales data on every single product sold in the stores that make up the sample (SKU, stock keeping unit). Likewise, in the media industry (television, newspaper and magazine publishing, radio, the Web) consumer panels are often used to measure the audience and market share of competing products, programs, or sites (Case History 6.2).

Unlike a survey designed and realized by an organization, the panel is usually owned by a research institute, which gathers data and then sells them to all interested parties. The institute's customers decide what type of data to buy (for example, only data on their own market performance or on competitors as well) and the level of detail (their overall sales and market share or a breakdown for every SKU; for all types of stores or only for certain categories, and so forth).

Normally for large European countries and for any number of product categories, a panel intended to represent the population (a consumer panel) or the retail universe (a retail panel) would call for a sample of several thousand subjects (up to 10,000). Instead, consumer panels in the media industry normally have around 3,000 to 4,000 subjects. Considering the fact that panel-based research investigates phenomena that are dynamic and evolving, maintaining the composition of the panel is critical. Consequently, properly managing a panel means adjusting the sample so it continues to represent the universe in question.

6.5.6 Experiments

This data collection method is typically applied in causal research. In fact, the primary objective with experiments is to capture and measure cause-effect relationships among different variables, in other words to explain the capacity of certain factors to impact specific aspects of the population under investigation. So experiments are studies conducted under controlled conditions, decided on by the researcher, with the aim of assessing the effect of these conditions (or factors) on the observable results of the experiment itself.

Case History 6.2

Ipsos Mediacell Radiometrics: an innovative tool for radio panels

MediaCell is an innovative tool that measures exposure to radio via a smart phone that captures a silent code inserted in the audio transmission of measured radios, thus allowing the automatic detection of radio audiences split by platform (with the distinction between FM, SAT, or DTT) and by real time versus time-shifted listening.

The decoder software is installed on cell phones, devices that have become a vital part of everyday life which people commonly carry at all times. This allows for passive measurement of radio listening without requiring participants to carry extra devices, change their behavior, or answer lengthy telephone interviews.

After an initial pilot phase in 2012, Ipsos Italy has launched 'Ipsos Mediacell Radiometrics 2013', the 2013 edition of the study, which consists in a panel of 4,000 individuals representative of the over-14 national population, equally divided between people who installed the MediaCell app on their mobile phones and those who substituted their mobile phone for an Ipsos mobile phone with a pre-installed MediaCell app. All main national radio stations and five local stations have agreed to participate to date.

Experimental design refers to the process that identifies: (1) the subjects who will make up the sample, along with sampling procedures; (2) the independent variables; (3) the dependent variables; (4) the methods for controlling variables that are not relevant to the relationships being investigated, but which can influence them nonetheless. In this sense, experiments are noticeably different from quantitative research based on surveys, where conditions aren't established by the researcher and the data are simply collected (not influenced *a priori*) to highlight any relationships that might exist among variables.

In experiments, the sample is called the *experimental group*. In this group, the independent variable is manipulated (to ensure that possible cause-effect relationships emerge) and later the dependent variable is measured. So any change in the second can be traced back to the variation in the first.

Here's an example. Imagine that a bookstore chain wants to modify store layout to improve customer interaction with the space and to increase sales. In this case the independent variable is the layout, and the dependent variable the overall sales in the store.

Before making a decision, the managing director of the retail stores decides to run an experiment. She selects a sample of stores that represent the universe of the entire chain, and changes the store layout (that is, she manipulates the independent variable). After a few months, she checks whether or not there's been any change in sales in the sample stores with respect to the ones that were not part of the sample (the so-called control group). If there was any variation (an increase or decrease) she can trace it back to the modified store layout; if not, she can conclude that changing the layout doesn't impact overall sales.

For further corroboration of this conclusion, the manager should make sure that there were no changes in other variables (*control variables*) that might have contributed in some way to the variation in the dependent variable. This of course applies to the experimental timeframe, from when she manipulated the independent variable to when she measured the effects on the dependent variable.

6.5.7   Structured observation

Although observation belongs to the tradition of qualitative research, it can also be used in research design that calls for a quantitative approach. In fact if observation is structured according to the canons of quantitative research and carried out on broad and representative samples with the aim of measuring phenomena, it can also serve to generate quantitative information.

Structured observation consists in a systematic process of recording the behaviors of the subjects targeted by the research, but with no direct contact between them and the researcher. The key to designing data collection via observation, as with the survey, is defining the behavior to be investigated. Clearly the nature of the observation directly relates to the research goals.

Structured observation has several advantages over surveys. First, it can be used to measure real behavior, instead of getting indications as to intentions or preferences. In this sense, the distortion can be eliminated in the interview process that derives from the difficulty of remembering or recording past or typical behaviors. What's more, observation-based research costs less than surveys if the phenomena in question occur frequently and last for a short time.

The main limitation lies in the fact that these methods 'record' behavior without providing any indication of the 'motivations' behind this behavior. Another downside worth mentioning is the distortion perceived by observers (with human, not mechanical, observation). This can lead to corresponding distortion in the information they gather. What's more, procedures relating to observation can be extremely time consuming, and give rise to myriad ethical and legal issues.

Due to the growing importance of virtual contexts in the different stages of the consumption experience, it's becoming common practice to use structured observation in studying online behavior (from the pages visited to the time spent on a site, from product reviews in blogs to tweets sent regarding a specific topic). All this information can be easily tracked, so researchers can measure these behaviors without having to interview the consumers (Research Focus 6.5).

Regarding data collection, structured online observation allows researchers to cut costs and time drastically. On the other hand, building a probability sample, or one that is representative to some degree, is no easy task seeing as participation in virtual environments is not a shared behavior across all consumer groups.

6.6   CONCLUSIONS

I began this chapter by asserting that an organization's market knowledge constitutes the map it uses to observe and interpret phenomena in its market. I also affirmed that the quality of the map depends on the breadth and depth of this knowledge.

Building broad, deep knowledge means using ad hoc methods and techniques that fall under the umbrella of marketing research. In this chapter we've learned that specific information objectives call for specific methods and techniques, which we can broadly classify as qualitative and quantitative. Each of these approaches allows the organization to attain certain objectives, but not others. So organizations that are familiar with these approaches can make more effective choices when deciding what kind of knowledge they need.

With this chapter we've come to the conclusion of the section of the book dedicated to the value analysis process. In the next chapter we'll begin to explore how companies and institutions that operate in creative industries create value for their customers. We'll start by identifying the type of market in which organizations offer their value propositions, and end by describing the levers that can contribute to creating these propositions.

REVIEW QUESTIONS

1. What are the main types of data and sources an organization can use for its marketing information processes?
2. What are the stages of a marketing research process? What are the main objectives of each one?
3. What are the main characteristics of quantitative and qualitative marketing research? How can they be complemented?
4. What are the research objectives that can typically be achieved through a qualitative research? What are the main methods and their specificities?
5. What are the research objectives that can typically be achieved through a quantitative research? What are the main methods and their specificities?

Research Focus 6.5

Sentiment analysis of Twitter audiences

Twitter is arguably the most popular microblogging service in the world. Thanks to its global status, both organizations and individuals make frequent use of Twitter to communicate with their audiences. Since the people with the biggest Twitter audiences are stars in creative industries (today Lady Gaga, Justin Bieber, and Britney Spears), the effectiveness of 'tweeting' is particularly interesting in these contexts.

Bae and Lee (2012) conducted *sentiment analysis* on Twitter users to see if the emotional tone of celebrity tweets to their fans would trigger retweets with the same or different emotional tone. Sentiment analysis involves structured observation of the opinions, judgments, and sensations expressed in non-structured texts (such as consumer-to-consumer communication). The aim is to understand whether the object or the subject being investigated triggers positive or negative opinions or sentiments.

Analyzing more than three million tweets sent in around two months as responses or retweets sent to the 13 top celebrities (from various creative industries) in the US, the authors underscored that the emotional tone expressed in the messages sent by the 13 celebrities was reflected in the tone of the responses and retweets. (In other words, tweets with positive emotional tones trigger positive retweets, and vice versa). This demonstrates that it's possible to elicit positive or negative emotions via Twitter by modulating the emotional tone of one's messages.

CASE STUDY

MUSÉE DU QUAI BRANLY: DESIGNING AND IMPLEMENTING A MARKETING RESEARCH SYSTEM

The Musée du quai Branly, founded in 2006 in Paris, offers a unique space for collections coming from two other Parisian museums, the National Museum of African and Oceanic Art, and the ethnographic section of the Museum of Man, specialized in non-European art (both visual and applied). The fundamental goal in creating this new museum was to place center stage certain cultures that were often relegated to the background in the West, giving visitors the chance to experience diverse perceptions of art and life. The quai Branly collections include more than 260,000 pieces with around 3,500 on display. The museum has a strong interdisciplinary accent, hosting art in a broad sense (painting, sculpture, music, textiles, and photography) presented from a transversal perspective. Thanks to its role in safeguarding intangible cultural heritage, the Musée du quai Branly has earned UNESCO patronage.

The building that houses the museum is a remarkable one. Designed by architect Jean Nouvel, it resembles a bridge surrounded by lush vegetation. This layout isolates the building from the rest of the city on one hand, and on the other turns visitors into true explorers who gradually discover the museum and its content.

Beyond the permanent collections, today the museum regularly hosts temporary exhibits, and fills the calendar with conferences, study days, and workshops. Theater and music performances and film festivals are also on offer in multi-purpose areas. In addition, the quai Branly houses a center for research on museum-related activities and a vast library.

Visitor data appear to confirm a growing interest in the museum's collections and activities, with nine million plus visitors since its opening, and 1.3 million in 2012 alone. This secures a respectable place for the Musée du quai Branly within the framework of the cultural offering of Paris, and France.

The Musée quai Branly and marketing research

From the outset, the quai Branly has distinguished itself by continually and comprehensively using information gleaned from marketing research to support decision making at various levels. In fact, this reliance on research was part of the life of the museum even before it actually opened. The governmental committee that assessed the feasibility of the museum project commissioned a number of studies, beginning back in 1995. Among these, one centered on visitors to the two museums that would feed into the new one, to verify their reactions and appreciation of the possibility of finding a single institution that would house the collections in question. Additional research was conducted on the museum's market potential to verify whether there was actually room on the market to attract visitors, in light of the already abundant offering of museums and culture in Paris.

Once opened, the museum management continued to rely on market information as vital input for decision making. Since its opening in 2006, a *permanent visitor observatory* was designed and implemented, which involves quantitative research based on surveys carried out during the year by means of personal interviews on a sample of roughly 2,500 visitors. By using tablets to conduct these interviews, the process is made more rapid and data collection far more accurate and efficient. Each year the observatory produces data on visitor profiles, satisfaction with the museum's offering, and specific use behaviors relative to various museum services. Relevant information allows management to tailor visitor segmentation and to pinpoint critical factors in the museum's value proposition.

Beyond the permanent observatory, the first years the museum was opened (from 2008 to 2010), three major 'strategic' studies were run ('strategic' because management realized that some of their initial choices would shape the image of the museum for years to come). To ensure as effective decision making as possible, management decided to collect information on the potential market. The three studies focused on the following:

○ *Museum-related choices*: In terms of the collections and how they were displayed, the aim of this study was to ascertain whether decisions regarding these aspects responded to the desires of potential visitors. So qualitative research was run to explore their perceptions, preferences, and behaviors in depth.

○ *Uses of the museum*: Here the aim was to verify the public's appreciation for a multi-media and multi-disciplinary offering that encourages the use of the museum for traditional visits and beyond, both as far as types of experience and time spent in the museum (attending performances, films, temporary exhibits, conferences, and so forth); to attain this objective a more complex research approach was used (both qualitative and quantitative).

○ *The museum's image*: This study sought to reveal visitors' perceptions of the museum, utilizing an exclusively quantitative format.

The three major studies described above guided choices as to museum products, communication activities, and public relations. But beyond this, the museum invests annually in marketing research with the aim of producing information relating to various decision-making contexts. These include behavioral studies on the use of specific services (for instance audio guides), satisfaction with individual exhibits or temporary activities (performances and workshops), and pre-tests to verify the effectiveness of communication activities, both external (advertising) and internal (explanatory panels describing the items on display). Below is a detailed look at the research done on a 2009 exhibit.

Research on *Le siècle du Jazz*

In March 2009, the Musée du quai Branly opened a temporary exhibit called *Le siècle du Jazz*. Although management was convinced that the theme was fitting in light of the museum's institutional mission, there was a possibility that it might not seem perfectly harmonious with respect to the exhibits the museum typically offered and the public had come to expect.

In actual fact, the intent behind this exhibit was to attract a pool of potential visitors who didn't normally come to the museum. So management thought it would be interesting to study the effect of the exhibit on the museum's 'traditional' public as well as a new set of visitors who would find the theme appealing. With this general goal in mind, management commissioned an external research institute to conduct a quantitative study during the exhibit. Specifically, the aim was to collect data both on visitors to the jazz exhibit, as well as participants in the numerous events offered during the same time frame and relating to the themes of jazz and New Orleans (concerts, workshops, conferences, performances). Two different methodologies were used for the two targets.

The goals of the study on the first target (visitors to *Le siècle du Jazz*) were:

- To profile exhibit visitors.
- To measure the congruence of a jazz exhibit with regard to the museum's image.
- To identify the main sources of information relating to the museum and the exhibit.
- To evaluate visitor satisfaction.
- To discover if there was any overlap between visitors to the temporary exhibit and participants in other events/activities during the same time frame.

The goals relative to the second target (participants in activities/events offered by the museum during the same time frame as the temporary exhibit) were:

- To profile participants and verify the difference between them and exhibit visitors.
- To identify the main sources of information relating to the museum, the exhibit (if this second target was aware of it), and other activities/events, and ascertain the difference with respect to visitors to the temporary exhibit.
- To discover if there was any overlap between visitors to the temporary exhibit and participants in other activities/events offered at the same time.

Methodology

Research was conducted over the three-month period during the temporary exhibit *Le siècle du Jazz*. The first target was interviewed personally using a structured questionnaire (included in the appendix). The sample was chosen by randomly selecting visitors as they left the exhibit (generally every third, fourth, or tenth person, depending on the time of day and the visitor flow). Interviews with 523 people were done using this method. For the second target researchers opted for self administration, distributing the questionnaire to all visitors on their way into the museum. The sample was compiled via self-selection by inviting respondents to hand in their questionnaires as they left the museum; a total of 915 visitors did so.

Main findings

The majority of visitors to the exhibit *Le siècle du Jazz* were French (82%, of which 23% were Parisian), equally divided in terms of gender (55% women); most (75%) were over the age of 31. Students accounted for 12.9 per cent of respondents, but 68 per cent of them were studying subjects unrelated to art. Similarly, of the visitors who worked for a living, 73 per cent had jobs that had nothing to do with art. Finally, 58 per cent of respondents had never visited the museum before, and 89 per cent of them had gone there specifically for the temporary exhibit. From a socio-demographic viewpoint, the research sample was aligned with the public, in keeping with the findings from the museum's observatory during the second trimester of 2009.

As for the congruence of the jazz theme with other activities/exhibits offered by the museum, 92 per cent of the sample expressed a favorable opinion. Of the remaining 8 per cent, 61 per cent thought the exhibit would have been more appropriate in a different venue (such as the Cité de la Musique). Satisfaction with the exhibit was recorded from 94 per cent of respondents (50% were very satisfied, 44% were satisfied).

As regards information sources, 21 per cent of interviewees found out about the exhibit from word of mouth, 15 per cent from posters advertising the event, and 13 per cent from press coverage. A majority of 88 per cent stated that someone they knew had recommended the exhibit, and these respondents also said they'd return for another museum event, while 77 per cent would come back to visit the permanent collections. Only 21 per cent of respondents said they were aware of other events taking place in the museum at the same time, and 70 per cent visited only *Le siècle du Jazz*.

The conclusion regarding this target was that the visitor profile for the temporary exhibit was similar to regular museum visitors. Yet a vast majority of visitors were only interested in the temporary exhibit, or weren't aware of the rest of the museum's offering. Two more crucial points: word of mouth was the main information source relative to the museum (more so than traditional channels or the web) and a clear majority of respondents were interested in visiting the museum in the future, and not only for temporary exhibits. Basically, this proves that temporary exhibits play a key role in enhancing awareness of the museum as a whole.

As for the second target, the participant profile was almost entirely French (92%, 40% from Paris); more than half were women (61%). The age of most participants (70%) was over 30 and 14.8 per cent were students. First-time visitors accounted for 48 per cent of respondents, while 42 per cent had been to the museum for other exhibits in the previous 12 months, just over half of them more than once (53%). With regard to behaviors relative to other activities/events running at the same time, 51 per cent of interviewees had already attended more than one event held at the museum, and 34 per cent planned on doing so.

Specifically regarding the temporary exhibit *Le siècle du Jazz*, 29 per cent stated that they had already visited the museum, while 54 per cent said they intended to do so. Lastly, 97 per cent of interviewees found the exhibit consistent with the museum. As regards information sources on *Le siècle du Jazz* with this target, 82 per cent of respondents stated that they had heard about it: 18 per cent from someone they knew, 18 per cent from media coverage, and 13 per cent saw posters advertising the exhibit.

Summing up, the profile of interviewees in the second group proved quite different from visitors to the temporary exhibit. Specifically, this group was French, with few exceptions, and a greater number of people had already visited the museum before and intended to come back for other events. Consistent with findings regarding the first target, however, for these visitors word of mouth was also the main source of information on temporary exhibits.

Comparing the results of the two groups, quai Branly managers could note interesting differences relating to visitor/participant profiles and their intentions and habits. Specifically, the study revealed that more foreign visitors went to the temporary exhibit (18% versus 8%) and a vast majority came to the museum for the sole purpose of visiting the *Le siècle du Jazz* exhibit (89%). Only a small number of visitors decided later to see the rest of the museum (70% said they wouldn't) or had already done so in the past (28% in the previous 12 months). On the contrary, participants in activities based on the jazz theme were more open to temporary exhibits (85% had visited more than one exhibit, or planned to do so) and tended to know more about the museum (48% had already visited during the previous year). Some findings were similar for the two targets: the perception that the museum's image was well-aligned with the exhibit, and the main information source (both groups cited word of mouth).

Summing up the strategic implications, temporary exhibits successfully draw in new visitors to the museum, giving them the chance to experience the other collections and activities, and encouraging them to come back again.

Appendix: The questionnaire

THE JAZZ CENTURY

- DATE DE L'INTERVIEW: |___|___|
  |___|___| 2009
  (9–12)

- HEURE DE L'INTERVIEW: |___|___| H
  |___|___| MN
  (13–16)

- NOM DE L'ENQUÊTEUR:
  _____ (17–18)

Good morning/afternoon Madam Miss/Sir. I work for the market research company TEST, which has been commissioned by the quai Branly museum to carry out a survey with the museum's visitors. Would you mind taking a few minutes to give us your opinion on the visit of the exhibition "The Jazz century" you've just made?

0. Are you definitively leaving this exhibition for today or do you plan to come back before closing time?

- Will not come back 1
- Will come back .... 2 → *Stop interview*

1. In which country do you live? *ENQ. : coder à partie de la carte pays*

Country code: I_____I   (19–20)

1b. – If France, write down the department: I____I____I____I   (21–23)

– If Paris: specify the last two figures of the zip code: I____I____I   (24–25)

2. Have you ever visited the quai Branly museum before today?

- No, it is my first visit 1   (26)
- Yes, I have within the last 12 months 2
  ↳ How many times ? I_____I times   (27–29)
- Yes, I have, but my last visit was previous to 2008 3
  ↳ How many times ? I_____I times   (30–32)

3. At what time did you begin your visit to the 'Jazz Century' exhibit?

I___I___I H I___I___I MN   (33–36)

4. Today, did you visit the quai Branly museum… *(Plusieurs réponses possibles)*

- Alone... 1   (37–41)
- With your husband/wife or partner 2
- With (your) children/grandchildren 3
- With other family members 4
- With friends 5
- With other acquaintances 6

5. How did you hear of this temporary exhibit 'The Jazz Century'?

ENQ : Question ouverte – plusieurs réponses possibles – bien relancer.
ENQ : Inviter l'interviewé à être le plus précis possible
→ Ex : si l'interviewé dit par la presse. Faire préciser par quel journal/magazine…
Si l'interviewé dit par la radio : faire préciser la station et l'émission…
Si l'interviewé dit par des affiches : faire préciser où étaient les affiches…

(42-49)

6. When you came to the quai Branly museum today, what were you intending to do?
ENQ : **Ne rien suggérer – plusieurs réponses possibles**

(50–59)

- To visit the temporary exhibit 'The Jazz century' 01
- To visit the temporary exhibit Mangareva – Panthéon de Polynésie... 02
- To visit the temporary exhibit Recette des Dieux – esthétique du fétiche...................................... 03
- To visit the temporary exhibit Planète métisse 04
- To see or see again the museum's permanent collections 05
- To see a movie.. 06

Specify the title : ↳ _____   (60–61)

- To attend a show 07

Specify the title : ↳ _____   (62–63)

- To attend a conference 08

Specify the title : ↳ _____   (64–65)

- To attend a lecture 09
- To study/do research in the mediathèque 10
- To spend time in the Jacques Kerchache reading room: relaxation, personal work...................... 11
- To spend time in the Jacques Kerchache reading room:
  event organized by the reading room 12

Specify the title: ↳ _____   (66–67)

- To take part in the festive event "A week in New Orleans" 13
- To attend a commentated visit or a workshop 14

7. And what did you see or do?	I did it before visiting "The Jazz Century"	I plan on doing it after visiting "The Jazz Century"	Exhibition only (nothing before nothing after)	
Visited the exhibition Mangareva – Panthéon de Polynésie	1	2	3	(68)
Visited the exhibition Recette des Dieux – esthétique du fétiche	1	2	3	(69)
Visited the exhibition Planète métisse	1	2	3	(70)
Saw or saw again the museum permanent collections	1	2	3	(71)
Saw a movie : _____ (73–74)	1	2	3	(72)
Attended a show : _____ (76–77)	1	2	3	(75)
Attended a conference : _____ (79–80)	1	2	3	(78)

Attended a lecture	1	2	3	(81)
Studied/did research in the mediatheque	1	2	3	(82)
Spent time in the Jacques Kerchache reading room: relaxation, personal work	1	2	3	(83)
Spent time in the Jacques Kerchache reading room: event organized by the reading room: _____ (85–86)	1	2	3	(84)
Took part in the festive event "A week in New Orleans"	1	2	3	(88)
Attended a guided visit or a workshop	1	2	3	(88)

8. In your view, does an exhibit like 'The Jazz century' belong in the quai Branly museum?

- Yes 1   (89)

- No 2

9. Why?

(90–97)

10. Before your visit what were you expecting to see in this exhibition?

(98–107)

11. We are now going to talk about the topics discussed during this exhibition. For each of them I will ask you to tell me if before your visit you considered yourself:

- **Little familiar with the subject → code 1**
- **Interested, but not very informed → code 2**
- **Well informed → code 3**
- **Expert → code 4**

	Expertise	Si codes 2, 3 ou 4 : In what current/movement/style are you particularly interested? **ENQ : Question ouverte**	Si codes 2, 3 ou 4 : Which practices do you have to satisfy this interest? **ENQ : Question ouverte**
Music	(108)	(109–111)	(112–114)
Cinema	(115)	(116–118)	(119–121)
Painting	(122)	(123–125)	(126–128)

12. You've just finished your visit to this exhibition. Would you say that you are... [1]

- Very satisfied.. 1   (129)
- Quite satisfied... 2
- Not very satisfied 3
- Not satisfied at all 4

13. The general intention/thread of 'The Jazz Century' exhibit is to reveal the signs of the influence of jazz on other fields (painting, photography, cinema, literature, graphic arts) throughout its history.

You've just finished your visit to this exhibition. Would you say that the thread of this exhibition...

Doesn't appear clearly through the works displayed/is confused 2	Appears clearly through the works displayed/is clear 1	(130)
Is convincing 1	Is a little convincing 2	(131)

14. And more precisely, how do you judge...

	Very good	Good	Average	Bad	
The visit's **circuit**/the **order** in which the works are displayed	1	2	3	4	(132)
The ease of **circulating** in the rooms, the fluidity	1	2	3	4	(133)
The **information** available in the rooms (texts on the walls, labels next to the works	1	2	3	4	(134)
The **choice of the paintings** displayed	1	2	3	4	(135)
The **lighting** and the **way the paintings are displayed**	1	2	3	4	(136)
The **choice of the music** broadcast	1	2	3	4	(137)
The **sound quality** of the music broadcast	1	2	3	4	(138)
The **choice of the objects** displayed (record sleeves, posters...)	1	2	3	4	(139)
The **lighting** and the **way the objects are displayed**	1	2	3	4	(140)
The **choice of the movies** projected	1	2	3	4	(141)
The **conditions of comfort** for watching the movies	1	2	3	4	(142)
The **quality of the soundtracks** of the movies	1	2	3	4	(143)
The **welcome in the exhibit rooms**	1	2	3	4	(144)
If you followed a guided visit: Quality of the **guided visit**	1	2	3	4	(145)

15. According to you, what are the **3 strengths** of this exhibition?

    1. /_____/   (146–147)

    2. /_____/   (148–149)

    3. /_____/   (150–151)

16. According to you, what are the **3 weaknesses** of this exhibition?

1. /_____/   (152–153)

2. /_____/   (154–155)

3. /_____/   (156–157)

17. Do you know that the quai Branly museum organizes different events related to the 'Jazz Century' exhibition?

- Yes 1   (158)

- No 2

18. Si Oui en Q17 :

Could you please name the events you've heard of?
Do you intend to take part in any of those events?
ENQ : ne rien suggérer – plusieurs réponses possibles
ENQ : Demander le titre précis de chaque manifestation citée

Title of the event	I took part in it	I intend to take part in it	I don't intend to take part in it	
_____(158-159)	1	2	3	(161)
_____(161-162)	1	2	3	(164)
_____(164-165)	1	2	3	(167)
_____(167-168)	1	2	3	(170)
_____(170-171)	1	2	3	(173)
_____(173-174)	1	2	3	(176)

19. Finally, do you intend to ... (177–181)

	Yes	No
Recommend this exhibition to someone in your circle of acquaintances	1	2
Visit this exhibition again	1	2
Come back to the quai Branly museum to take part in an event related to this exhibition	1	2
Come back to the quai Branly museum to visit another temporary exhibit	1	2
Come back to the quai Branly museum to visit the permanent collections	1	2

20. How old are you?

|___|___| years old   (182–183)

21. What is your occupation?

- Pupil (secondary school or high school) 01 (184–185)
- Student (tertiary level, college, or graduate student) 02
- Artist 03
- Teacher in primary school 04
- Teacher in secondary school or high school 05
- University professor 06
- Upper management, senior level executive 07
- Freelance worker/professional (doctor, lawyer, dentist) 08
- Craftsman/storekeeper/head of company 09
- Middle management, executive 10
- Employee/worker 11
- Retired 12
- Looking for a job 13
- Other unemployed 14
- Other *(specify)*: _____ 15 (186–187)

22. Si Actif : Is your occupation related to…

	Yes	No	
Music	1	2	(188)
Cinema	1	2	(189)
Plastic arts – heritage	1	2	(190)

23. Si vous êtes étudiant : Are your studies related to…

	Yes	No	
Music	1	2	(191)
Cinema	1	2	(192)
Plastic arts – heritage	1	2	(193)

24. ENQ. : *Write in the gender:*

- Male 1 (194)
- Female 2

THANK YOU FOR HAVING SPENT TIME ANSWERING OUR QUESTIONNAIRE.

REVIEW QUESTIONS

1. Musée du quai Branly relies on a rich system of marketing research to take strategic and tactical decisions. How do these studies interconnect? Why are some considered strategic and others more tactical?

2. *Le siècle du Jazz* temporary exhibition was organized with the objective to attract a new audience to the museum. What characteristics of the exhibition would make it possible to achieve this objective? Were they effective?

3. The museum management opted for research design with different methodologies to investigate two targets: traditional museum visitors and new ones. Was this choice appropriate? And was it effective?

Part III

CUSTOMER VALUE CREATION

Chapter 7

IDENTIFYING TARGET MARKETS AND CREATING VALUE PROPOSITIONS

LEARNING OBJECTIVES

After reading this chapter you should be able to:

- Define a market, identify the stages of its lifecycle, and measure its current size and its potential.
- Segment a market and profile the customers belonging to each segment.
- Assess the attractiveness of market segments and choose a targeting strategy accordingly.
- Identify the components of a value proposition and design a proposition able to meet customer expectations.
- Build a positioning for a value proposition.

OVERVIEW

The process of value analysis generates market knowledge that provides a solid foundation for value creation. The end result of this latter process is a series of value propositions capable of satisfying customer expectations. To achieve this, the organization faces two critical choices: what type of customers it wants to serve, and how to match value propositions to expectations in order to win customer preference. The first choice leads to identifying target markets; the second, to creating value propositions with a strong market positioning. Both indelibly inform the role that the organization plays in its markets. In this chapter, I'll address two topics underlying these choices: how to choose a target market, and how to create value propositions that customers prefer over the competition.

The choice of target market calls for decision making on several levels because a market can be defined in various ways. More importantly, it can be broken down into sub-markets that have similarities and dissimilarities. As we'll discuss in this chapter, the first step on the decision-making path is to delineate the boundaries of the market in question, which allows the organization to estimate both its current size and its potential. With market estimates in hand, it's also possible to comprehend and measure the organization's 'weight' in the market compared to its competitors, and use this information to set market objectives: to tap into latent market potential, to grow in the current market, or to pursue the most courageous and risk-laden strategy: to create an entirely new market.

After the market has been mapped out, it can be broken down into homogeneous groups of customers, also known as market segments. Next the attractiveness of each segment is evaluated to determine which ones can be served sustainably, both in productive and financial terms. This path ends with the organization choosing its target segments and staking out its operative and competitive field of action. But what's the point of choosing specific segments to serve? Why not operate in all segments, across the board? After all, the whole pie is bigger and more appetizing than a single slice. We'll explore the answer in this chapter.

Moving on, assuming that expectations differ from segment to segment, the choice of the number and type of segments to serve hinges on the question of personalizing the offering, a decision that involves investments and costs. If an organization wants to serve different segments, the only way to do so is to create diverse value propositions, which call for varying levels of effort and investment. At the other extreme, if the organization opts to offer a single value proposition, the decision-making process is greatly simplified and investments are drastically reduced, but the risk is that some customers won't find the offering attractive. So by clearly identifying segments and deciding which ones to serve, the subsequent choices as to the type and variety of value to offer will be more effective and efficient.

Creating value propositions is another process that involves multi-level decision making. In fact, every proposition can offer different attributes that serve to provide different benefits. So the design stage entails choosing the right combination of tangible and intangible attributes to satisfy the expectations of target customers. After design comes positioning, which calls for decisions pertaining to carving out market space that's separate from other organizations, to prompt customers to prefer a given value proposition over the competition. Figure 7.1 offers a detailed description of the pertinent decisions for identifying target markets and creating value propositions that we'll discuss in this chapter.

As I said before, the process of value creation consists of decisions that profoundly inform the position of the firm or non-profit in the markets where they operate, decisions that form the basis of *strategic marketing*. Why use 'strategic' to refer to these decisions? For two main reasons:

- They have *medium- to long-term effects*, dictating the organization's market position in the long run and

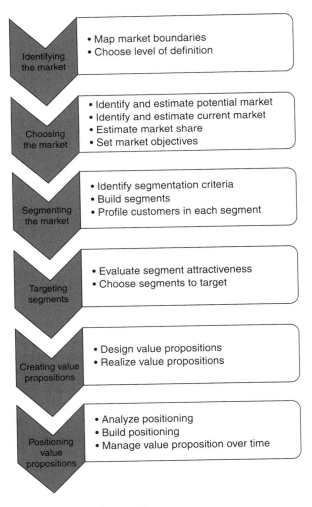

Figure 7.1 – Strategic marketing decisions in the value creation process

necessitating investments with returns that are not immediately evident, but that gradually materialize over time.

- They provide a frame of reference for *subsequent decisions* pertaining to what's called tactical or operative marketing; if strategic marketing decisions are ineffective or inaccurate, subsequent decisions will be too.

7.1 IDENTIFYING THE MARKET

A market can be defined from a variety of perspectives. A legal expert, a sociologist, and an economist all have diverse viewpoints, so they would probably come up with different definitions. However, as far as marketing is concerned, *a market consists in a) a set of actors who interact to exchange goods, services, reputation and information, b) the activities that form the basis for this interaction, and c) additional actors who exert their influence* through regulatory action (trade associations, supervisory committees, legislative bodies), infrastructure management (transportation, technology, communication, and so forth), and support for all of the above (providing services such as marketing research, consulting, sales, and others).

The focus of marketing is on the first set of actors, that is, both customers and the organizations that compete to win customer preference. And as far as defining the market, it's this viewpoint that to some extent shapes how companies and non-profits do so. But what's the purpose of defining the market? After all, don't all organizations know exactly what their market is? Admittedly, the exercise might seem purely academic, but let's think for a moment: What's Amazon's market? Online book sales, book sales in general, or online sales in general? And what about Amazon's sales territory? Or take another example, like Louis Vuitton: Is the market in this case clearly accessories? Or luxury goods? Or how about a publisher of children's books: Again, what's the market? Children's books? Publishing in general? Leisure for children? And who qualifies as 'children' anyway?

So clearly defining a market isn't the simple exercise it might initially appear to be. But still, some might say, it serves no practical purpose. Why should an organization bother to define the market it operates in? What's the point?

Actually, defining a market is a complex but necessary undertaking for all organizations. Why? Because

marketing decisions call for investments, and to ensure these investments are financially sustainable, the organization has to assess potential returns. Is it worthwhile for Amazon to build hundreds of thousands of square meters of new warehouse space in Finland? And how does Prada decide between two communication campaigns that use different vehicles and come with different costs? And as the children's book publisher (let's say it's located in Germany), is it worthwhile to buy the copyright on the German translation of a Spanish bestseller? How can these companies make similar decisions?

To do so, firms and non-profits need a set of market measurements to assess whether or not investments are potentially sustainable or even profitable. To get these metrics, first they have to define and demarcate the market they have in mind. Without this input, any assessment is based solely on instinct and chance, and the risk is that the final output will prove ineffective and inefficient.

So mapping the borders of a market is a critical task. What's more, it's also a highly complex one, because there are no objective boundary markers to use as reference points. The conclusion to be drawn here is that for any organization, *delimiting the confines of a market is a subjective exercise*, based on the assumptions of that organization, and the information it can access.

The children's book publisher mentioned above might define the market as the set of books for children sold in Germany a given year, according to a publishers' association bestseller list, but another domestic publisher might consider the set of books read by German 10- to 14-year-olds. Which means the first publisher wouldn't include a title like Kafka's *Metamorphosis* in its market, but the second publisher would. Neither one of these firms is right; neither will come up with a 'better' parameter than the other. They probably simply have different objectives, so they base their perspective on diverse assumptions and information.

The standard method for defining a market is to consider *sales of certain product categories*. So there are markets for lighting fixtures, men's trousers, sports sponsorships, and product placements in movies. But this definition is shaped by the traditional product orientation, which should be avoided by organizations seeking to satisfy their customers (Chapter 2). If in fact the market is defined in terms of product categories, the risk is neglecting products that offer similar benefits, in other words, items which consumers consider product substitutes. The final outcome is an extremely narrow view of the market.

Since products are the building blocks of value propositions that serve to provide benefits to customers, the definition of a market should start here – with benefits – in keeping with a more market-oriented approach. So there's a market for free time, which breaks down into free time on weekdays, or on weekends, or on vacation. Competing in the first two subdivisions are product categories such as cinema, TV, theater, and sport; the third one would include tourist destinations, training courses, and volunteer activities. But there's a risk here too, albeit the opposite of the previous approach: generating a vision of the market that's too broad, that encompasses products and competitors that vary too much.

Summing up, then, a market can be represented as a system of different-sized concentric spheres, structured in such a way that at the outer fringes there are single product sub-categories and more broadly defined needs, and inside there are other possible ways to group together categories of products and the benefits that customers seek. Moving from a single product to a need means shifting from a product orientation to a market orientation. For the organization, the choice of approach is subjective and depends on its specific objectives.

7.2   THE MARKET LIFECYCLE

As far as mapping out a market and measuring its size, the ability to do so accurately is highly contingent on the *evolutionary stage* of that market. It stands to reason that a new or emerging market would be terribly difficult to delineate because it takes time for the supply–demand dynamic to give this market its shape. On the opposite end of the evolutionary spectrum, it's easy to mark out a mature market because the factors that drive evolution are already evident, and can be observed with greater precision.

A classic marketing concept is *market lifecycle*. (The lifecycle concept also refers to products, as described in Section 8.1.2.) This relates to different stages in the life of a market based on a time unit (weeks, months, or more often years) and the supply-demand dynamic, that is, sales. The latter can be expressed in product units or values (taking into account fluctuations in

market price). There are normally four stages in the market lifecycle:

1. Introduction.
2. Growth.
3. Maturity.
4. Decline.

7.2.1   Introduction

Normally a new market emerges thanks to an innovation[1] that succeeds in satisfying benefits that were not previously addressed to the fullest, or transforming implicit benefits into explicit ones. In this stage sales are usually limited and sales growth is slow. There are only a few competitors (in some cases only the innovator who created the market) and not many more customers: the people who are more keenly aware of their unsatisfied needs and/or more sensitive to the shift from implicit to explicit benefits. The objective of competitors in the market creation stage is *customer education*, in other words disseminating knowledge about their value propositions.

This should set in motion further dissemination of knowledge and awareness of unsatisfied (or potentially satisfiable) benefits, spurring demand and accelerating sales growth. If this mechanism isn't triggered, the market will probably end up spending too much time stalling in the introduction stage, preventing competitors from making their market presence financially sustainable. As a result, most likely after a number of competitors abandon the market, it will languish in a long period of stagnation, or transition from introduction directly to decline.

7.2.2   Growth

If instead the dissemination mechanism is activated, the market begins to grow, sales rise to a peak, and then start to level off as the market reaches maturity. Growth is the result of the combined effect of new customers, who can take advantage of the experience and word of mouth of original customers, and new competitors who are prompted to enter the market thanks to growth opportunities. To carve out a market position, these new entrants will offer differentiated value propositions, activating new market segments. In this stage the objective of competitors is to follow market expansion, facilitating further dissemination of product knowledge and building a differential image that allows them to defend the market share they've won.

7.2.3   Maturity

The growth stage ends when the majority of potential customers have become buyers, and the market enters the maturity stage, when sales stabilize and sales growth by and large stops. Since potential customers are now actual customers, product purchases tend to be substitutions and entirely new customers are few.

Maturity for most markets is the longest stage, so sales may fluctuate somewhat due to changes in the macro-context. (An increase in a country's birth rate leads to a large new generation of readers, for example.) A similar effect might be caused by an innovation launched by a competitor that reactivates new demand. An example here is the e-reader, which could lead to a new market growth spurt if this innovation prompts infrequent readers to read more, or so-called 'hot readers' to buy books in digital format, in addition to the hardcover or paperback.

The maturity stage of a market can last decades, even centuries (as with classical music or opera). To aid in decision making, organizations operating on mature markets find it useful to divide this stage into sub-phases, characterized by new periods of sales growth or temporary decline.

7.2.4   Decline

This stage occurs when market growth decelerates more and more rapidly, dropping to the levels of the introduction stage and dipping lower, even to the point of disappearing entirely. Decline in this context is mainly theoretical, because after expansion and contraction, along with competitors relaunching and revitalizing their products, very rarely does a market actually reach this stage. This is particularly applicable for creative industries, where products supply hedonic, communicative, and ethical value, which relate to benefits that people rarely fully satisfy. If they do, and they no longer have any need or desire for the products sold on this market, they'll have no more motivation to buy (any product at all, not just certain products).[2] The history of movie theater attendance in Europe from the 1950s through 2012 is one example. At the end of the 1950s and through the 1960s and 1970s in most countries attendance dropped so dramatically due to the advent of television that one could advance the hypothesis of the decline of the cinema. However, some innovations introduced in the 1980s have brought about a new growth stage that has been in effect since the 1990s.

If we just focus on this time period the cinema appears to be a market with a bright future.

It's safe to assume that the objective of competitors in this stage is to avoid allowing the market to slip into decline. If in fact their market disappears, either they'll do the same, or they'll have to move into other markets and stake out new competitive territory.

7.2.5   The relationships between market lifecycles and product lifecycles

Throughout a market's lifecycle, evolution is driven by the dynamic relationships between customers and producers, along with variables inherent to the macro-context (Section 4.2.2.1). Factors such as technological developments, demographic changes, and new norms and regulations can impact market evolution significantly, determining how long any given stage lasts with respect to the others.

As for market variables shaping evolution, the *imitation-differentiation dynamic* is key. The market expands as long as there are new customers who imitate their predecessors while differentiating themselves in some way; likewise with competitors, new entrants have to imitate but also try to innovate with respect to incumbents.

When this dynamic slows down, the market shifts into a stage of stability: imitation takes precedence over differentiation; customers come to expect similar benefits; and competitors differentiate less and resemble one another more, which doesn't give customers much motivation to prefer one over the other. At this point, if market segments express different needs and desires and some competitors launch value propositions designed to satisfy them, this reignites the dynamic and a new growth stage begins. As a result the actual configurations of the various market lifecycles (the shape of the curves) can differ a great deal depending on these dynamics. Now, since the imitation-differentiation cycle materializes when competitors launch different value propositions on the market, and since the basis of these propositions is the product, the lifecycle of a market encompasses the lifecycles of the products sold there (Section 8.1.2).

Typically a market is born from an innovation that takes the form of a new product and then the resulting competitive dynamic pushes this market toward a greater variety of products. So in a sense the market is 'supported' over time by systematic new product launches, some of which might be so innovative they capture sales from other products. For example, many believe that digital music will be the death of recorded music, or that e-books will lead to the extinction of printed books. Even if this weren't the case, for some customers the two types of products substitute one another, so clearly more sales of one mean less of the other. Extrapolating from this consideration, the life-cycle of one product impacts the lifecycle of the other, even though overall sales appear stable, or may even seem to rise, when looking at the market as a whole. The product lifecycle is a model used to make various product-related decisions, a topic I'll delve into further in Chapter 8.

7.3 THE POTENTIAL MARKET, THE CURRENT MARKET, AND THE MARKET POTENTIAL GAP

Defining a market and pinpointing the stages in its lifecycle are prerequisites to measuring its size. And it's this measurement that enables an organization to make a number of marketing decisions and subsequently to assess their effectiveness. Without objective criteria for setting the boundaries of a market, the organization can do no more than estimate its size on the basis of subjective assumptions and available information.

But what is it that the organization has to estimate? Simply the size of the current market? The answer is no, at least not always. To make certain decisions (to change specific features in the value proposition, for instance), it's enough to gauge the dimensions of the current market. For others (creating a whole new value proposition), it's necessary to take a broader perspective, and estimate the potential market. So depending on the decision it's facing, the organization has to make different estimates, and these estimates relate to different interpretations of the concept of 'market'.

7.3.1 The potential market

Market potential consists of the *maximum sales level attainable in the market, in a specific time and place, and under specific macro-environmental conditions*. In other words, it's the level of demand that would result if all customers who had the need/desire were to buy and use the maximum number of products that they could.

For example, the market potential for non-academic publishing in certain countries equals all the books that could be sold if all the people who knew how to read were to purchase and consume the maximum number of books they could possibly read in a year (excluding textbooks).

Here is the mathematical formula for market potential at time t:[3]

$$MktPot_t = N_{max_t} \times Q_{max_t}$$

where $N_{max\ t}$ is the maximum number of purchasing units for the products on the market at time t, and $Q_{max\ t}$ is the maximum quantity that can be bought by single purchasing units (individuals or families in consumer markets, or firms, local administrative bodies, or institutions in business markets).

One way to understand potential market is as the capacity of the market to absorb relative product categories over a certain period of time, so in a sense it's an expression of the degree of possible saturation. This interpretation helps underscore a vital aspect of defining potential market, one that also holds true when defining a market: it's *relative*, not absolute. In fact, potential can take on vastly different configurations, depending on the definition of the market (the various levels illustrated in Section 7.1), the breakdown of the context/market (by segment, distribution channel, usage occasion, and so forth) and the time horizon (multiple years, one year, months, weeks, or days).

Let's consider the potential market for movies playing in the cinemas in a certain city. Different ways to define the market are by the 'film in the cinemas' product, or by the need to spend free time in a satisfying way (competing with other cultural or artistic pastimes, or sports activities). Depending on which definition is applied, this potential takes on entirely different configurations: from the number of tickets that could be sold in the city's cinemas to all the purchases residents could make on ways to spend their free time. The definition of the market could go even further and consider not only films distributed at the cinema, but alternative distribution formats as well (DVDs, television, Internet downloads). That would yield yet another configuration for potential. In light of all this, an organization should always consider – and measure – the potential of a market by clearly establishing certain basic assumptions, keeping in mind that if these change, potential changes too.

A fairly reasonable assumption underpinning every measure of potential is that *present market potential is not dependent on the investments and marketing decisions made by organizations competing on that market*, while future market potential can very well be. In other words, in the short term the maximum quantity of products that customers in a market can purchase is determined by objective context conditions. These include the laws that regulate trade, the general economic situation at a national and international level, the level of technology use among companies and customers, and the size of the population of individuals or organizations in the market. (So the number of consumers who make up the market today is certain, but what that number will be tomorrow is unknown.)

Instead, it's easy to see that in the future, organizations that operate in the market (together with any new entrants) can modify some of these conditions, and consequently enhance or diminish the potential of that market. This happens, for instance, when companies hire lobbyists to encourage lawmakers to pass favorable legislation for product sales, or when organizations launch new technologies permitting market access to new customers, or when all competitors join forces in customer education initiatives.

What becomes clear from this discussion is why the potential of a market at time t is represented as an asymptote with respect to the x-axis in the graph that plots sales against marketing investments of competing organizations.

7.3.2 The current market

The current market (also known as the actual market, market demand, or primary demand) is the *sum of all products purchased in the market during a given unit of time* (which here too can be years, months, weeks, and so on). This corresponds to the total sales of all the organizations that operate on that market. The mathematical formula for the current market is:

$$Mkt_t = \sum_{n=1}^{n} q_{i_t}$$

where q_{it} represents sales of organization i operating in the market at time t, and n the number of organizations.

Unlike market potential, the current market is a function of the marketing investments made by organizations. In fact, if these organizations launch new products, modify their prices, run communication campaigns, or expand distribution, there's a very good chance that their sales will increase and their current market will grow. This applies for the market as a whole as well as for purchases of the products offered by the individual organizations that actually make investments, which constitute a portion of the overall market. Figure 7.2 shows the relationships between potential market, current market, and the market of an individual organization.

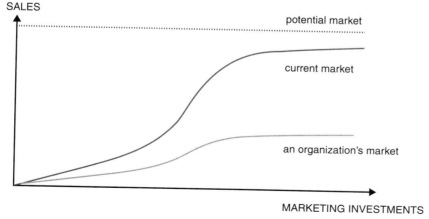

Figure 7.2 – Potential market, current market, and an organization's market

7.3.3   Market potential gap

Integrating all three concepts gives rise to a new one, which proves essential for making marketing decisions: the market potential gap. This represents the portion of the market that isn't satisfied by individual organizations. Analytically, the gap looks like this:

$$PotGap_t = MktPot_t - q_{i_t}$$

where q_{it} expresses the sales of organization i^4 at time t.

So the gap concept highlights the maneuvering room that each organization can exploit to meet a portion of the demand that isn't yet satisfied. There are four types of market gaps:

- The *non-usage gap* derives from the existence of a number of potential users (as opposed to current users) of certain products, among those sold on the market. With the reading market, the non-usage gap would be the quantity of books that are not read by people who read no books at all during the time unit in question, despite having no impediments preventing them from doing so. In other words, this gap is the number of books non-users could read if they chose to do so.
- The *usage gap* relates to the fact that consumers use the product only on certain occasions, rather than on all possible occasions. Continuing with readers, for people who only read when they're on vacation, the usage gap would include the quantity of books they don't read during other times of the year. So the usage gap in this case is the difference between the number of books they read in the summer, and the number they could read if chose to read all year round.
- The *light usage gap* is due to a reduced quantity of the product used in single use occasions (naturally if product use is divisible). Again with reading, this refers to the quantity of books that are not read by people who do read regularly, but only a few pages at each sitting, so they actually only finish a few books during the timeframe under consideration. In other words, this is the difference between the number of books they currently finish, only reading a few pages at a time, and the number they could finish if they read more pages every time they picked up a book.
- The *competitive gap* equates to the difference between the total current market and the organization's market, and is made up of the portion of the market satisfied by competing organizations through their products.

Every one of these gaps between the potential and actual market may be caused by other types of gaps linked to various components of the value propositions offered by the organizations that operate on the market:

- *Product gap*: when none of the products currently available on the market adequately satisfies demand.
- *Distribution gap*: when the product is difficult to access, via online or offline distribution channels.
- *Price gap*: when prices of all products are too high for a portion of the market.
- *Communication gap*: when there is little information on the product alternatives available on the market, which prevents consumers from purchasing.

The entire discussion up to this point has encompassed the market as a whole. But it's clear that to address its specific needs, an organization can measure the potential and current market as well as its own market at different levels: for example, according to geographic areas, market segments (Section 7.6), distribution channels, or even the market of a single customer or group of customers (typically in business markets).

7.3.4   Market estimates

Before measuring potential or current market, it's necessary to clarify the assumptions with regard to the relevant boundaries, levels, and time units. The next step is to take into consideration the specificities of the market in terms of its constituent customers, differentiating between consumer markets and business markets. In fact, purchase and use processes for consumers (Chapter 4) differ from those of corporate clients (Chapter 5), in terms of timing on repeat purchases and processes for extracting value. As a result, the formulas for estimating these markets differ as well.

7.3.4.1   *Estimating market potential*

This is the formula for estimating the market potential for *consumer nondurable goods*:

$$MktPot_t = N_{max_t} \times F_{max_t} \times Q_{max_t}$$

where $N_{max\ t}$ stands for the maximum number of customers who could purchase market products in the unit of time in question, having no objective impediment to product purchase or use ('objective' meaning physical, technical, technological, so basically anything independent of organizational decisions). With reading, to refer back to the previous example, an objective impediment might be a lack of fluency in German, say, preventing a person from being able to read a book written in that language, or serious visual defects that make reading impossible, or illiteracy. When calculating $N_{max\,t}$ the normal procedure is to consider people who live in the area where the potential market is being measured (a country, region, city, and so forth).

The indicator $F_{max\,t}$ refers to the *maximum frequency of purchase or use* of the product during the time unit in question. This frequency is linked to various product usage occasions. Q_{maxt} indicates the maximum quantity of product that can be used in every usage occasion, if this quantity is divisible: with reading, this might be the number of pages that can be read every time a person opens a book, which would be a function of the time she dedicates to reading.

When calculating potential market, especially if the objective is to reveal possible gaps, the recommended method is to utilize the maximum measurements for each parameter. That said, it's up to the analyst to take a prudent approach to estimating parameters if they deviate too far from reality. But by the same token, using the actual situation as a starting point runs the risk of generating a projection for the potential market that resembles the current market too closely, reducing the informational scope of the very concept of potential. An example will help clarify this point.

Imagine having to estimate the potential market for newspaper reading in a medium-sized European country in 2015, with reference to dailies published in the native language of that country, expressed in volume (that is, number of copies). Here are the necessary parameters:[5]

- The number of residents in the country in 2015 who don't have any impediments that prevent them from reading. That excludes children who don't know how to read, people who are visually impaired, or anyone who doesn't know the language. Let's say that the number of residents is 40 million, and the people who don't have any of the impediments listed above number 30 million.
- The maximum frequency. Assuming that newspapers are published on a daily basis, this would coincide with the number of days in the year (365).

- The maximum quantity. Based on people's free time, and considering a certain level of saturation that prevents them from reading more than a certain number of newspapers in a day, a reasonable maximum is two a day (naturally to be corroborated with relevant data).

Now comes the following calculation:

$$MktPot_{2015} = 30\,ml \times 365 \times 2$$
$$= 21,900,000,000\,copies\,read$$

Adopting a more cautious perspective, in light of the fact that a family is made up of more than one member, it's safe to assume that they all read the same newspaper. So rather than consider individuals, family units should be used, which would sharply reduce N_t. But a counterpoint to this argument might be that all the members of the same family don't necessarily read the same paper, so an estimate is needed of how many families read the same paper and how many read different papers. What's more, although people can read a paper a day, there will probably be some days when they don't have the time, so the frequency would decrease. And last, while it's true that there's the potential for reading two papers a day, for a number of reasons relating to culture and values it's more reasonable to assume that people would only read two newspapers on certain days, but not every day of the year.

So now let's say that there are 10 million family units (with more than one member or singles); a reasonable number of days that people dedicate to reading the newspaper is 250; people read two newspapers a day when they're on vacation, so that might be 30 days a year, for example. The calculation based on these new parameters would be:

$$MktPot_{2015} = 10\,ml \times [(220 \times 1) + (30 \times 2)]$$
$$= 2,800,000,000\,copies\,read$$

That's around one-tenth of the previous estimate.

Our discussion up to this point has centered on consumer nondurables that provide value with a single use. But it's essential not to forget *consumer durable goods and services* that provide value over time through repeated use experiences. Examples are videogames, e-readers, works of art, clothing, lighting fixtures, or residential property. For these products frequency of use or maximum quantities don't apply. Instead common sense dictates that each individual product category should be considered for its specificity.

The first general consideration has to do with the purchasing unit, whether it's better to consider individual consumers, family units, or some other more salient variable. It's reasonable to assume that for some durable goods such as e-readers or shoes, the purchasing unit can be the individual; for others like an HD television set, the family would make more sense. For still others, like a painting or photograph, the purchasing unit might refer to the number of rooms in a house.

The second general consideration is whether to take product units that are already in use, and separate out the ones that need to be substituted. In fact, if an individual or a family already has the product, they can't be factored into the potential market (if, obviously, there's no point in having more than one, as is often the case). The exception is if the product has to be replaced because it no longer functions, either in technical or communicative terms (a console that doesn't work properly or an article of clothing that's no longer in fashion).

The formula for this calculation is:

$$MktPot_t = N_{max_t} - U_{used_t} + U_{subs_t}$$

where $N_{max\ t}$ stands for the maximum number of potential buyers; $U_{used\ t}$ stands for the product units already in use at time t, which exclude their owners from the calculation of potential buyers; $U_{subs\ t}$ indicates the units that are nearing the end of their technical or communicative utility and will have to be replaced.

Regarding the *market of corporate clients*, there are two possible approaches. The first corresponds to the calculations used for consumer markets, as above, for example if corporate clients buy nondurable or durable creative products (for example, a newspaper subscription for the office or an e-reader for every employee). When business customers buy property rights on creative products (Chapter 5), they're considered investments. So it's more useful to estimate market potential in terms of value rather than volume. (Put another way, it's more relevant to gauge the potential of investments in product placements rather than the number of possible placements.)

Second, the organization needs to build the estimate as a *percentage of investments* made in all products for which creative products serve as production factors, or in communication vehicles for which creative products are used as communication factors. For example, to estimate the market potential of property rights on music to use as the soundtrack on a videogame, the first step is to estimate the investments needed to produce this videogame, and then the maximum percentage that can be earmarked for the soundtrack.

7.3.4.2   *Estimating the current market and the market potential gap*

To estimate the current market (that is, actual market demand), all the required parameters relate to actual customer habits as far as product purchase and use. Generally, for the variables in this calculation (consumption frequency, quantities consumed per usage occasion, technical product life), the market *average* applies.

So for nondurables, the formula is:

$$Mkt_t = N_t \times F_t \times Q_t$$

With the three indices referring to the number of actual customers, the average frequency of use, and the average quantity per usage occasion. With the markets for durables or business clients, the same principle holds and actual averages apply. Measuring the *market potential gap* means simply calculating the difference between potential and actual values, relative to all the parameters in the specific formulas. Figure 7.3 shows calculations for measuring the gap for the newspaper example above.

7.4   MARKET SHARE

The portion of the market served by a single organization is equal to its sales. The indicator most often utilized in marketing to estimate the weight of a company's sales on the market as a whole is *market share*, defined as the total sales of a company or institution expressed as a percentage of total market sales. The mathematical expression is:

$$MktShare_{i_t} = \frac{S_{i_t}}{S_{tot_t}}$$

where S_{i_t} stands for the sales of organization i at time t, and $S_{tot\ t}$ the total sales on the market in question, that is, the actual market. As with all the other market measurements and estimates, market share can also be expressed in volumes (units, cases, kilos) or value (euro, dollars, yen). The comparison between share

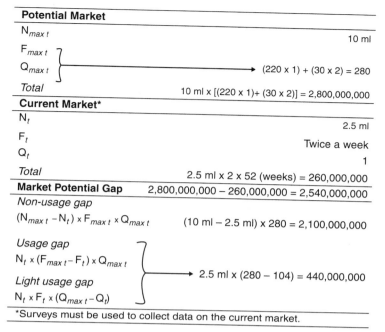

Figure 7.3 – An example of the calculation for the market potential gap

and value provides the organization with useful input for making pricing decisions. If the market share in volume is greater (or less) than the share in value, then the organization is selling its products at a lower (higher) price than the market average; if instead value equals volume in terms of market share, then pricing is in line with the market.

As with the previous parameters, market share measurement also always relates to a specific context (space and time). As we now know, defining the confines of a market is a highly subjective exercise.[6] This explains why, unless it's done by a third party, it's not uncommon to find several organizations claiming the title of market leader, or market shares that add up to more than 100 per cent.

7.4.1 Relative market share

Beyond absolute market share, another indicator used to represent the position of an organization with respect to its competitors is the relative market share, calculated as ratio of the market share of organization *i* over that of the largest competitor(s) (either the biggest on the market or the average of a benchmark group). Table 7.1 provides an example of the calculation for the relative market share for four multiplex

Table 7.1 – A relative market share calculation

	CITY 1	CITY 2
COMPANY 1	40	40
COMPANY 2	30	5
COMPANY 3	15	50
COMPANY 4	15	5
RELATIVE MARKET SHARE (COMPANY 1)	40/30 = 1.33	40/50 = 0.8

cinema chains competing in two large cities. (For simplicity's sake, we'll say that there are no other cinemas competing on the market.)

So let's take Company 1. In both markets it has 40 per cent of the market share. Looking no further, this company would come to the conclusion that it has a strong position, having secured nearly half of the two markets. But going on to analyze relative share, what becomes clear is that while Company 1 is the market leader in City 1, with a relative share of 1.33, this isn't the case in City 2, where with a relative share of 0.8 Company 1 ranks second after Company 3.

This shows that there are actually two different competitive positions.

7.4.2   Breaking down market share

Although market share is a very effective measure for giving an instant snapshot of an organization's position with respect to the competition, it's too superficial an indicator if the market is fragmented into several customer segments (geographic areas, distribution channels, and so forth, which we'll discuss further in Section 7.7). For example, imagine trying to analyze the market position of a publisher specialized in guidebooks. Simply measuring the company's share on the guidebook market would probably lead to overestimating its position. The reason is that a wide range of travel-related books are available which for some consumers may represent substitute products, even they don't provide the exact same benefits as guidebooks. On the other hand, considering the entire publishing market, the specificity of the company would generate a negligible share with respect to giant non-specialized publishers, and the end result would be underestimating the strength of its specialization.

Clearly, these factors reveal two different aspects of the competitive position of organizations. To capture them both simultaneously two additional indicators can be used, obtained by breaking down the market share: penetration rate (or simply penetration) and weighted coverage (or simply coverage). The *penetration rate* refers to the sales of the organization relative to the total purchases for the entire product category made by the organization's clients (defined as *purchases by served clients, P_{sc}*). *Weighted coverage* is the weight of purchases by the organization's clients relative to the total purchases in the product category. Multiplying these two factors yields market share:[7]

$$MktShare_{i_t} = \frac{S_{i_t}}{P_{sc_{i_t}}} \times \frac{P_{sc_{i_t}}}{S_{tot_t}}$$

The first factor is penetration, and the second weighted coverage.

Breaking down weighted coverage even further gives rise to two new factors:

- n_{i}, which represents the number of customers served by organization i.
- N_{t}, which indicates the total number of customers who purchase the product category.

So the resulting formula is:[8]

$$MktShare_{i_t} = \frac{S_{i_t}}{P_{sc_{i_t}}} \times \frac{P_{sc_{i_t}}}{n_{i_t}} \times \frac{n_{i_t}}{N_t} \times \frac{N_t}{S_{tot_t}}$$

The first index deriving from the calculation (Psc_{i_t}/n_{i_t}) represents the *average size of served customer purchases*; the second (n_i/N_t) is the *numerical coverage*, in other words, the percentage of customers served by the organization relative to the total number of customers in the market; the third (N_t/S_{tot_t}) is called the *dispersion index*, the reciprocal of the average size of market customer purchases, basically expressing the average market customer size. This can be compared to the average size of served customers to ascertain whether the organization sells to customers who are bigger or smaller than the market average.

Table 7.2 provides a fictitious example of cinemas and a breakdown of market share in 2015 for a average-sized movie distributor; calculations are made in value.

Table 7.2 – A breakdown of market share

Company sales (S_i)	100 ml/€
Total sales on the market (S_tot)	800 ml/€
Market share (MktShare)	100 ml/800 ml = 12.5%
Purchases of cinemas served (P_sci)	500 ml/€
Number of cinemas served (n_i)	2400
Total number of cinemas (N)	4000
Penetration (S_i/P_sci)	100 ml/500 ml = 20%
Weighted coverage (P_sci/S_tot)	500 ml/800 ml = 62.5%
Average size of cinemas served (P_sci/n_i)	500 ml/2400 = 208,300 €
Numerical coverage (n_i/N)	2400/4000 = 60%
Dispersion index (N/S_tot)	4000/800 ml = 0.0005%
Average cinema size (S_tot/N)	800 ml/4000 = 200,000 €

In the example, the company's market share is 12.5 per cent, corresponding to a 20 per cent penetration and weighted coverage of 62.5 per cent. Underlying this percentage is a numerical coverage of 60 per cent and an average size of cinemas served that's in line with the market average. So, as we'll explore further in Section 7.5.1, if a firm wants to boost its market share (and if it doesn't have any other information), increasing penetration looks like a good choice, so the distributor could try to convince the cinemas it already serves to show more of its movies, rather than competitors' films. Also, since the weighted coverage is high but there is room for expansion, increasing the numerical coverage also appears to be a promising strategy. For the distributor this means selling its movies to more cinemas.

7.5   CHOOSING THE MARKET AND SETTING MARKET OBJECTIVES

Delineating the boundaries of the market and drawing a distinction between the current and potential market are tasks that lay the groundwork for one of the most critical strategic marketing decisions for an organization: choosing the market where it wants to offer its value propositions.

In keeping with the marketing model described in this book, the prerequisite for creating value is identifying customers by their key descriptors through the value analysis process, and then selecting them during the value creation stage.

The organization can concentrate its efforts on:

- The current market.
- The potential market.
- An entirely new market.

The decision to focus on the current market basically equates to creating value for existing customers, whose expectations are explicit and well known to the organization. To do so it is essential to follow the evolution of customer expectations and strive to provide value propositions that respond to these changes, and that customers perceive as different from competitors' offerings.

On the other hand, focusing on the potential market for the organization implies activating a market that hasn't completely materialized, one where there are gaps with respect to the current market. The potential market consists of customers who use only a few products (if any at all). So the organization has to gain

a thorough understanding of the expectations of these customers, and will probably need to create different value propositions with respect to current offerings, or find different ways to deliver these new propositions.

Lastly, deciding to focus on a new market is the most innovative, courageous, and risky choice. Here the organization actually creates a market that has never existed before. Customers' value expectations are implicit, for the most part, so the challenge lies first in understanding and then satisfying them. What's more, often even identifying potential customers proves problematic because, with needs that aren't explicit, these customers are hard to 'see' and win over.

Here are some examples. Cirque du Soleil is unanimously recognized for having creating a new market through a new product category, blurring the confines between a circus and a musical. Disney is credited with founding the first ever theme park – Disneyland – in Anaheim, California in 1955. Universal Studios opened the first movie studio theme park in Hollywood in 1963. What do all these groundbreaking initiatives have in common, and what makes them different from the followers who launched similar shows or amusement parks on the market?

The difference lies in their strategic approach to the market. Cirque du Soleil, Disney, and Universal Studios have taken a risk and created new markets through innovation that has emerged unexpressed needs and desires. This is called a *market-driving* approach. On the other hand, entering an established market or deciding to focus on the current market equates to a *market-driven* approach, letting the market serve as a guide for organizational decisions. In other words, the organization formulates the value proposition to offer to the market by analyzing needs expressed (more or less ambiguously) by current and potential customers. But the questions are how to decide which strategic approach to adopt, which markets to focus on, and where to offer value propositions.

Obviously there are several things to consider, but the market lifecycle model helps find the answers. During the *introduction* stage, the market potential gap is sizeable. Many potential customers have yet to make their first purchases, and there are only a few organizations offering products. This stage is when the most interesting opportunities can be found in the potential market as opposed to the current one, which is still small. In fact, the current market may be so small that if competitors were to focus exclusively on present customers, they'd be battling over negligible sales, and this would probably prevent the market from progressing to the next stage.

As for the *growth* stage, the current market is now reaching a size that makes it attractive for organizations that compete here, but the market potential gap is still interesting enough to warrant ad hoc strategies. This is the time to pursue a dual strategy, centering in part on activating the potential market with specially developed value propositions, and in part consolidating relationships within the current market via propositions that follow the evolution of customer expectations.

The *maturity* stage sees a shrinking market potential gap, so at this point organizations have to secure a strong competitive position and a solid base of loyal customers who guarantee stable sales. This means systematically refining current value propositions, and at the same time attempting to create innovative ones to trigger a new growth stage. But under these market conditions, the biggest growth opportunities are probably not inside the market. So this is the time when the organization should consider investing in creating a whole new market, with an innovative value proposition that can serve as the launch pad for a new lifecycle.

In choosing a market as the focus of its value creation efforts, an organization needs to formulate marketing strategies and set strategic objectives. Since the configurations of current, potential, and new markets differ, so do the strategies that are best suited to each one.

7.5.1   Growing in the current market

Organizations that choose to focus on this market concentrate on current customers and competitors. To stake out growth paths here, the concept of market share and its constituent components is a useful tool. At any given moment, an organization has a certain market share, so logically the remainder of the market is served by its competitors (we've called this the competitive gap). If an organization's objective is to grow in its current market, it aims to appropriate market share from its competitors to expand its own (unless the market is still growing at a rate that allows all competitors to grow while maintaining respective market shares).

Two market objectives enable organizations to boost market share: increasing penetration or expanding coverage (or, obviously, a combination of the two). *Increasing penetration* is the right choice when the organization covers a sufficient slice of the market, but the customers it

serves only source the organization for a limited portion of their purchases. In this case, the focus should center on served customers, attempting to understand what conditions would prompt them to buy more, and then revamping the value proposition accordingly.

So for a performing arts institution or a sports club, this equates to turning occasional spectators into season ticket holders. To achieve this aim, these organizations could modify components of the value proposition, for instance making it more affordable by discounting tickets, or more accessible by creating 'fast track' entrances to venues. A nature reserve, however, might decide to design a network of walking trails that encourage visitors to come again, exploring a new path each time. Or a shoe manufacturer could create a loyalty card that gives customers discounts once they've purchased, say, ten pairs.

Expanding weighted coverage is a winning move when high penetration doesn't allow for much room to grow, but coverage does. Organizations can pursue this strategy by upping numerical coverage (selling their products to more customers) or augmenting the average size of their customers, as compared to the market average. Increasing the weighted coverage shifts the focus onto people who are not currently customers. Often this involves revising the product component of the value proposition, making it more attractive for people who buy from the competition, or changing up distribution, making it easier to reach a broader portion of the market, and offering better logistics and distribution services.

For example, an architecture studio that wants to increase its weighted coverage might invest in communication to enhance awareness among customers on the market. A design company could focus on improving delivery time for large retailers, whose priority is optimal warehouse management.

7.5.2   Activating the potential market

When organizations opt to focus on the potential market, their implicit objective is to reduce the market potential gap. Their initial efforts should center on gleaning knowledge to get a grasp of the causes behind the gap. Is it because there are many potential customers who don't buy any products on the market (nonusage gap)? Or because customers don't use the product often, or they don't use many products (usage gap or light usage gaps)? And do these gaps in turn depend on other gaps (product, distribution, communication, or price gaps)?

Finding answers to these questions is the key to channeling efforts to create value propositions that enable organizations to close these gaps. And each answer translates into different market objectives: *to turn non-users into users*; *to increase the average frequency of purchase and use*; *to augment quantities of products that are purchased and used*. The first means focusing on non-users, people who have no direct product experience, or insufficient knowledge of product categories. So communication investments are clearly indispensible to encourage them to try out the value proposition in question. For the organization, this might also require innovating the constituent products, seeing as potential customers don't seem interested in current ones.

As for the other two objectives, organizations have to focus on customers who do use the products in question, but not as often as they could. Here investments should probably be concentrated in making the value proposition more accessible and improving value delivery in general, seeing as these customers already have some product experience. To pinpoint the investments and actions it should take, the organization first has to link frequency gaps in product usage to gaps relating to components of the value proposition. It's easy to see that if there's a product gap, the organization has to concentrate on the product component of its value proposition, for example, by enhancing the quality, varying assortment, or proposing new products. When faced with a distribution gap, however, an upgrade of the distribution network is the right move with maneuvers on margins, promotions for trade, more engaging incentives for the sales force, and so on. When the gap comes from pricing, revising the price list can make the product more accessible to a larger portion of the market. Finally, if there's a communication gap, relevant policies need to be reworked, with an eye to product awareness in the market.

Let's look at some examples. A publisher realizes that a group of older consumers are reading less than they'd like to because they have a hard time reading small print; this information could lead the publisher to print books using a larger typeface, or to promote e-readers for this market segment. A sports club discovers that many companies hesitate to invest in sponsorships because they're not clear on the returns that they could gain. The club could invest in marketing research among its fans to analyze their characteristics and preferences, along with their perceptions of the team, and then communicate to potential sponsors what they can expect in terms of enhanced awareness and image transfer.

7.5.3 Creating a new market

Creating a new market is the riskiest option for an organization. The basic difference between a new market and a potential one is that the latter is made up of customers who are aware to some extent of what they want and need, but are only partially satisfied, if at all. With a new market, instead, customers aren't even aware of their needs and desires, much less the fact that there is any way to satisfy them.

Creating a new market means identifying new customers, designing an innovative value proposition that can make their needs/desires emerge, and motivating these customers to satisfy these needs/desires. The first major investment that the organization should make is in marketing research, initially exploratory, and then qualitative. The aim here is to generate knowledge on possible latent needs as well as trends that characterize the market's macro-context. The next investment is innovation, that is, designing and implementing a value proposition that offers content that's original enough to be recognized as distinctive and attractive by customers who have yet to perceive certain needs/desires.

An example could be an opera house that partners with an international cinema chain to stream live opera performances all over the world. Opera fans in many countries have probably never dreamed of seeing a live performance at the Metropolitan Opera or the Teatro della Scala, because many of them can't afford to make the trip to New York or Milan, nor do they realize that the quality of today's digital technology makes the streaming experience 'just like being there'. Consequently, through the new value proposition, these customers discover that they have a desire that they didn't realize they could satisfy, so it's never before been explicit. This gives rise to a new market: streaming live opera performances at the cinema.

7.6 MARKET SEGMENTATION

Once the organization has chosen to concentrate and compete on the current or potential market, or a completely new one, the next decision is a crucial one: To what extent should the value proposition be personalized? The answer to this question calls for a comparison of an efficiency–effectiveness trade-off.

Since the market is made up of customers (consumers or businesses), each with different motivations and preferences, one option for the organization would be to design an ad hoc value proposition for every single one. If this were the case, every customer's expectations would be completely satisfied. But it's easy to see that when referring to a market that's a thousand or even a million strong (as with many consumer markets) this path would be nearly impossible to follow, because the organization would have to create and manage an unimaginable number of value propositions. Implementing the extremely effective solution would lead to sacrificing efficiency, making this option unsustainable, both productively and financially.[9]

On the other end of the spectrum, an organization might decide to offer one single value proposition to the entire market, despite the realization that its customers have a variety of motivations and preferences. The advantage here would be to simplify the offering to the maximum, making it sustainable from a production and financial standpoint. But this extreme efficiency would prove detrimental to effectiveness. With a single value proposition, in fact, some customers will find that it meets their expectations, but others won't. This second group may decide not to buy the product at all, or if they do they may end up only partially satisfied. So basically, once a company or non-profit has identified the market where it wants to operate, it faces difficult decisions that have an enormous impact on the sustainability of its activities and its prosperity – even its very survival.

The two options described above can be placed on either end of a continuum. *One-to-one marketing* involves personalized offerings that give every single customer exactly what she expects; *mass marketing*, which is standardized, entails asking all customers to accept the same offering. An interesting example is provided by the world of fashion, where one-to-one is custom made, hand-sewn garments, and mass marketing can be found in chains like H&M, which offers a standard assortment of lines and styles in all its stores.

The pros and cons of standardization and personalization are similar though inverted, giving rise to a trade-off for the organization. To strike a balance between both approaches, the tool to use is *market segmentation*. According to Smith's traditional definition (1956, p. 4): 'Market segmentation [...] consists of viewing a heterogeneous market (one characterized by divergent demand) as a number of smaller homogeneous markets in response to differing product preferences among important market segments. It is attributable to the desires of consumers or users for more precise satisfaction of their varying wants.'

In other words, segmentation is based on the realization that as different as customers are, they can be grouped together by similar value expectations. This equates to *subdividing the market into groups of customers who have homogeneous value expectations, but who are heterogeneous with respect to customers who belong to other groups*. Each group is a market segment, and every segment is defined by a preference for a different combination of benefits that customers expect to obtain and sacrifices that they expect to make.

Smith's definition underscores a key aspect of segmentation. Contrary to a common conviction in managerial practice, markets aren't 'naturally' or 'objectively' segmented. Instead, segmentation is a way to 'see' a market as if it were made up of smaller 'submarkets'. As a result, *segmentation is the outcome of a choice made by the individual organization*. So various organizations operating on the same market 'see' that market from diverging viewpoints, because they segment it in different ways.

From the previous discussion what should be clear is that this choice is contingent on the stand the organization takes in terms of the effectiveness-efficiency trade-off. The options are to divide the market into several segments, each one made up of a limited number of customers, or into a few macro-segments made up of far more customers. In the first case, the organization tends toward one-to-one marketing; in the second the approach is closer to mass marketing, with all the advantages and disadvantages that ensue.

By moving toward the mass marketing endpoint (dividing the market into just a few large segments) the organization can leverage greater *scale economies*, competing on the market with a small number of value propositions. This translates into the standardization of several production, distribution, and communication processes, with resulting savings on unitary product costs. Likewise, *decision-making processes are simplified*; fewer propositions to offer means fewer decisions to make. Last of all, competing on a few large market segments usually leads to greater *market power* with distributors, which in turn leads bigger profit margins.

At the other end of the spectrum, an organization that moves towards one-to-one marketing, with numerous smaller segments, can enjoy *scope economies*. This refers to cost advantages that arise from producing a variety of value propositions, but ones that can still share some production factors. This approach would also be more likely to win *greater customer satisfaction*, because the organization can offer single segments certain value propositions that are much more closely aligned with their needs. Last of all, serving many segments may lead the organization to *learn from the market more quickly and accurately*. This thanks to the fact the organization is better equipped to capture signs of change from the market, because it has to gather information on several different segments.

Let's look at an example. Imagine two newspaper publishers competing in a market where one of the benefits that readers seek is adequate coverage of local news and events. The first paper prints a single national edition with ad hoc supplements for the major cities and the regions of the country; the second publishes a number of local papers, each with a standard section dedicated to national and international news.

Readers of the first paper would be satisfied in terms of their need for national and international news, but entirely dissatisfied if they live in cities or regions that aren't covered by the local supplements. In this case, they probably wouldn't buy the first paper, and may opt to purchase a local daily instead. What's more, national advertising investors would no doubt find the first paper an interesting vehicle, while investors who only want to reach local markets would not. Publishing a single national paper would only require a single national news desk, and agencies or small local bureaus for inserts. This would lead to lower production costs on average, fewer decisions on how to realize and price the product, and how much ad space to sell, again at what price. Last, thanks to national circulation the company can use a single distributor and enjoy greater market power and preferred customer status.

People who read the second newspaper will be very satisfied as far as local news goes, but to the detriment of coverage on national and international events. What's more, local advertisers would be very interested in this publisher's local dailies for their communication campaigns, but investors targeting a national or international audience would not. Publishing several local papers would call for a number of local desks, which is likely to boost costs and complicate decision making; seeing as the products are different, pricing would also vary for both the papers and relative ad space.

But the chance to communicate more effectively with a number of local communities would make the company attractive to investors who want to reach these audiences. What's more, the publisher could compile news modules to print in all its papers that would help to trim the average product cost. And last, the company could build strong ties with local communities, enabling it to scoop local news stories and to position itself as a supplier of relevant articles to the first publisher.

In conclusion, neither of the two companies has come up with a 'better' way to segment the market, but both will contend with considerable – albeit converse – advantages and disadvantages.

7.7 THE SEGMENTATION PROCESS

The point of segmenting a market is to come up with a constructive categorization of customers that the organization can use to develop value propositions that match expectations as closely as possible, segment by segment. An effective segmentation process is one that enables the organization to draw a map that serves as a guide in designing and realizing specific sustainable value propositions for each segment. There are three different stages in this process: identifying segmentation criteria, building the segments, and profiling the customers that belong to each segment.

7.7.1 Identifying segmentation criteria

Segmentation criteria are *variables that form the basis for distinguishing between various segments* (which is why they're also known as *segmentation bases*) and *assigning individual customers to the most appropriate one*. Since each segment differs from all the others as far as value expectations, segmentation criteria can be generated:

- Directly, from different combinations of expected benefits and sacrifices that constitute value expectations.
- Indirectly, from different combinations of the determinants or consequences of those benefits and sacrifices.

In both cases, identifying segmentation criteria calls for collecting data on customers that allow the organization to assign them to one segment or another. Since these criteria serve to describe and differentiate between various segments, any marketing research conducted to obtain these data has to follow a quantitative approach.

7.7.1.1   Value-based or benefit segmentation

With this type of segmentation, the direct question the organization has to ask is: 'What are the benefits and sacrifices that customers are looking for?' To find an answer, the organization should carry out a marketing research to come up with segmentation criteria. Here are the stages in a typical market segmentation research project:

1. *Create a list of benefits that customers are looking for* (and related sacrifices, or negative benefits). There are two ways to do this. If the organization doesn't have a solid information base, qualitative research is the best way to go (Section 6.4), exploring possible benefits and their determinants. In some cases, the organization might already know what these benefits are thanks to past research or prior market experience of its managers, so it can compile this list without additional investigation.

2. *Measure the relative importance of these benefits.* This stage necessitates quantitative research with a descriptive goal, normally conducted via surveys (Section 6.5). Ultimately the aim is to get an indication from every customer as to his or her value expectations, evidenced by the relative importance of certain benefits over others.

7.7.1.2   Segmentation by individual characteristics

In this case segmentation criteria consist of the individual customer characteristics that have been identified as determinants (Section 4.1) or consequences (Section 4.4) of value expectations. In fact, since certain combinations of benefits are determined by a specific set of variables, and from these benefits follow specific behaviors, by revealing either the variables or behaviors (or a combination of both) organizations can also identify related benefits that then serve as differentiators of various market segments.

Specifically, segmentation is based on the characteristics that qualify either individuals in general (demographic, socio-economic, cultural, or psychological factors) or their relationships with the product categories that constitute the market (product purchase and usage behaviors, purchase frequency, repeat purchases, purchase quantities, and so forth). Table 7.3 details the main segmentation criteria for consumer and business markets.

Table 7.3 – The basic principles of segmentation: individual characteristics

CHARACTERISTICS	CONSUMER	BUSINESS
DEMOGRAPHIC	Age Gender Residence Marital status Stage of family lifecycle	Years in business Size (trunover employees, factories, subsidiaries, and so on) Location of headquarters/ subsidiaries
RESOURCE-BASED	Disposable income Profession Membership in social groups Status Reputation Aesthetic tastes Education Consumption of cultural products	Financial performance Growth rate Type of business Membership in trade associations/financial groups Prestige Type and quality of managerial competences
VALUE-RELATED	Terminal values Instrumental values Lifestyle Level of involvement	Organizational Competitive style Dominant managerial style Level of involvement

continued

Table 7.3 – *continued*

CHARACTERISTICS	CONSUMER	BUSINESS
PSYCHOLOGICAL	Self–image Personality traits	Self-image and personality traits of key decision makers
BEHAVIORAL	Frequency of purchase/consumption Quantities of products purchased Purchase habits Variety of products purchased Consumption habits Brand loyalty Store loyalty Media habits Preferred information sources	Frequency of purchase/investment Average investment Variety of product purchased Investment habits Supplier loyalty Preferred information sources

7.7.2　Building the segments

This involves grouping customers together into different segments according to the criteria established in the previous step. To assign each customer to the proper segment, the *principle of exclusivity* applies: each customer belongs to one – and only one – segment. If a customer can be classified in two different segments, that means the segmentation criteria don't work. Organizations can use two approaches to build their segments: a priori or a posteriori.

7.7.2.1　A priori segmentation

In this case, the researcher or manager chooses segmentation criteria before collecting data on customers, on the base of her previous knowledge of the market and her assumptions regarding the market. This is why a priori segmentation always uses individual customer traits as relevant criteria. Instead, as described above, value-based segmentation involves listing and measuring the importance of benefits, irrespective of individual characteristics.

To give an example, it's generally accepted that viewers' taste in television shows depends on a combination of factors (age, gender, profession, cultural capital, temporal resources). So a television company wanting to segment its market to put together next season's schedule could build segments based on combinations of the variables listed above. Here's what the segments might look like: women over 55 who work in the home and can spend much of their time as they please, with low cultural capital and limited economic capital; men from 35 to 45 years old who are self-employed or work in large companies with high economic and cultural capital and little free time; and so forth.

Once the organization has constructed the segments, the next step is to conduct quantitative research to link different segments to the various combinations of benefits/sacrifices that lead to certain expectations. Continuing with the example above, the television station could conduct a viewer survey on a sample built with the same segmentation criteria, and use a questionnaire to find out what viewer expectations are for programming.

The advantages to the a priori approach are undeniable, but there are also disadvantages that can't be overlooked. First, for the *advantages*, this approach is an altogether simpler process. Since segmentation criteria refer to personal traits of customers, relevant data are easier to access. In fact, they're often available from institutional sources (for socio-demographics), or even the organization's own archives, from prior research for instance. In any case, with a simple, easy-to-administer questionnaire the company can get all the relevant data it needs. So another plus is that research costs are normally quite low.

But there are also *disadvantages* to the a priori approach that could jeopardize its effectiveness. The first is that the combination of segmentation criteria the organization uses might not reveal value expectations or preference structures characterizing each segment. In other words, what could happen is that customers who are similar from a demographic and socio-economic standpoint might have very different expectations of value, or vice versa.

The second major disadvantage is that the a priori approach relies a great deal on previous market knowledge. In other words, the organization bases segmentation criteria on what its managers have learned from the market in the past. So with rapidly evolving markets, using criteria that were once highly effective might no longer reflect the current market or, more importantly, the future market.

7.7.2.2   *A posteriori segmentation*

Here it's marketing research that makes segmentation criteria emerge. In fact, the manager or researcher doesn't start with a preset list of criteria; instead she relies on marketing research findings. This approach is typical of value-based segmentation. In fact, the same study used to compile a list of benefits and their relative importance (the first two stages outlined in Section 7.7.1.1) also serves to pinpoint which customers attribute similar importance to the same combination of benefits.

Cluster analysis is normally used to build segments. This multivariate statistical analysis technique creates groups (defined clusters) within an observed population, highlighting variables (the segmentation criteria) that guarantee that members of each cluster are very similar to one another, and very different from members of other clusters. So basically each cluster is characterized by a distinctive combination of benefits.

The advantages and disadvantages of a posteriori analysis are comparable albeit converse with respect to a priori. To begin with, the *advantages* of a posteriori undoubtedly include immediate and accurate evidence of the different value expectations of various segments, without the risk of multiple segments expressing the same preferences. Also, the a posteriori approach doesn't resort to prior information, so it generates an updated snapshot of the market under investigation.

But there are *disadvantages* too, the first being that the a posteriori approach relies entirely on an initial list of benefits. But what if the list is incomplete? (The manager who compiled the list may have underestimated the importance of some benefits, or the qualitative research that generated it may have failed to make all the benefits emerge, for example.) There would be negative repercussions on the precision of the results.

Also, the process of coming up with a description of the segments is more complex: it can't be done without marketing research, which often consists of a qualitative and a quantitative stage (a combination that pushes up costs) and calls for sophisticated data-gathering techniques. (For example, the quantitative questionnaire for this research would normally be longer, using several scales, revealing multiple variables with respect to the questionnaire that would be used for a priori segmentation.)

To sum up market segmentation, this process is the outcome of a decision the organization makes based on its objectives and resources, which in turn dictate the choice of approach to take. With limited financial resources and analytical competencies, and the desire to identify a few macro-segments, the a priori approach is best. If, however, resources don't represent an obstacle, and the organization wants to pinpoint several smaller segments, an a posteriori approach would be a better fit. Figure 7.4 compares the two approaches with a fictitious example based on the performing arts.

7.7.3   Customer profiling

What are the expectations of the different customers on the market? What combination of benefits do they prefer? Building segments reveals the answers to these questions, but segments don't provide all the information if a firm or non-profit needs to design value propositions that guarantee satisfied customers. One final question remains: Who are the customers in each of the different segments?

The answer can be found through customer profiling, which involves *describing the customers in each segment based on their most distinctive individual characteristics*. So the same type of individual variables that work as the basis for segmentation typically apply for profiling as well, but clearly if some of these variables have already been used as segmentation criteria, different ones are employed for profiling. It's important to point out that the variables needed for profiling are the ones that are most distinctive to the customers of each segment, in other words, the dominant traits of one segment with respect to the others.

So in a consumer market, analysis can profile customers by purchase frequency if one segment scores much higher or lower than average on this variable; disposable income works if income in some segments varies significantly from the average. But if the segments are very similar on certain markers (that is, more or less in line with the average) then those variables won't work for profiling.

A PRIORI SEGMENTATION

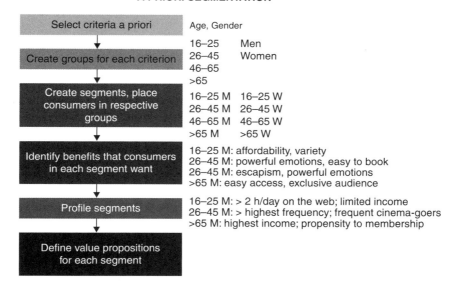

Select criteria a priori — Age, Gender

Create groups for each criterion

16–25   Men
26–45   Women
46–65
>65

Create segments, place consumers in respective groups

16–25 M   16–25 W
26–45 M   26–45 W
46–65 M   46–65 W
>65 M   >65 W

Identify benefits that consumers in each segment want

16–25 M: affordability, variety
26–45 M: powerful emotions, easy to book
26–45 M: escapism, powerful emotions
>65 M: easy access, exclusive audience

Profile segments

16–25 M: > 2 h/day on the web; limited income
26–45 M: > highest frequency; frequent cinema-goers
>65 M: highest income; propensity to membership

Define value propositions for each segment

A POSTERIORI SEGMENTATION

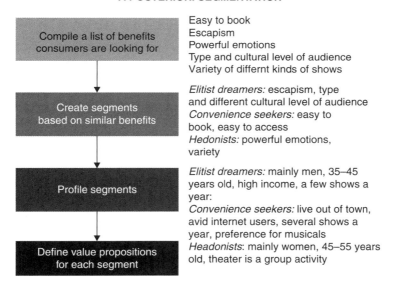

Compile a list of benefits consumers are looking for

Easy to book
Escapism
Powerful emotions
Type and cultural level of audience
Variety of differnt kinds of shows

Create segments based on similar benefits

Elitist dreamers: escapism, type and different cultural level of audience
Convenience seekers: easy to book, easy to access
Hedonists: powerful emotions, variety

Profile segments

Elitist dreamers: mainly men, 35–45 years old, high income, a few shows a year:
Convenience seekers: live out of town, avid internet users, several shows a year, preference for musicals
Headonists: mainly women, 45–55 years old, theater is a group activity

Define value propositions for each segment

Figure 7.4 – Comparison between a priori and a posteriori segmentation: a fictitious example in the performing arts

Customer profiling plays a key managerial role in *rendering segmentation actionable*. When organizations can distinguish between segments both in terms of expected benefits/sacrifices, and distinctive individual characteristics, they can design value propositions that are aligned with expectations, and distribution and communication processes that are consistent with the purchasing and consumption habits of the people in different segments. Research Focus 7.1 describes research on a posteriori segmentation regarding members of four Australian art museums.

Research Focus 7.1

Segmentation of museum members

Many non-profits in creative industries offer their customers membership, which can take a variety of names ('clubs', 'friends of', and so on), signaling a special relationship with the institution. Members get the chance to have a voice in organizational decision making, and the institution gains a pool of people it can tap for carrying out certain activities or donating time or money.

The mechanism underpinning the close connection with the institution is the identification that members feel with its values, mission, and activities. But there can be a variety of motivations behind this identification. In other words, members (like all the customers in a market) can be seeking different benefits in their relationship with the institution. That's why it's important to understand the range of benefits members expect, so as to design value propositions suited to each group, strengthening member relations over time.

Kleinschafer and colleagues (2011) conducted research on members of four regional art museums in Australia to identify possible clusters characterized by the search for different benefits. The procedure the researchers used was typical a posteriori segmentation, as follows:

1. Identifying the list of potential benefits based on prior research on the topic along with qualitative research carried out via in-depth interviews with 11 people (two museum employees and nine members).
2. Conducting a survey on 433 members of the four museums, in order to build the segments using cluster analysis.
3. Profiling customer clusters via socio-demographic and behavioral variables.

The study revealed the following benefits: participating in museum activities, reinforcing high involvement in the art world, personal growth/enrichment, contributing to the well-being of the community, the pleasure of positive experiences, the pleasure of interacting in a non-elitist environment; social visibility, prestige.

Based on these benefits, the analysis identified three clusters: promoters, donors, and committee members. *Promoters* scored high on reinforcing involvement with the art world, and the pleasure of interacting with a non-elitist environment. Next came social visibility, pleasant experiences, and contributing to community well-being. On average, promoters had a higher income than other members, a higher level of education, and more instruction in art in the form of art courses. Compared to other members these people made fewer donations and fewer museum visits, but were very active in promoting museum activities.

Donors scored lower on all benefits with respect to other members. This may indicate that the benefits they were looking for weren't on the list that was used in the analysis, or, as the authors themselves suggest, their level of identification was lower than the others. This cluster had relatively newer members, the highest percentage of men, with a lower average age and lower income than promoters. Donors made the most consistent donations both in time and money, but undertook fewer promotional activities for museum initiatives.

Committee members had the longest membership and scored the highest in measuring identification. They looked for more benefits than members in the other clusters: participating in museum activities, personal growth/enrichment, contributing to community well-being, social visibility, prestige. On the contrary, they scored lowest on the pleasure of positive experiences and of interacting in a non-elitist environment. Members of this cluster on average were older and had a lower income and education level. These people participated more actively in decision making, and were more likely to be members of other organizations as well.

7.7.4   Evaluating the effectiveness of segmentation

At this point, after drawing up a map depicting several market segments and adequately profiling each one, the organization can't necessarily start using this map right away to make decisions. As we now know – and this bears repeating – there's not one unequivocal way to segment a market. The map generated from segmentation has to serve the organization in reaching its objectives, in line with its available resources. Otherwise, this map provides a detailed snapshot of the market, but one that can't be used for decision making.

This explains the need to evaluate the effectiveness of the segmentation, and modify it if need be. If the segments that emerge enable the organization to design and realize value propositions that are sustainable from a financial and productive standpoint, then segmentation is effective. To clarify with an illustration, the segmentation process might provide a map made up of several small segments, each clearly profiled and distinctive with regard to benefits. But this map is useless if the organization's cost structure is so inflexible that it's impossible to realize value propositions targeting small segments in any financially sustainable way.

For segmentation to be effective, segments must be:

- *Measurable*. As we saw in Section 7.3.4, measuring the dimensions of a market or a segment requires information on customers' purchase behaviors that is then translated into estimates for sales volumes and revenues. Without this information, there's no way to make measurements, and the organization won't be able to assess the productive and financial sustainability of the value propositions intended for the different segments.

- *Significant in size*. Organizations that strive to personalize their offerings sacrifice efficiency for effectiveness. But the choice of how far to go in personalization depends on the investments needed to produce a value proposition for the segments in question. Some investments are sustainable and others are not depending on segment size (in terms of volume and value). For a segment that's too small, the value proposition may not be sustainable productively or financially.

- *Stable*. Sustainability also has a time element, seeing that some decisions underpinning the realization of a value proposition call for investments that generate returns over time. As a result, the segments in question have to be stable enough to allow for the organization to recover this outlay. If, however, segment size or demands are very changeable, the value proposition designed to satisfy these customers would quickly be without a market, and without having generated adequate revenues to ensure a return on investments.

- *Diverse in customer preferences*. Customers from different segments must be attracted by different value propositions. If this isn't true, more than likely the bases of the segmentation are inadequate in some way. There are a number of possible explanations for this, depending on the method that's used. With value-based segmentation, analysis may have missed out some of the benefits people are looking for, or failed to accurately grasp the relative importance of these benefits. If segmentation is based on individual traits, on the other hand, then the ones chosen for segmentation may not be the true determinants of the benefits customers expect.

- *Accessible*. Once an organization designs and realizes its value proposition, it has to make sure this proposition gets delivered to targeted customers. This means accessing distribution and communications channels that are able to reach these customers in a financially sustainable way. If accessibility is lacking or simply too expensive, this will make it impossible to deliver in its entirety to its customers the value the organization has created, which may result in lost sales or unsatisfied customers.

What happens if an organization comes to the conclusion that its segmentation is productively or financially unsustainable? Clearly the answer to this question depends on the underlying causes. If the segments can't be measured, the organization needs to invest in gathering additional information on the purchase and use behaviors of its customers. (With consumer clients: How often do they buy and consume the products in question in an average month or year? With corporate sponsors: How much do they normally invest in sponsorship activities in a year?)

If, however, the problem can be ascribed to small or unstable segments, the organization could group together segments that show some degree of similarity as far as benefits. The aim here would be to increase segment size and attenuate instability (if for some benefits the relative importance is fairly similar among different segments). In this case the organization would move toward the mass marketing end of the continuum. As a result, it's vital to realize that the value proposition the organization will offer won't necessarily be aligned with the expectations of all the customers in the new larger segment it's created. But the hope is that greater financial/productive returns deriving from fewer value propositions will more than compensate for the customers who might be lost.

Let's say that the segments the organization identifies don't actually show different preferences because all the customers tend to choose the same value proposition. In this case, the problem is more serious, and doesn't relate simply to the segmentation process but rather to gaps in value analysis, creation, or delivery (Section 2.2.4). The organization hasn't identified the real benefits customers are looking for, or it hasn't been able to translate its knowledge of these benefits into truly differential value propositions, or it hasn't delivered these propositions to the market intact. The solution to this problem lies in reviewing the value creation processes, with an eye to detecting possible gaps that have led to ineffective segmentation, and deciding how to fill in these gaps.

Last, if the obstacle is accessing segments in a financially sustainable fashion, beyond regrouping the segments (as recommended above) the organization could verify whether different communication media can provide an acceptable level of effectiveness and at the same time cost savings that would render the investment sustainable (Chapter 9).

7.8   TARGETING

Targeting is the crux of all strategic marketing decisions. In fact, after identifying and profiling the segments, and verifying the effectiveness of this segmentation, firms and non-profits have to decide *which segments to serve through ad hoc value propositions*: that's what targeting is all about.

It's essential to remember that through market segmentation an organization positions itself along the marketing continuum (one-to-one versus mass marketing), in an attempt to strike a balance between the pros and cons of these strategies. But since there are a variety of available options, before making a choice the organization has to assess segment attractiveness to verify whether or not it has the right resources and competences to create

value propositions that are aligned with corresponding expectations.

7.8.1   Assessing segment attractiveness

The point here is to verify whether designing and realizing an ad hoc value proposition for the segment in question is sustainable for the organization in productive and financial terms. Sustainability centers on two main issues:

- Estimated returns (sales, profitability, image, reputation, and so on) that justify investing in an ad hoc value proposition.
- Availability of resources and competencies that enable the organization to realize a value proposition that generates customer preference.

Consequently, the *criteria* can relate to the following assessment areas:

1. *Potential sales.* As we've seen (Section 7.3.4), volumes and values associated with a segment are contingent on customers' purchase behavior (and with corporate clients, product usage) in terms of frequency and quantity, as well as willingness to change their choice processes and purchase/consumption habits; the propensity toward innovation; sensitivity to specific aspects of the value proposition. Organizations also need to consider the actual and potential size of the segment, and the current stage in the market lifecycle (Case History 7.1).

Case History 7.1

Musei Civici di Venezia: calculating the potential of the student visitors segment

Musei Civici di Venezia Foundation (MUVE) is a public institution established by the City of Venice in 2008 to manage all the museums owned by the city. (Public museums in Italy are owned and operated either by the city or region where they are located, or by the national government.) MUVE was created by absorbing the municipal department that had previously been tasked with museum management. The Musei Civici di Venezia represent an example of excellence among public museums in Italy, one of the extremely rare cases of public museum management that has, from the outset, consistently generated positive financial returns solely with ticket sales.

According to its statute, the Venetian Foundation is responsible for managing and enhancing the extensive cultural and artistic heritage of city-owned museums, for contributing to strategic development plans, and for promoting the participation of other public and private institutions in the life of the Foundation. The municipal museum system counts 11 sites, grouped together in different theme-based sectors: the area in and around Piazza San Marco (Palazzo Ducale, the Correr Museum and the Torre dell'Orologio); Eighteenth Century Venice (Ca' Rezzonico, Palazzo Mocenigo and the House of Carlo Goldoni); the modern and contemporary sector (Ca' Pesaro and Fortuny Museum), and the nature and ethnographic sector (the Natural History Museum, the Glass Museum, and the Lace Museum).

MUVE is able to segment its visitors in a number of ways, depending on the information needs that arise within the framework of specific research. One macro-segmentation differentiates individual visitors from groups; Table 7.4 shows the relative sizes of these two macro-segments in 2011.

Table 7.4 – MUVE: Number of tickets issued in 2011 per segment

Segments	N.tickets	%
Individual visitors	1,293,325	72.1
Groups	502,372	27.9
Student groups	104,720	5.8
Non-Student groups	397,652	22.1
Total	1,795,697	100.0

For groups of students, MUVE proposes quite a wide range of ad hoc products, with initiatives targeting both students and teachers: guided tours, interactive visits, workshops, and extended didactic packages (over multiple days). These offerings are available in all the museums at an extra charge in addition to the ticket price, providing an additional source of revenue for MUVE. As for the school categories, 9.6 per cent of the initiatives target pre-schools, 36 per cent elementary schools, 36 per cent middle schools and 18.4 per cent high schools.

Although the student visitor segment is the smallest, it's still a strategic one for MUVE both due to its institutional mission (disseminating knowledge of Italy's patrimony among the younger generations) and for financial reasons (creating an interest that can lead to repeat visits). This is what prompted the Marketing Department at MUVE to conduct marketing research, in collaboration with the Fitzcarraldo Foundation, in 2011. The aim of this study was to estimate the potential market for the Italian student segment for municipal museums in Venice, both at an overall level and for each student age group. A follow-up study would provide profiles of sub-segments to help the organization redefine product and communication strategies for each target.

To calculate the potential market, the first step was to distinguish a priori between two macro-segments: Italian students who live nearby (those who can take a day trip to visit Venice, without having to stay overnight) and Italian students visiting the city for multiple days (those who live farther away, necessitating at least one overnight).

LOCAL ITALIAN STUDENTS

To estimate the potential of this macro-segment, the population was broken down by age: from six to ten for elementary school, 11 to 13 for middle school and 14 to 18 for high school, according to data provided by ISTAT (the Italian Statistics Institute). These students live in the Veneto region or in cities nearby, specifically within two hours of Venice by train or bus. (For elementary schools maximum travel time was one and a half hours, since a longer distance was considered too tiring for six to ten year olds.) Table 7.5 shows the relevant data.

Table 7.5 – MUVE: The potential of the student segment, broken down by scholastic level

Geographic area	Elementary school	Middle school	High school	Total
Veneto Region	231,066	135,732	199,809	566,607
Within 1.5 hours travel time	6,444	6,266	3,612	16,322
From 1.5 and 2 hours travel time	–	–	49,432	49,432
Total	237,510	141,998	252,853	632,361

ITALIAN STUDENTS WHO TAKE MULTIPLE-DAY VISITS

Estimates for the potential of this macro-segment were based on data from the *Touring Club Italiano* (which has a research department that monitors tourist flows in Italy), ISTAT (the Italian Statistics Institute), and MIUR (the Ministry of Education). These data showed that the number of high school students who went on multiple-day field trips in Italy in 2011 numbered 372,400, and middle school students were 497,794. Breaking down these results by number of students per year (assuming that it would be very unlikely for the same class to go back to the same destination) and subtracting the number of students from schools nearby (included in the previous macro-segment), the result is a potential estimated at 232,100 students.

Tallying up all the students who visit the city in one day with those who visit for multiple days, the potential for this market segment is estimated at 864,461 visitors every year. Seeing that the actual number of visitors in this segment is 104,720, the market potential gap equals 759,741 students, signaling ample room for growth.

2. *Potential market share*. Irrespective of market size, an organization's sales are determined by the market share it can secure. So a key consideration pertains to *competitive pressure* from the number and strength of organizations competing on the market. Obviously, the more numerous the competitors and the stronger they are, the more difficult it will be to transform potential sales into actual sales. Resources and competencies are what make competitors strong: the loyalty of their customers (which can be expressed in terms of switching costs), reputation, the quality of their competences, and the solidity of their commercial relationships.

But Porter (1980) suggests that the competitive pressure in a sector (and by analogy in a market segment) depends not only on the intensity of the current competition, but also the presence and power of competing products that, though they may belong to different categories, might be perceived by customers as valid substitutes. Suppliers upstream and customers downstream can intensify competition as well. Think of a small organization that decides to become sponsee in a segment where large companies compete. The disparity in size between the organization and its potential clients could create a power relationship that is so skewed toward the latter it would lead to an extremely risky waste of resources by the organization, canceling out the attractiveness of the segment.

3. *The potential for other returns*. The decision to compete in a segment with a certain value proposition might be justified by other returns (beyond sales) that don't immediately translate into positive financial results, but that may do so in the future. Serving a segment of customers with an excellent image and reputation may transfer these qualities to the organization itself. And serving a segment that has demanding, sophisticated expectations necessitates developing operations capabilities and earning a reputation as a competent supplier that can satisfy these expectations. This means that in the short term, the financial returns on the segment may be limited or even negative, but serving those customers is a way to accumulate resources and competences that the organization can leverage to operate in other segments or to gain financial returns in the future when operations become more efficient.

4. *Investments and costs*. The three areas analyzed above will determine the potential for returns that the organization can expect from serving a certain market segment. But returns are also contingent on the investments required to design and realize a value proposition that meets the expectations of the segment. So the first thing to consider is the total investments required, and the costs that these investments will generate over time. If these numbers are comparatively high in light of the potential returns, then the segment won't be very attractive for the organization.

5. *The strengths and weaknesses of the organization compared to its competitors*. Regardless of the size of investments, the quality of the organization's resources and competences are what determines the quality of the returns on these investments. Put another way, all investments being equal, the organization that has higher quality resources than its competitors (know how, brand image, strong relationships with distributors, and so forth) will be able to transform these investments into higher quality value propositions. This is why every organization has to carefully evaluate its *strengths and weaknesses*, compared to its competitors, to weigh

Table 7.6 – Criteria for segment attractiveness

Assessment area	CRITERIA
SALES POTENTIAL	Current sales volume Current sales value Average frequency of purchase/use Average quantity purchased/utilized Customer propensity to innovation Stage in lifecycle Potential sales volume Potential sales value
MARKET SHARE POTENTIAL	Number of competitors Customer loyality of brand/supplier Switching costs Funtional competences of competitors Reputation of competitors Existence and market power of 　producers of substitute products Market power of suppliers Market power of distributors Market power of customers
POTENTIAL FOR OTHER RETURNS	Possibility to enhance image Possibility to earn a reputation Possibility to develop competences
INVESTMENTS REQUIRED	Ad hoc production investments Ad hoc distribution/commercial investments Ad hoc marketing investments
STRENGTHS AND WEAKNESS COMPARED TO COMPETITORS	Resources and operation capabilites Brand/company image Strength of distribution and commercial 　realtionalships Availability of financial resources

up its chances for realizing value propositions that stand out from the rest. Table 7.6 details the most common analytical criteria used for assessing the five areas listed above.

7.8.2　Choosing target segments

Once the organization has made its assessments of the attractiveness of various segments, it can choose which ones to serve and how. The myriad possible strategies either tend more toward the personalization of one-to-one marketing or the standardization of mass marketing (Section 7.6).

Niche marketing entails focusing on one small segment. In this case, all the organization's marketing efforts and investments are concentrated on realizing a value proposition that can fulfill the value expectations of this segment alone. An art gallery that exclusively sells seventeenth-century Flemish paintings, or a record company that only produces LPs, a clothing manufacturer whose only raw material is cashmere, an architectural studio specialized in building structures on water: all these are examples of organizations that pursue a niche strategy (Case History 7.2).

This strategy is sustainable if the limited size of the segment is compensated by the willingness of the customers in that segment to pay a premium price to fulfill their expectations. To satisfy niche customers, the organization has to develop highly specialized competences that can rarely be used to produce other value propositions, nullifying any possibility of scale or scope economies.

Case History 7.2

Persephone Books: books by women for women

'Persephone prints mainly neglected fiction and non-fiction by women, for women and about women. The titles are chosen to appeal to busy women who rarely have time to spend in ever-larger bookshops and who would like to have access to a list of books designed to be neither too literary nor too commercial. The books are guaranteed to be readable, thought-provoking and impossible to forget.' (http://www.persephonebooks.co.uk/) This British publishing house specializes in resurrecting out-of-print books by women authors written during the decades between the two World Wars.

The excerpt from the publisher's website sounds like a very precise description of the target Persephone aims to satisfy, and the kind of value proposition it proposes to do so. The end result is a catalogue with a limited number of titles, different from more famous publishers, and categorized by topics that may be of interest to a female readership.

But most importantly, this proposition offers the chance to take part in a community of women who share the same passion. In fact, Persephone organizes a number of events at which readers can meet and visit significant places that serve as the settings for some of the books, go to exhibits or attend lectures, or simply pass the time together over a cup of tea. The publisher has also set up two reading groups, and hosts a forum on its website where every month readers and Persephone employees can discuss one of the publisher's titles.

Segment specialization differs from niche marketing in terms of segment size, which can be considerable. An apparel company that specialized in men's clothing, a publishing house that focuses on children's books, a radio station that plays uninterrupted music, an online store that exclusively sells sports equipment: all these are examples of companies that target a single segment, but the size of this segment is comparable to an entire market.

Organizations that pursue this strategy normally satisfy a wide range of demands that emerge, in doing so becoming *segment specialists*. As a result, these companies probably deal with sub-segments within their specialty segment. The men's clothing company might have classic and casual product lines to satisfy the expectations of men with different tastes; the children's book publisher could organize its catalogue by age bracket, or by educational and recreational divisions; the radio station may offer programs dedicated to various musical genres in different time slots, and the online store could have different virtual departments for various types of sports.

The *multi-segment strategy* involves offering a specific value proposition for each target segment. A pay TV company could offer channels broadcasting news, and others showing cartoons, sports, films, or documentaries, in an attempt to serve diverse segments in the market of television entertainment. A publisher that offers a number of men's and women's magazines might also print periodicals dedicated

to gardening, sailing, cooking, and other hobbies to appeal to a broad range of segments in the information market.

To pursue this strategy the organization has to manage a vast product/brand portfolio and deal with all the challenges this implies, which mainly center on preventing the products/brand from competing against one another (Chapter 8). More than any other the multi-segment strategy recognizes and leverages the differences in the market. Here success depends on the ability of the company or non-profit to maximize effectiveness by offering specific value propositions for each segment, while guaranteeing efficiency by developing productive and commercial synergies.

Going back to the examples above, the pay TV company could set up multi-purpose television studios for recording programs produced in-house, and communication campaigns promoting various types of subscription packages. The publisher could have a staff of reporters who write articles for publication in various magazines, and organize distribution so that the entire product portfolio is channeled through a few distributors.

Macro-segmentation strategy calls for aggregating various segments and satisfying them all with a single value proposition. This is often the strategy of choice when an organization views its productive and financial capabilities as inconsistent with the characteristics of the different market segments; the solution is to regroup them to come up with larger, more stable segments that show a similar sensitivity to certain marketing levers. As we saw in Section 7.7.4, the effectiveness of this choice is less than optimal because it involves offering the same value proposition to segments whose value expectations differ. Clearly the risk here is leaving some customers dissatisfied, or even losing them to competitors.

Macro-segmentation most closely resembles mass marketing: offering a single value proposition for the entire market, capitalizing on efficiency through standardization, and sacrificing alignment of this proposition with various value expectations. Although this strategy may appear to be a far cry from the fragmentation and dynamism of today's markets, it's not as rare as one might think in creative industries. Take mass media, for instance, where public television and radio stations have to target the entire population for institutional reasons with programming that appeals to the majority of viewers and listeners. (This explains why these operators are often called 'generalists'.)

But other sectors also follow the same path: historical monuments, national parks, and tourism, where standardized offerings target the broadest possible market, without acknowledging any differences in the expectations of diverse segments of the user population. The same is true (and even more evident) in the business market where countless creative products are offered in an identical manner across the board. How many properties in a sports or cultural context are proposed for sponsorship without the slightest consideration of the different needs of potential clients? And how many creative products are promoted for possible placements without a preliminary evaluation of the diverse expectations investors may have?

7.9 CREATING VALUE PROPOSITIONS

There are two stages to creating a value proposition: design and realization (Section 2.2.3). During the *design* stage the organization identifies the benefits it wants to offer through the value proposition and the relative sacrifices that customers will be asked to make. During *realization*, Marketing works with other organizational units to translate the value proposition into a sellable offering. Marketing's contribution to this process lies in a series of decisions that come under what is termed the *marketing mix*, traditionally consisting of four decision-making areas: the product, the price,

distribution, and communication (which we'll discuss in the following chapters).

Integrating the decisions made by Marketing and by other business units ensures that the value offered is aligned with the market knowledge gleaned in the value analysis process (Section 2.2.4).

When creating a value proposition, the first question is: What benefits should the organization offer to the customers that it wants to serve? To find an answer, it's essential to keep in mind that *an offering is made up of attributes, not benefits* (whether referring to a theatrical season, a publisher's magazine, a tour operator's vacation packages, or a fashion house's clothing collection). So to reformulate the question above to make it actionable for the organization: What attributes should the offering have? From the discussion on targeting in the previous section, and the description in Section 4.4.1.1 of the means–ends relationships customers use to evaluate products, the answer should be clear: *The attributes to offer are the ones that the customers in the target segments associate with the benefits that are important to them.*

Let's take an online newspaper. If a customer segment expects free, frequently-updated content that's easy to access with various devices, which also provides links to other sources for in-depth information, a publisher who wants to serve this segment should design an online newspaper with attributes that are associated with these benefits. Or take a sports property. If a segment of sponsors wants to shore up customer loyalty, offer hospitality to special guests during events, and have exclusive sponsorship rights, the sports club interested in attracting this segment has to design a sponsorship package that can fulfill these expected benefits.

From this description, it may sound like designing a value proposition is a fairly simple stage in the process, and any problems that might arise would come in realizing this proposition. But unfortunately the design stage has its own share of complexity. And this mainly revolves around the *diverse nature of benefits and the differential effect they can have on customer satisfaction*. To illustrate this point, let's imagine a survey conducted by a theater inquiring into what benefits spectators expect to obtain.

Respondents would probably list things like emotionally moving performances, variety of types of shows, flexibility in the type of ticket package, and so on. But it probably wouldn't even occur to

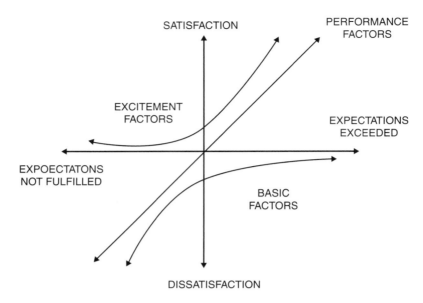

Figure 7.5 – Differential impact of benefits on customer satisfaction

interviewees to mention the temperature inside the theater. But what if they go to a show and find the theater stiflingly hot? How would they react? Would they feel satisfied?

Now let's imagine spectators arriving the theater and being greeted by staff members, who offer to take their coat so they don't need to wait in line at the coat check. Then when spectators present their ticket they get a coupon for a free drink at the bar in the theater. And after the show when they pick up their coat they get a free DVD of the show they've just seen. None of these attributes refer to the benefits they cited in the survey, but what influence would they have? Would they affect their satisfaction? Clearly all these benefits would have very different impact.

Useful indications that help the organization answer these questions are provided by the *three-factor theory of customer satisfaction*, initially proposed by Kano (1984) and later elaborated on by other authors (Arbore and Busacca, 2011; Brandt, 1988; Johnston, 1995; Oliver, 1997; Vavra, 1997). According to this theory there are three different categories of benefits (and related attributes), classified on the basis of impact on customer satisfaction (Figure 7.5).

- *Basic factors* (also known as dissatisfiers, must-haves, or hygiene factors) are benefits that are seen as minimum requirements of the offering. They have no impact on customer satisfaction if they're aligned with or exceed expectations, but they trigger dissatisfaction if they're below par or lacking or altogether. In other words, these factors have more potential impact on dissatisfaction than on satisfaction. So basics are things that customers take for granted: they are necessary, but not sufficient, to guarantee satisfaction. Example: a comfortable room temperature inside the theater.
- *Excitement factors* (satisfiers or nice-to-have factors) are those benefits that have no impact on dissatisfaction if they're missing, but they positively impact satisfaction if they're present by eliciting surprise and positive emotions. So they have greater potential impact on satisfaction than on dissatisfaction. Examples: welcoming people at the door and taking their coats at the theater (customer care).
- *Performance factors* are benefits that have a linear and symmetrical impact on satisfaction: as performance factors increase, satisfaction increases and vice versa. Examples: powerful performances, variety of shows, flexibility in ticket packages (Research Focus 7.2).

Research Focus 7.2

Satisfaction among opera-goers

The opera has a number of special features compared to other performing arts. From a production standpoint, an opera performance is one of the most complex and costly because it combines various artistic forms (music, theater, dance) with numerous artists (singers, musicians, dancers), and in many cases elaborate scenery. What's more, some opera singers are stars in their own right who must be paid accordingly.

From a consumption standpoint, the opera elicits complex emotional responses: the combination of different art forms creates a rich multi-sensorial experience. The story draws spectators in, letting them identify with the characters and often, in countries with a long operatic tradition, evoking powerful associations with that country. A host of experts in the opera community are vociferous in expressing their appreciation or disappointment in artists and performances. As a result, spectator satisfaction is a complex phenomenon to investigate and to manage.

Jobst and Boerner (2011) analyzed spectator satisfaction at the Dessau Opera House, one of the biggest venues of its kind in Germany. These researchers conducted a survey with a structured questionnaire on a sample of 116 spectators at Mozart's *Magic Flute*, one of the most often performed and representative works in German opera. The majority of the people in the sample were women (58%), 49 years of age on average (minimum 18, maximum 75), with a high level of education (66%): these characteristics made the sample representative of the population of opera-goers in Germany.

The aim of the study was to identify the benefits capable of creating satisfaction in opera-goers. Building on previous studies, the researchers came up with six categories of benefits:

- Aesthetic appreciation for artistic qualities.
- Positive emotions elicited by the experience.
- Positive and negative memories triggered by the experience.
- Identification with the characters and the artists.
- Comfort during the performance (acoustic, visual, seating, temperature of the venue, and so forth).
- Customer care before and after the performance (parking, the coat check, the foyer, and similar).

The study found both performance factors and basic factors, but no excitement factors. The former, in order of importance, were positive emotions, aesthetic appreciation, identification with the characters and the artists, and memories. While positive emotions have a positive impact (as they increase so does satisfaction), memories have a negative impact (as they increase, satisfaction decreases). This finding might indicate greater appreciation for operas that allow spectators to escape from their daily lives, and less for operas that immerse spectators in their daily worries and cares.

Comfort during the performance and customer care received before and after the show had no impact on satisfaction: if these factors were present, they didn't increase satisfaction; if they were negligible or lacking entirely they didn't increase dissatisfaction.[10] This is typical of basic factors.

In light of the different nature of these three types of factors, it's reasonable to assert that performance factors represent explicit benefits (Section 4.4.1.1.1). Instead, basic and excitement factors are more implicit. The former (basic) customers take for granted, so they tend to forget to mention them; the latter (excitement) customers don't expect, so they don't consider these factors as evaluation criteria and don't include them with the other associations they recall when thinking about the product category in question. Consequently, when analyzing value, instead of stopping with specific explicit benefits, it's essential to *dig deeper to find out what customers take for granted, or what might surprise them or elicit positive emotional reactions*.

All this means that when creating value propositions, the organization has to keep in mind not only the type, but also the nature of benefits/attributes that customers associate with its offering. First the offering has to achieve the level of satisfaction customers want for the benefits/attributes they take for granted: the must-haves. Second comes the decision regarding the benefits/attributes that customers believe are vital to their satisfaction, that is, performance factors. How should the organization provide them? How far should it go to do so? Last, the organization should also think about how to connote its offering with benefits/attributes that are seen as excitement factors, while keeping in mind that these are nice-to-haves, and as such can't compensate for a lack of basics or inadequate performance factors. No opera lover would be satisfied by a warm welcome and a second-rate performance!

The distinction used up to this point between basic, performance, and excitement factors refers to a precise moment in the lifecycle of a market. But what happens as the market gradually evolves from stage to stage, from introduction to growth to maturity? Intuition tells us that thanks to differentiation–imitation dynamics, in time all competitors will tend to include certain components in their value propositions that are currently considered excitement factors. This will lead customers to consider them vital aspects of value, and gradually come to class former excitement factors as performance factors. And once today's performance factors are satisfied systematically, they will be taken more and more for granted and eventually become basics.

So essentially in every market little by little the different factors slide downward and toward the right on the curve illustrated in Figure 7.5. To sum up: *the frontier of value is dynamic, never static*. In the initial market lifecycle stage, customers perceive value propositions as containing mostly excitement factors; then in the growth stage the first basic and performance factors emerge. Finally, in the maturity stage, these factors consolidate and trigger a systematic shift of the value frontier: the competing organizations attempt to innovate their value propositions continuously, to include new excitement factors so that they become distinctive in the eyes of consumers. And so it goes until some competitor or newcomer in the sector launches a value proposition that's so innovative it gives rise to an entirely new market, activating an entirely new lifecycle.

7.10   POSITIONING THE VALUE PROPOSITION

For an organization to effectively align itself with market expectations and fulfill them, it must create a value proposition. But that's not all it takes. Let's consider a theater that offers a season with an exciting variety of shows, flexible ticketing options, and a comfortable atmosphere. Now let's ask ourselves: By doing all this, will the theater be able to secure the preference of a part of the potential market of spectators? The answer, as we can easily predict, is no. And the reason lies in the fact that the theater has to contend with competitors.

The basic principle to keep in mind is that *preference requires difference*. Customers buy and appreciate value propositions that they perceive as different from the others, with respect to the benefits they think are important; in other words they prefer the propositions which they believe are better able to satisfy their expectations.

So once the organization has created a value proposition, the next necessary step is to position it on the market. Positioning means creating market space for the value proposition, and the first place to do this is in the system of customer perceptions. A *distinctive positioning* consists in customers recognizing *a series of differential characteristics in the organization's value proposition compared to the competition*. Building a distinctive positioning equates to constructing the perception of difference.

7.10.1   Positioning and differentiation

So the concept of positioning is closely related to the concept of *differentiation*: for positioning to be effective, it must be distinctive, and it's distinctive if customers recognize something different about it when they measure it up against competitors' offerings. Put another way, building positioning necessitates building differences with respect to competitors that motivate target customers to prefer a given value proposition. But positioning – and differentiation! – is never absolute, it's always relative with respect to three markers: target customers, competitors, and the organization offering the value proposition.

Target customers are the foundations for positioning. They're the ones with expectations that the organization needs to satisfy and perceptions about various value propositions. The positioning of these propositions isn't absolute, but relative to every segment: as the segment changes, so does the positioning for the same value proposition. For instance, imagine a company that produces designer lighting fixtures in a relatively high price bracket. This positioning would be seen as luxury for a customer segment with a low average income, and accessible for a high-income segment.

Different customers will have different knowledge about various *competitors* and value propositions (Section 4.3); what they perceive in their evoked set is a variety of products, brands, and suppliers that represent various value propositions. So the perception of each product, brand, or supplier is always relative to all the others. Customers with different knowledge perceive an organization's value proposition differently, because they're comparing a different set of competitors. As the competitors taken into consideration change, so does positioning. Some customers might only know about other companies with lower-priced products (beyond the lighting company in our example); in their eyes our example company will be very expensive. Other customers who are familiar with lighting manufacturers with higher prices will consider the prices of the example company as average.

Last comes the *organization*. Depending on public awareness, reputation, and overall image, every organization is more or less legitimate in the eyes of its customers when it comes to proposing and sustaining a given value proposition on the market. As the company offering the proposition changes, so does the positioning. Continuing with the example above, if the company produces lighting fixtures with a perceived average price that's high, and decides to launch a new 'budget' offering with far lower prices, its prior image will shape the perceptions of customers who know the company, and they probably won't find it legitimate for this producer to offer a lower quality, lower priced offering.

7.10.2 Characteristics of a strong positioning

If an organization's positioning strategy is effective, it leads to a strong positioning, and a strong positioning leads targeted customers to prefer the organization's value proposition over that of the competition. A strong positioning is built on elements that are:

1. Favorable.
2. Relevant for the target.
3. Different from the competition.

The first point might seem obvious, but it's always an essential one to remember. For customers to prefer one value proposition over all the others, it has to have favorable elements. In some cases, the target customers might be very familiar with the offering of an organization, but their connotations are negative. So it stands out from competitors' offerings, but not a way that would lead to customer preference.

Positioning is strong (and induces people to purchase) if it's built on elements that are very relevant for customers and perceived as very different with respect to competitors. The first quality generates alignment with expectations, the second leads to preference. A positioning consisting of components that are neither relevant nor differential is not only weak, it can't even

be considered true positioning, because it occupies no clearly defined space in customers' system of perceptions.

Positioning that is different from the competition but in ways that are not relevant won't win customer preference. Let's take an example of a theater that uses oriental perfume to scent the air and create ambiance. The theatergoers will probably perceive a difference (assuming that no other theater does the same thing), but one that has little or no relevance as far as their satisfaction. Essentially, the organization is investing in something that won't be transformed into customer preference, so it's wasting resources. By the same token, positioning that has components that are relevant but not differential isn't distinctive: it's built on the right foundations, but being aligned with the competition, customers have no reason to prefer it over all the rest.

So in attempting to build a strong positioning, what's vital to keep in mind are *points of parity* and *points of difference*. The first are non-differentiating, because these are characteristics of the positioning that customers attribute to the value propositions of various competitors. Points of parity, which coincide with basic factors (Section 7.9), are often characteristics of an entire product category.

For instance, a theater would find it hard to establish a distinctive positioning based on the fact that space for actors and spectators is separated, and that spectators watch the show while sitting in seats, because these features are standard for almost all theaters. An attempt at differentiation might be to eliminate the separation between actors and audience, and provide no seats, making spectators stand while they watch the show (see the examples in Section 2.3).

In other cases, there are points of competitive parity that all competitors offer because over time they've integrated these components into their offerings. Often factors that were once placed in the excitement or performance category are basics today because everyone offers them. For the theater an example would be online ticketing services.

Points of difference are elements that customers associate specifically with a given offering, and these are what form the basis for a truly strong positioning.

7.11 POSITIONING ANALYSIS

Analyzing the positioning of a value proposition is the key to effectively managing it. In fact, this analysis enables

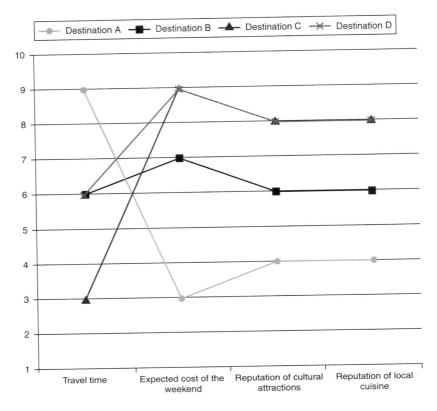

Figure 7.6 – An example of a snakeplot

the organization to discover the current positioning and, indirectly, the effectiveness of the strategy that brought it about. To analyze positioning the organization needs to conduct quantitative marketing research, and the most effective way to go about this is with a survey (Section 6.5.4). Using a structured questionnaire, analysts would interview a sample of target customers to reveal their perceptions of various competitors and the constituent elements of their value propositions (averaged for the market as a whole and broken down by segment).[11]

For an initial analysis, researchers can compare opinions on different value propositions regarding each constituent element. A very popular tool for representing these findings is the *snakeplot*, illustrated in Figure 7.6 (which graphs the data relative to the example on tourist destinations discussed in Section 4.4.1.3.1.1).

The advantage of the snakeplot is that it provides an instant snapshot of the similarities and dissimilarities of the competing value propositions, as perceived by customers. But the major disadvantage is that it can't give a comprehensive picture because each component of the value proposition is plotted on the graph individually. So the snakeplot is a useful tool if the aim is to identify the distinctive elements of a given value proposition with respect to every single competitor. But it's much less effective if the organization wants an overall view of its positioning, something it can only get from integrating its customers' opinions.

7.11.1 Perceptual maps

A perceptual map is the tool normally used to get a comprehensive representation of positioning. Through multivariate analysis (see note 11 to this Chapter) this map represents customers' perceptions of various competitors in a multi-dimensional space. Figure 7.7 illustrates a perceptual map created from the same dataset as the

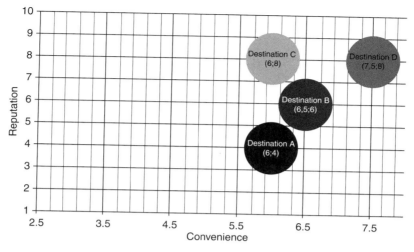

Figure 7.7 – An example of a perceptual map

previous figure. The variables 'convenience' and 'reputation' are built by factoring in the benefits 'travel time' and 'total expected cost' for the first, and 'reputation of attractions' and 'reputation of local cuisine' for the second (assuming that this combination is justified by the correlation between variables that have emerged from the data).

What can a perceptual map reveal about positioning? First, the positionings of all competitors are plainly visible, based on the components of their value propositions. So, for example, customers perceive Destination D as having excellent attractions and quality cuisine, which they can travel to with little time or expense. Second, the map shows the distance between competitors, and the distinctiveness of each one's positioning. So Destination D stands out among the other options, which all appear quite similar as far as accessibility (in terms of distance and cost). But each one has a different reputation: low for Destination A, intermediate for B, and high for C. The map also gives an indication of where there are direct or indirect competitive relationships from the distinctiveness of every positioning. Destination D's seems very different from the others', and as such is subject to less direct competition. But if there are consumer segments who value reputation above all else, then Destination C could be a formidable competitor.

But can the perceptual map tell managers whether or not positioning strategies are effective, and whether a competitor's positioning is strong? Unfortunately

the answer is no, because this map reveals nothing at all about the relevance of the benefits that differentiate one competitor from the other, and, as we know, relevance is one of the three requisites of a strong positioning. To get this information the organization needs to find out customer preferences regarding the constituent elements of the value proposition under investigation.

Basically, with the same survey managers can inquire into customers' preferences as well as their judgments on competitors. Another way to uncover this information is by asking respondents to indicate the relative importance of the constituent elements of value propositions or to describe their ideal offering (using those elements). With the resulting data a preference map can be drawn up. (Figure 7.8 shows a fictitious map based on the tourist destination example from above.)

This map doesn't show competitors but rather customer segments, with customers positioned on the map according to the preferences they expressed regarding the single components of the value proposition. In other words, customers who have similar preferences are obviously grouped together in a single segment, with each segment differing from all the others. In the figure, for instance, four different segments emerge (with segment size corresponding to the dimension of the relative bubble).

Segment 1 includes customers who prefer accessible destinations with a high reputation; the priority

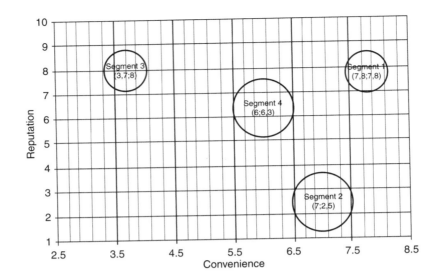

Figure 7.8 – An example of a preference map

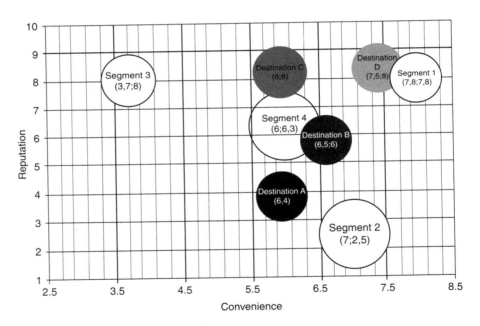

Figure 7.9 – Superimposing a perception map and a preference map

of people in Segment 2 is accessibility, with reputation being far less relevant; on the other hand, Segment 3 doesn't seem to place much importance on accessibility but is very keen on reputation; finally Segment 4 is made up of customers who take all the factors into consideration, without particular emphasis on any single one. To provide an answer to the question of the strength of competitors' positioning (and consequently the effectiveness of their positioning strategy) the two maps are superimposed (Figure 7.9).

By superimposing the two maps, the organization can discern whether or not distinctiveness corresponds to relevance, more clearly capturing direct and indirect competitive relationships. As the figure plainly shows, for example, Destination D has a strong positioning, because it's different from competing destinations and it's aligned with the preferences of Segment 1. Instead, Destinations B and C seem to compete for Segment 4. Finally Destination C, which might have been a competitor for D, seeing as both have similar reputations, appears to contend more with B because there's an intermediate segment that's close to them both. Finally, Destination A doesn't have a strong positioning, according to the map. In fact, it's far away from any market segment, indicating that it hasn't built a distinctive positioning on relevant aspects of its value proposition, so it's not aligned with the preferences of any group of customers.

What indicates that there are no competitors near or overlapping Segments 2 and 3? The fact that there are *offering voids*, that is, market segments with expectations that aren't satisfied by any of the current competitors. This is another invaluable indication that emerges by overlaying the two maps: the existence of potential market segments that are not being adequately served. These voids represent opportunities that organizations can exploit either by creating ad hoc value propositions or by repositioning one of their current propositions. In the example, Destination A could decide to make investments to become more closely aligned with Segment 2 by improving the perceptions of accessibility. Different ways to do this include creating transportation links that cut down on travel time or discounting tourist services.

7.12 MANAGING THE VALUE PROPOSITION

At the beginning of the chapter we saw that every market evolves through a series of stages, from its initial creation to growth and finally to maturity, which can encompass temporary expansion or contraction of sales. We also discussed how the transition from one stage to the next comes about through competitive dynamics consisting of differentiation and imitation, which, in turn, are powered in a continual cycle by changes in customer expectations. Since value propositions are designed and realized to satisfy the expectations of customers in different market segments, clearly the only way to manage these propositions is to keep pace with market evolution. Combining the concepts of segmentation and positioning enriches the representation of market evolution, giving rise to a more detailed description of what it means to manage value propositions over time.

When one or more organizations create a new market, that market is made up of customers with very similar expectations. In fact, activating a market essentially means transforming implicit benefits into explicit ones by introducing innovative offerings and by initiating a process of customer education. All this is done by the innovators themselves. So it's very likely that in the early stages of the market's lifecycle, competing value propositions are few and pioneering consumers won't find much that differentiates available offerings, so their expectations will be extremely homogeneous. Essentially the market coincides with one small segment (or just a few), and the organizations that do business here are all competing to win the preference of these customers.

As the market gradually grows, it attracts new competitors. To win market share, these organizations have to fulfill certain basic expectations, and on top of that create distinctive positionings for their value propositions, innovating the constituent elements. At the same time, incumbents defend their positions by innovating their propositions. This process transforms certain excitement factors into performance factors (and some of these in turn into basics), with new excitement factors being launched by organizations seeking to stand out among the competition.

Market growth comes from transforming potential customers into new adopters. These new customers can access more and more sources of information, and by tapping into the experiences of pioneers they can better define their own expectations. And veteran consumers who repeat their product use experience can refine their expectations as well. The outcome of all this is that the market gradually separates into segments, with organizations vying for market share in each one. This process continues in a similar fashion in the maturity stage, which sees progressive segmentation and re-segmentation of the market, due to strategies of competitors who create innovative value propositions to satisfy new customer expectations.

By observing this evolution from the viewpoint of a single organization, it's easy to intuit how to manage a value proposition over time. In the initial stage of *market creation*, since there are only a few customers and their expectations aren't particularly well defined, every organization competes with a value proposition centering on a few relevant benefits, with no single offering clearly standing out from the rest. In fact, excessive differentiation in this initial stage would prevent the creation and diffusion of a basic knowledge set shared by customers, which is necessary to establishing market boundaries.

So managing a value proposition means creating an innovative offering that activates a new market and triggers a growth trajectory. For example, consider the e-reader/e-book, a market created by Amazon with the Kindle.[12] Initially there were only a few competitors on the market (with Kindle alone achieving some level of awareness) and few users, grouped into a single segment, who were attracted by the benefits of portability and the storage space to accommodate a huge number of digital books.

Gradually with *market expansion* comes the need for differentiation. Basic factors become stable, so market strategy centers on points of difference. What's more, gradual segmentation increases the number of value propositions offered by every competitor that decides to serve several market segments rather than focusing on just one. Consequently, managing a value proposition also means creating and positioning new propositions for the targeted segments, while systematically refining existing propositions, building a rich and varied portfolio.

This is the current stage for the market of digital books. The initial success of Amazon has attracted other competitors (Barnes & Noble with the Nook, Kobo Inc. with the Kobo, and others), some of whom launched products with different technological platforms, such as tablets. This triggered the emergence of various market segments with customers looking for different benefits: being able to read in the dark or outdoors in the sunlight, having enough memory to store hundreds of books, Internet connectivity, transferability onto other devices, and so forth. Consequently a number of competitors are currently offering a variety of value propositions, each one aiming to satisfy the needs of different segments.

When a market reaches the *maturity stage*, the process described above intensifies. Since the market potential gap is very narrow, competition is primarily oriented toward repositioning value propositions through innovations that give rise to differentiating new excitement factors. So managing a value proposition now is all about innovating and repositioning, at least until a competitor comes up with something so innovative as to spur a new growth stage or even to activate a whole new market, recreating the characteristic conditions of the introduction stage of the market lifecycle.

To summarize the evolutionary paths of managing value propositions, a matrix in Figure 7.10 can be used that combines the value proposition's degree of innovation with competition across several segments.

Taking a newly-created market as the starting point, the organization offers a specially designed value proposition to serve a segment that coincides with the entire market (Quadrant I of the matrix). As the market grows and new segments emerge, the organization can continue to serve its satisfied customers with the original value proposition, but at the same time it can expand its market by offering the same proposition to other

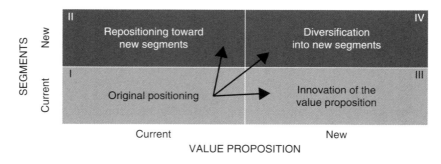

Figure 7.10 – Evolutionary paths for managing a value proposition

segments (probably with a few variations, but keeping the basic design intact) (Quadrant II).

At this point, customer evolution might prompt the organization to propose original new value propositions to its market segments, offering innovative excitement factors that satisfy different expectations (Quadrant III). And if there are other segments with entirely new expectations, beyond the segments the organization currently serves, it might opt to design and realize value propositions that differ substantially from the original one, incorporating cutting-edge technology or novel symbolic or experiential elements (Quadrant IV).

7.13   CONCLUSIONS

My aim in this chapter was to describe the strategic component of the process of creating value for the customer, also known as strategic marketing. Value creation calls for choices that determine the long-term market positioning of an organization to a great extent. Salient questions that managers should ask themselves are: 'Which customers do we want to serve?' and 'How do we want them to perceive our offering compared to the others, and to prefer it over the others?' Answering these questions entails making choices about which market the organization wants to target and how to design appropriate value propositions.

Throughout the chapter I've analyzed the different steps in the decision-making process regarding the target market, from more abstract stages of identifying and delineating the boundaries of that market, to more operative steps such as identifying different segments, and evaluating the size and attractiveness of each one. Summing up, the strategic decision pertaining to identifying a target market can be stated simply as choosing to serve one, a few, many, or all of the constituent segments.

This choice is closely connected with the decision regarding personalizing the offering, that is, designing value propositions that are specifically adapted to clearly defined groups of customers. As we now know, this decision consists in positioning the organization on a continuum with the end points being mass marketing strategies and one-to-one marketing. Through market segmentation, organizations attempt to strike a balance between the advantages and disadvantages of both in order to satisfy their target customers in a way that's productively and financially sustainable for the organization.

After choosing the target market segments, next comes creating and positioning the value proposition. For these stages too I pointed out the specific decisions or evaluations organizations need to make so that their value propositions are capable of satisfying the expectations of target customers, while standing out among competing propositions.

In describing the creation of value propositions, our exploration has covered the strategic issues relating to design, but we haven't yet touched on choices relating to the constituent components. The benefits provided by a value proposition depend on the tangible and intangible attributes of the relative products, brands, prices, and communication and distribution channels. In Chapter 8 we'll take a closer look at decisions regarding the first three factors: products, brands, and pricing. However, choices about communication and distribution have to do with making the value proposition accessible to customers, so these decisions are more germane to the process of value delivery, and warrant a separate discussion, which will be the topic of Chapter 9.

REVIEW QUESTIONS

1. What are the different stages of a market lifecycle? What are the differential characteristics of each stage as far as supply-demand dynamics?

2. How can a potential market be measured? Which indicators are necessary? And what about potential market gaps?

3. What are the components of the market share indicator? What insights can be gained by breaking it down?

4. What are the segmentation criteria an organization can use? Do they differ in consumer or business markets? In building market segments, what are the advantages and disadvantages of a priori and a posteriori approaches?

5. How can the attractiveness of target segments be assessed? How can this information guide targeting choices?

6. What are the components of a value proposition? How should they be chosen in order to meet customer expectations?

7. Why is it important to build a positioning for a value proposition? What are the characteristics of a strong positioning?

CASE STUDY

MTV ITALIA: DESIGNING AND IMPLEMENTING A MARKET EXPANSION STRATEGY

August 1, 1981 marked the first-ever broadcast of the US television station MTV. From the very start, the channel's value proposition was clear-cut and highly differentiated from its competitors: all-music programming with music videos presented by *video jockeys* (VJs).

This innovative use of a television channel (as compared to traditional means for broadcasting music), along with a strong accent on pop culture, propelled MTV to a strong positioning among a very specific television audience: 15- to 34-year-olds.

The success and influence of MTV was such that wherever it was broadcast, sales soared for many albums that wouldn't normally get air time on radio stations (previously the music industry's most effective distribution channel). The MTV effect in later years actually labeled an entire generation – the MTV Generation – with its programming and its light, transgressive style: it was a lifestyle icon.

Viacom acquired MTV in 1985 and created *MTV Networks*. In the wake of its incredible popularity in North America, Viacom decided to launch MTV in the rest of the world and opened its European headquarters in Amsterdam, later moving to London. In 1988 the channel started broadcasting in Switzerland, Belgium, and Greece, and the following year in Germany.

In 1991 it was Italy's turn. At first MTV Europe's programming was aired only by a few local stations for six hours a day. Thanks to the initial success this generated, in 1995 MTV Italy was established, with the aim of producing programming especially for Italy, broadcasting for 13 hours a day.

In December 1996 the first program in Italian debuted, and in September 1997 the channel reached 22 hours a day of air time through an agreement with a local network. The event was celebrated with the first *MTV Day* (replicated every year), consisting of non-stop concerts organized in a single day in an Italian city to mark the channel's birthday. In later years MTV programming continued to expand to include local production of certain programs.

In 2001 Telecom Italia acquired 51 per cent of MTV Italy from Viacom and continued the process of adapting content to local audiences with more determination than ever before. Following this, the new decade brought radical changes. In 2003–2004, MTV Italy split its offering into multiple channels, with *MTV Hits* offering music videos, and *MTV Brand New* alternative music, leaving more general music programming on *MTV*. This last channel also broadcast local and international non-musical shows (news, reality, fiction and other entertainment), such as *Loveline, The Osbournes*, and *Scrubs* during prime time and late night slots as an Italian free to air exclusive.

The need to expand the market

From its debut until the mid-2000s, MTV Italy built *a solid competitive positioning on its target audience* (15- to 34-year-olds, with special focus on 15- to 24-year-olds). The success of the brand and the channel was so apparent to market players that sponsors and advertising investments were guaranteed, even without data on viewer numbers. (In fact, MTV didn't take part in the national ratings survey for television audience (Auditel), an anomaly in the Italian television industry.)

But since the mid-2000s, the characteristics of the competitive context have changed, and changed very rapidly. Besides the limited size of the core target (15- to 24-year-olds) additional elements negatively impacted the competitive positioning of MTV Italy, eroding the distinctiveness of its value proposition.

1. There were far more opportunities to access a profusion of music video content online, and at the same time an explosion in the popularity of YouTube among young people.
2. There was a switch-over from analog to digital television, which began in 2008 in Italy (and concluded with the definitive switch-off in 2012), exponentially multiplying the number of channels available to television viewers; dozens of new channels were created specifically targeting young people and the competition of the Sky satellite digital platform on this target was increasing (with channels like Real Time, Dmax, Sky Uno, Cielo, and Fox).
3. Large ad spenders had many more channel options to allocate their investments after the switch-off.
4. Those same spenders were more eager to measure their return on communication investments, which penalized MTV since its audience numbers were not measured in the national survey.

In 2009, the Viacom Group (owner of MTV Networks and 49 per cent of MTV Italy), recognizing that the global competitive landscape of the industry was undergoing dramatic change, fostered the repositioning of the MTV network internationally, with the clear aim of expanding content beyond solely music while continuing to focus on a young target.

In May 2010, MTV Italy started broadcasting on a new digital terrestrial platform, with an offering covering two channels, reinforcing its existing positioning: *MTV+* (rebranded *MTV Music* in 2011), entirely dedicated to music and video clips, and *MTV*, with more generalist programming.

But by this time the competition for young viewers, both from other television stations and other media, was so intense that for the first time since its inception MTV Italy perceived the danger of a drop in sponsorship and advertising revenues and the need to strengthen its reputation and positioning. The risk to avoid was to be perceived as a channel anchored to a format of content that was no longer keeping pace with the evolution underway in the media system and the target audience.

The first move MTV Italy made to rectify the situation was to launch new products and innovate the transmission platform. To this end, 2011 saw the launch of new satellite channels distributed on the digital platform owned by Sky, alongside the old *MTV Hits* focused on the top selling tunes in Italy: *MTV Classic*, dedicated to hits spanning the last three decades; *MTV Rock*, with an accent on rock and alternative music; *MTV Dance*, offering all dance tunes; and *MTV Live HD*, exclusively broadcasting live events in high definition.

However, management at MTV Italy realized that product innovation alone within the music context wouldn't be enough to defend the competitive positioning of the MTV system. In fact, it was becoming more and more obvious that to contend with the proliferation of competitor offerings, the network had to expand its market, turning to a *multi-segment strategy* with value propositions shifting away from music content. Although various media were vying for MTV's preferred target, the network's true positioning was built on a distinctive communicative style that could represent value for different (albeit related) targets.

The repositioning strategy: a new targeting and a new value proposition

The aim of the repositioning strategy was to revamp the network's image: from television offering almost exclusively content for young people to more generalist television with the potential for attracting a broader age group: young adults. Repositioning meant expanding content to include a greater variety of entertainment while keeping a firm hold on musical content.

To make the plan more credible, and to generate the resources from sponsors and advertising investors needed to support the new positioning, MTV opted to take part for the first time in the national ratings survey for television audiences. The decision was a risky one, but management felt confident that the channel would prove capable of covering its traditional target and also expanding to encompass the broader repositioning target.

With the new strategy, *MTV* became the flagship channel, conveying the image of the network. As such, it replaced *MTV+* (renamed *MTV Music* in 2011 for this reason), which in turn became the channel with a strong focus on traditional content – music – gaining a more precise positioning for its value proposition.

The *new value proposition* of the network would be more generalist, based on *intelligent entertainment*, with MTV's typical communicative style. Music was part (but not all) of the offering, broadcast on various channels (free to air and pay TV) according to genre and format. To reinforce this message, the traditional tagline – 'Music television' – associated with the MTV logo from the start, was eliminated (Figure 7.11).

In Summer 2012 the new station presented its lineup along with a communication campaign designed to create a new positioning with viewers. The key message was not only 'MTV is changing,' but also 'How to do television is changing too,' with a new kind of entertainment, different from competitors' offerings, available to the audience for the first time.

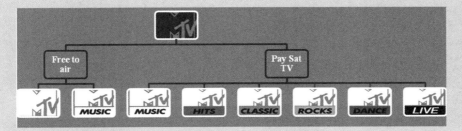

Figure 7.11– The MTV Italy network

The strategy for the new channel consisted of two sequential stages. The first, lasting the whole of 2012, focused on the core target: 15- to 34-year-olds. Implementation in this stage impacted afternoon programming, with major product innovation including new formats:

- *Docureality shows* dedicated to disciplines such as dance, gymnastics, and football; the lives of promising young athletes are presented in these shows using a typical reality format.
- *Sit-coms,* including shows such as *Awkward* and *Modern Family*.
- *Transformational documentaries,* spotlighting life-changing events or processes experienced by young people; examples are *16 and Pregnant* and *Teen Mom.*

The second stage of the strategy was initiated in the spring of 2013, when actual *market expansion* took place, focusing on the 25- to 44-year-old target. Innovation here meant renewing content and resetting the prime time slot from the traditional 9:00 pm to 11:00 pm, to more effectively intercept the needs of the broader target. The new lineup offered an array of different formats, tailoring new shows to the target, and improving on previous products. Here are some examples:

- *TV series*, exclusives for Italy, such as *Girls*.
- *Films*, both prime time and late night, in particular action and horror genres.
- *Comedy shows*, giving air time to comedians who've made their mark on other media;
- *Il Testimone* (*The Witness*), a show offering investigative reporting on current events that attracts quite a transversal audience.

The positioning of the new value proposition

MTV chose to expand its target in response to competitive pressure, repositioning itself in the perceptions of Italian TV viewers. This choice might seem more risky than simply securing the original target, because with a generalist proposition targeting a wider audience the competitive arena is much more crowded. But MTV Italy's strategy was to establish a distinctive positioning built on new shows and original programming, and all this, as always, with the station's signature television style: young, intelligent, light, and transgressive.

Proof of the success of this strategy, and the new positioning, is corroborated by 2013 data on MTV's viewership and share, in addition to ad hoc research on its audience. Today MTV viewers mainly fall into the 15-to-44 age bracket; they enjoy substantial spending power and have a high level of education. This group is very demanding and selective, showing an appreciation for experimentation and innovation in terms of content.

What's more, MTV viewers don't access content solely on television, but via mobile devices as well. In fact, alongside the repositioning, MTV Italy has implemented a strategy of content delivery through other platforms: on the web, with the www.mtv.it website and its full length, on demand, for free section, and via the new MTV app that allows access to all contents from mobile devices and simultaneous social interaction.

The new multichannel content delivery is supported by a dedicated communication strategy. As a result of the success of this strategy, data show that a sizeable slice of the target watches programs exclusively online, an audience that isn't counted in the national survey system.

REVIEW QUESTIONS

1. The decision to reposition MTV Italy was rooted in a number of facts regarding both the competitive arena and the broader macro-environment. What are the major events that affected MTV Italy's market position?

2. The first reaction of MTV Italy to these changes was to launch new channels. But the company's management believed this strategy was not sufficient. Which kind of objectives could that strategy achieve and which ones were out of reach by investing only in product innovation?

3. MTV Italy seemed to have two strategic options: to consolidate its traditional positioning toward the young segment, or to broaden its market to include a wider audience. What are the benefits and risks connected with these two options? What are their repercussions for the other products in the MTV Italy portfolio?

CREATING VALUE WITH THE PRODUCT, THE BRAND, AND THE PRICE

LEARNING OBJECTIVES

After reading this chapter you should be able to:

- Understand the contribution of product management, brand management and price management to customer value creation in creative industries.
- Identify the various stages of a product's lifecycle and detail the most important product decisions for new products and for established ones.
- Understand the peculiar role of brands in creative industries and their value for consumers and producers, and detail the most important decisions in the various stages of a brand's lifecycle.
- Identify the reference points for setting a product's price, and changing it over the product lifecycle.
- Interpret the complex effects of product price on product sales.
- Distinguish different price setting methods, and choose the most appropriate one according to the market objectives to be achieved.

OVERVIEW

Value creation is all about designing a proposition made up of benefits and their corresponding sacrifices, as I emphasized in Chapter 7. Now we'll turn our attention to three components of the value proposition that have the most evident and immediate impact on these benefits and sacrifices: the product, the brand, and the price. The first two more than anything else are what shape the consumption experience and product use as a factor of production or communication, while the last represents the most obvious sacrifice (although not the only one, and not even necessarily the biggest one, as we saw in Section 3.1.6).

These three components play a very particular role in the value proposition. As I said in the first chapter, if creativity is what connects the production and consumption systems, the product is where this creativity primarily emerges. On one hand, authors, artists, journalists, designers, stylists, and athletes use their creative resources and skills to make products; on the other, customers buy these products to experience or exploit this creativity.

What we also discussed in Chapter 1 is the vital role that brand plays in the relationships between producers and customers in creative industries. There are two main reasons why brand is so essential. For producers, brand is an asset they use to capitalize investments that can't be recovered from individual products due to the length of their lifecycle, which is normally much too short. For customers, the brand represents a quality clue that minimizes the risk inherent to buying and using an experience product.

Finally, price also has a very similar part to play, especially because it's one of the few objective indicators people can utilize to compare very different products (a customer contemplating the purchase of either a painting or a vacation; a firm debating between sponsoring a sports team or funding the restoration of a historical monument). Put another way, price is one of the few parameters of vertical differentiation that customers can quite confidently use as a point of reference when positioning different products on a comparative scale. What's more, price is also a handy quality clue; it's logical to assume that a higher list price equals higher quality. For producers, this means that price is a powerful tool for positioning a value proposition.

In this chapter we'll discuss topics relating to product, brand and price from a producer's point of view, in other words, in terms of product management, brand management, and price management. Customer satisfaction, as always, is the litmus test for ascertaining whether or not these components are managed effectively. But beyond effectiveness, the aim of this chapter is to provide a perspective that accentuates efficiency as well. In other words, we'll explore how to strike the proper balance between the two.

Specifically, the two questions I'll try to answer are: How do the product, the brand, and the price contribute to creating value for the customer? And on the other side of the coin, how do choices regarding product, brand, and price contribute to generating value for the producer? The answers, naturally, are interrelated. In fact, it's the organization's ability to adopt a win-win rationale, that is, value for the customer combined with value for itself, that guarantees productive and financial sustainability for creative products and activities.

In this chapter we'll discover that effectiveness and efficiency can be pursued by coordinating and integrating a series of decisions that have to do with both individual products and brands and their relative prices, as well as portfolios of products and brands. In particular, we'll see that the decisions relating to these three components of the value proposition differ on a very basic level when considering the moment of innovation (creating and launching a new product or brand) or later on in the lifecycle (when products and brands have already won a market share). To comprehend this difference, I'll use product and brand lifecycle models to frame the analysis of key decisions.

8.1   PRODUCT MANAGEMENT

Let's take the example of managers of a radio station. What's their product? The answer is less obvious that it might initially seem. The first response would be their programming. But when – on a daily or a weekly basis? And if the weekend schedule is different, what time frame should be used? And considering advertising investors, airtime is sold on an hourly basis, so time slots are the true products. But what about individual programs? Aren't these the basis of creative choices in terms of content, format, and guests? And if the critical success factor of an individual program is the host or DJ, isn't this a product in and of itself? So the answer to the question about the product is not simple or pointless. And it's even less so if

the company owns a number of different radio stations, and it has to manage them all while exploiting synergies and avoiding cannibalization.

So the first point to consider is the unit of management to apply, in other words, the product on which the organization bases its decisions.

8.1.1   Establishing a product hierarchy

A product hierarchy is made up of the *different levels of aggregation of an organization's products*. Each level can be managed as a separate unit. Specific creative industries often have their own ways to denominate various levels. For consumer markets, for example, publishing houses have books and series; clothing manufacturers have lines and collections; theaters have shows and season tickets; radio stations have programs and schedules; and so on. Generally speaking, the main hierarchical levels are:

- The *individual product*. This is the minimum level on which to base specific marketing decisions (the individual radio program, book, or issue of a newspaper or magazine, for example). For each of these products an organization can make specific product-based decisions (format, content, and so on), and pricing decisions (list prices, discounts, freebies); these products can have communication campaigns (ads, web banners, and so forth) and specific distribution strategies (only online or offline, or a combination of the two).[1] In the world of consumer products centering on physical retail stores (books, CDs, DVDs, clothing, for example) this hierarchical level is normally called an *SKU* (*stock keeping unit*).
- The *product line*. This is made up of a set of products belonging to the same category and targeting the same consumers. In the clothing industry, for instance, a company would have lines for men, women, and children. In publishing, there might be a line for children and for teens, or mystery, romance, and so forth (usually grouped together in series). With periodicals, there are men's and women's magazines, and professional and lifestyle publications.
- The *product category*. This consists in the set of products that share the same production processes and satisfy the same generic needs/desires. For example, a museum can offer various product categories to final consumers: visits to the collections, workshops, conferences, and so forth. A fashion company can sell clothing, shoes, bags, eyewear, and more.

As I just mentioned, every one of these levels calls for explicit decisions made by specific roles within the organization and then coordinated with other functions to increase effectiveness without losing efficiency. For instance, companies that do business in creative industries might have a product manager who is responsible for individual products, a group product manager who heads up several products or lines, and a category manager or marketing manager who handles entire product categories. With the BBC, for example, the product category (which they call an 'operational area') is headed by a Director; the lines or products that make up the category are the responsibility of a Controller.

As detailed in Section 8.2.4, various brands can be associated with each hierarchical level. Naturally, if the organization has a brand management structure (as opposed to a product management structure), it will have brand managers instead of product managers.

8.1.2   The product lifecycle

In the previous chapter, I introduced the model for the market lifecycle, which is helpful in explaining market evolution and dynamics that drive it. I also mentioned that the market lifecycle is fueled in part by the lifecycles of different products that are sold on that market (Section 7.2.5). Consequently, there are noteworthy interrelations between the two cycles.

In this section I want to delve deeper into the product, to explore the factors that determine the form and the duration of a specific product's lifecycle, and the decisions in the various stages that are made by companies and institutions in creative industries. To this end, I'll base my explanation on the assumption that the cycle has a standard structure with the same four sequential stages found in the market (introduction, growth, maturity, decline), and the same growth dynamic for sales.[2] So what determines the form and duration of the lifecycle of a product?

8.1.2.1   *The unit of analysis: the hierarchical level of the product*
The form and the duration of the cycle depend primarily on the hierarchical level of the product that the organization uses as a reference point for measuring sales. It's easy to see why, keeping in mind that the lifecycle model is one that describes a relationship: time versus product sales.

Take music, for instance. Singles or CDs by a hip-hop artist have a certain lifecycle that can be measured in

weeks (or months, for songs that become hits); but overall sales by the artist have a different lifecycle depending on both her artistic production and the effects of the sales of her latest releases on her previous work. (A consumer who buys one of her new songs might want to check out her old ones too.) Extrapolating even further, there's yet another lifecycle for the sales of the entire sub-category (the hip-hop musical genre, in our example), which consists of sales of all the tracks/CDs of all the artists categorized as hip-hop. So continuing in terms of abstraction along the levels presented in the previous chapter (Section 7.1), this leads to the lifecycle of the entire market, which, as we've seen, is hard to break down since it's made up of products and categories that undergo systematic revitalization.

8.1.2.2   *The differentiation–imitation dynamic among customers*
I've already mentioned the differentiation–imitation dynamic that emerges among competitors and among customers (Section 7.2.5). The model that illustrates the impact of this dynamic on the form of a product's lifecycle is called the *diffusion of innovation*, first proposed by Rogers (1962). This model classifies customers according to their attitudes and behaviors toward adopting a new product.

When a new product is launched, customers don't know much about it; perceiving a high risk, not many are motivated by buy. The few who do, the *innovators* or *pioneers*, have distinctive traits: a low aversion to risk, a tendency to be non-conformists (they don't need reassurance from the fact that other consumers are making the same choices) and a strong desire for social distinction, close connections with sources of innovation, and marked interest in new trends in general. Obviously these people are a minimal percentage of any market, but they play an essential role: they provide proof of the product to other customers, activating the first imitation phenomena.

Innovators are followed by *early adopters*. These people are more numerous than the previous group, yet share many of the same traits. Generally speaking, though, early adopters have a greater aversion to risk (especially social risk), and more intense social connections with other customers; they are more often opinion leaders. These are the people who set in motion the much more powerful imitative dynamic: the *bandwagon effect*. Their social visibility makes them particularly suited to engendering a demonstrative effect on other customers. In other words, by consuming a certain product, they demonstrate that its quality is high. So in a sense these consumers actually represent quality clues.

Next come the *majority* of customers, to include the *early majority* and the *late majority*. Both these groups, at varying levels of intensity, are adverse to risk and as such not particularly taken in by innovations; they tend to be conformists, and need to see that other people have already adopted the product before they do the same.

The last category is the *laggards*. They represent a minority of the market (numbering about the same as the innovators and early adopters put together). These consumers are very resistant to change; for the most part they are not opinion leaders and are very strongly tied to tradition and habit. With final consumers, the laggards tend to be older and often continue to use very out-dated products, in part because they have a hard time accepting more advanced technologies. This explains the lower degree of penetration among older consumers in terms of digital products or more innovative art forms and vice versa.

To express the innovation-imitation dynamic the following mathematical formula applies (Bass, 1969):

$$n_t = \left[p + q\left(\frac{N_{t-1}}{MP}\right) \right](MP - N_{t-1})$$

where n_t is the number of customers who adopt the product at time t for the first time; p is the coefficient of innovation which represents the probability that a customer will buy the new product on the basis of information gleaned directly from the producer; q is the imitation coefficient (always greater than p), which represents the probability that a customer will buy the new product thanks to word of mouth from other consumers (so this is a measure of the bandwagon effect); MP is the market potential; N_{t-1} is the number of customers who've already adopted the product at time t-1.

Sales during the lifecycle represent the total purchases by various types of consumers. As the later groups buy for the first time, the previous groups are already in the repeat purchase phase (if the product allows and the customers benefit).

8.1.2.3 The investment cycle

The model for the diffusion of innovation represents the standard dynamic of distinction–imitation among customers. But the actual shape of the curve of this cycle depends on how quickly this dynamic emerges, which in turn depends to some extent on the actions of organizations that do operate on the market. Also connected to sales as represented in the cycle are the investments that organizations have to make in order to operate in the market. Obviously many investments pre-date an organization's initial sales: payments made to property rights holders, investments in product development and communication campaigns connected to launching the product, and training the sales network, for instance. So from a financial viewpoint, clearly the product first generates costs, and later sales revenues, so in the initial lifecycle stages cash flow will be negative.

Generally speaking, the greater the investments that an organization has to incur before launching a new product (generating cash expenditures), the faster sales should grow (generating cash earnings) to render the product financially sustainable. If instead sales are slow taking off subsequent to major investments, the organization may find it impossible to support the product over time, which could lead to the decision to pull it off the market to avoid further financial losses.

This would be the case, for example, for various television programs, designed without much consideration for spectators' expectations. When the first few shows attract a very low audience, they lose their appeal for advertising investors. This means they are not sustainable in the long-term, and they'll inevitably be cancelled.

So when a product calls for heavy investments, the organization will try to jump start sales; if instead investments are relatively limited, the timing for the return on investments can be slower. It's easy to see that the first case is more typical of mass marketing strategies, while the second comes into play with niche marketing (Section 7.6). The investments–returns dynamic sharply impacts the shape of the cycle and the duration of the different stages.

In fact, a strategy aimed at a quick recovery on investments will attempt to compress the introduction phase, or even skip it completely, driving forward directly to the growth stage and saturating the market as rapidly as possible. Maturity is the next step, with systematic repeat purchases or rapid decline (if this product has to make way for other new ones). An approach with far less pressure on recovering investments would involve more traditional introduction and growth stages, with sales probably peaking at a lower level, and a much slower purchase–repurchase cycle. Here are some examples. In movies, music, books, or art exhibits, the first strategy described above would correspond to blockbusters, which immediately rise to the top of the bestseller lists thanks to intense communication campaigns and blanket distribution. Then these products are left to drop in popularity just as rapidly to vehicle content in other ways (films in DVD or on TV; singles in compilations or sound tracks; books in paperback; art exhibits on tour). The second strategy would apply to connoisseur products, which generally have a more limited potential market. These are launched with more selective communication and distribution strategies, and reach their sales peak thanks more than anything to word of mouth (Figure 8.1).

8.1.2.4   The competitive dynamic

Section 7.2.5 described how the differentiation-imitation dynamic doesn't only affect customers but organizations as well, perhaps to an even greater degree, giving shape and duration to the stages in the product cycle. In fact, if one organization launches a new product and it performs well, the others will quickly follow suit with their own versions in an effort to imitate the first mover. Some of the product features will be the same (so that customers will associate the new products with the originals and appreciate the similarities) and some different, to create customer preference. With this wave of new products, sales in the category rise significantly, benefiting the pioneer product all the more (Research Focus 8.1).

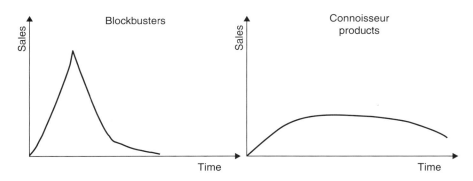

Figure 8.1 – Different strategies for managing the product lifecycle

Research Focus 8.1

The lifecycle of style trends in the fashion market

In the fashion market there are very particular dynamics of distinction and imitation among customers. In fact, people use fashion products, perhaps more than anything else, to express their identity. But the true product is *style*, that is, the combination of specific pieces that make up a collection (shirts, trousers, jackets, skirts, and so on), and their distinctive attributes (size, color, trimming, fabrics, and other materials).

If consumers use fashion not only to show that they belong to a certain social group, but also to distinguish themselves from the masses and to stand out in a crowd, how can companies satisfy this dual desire? How can they create styles that are both the same and different? Styles that can be found in competitors' collections (ensuring social acceptance), but which at the same time are distinctive (winning customer preference)?

Cappetta et al. (2006) studied the evolution of styles in the fine fashion market (also known as *prêt-à-porter* or *ready to wear*) from the 1980s to the 2000s. Fine fashion refers to the market of products that are not tailor made (unlike high fashion or *haute couture*), but still considered high end in terms of both quality and price. (Competitors in this segment include Armani, Dior, Gucci, Louis Vuitton, and Prada, among others.)

The authors demonstrated that in this market over the years, the succession of style lifecycles follow a peculiar innovation process. At times, various styles vie for social acceptance by consumers, and eventually one style finally predominates over the others (also thanks to the critical contribution of specialized media). This period the authors call 'ferment'. Then competitors start trying to better one another by innovating this style. Here the authors refer to 'incremental change'.

Here's an example. In the mid-1980s, most companies adopted the masculine style in women's wear introduced by Armani a few years before. This style gradually fell from grace in the later part of the decade, which was a time of ferment, to the point where a minimal style emerged, with more feminine garments (with skirts replacing trousers), more neutral tones, and unusual fabrics. The early 1990s were a time of incremental change that eventually turned back into ferment during the second half of the decade, with the kitsch style emerging, with combinations of traditional and new materials (PVC, plastic) and loud, colorful trimming.

Cappetta et al. show that, unlike many high-tech markets where ferment ends when one *dominant design* becomes the standard, in the fine fashion market *convergent design* emerges that attracts creative efforts of the majority of firms, but that never definitively substitutes other more niche styles.

If for example an art gallery organizes a successful exhibit of young artists from a developing country, very likely other galleries will go scouring the same country for other artists to set up their own exhibits. This would spark greater public interest in artists from that country, and the gallery that hosted their debut could continue to organize exhibits, being credited as the expert and leveraging the benefits of reputation. But if sales of this new product are disappointing, other organizations would lose interest in launching similar products. As a result, sales of the product category as a whole would stall, and this would further penalize the innovator, who would end up acting alone to promote the new category.

8.1.2.5   *Product specificities*

Aside from the supply and demand dynamics that come into play in a market, the shape of the lifecycle and the length of the individual stages also depend on the specific features of the product. A temporary exhibit has a opening and closing date, and may be offered again in a different venue. The same is true with a ballet, a play, a musical tour, a fashion collection, and a sports season. On the other hand, a city, a country, an archeological site, a national park: all these have practically infinite lifecycles.

When there is a pre-established end point, the overall cycle of single products may last years if it consists of a succession of sub-cycles in sales. Clearly, previous product sales impact later sales, shaping the form and duration of cycles. When an art exhibit goes on tour, for instance, success in one city will have positive repercussions in the next city (in fact, the communication campaign will play up this success). In this case the first exhibit will probably have a fairly standard cycle, while later exhibits will look more like blockbusters.

But the opposite can happen too. For instance, a certain play might be offered as part of a season's programming, so there is a high and pre-defined number of potential customers (season ticket holders). But in the years to follow, the show probably won't be offered again in the same package, so it will have to attract spectators who are not season ticket holders, clearly giving rise to a different cycle.

Summing up, the lifecycle model is useful to organizations in understanding trends in the supply–demand dynamics within a market, and in providing input for making decisions regarding the product and other components of the value proposition. As for the specificities of creative industries, this model helps show how creating value for customers (be they consumers or businesses) is very different with a new product as opposed to one with a track record.

This implies that the decisions an organization needs to make are different too, as we'll see in the following sections. But before detailing these decisions, it's essential to clarify exactly what the various components of a product are, because product innovation is all about creating new attributes and combining them in different ways or creating new relationships between attributes and benefits/sacrifices.

8.1.3   Product attributes

Every product is made up of a set of attributes that serve to provide certain benefits or to minimize possible sacrifices. Marketing has a different perspective on product attributes as compared to, say, production. In fact, production considers attributes from a technical standpoint, while Marketing sees them as elements that customers can perceive and evaluate to make their purchase decisions. A product attribute often consists of numerous technical attributes.

For instance, from a production standpoint, a film is made up of a screenplay, a director, a cast, a set, scenery, photography, editing, post-production, a soundtrack, and more. What consumers see in a film instead centers on the story, sometimes the director, perhaps famous actors, awards, the sound track, and so forth (Research Focus 8.2). For a corporate client a film is a plot that can provide an effective placement opportunities, or a group of actors or a director who can provide access a given target market.

Creating and modifying a product during its lifecycle means combining the attributes that customers believe are capable of fulfilling their explicit expectations, or drawing out their implicit ones. It's worth reiterating that by adopting the customer's perspective, within the framework of a market orientation, a product is always the set of benefits that can satisfy her needs and the related sacrifices that she has to make.

Seeing that product attributes are meant to provide benefits and that these benefits must be differentiating to create customer preference, a useful way to classify them is based on their contribution to the differentiation of the value proposition. Two aspects factor into this classification: the nature of the attributes and their current and future uniqueness.

As far as *nature* is concerned, there are tangible and intangible attributes. The first can furnish vertical differentiation, the second horizontal (Section 1.2). The style (of a novel, newspaper report, fashion collection), the genre (in literature, film, music), design, brand awareness, and reputation – these are all examples of intangible product attributes. The size, weight, duration, or inclusion/exclusion of certain features are tangible attributes (Case History 8.1). For a national park, for instance, these would consist of the number of square miles, the number and average length of hiking trails, the availability of mountain bike rentals; intangibles might include awareness, reputation, history, and atmosphere. Generally speaking, tangible attributes tend to provide utilitarian value; intangibles hedonic and communicative value.[3]

Research Focus 8.2

The value of stars in films

The movie industry is and always has been a star factory. Although the thousands of movies in any given year are made thanks to millions of actors, very few enjoy the status of the likes of Johnny Depp, Helena Bonham Carter, Tom Hanks, Julia Roberts, Tom Cruise, or Kate Winslet, who can excite the passions of millions of fans and actually make or break a film. But beyond the conventional wisdom in the industry, is it really true that the box office performance of a film can depend on the stars in its cast?

To answer this question Elberse (2007) carried out an experiment using HSX, a virtual market in which about half a million registered users can buy and sell shares in new feature movies, predicting box office success on the basis of information on the director, the cast, the screenplay among others. Previous research has demonstrated the reliability of HSX in predicting whether new releases will become box office hits.

The author measured the impact of 1,200 star casting announcements on the box office projections of corresponding films. All the stars were defined in terms of their economic reputation, measured as average box office results from previous films, and their artistic reputation, quantified as the number of nominations and wins at the Academy Awards and the Golden Globes. The results show that both the economic and artistic reputation of the stars have a positive impact on the film's box office revenues, the latter having a far greater effect. What's more, Elberse shows that having an A-list cast multiplies the positive impact of including a newly recruited star, confirming the hypothesis that in a high-ability group of people, the creative performance of each individual improves thanks to the talents of fellow group members.

The study's last finding is that the positive impact on the box office of big name stars in the cast does not translate into comparable financial results for the producer. Essentially, additional revenues accredited to the presence of stars are offset by the greater costs deriving from their fees, so basically the effect on profits is nil. The conclusion is that 'stars may not add more value than they capture' (p. 117).

Case History 8.1

Etiqueta negra: a mix of highly differentiated tangible and intangible attributes

Etiqueta negra is a Peruvian monthly magazine considered by many to be one of the best in the world. Founded in 2002, its slogan is: 'a magazine for distracted people'. What makes it distinctive in every sense is an effective mix of different kinds of attributes. As for intangibles, first and foremost is a daring publishing approach: every issue covers a single topic from a variety of creative perspectives: photographs, essays, investigative reporting, interviews, or graphic novels. It's the chosen strategy for attracting the attention of the 'distracted' segment and to satisfy their need for in-depth exploration. Tangible attributes, instead, include contributing authors, who are often well-known names at an international level from the world of literature, music, investigative journalism, and art. The number of articles in each issue is very limited, no more than a dozen. The graphics are exceptional quality, and are just as vital as the content. The quality of the paper is excellent, making the magazine stand out from similar products.

Case History 8.2

Product differentiation in automobile racing: *Formula 1* versus *NASCAR*

Automobile racing attracts millions of fans the world over making it (combined with motorcycle racing) the sports sector that wins one of the largest market shares of sponsorships, on a par with football. Nearly as intense as the rivalry between drivers is competition among the organizers of races and championships to attract both live spectators and, more importantly, television viewers. The winning strategy is to differentiate the championships on a series of attributes.

The two most successful championships are the Formula 1 and NASCAR (National Association for Stock Car Auto Racing) (www.formula1.com; www.nascar.com). The first is more widely known, even among people who aren't racing fans, thanks mostly to the fact that the races are held in several different countries. NASCAR, instead, is concentrated in North America, mainly in the US. To get an idea of its popularity, simply consider that NASCAR is one of the most watched sports events in that country, second only to the Super Bowl, and is broadcast in hundreds of countries around the world.

The products in these two championships differ on a number of attributes, specifically (Maggi, 2012): the scope (national or international), the type of vehicle, the format, and public participation. First, while Formula 1 is a global event, NASCAR is deeply rooted in North American culture. Second, F1 automobiles with open wheels are designed especially for the race; in NASCAR, competitions pit ordinary automobile makes and models with covered wheels against one another. The thrill of Formula 1 racing comes from the extraordinary performance of the vehicles; with NASCAR, the excitement comes from continual contact among the contenders.

As for the format, the Formula 1 championship consists of 20 races held on Sundays, with 24 vehicles racing in less than two hours. With NASCAR, there are 40 races, many mid-week, with 40 contenders racing from three to five hours. Public participation also differs in the two championships. With F1 the audience watching the race at the track has no opportunity to interact with the drivers or the teams, except for the few who can afford a 5,000-plus-euro ticket for the Paddock Club, or much more likely, who are guests of one of the sponsors. On NASCAR race days, instead, spectators can buy a 'pit pass' so they can access the garages where the race cars are prepped and interact with the pit crews and the drivers. Finally, with regard to ticket prices for races and passes to the paddock or pit, Formula 1 costs more than double NASCAR.

With regard to *uniqueness*, it's possible to draw a distinction as far as current attributes between *points of parity* and *points of difference*, and still other attributes that might become future points of difference. The first are factors that signify that a given product belongs to a specific product category (it's taken for granted that a national park has hiking trails); the second are the basis for the differentiation of the current value proposition (the national park with the most extensive network of hiking trails in the country for all abilities). The third kind of attribute isn't part of the product at present, but the organization may be making investments in this direction to enhance future differentiation (for instance, a shuttle bus linking the park to the major cities in the neighboring region).

For the product to be able to create value, the combination of attributes has to be selected so that beyond basics, there are also differentiators. What's more, considering future developments, there should be room to add attributes that allow for further differentiation (Case History 8.2).

8.1.4   Creating value with new products

Creating and launching a new product are processes that call for some of the riskiest decisions any organization will ever make, be it a for-profit or a non-profit.

Investments are so high, both for production and launch, that failure can jeopardize the very survival of the organization. History is replete with cases of film production companies, publishers, music labels, and performing arts institutes that have gone bankrupt because they've failed to recover on investments in new products.

That said, it's worth remembering that systematically launching new products is the order of the day in creative industries, and that the failure rate of many of them is a natural part of all this (Section 1.2.4). In other words, *product innovation is the typical method for creating value in creative industries*. So for organizations, careful management of value creation contributes substantially to success.

8.1.4.1 New product development

A new product launch is the end result of a process that starts with an idea. This idea goes through a series of stages to be transformed into a product, which is a component of a value proposition.

There are typically five stages in product development from idea to product launch.

- *Identifying market opportunities*. During this stage the organization searches and quantifies areas on the market that aren't adequately covered by existing products. Opportunities are obviously much harder to identify in future markets as opposed to existing ones. In fact, with a market that's currently in any given lifecycle stage, the organization has to gauge the size of the potential market that has yet to be activated or identify possible supply voids (Section 7.11.1). Within the framework of a market-driven strategy, to get a good idea of the approximate dimension of the opportunity in question, the proper approach is to analyze the positioning of current products and how well they match customer preferences (Section 7.5.1).

But when it comes to creating a completely new market, that is, a market-driving strategy, opportunities are much more ambiguous. Customer expectations are unclear and the benefits they're looking for are implicit. Even identifying who potential customers are is no mean feat. Building a map of product positioning is impossible, and spotting competitors complicated. So the organization's creative efforts in these circumstances focus mainly on piecing together weak signals, captured by analyzing various trends (socio-cultural,

demographic, technological), predicting institutional and regulatory changes, and trying to put all these pieces together in the right combination to construct future market scenarios.

- *Generating ideas and developing product concepts*. By identifying market opportunities, organizations get some notion as to the area on the market their new product should occupy. Now it's time to start thinking about the product itself. In this stage the organization needs to come up with a number of ideas that will form the original nucleus of what will become the product launched on the market. Ideas can come from individuals or from teams. The latter often use structured techniques such as *brainstorming*, when eight to ten people use free association and analogical thinking rather than logical reasoning to draw out new product ideas.

Normally at this stage a vast number of ideas come up, a number that is then pared down through a selection process to provide fuel for the successive phase: transforming ideas into product concepts. Here a variety of selection criteria can be applied: intrinsic quality; alignment with organizational objectives and strategies; alignment with the target market; degree of innovation and related level of market risk; the possible challenge in getting the rest of the organization to sign off on the new idea; productive feasibility; and initial ballpark estimates of investments.

The *product concept* is a description of the idea that can then be submitted to the other people not involved in product development. This description can be verbal (a synopsis of the plot of a film or book, for example) and/or visual (a sketch of a designer object or a garment). Developing the concept is usually the responsibility of the individual or team that generated the original idea, and takes more detailed elaboration to give a clearer picture of what the product will actually end up looking like.

The product concept also includes the positioning the organization hopes to achieve. In fact for the product to secure a place on the market, from the moment the idea is conceived it must be clear which customers it's intended for, which alternative products they might compare it to, and how this product will be differ from other alternatives.

For most creative industries, the two stages described so far, identifying opportunities and generating ideas, happen continuously. Since the systematic launch of new products is the normal modus operandi in these industries, by regularly monitoring market trends it's possible to detect where market opportunities arise. At the same time, some organizational units work incessantly on developing product concepts to transform into finished products. So often it's hard to tell which of the two stages comes first. Is it identifying opportunities that generate new ideas, or is it the continual work of developing new concepts that leads the organization to verify whether there are market opportunities for these ideas? But this debate is secondary to the much more relevant question of integrating the two processes (Chapter 11), which is what ensures that the output of creative effort is a product that actually has a market.

In the media industry, like with visual and performing arts, analyzing market trends can reveal opportunities and provide insights for organizational units that deal in products. For instance, the success of a film that's based on video games or a television series based on politics and power might suggest scouting video games and scripts for these kinds of shows. At the same time, since organizations in these industries constantly get countless pitches for new books, songs, series and others, they can come across original ideas that don't have an obvious market opportunity, but careful verification may reveal that such an opportunity actually exists.

In any case, regardless of which step in the process comes first, after being analyzed in light of the same criteria used for ideas, not all of the product concepts make the cut to continue on to successive stages. What's more, and here's the big difference, customers themselves can give their opinions on concepts, as we'll see in the next section. Concepts that pass the evaluation process are the ones that will be transformed into final products.

● *Developing the product*. This transformation calls for an intermediate step: realizing a pilot (sometimes called a prototype). The *pilot* is very close to a definitive version of the product, created to verify the productive capabilities of the organization and to get an idea of actual production costs. For example, with a television series, a pilot is one entire episode, complete with the director, actors, scripts, and sets. The pilot provides invaluable input for pinpointing possible production problems and estimating costs, which allow the organization to undertake corrective measures or to drop the entire project if it proves to be too risky or costly.

● *Designing marketing strategies programs*. By analyzing the pilot the producer can adapt, modify, and improve certain attributes to come up with a final product. At this point the organization builds the rest of the value proposition and formulates its positioning strategies. If market opportunities are identified accurately, there should be no need to reset the target or the positioning for the value proposition, unless during development market conditions have changed (a competitor has launched a similar product, or relevant regulations have been amended).

The positioning strategy also calls for the making of choices pertaining to other components of the value proposition: first, the price of the product and second, communication and distribution. In other words, this is the time to set up the entire marketing mix that defines an organization's market offering. Price setting and communication/distribution activities make it possible to analyze the product by the numbers, verifying its financial sustainability.

A critical issue at this stage is *sales forecasts*, that is, the revenues that the organization can expect from product sales, both during and after the launch.[4] Subtracting production and marketing costs from these revenues gives a measure of the financial results that the product can generate.

There are myriad sales forecast models (Ainslie et al., 2005; Sawhney and Eliashberg, 1996). Whichever one the organization chooses, it has to give an indication of the portion of the target market the new product can win, in other words, its *sales potential*. Once again, it's obvious that to correctly predict sales, a clear definition of the target market is essential (Section 7.1). Here's the mathematical formula that expresses the rationale behind estimating sales volumes:

$$V_P = MP_P \times PI$$

where V_P represents estimated sales volumes of the product P, MP_P is its market potential, and PI the estimated purchase intentions of target customers. Factoring in the sales price results in predicted turnover. It's important to keep in mind that the variables in this formula aren't independent. (If the price increases, most likely the product's potential market and customers' intention to purchase will be impacted.) But it can still be used to carry out simulations based on the actual price sensitivity of the target in question (Section 8.3.2.2).

● *Launching the product.* During this stage the organization executes the launch-related activities following the previously established plan. But before actually doing so, a network of relationships that contribute to creating product value must be activated (Section 2.1.1): presenting the product to critics and experts (a movie or fashion collection preview, an invitation-only art exhibit pre-opening) and giving early adopters the chance to sample the product before it's released (sending a new book to a group of readers before it hits the bookstores). These are both ways to facilitate the process of categorization and interpretation as applied to the new product. What's essential for creative products is creating a space within the perceptions of customers to prompt them to consider the product in question in their choice processes (Section 4.4.1.2).

8.1.4.2 The role of Marketing in the process of new product development

Given the specific function of new products within the context of value creation processes in creative industries, the development stage is when the dialogue between Marketing and other business units becomes the most confrontational, but also potentially the most productive. In Section 2.2.2 I emphasized that the role of Marketing essentially depends on organizational culture. In market-oriented companies, Marketing has a voice in all organizational processes, while respecting departmental responsibilities. With product orientation, Marketing is relegated to managing a few tools for market relations. As a result, the part that Marketing plays in developing new products is also highly contingent on organizational culture. Now let's try to analyze Marketing's role in general terms, and then we'll explore how this changes in light of organizational culture.

Marketing has a dual role in new product development: informational and decisional. The *informational role* entails representing the viewpoint of customers (their expectations, attitudes, perceptions, and preferences) during the various stages of the process by generating market information. The *decisional role*, instead, calls for decision making typical of strategic or operative marketing pertaining to product launch: targeting, positioning, communication, and distribution.

Regarding the informational role, Marketing can help identify opportunities by providing data that reveal several critical market characteristics: the most attractive segments of the market at present, and more importantly, in the future; possible supply voids; strategies and actions of competitors, which can serve as a launch pad for imitation or differentiation maneuvers; macro- and micro-environmental trends that could pave the way for future market evolution; and changes in related sectors, or even in unrelated ones that can be used as models for anticipating the evolution in the relevant market. What's more, working in conjunction with Sales, Marketing can offer interpretations of sales trends for the organization's current products, to assess what stage in the lifecycle they're in and if and how new products can impact these stages.

Marketing personnel can sit on inter-departmental teams responsible for different stages of product development (Section 11.2.1). But even in organizations that have specially designated units to handle these stages (made up of editors, curators, stylists, and designers, to name a few), Marketing's informational role is to bring the customer's viewpoint to the table. With consumer markets for creative products, this can be done by running tests to get feedback from consumers throughout the process of transforming ideas into products. The point of these tests is to glean information on three areas: customer perceptions, preferences, and behaviors.

Perceptions relate to the categorization and interpretation processes customers implement during various development stages; the degree of innovation and the differences as compared to existing products; and the elements of uniqueness or similarity. *Preferences* have to do with what customers think of the attributes of the idea/product, in other words, their likes or dislikes. *Behaviors* center on their intentions to purchase the product; followed by the opinions they express; the specific ways in which they use the product (with a television series, do they watch it alone or with family or friends?); purchase methods and points of sale; and the intention to recommend the product to other potential customers.

8.1.4.2.1 The concept test
With a concept test, customers are asked to express their opinions on various product concepts put forward by the organization. This is generally done via qualitative research with in-depth interviews or focus groups. If the concept can be described in detail and represents no radical break from existing products, the test can also be done with a quantitative approach using an experiment-based research method. For instance, a sample of readers could be given a synopsis of several different novels being considered for publication. Or a sample of television viewers might be asked to give their feedback on a description of characters and plot for a proposed series.

The concept test takes place during the initial stages of the development process, when there's still relatively ample maneuvering room for possible changes and improvements. But at the same time it's vital to remember that what's being testing is a *description* of a product idea; the producer is asking customers to add a generous dose of imagination to envision the end result.

This is why the most interesting information generated from this test relates to perceptions and preferences; input about behaviors is not usually very reliable, seeing that the concept is still quite a vague rendition of the product idea. Another element to keep in mind is that the experiential nature of creative products makes it hard for consumers to leave too much to the imagination before actually trying the product personally.

8.1.4.2.2 The product test

With a product test, consumers are asked to try out the pilot. For example, a sample of readers or a reading group could be given a few chapters of a book, or television viewers could be shown the pilot episode of a new series. The timing for a product test is very close to the realization of the final product. So the customers get the chance to experience a version that's still not complete, but that does contain most of the distinguishing attributes.

This explains why the most interesting information here primarily pertains to preferences and behaviors. The product test can be done with a qualitative, quantitative, or integrated approach. The first generates in-depth qualitative information, the second makes it possible to measure certain key variables such as reasons for customer preference for a given product over competitor products or vice versa; intention to purchase the given product; intention to recommend this product; and so forth.

8.1.4.2.3 The market test

This encompasses the entire marketing mix; that is, the product, the list price, and the communication and distribution campaigns. Market tests are very common in non-creative sectors, but less so in creative industries, because of the time it takes for consumers to fully experience the product (Section 1.2). This kind of test can take various forms, all based on a quantitative research approach. The two most common are area tests and simulated test markets. With an *area test* the product is actually launched in a limited geographic market (certain cities or regions) where communication is channeled through local media. Consumers aren't aware they're being tested, they simply make their usual purchases.

With a *simulated test market* (STM) everything is simulated, as the name suggests. Traditionally for mass market goods, consumers are invited to a place that's set up like a regular store stocked with the new products to be tested.[5] Consumers then make their purchases, like they normally do, with a set amount of money provided by the research institute that organized the test. Before the purchase session, they may also be shown advertising for a variety of products, including the ones being tested.

What should be clear is that the primary purpose of market tests is to measure purchase behaviors and estimate potential sales of a new product. But the specificities of many creative industries make this kind of testing quite complicated. That's why in some sectors (television, cinema, publishing, fashion), products are often launched in different sequences in different countries, and wherever these products debut is considered the testing ground for later launches.

The function of these different tests is essentially to reduce uncertainty and market risk linked to new products. But since tests call for investments, before running them it's critical to weigh costs and benefits carefully. In any case, if the organization is market oriented, it will almost certainly want to get feedback from its customers before the actual product launch. And this consideration brings the discussion back to the question I posed at the beginning of this section regarding the specific organizational culture.

If this culture is product-oriented, very likely the organization will not run any consumer tests at all. This doesn't mean that no other assessments are done during the different stages in the process, but simply that they are structured in different ways. If an organization operates on the premise that it must achieve technical excellence, and that the only qualified judges of this excellence are experts, it's nearly certain that these are the people who will participate in product tests, in lieu of potential customers. This decision is based on the assumption that the technical quality equals commercial success, an assumption that is not corroborated by research, as I've already pointed out (Section 2.2.2.2).

In this type of organization, Marketing has a less informational and more decisional role, and is called on to participate after product development and during product launch. Basically, it's as if value creation were assigned to the organizational units that handle the product, while Marketing is simply tasked with delivering that value to the market.

8.1.5 Creating value with existing products: managing products throughout their lifecycle

A new product's lifecycle begins with its launch and continues along a specific trajectory plotted by the variables discussed in Section 8.1.2. In managerial practice, in creative industries new products and product development processes take center stage. But as vital as these new entries undeniably are, it can't be forgotten that more often than not an organization's existing products are what guarantee greater sales revenues and income – hence financial equilibrium. Proof of this can be found in the catalogues of countless publishers and recording labels, iconic pieces from clothing and design collections, the role of repertory in performing arts, and with permanent collections for myriad museums and art galleries.

It's safe to assume that much of the attention trained on the newness of a product is due mostly to the communicative effect – the buzz – it creates on the market, which sparks criticism, debate, and discussion among experts and customers. This obviously has a ripple effect on the self-perceptions of everyone who has a hand in new product development and launch, people who are constantly under the scrutiny of the critics and the market.

That said, once a new product has reached maturity, it's time to set up a strategy for the future. What often happens is that after a period of growth in which the product sales peak, a decline sets in that may be followed by new growth. Chandrasekaran and Tellis (2011) studied this 'saddle', analyzing sales data on ten durable product categories in 16 countries from 1950 to 2008. None falls under the definition of creative products used in this book, but four of them are traditional devices for using creative products: TVs, DVD players, VCRs, and camcorders. In any case, the conclusions of these authors can readily be extended to creative products as well, whose sales systematically showing this same saddle.

The researchers found *three different reasons behind the saddle phenomenon*. The first two are the evolution of technology and trends in the economic cycle, so they have to do with the macro-environment surrounding the market. The third relates to specific characteristics of the market, so it can be affected by the decisions of organizations that operate there: the temporal shifts in the bandwagon effect found among early adopters and the early majority.

In the model developed by Rogers (1962), presented in Section 8.1.2.2, the diffusion of innovation in a market is represented in a continuous fashion, as if the imitation dynamic among various groups of customers progressed in a linear way. Chandrasekaran and Tellis (2011), however, demonstrate that imitation of early adopters by the early majority happens discontinuously (resulting in what they call a 'chasm'), in particular for devices used to experience creative products. Because early adopters are few in number, and they often have different expectations than the majority, when the purchases made by this first group begin to stabilize, the majority haven't yet made their first purchase, so overall there appears to be a sales slump.

The evidence of this slump following an initial peak in sales suggests that the organization finds itself facing two strategic alternatives: to go along with the drop in sales and the decline of the product, or to trigger the saddle and push new sales growth. The first refers to planned obsolescence, the second, product revitalization.

8.1.5.1 *Planned obsolescence*

This strategy involves actually planning for the drop in sales when launching the product on the market, in anticipation of a relaunch in other markets. This gives rise to multiple lifecycles that characterize numerous creative products (Section 1.2.7). With planned obsolescence the product stays on the market, supported by communication and distribution activities, until it hits sales targets and generates financial returns. When this happens, communication investments are reduced or stopped altogether, the product is slowly taken out of circulation, and sales fall to zero.

The justification underpinning planned obsolescence is that the product can be relaunched on other markets where there is potential, either the same version or a modified one. In many creative industries this strategy is used to sell a product sequentially in various geographical markets (Case History 8.3).

What's more, in all the industries where the main product consists of content with planned obsolescence, the underlying aim is to migrate the product from one channel

Case History 8.3

Yo soy Betty, la fea: a local product for a global market

Yo soy Betty, la fea is one of the biggest hits in the world television market. The original series was produced by RCN (Radio Cadena Network), a Colombian television network, and broadcast in Colombia daily from 1999 to 2001 in half-hour episodes. The show tells the story of Beatriz Pinzón Solano (Betty), a brilliant but shy Colombian girl, a university graduate with a Master in Economics but whose lack of good looks makes it hard for her to find a job. Finally, almost by chance, she gets hired as an executive secretary in a fashion house, and begins to discover her own assets, gain self-confidence, and embark on a path in her career and her life that will culminate with a position at the head of the company and marriage to the President.

Compared to the traditional soap opera format, which tells the story of a modern-day Cinderella whose life is transformed after she meets her Prince Charming, Betty is a character who makes her own way thanks to her own talents. What's more, the fact that she's ugly isn't seen as something to pity her for; instead, it's a topic of sarcastic and self-deprecating humor. Betty instantly became a model for millions of Colombian women. In 2000 *Yo soy Betty* won the highest rating for Colombian television series, peaking at 3.3 million viewers and winning a 72 per cent market share.

While the series enjoyed its greatest popularity in Colombia, it was sold to other national networks in various countries in South America and in the United States on a Spanish language network. After the series had already concluded in Colombia, a dubbed version was sold to networks in countries like Brazil, Hungary, the Czech Republic, Italy, Turkey, Malaysia, and Japan. Remakes were later acquired by national networks in Germany, India, Mexico, and Russia.

In 2006, a remake of *Yo soy Betty* (*Ugly Betty*) was launched in the US by the network ABC, with weekly half-hour episodes. Although it was broadcast in the same time slot as popular shows like *Survivor*, or hits like *My Name is Earl*, the first episode of *Ugly Betty* broke the record for viewers for a series premier – 16.3 million – and the show is still an American favorite. Considering the original Spanish-language series, the dubbed versions and remakes in English and other local languages, *Yo soy Betty, la fea* has been broadcast in 25 countries.

to another, with an eye to a multichannel approach (Chapter 9). For instance, a film is distributed at the cinema first, then in DVD, then broadcast on pay TV, and finally on free to air TV (this strategy is called *windowing*). In some cases, for example with animated features, the cycle continues with the sale of property rights on the characters in the film as endorsers of other products.

According to this strategy, the previous cycles also serve to create awareness and communication for activating later cycles. Likewise, often the business market emerges after the cycle has run its course on the consumer market. An interesting example in the music industry is when the copyright on a song is sold as part of a soundtrack or an advertising campaign.

8.1.5.2   Product revitalization

The aim of this strategy is to spur new growth stages within the same market. So when there's a saddle after the first sales peak or when the market reaches maturity definitively, the organization tries to modify the product so it becomes attractive to the market once again. A market that's moving toward maturity shows certain unique characteristics.

First of all, on any given market there are both customers who are already making repeat purchases

(product permitting) and others who have yet to buy the product (Section 8.1.2.2). The first group includes early adopters and a portion of the early majority, and the second are the late majority. These two types of customers have different product experiences, which translate into different expectations. Second, other competitors have entered the arena and won their market share by offering products with points of parity and points of difference.

So the organization is facing the same decision as with the product launch: which market segments to serve, and whether to use the same product positioning or a new one. There are various options on the table, but all of them center on relaunching the product and triggering new sales growth.

8.1.5.2.1 Product improvement   The first option is to consolidate the product's strengths and improve on its weaknesses. Leveraging the experience of customers who've already used the product, the organization can build an *importance–performance matrix* (Figure 8.2) and decide which product attributes to improve, which to leverage, and which to continue to use as points of difference, if no other competitor is capable of realizing an effective imitation.

On this matrix, various product attributes are classed on the basis of their importance for customers, and the performance perceived by customers relative to competitors.[6] So the attributes that score high on importance and performance are the ones to continue to build on with respect to differentiation (Quadrant I); attributes that have low importance and performance should be monitored in case they become important in the future or if some competitors attempt to innovate them to boost their relevance (Quadrant III). Attributes with high importance and low performance need improvement (Quadrant II); for those with low importance and high performance the producer has to work harder to demonstrate their value or, if they truly don't meet customer needs, eliminate or downgrade them to simplify the product (Quadrant IV).

In fact, contrary to the way improvement is often interpreted in managerial practice, this strategy can sometimes come about through *simplifying the product*, eliminating or minimizing the intensity of certain attributes. With a radio program in which several guests are invited to speak, an improvement might be to reduce the number of guests (which is a product attribute) and dedicate more time to each one.

8.1.5.2.2 Versioning With versioning, the organization launches a different version of the original product, one that can be attractive either for people who've already purchased the previous product, or for new customers. Clearly for the first group the new version would probably offer added or improved attributes, and for the second group simplified ones. With a book that's already been published, a new version might be a limited edition, printed on high quality paper or with a special cover; a version celebrating the anniversary of the book or the author, with a foreword or an afterword by the author herself or by prominent critics; or an economical version in paperback or an e-book (Case History 8.4).

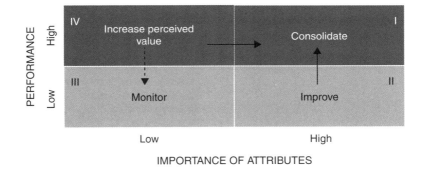

Figure 8.2 – The importance–performance matrix

Case History 8.4

A 60-year long versioning: *Tex Willer*

Tex Willer is enjoying one of the longest life spans of any character in the history of comic books anywhere in the world. Published by Sergio Bonelli Editore, Tex debuted in Italy in 1948, and since then has thrilled adventure-seekers for generations, in Italy and beyond. The comic book was launched in Brazil in 1951, Finland in 1953, Norway in 1961, and debuted in 1967 in former Yugoslavia, and in 2000 in Turkey. In all these countries Tex is still being published regularly and successfully. (Tex has appeared in many others countries, such as Sweden, Denmark, Germany, India, Indonesia, but with less continual publication.) Sergio Bonelli Editore, leader in the Italian market, has made history in Italian comic books in the twentieth century. In addition to Tex, Bonelli's creations include characters such as Zagor, Dylan Dog, Nathan Never, some of whom are almost the same age as Tex.

Tex Willer is a Texas Ranger who lives in the mid-1800s, a lawman in the American South West (in particular Arizona, Utah, and Texas) along with three other pards. As a white chief of the Navajos, he fights to defend the rights of Native Americans against the white colonizers of the new Western frontier. He's a typical character from an adventure comic, who personifies justice and honesty, combating and overcoming oppression and injustice. The regular series of the comic book (which comes out on a monthly basis) is published in 16 by 21 centimeter collector's albums with just over one hundred black and white pages.

On the Italian market, one of the largest comics book market in the world, Tex has had the longest-running success, even though the variety of publications in Brazil is equal to if not more ample than the Italian offering. The regular series now boasts more than 600 issues. Through the years several versioning initiatives have aimed at increasing purchase frequency by fans.

Because later generations didn't have the chance to read the early Tex comic books, over the years the publisher has launched three reprints of old issues (in 1964, 1985, and 1996). Special series have also been created (with annual issues or similar): in color (Color Tex); with longer story lines, double the number of pages (Maxi Tex); larger formats (20 x 30 cm), often with guest artists (*Speciale* Tex) and that have also been reprinted (Tex Stella d'Oro); the Historical Collection in color, with past color comics reprinted in a larger format; and finally some collections with stories published in bundles from different periods but with the same themes (for instance, run-ins with Tex's eternal nemesis Mefisto).

With this strategy Sergio Bonelli Editore has successfully and repeatedly revitalized the product, making Tex Willer the longest-lived character in the comic book sector. With sales peaking at a million copies and today leveling out at more than 200,000 copies per month, today Tex is still the company's leading title. (By comparison, for the most popular American superheroes, monthly comic book sales run to around 5,000.)

8.1.5.2.3 *Bundling or unbundling*   Bundling means *selling several products together that can also be sold separately*, usually at a discount on the sum of the prices of each individual item. Unbundling, obviously, is the opposite. A book or DVD sold with a newspaper is an example of bundling. Guides dedicated to different regions of a country that are excerpts from a comprehensive guidebook are examples of unbundling. Both strategies call for a specific pricing strategy to make it more convenient for customers to buy the bundled (or unbundled) products with respect to the individual products (or set). Section 8.3.6.2 provides further details.

At times with both strategies the end result is actually a new product, with the previous products serving as components or sources, so it wouldn't be accurate to say that the original product continues on its lifecycle. By the same token, however, since the new products that emerge are closely linked to the originals, the argument could be made that they are relaunches of the original product (or that they serve to help relaunch it), if the aim is to keep it on the market.

8.1.5.3 *Eliminating the product*
When the product starts to decline, the last resort is to eliminate it from the production process and the market. This is an extreme scenario that organizations normally implement for one of only two reasons. The first is the market: there are substitute products that can satisfy customers' expectations that are so far superior to the product in question that there's no way to catch them up by implementing improvements or other

Table 8.1 – Product P&L: a fictitious example

	Per unit	Total (10,000 units)
Sales revenue	100	1,000,000
Cost of goods sold	(30)	(300,000)
Gross margin	70	7000,000
Other variable costs (sales, marketing, etc.)	(20)	(200,000)
Margin	50	500,000
Direct fixed expanses	(10)	(100,000)
Allocation of over heads	(5)	(50,000)
Operating earnings	35	350,000

strategies. The second is financial: the losses on the product are such that sales are no longer sustainable.[7]

To assess the financial sustainability of a product, the most common tool is the *product profit & losses* (P&L), which itemizes all the revenues and costs relating to the product to highlight whether or not the first outweigh the second. A breakdown of both shows sources of revenues and cost-generating objects and activities (Table 8.1).

During the course of the lifecycle of a product, there may come a time when it doesn't generate satisfactory financial results. (In the introduction stage, for example, costs incurred before and during the launch often exceed sales revenues.) But it's not temporary slumps that prompt the decision to eliminate a product; this is motivated instead by the obvious inability to generate adequate returns for a protracted period of time.

But even when sales slide or financial results are negative, the organization may opt to keep a product on the market and continue producing it. Normally this is due to the specific role the product plays within the context of the organization's strategic objectives. For instance, some products contribute to the organization's image, or satisfy certain specific needs of market segments that the organization wants to serve. These circumstances might lead to the decision to produce the item in question at a loss and use financial resources generated by other products to cover those losses.

This choice falls within the broader framework of product portfolio management (Section 8.1.7). But whatever the motivation for keeping a financially unsustainable product on the market, it can't be made without carefully analyzing costs and sales revenues, in an attempt to reveal unexplored potential markets or to discover more efficient production or commercialization methods.

8.1.6   Consumer participation in product creation processes

Up to this point we've talked about creating new products and modifying existing ones, as if the organization had full control over the entire process and customers were mere recipients of these products. But referring back to Chapter 2, I pointed out that consumers are taking a more and more active part in creating value in creative industries, and in Section 2.3 I detailed the various forms that this value co-creation can take.

In the same chapter we saw how this phenomenon is by no means a recent one. Way back in the analog world of 1975, Bruce Springsteen invited his fans to record his concerts and radio programs and produce bootleg copies of his music. What's changed today is the diffusion and intensity of the co-creation trend, all thanks to digital technologies.

Remaining in the world of rock music and fast-forwarding 35 years, in 2008 the group Nine Inch Nails released *Ghost I–IV* online. The new album consisted almost entirely of instrumental tracks, and the group invited their fans to use the instrumentals to create new music, share it online, and post it in the remix section of the band's site nin.com. Another popular trend is the *remix culture* (Tapscott and Williams 2006): 'The phenomenon of consumers' using bits and pieces of existing popular culture to create new meanings and artifacts' (Wikström, 2009: 157).

All this begs the question: Why should companies and non-profits in creative industries give up any degree of control over the processes of inventing and creating products and put it in the hands of consumers? And looking at the other side of the relationship: Why should consumers be motivated to participate in the process of creating new products and revitalizing existing ones? What prompts them to spend their time and energy doing so?

The short answer is also the most obvious one: because this is where the world is heading. And even if this makes sense, it still doesn't justify the choices of every single organization. An answer that's more aligned with the theoretical framework I've established in this book is that value in creative industries is created through a network (Chapter 2), and consumers are by no means disconnected from this network. So organizations that figure out how to effectively leverage this connection can tap into consumers' competences and creativity.

But there's a fundamental difference with respect to the past. In 1975 Springsteen could invite thousands of fans to produce bootleg copies of his music; today he can extend the invitation to millions, and they can create much higher quality copies thanks to digital technologies. What's more, as to the motivation behind consumer co-creation, value in creative industries is experiential (Chapter 2). Participating in creating products is actually a form of experience that enhances value for consumers (at least for the ones who acknowledge the value of co-creation). And a part of this participation is also the experience of sharing with other consumers (Case History 8.5).

Case History 8.5

Espacio Fundación Telefónica: Participation as an element of differentiation

Fundación Telefónica was established by the Spanish telecommunications group of the same name. Its mission statement lists, among other objectives, spreading knowledge and providing training on the role of technology as an instrument of social progress.

The *Espacio Fundación Telefónica,* a 6,000-square-meter company-owned exhibition space, was opened in May 2012 in the heart of Madrid. This is where Foundation-owned Cubist artwork is exhibited; education and training activities take place in an open multi-purpose space where culture and knowledge, art and technology, and learning and teaching coexist.

Among the wide range of initiatives, particularly popular is *Friends of Talent*, a cycle of events offering young Spaniards who've achieved success in various creative industries the chance to share their stories. The *Thinking Party* is also a major draw, an annual event hosting both experts and laypeople, who are invited to tell about the transformations they've experienced thanks to the use of technology.

The point of difference in the *Espacio Fundación Telefónica* program springs from the participatory use of space. Everything that happens here, from small monothematic conferences to big events like the *Friends of Talent* and the *Thinking Party*, is designed to encourage public participation, idea sharing, and open debate. Both the format of the events and the layout of the space help to achieve these results.

As for the format, it's more like a talk show than a classic conference with one or two speakers presenting and the audience listening. In fact, a speaker is only given a few minutes to introduce the topic of discussion, and then the rest of the time is dedicated to questions and answers. The space itself is also designed to encourage communication among the participants, consisting as it does of a low, semi-circular auditorium, a small amphitheater where the presenter is separated from the audience by a short distance.

In the meeting rooms, even the lighting is non-traditional, and continuously changes color. The video screens in the back of the room don't show classic Powerpoints, but illustrations, photographs, slide shows of images, and video clips. For instance, at the start of the *Friends of Talent* meeting, a video is shown recapping the meeting from the previous month, just like television talk shows. So for *Espacio Fundación Telefónica*, public participation is what creates differentiation.

An organization that wants to gets its customers on board as product co-creators has to take two critical decisions: how much control to give them and how much sharing to elicit among them. Granting control and encouraging sharing are both ways to get good ideas for products, concepts, and even pilots, which, with little additional work, can be launched on the market (see the Threadless case in Section 2.3.1).

There are a number of different paths to activating this exchange, like setting up creative competitions and contests, and establishing platforms to support brainstorming. The quality of the resulting ideas depends on the quality of the participation these initiatives stimulate. This brings up the question: How can an organization encourage talented people to share their ideas?

Several studies have shown that a determinant of the quality of participation is the *quality of the creative experience* as perceived by consumers (Dahl and Moreau, 2007; Füller et al, 2007; Füller et al, 2011; Prahalad and Ramaswami, 2003): the higher quality the experience, the higher quality the ideas that will emerge. There are four components to the quality of a creative experience:

- *Competence*, the satisfaction deriving from the ability to complete the creative task.

- *Autonomy*, the pleasure from the freedom to choose the process and method for performing the task.
- The *pleasure of the task*, the perception that it's stimulating, challenging, and engrossing.
- The *sense of community*, the willingness to exchange information, give feedback, and accept criticism from other participants in the community of co-creation.

The more successfully the organization designs a consumer participation process that encompasses these four components, the higher the quality of the ideas that will be generated by participants (Case History 8.6). As an example, a sense of competence could come from providing participants with adequate information and tools to carry out the project, and a sense of autonomy from eliminating any unneeded restrictions on the creative process. To ensure a task is pleasurable, it mustn't be busywork that's repetitive and unchallenging. Finally, a sense of community emerges from encouraging open discussion among participants and providing the necessary community-building tools.

Case History 8.6

The Swarovski Enlightened Design Competition

In 2008 Swarovski initiated its Enlightened Design Competition for jewelry designers (professionals, students of design, or simply creative consumers) to generate new concepts in jewelry. To run this competition, the company established a virtual platform that provided both a toolkit for creating jewelry (to promote a sense of competence) and typical interactive instruments for community members, enabling them to comment on and vote for projects submitted by other members (to build a sense of community) (Fuller et al., 2011). As for a sense of autonomy, there were two different paths for joining in the competition: one was completely open-ended, allowing participants to propose any jewelry they had in mind, and the other was more guided, with participants assembling pieces from a preset series of components and crystals. The 1,700 designers who took part in the competition came up with 3,000 jewelry concepts. The members of the community offered more than 23,000 evaluations with around 3,000 comments. The best ideas from the competition were collected in a trend book presented at the sector's most prestigious fair in Basel, where the company also debuted jewelry based on the winning concepts.

8.1.7 Product portfolio management

Although it's theoretically possible, it rarely happens in practice that organizations – especially in creative industries – do operate with a single product; far more often they have one or more product lines. The product portfolio (also known as the product mix, assortment, or range) consists of the *set of product lines sold by the organization*. Dealing with a portfolio of products gives rise to obvious management issues that aren't there when selling a single product. So what is it that drives organizations to diversify their product offering?

Keeping in mind the discussion on targeting options (Section 7.8), the motivation underlying a product portfolio is the desire to serve various targets by offering each one a specific value proposition. So as a general rule, the broader the market that the organization wants to serve, the more likely it is it will offer a portfolio of products. To be more specific, the various reasons behind this choice revolve around increasing the effectiveness and the efficiency of the organization's offering system (Picard, 2005).

First of all, by selling several products the organization can *operate in markets that are in different stages of their lifecycles*, offsetting the stability or the decline of one with the growth of others. This serves to mitigate risk because if one product is performing poorly, the financial equilibrium of the organization is preserved by the solid performances of the others. By the same token, with a product portfolio the organization can better *grasp opportunities that arise on various markets* and, at the same time, offer its customers superior value propositions. Lastly, producing several products makes it possible to *access scale or scope economies*, if part of the production process or some of the components can be shared among different products.

If an organization produces and/or sells one or more product lines, coordinated and integrated management is the path to maximizing the capacity of the different lines to provide joint value while preventing them from competing against one another on the same market segments.

Decisions regarding the product portfolio basically tie into three dimensions of the portfolio:

- *Breadth*: the total number of lines offered by the organization.
- *Depth*: referring either to the single line, in which case it means the number of products in the line, or in the entire portfolio, meaning the average number of products per line.
- *Length*: the total number of products offered by the organization.

Clearly if the first two dimensions change, the third will too.

8.1.7.1 Designing the breadth and depth of the portfolio

Choices regarding these two dimensions tie closely into targeting decisions (Section 7.8.2). Portfolio breadth depends on the number of segments the organization wants to serve, and depth on the level of personalization it seeks to provide. A fashion house that offers both men's and women's lines can decide how many pieces to include in each one to fulfill the more specific expectations of the two customer targets. Generally organizations that adopt a niche strategy have portfolios that are fairly narrow but very deep; segment specialists have a variety of lines to satisfy a range of segment expectations, with portfolios that are quite deep; organizations pursuing a multi-segment strategy have broad portfolios that are relatively less deep; and mass-marketers tend to have the broadest portfolios of them all, but with the least depth.

Portfolio management determines how the organization creates new products and manages existing ones. Every product variation affects its breadth and depth. Launching a new product line may be justified by the drive to enter a new market segment or to satisfy an additional need in the original segment (if it involves a new product category). Instead, presenting a new product within an existing line might be motivated by a desire to personalize the offering in order to fulfill the more specific needs of the customers in the segment served.

8.1.7.2 *Assessing portfolio equilibrium*

Choices relating to lines and products don't simply involve selecting targets and personalizing an offering. As discussed in the previous section, how each product or line is managed has a ripple effect on all the others, simply because the overall financial sustainability of the organization is the sum of the sustainability of the single components of the product portfolio. When some lines or products fail to generate adequate financial resources (or they absorb more resources than they generate), this can affect how the organization manages other profitable products. In fact, these will be expected to produce surplus income to safeguard the financial equilibrium of the organization.

Since each stage in a product's lifecycle is marked by a different propensity to absorb and generate resources, a general rule is that a balanced portfolio has to contain products in different lifecycle stages. In particular, products in the introduction and growth (or revitalization) stage are the ones that should guarantee a market position and positive cash flows in the future, while mature products should secure current resources to support the ones going through earlier stages. Again, this rule is a valid guideline, but a number of other variables also come into play that can impact market position and resource generation.

To assess portfolio equilibrium, an effective tool is represented by a matrix that categorizes products based on two dimensions: the attractiveness of the market where the products are sold and the position of the organization in that market. The *attractiveness of the market* indicates that the market can potentially offer returns in terms of sales, financials, reputation, and image. The *market position*, on the other hand, relates to the capacity of the organization to take in a portion of those returns, expressed as market share, profitability, reputation, and image.

To build this matrix, each product (or line) is evaluated on the basis of a series of indicators that represent the two dimensions (Table 8.2). Each indicator calls for a quantitative judgment by the manager making the evaluation (or the team involved in the process, in which case an average is used) on a rating scale (generally from one to five, or one to seven), weighted by importance (with each indicator weighted as a percentage).

Table 8.2 – Attractiveness and market position indicators

MARKET ATTRACTIVENESS	MARKET POSITION
POTENTIAL SALES	CURRENT POSITION
Current market size (volume and value) Lifecycle stage (rate of market growth) Size of potential market (volume and value) Number of competitors Customer loyalty to brand/supplier Switching costs Functional competences of competitors Reputation of competitors Existances and market power of producers of substitute products Market power of suppliers Market power of distributors Market power of customers	Current sales (volume and value) Market share (volume and value) Growth rate of trunover Variation in market share over time Penetration Weighted coverage Market power with respect to customers Market power with respect to distributors
POTENTIAL FINANCIAL RETURNS	STRENGTHS AND WEAKNESS COMPARED TO COMPETITORS
Ad hoc production investments Ad hoc distribution/commercial investments Ad hoc marketing investments	Production resources and competences Brand/company image Stability of relationships with distibutors/retailers Availability of financial resources

There are four product categories:

- *Strategics*: The organization has a strong position in attractive markets with these products; they'll serve as the foundation for sustainability in the years to come.
- *Contributors*: The same strong position, but in less attractive markets; the first dimension indicates that these products generate sizeable resources (financial, reputation, and image), the second that the type of market doesn't absorb all of these resources, so they can be reallocated to shore up the rest of the portfolio.
- *Absorbers*: Since the organization has a relatively weak position in attractive markets with these products, they currently absorb substantial resources from the rest of the portfolio.
- *Indefinites*: Neither the organization's position nor the market's attractiveness are definitive as of yet, so the contribution they make to the equilibrium of the portfolio is not clear.

A balanced portfolio contains strategic products supported by contributors. If there are indefinite products this may be an indication that investments in products/markets still need to realize their potential, while absorbers might be justified for non-financial reasons. A portfolio that is rich in the upper quadrants and poor in the lower ones is not balanced. Specifically, it belongs to an organization that's capable of selecting more attractive markets, but less skilled at building a solid position. This might jeopardize sustainability, seeing that the product portfolio requires more resources than it's capable of generating.

The opposite happens for a portfolio that's strong in the bottom half of the matrix and weak in the top half, signifying an organization that bases its business on past results but pays little attention to the future. It will be subject to similar problems of sustainability as described above, but for opposite reasons.

Ideally, the matrix is linked to the product lifecycle model. In fact, a product should begin as an indefinite in the introduction stage. Then, if the organization is able to carve out a solid market position, the item should become strategic, and later turn into a contributor. If instead the organization isn't capable of establishing a strong position, the indefinite product risks turning into an absorber, eventually moving toward elimination.

In many creative industries organizations have endless portfolios containing products that are mainly absorbers, with the sustainability of the entire portfolio resting on a few strategics and contributors (Section 1.2.4). What ensures the long-term survival of these organizations is their ability to select products (even just a few) that have these characteristics.

8.2 BRAND VALUE MANAGEMENT

The brand is a *name, symbol, or sign that distinguishes the products of a company or institution from all the others*. In this sense, the brand is a designation, a kind of signature affixed by producers on their products. In creative industries, producers can be individuals who actually create products (authors, artists, and athletes, for instance) or the organizations that produce them (publishers, television stations, sports teams, and so forth). But when and how does the brand create value for the customer?

The brand constitutes an intangible attribute of the product and the value proposition. Consequently, *the brand can create value not in the way it performs, but through its capacity to transfer meaning*. This clearly goes beyond a pleasant-sounding name or an eye-catching symbol that denotes the brand (although these factors do play their part). A very stimulating question to ask is: What does a well-known brand (artist, museum, newspaper, or director) add to a product (work of art, exhibit, article, or film)? There may be a wide array of answers, but all of them tie into two things: awareness and image.

Brand awareness is the extent to which customers are aware of the brand's existence, and how much and what exactly they know about it. *Brand image*, instead, refers to the associations customers attribute to the brand; their opinions, which come from firsthand experience (what they themselves think) or word of mouth (what others customers think). Both awareness and image are components of brand knowledge: the first is descriptive, the second interpretative–evaluative.[8]

Now we'll turn back to our earlier question, and clarify it further: What does knowledge of the brand add to the value of the product (and the entire offering) for the customer?

8.2.1 The value of the brand for the customer and the organization

To comprehend the value of the brand for the customer, it's necessary to consider the various steps in the decision-making process that lead to purchasing and using the product (Chapter 4). Also relevant is the role of benefits and sacrifices in the configuration of expected and perceived value (Chapters 2 and 3). Now, the first way in which a well-known brand creates value is by playing an *identifying role*. If a brand is widely recognized it means that customers have memorized it in their evoked sets. As a result, this knowledge reduces the cognitive sacrifices connected to recalling the information during the choice process. What's more, knowledge of the brand's distinctive symbols facilitates brand recognition in stores (online or offline), streamlining and simplifying this process even further.

Second, a well-known brand creates value thanks to its *evaluative role*. As I've often reiterated in previous chapters, the brand serves as a quality clue, making it easier to compare alternatives and make choices, limiting some of the typical challenges of choosing among experience products. So basically the brand constitutes a value agent, like any other actor involved in the network of value production.

Finally, a well-known brand creates value through its *communicative role*. In fact, brands that people are familiar with can be topics of conversation, serving as links within social networks (Section 3.1.3). Also, brands can be used as communicative elements of self-identity (Section 3.1.1.2). Or they can represent the building blocks of a community, activating a process of value creation via specific practices (Section 3.3.5.1).

Summing up, there are a variety of motivations that can prompt a customer to prefer a well-known brand over an unknown brand (all other conditions being equal, obviously). All of them taken together constitute the differential value of the brand, as compared to value generated by the product itself. These motivations also underpin the value that the brand is able to generate for the organization, which is referred to as *brand equity*, a common term in financial jargon that marketeers have made their own.

8.2.1.1   Brand equity

This is the fruit of customers' knowledge of the brand. The greater the knowledge (awareness), and the more positive the perceptions of the brand they have (image), the greater the equity. One way to represent equity is as the productivity of investments. A given amount of resources invested by an organization in a high-equity brand produces a greater customer response (in terms of preference and purchases) than

the same amount invested in the same way in a brand with lower equity. The explanation for this is that customers recognize a value differential in the first with respect to the second. But what exactly is value for the organization? What produces the value differential that customers associate with the brand?

A brand that enjoys high awareness and a positive image has a competitive advantage over other organizations that operate on the market. This generates better market performance and financial results for a number of reasons. First, for the organization it will be easier to win *market acceptance for new products*. Seeing as the brand serves as a quality clue, customers perceive fewer risks when they select this brand, and they can anticipate to some extent the experience they'll have. Second, the organization can set a *premium price*, that is, a positive price differential with respect to a comparable offering. This is thanks to the fact that customers recognize the value of the brand and are willing to pay for it.

In addition, a well-known brand can be leveraged to implement *cross selling* initiatives, in other words, selling various products in the portfolio to the same customers. For instance, a customer who buys a sofa can also purchase a coffee table from the same brand; a visitor to an art exhibit might also buy the catalogue; a spectator who goes to see a movie at the cinema buys the DVD too. Cross selling is also made possible thanks to brand awareness and image, both of which reassure the customer as to the quality of the product, reducing perceived risks.

Another value provided by a brand with high awareness and a positive image is *customer loyalty*. The capacity of a brand to satisfy the expectations of customers prompts them to purchase and use the offering of the same brand repeatedly, stabilizing the relationship over time and generating positive effects for the organization (detailed in Chapter 10).

All the possibilities I've just described give the organization an additional source of value, which it can tap through *brand extension strategies*. A well-known brand with a positive image is the key to entering diverse product categories and markets that are new to the organization, making it possible to capture the opportunities in these fresh contexts. Since brand extension is a very common strategy in creative industries, I'll dedicate a separate section to this topic (8.2.3.2.2).

These are all reasons why an organization might decide to invest in creating and developing a brand. And this also explains why in creative industries numerous organizations spend the same energy and financial resources on building brand equity as they do on production: The Louvre, Teatro alla Scala, the *Frankfurter Allgemeine Zeitung*, the BBC, and the city of Amsterdam (Case History 8.7) are very widely known brands that all enjoy an excellent image, and that are managed by their 'owners' in keeping with the principles of brand management.

If a company or institution decides to invest in brand management, a variety of decisions arise throughout the brand's lifecycle. Keeping in mind that the stages are the same as for the product lifecycle, the next few sections explore typical decisions that organizations face, from the introduction stage to beyond.

8.2.2   Creating a new brand

Creating a new brand that generates value both for the customers and the organization means building awareness and a positive image. This calls for decisions pertaining to two main areas: a system of brand elements and a network of associations that customers attribute exclusively to the brand in question.

But first, a critical preliminary step is to clearly define the *brand identity*. This term refers to the *ultimate purpose that the brand serves for the organization*. So basically brand identity is about objectives, both in the market and in the organization. Some relevant questions for determining brand identity are: Who is the brand intended for, the mass market or a niche? What brands can be seen as comparable or as competitors? How is this brand different from the others in the portfolio? What (if any) are the relative objectives as far as sales? Profit? Image? This is why brand identity determines *brand mission* (and why the two terms are often used interchangeably).

Pinpointing a clear identity enables the organization to select both identifying elements and the associations it wants to elicit in the perceptions of its customers (Case History 8.8). For a mass market brand, for instance, where the aim is to prompt a huge number of customers to purchase products, the brand has to have distinctive elements that are easily decoded and associations that are aligned with the expectations of a sizeable percentage of consumers. At the other end of the spectrum, a niche brand can be denoted by distinctive elements and more complex and exclusive associations.

Case History 8.7

Amsterdam: the city branding strategy

Cities, regions, and even entire countries can be considered and managed as brands with regard to certain factors. The generic term *place branding* simply means treating a place like a brand, working to give it a clear identity, image, and distinctive signs to make it attractive to target audiences: visitors, investors, and even residents themselves. More specifically, it's common to talk of *city branding*, *region branding*, or *nation branding*.

The city of Amsterdam has always enjoyed an image associated with culture and innovation, thanks to its museums and its long tradition of commerce, combined with an atmosphere of freedom and transgression, mainly linked to a tolerance for drug use and prostitution. But in the mid-2000s, Amsterdam started coming up against stronger competition from other Dutch cities vying to pull in tourists and investors (such as The Hague and Rotterdam) and major European capitals. This trend prompted the decision to design a city branding strategy that would shore up the city's image among its targets.

The strategy was implemented by organizing ambitious international cultural events (like the Uitmarkt Festival, the biggest cultural happening in the Netherlands), leveraging the communicative power in major architectural projects (see Zuidas: www.zuidas.nl), and creating a new information system for visitors to render the city more hospitable and user-friendly. The logo created for the new strategy, 'I amsterdam', encapsulates all these messages (www.iamsterdam.com).

Case History 8.8

South Korea: identity building through a nation brand

In 2009 South Korea established the Presidential Committee on Nation Branding, under the direct control of the President of the Republic (www.koreabrand.net). This committee was tasked with designing and implementing the most effective strategies for promoting the image of South Korea in the world; disseminating knowledge about its culture, traditions, people, and products; enhancing respect and positive attitudes toward the country on a global level; and encouraging acceptance and appreciation for Korean companies and products.

Underpinning the Committee's work was a clearly-defined vision: 'to create a reliable and dignified Korea', with the specific aim of becoming one of the top 15 countries in the *Nation Brand Index*,[9] placing higher than the average OECD country. The vision is summed up in the motto: 'Korea. A loving embrace', which conveys the identity of a nation that seeks to contribute to the progress of the entire planet through its citizens, businesses, and a society built on the principle of inclusion. To achieve the aim, the Committee drew up a set of strategies based on four pillars grounded in the fundamental values of the country:

- Augmenting the contribution of South Korea to the international community, to demonstrate to the world that the country was capable of taking on various kinds of responsibility on the international scene (for instance, by hosting the 2010 G20 in Seoul).
- Disseminating the values of the traditional culture, with the aim of creating an image of an economically advanced country while enhancing knowledge of the South Korea's basic values.
- Reinforcing the country's global communication to improve reciprocal knowledge of South Korea and the international community.
- Pursuing social integration inside the country to encourage active participation of citizens in public life and to build their self-esteem.

Specifically, the role of the Committee was to coordinate and fund initiatives proposed by various organizations, both public and private. In 2013, having realized the aim of placing higher than the average OECD country in the Nation Brands ranking, the Committee was disbanded.

8.2.2.1   Creating brand elements

These include *a variety of signs that can have a unique and distinctive association* with the brand: the name, the logo and other visual symbols, the jingle used in the communication campaign or any other identifying sound, famous people linked to the brand, the package (with physical products), the slogan, and the URL (the web domain).

Distinctive brand elements serve two different purposes: to enhance awareness and to facilitate the construction of a network of brand associations in the perceptions of customers. For this reason, brand elements have to be chosen very carefully, to ensure that they have the following properties (Keller, 2012):

- *Memorizability*. Brand elements must be readily recognized and recalled from memory; the name has to be easy to pronounce and write, the logo and symbols have to be simple, the jingle catchy, and so forth.
- *Being a conveyor of meaning*. Brand elements shouldn't be an end in themselves; instead they should mean something, tell a story. The name of the organization might represent its story; the logo and the symbols can be composed of colors, shapes, and fonts that have meaning beyond aesthetics; the celebrities associated with the brand can serve as endorsers, transferring corresponding meanings (Section 5.7); and the package itself can convey meaning too.

- *High aesthetic quality*. This depends on the brand's target. Brand elements have to be eye-catching and attractive, capable of capturing the target's attention and conveying positive sensations.
- *Adaptability*. This means being able to use brand elements in myriad ways and in a vast range of contexts. Many visual elements are part of innumerable communication materials (websites, catalogues, advertising, flyers), so when choosing colors, fonts, sounds, and images the organization has to consider a variety of uses, which can also lead to substantial technical restrictions. (If the logo is white, it always needs to be reproduced on a dark background.) What's more, if the target market is international, elements have to convey the same meanings across different languages and cultures.
- *Defendability*. The brand owner must be able to defend respective brand elements from illicit use. For brand elements to be distinctive they can't be used by anyone else, so they must be registered to guarantee exclusive rights to the brand owner.

As we'll see shortly (Section 8.2.3), brand elements can't always stay the same if the brand itself evolves throughout its lifecycle. These elements, as we now know, serve as memory aids and as vehicles of brand associations. When the latter change following a repositioning, the identifying elements have to change too.

It's easy to imagine that creating brand elements isn't all it takes to generate awareness and build a positive image. To reach these objectives, the organization has to incorporate brand elements in communication activities in such a way that customers are exposed to them, pay attention to them, and store them in their memories.

8.2.2.2 Building brand image: creating a network of associations

Brand image is made up of a *set of associations* that customers attribute to a given brand. Associations are the result of interpretations and evaluations that customers make based on information on the brand and on their personal experiences (if they've already purchased or used the brand). It follows that building an image means creating in the perceptions of customers a set of associations linked to the brand that are as distinctive as possible with respect to associations attributed to other brands.

This description makes it clear that image is conceptually similar to positioning. So following this line of reasoning, it's possible to say that building an image basically means building positioning. *Image is the outcome of a positioning strategy*. It's the impression that customers get from a brand. As mentioned in the previous section, since identity should precede both, it's logical to conclude that defining brand identity precedes defining brand positioning, which, once enacted via market strategies, results in a brand image (Figure 8.3).

Everything that's been said about positioning the value proposition (Section 7.10) and the product (Section 8.1.4) also holds true for the brand. A strong positioning has to be built on positive associations that are relevant for the target market and distinctive with respect to competing brands. So building positioning means identifying a set of possible associations and then selecting the ones that represent points of difference, which can give rise to a strong image.

With regard to identifying and selecting associations, these can be broken down into two different levels: primary associations, which are directly connected with the brand, and secondary associations, which have an indirect connection because they are attributed to other subjects who have relationships with the brand (Figure 8.4).

Primary associations include the attributes of the products sold under the brand in question, the benefits these products provide, the values that the brand communicates, the personality that the brand conveys, the category of the products sold under the brand, the brand's specific usage occasions; target customers the brand is best able to satisfy, and other brands that may give rise to associations either due to similarities or differences.

Secondary associations encompass the organization that owns the brand, other related brands, third parties that certify the quality of the brand (via awards and certification, for instance), celebrities who may act as endorsers, characters created especially to represent the brand, distribution channels through which the brand is sold, the country of origin, and last of all the events that are specifically associated with the brand.

The basic difference between primary and secondary associations lies in the *control* that the organization has over elements that constitute image. So if brand image is built on the first (attributes or benefits, for example), the final result depends to a great extent on the capacity of the company to produce the products in question. If instead image is built on the second, this control is shared with third parties that have some connection with the brand.

If the image of a city is anchored on an event, for instance, and the event creates conflict or fails to draw big crowds, the fallout may tarnish the city's image. If an author builds her image on the literary

Figure 8.3 – The relationships between the brand identity-positioning-image

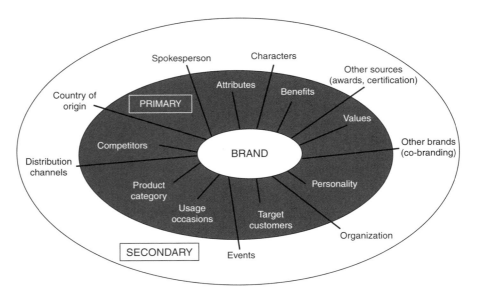

Figure 8.4 – Types of brand associations

prizes she's won, and then it comes out that the jury awarding the prizes isn't impartial, this would reflect badly on her image. If the image of a theater is built on the testimonial of a celebrity, and this person causes a scandal through objectionable or even criminal behavior, the image of the theater would be damaged as a result.

8.2.3   Managing the brand over time

Brand positioning must be monitored and managed throughout the brand's lifecycle (Whan Park et al., 1986) (Figure 8.5), as is the case with positioning the value proposition (Sections 7.11 and 7.12). If an organization has successfully introduced a new brand and sales start to rise, at this point other companies or institutions will probably try to launch brands with similar characteristics to exploit the market opportunities it has created. As a result the points of difference used to build the initial positioning may become points of parity, eroding the image of the brand in question.

8.2.3.1   *Strategies in the growth stage*

From the outset of the growth stage the organization has to invest in *reinforcing brand image*. This means consolidating the brand associations in the perceptions of customers. To do so, the first step is to *keep brand awareness high* through constant communication activity. Awareness serves as a vehicle for entrenching image. As the market grows, so does the intensity of competitors' communication, so the organization must avoid the risk that recall and recognition of its brand decline to the benefit of its competitors.

There are two basic strategies for reinforcing brand image:

○ *Reinvigorating associations*. This entails rejuvenating positive associations and neutralizing negative ones. If a book series has the image of showcasing talented new writers, the publisher needs to keep investing in scouting. If an archeological site has a distinctive image based on the quality of the educational activities and the interactive technologies it offers, it needs to continue its pioneering offerings in both areas.

○ *Renewing brand associations*. To do this, an organization might want to explore new points of difference. This would be the path to take if competitors have drawn the original points of difference into their image as well, turning them into points of parity. But what's critical to keep in mind are weaknesses. Every brand has them, and one brand's weakness is a competing brand's strength to be leveraged to build differentiation. This explains why every

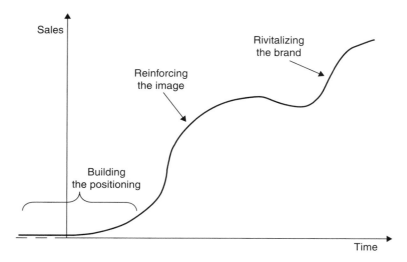

Figure 8.5 – Managing brand positioning throughout its lifecycle

organization not only has to be aware of its brand's weaknesses, but actually implement strategies that can mitigate or even neutralize the resulting negative effects, perhaps through communication campaigns that highlight the relative importance of other factors.

- *Revitalizing brand elements.* Brand elements represent the components of a brand that are readily visible, the ones that customers can most easily interact with, and which they store in their memories as fragments of information on the brand (Section 8.2.2.1). An easy way to communicate the fact that the organization is revamping or recharging a brand is to restyle respective brand elements with a new logo, a new jingle, a new package, and so on.

8.2.3.2   Strategies in the maturity stage

To prevent the decline of a mature market, *brand revitalization strategies* are needed. The aim of these is to spark a new growth stage for brand sales and to expand the current market.

The different options aren't mutually exclusive, and several can be used simultaneously as long as they're properly integrated to maximize effectiveness and efficiency. Generally, a distinction can be drawn between the underlying aims: boosting sales to current customers or expanding the customer base (Case History 8.9). So using the terminology introduced in Section 7.5.1, the organization seeks to increase penetration to achieve the first, and weighted coverage for the second.

8.2.3.2.1 *Increasing penetration among current customers* This can be achieved by increasing either product quantities sold to current customers, or purchase frequency and/or usage frequency. For example, bundling several products (Section 8.1.5.2) might be a way for a clothing manufacturer to drive up sales among current customers; the same is true for a promotion offering discounts for purchasing multiple products (three for the price of two and price cuts, for example). As for the business market, a sports team could offer its sponsors the chance to support both the team and the stadium. Here are more examples: rotating the pieces on display in a permanent collection could increase the frequency of visits to a museum; creating theme-based trails or special events could increase the frequency of visits to an archeological site or national park; organizing friendly matches may be a way to increase the frequency of ticket purchases for a sports team.

8.2.3.2.2 *Expanding the customer base* The aim here is to reach different targets. An organization can achieve this by using current segmentation and focusing on other attractive targets, or by formulating new market segmentation to emerge targets that were previously overlooked.

Case History 8.9

The long life of Havaianas: a repositioning success story

Havaianas: undeniably an icon of Brazil, its people, and the Brazilian lifestyle. But beyond this, these flip-flops represent an enormously successful case of brand management, seeing as the brand is more than 70 years old and makes a sizeable contribution to the turnover and profitability of Sao Paulo Alpargatas, the biggest footwear manufacturer in Latin America.

It all began in 1962 when the company launched the first model of rubber sandals with white soles and two colored straps. The first Havaianas were inspired by *zori*, traditional Japanese sandals made of straw; the name derived from the Hawaiian Islands, to call to mind easy-going footwear suitable for hot climates. With a very low price, the sandals were big sellers from the start, especially among the lower socio-economic classes, becoming so popular that after a year the company was producing 1,000 pairs a day.

For nearly 20 years the company focused on expanding the domestic market without paying much attention to creating brand value. In fact, there was only one basic model in four different colors. In 1988 sales peaked at 88 million pairs; the product had become a part of Brazil's popular culture.

In the early 1990s the situation began to evolve. Brazil was beginning to see the growth that has made the country an economic powerhouse today, and Brazilians were enjoying a better quality of life. Havaianas, with their image as a poor product for the masses, were no longer seen as congruent with the ambitions of the country. What's more, over the years the huge success of the originals had spurred numerous imitations. The combination of these two factors triggers a drop in sales.

The company realized that a major change was needed, and it opted to start investing in repositioning the brand image with an eye to expanding the market. The strategy was based on two basic tactics: increasing the number of models (currently 80) and more importantly the colors (now 60,000). This gives every consumer the chance to choose the flip-flops that best fit his or her style. Another component of this repositioning was a revamped communication strategy to create the image of a product that was less functional and more fashionable, meaning more aspirational.

The new models varied in terms of styles, colors, and prices, to continue to ensure that everyone could afford a pair of Havaianas, but at the same time to project a clearer distinction between consumer targets and to encourage impulse buys. What's more, the new communication campaign featured young Brazilian artists and celebrities sporting Havaianas as they enjoyed relaxing or socializing.

The strategy successfully reignited sales, which continue on an upward trajectory today. One driver for this trend was the launch of Havaianas on international markets in the late 1990s. This move reinforced the new positioning as a fashion brand, confirmed by the appearance of the flip-flops on the catwalks of world-famous designers.

○ *Brand repositioning:* Assuming that different segments have different expectations, the organization needs to reposition its brand, creating an image that's consistent with the expectations of the new target. But this strategy can have repercussions on current customers as well, so the key is to be very careful to avoid the risk of becoming attractive to new targets while losing appeal with the existing customer base.

For instance, if an opera house with a strong tradition-based image begins to perform contemporary works with innovative sets and costumes, it would probably succeed in attracting new spectators but may lose its more traditional-minded audience. Obviously such a decision may be an intentional one, if the organization has opted to modify its brand identity. Moreover, undertaking brand repositioning can also be a way to give new inspiration to current customers. Seeing as their desires and needs may have evolved over time, the brand image should do the same.

○ *Breaking into new segments:* An additional option for expanding the customer base is to break into new segments with the current offering, without making any major changes to the brand image. Let's say, for example, that the opera house mentioned above has always targeted music buffs, in keeping with its mission. At this point it may decide to focus on under-30s by offering discounted tickets to special evening events, expanding the target market. This choice may also make the opera house attractive to new potential sponsors, and pave the way into new segments of the business market.

In this scenario, when launching its brand the opera house may not have considered under-30s an attractive segment, or may not have had access to the resources it needed to adapt its product offering to this segment or design an ad hoc communication campaign. But imagine what might happen later: after the brand is launched and it has won a share of the market, the organization has accumulated the resources it needs to broaden its target market, and some segments have become more attractive. In this case, the organization should invest in adapting its products or its communication campaign, rather than changing the brand image.

○ *Brand extension:* This strategy entails using the brand to sell products other than the originals, both within the same product category and in different ones. The first is called a *line extension*, for example when the Guggenheim in New York opened new museums in Venice, Bilbao, and Abu Dhabi; the second is a *category extension*, as was the case when the daily newspaper *Frankfurter Allgemeine Zeitung* launched a collection of books. Actually, a brand extension can be used both to increase penetration among current customers, and to expand the customer base. Thanks to its dual nature, this is one of the most commonly implemented strategies among organizations with strong brands, in creative industries and beyond.

It's also worth noting that while innovation in line extensions mainly ties into products, the more risky and innovative strategy is category extensions, where product and market innovation are combined. With a category extension, the brand is associated with products that belong to a different category from the original one, so the organization uses the value of its brand to branch off into a new market.

This market may already exist, or it might be an entirely new one that the organization wants to create via the brand. The difference lies in the fact that in the first case the brand is extended into a market where there are already other organizations with their own brands, products, and images. In the second case the market is actually created, with all the risks and opportunities outlined in Section 7.5.3.

To design an effective category extension strategy, the organization must ascertain that certain conditions are in place:

1. *The potential for an extension.* The critical condition in the new market is that *customers know the brand*. Logically if there is limited brand awareness, the organization can't leverage the repository of positive associations needed to insert the brand into customers' evoked set. Clearly this condition draws a very clear distinction between extensions that are meant to increase penetration among current customers and extensions that serve to augment the customer base. In the first case brand awareness is a given; in the second this awareness must be carefully corroborated by quantitative market research.

2. *The potential for acceptance of the extension.* One thing that can't be taken for granted is that customers will accept the extension. In fact, if the brand enjoys a clear, distinctive image, this is also thanks to the characteristics of the current products. So when people see the same brand applied to different products in a different category, they may think it's incongruent or out of line, so they won't have any desire to buy or use the new products.

Research on this issue (Aaker and Keller, 1990; Keller and Aaker, 1992; Völckner and Sattler, 2006) suggests that customers more readily accept a brand extension if there is a high *perceptual fit* on two levels: between the original and new product categories and between the brand and the new category.

Since every product category is represented in the perceptions of customers by means of a series of factors (Section 7.9), the ones that characterize the two categories may be seen as incongruent. As an example, just think of the product categories of 'apparel' and 'theatrical productions'. Very likely most customers won't see a fit between the skills and competences needed to produce a show at the theater and those required to produce clothing. On the contrary, a fit would be very apparent between the categories of apparel and accessories or design. Likewise with radio and television programs, or daily newspapers and monthly magazines.

So the organization first has to assess the perceived *category-to-category fit*. Next, it should scrutinize the *brand-to-category fit*. The brand already has its original image, which determines its position within the current category. But this image may not have much to do with the basic characteristics of the new category. Here's another example: a brand of high-tech sportswear may not seem like a good fit with casual accessories.

3. *The potential of the market.* Even when there's a promising fit in terms of categories and brand, this is no reason to assume that there's room for the brand

on the new market. In fact the organization has to ensure that the brand's current associations correspond to *benefits that customers in the new market believe to be relevant*. If this isn't the case, the brand won't possess performance factors and won't be perceived as on par with the market's current brands.

4. *The competitive differential.* The assessment in the previous points refers to the capacity of the brand to be relevant. Now the organization needs to make sure its brand has *points of difference* with respect to established brands. As often reiterated, it's difference that creates preference. So if there is brand awareness, fit, and relevance, but no difference, customers in the new market will have no convincing justification for shifting their purchase and use choices from their current brands to the new one.

When considering a brand extension into new categories, organizations should always analyze the potential risks for the brand. If such an extension penetrates categories that are seen as too distant from the original, or, as is more often the case, simply involves too many new categories, the brand's image may end up tarnished, resulting in what is known as *brand dilution*. For instance a celebrity (a personal brand) who endorses several different brands of a wide range products may see her image diluted among her fans. Likewise, in the fashion world if a brand is extended to less prestigious product categories, the result is negative fallout on the brand image (Albrecht et al., 2013).

8.2.4   Managing a brand portfolio

Organizations that adopt a brand management approach very likely don't sell a single brand but an entire brand portfolio instead. Most of the considerations already discussed about product portfolios in Section 8.1.7 apply to managing brand portfolios too. Specifically these pertain to motivations behind a portfolio versus individual brands, decisions relating to portfolio breadth and depth, and assessing portfolio equilibrium. In this section I'll address the main differences between the two types of portfolios.

The two key objectives of managing a brand portfolio are maximizing effectiveness (that is, the capacity to cover various market segments) and at the same time minimizing inefficiency (possibly due to similar or overlapping images of various brand), which might create confusion in the minds of customers and internal competition among the brand, also

known as *cannibalization*. These two objectives lead to the ultimate goal of optimizing the value of the entire portfolio for the organization.

The most common tool utilized for managing a brand portfolio with these objectives in mind is *brand architecture*: an organized structure for the brand portfolio. Brand architecture establishes:

- The role of individual brands in the portfolio.
- The relationships among brands in the portfolio.

8.2.4.1   *The role of individual brands in the portfolio*

The decision to create a new brand to add to a portfolio is normally the outcome of an organization's desire to serve a certain market segment that has characteristics and value expectations that differ from the other segments served. To do so, the organization comes up with a specific offering that's distinctive from the offerings earmarked for other segments. Ultimately this decision springs from a prior assessment of the attractiveness of the new segment.

But beyond the external function on the market, every brand also plays a part in the organization's portfolio, a role that varies primarily in light of specific objectives set for that brand. So from this perspective it's possible to differentiate between brands that are (Keller, 2012):

- *Strategic*: These represent the future of the portfolio in terms of target market size, growth rate and awareness. Often these are the brands that customers identify most with the organization.
- *Cash cows*: These generate financial resources for the entire portfolio. Often cash cows are long-standing brands with a loyal, consolidated customer base; they generally require few investments for revitalization or repositioning, so they can contribute with the surplus resources they create to supporting other brands in the portfolio.
- *Image-enhancers*: These brands elevate the image of the entire portfolio or organization. The related image is normally high-quality, exclusive, and prestigious. Often image brands absorb rather than generate financial resources because, despite their high prices, sales revenues don't cover production and distribution costs.
- *Flankers*: Alongside the rest of the portfolio, these brands close off the market to competitors. They're tactical brands created to restrict the maneuvering room of competitors in attractive segments where the organization doesn't have a strong position. Alternatively, these brands are created to protect

strategic or image brands from competitors who want to appropriate market share by connoting their own brands with similar attributes.

- *Entry level*: These brands allow access into the portfolio because they're more economical. Brands in this category are sold at lower prices with the aim of allowing segments with less spending power or more risk aversion to establish a relationship with the organization, to then push them toward other brands in the portfolio.

8.2.4.2 *The relationships among brands in the portfolio*

The choice of having several different brands in a portfolio as opposed to doing business with a single brand depends on whether the organization's priority is effectiveness or efficiency. This choice intersects an issue that brand management has to address: whether to communicate the fact that the different brands belong to the same organization and if so how. More specifically, the question is whether or not to highlight the link with the name/brand of the organization (also called corporate brand, master brand, or parent brand). The combination of these two decisions lies at the heart of the *branding strategy*. These branding strategies can be positioned on a continuum, with the end points being maximum effectiveness and maximum efficiency.

- *The branded house.* With this strategy, a master brand is used for all the organization's products, and each one is distinguished only by its name. For instance, Frieze differentiates between its art fairs only by the name of the city that hosts each one (Frieze London, Frieze New York, for example). Or for another example, Abercrombie & Fitch uses its parent brand on all the items in its clothing collections. The aim of the branded house strategy is to maximize efficiency, exploiting communicative synergies generated by communication based on a single brand that have positive repercussions on all the products. Specifically, this strategy makes it possible to utilize the same brand elements for all the products, reinforcing awareness and facilitating memorization. The organization can also keep tight control over image, since image revolves around the master brand. However, efficiency here goes to the detriment of effectiveness: if there are market segments that differ widely in expectations, the closer the brand is connected to a single segment and the less appropriate the other segments will consider it.

- *The house of brands.* This strategy is diametrically opposed to the previous one. Here the organization owns several brands and manages each one separately, without making their shared origins public. An example is the Universal Music record label, owner of dozens of brands, each specialized in a specific genre: Island, Def Jam, and Republic for more commercial music, Deutsche Grammophon and Decca for classical music, Verve and Blue Note for jazz. The point of this strategy is to maximize effectiveness by attempting to build a positioning for each brand in every single market segment, sacrificing efficiency. Each brand has its own brand elements, communication strategy, managerial team, and other specific costs.

- *The sub-brand strategy.* Here a master brand is used with a sub-brand (which occupies a less prevalent position). In the radio industry, for instance, the BBC in addition to its corporate brand has a number of sub-brands representing 18 different stations, such as BBC 1, BBC 1xtra, BBC 5 Live, and BBC Wales. By implementing this strategy the organization seeks to build a strong image for the parent brand that can be transferred to each sub-brand, every one with specificities that render its image more attractive for its target segment.

  The sub-brand strategy is effective when the differences between segments aren't so dramatic as to call for ad hoc brand positioning, but at the same time not so negligible as to be covered with a single brand. The association between the parent brand and the sub-brands is also conveyed by the structure of brand elements that encompasses certain differences for each sub-brand. A final note worth mentioning is that the sub-brand strategy can be incorporated into a house of brands approach, if some of the brands in an organization's portfolio have sub-brands.

- *The endorsement strategy.* Here too the master brand is used with another brand, but the latter actually predominates over the former. This means that the master brand serves as endorser, presenter, and certifier of quality of the second brand. The organization's efforts center on building a strong image for the endorsed brand, with positive associations also linked to the master brand. So an endorsement strategy is effective when the organization wants to serve segments that necessitate ad hoc brand positioning, where a single brand or a sub-brand isn't effective enough.

Generally speaking, this also leads to the creation of distinctive brand elements that are associated in some way with the parent brand. For instance, endorsement strategies are commonplace with brand extensions in the fashion and luxury business. Dior in the perfume market builds brand value by endorsing brands like Poison, J'Adore, Dolce Vita, and Dune.

8.3   PRICE MANAGEMENT

It may sound strange to include price as one of the components of value for the customer. But by now it has become clear that there's both a negative and positive side to value (sacrifices and benefits). As for the first, price is the most readily apparent. Customers might not be fully aware of other sacrifices, such as the time they'll have to spend on the choice process, or the cognitive effort in making a final selection. But as for price, that's something people are rarely oblivious to (except of course with gifts). All this means that organizations face momentous decisions when it comes to pricing, for three main reasons:

- Price has *an (often immediate) impact on both revenues and costs*, which means on the financial sustainability of the value proposition as well. The price level directly affects product sales and costs, in particular if sales in turn generate economies of scale and scope.
- Price *conveys product quality*. For experience products, price represents one of the few tangible attributes on which customers can form their expectations as far as the product's capacity to satisfy their needs or desires.
- Price *allows customers to compare alternative value propositions*. Following on from the preceding point, customers can compare value propositions both within the same product category and among different categories.

Simply stated, from a marketing viewpoint, *price is a variable of positioning*. In other words, price can be leveraged to communicate to the market the value of an offering and to make it stand out from the competition. So for the organization, effective price management means considering three distinct factors carefully and concurrently: the costs of producing and selling the offering (which calls for evaluating production and distribution processes from a financial and organizational standpoint); the value that customers attribute to the offering (which requires analyzing current and potential demand); the price – and therefore the value – of competitors' offerings (competitive analysis of alternative offerings).

Cost represents the minimum price threshold; pricing a product below cost is tantamount to sacrificing the financial sustainability of the value proposition. The value attributed by target customers, instead, marks the maximum price threshold; exceeding this ceiling would mean risking lost sales because customers aren't willing to pay a higher price than the value they perceive. Finally, competitor prices provide benchmarks for positioning, as price is directly proportional to the perception of value.

The three criteria for pricing decisions form the basis for three methods for price setting, each with a different focus: cost-based, demand-based, and competition-based. The most common methods are described in the following sections. But first, one thing to keep in mind is that to use them effectively, the organization has to be aware of the complexity of customers' perceptions of price in relation to the various stages of the consumption experience. We'll explore this complexity next.

8.3.1   Price and cost in customer experience

Imagine a person's favorite band is going on tour, and they're performing in a city far from where she lives. Beyond the benefits she knows she'll get out of the experience, she can anticipate making quite a few sacrifices as well: finding tickets, travelling to the venue, and finding a place to stay, among others. But let's focus on the economic sacrifices, the most immediate of which is the ticket price. Say there are three price options based on proximity to the stage: 50, 70, and 100 euro. On the official tour site, she can buy tickets online with a 5 per cent service fee; there's also a 10 per cent discount for early ticket purchases.

Now about the trip. From the official tour website she discovers that when she buys her concert tickets she gets a 10 per cent discount on the cost of the train ticket from her city to the host city. According to the train company's site, today the cheapest return ticket costs 45 euro. Surfing the websites of the major airlines, the cheapest return ticket she finds is currently going for 85 euro, but she'd need to add a train ticket from the airport to the city center, which costs 11 euro. Finally on a hotel booking site she finds a room for 40 euro a night. So what's her final cost for going to the concert?

What becomes apparent from this example is that there are many things to consider as far as price goes. This is true both for the organization, which has to decide how to price its products, and for consumers, who have to tally up all the expenses related to the consumption experience.[10]

From the standpoint of the *organization*:

- *The list price (that is, the official sales price) doesn't always coincide with what the customer actually pays*, which factors in discounts and extras too. To calculate the actual price, a price equation should be applied:

Price = List price − discounts and allowances + extra fees

So price management involves both setting the sales price (Section 8.3.5) and making decisions that will affect the actual price that customers pay, which is where pricing strategies come into play (Section 8.3.6).

- *Different market segments can pay different prices* for the same product. A product that provides a series of benefits and sacrifices can elicit diverse expected value among various segments, depending on the specific combination of benefits and sacrifices that customers prefer. Consequently, price management calls for meticulous market segmentation, based on desired benefits.

All this is clearly illustrated in the concert example. If the fan's willing to sacrifice the quality of the experience with seats that are further away from the stage, but she likes the convenience of buying online and she's looking to save money, she'd probably want to pay 47.50 euro for a 50-euro ticket with an advance purchase discount $\left(\text{P} = 50€ \times (1 - 10\% + 5\%)\right)$. On the other hand, if her priorities are the quality of the experience and the convenience of buying online, but she wants the freedom of being able to decide at the last minute whether or not to go to the concert, she'd be prepared to pay 73.50 euro $\left(\text{P} = 70€ \times (1 + 5\%)\right)$.

From the standpoint of the *customer*:

- *The price of the product doesn't necessarily equal the total cost* of getting value out of the consumption experience. In fact, as we know, this experience is made up of stages, and in each one customers will probably have to face other expenses to ensure a satisfying consumption experience (Section 3.1.6). For the concert, these would include the cost of travel and accommodation. So the takeaway here is that the organization has to have deep, detailed knowledge of the different stages of the experience and the related sacrifice-generating activities.
- *Different market segments can incur disparate overall costs depending on the specific consumption experience*, which is the result of a set combination of products and services

that consumers activate within the context of that experience. The main product is only one component.

- Going back to the concert example, depending on the fan's travel arrangements, the overall cost can vary a great deal, from 128 euro on a train ticket if she's money-conscious $\left(\text{Cost} = 47.5€ + 45€ \times (1 - 10\%) + 40€)\right)$, to 220.50 euro if flexibility is a priority and she decides she wants to fly $\left(\text{Cost} = 73.5€ + 85€ + 11€ \times 2 + 40€)\right)$. What all this means is that the organization needs accurate knowledge regarding customers' possible sources of value, both the ones that the organization controls and those that depend on others subjects and organizations.

These considerations highlight the fact that pricing decisions are far-reaching ones, more so than it may seem at first. Deep knowledge of the entire cycle of customer experience provides the foundation for effective decision making. Equally essential is an understanding of the impact that price can have on the choices customers make, which taken together constitute market demand.

8.3.2 Price–demand relationships

Information on the impact of price on customer choice is contained in what's known as the *demand curve*.[11] This represents the maximum quantity that customers purchase for every product price level. The demand curve provides three basic pieces of information:

- The *shape* indicates the number of units sold for every price level.
- The *slope* shows how sensitive consumers are to price variations.
- The *sign* refers to the direction of the relationship between demand and price, either positive or negative.

Shape and slope depend on customers' preferences and financial resources, the availability and price of substitute products, and environmental factors that might impact demand such as laws, regulations, and infrastructures. With regard to sign, the demand curve is normally depicted as negative based on the assumption that as the price rises, sales fall and vice versa. But as we'll see, this assumption doesn't always hold true.

The hypothetical example in Figure 8.6 shows the demand curve for a monthly magazine. When the price is set at 6.00 euro, it's generally considered to be too expensive and not a single copy is sold; if instead it were distributed free of charge the market would absorb up to 12 million copies.

8.3.2.1   The shape of the demand curve

The shape of the curve provides clues as to the optimal price level for a given product in terms of impact on sales. Taking a very superficial stance, the temptation would be to assume that the optimal price is the lowest, because this would maximize sales volumes. But such is not the case. In fact, price represents unit revenues, in other words, the amount that the organization earns from each unit it sells. So cutting the unit revenue has a negative effect on overall revenues. If instead the organization wants to maximize the latter, it needs to discover the lowest possible price level. Below this threshold, the increase in the number of units sold won't compensate for the loss in unit revenues, and overall profit will suffer.

Put in formal terms, this price level is where marginal revenues equal zero, because *marginal revenues are* *the variation in total revenues deriving from the additional sale of a unit of product:*[12]

$$MR = \frac{\varDelta TR}{\varDelta Q}$$

where $\varDelta TR$ is the variation in total revenues, and $\varDelta Q$ the additional unit of product sold. Figure 8.7 shows the curve for total revenues and tables with calculations for the magazine example in Figure 8.6. As the figure shows, the price level that maximizes revenues is 4.00 euro (the point at which marginal revenues equal 0).

8.3.2.2   The slope of the demand curve

The slope of the demand curve indicates consumer sensitivity to price variations, which is defined as *price elasticity of demand* (PED). Elasticity indicates the

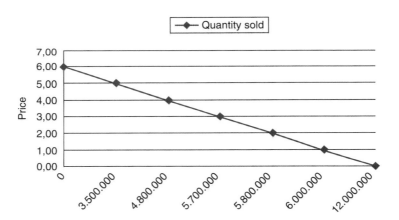

Figure 8.6 – The demand curve

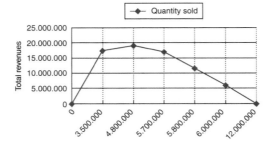

PRICE (in £)	QUANTITY SOLD	TOTAL REVENUES (TR =P x Q)
6.00	0	0
5.00	3,500,000	17,500,000
4.00	4,800,000	19,200,000
3.00	5,700,000	17,100,000
2.00	5,800,000	11,600,000
1.00	6,000,000	6,000,000
0.00	12,000,000	0

Figure 8.7 – The curve for total revenues

effectiveness of raising or lowering the price of a product. The formula is:

$$E = \frac{\%\Delta Q}{\%\Delta P}$$

where $\%\Delta Q$ stands for the percentage change in demand for the product, and $\%\Delta P$ is the percentage change in price.

If the sign of the slope of the demand curve is negative, the elasticity formula yields a negative number, but normally the absolute (positive) value is considered. Demand is referred to as *elastic* when a price variation triggers a more than proportional variation in demand. When the opposite occurs, demand is *inelastic*, that is, the change in demand is less than proportional to the change in price. With an elastic curve a lower price generates higher revenues and vice versa (since total revenues equal the unit price multiplied by the quantity of product sold). With an inelastic curve the opposite is true.

PED is caused by several factors. First, the *less differentiated the product* (that is, the more substitute products there are), the more elastic the demand. The reason for this is that customers have the option of buying other relatively similar products if the price of the original one rises. With regard to creative products, the more they're perceived to be unique, the less sensitive customers will be to price.

Second, the more *the product is seen as a necessity*, the more demand for that product will be inelastic, because customers can't go without it. (This would include certain foods, items of clothing, and so forth.) With creative products, the ones that satisfy identity-related needs could be considered necessities, since consumers can't give them up without sacrificing their sense of self. Last, *the greater the customer loyalty to the product*, the less elastic the demand, because loyal customers recognize that the product is better suited to satisfying their needs and desires than any other. That means they are willing to pay a higher price for it.

8.3.2.3   *The sign of the demand curve*
Up till now, the discussion has centered on demand curves with negative slope, but this isn't the case with all products in every market. In fact, in markets where customers associate price with product quality, it's likely that *the demand curve slope will be positive*, especially with creative products. Since it's hard to predict the quality of such products before actually experiencing them, customers look for quality clues, and the price is the simplest and most readily apparent. In other words, the higher the product price, the higher the quality that customers perceive.

This same condition is associated with all products with high distinction value. Traditionally, demand for these goods is represented by the *prestige pricing* curve (Hawkins, 1954; Leibenstein, 1950) (Figure 8.8(a)). The underlying reason for the non-standard shape of this curve is that a high list price sends the message that the people who possess that product belong to an exclusive social circle, seeing that the price makes it inaccessible to all but a few. (This is the case with all luxury brands.)

So within a given range, as the price decreases, demand increases, as per the norm. But once the lower price threshold is reached, the product becomes accessible to so many customers that it loses its distinction value. This leads many customers to stop buying it, and as a result demand decreases as the price falls.

In actual fact, for all products where there is a customer perception of a positive relationship between quality and price (including distinction value as a component of quality), what most often happens is that the demand curve has two thresholds, an upper and lower one (Costabile, 1992) (Figure 8.8(b)). Within these two boundaries, product demand increases as the price rises because customers connote those products with higher quality (or distinction value) and buy larger quantities (or a greater number of customers are prompted to buy). Clearly, for the opposite reasons, as the price drops, sales volumes decrease.

Once the price exceeds this upper threshold, customers continue to associate the product with higher quality, but for some the price becomes unaffordable. At this point sales volumes decline and the curve becomes negative once again. Below the lower threshold, the product is so cheap that it attracts other customer segments, or it becomes suitable for additional use occasions. So demand realigns with the standard trend: as the price falls, sales volumes rise. If for example, the ticket price for a Lady Gaga concert dropped below a certain level, many fans would begin to think she was no longer a world-class performer and would probably not go to the concert, but many others could afford to have her sing at their birthday party!

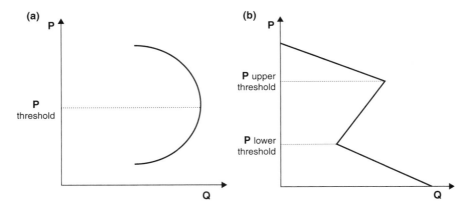

Figure 8.8 – Price thresholds along the demand curve

So for organizations it's critical to know the shape, slope and sign of the demand curve for their products. The first provides input on the optimal price level, in light of relative sales targets; the second marks out the maneuvering room on pricing; the third indicates where demand may show discrepancies with respect to price. Section 8.3.4 details some marketing research methods that are useful in providing all this information. By using a combination of these, organizations can identify the minimum and maximum boundaries for the price of their products, as well as the optimal price point within this range.

8.3.3   Revealing the minimum price threshold: the level of sustainable costs

If the price of a product is too low, sales revenues can't cover product costs. Obviously, this would jeopardize the product's financial sustainability and, in extreme cases, the survival of the entire organization (Section 8.1.5.3). There can be justifications for keeping a product on the market even when sales revenues don't cover costs (Section 8.3.5.3), but such a scenario must be an exception and not the rule.

The technique used to determine the price level needed to ensure that sales cover costs is called *break-even analysis*, which ascertains the relationship between total revenues and total costs of a product at different sales levels. The *break-even point* (BEP) is the quantity of product sales at which revenues equal costs; in other words, when profit is zero.[13] To calculate the BEP, the starting point is the profit equation:

$$Profit = Total\ Revenues - Total\ Costs = (PxQ) - (FC + TVC)$$

where P is product price, Q is quantity sold, FC is fixed costs, and TVC is total variable costs. (Fixed costs stay the same regardless of production volumes; variable costs change.) For a book, for instance, the cost of the communication campaign for the launch doesn't vary whether one thousand or one million copies are sold, but the cost of the paper the book is printed on obviously does. For a sports team, the costs of players' salaries are fixed with respect to the number of matches they play; the travel expenses for away games are variable.

Keeping in mind that total variable costs equal the unit variable costs multiplied by the quantity sold ($TVC = UVC\ x\ Q$), to calculate the BEP these steps need to be followed:

$$\begin{aligned} Profit\ &= (PxQ) - (FC + TVC) \\ &= (PxQ) - \left[FC + (UVCxQ) \right] \\ &= (PxQ) - FC - (UVCxQ) \end{aligned}$$

BEP, as we said, is when profit is 0, or total sales revenues are equal to total costs:

$$(PxQ) = FC + (UVCxQ)$$

$$(PxQ) - (UVCxQ) = FC$$

$$(P - UVC) x Q = FC$$

$$Q = \frac{FC}{(P - UVC)}$$

Since the contribution margin of the product is the difference between product price and unit variable costs, the BEP is derived from the relationships between fixed costs and the contribution margin. The same calculations provide the price level that corresponds to the BEP. Dividing all the terms in the equation below by Q:

$$(PxQ) = FC + (UVCxQ)$$

$$P = \frac{FC}{Q} + UVC$$

This means that the minimum price level possible for a product is one that covers both variable costs attributed to the product, and a portion of fixed costs allocated to the product.

In the magazine example from Figures 8.6 and 8.7, let's say the fixed costs total one million euro, variable costs per unit run to 0.50 euro, and the publisher estimates sales at 4.8 million copies. In this case, break-even would be:

$$P = \frac{1 ml / \text{€}}{4.8 ml / \text{€}} + \text{€}0.50 = \text{€}0.21 + \text{€}0.50 = \text{€}0.71$$

Break-even analysis is often plotted on a graph to get a snapshot of the total losses (or profits) the organization would sustain if sales go below (or above) the BEP.

What is readily apparent from the illustration of break-even analysis is the relationship between costs, prices, and profit. If the fixed costs of a product are high (or if they rise over time) the BEP shifts to the right. This leaves the organization with two options to avoid incurring losses: either sell more units of product at the same price, or raise the price while keeping sales volumes constant. (Graphically, the slope of the revenue curve rises, becoming steeper as it moves toward the left.)

So with break-even analysis, it's quite intuitive that in creative industries where fixed costs are high, to ensure

financial sustainability and keep prices accessible to more than just a happy few, organizations have to target a much larger number of consumers to sell significant quantities of product. (Examples of creative industries with high fixed costs are archeological sites or national parks where maintenance costs can be extreme; sports teams that face skyrocketing salaries for athletes; or performing arts organizations with legions of actors, dancers, musicians, and singers.) But more often than not, this isn't possible because public access must be restricted: a precious artifact has to be protected from excessive exposure to ensure its preservation; the layout or size of an archeological site may allow for only small groups of visitors; an artist is physically capable of producing only so many works of art.

Looking more closely at the performing arts, for instance, Baumol (1967) underscores the fact that in this industry there is no way to offset the dynamic of production costs with an increase in productivity. This contrasts with other industries, where many businesses can avoid increasing costs (and in turn prices) through innovations that either boost production while using the same production factors, or cut production time, or even utilize fewer production factors (workers, for instance) to output the same quantity of product.[14] But these solutions don't apply in the performing arts (or in many other creative industries).

Here often the specific creative choices of the artist determine the quantity of production factors used: a Mozart symphony for violin and orchestra involves a specific number of instruments; any fewer would be a radical deviation from the original work. The tempo is set as well, so playing it more quickly to exploit the performers' production capacity several times over isn't an option. In light of these innate constraints, the most reasonable solution for ensuring financial sustainability would be to set the price high enough to cover costs. But in many creative industries that price would be far beyond the pocketbook of many potential consumers. The solution? Tapping alternative sources of revenues, especially from the business market.[15]

For these markets, in fact, creative products constitute production factors, and provide benefits that differ from those of the consumer markets (Chapter 5). This means relative price levels vary a great deal. (Sponsoring a season of the Bolshoi is a very different thing than buying a season ticket to the ballet.) More importantly, corresponding costs are extremely low – in some cases even nil – for the organization offering the creative product.

The chance to access sources of revenues other than product sales in consumers markets allows organizations in creative industries to have more maneuvering room for setting the price and the relative BEP target. Most of the time, total revenues are fixed with respect to volumes sold.[16] This explains why many organizations view revenues from business markets as solutions for covering fixed costs and for mitigating the effects of this outlay on their financial equilibrium. These effects can be represented in the following formula, where *RBM* stands for revenues from business markets:

$$(PxQ)+RBM = FC +(UVCxQ)$$

$$P = \frac{FC-RBM}{Q}+UVC$$

In the example from Figures 8.6 and 8.7, assuming that the magazine can generate 2.8 ml/€ per issue from advertising, the break-even price becomes:

$$P = \frac{(1-2.8)ml/€}{4.8ml/€}+€0.50 = -€0.375+€0.50 = €0.125$$

8.3.4   Determining the maximum price threshold: the value for target customers

The maximum price threshold for a product corresponds to the perceptions of value of target customers. Beyond this limit, many customers will probably think that the product price exceeds its value, so they'll look for substitute products or other ways to obtain the item (putting it on their personal wish list, or buying it used, if possible). Or they may simply resign themselves to the fact that they can't afford it.

Discovering the maximum price threshold implicitly means reconstructing the product's demand curve. Keeping in mind that the value expectations of each market segment differ, because of diverse motivations and knowledge sets, the logical assumption is that each segment has a different maximum price threshold for any given product,[17] which corresponds to varying levels of demand. There are a variety of methods for determining the maximum price threshold.

8.3.4.1   *The value expectation method*

This is based on a fundamental premise: that customers are willing to pay a price that corresponds to the perceived value of a given product, relative to substitute products. Consequently, to use this method the organization needs to find out which products are actually alternatives (other products of the organization or of competitors) and use them as benchmarks. Quantitative marketing research typically generates the necessary data through a survey (Section 6.5.4). To reveal the price threshold, the following formula applies:

$$P_a = \frac{V_a}{V_b} \times P_b$$

where P_a is the price of product a, P_b is the current price of the benchmark product, V_a and V_b are the perceived values of product a and the benchmark. In actual practice, the maximum price can be interpreted as the indifference price, in other words, the price that would make customers indifferent as to which product they end up purchasing, because paying less money would mean getting relatively lower value, and vice versa.

As an example, let's go back to the four alternative destinations presented in Chapter 4, Table 4.3. Imagine that the managers of Destination B are using Destination A as their benchmark, which offers a weekend package for 600 euro. Applying the formula above, the maximum price that they can apply for their destination is 660 euro (6.3/5.7 x €600), because customers perceive Destination B as having 10 per cent higher value than Destination A.

But what would happen with a different benchmark? Using Destination C, for instance, with a weekend price of 400 euro, the most Destination B managers can charge is 400 euro because the perceived value is identical. Continuing on, with Destination D as the benchmark, priced at 500 euro for a weekend, the maximum price would only be 420 euro, because the perceived value of Destination B is 84 per cent of the benchmark. So depending on the benchmark, there are three possible price thresholds. How do managers decide which one to apply?

Beyond the necessary cost considerations, to make a pricing decision, the positioning map in Figure 7.8 in Chapter 7 comes in handy (along with the relevant comments). It's clear that the direct competitor for

Destination B is actually Destination C, seeing that both compete for Segment 4. But Destination A doesn't have a clearly defined positioning, perhaps in part because the price is too high with respect to the attributes it offers. Destination D, instead, is more focused on Segment 1, whose customers place a higher priority on benefits that they don't see Destination B as adequately satisfying.

All this shows that the best benchmark is Destination C. At this point, to come up with a final price other factors come into play, as detailed in the next section. Here suffice to say that if the managers of Destination B decided to set the same price as Destination C, they would effectively neutralize the effect of price on choices of potential customers. Instead, if Destination B cost less, the price could be leveraged to attract the target customers; setting a higher price, on the other hand, would connote the destination with prestige.

In any case, what's clear from the example above is that in order to apply the pricing method based on value expectations, managers need to carefully analyze positioning and clearly define targeting strategies. Neglecting to do either of these things could lead to what customers may perceive as the wrong price: either too cheap (creating doubts as to the quality) or too expensive (resulting in lost sales volumes).

8.3.4.2   *The willingness to pay method*

With this method, target customers are asked directly the highest price they'd be willing to pay for the product. Here, too, quantitative research via surveys is used. But since customer responses refer to future behaviors, reliability isn't high. To compensate, data should be collected on various *price points*, indicative of diverse thresholds within the price band that customers have memorized.

Memorization depends on several factors: once they've made repeated purchases in a given product category, customers commit to memory price information, along with an assortment of details on various product attributes. They also 'store' communication on various products/brands, and information gleaned informally via word of mouth. For example, it's likely that for the reasons mentioned above, consumers know that a season ticket for the theater in their city can cost anywhere from 150 to 250 euro, that they'll probably pay from 15 to 35 euro for a best-selling novel, and that for a pair of brand-name or prêt-à-porter trousers they can expect a list price ranging from 150 to 300 euro.

Identifying various price points usually means finding the *right* price or a *fair* price for a product; a *high but acceptable* price; and the *maximum* price, that is, a level above which would be excessive and unacceptable. With the same method it's also possible to identify the lower price range, that is the price consumers would consider *low but acceptable* and the *minimum* price. In addition to these price points, the price that customers are used to paying can also be added, to position it with respect to the other price bands.

It's important to remember that with both procedures (considering only willingness to pay or establishing different price points) this method has a limitation: data reliability. In the first case, this is due to the fact customers make assertions about their future behaviors, and in the second, distortions can emerge in the process of recall.

8.3.4.3   *The customer behavior method*

Organizations can overcome the above limitations by utilizing data on the actual behavior of customers. In this case, an experiment is used instead of a survey, specifically a version of a *market test*: either an area test or a simulated test market (Section 8.1.4.2.3). For the first, the product is rolled out in a select number of geographical areas of the market during a timeframe that allows customers to purchase and repurchase the item being tested. These areas have to be homogeneous (in terms of customers and competitors) so they can be compared and additional factors (beyond the price) that impact sales can be excluded. The price is set at a different level for each area, so the resulting data will show quantities sold for each level.

But area tests are quite complicated and expensive to organize, and more critically, they show alert competitors the retail price alternatives the organization is contemplating for its product. So another option is to set up a simulated test market, in physical or virtual stores specially created for testing purposes. Here too the same procedure as the area test applies: groups of different customers are offered the same product with different list prices and in some cases alongside the relevant communication campaign.[18]

Each of the three methods we've just discussed for pinpointing the maximum price of a product actually identify a number of thresholds that can be associated with the maximum volume of product sales. Consequently, these methods make it possible to

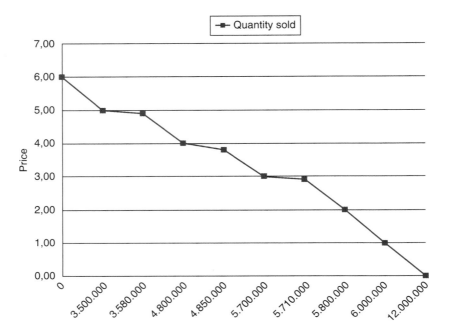

Figure 8.9 – Example of an actual demand curve

determine the percentage of target customers willing to buy at each price level, generating a demand curve for the product in question.

When managers actually apply these methods in real markets, what becomes apparent is that the demand curve in many cases doesn't have a continuous, regular shape, as textbooks on Economics and Marketing would suggest. Instead there are *kinks*, signs of irregularities, with some price bands showing extremely elastic demand, and others where price variations appear to have no impact at all on sales, and portions of the curve that actually change sign (Figure 8.9).

In these circumstances, it's crucial for organizations to discover if there are any kinks on the curve, and where they appear. These correspond to market segments with varying levels of price sensitivity; at or around these points, sales are expected to have a greater impact on revenues.

8.3.5 Methods for determining the final price

With information on costs, value for target customers, and the demand curve in hand, the organization

is well-equipped to make decisions on the list price for its product. As we've seen, cost and value provide the minimum and maximum thresholds, and the final price should fall within this range. Logic would dictate that the minimum (cost) threshold is lower than the maximum (value), but unfortunately, this isn't always the case.

In fact, it's entirely possible that for some products costs are so high that the price needed to cover them exceeds the corresponding value for customers. The reasons for this are many, but generally speaking they fall into two main categories: the efficiency of production and distribution processes, which are cost-determinants, and the organization's capacity to generate higher value than its competitors and transfer that value to its customers.

If costs necessitate a price level beyond the value customers perceive, the pricing decision must be made within the broader strategic framework of reengineering organizational processes. In fact, this situation signals a misalignment between the capabilities an organization has and the ones it needs to operate effectively on the market. The solution to this problem is to map out a path to recovering efficiency and productivity, and at the same come up with a plan of action for enhancing the value proposition. If not, the risk is jeopardizing the long-term survival of the product – and in extreme cases even the entire organization.

With creative products, there are fascinating examples of ways to contain production costs and increase efficiency that can actually enhance value. Looking to contemporary theater, for example, hit productions have been proliferating that are realized with minimal sets and staged in unorthodox performance spaces (garages, abandoned buildings, and so forth) (García, 2013).

Assuming that an organization finds itself in a normal situation, with product costs that correspond to a minimum threshold that is lower than the relative value perceived by target customers, the price would naturally fall within this range. Managers might be tempted to assume that price-setting in these circumstances is quite straightforward: the price should be set at the highest possible level, that is, at the value that customers attribute to the product. But this conclusion would be too hasty. As we've seen, the price is above all a positioning lever, which means pricing decisions can't be made without considering customers and competitors, in addition to revenues and profit targets.

So there are many considerations to make before deciding on a final price, and several possible methods to use. As I mentioned before, these methods differ depending on the central focus of the decision-making process, be that demand, costs, or competition.

8.3.5.1   Demand-based methods

These methods share an emphasis on the variety of expectations and perceptions of diverse customer segments, which give rise to different prices.

- *Price lining.* This method is product versioning translated into pricing choices (Section 8.1.5.2.2). The underlying reasoning here is the recognition that the demand curve is irregular, and its kinks show various price points where there are segments with different value expectations and price sensitivities.[19] With price lining, a series of price levels are set in relation to a number of different versions of the product. With the pertinent information to hand, each level should correspond to various points in which the demand curve shows changes in elasticity. A common example of price lining happens at the theater box office, where different ticket prices are offered depending on the location of the seats (Case History 8.10).

- *Auction.* At an auction, products are sold to the highest bidder. Usually, the seller sets a minimum (or starting) price, and potential buyers bid against one another, each bid higher than the previous one until no buyer is willing to bid further. An auction can be a very rapid process (for instance with a work of art sold by an auction house) or last days or even weeks (as with items sold online via *eBay*).

With an auction, the clearest possible picture of the different value expectations on the market emerges, because each customer bids the maximum price she's willing to pay, and the actual buyer is the person who attributes the highest value. To set the starting price and estimate a reasonable sales price, the organization should know the determinants of the value expectations of potential customers, and the product attributes that they associate with this value (Research Focus 8.3).

Case History 8.10

'Pay as much as you want': In Rainbows by Radiohead

In 2007, after cancelling their contract with the label EMI Group, the band Radiohead launched their *In Rainbows* album by posting it on their website, making it available for download to all their fans, who could pay whatever amount they thought it was worth, even nothing at all. The response was one million downloads, of which 62 per cent paid nothing, while the remaining 38 per cent paid an average of 6.00 US dollars, generating average unit revenues of 2.28 dollars per album (Naughton, 2007). This is more than the amount the band would have earned from EMI for copyright. Two months after its Internet debut, the album was offered through offline channels for a price, and after a year time sales hit the three million mark. This approach represents a near perfect case of price lining for Radiohead, who let their individual customers decide for themselves what price to pay for the product.

Research Focus 8.3

Price setting for contemporary art

What it is that determines the price for a work of art sold at auction? The easy answer is the artist, and this is true. But is that all? After all, the price of a product represents the value that customers attribute to it, so it stands to reason that they should consider other things beyond the artist.

To explore this question, Marinelli and Palomba (2011) conducted a study of the prices fetched at auction of 2,817 works of contemporary Italian art sold in 19 auction houses around the world from 1990 to 2006. In addition to the name of the artist, the authors sought to understand the influence on the sales price of other variables linked to the physical qualities of the piece (the size, the support (canvas, paper, and so on), the medium (oil, acrylic, or other); the prestige and popularity of the work (whether it's signed by the artist, or included in catalogues and monographs, reviews from art critics, citations in literature, the number of exhibits featuring the work, the number of previous owners, the date of the work); and information regarding the sale (the auction house, the year and month the auction was held, the city hosting the auction, and the auction house's pre-sale estimates of the value of the work).

The results of the study show that the greatest impact on the sales price of art work, beyond the artist and auction house estimates, comes from the size of the item (the price increases up to a certain size threshold, and then tends to diminish again), the support (with canvas pushing the price up and paper doing the opposite), the date of the work, and whether or not it's included in a catalogue or cited in the literature. Some factors that have less (albeit positive) influence on the price include the number of exhibits in which it was displayed and the number of previous owners; however, reviews from art critics drive prices down. No effect at all was measured with regard to the medium (oil, acrylic, and the like). What's more, while the type of auction house didn't affect the price, the city hosting the auction did, with prices going up London and New York, and down in Milan.

○ *Prestige or image pricing*. This method leverages price as a factor of product distinction (Section 8.3.2.3). Here the price is set very high relative to the product category, to build an image of exceptional quality, prestige, or status. Often the price level exceeds the maximum threshold (which the organization discovers by analyzing perceived value among target customers). But the move is a deliberate one, to make the product particularly exclusive, even if that means limiting the number of customers who will actually buy it.

Naturally, this method is associated with any creative product that falls into the luxury category (be it fashion, design, a tourist destinations, or art). But the essential thing to remember is that this pricing policy can be applied to any product category, keeping in mind that the prestige price will be much higher than the habitual price level for the category.

In 1994, for example, Viking-Penguin published *Blue Dog*, a book illustrated by the artist George Rodrigues. The price initially proposed by the team handling the US launch fell within the 17.95 to 19.95 dollar range, in line with similar publications. However, the company's CEO insisted on publishing a basic edition of the book for 45 dollars, and a special edition for 250. The sales performance proved the CEO right: first-year sales hit 60,000 and 2,000 copies, for the basic and special edition respectively (Tabor, 1995).

○ *Skimming pricing*. Skimming is a technique used when launching (or relaunching) a product. The price is set at the maximum threshold for the segment most interested in the new product. These customers are typically innovators and early adopters (Section 8.1.2.2), so they are less sensitive to price. Once demand in this segment is satisfied, the product price can be gradually lowered to attract more price-sensitive segments, leaving the product intact (and justifying the price reduction with a decrease in innovative product value) or launching a simplified version of the original product. In publishing, for example, this is what typically happens with hardback and paperback editions of books.

There are three prerequisites for effective skimming pricing: 1) demand of the initial segment that's broad enough to ensure an adequate return on sales; 2) a high price that doesn't attract too many competitors, making individual market share for each producer too small; 3) customers who associate a high price with high quality.

- *Penetration Pricing.* This technique is diametrically opposed to the previous one. With penetration pricing, the new (or relaunched/repositioned) product is given a very low list price, with the aim of immediately attracting as many customers as possible and building a hefty market share. Some tourist destinations in the Caribbean or on the Red Sea are excellent examples of penetration pricing.

Here are the essential conditions for effective penetration pricing: 1) a broad segment of price-sensitive customers; 2) a low price, which squeezes unit margins and serves as a deterrent to competitors, permitting the organization to quickly secure a solid market share; 3) unit product costs that decrease as production volume rises, increasing the unit margins.

- *Odd-even pricing.* This method is based on empirical evidence proving that customers perceive prices that have odd numbers as end digits, or are slightly less than round numbers as more economical, as compared to even or round numbers. So if a work of art costs 975 euro, a buyer would perceive it as a bargain compared to 1,000 euro, even though the actual difference is minimal. The explanation for this phenomenon is a cognitive one: since paying for something entails a sacrifice, the customer memorizes price as an approximation, to make it more acceptable on an emotional level. This happens both when she associates the price with a class identified with the initial digit (975 belongs to the 900 class, 1,000 to the next class up), and when she perceives the better bargain as a number composed of fewer digits (975 has three, 1,000 has four). In any case, odd numbers represent price points where the demand curve shows a dramatic change in elasticity. So setting the price just above or below these points may have an appreciable impact on product sales.

8.3.5.2   Cost-based methods

Pricing a product by using these methods means adding up production and marketing costs, plus a share of fixed costs and, when applicable, the profit that the product must generate.

- *Cost-plus pricing.* In this case, the calculation starts with the unit cost of a product, adding on a sum earmarked to cover direct fixed costs, overhead, and expected profit. With a ticket for a guided tour to an archeological site, for example, the price should cover the guide's salary (direct fixed cost) and a share of the cost of restoration and upkeep of the site (overhead).

The most common cost-plus pricing technique is to express the amount added to the unit cost as a percentage, called the *markup*, using this formula:

$$P = C(1 + m)$$

where P is the product price, C costs attributed to that product, and m the markup.

With this method, either current or future product costs can be used. The latter case is often called *experience-curve pricing.* Using future costs allows for wider maneuvering room in price setting. The assumption here is that future costs are lower than initial ones, because experience garnered over time enables the organization to improve process efficiency, and in doing so, cut costs.

Instead of basing the product price on current costs, the organization predicts the future cost level it will be able to achieve; the resulting price is potentially lower. An organization would opt for this approach when it wants to make a push for a rapid rise in process efficiency, but failing to do so would mean incurring losses.

- *Target profit pricing.* This method is similar to the previous one, the primary difference being a shift in focus from costs to profit.[20] Basically, the organization defines the product price by setting a clear profit target. Returning to the break-even formula from Section 8.3.3, and using TP as total profit expected from the product, the resulting price would be:

$$P = \frac{FC}{Q} + UVC + \frac{TP}{Q}$$

Often profit is expressed as a percentage of sales, in other words, Return on Sales (ROS), and this method is referred to as *Target ROS Pricing.* The formula for this calculation is:

$$TgtROS = \frac{TR - TC}{TR}$$

where TR stands for total revenues and TC total costs.

8.3.5.3   Competition-based methods

The key reference points for these methods are the prices of competing products. In other words, price is used primarily with an eye to positioning the product, to convey its value in relation to competitors. The basic assumption here is that customers are aware of the prices of competing products, and use them to draw comparisons. To ensure that they do so, this pricing method is often supported by communication campaigns that highlight price differences.

- *Above-, at-, or below-market pricing*. These methods are self-explanatory. The motivations behind each are either conveying a higher value (above-marketing pricing), neutralizing the effect of price on choice processes by aligning it with the competition (at-market), or communicating the economic advantage of paying less for the same benefits (below-market).
- *Loss-leader pricing*. This method is more commonly utilized by retailers rather than producers, and involves setting a price level that's lower than that of competitors, even below cost (which obviously means taking a loss). Retailers apply loss-leader prices on well-known products or brands (again called loss-leaders) with the aim of connoting the entire assortment with the concept of 'economical', prompting consumers to buy other products/ brands in the offering as well. For instance, a design company's online shop might offer a brand or an item at an extremely low price to attract visitors and give them exposure to the entire product assortment.

As for producers, beyond the motivation described above, they may also try to drive competitors to lower their prices to a level that they can't sustain in the long term, effectively forcing them out of the market. Such a strategy was implemented in the Italian pay TV market when a newcomer, Mediaset, entered the market and quickly tried to capture market share from the sole leader, Sky, compelling this company to spend disproportionate resources defending itself from the attack.

8.3.5.4 *Prices and distribution channels*
Up to this point I've implicitly assumed that the organization sells directly to its customers, with no intermediaries involved in the transaction. In this case, the price the customer pays equals the unit revenues the organization takes in. But what happens if the organization uses commercial intermediaries to distribute its products?

These intermediaries, detailed further in Chapter 9, are all the subjects that participate in the process of distributing products on the market. They can be found in

all creative industries: agents and sales representatives of the organization who earn commissions on the products they sell; wholesalers who sell to retailers; and retailers who sell to end consumers.

For example, a museum sells entrance tickets through a tour operator that organizes trips to the host city, with a museum visit as part of the package; a TV producer sells the format for a new series to a TV channel, which in turn sells it as part of a package to a Pay TV platform; a magazine publisher sells its publications to area newsstands through a wholesaler. Moving upstream there are agents who act on behalf of writers, athletes, musicians, and artists, selling property rights for their creative works.

Clearly there can be any number of links in the distribution chain; every subject along the way buys a given product and then resells it to the next one in line. So organizations have to take into account all these transactions when setting the product price, adding further complexity to an already complicated decision. What's more, an organization will lose some or all control over the final price when it entrusts distribution to intermediaries, because they are free to set a price that they feel is in line with their markets and their profit expectations. But that doesn't mean that the producer can or should ignore what happens to the price as the product moves through the distribution channel.

The method used to factor in all the subjects involved in distribution is *demand-backward pricing*. The starting point in this case is an estimate of the final price that customers are willing to pay, either based on their perceptions of value, or in light of price levels of direct competitors. Then, by subtracting the markups tacked on by various intermediaries along the way, the producer comes up with the price to charge the first intermediary in the chain. This price is the basis of the producer's evaluation of financial sustainability, but it is nowhere near the final price paid by the end consumer (Figure 8.10).

8.3.6 Pricing strategies and tactics

As we've seen, costs, customers' perceptions of value, and competitors' prices are three factors to consider jointly when making assessments that form the foundations of pricing decisions. Setting the final sales price of a product might also be impacted by the organization's objectives on the market in question.

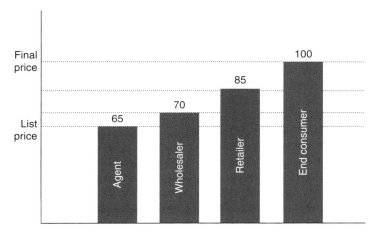

Figure 8.10 – Example of demand-backward pricing

These objectives may call for more general strategic choices, or tactics put in place to reach specific short-term aims. Some of these tactics are typical of creative industries.

8.3.6.1   Dual market pricing

Creative products are usually sold on two markets: consumer and business. In some cases customers in the two markets have motivations to buy that are independent of one another; this normally happens when a creative product is purchased on the business market as a production factor. A tourist destination chosen as the setting for a film, a song used as the soundtrack for a videogame, designer furnishings for the interior décor of an embassy: all these are examples of corporate customers purchasing creative products (or property rights for these products). But their motivations have nothing to do with the fact that consumers purchase these products as well.

Instead, when property rights for certain creative products are purchased as communication factors, the motivations of corporate clients are closely linked to demand in specific segments of the consumer market. As discussed in Chapter 5, an advertising spender who wants to run a print campaign would take into account the GRPs of various newspapers. A company that wants to sponsor a sports team would make its choice based on the team's reach and image. A firm looking to use a testimonial for its communication campaign would consider the image of the potential spokesperson. So strategic choices regarding targeting and positioning that creative

product providers make for the consumer market also have repercussions on the business market and vice versa. And this holds true for the subsequent pricing choices as well.

These are justified not only by specific conditions of demand and competition on one of the markets, but also by the organization's objectives with regard to the other. For example, let's say a publisher wants to create a magazine with an exclusive target, with an eye to selling advertising space to spenders interested in an elite image and a select audience. Obviously content is key to attracting a certain readership, but another effective tactic would be to set a prestige price to render the product less accessible to the mass market. On the other hand, if the publisher wants to have a magazine with enormous reach, which could make an attractive advertising channel for mass producers, a very low price (or even offering the product for free) would guarantee a much wider circulation. And the same can be said for a television channel, a radio station, a newspaper, and so forth.

8.3.6.2   Bundle pricing

This tactic involves setting prices that correspond to product bundling, described in Section 8.1.5.2.3. Basically a bundle of products is offered for less than the sum of the prices of each individual item. That way the customer pays less and can afford to buy more products, so the producer boosts overall revenues. Beyond increased revenues, bundling products and pricing are practices that are becoming more and more common in order to generate additional reciprocal advantages in all sectors with a potential for digitalization.

In fact, in these sectors, producers can create differentiation by generating multiple bundling offers, increasing the chance that they'll be perceived as distinctive from competing products. Customers, both individually and as a segment, can satisfy a broader set of needs as compared to individual products, opting for the bundle that best fits their value expectations (Case History 8.11). In light of this phenomenon, it comes as no surprise that an artist with millions of fans like Justin Timberlake launched an astounding 115 versions of his 2006 album FutureSex/sound in the form of countless bundles, generating volumes totaling 19 million copies (Wikström, 2009).

8.3.6.3   Price promotions
This term refers to any discounts on the list price that producers offer to their customers as a form of remuneration or reward.

○ *Discounts.* This is the most obvious type of price promotion: giving customers the chance to buy a product at less than the list price. In operational terms, there are a variety of ways to discount products. The most obvious is to sell the product at a *lower price* for a specific time period or through a specific channel. The discount, generally a percentage of the sales price, is applied upon payment. For instance, a publisher might offer 25 per cent off the cover price of a book if purchased before a certain date; or concertgoers might get a discount on tickets when they purchase online.

A similar tactic is to discount successive purchases. The standard procedure here is for customers to get a *coupon* when they purchase a product, which they can cash in on their next purchase. An interesting example of bundle pricing with coupons is the launch of the U2 iPod, priced at 50 US dollars above the standard iPod, with autographs of all the band members engraved on the back and a 50-dollar iTunes coupon to download all the band's music.

Case History 8.11

Pricing models in digital music distribution

Of all the creative sectors, the bundling phenomenon (both for products and pricing) has permeated the music industry, perhaps more than any other. In fact, the traditional music product – the album – is a perfect example of a bundle (whether on vinyl, tape, or CD). When consumers buy an album they get a combination of tracks selected by the artist or the record company, irrespective if consumer preferences and purchase intentions. But with digitalized content, music consumers are no longer 'forced' to buy entire albums, and at the same time, producers can offer a far greater variety of bundles.

All these new possibilities have given rise to a series of pricing models used by online music retailers. Their aim is to satisfy diverse needs, and at the same time to stand out among the competition. Here are some of the most popular models (Wikström, 2009):

○ *Single-song download pricing.* This is the model adopted by iTunes and Amazon, leading retailers with the largest market share. The smallest sellable unit is a single track, which has a pre-set price. Initially iTunes used uniform pricing, at .99 cents per single, but that evolved into a small number of different price points, which is the dominant model today.

○ *Membership pricing with limited downloads.* This is the model used by eMusic, another market leader. Consumers pay a set membership price for the music downloading service, and later they choose which songs they want. So the product is essentially access to a music library. Generally membership involves price lining, giving consumers the chance to choose among different plans, each allowing a different number of downloads per month.

○ *Membership pricing with unlimited downloads/streaming.* Spotify, MelOn, Rhapsody and Omnicome utilize this model, which is identical to the previous one except with no limit on monthly downloads. Here too various bundles are offered, but the variable is the number of devices members can use for downloads or streaming, rather than the number of tunes.

○ *Ad-based pricing.* Pandora and last.fm are among the most famous online retailers who apply this model. These sites are exactly like traditional radio stations, so instead of consumers paying to listen to music, it's the advertisers who pay. And just like traditional radio, most retailers who use this model have preset playlists that can't be changed, although some do offer a certain level of on-demand listener interaction. Unlike the models described above, here the accent is on streaming instead of downloading. The ad-based model is often offered within the framework of competing plans that use other models as basic options, for instance allowing customers to download rather than stream their favorite tunes.

Discounts can also be linked to the amount of product purchased (also known as *quantity discounts*), resulting in a lower unit price. Examples here are BOGOF (buy one get one free) or three-for-two. In the business market, this kind of discount is common practice with advertising space. For instance, an advertiser that buys airtime on a radio station might get a discount based on the minutes it purchases, or free advertising space on other media owned by the same company that runs the radio station (a newspaper or magazine, for instance).

Going further, discounts can be *seasonal*. This is typical in sectors where planned obsolescence is common practice (Section 8.1.5.1). Fashion is a typical example where prices are cut when products come to the end of their life cycles. Likewise, in some cases prices fall in *off-peak times*; the performing arts and amusement parks, for instance, typically offer discounted prices during low season. On occasion, discounts are offered based on *terms of payment*: if consumers pay for the product in question by a certain date, they get a discount, but after that the price reverts back to normal. This kind of discount is very common when the customer is an intermediary or business client. In these situations, the customer can normally pay after acquiring the product (with a 30-day or 60-day billing cycle, for example), but this means it's the producer who basically extends a line of credit to the customer. To avoid this financial burden, the producer can offer the product at a lower price if the customer pays up front; this is referred to as a *cash discount*.

- *Allowances*. These kinds of promotions involve reducing the list price without actually intervening directly on the price, but by rewarding customers in other ways. A very popular formula is when producers pay intermediaries (in cash or with surplus quantities of product) to carry out specific activities: advertising in points of sale, placing the product where it has the greatest visibility (this applies to websites for online stores as well) or in specially-designed displays. These are generically called *promotional allowances* or specifically *off-invoice promotions* or *co-op advertising*.

  Another kind of allowance is the *trade-in*, when customers get the opportunity to return their old product in exchange for a discount on the new one. Typically used with durables (cars and household appliances, for example) trade-ins are very common in many creative industries as well. Some booksellers use trade-in promotions, from traditional businesses to Amazon, and these initiatives are becoming

popular in the clothing and design sectors too (for instance, from accent pieces to furniture to whole houses).

- *Free trials*. Free trials are meant to encourage customers to test new products and then (hopefully) buy them. This tactic can also be considered a price promotion, even though the price in this case is zero. Since creative products are experience products, one way to generate anticipation of their full experience is to give customers a 'sneak peak' before they actually make a purchase (Section 1.2). Obviously, if this is free, the perceived sacrifices will be negligible, so the trial will be even more accessible.

  In sectors that produce content, digitalization facilitates an infinite number of free trials. The chance to read an excerpt from a book before it's published, or to listen a few bars of a new tune or a track from a new album: these kinds of free trials have become commonplace today. What's more, in some sectors digital content can be used as proof of purchase for complementary products. The American musician Prince represents an amazing example. He launched the album *Planet Earth* in Great Britain on July 15, 2007, offering it free of charge with the purchase of the newspaper *Mail on Sunday*. The aim was to promote a series of 21 shows scheduled to take place at the O2 Arena in London.

8.3.7   Price management over time

The role of the price of a product changes during its lifecycle. In fact, competitive dynamics evolve throughout the different stages (Section 8.1.2.4) and the price, as a positioning tool, evolves as well.

In the *introduction* stage, right from the product launch the organization can set the most suitable price for the target segment depending on the desired positioning. But skimming pricing might also be an option if the strategy is to recover on pre-launch investments as rapidly as possible; another possibility is prestige pricing to give the product an exclusive image. On the other hand, with substantial sales targets or market share, penetration pricing or experience-curve pricing are both feasible, setting a price that's low enough to pull in substantial numbers of customers straight away. Whatever the method, the organization can leverage promotions based on free trials to encourage initial contact with the product.

In the *growth* stage price plays a less prominent role. Now product sales are rising, showing that customers accept the current price. If the competition is already intense at this point, the organization may want to build a solid market position and attempt to cover several segments by following a product versioning strategy, which would call for price lining.

The *maturity* stage usually comes with a strong accent on price as a tool for competitive positioning. In fact, this is the time when competitive intensity reaches an apex, and price can be used as a way to stand out from the competition. What's more, during the maturity stage, organizations need to determine whether it's worth investing in revitalizing the product, as opposed to allowing a controlled decline. Price promotions are also usually very intense in this stage.

With the pricing tool an organization can try to boost floundering sales or cordon off a market from its competitors. Whatever the intention, a competitive strategy that leverages low prices for extended periods risks sparking a *price war*, with competitors aggressively and systematically cutting their prices. These actions in turn shrink unit margins to the point where the price could potentially dip below the minimum cost threshold. The risk of a price war lies in incurring losses that are difficult to sustain in the long term.

Opting to undertake a *revitalization* strategy leads the organization back to a stage that's analogous to product launch, because the ultimate aim is to carve out a new market position for the product. Consequently, everything discussed with regard to the introduction stage also applies now. If, however, the organization decides to allow the product to enter the *decline* stage, following a strategy of planned obsolescence, then price promotions become crucial. These accelerate the decline, paving the way for the introduction of a new product, or maximizing financial returns on the outgoing product, while lowering all the related costs.

8.3.7.1   The relationship between product price and contribution margin

If at any time during the product lifecycle the organization opts to raise or lower the price, it needs to reflect on the financial repercussions of such a move. Specifically, it's vital to evaluate the impact that a price variation will have on the total contribution of the product to the profit margin. The aim in doing so is to anticipate whether or not the decision is consistent with the organization's profit expectations and the product's financial sustainability.

Modifying the price has a dual effect on the overall contribution to the profit margin. The first is on the unitary contribution margin, because the price

constitutes a positive component of the margin. The second pertains to product sales, because they are contingent on price. If the demand curve has a negative sign (or turns negative between two price bands) clearly the effects are inverse: cutting the price lowers the unitary contribution margin, but boosts sales; increasing the price does the opposite. So the question is: How much of a variation in price is worthwhile?

To envisage the dual effect on the margin, managers can apply the two formulas below. If the demand curve is negative and costs don't vary as quantities change in the short run, these formulas indicate the variation in sales volumes needed to offset the impact on the unit contribution margin, and to neutralize the effect of the pricing decision on the total contribution margin.

With a price cut:

$$\%_\Delta Q = \frac{\%_\Delta P}{\%CM - \%_\Delta P} \times 100\%$$

where $\%\Delta Q$ is the percentage variation in sales volumes, $\%\Delta P$ is the percentage variation in the intended price (absolute value), and $\%\Delta CM$ is the current contribution margin as a percentage of the current price. For instance, if the current margin is 50 per cent, and the organization wants to cut the price by 10 per cent, the added volumes that should be generated to avoid penalizing the total margin are 25 per cent of current volumes: 10%/(50% - 10%) x 100% = 25%. An increase in volumes over 25 per cent would boost the total margin.

With a price increase:

$$\%_\Delta Q = \frac{\%_\Delta P}{\%CM + \%_\Delta P} \times 100\%$$

For example, with the same margin as in the example above, if the organization wants to raise the price by 10 per cent, the volumes that the organization could afford to lose without penalizing the total margin would be 16.6 per cent of current volumes 10%/(50% + 10%) x 100% = 16.6%. A drop in volumes of less than 16.6 per cent would translate into a possible increase in the total margin.

Utilizing these formulas, managers can simulate the product's effect on the total contribution. What's more, with input as to price elasticity to demand of their product, they can verify whether the outcome of increasing/decreasing the price is consistent with organizational objectives. In the first example above, if demand is fairly inelastic, the risk is that cutting the price by 10 per cent would correspond to an increase in volumes of less than 25 per cent, shrinking the overall margin. On the other hand, in the second example when demand is sufficiently elastic, a drop in volumes of more than 16.6 per cent would mean a loss in the total margin.

8.4   CONCLUSIONS

In this chapter I've described the three main components of the value proposition that an organization can offer to its target customers: the product, the brand, and the price. Specifically, I've underscored how these three components contribute to providing value to customers. At the same time I've outlined the typical decisions pertaining to product management, brand management, and price management that organizations operating in creative industries face.

These decisions give concrete form to positioning choices. Integrating them coherently guarantees the organization a sharp image and a solid competitive position in its target markets. In analyzing these three factors, I've consistently referred to the lifecycle model, because integration depends on the specific stage in the life of the product or brand. The quantitative evolution of demand and of its distinguishing features, along with the evolution of competitive dynamics – all these phenomena shape the type of decisions organizations need to make with regard to these three factors.

This chapter concludes our analysis of the customer value creation process. As we've discovered, this process initially involves identifying the market segments the organization wants to serve, and then building and positioning a value proposition to offer to these segments, and finally making specific decisions that lead to the realization of this proposition.

If an organization's value creation process is effective and efficient, the resulting value will be aligned with the expectations of its target customers (Section 2.2.4). The next step is to transfer this value intact to customers by means of appropriate mechanisms, which call for specific decisions. This is the topic of the next chapter.

REVIEW QUESTIONS

1. What is the differential role played by products, brand and prices in the creation of customer value? How do they interact?
2. What are the determinants of the length and the shape of a product's lifecycle? How do supply and demand interact and influence this lifecycle?
3. What are the typical decisions to be taken to create customer value through new products? What is the specific contribution of Marketing? And what are the decisions regarding existing products?
4. How does a brand create value for customers and for organizations? What are the most typical decisions when creating a new brand or when managing it in its growth or maturity stages? What are the differences between brand identity, brand positioning and brand image and how do they impact brand management decisions over the brand lifecycle?
5. What information can a demand curve provide to a manager who has to decide on product price?
6. What methods are used to set the minimum price level and the maximum one? How do competitor prices affect pricing decisions? What are the methods for determining the final price? How do these methods differ?

CASE STUDY

SHAKHTAR DONETSK: THE CREATION OF A NEW EUROPEAN FOOTBALL BRAND

In 2009, Shakhtar Donetsk became the first Ukrainian football club to win a European trophy, the UEFA Cup (since then rebranded as the UEFA Europe League).

The achievement of such a long-awaited result strengthened the belief of the club's management that they were on the right path to firmly establish Shakhtar among the ranks of Europe's top teams. In light of this, in 2010 three new strategic goals were set, for the four years to follow:

○ *Sports results*: stay on the track of the recent prestigious result achieved at the European level, by playing a leading role both in the Ukrainian championships and in the major European leagues.

- *Supporters*: increase the fan base and expand the portfolio of business partners.
- *Revenues*: continue to grow revenues, also by searching for new revenue sources.

The starting points, as of the 2010–2011 season, were the following.

- In terms of sports results, the club had won the Ukrainian League and Cup and reached Champions League Round of 16; in terms of supporters, the club had an average Premier League match attendance of about 34,000 people and 17,795 season ticket holders.
- In terms of revenues, Shakhtar's overall revenues amounted to 500 million Ukranian Hryvnav (UAH), 169 million of which from commercial activities.

The results presented in the 2013 Annual Report show that all goals have been achieved. As for sport results, Shakhtar won the Ukranian League and Cup both in 2011–2012 and 2012–2013, and in this last season once again made it to the Champions League Round of 16. As for supporters, the average Premier League match attendance reached a peak of 41,199 people; in addition the number of season ticket holders broke the record of 24,500; the number of fans who attended more than 10 games was 18,404 for 2012–2013, up 19 per cent from the previous season.

The financials (Figure 8.11) show an impressive record of revenues, 2.6 times higher than the 2010–2011 season, with a 34 per cent rise in revenues from commercial activities. Specifically, income from sponsorships and advertising (up 56%) and leasing for corporate boxes (up 25%) have consistently exceeded ticket sales – and this in a season drawing record-breaking crowds.

CLUBE INCOME (min, UAH)

Items of income	2010–11 season	2012–13 season
Players sales and loans	136	908
Revenue from UEFA	195	194
Business revenue	169	227
Total	500	1329

BUSINESS REVENUE (min,UAH)

Items of income	2010–11 season	2012–13 season
Sponsorship and advertising	54	84
Sale of tickets and season tickets	49	49
Corporate boxes	40	50
Sale of merchandise	22	22
Revenues from the Premiere League (advertising+TV rights)	4	22
Total	169	227

Figure 8.11 - Shakhtar Donetsk: Main revenue sources for 2010–2013

The club's financial results suggest that Shakhtar is in step with its international counterparts in the way it's run as well: it's no longer just a football team, but a business with diversified revenue sources, an undisputed reputation for first-rate management, and a variety of assets (including one of the best stadiums in Europe, a football academy for talented new players, and a strong relationships with the host community).

Shakhtar's success can be attributed to a combination of factors. Beyond an impressive improvement in the team's athletic performance, noteworthy is the quality of management throughout the organization, and the creation of a brand with an identity and a positioning that stand out in the world of football, at both national and international levels. The fact that all these aspects have come together is no coincidence, but rather the result of strategic revitalization initiated by the club in the mid-2000s.

Formulating a new strategy

Shakhtar was founded in 1936 with the name *Stachanovets*, in memory of Aleksei Stachanov, a legendary miner from the Donets Basin, famous for his dedication to the job. From the start the team was a powerhouse in the Soviet football championship. In the 1990s, when the national Ukrainian championship was established, Shakhtar vied for the top spot against its historic rival: Dynamo Kiev. In 1996, the sports club changed hands. The new President, Rinat Akhmetov, had plans for Shakhtar and was willing to provide the investments needed to realize them. Akhmetov's ambition was to see his club compete on the same level as the great European clubs, not only in the quality of play, but the managerial approach as well.

The first investments were concentrated on raising the bar for technical skills: hiring foreign coaches, trainers, and players from world class championships, in particular from Brazil, and establishing an Academy where promising young native players could train. The next step was to put together a management team tasked with drawing up a long-term strategy to better leverage past and potential investments.

In the mid-2000s, the new management team set out two *strategic objectives* for the five years to follow:

1. Augment the weight of the team on the international scene, ensuring that Shakhtar would become a regular in European competitions, aiming to bring home the top European trophies.
2. Consolidate the role of the club on a local level, establishing Shakhtar as major promoter of the culture of football in the Ukraine.

Management was convinced that to reach these objectives a cultural revolution was needed, not only inside the organization but also among the key external stakeholders: fans, supporters of all kinds, and residents of the city and the entire region. Basically, the image of Shakhtar had to evolve from a post-Soviet era football team into the pride of all of Eastern Europe, a contender that could hold its own against the best teams on the continent.

When the strategic overhaul began, the club could count a number of valuable assets:

1. More than 70 years of history, deeply rooting it in the local community and the surrounding region.
2. State-of-the-art facilities (including a training center and the Academy) on a par with the top European clubs.
3. A new stadium for the 2012 European Championship (built and opened in 2009, earning five stars from UEFA, the top rating).
4. A team of managers and employees highly committed to the club, motivated to take part in the revitalization project.

Despite all these advantages, the management team realized that what was lacking was knowledge about the fan base and more specifically about the team's image among the Ukrainian football fans. This knowledge would provide the foundations for designing a strategy that would make the team's objectives attainable. What followed was the club's decision to invest in market research to fill this knowledge gap.

The study, designed and conducted by the Masmi Research Group, set out a series of information objectives relative to:

○ Attitudes toward football among adult Ukrainians.
○ Distinctive attitudes toward football among people who consider themselves fans (useful for identifying various market segments).
○ Behaviors of football spectators, with regard to how they normally experience the sport (at the stadium, at home on TV, outside the home on TV).
○ The image of Shakhtar and its direct Ukrainian competitors.
○ The general opinion of the club's current brand elements.
○ Shakhtar's market potential, should its strategic objectives be achieved.

These informational objectives called for integrated research design: an initial qualitative phase via focus groups in four Ukrainian cities and in St. Petersburg, and a subsequent quantitative phase. This involved a survey with a sample size of 2,000 representing the Ukrainians who claimed to have an interest in football, and who lived in cities with populations over 200,000.

The findings were encouraging. Shakhtar enjoyed a positive image both among its own fans and football fans in general. The team was recognized as having ambition, technical quality, a desire to grow, willingness to invest, and a forward-looking attitude – all associations that the new strategic plan could leverage. At the same time, though, the perception emerged that many of these positive factors had not yet translated into success, at an athletic or managerial level. As a case in point, opinion on the most recent team logo (Figure 8.12) wasn't particularly flattering; it was seen as quite traditional, predictable (with its round shape, a football in the center, and a green pitch), and muddled (using three different languages: Ukrainian, Russian, and English).

Figure 8.12 – Shakhtar Donetsk: The team logo (2006)

Overall, the interviewees acknowledged the team's potential for success, but didn't recognize a clear image, which was a must-have if the club wanted to be perceived as the ambassador of Ukrainian football culture to the rest of the world. After some reflection the management team came to realize that *the lack of a clear brand identity* was the main reason why the team didn't have a distinctive positioning among football fans. This prompted the club to turn to a consulting company specialized in branding, Interbrand, which would develop a branding strategy to establish a new brand identity, complete with a new set of brand elements and an appropriate brand architecture.

The new brand identity

Developing a branding strategy is a process that begins by clearly determining what the brand is meant to represent, which positioning it will have within the relevant context, and how it can serve the business objectives. The brand identity formulated by the management team consisted of a brand vision and a brand mission:

a. *Vision*. To be the ambassador of Ukrainian football in the world and of international football in Ukraine, promoting the culture of the sport in the country.
b. *Mission*. To be the team that redefines the boundaries and the standards of excellence in football in Ukraine.

The next step was to identify the values underpinning this identity, values that would serve to more clearly delineate brand positioning.

a. *Youth*. The club believes that this value represents ambition, as well as change and the ability to realize it. Youth is the age of talent, the apex of personal potential. Football has a major influence over young people, what they think and what they do, and Shakhtar intends to set a positive example for them. Youth also relates to Ukraine, one of the 'youngest' countries in Europe, where football can engender unity, pride, and prosperity.
b. *Loyalty.* The club's history is part of both the past and the future, so the brand should never forget yesterday, yet always move toward tomorrow.
c. *Determination*. There's no need to be afraid of growing up. Never stop believing; nurture new hopes and constantly set new objectives. As soon as one target is hit, new ones must be set.
d. *Knowledge*. This is seen as a driver of growth and development. There's always new and better knowledge that can be used to realize future projects.

To make the new identity easy to communicate, management came up with a slogan that captures and conveys brand values and stakes out the terrain for building its positioning: 'Beyond boundaries.'

New brand elements: the name

The club already has a name, of course: 'shakhtar' means 'miner' in Ukrainian. This name has always been a point of pride for the club, underscoring its origins in mining country. In keeping with the research findings, the first objective of the project was to sort out the confusion surrounding the languages and lettering used in the logo: Russian or Ukrainian? With Cyrillic or Latin script? There were four options, as shown in Figure 8.13, each with pros and cons. Using Ukrainian would obviously convey national identity. But the Donbass region is Russian-speaking; in fact, for years the club's Russian name was used (Shaktyor). So this language would help communicate the club's longstanding tradition and its ties to the entire region. With regard to the script, using the Cyrillic alphabet would do the same, but Latin script would be more easily understood abroad.

Figure 8.13 – Shakhtar Donetsk: Lettering options

In the end, management opted for the Ukrainian version of the team's name written in Cyrillic script (shown in the lower right-hand quadrant). The reasoning was the desire to underscore the dimension of meaning, that is, the use of lettering that's specific to – and descriptive of – the brand, and at the same time evocative of the team's homeland. In fact, the evocative aspect is a critical one: by using Ukrainian-Cyrillic, the brand is setting down its roots in the region and openly embracing its origins. The aim was to make the name appealing, recognizable, and easily understandable to the greater public; at the same time, this would strengthen the vision of Shakhtar being the ambassador of Ukrainian football.

New brand elements: the logo

Between 1936 and 2007 the team logo changed various times: a blue hexagon with a red 'C' in the center and a jack hammer on top (1936); a black and white symbol with the club's name (1946); two crossed hammers inside a circle with the name 'Shakytyor Donetsk' (1965); and the most recent logo (Figure 8.12), which didn't get favorable reviews from the sample of fans interviewed for the study.

The new logo proposed by Interbrand encompasses myriad symbols (Figure 8.14):

1. Traditional colors: orange and black. Since the club's beginning, these colors have represented the contrast between the darkness of the mines and the brightness of sunlight.
2. The black portion at the bottom makes several allusions to the origins of the club, with crossed hammers, the symbol of miners, and the year the club was founded.
3. The flame burning in the upper part of the logo symbolizes the natural energy found underground in the Donbass mining region, as well as the 'flame of passion' that drives the fans, the players, and the managers of the club. The flame bears a slight resemblance to a trident, the national symbol of the Ukraine, reflecting Shakhtar's ambition to become the pride of the entire country.
4. The upper part of the logo depicts the sun on the horizon: the dawning of a new era.

The logo's unique pointed shape reflects the value of determination, calling to mind the team's reputation as an aggressive competitor and conveying a strong sense of direction. The shape is a very courageous break from standard football team logos. Summing up, the logo is meant to communicate a deep sense of club history and pride. What's more, Shakhtar has ambition and strives for excellence, taking the lead for past and future generations.

The next step was to align the club's overall product and communication strategy with the new branding strategy. To achieve this, brand architecture was built on three hierarchical levels, to simultaneously achieve both effective and efficient communication. First comes the *master brand*, which represents the corporate dimension. Using a master brand makes it possible to create a set of positive brand associations which can by extension be used in broader contexts. The second and third levels consist of sub-brands and endorsed brands.

Figure 8.14 - Shakhtar Donetsk: The new logo

The new brand architecture

Specifically, *sub-brands* identify specific activities that the club manages either directly or by partnering with other organizations. Sub-brands are used in the following contexts:

a. *Business partnerships.* Beginning in the 2011–2012 season, the club established a number of partnerships to shore up brand awareness and reinforce the new brand image. An example is the 'FCSD Clothing Collection' for men, women and children created by young designers inspired by the slogan, 'Wear with pride every day'. Another is the promotional campaign with Parallel, a petrol distribution company, with reward programs for loyal customers (not just Shakhtar fans).

b. *Partnerships with other football clubs.* For instance, during the 2011–2012 season, Shakhtar teamed up with AC Milan, Arsenal, and PSG to take part in a Europe-wide event promoted by Indesit, a household appliance producer, called 'Indesit Football Talents', with the aim of discovering and encouraging tomorrow's young football stars through photos and videos posted on the official company site and on social networks.

c. *Specific communication activities.* The club owns: an official site (around 14.7 million hits during the 2011–2012 season), a club newspaper (150,000 copies sold during the same season), an in-house newsletter, pre-match distribution programs (letters and flyers), and an online television channel (FCSD.tv), all marked with the corporate logo.

d. *Outlet.* The club has been selling collaterals, with the aim of giving the fans closer contact with the club, promoting a sense of membership, and providing a way to remember the experience. The sales strategy exploits online and offline channels. Some of the commercial initiatives are realized by selling comprehensive brand property rights for merchandise

The third and final level is made up if *endorsed brands*, that is, brands with their own unique images but that tap into the positive associations of the master brand. An example is the Donbass Arena, which has its own logo resembling the club's in shape and color (Figure 8.15). The club has strategically chosen to use the stadium, its crowning achievement, for initiatives not only from within the world of football (the 2012 Champions League and European Championships), but also outside. Specifically, this venue has hosted a number of rock concerts, as well as the European Club Association meeting and the National Boxing Championships (both in 2012).

Figure 8.15 - Shakhtar Donetsk: The Donbass Arena logo

REVIEW QUESTIONS

1. Shakhtar's top management team identified the lack of a clear brand identity as one of the issues to be tackled in the formulation of the new strategy. What elements did they decide to build the new identity on? Why?

2. The heritage of a brand may constitute a repertory of associations to be leveraged when building its positioning, or a constraint if managers want to change this positioning. When the new brand identity was formulated, which associations with the Shakhtar brand represented opportunities and which were constraints?

3. The new identity gave life to an entirely new Shakhtar brand system. What are the main components of that system?

Part

IV

CUSTOMER VALUE DELIVERY

Chapter 9

DELIVERING VALUE TO THE CUSTOMER: MANAGING A MULTI-MEDIA, MULTI-CHANNEL ENVIRONMENT

LEARNING OBJECTIVES

After reading this chapter you should be able to:

- Detail the main characteristics of a multi-media, multi-channel environment.
- Distinguish among Paid, Owned, and Earned touchpoints.
- Understand the main managerial issues related to the design, implementation, and assessment of communication campaigns.
- Distinguish among the different channels of distribution and the relative strategic and tactical decisions.
- Understand the rationale of a multi-media, multi-channel integration strategy.

OVERVIEW

As I pointed out back in Section 2.2.3, the aim of an organization's value delivery process is to facilitate *access* for its target customers to the value propositions it has designed for them. Effectively managing this process ensures that the value in question arrives at its destination intact. The final goal is to avoid the risk of a misalignment between perceived and expected value, which in turn leads to customer dissatisfaction.

Access isn't just *physical* (customers actually possessing and using products or partaking in services) but *cognitive* and *economic* as well. In other words, people have to realize that a value proposition exists, know what features it has, and understand that they can purchase it without too many sacrifices, beyond the ones they've already anticipated.

What this means for producers is that value delivery involves two main processes: *communication* and *distribution*. The first is about providing information on value propositions and building their positioning; the second, making these propositions available, where and when customers want them, while also contributing to this positioning.

An entirely digital world is arising out of recent technological transformations, which are revolutionizing these two processes. What's emerging is a new reality where media that supply content and channels that provide access to offerings are multiplying, giving rise to a multi-media, multi-channel environment.

One of the more palpable outcomes of these changes is that the boundaries between communication and distribution channels are becoming more and more blurred. As a result, any conversation about value delivery, which until recently would have taken on distribution and communication processes separately, must now address them together. In fact, handling value delivery today means managing these new multi-media and multi-channel environments.

Following this line of reasoning (and keeping in mind what we said in Chapters 3 and 4 on the various stages of customer experience), we might wonder if the value delivery process is any different from value creation, seeing that the latter is more and more impacted by the same technologies that drive communication and distribution processes. Is the sole aim of an online communication campaign to inform customers on the features of offerings, or is it an essential part of the brand experience? Does store design serve only to make the shopping experience a pleasant one, or is it a vital component of the brand image?

The answers are quite simple. If customer experience is made up of different stages, some that come before and some after actual product consumption, and if value for the customer springs from the entire cycle of experience, there's no doubt that communication and distribution are also components of customer value. And this is true if for no other reason than the fact that these processes can affect the sacrifices that customers have to make to enjoy benefits, sacrifices that are an integral (albeit negative) element of value.

So the separation between value creation and value delivery processes is a somewhat artificial one, though granted it's justified by how things really work. Today product and brand design is separate from (and antecedent to) distribution and communication, because there can't be one without the other. There wouldn't be anything to communicate or distribute to customers if there were no products or brands in the first place!

There will probably come a time when this separation becomes ineffective and totally obsolete, but today it's still the predominant management approach. That's why I'll assume that there's a line between value creation and delivery, even though I'll remind readers from time to time that this line is a very blurry one indeed.

In this chapter, I aim to answer two questions: Which channels can organizations in creative industries utilize to facilitate customer access to their value propositions? And how can they use these channels to guarantee a seamless experience and effective value delivery?

The answer to the first question calls for an analysis of various *touchpoints* that the organization can design and implement. As we'll see, selecting the most appropriate ones depends on the target as well as the organization's budget constraints and performance expectations (both market performance and return on investments), as always with an eye to effectiveness and efficiency.

As for the second question, the key is the *integration* of management processes. The environment in which customers find themselves today allows them far more access to value propositions, and more importantly, greater control than ever before over how they interact with producers (Section 2.3.1). This means that companies and non-profits have to guarantee an unequivocal message and a uniform experience through touchpoints, or risk eroding their positioning and disappointing their customers.

To deal with these issues, I think the best place to start is with a brief description of the main transformations in distribution channels and communication media that are revolutionizing value delivery processes.

9.1 CHARACTERISTICS OF A MULTI-MEDIA, MULTI-CHANNEL ENVIRONMENT

In a pre-digital world, the most effective and efficient way for organizations to guarantee access to their products and brands to a wide range of customers was to turn to specialists who made up the system of communication media and the system of distribution channels.

A government body that ran nature reserves, for example, would buy advertising in tourist magazines to communicate its offerings, and encourage tour operators to include visits to the reserves in the vacation packages they offered. Likewise, a design company would use specialized agencies to advertise the debut of its new collections, and set up distribution contracts with independent stores or chains to make its products accessible to its target. For many years, these examples represented typical ways to manage communication and distribution processes.

The reason for this approach was that the socioeconomic context in which organizations traditionally interacted with their customers was a rigid one in many ways. Let's look at an example. Up until not so very long ago, for an opera fan living in Austria, it would have been hard to find out what was playing at Covent Garden in London. Unless she actually travelled to London in person, she'd have to wait for a specialized magazine to publish an article on the season's programs at major European opera houses, or call the venue directly, or ask a friend who happened to be going to London to pick up a brochure. Covent Garden was far away, both in terms of distance and time. What's more, our opera fan could only share her passion with a small circle of fellow opera lovers and with people she met at the operas she went to see. Just think of how different things are today.

We can easily picture this same opera lover sitting in a café in Salzburg, listening to an aria on the radio that the announcer says is playing at Covent Garden. With her smartphone she can instantly access the theater's website, check if there are any tickets left for a specific date, and buy one. Then, between sips of coffee, she can book a flight and a hotel online. And as soon as she's done, she'll probably post or tweet her plans on her favorite social networks to see if any of her friends want to join her. Covent Garden has moved much closer, both in space and time, and this personal passion for opera is much more public than ever before.

Reflecting on this new reality, Boyd (2011) suggests that we're experiencing a 'collapse of contexts'. In other words, the concepts of near–far, present–future, public–private, and even real–virtual are blurring together and becoming more firmly anchored in subjective choices of every individual. But what impact does this collapse have on value delivery processes?

In the traditional context, relationships between organizations and customers are determined by spatial, temporal, and social categories structured along rigid dichotomies. This gives rise to the need for a *system of mediation* between the production and consumption systems to reconcile these differences, in terms of space, time, and sociality. And this is where communication media and distribution channels come in. The first system conveys information and symbols, the second products and services (and actually information and symbols too). This type of traditional mediation is continually losing ground with regard to significance and convenience, utility and power, both for producers and customers: it's turning into something else.

9.1.1 Trends in the use of mediation systems

The transformation of mediation systems is driven by three trends in how they're used by consumers: ubiquity, sociality and multi-tasking.

Ubiquity lies at the root of all these transformations, that is, so-called *ubiquitous computing* (Weiser, 1991). Generically speaking, this term means that *anyone anywhere can connect to a set of computer networks, which in turn are interconnected*. This is possible thanks to the evolution of devices such as smartphones and tablets that can be used to communicate information, receive and send data, work, and socialize.

Connectivity can also happen directly between objects and computer networks, without human intervention. This is what's called the *Internet of Things*, where 'intelligent' objects and devices can interact with the surrounding environment autonomously, thanks to their ability to interface with other networks. Examples are product labels that activate communications via a quick response code (QR), or cars, appliances, and computers that communicate their status to a control device.

Combining ubiquitous computing with social media results in *ubiquitous social media* (Mandelli and Accoto, 2012). This basically means that anywhere people go, they can use portable devices to activate social networks connected to computer networks. This social network might be extremely 'local' and 'temporary', as with *social check in* systems (such as FourSquare) that signal users' positions through their mobile device and activate nearby social networks.

What was once far away is close by; what was public is now private; the future is the present. For example, in a 2013 UK study run by Ispos Mori on a sample of around 1,000 people representing the adult population (over 15), results show that the percentage of people who connect to the web via broadband from their homes is on the rise (72%), but is only slightly higher as compared to 2011. On the contrary, the percentage who use their mobile devices to do the same has risen from 34 to 46 per cent, with more people accessing social networks through their smartphones or tablets than their computers (Ipsos MediaCT, 2013a).

Closely related to the previous points is a third dimension of the transformation of mediation systems: the tendency of individuals to *multi-task*, that is, to use more than one communication medium at the same time, which is now possible with the latest mobile devices. Proof of this phenomenon is shown in Figure 9.1, which illustrates the findings of a 2013 US study conducted by Ipsos Mori (Ipsos MediaCT, 2013b). The sample in this case consisted of 2,000 people representative of the over-18 population with an annual family income of over 100,000 dollars (labeled 'affluent'). What emerges from this research is that the consumer who uses one communication medium at a time is no more than a figure from the distant past.

These three trends are radically altering the way consumers utilize communication and distribution channels. Once upon a time, if a consumer wanted to use a communication medium or a store she would have to accept space–time restrictions: watching a TV show meant having to go home and turn it on at a specific time; buying a product meant finding a store that sold it. What's more, there was a set sequence to the use of media and channels: if a consumer read something interesting about a product in a magazine, to find out more she'd have to go to a store; once in the store, after checking the product price, she'd have to look for another similar product to compare the two and see which one was cheaper.

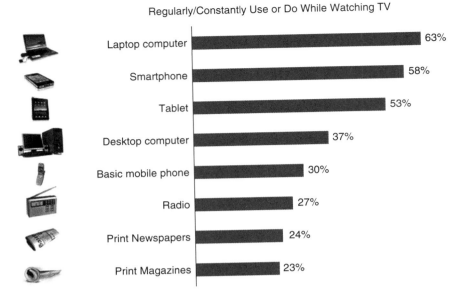

Figure 9.1 – Multi-tasking among the affluent in the US
Source: Ipsos MediaCT (2013b)

Today none of this is necessary. If a consumer reads about a product in magazine, she can instantly ask the people in her social network what they think, and simultaneously access a blog to find more product reviews while surfing the official company website for more information. And she can do the same in a store too, using her smartphone to access comparison shopping websites to find the nearest location offering the lowest price on the item she's looking for.

9.1.2   Effects on value delivery processes

At this point a logical question is: What impact do the transformations described above have on value delivery processes for producers?

First of all, there's a *proliferation of channels* that give consumers access to value propositions and relevant information. Today's digital web-based world is easily accessible to nearly everyone at a minimal cost. Just think of any kind of content, and the difference between what's published online versus offline. With respect to architecture and design, for instance, offline content production was once limited to a few specialized magazines that only reached a few thousand readers. (The circulation of magazines like *Casabella* and *Domus* is just over a hundred thousand.) Today, instead,

bloggers and sites such as www.yatzer.com, www.dezeen.com, and www.designboom.com count millions of users every month. Likewise, online shops can serve an inconceivable number of customers, compared to offline retailers. Case in point: In 2013, the fashion and design site www.yoox.com surpassed the one million mark in its number of active clients.

The second effect is an *enhanced ability to interact directly* with customers. In the past, big companies and institutions were the only ones who could afford to establish direct relationships of this kind, by investing in sales networks, owned stores, and advertising campaigns that could reach a vast target. Other businesses and non-profits faced the perennial choice between relying on distribution intermediaries or concentrating their efforts on a local market that they could access directly at little cost.

Internet and digital web-based communication tools empower all organizations to have direct contact with their customers on a broad scale. Today absolutely anyone can create a website or blog and build relationships with an audience scattered all over the world, securing a reasonable flow of revenues. A small-town museum, an out-of-the way nature reserve, a tiny tailor's workshop, a niche publisher specialized in art books, as well as any individual artist, author, musical group – the list is endless. For a real life case, see the video *Beautiful Onyinye* by the Nigerian duo P-Square, which has garnered more than 16 million hits on YouTube (Bright, 2013), an audience unimaginable in the pre-digital era.

The third noteworthy effect is the *loss of control* over the market, the individual customer, and even the producer's own products and brands. In fact, these same digital, ubiquitous, and social communication tools are primarily responsible for giving consumers so much leeway in participating in value production processes, becoming in turn autonomous producers of both products and information (Section 2.3). In the past, distribution and communication flows were essentially mono-directional or one-to-many, even though with the development of direct marketing tools many organizations also added one-to-one flows. But all these share a common source – that first 'one' was always the same, always the organization.

Today, however, the starting point can be the individual customer or a community of customers who activate communication flows regarding an organization, a product, or a brand. These consumers create content, make recommendations to try or buy a given product, and offer suggestions on how to use it. And all this can be beyond the control of the organization. So the bottom line is that the digital world favors the creation of a plethora of players who can take part in communication and distribution.

To conclude, the transformations occurring in the system of mediation on one hand give rise to tremendous opportunities for producers of creative products, because they expand the possibilities for delivering value to the market in every direction, potentially more effectively and efficiently than ever before. On the

other hand, these advantages are counterbalanced by a loss of control over delivery flows, in which customers and countless other players can intervene directly (be they intermediaries, infomediaries, bloggers, or others).

So another logical question is: What effects do the changes detailed above have on players in traditional communication and distribution systems? They too are finding that their roles – and their power – have been downsized within the context of value delivery processes. In fact, role and power are directly proportional to the capacity to mediate between production and consumption in terms of bridging distance – temporal, spatial, social, and cognitive.

But when consumers are empowered to bridge these distances themselves with little or no need for intermediation, and when they have far more direct paths by which to access producers, clearly a revolution in the role of communication media and distribution channels is inevitable. From the viewpoint adopted in this book, this role changes from *product mediation* to *experience mediation*, with a tremendous impact on the processes of delivering value from producers to the market.

9.2   TYPES OF TOUCHPOINTS

The value delivery process consists of *designing, realizing, and managing a system of touchpoints* between the organization, its products and brands, and its target customers. Myriad touchpoints can give current and potential customers access to value propositions. One way to classify them is by the degree of control that the organization has, that is, whether they are *paid, owned, or earned* (POE)[1] (Case History 9.1).

Case History 9.1

La Gazzetta dello Sport: expanding touchpoints to shore up a new positioning

La Gazzetta dello Sport is the best-selling sports newspaper in Italy, and overall the most widely read daily in the country, with a circulation[2] of around 250,000 per day and more than four million readers (www.rcsmediagroup.it). RCS Group, the owner, counts many other newspapers in its portfolio, both in Italy (such as *Corriere della Sera*) and in Spain (*El Mundo, Marca ed Expansión*).

The Gazzetta (as Italians usually call it) was published for the first time in 1896, and has since earned its reputation as a mainstay of the country's sports culture. One of its distinguishing marks has always been the color of the paper – pink – in keeping with the tradition of French sports newspapers, when each one was printed on a different color paper.

Over the years the Gazzetta has expanded its product portfolio to include a sports magazine (*SportWeek*), collateral products (book series, DVDs and calendars), Italy's most popular website for sports information (www.gazzetta.it), and even one of the biggest international cycling races: the *Giro d'Italia*.

Around the close of the first decade of the 2000s, a series of market transformations led Gazzetta's management to reflect on the paper's actual strengths and weaknesses and to come up with a new strategy. If on one hand the Gazzetta was the undisputed market leader, with nearly 100 per cent awareness, on the other the sector's digital revolution was starting to have a negative impact on sales. Marketing research showed that although the paper's authority was uncontested, the Gazzetta was perceived as being quite 'old style', still firmly anchored in a traditional concept of information.

Hence the decision to create a new positioning, conveyed by products that were diverse but integrated at the same time, focusing more on sports entertainment and less on pure information. The payoff was: 'Tutto il rosa della vita' ('Everything rosy in life') conveying a positive approach, with sporting values representing a lens for looking at life through rose-colored glasses, even life beyond sports.

To shore up the new brand positioning, management invested in more consumer touchpoints. Today, beyond the traditional product, these include mini-events staged during bigger, non-sporting events, fantasy football, apps for smartphones and tablets, and even a physical store for sports fans in Milan selling sportswear, books, DVDs, comic books, memorabilia, and more.

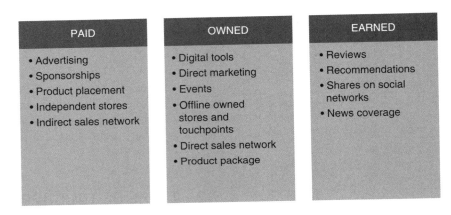

Figure 9.2 – Major touchpoints

Paid (or *bought*) touchpoints are ones that the organization buys for a limited period of time. Examples are ad space on a television channel, newspaper, or website, or independent stores used to distribute products.

Owned touchpoints are self-explanatory, and obviously afford the organization complete control. Although there is no pay-for-use fee as with the previous type, there are design and management costs to consider. The most obvious examples here are owned stores, owned sales networks, company websites, social media accounts, and so forth.

Finally, *earned* touchpoints are beyond the organization's control and are fueled by third parties (experts and consumers, among others). Here content regarding the organization and its products/brands is delivered because it's considered interesting and captivating. Some examples are expert reviews, word of mouth among consumers, 'retweets' and 'shares' on social media, and so on.

Figure 9.2 shows the main touchpoints bridging organizations and customers, broken down by the previous categories. In the following sections we'll take a closer look at how organizations need to manage these touchpoints, focusing on the specific decisions pertaining to managing communication campaigns and distribution channels.

9.3   PAID TOUCHPOINTS

9.3.1   Advertising

This represents one of the most traditional means of contact between producers and customers. In fact, advertising has been so prominent for so long, in particular for consumer goods, that many lay people take advertising and marketing to be synonymous.

Organizations use advertising to deliver content to a target audience via media owned by third parties.

There are three characteristics of advertising that distinguish it from other communication tools:

- It's *paid*. To utilize space within a given communication channel, the organization has to pay the owner of that channel. This distinguishes advertising from public relations, which involves providing content to the media in the hopes that, if it's potentially attention-grabbing, they'll publish or spotlight it in their information channels.
- It's *impersonal*. Communication used in advertising is typically mass media, so customers aren't recognized as individual targets, which precludes the possibility for personalized interaction, either in content or response.

  This is the main differentiator from direct marketing, which can be highly personalized. Classic examples are television or radio spots or newspaper ads.
- It's *temporary*. In other words, advertising covers a limited timeframe. No organization can afford to advertise every day of the year; the costs would be astronomical and the effort would be wasted. As we'll see in Section 9.6.3.1, with an advertising campaign, content (in the form of advertising space) is transmitted for a pre-set period of time to achieve specific organizational objectives with the target audience.

  In creative industries, for instance, ad campaigns often accompany a new product launch (a new season at the theater, a new book, a new album) or the repositioning of a value proposition (a museum that opens a children's section, an archeological site that offers a new access route for disabled visitors). The timing for these campaigns coincides with these activities. So this need for scheduling is another difference with respect to other communication tools like websites or sales networks, which the organization can leverage to deliver content on a daily basis.

The *object* of advertising is content related to the organization, its products or brands, depending on specific objectives. An art gallery might run an ad campaign in a specialized magazine to reinforce its image as an international venue, or to publicize an upcoming temporary exhibit, or to raise awareness of a sub-brand associated with a new consulting service for collectors.

As regards *communication media*, advertising is a highly flexible tool that can be transmitted via mass media to reach millions of customers (on global platforms like Google, Yahoo, Bing, and Baidu; national radio and television platforms, national newspapers, and magazines; search engines; and so on), or via niche media, covering a limited geographical area (local radio, television, or print media, or posters and flyers) or an exclusive audience (theme-based magazines, specialized websites). Organizations choose the best media mix in light of the target audience they want to reach and the type of content they want to convey (More on this in Section 9.6.4).

9.3.2 Sponsorship and product placement

In Chapter 5, we discussed the fact that organizations operating in creative industries actually represent the ideal media for delivering content in the form of sponsorships and product placement. Readers can refer back to that chapter for details.

However, here it's worthwhile to point out that many creative companies use sponsorships and product placements as tools for creating touchpoints with their current and potential customers. Media firms often act as media sponsors for charity events or non-profit initiatives, providing free ad space to deliver content publicizing these projects. Fashion houses frequently sponsor sports teams, or fund restoration projects for artwork and archeological sites, or serve as corporate members of various kinds of cultural institutions.

9.3.3 Sales promotions

As the name suggests, the range of activities that fall under the heading of sales promotions have the primary aim of eliciting specific behavioral responses from customers specifically related to purchasing products or brands: first-time buys, repeat purchases, bigger purchases, and so forth. At the same time, through sales promotions organizations can create touchpoints with their customers, and convey various types of content to their target audiences. Although some initiatives can be run by the organization itself, in most cases distribution gets involved, so sales promotions are considered paid.

The specificity of sales promotions as compared to other tools lies in *offering an advantage or incentive* either to consumers or retailers in the organization's sales network when they adopt certain purchase behaviors. *Promotional mechanics* are the specific ways these advantages are provided.

There are two macro-categories of mechanics depending on what they offer: either an economic advantage or a gift, either immediate or deferred (Figure 9.3).

The first type that offers an *economic advantage* is the price promotion, discussed in Section 8.3.6.3. A promotion involving a *gift* can be classified by the mechanic: either the gift is a sure thing, given to everyone who takes part in the initiative, or it depends on the customer's ability or luck.

Guaranteed, immediate gifts might include complementary products or services to mark special occasions (a book gifted to celebrate the opening of a new book shop, a poster given to visitors to commemorate the opening of an exhibit, a free performance offered on a special anniversary). Other gifts are guaranteed but deferred, for instance when customers repeatedly perform certain actions (collecting points or proof of purchase seals, for instance) and reach certain results they earn the right to receive a gift. Uncertain gifts linked to customer ability include games and contests, while typical gifts based on luck are drawings, scratch cards, sweepstakes, and the like. Clearly dependent on the relative mechanic, some promotional initiatives are better than others at delivering content (Research Focus 9.1).

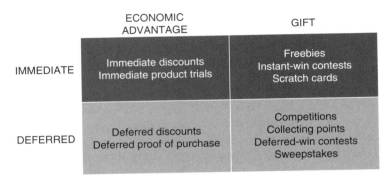

Figure 9.3 – Promotional mechanics

Research Focus 9.1

The perceptions of various kinds of promotions in performing arts

Consumers have come to view the use of sales promotions outside of creative industries as completely normal. But some doubt arises about the actual effects of this form of communication within creative industries, given the cultural, symbolic and identity value of so many creative products. In fact, managers of creative organization may think that these effects are minimal, or even counterproductive, because promotions would give a decidedly 'commercial' flavor to products whose value lies in a totally different direction.

To clarify this question, d'Astous et al. (2004) investigated the effects of various promotional mechanics on performing arts spectators in terms of their appreciation of the promotional offer and their perception of the organization's intention to manipulate (meaning the sense that the organization was using the promotion to manipulate their judgments on the performance). Specifically, the authors hypothesized that these effects depend on the mechanic in question (in this study a lottery, a discount, and a gift), as well as the type of performance (a play, a concert, and a comedy show), the attraction of the performance, and the perceived fit between the specific mechanic and the performance in question.

Through an experiment (Section 6.5.6) they ran in Canada, the authors demonstrated that individual mechanics produce different effects on appreciation and the perception of manipulation, depending on the interaction with the other variables in the study.

Their findings showed that the better the fit between the promotional mechanic and the type of performance, the higher the appreciation of the mechanic. What's more, when spectators perceived the performance as attractive, this further enhanced their appreciation of the mechanic; the less attractive the performance, the lower this appreciation. In other words, the greatest possible effect in terms of high appreciation for the promotion along with low perception of manipulation came about when the performance was attractive and the mechanic fit the performance; the opposite was true with an unattractive performance and a poor mechanic–performance fit.

The authors concluded with the recommendation to performing arts managers that they shouldn't consider a promotional offer as compensation for a performance with little audience appeal. What's more, if there's no way for spectators to anticipate a show's attraction, as is the case with something completely innovative, then it's worth selecting a promotion that fits well with the type of performance.

Case History 9.2

RED: A new concept in bookstores

The largest bookstore chain in Italy is la Feltrinelli (with 123 stores – 108 owned and 15 franchised), one of the few cases in the world of publisher-owned booksellers. What started as Giangiacomo Feltrinelli Editore has gradually grown into the Feltrinelli Group, an Italian media conglomerate whose current operations include television (la Effe), e-commerce (laFeltrinelli.it), and even a restaurant chain (Antica Focacceria San Francesco). The Group also owns La Central, a chain of Spanish bookstores.

From the very beginning, in the mid-1950s, the entire group has been driven by a strategy anchored in innovation. With its first bookstores opened in 1957, la Feltrinelli introduced never-before-seen concepts in Italy in book distribution like self-service, areas where customers could browse and read books, a regular calendar of events, an expanded assortment beyond books, new retail formats, and children's areas: basically la Feltrinelli created a category of bookstore that wasn't centered solely on selling, but instead offered an open space dedicated to culture.

Today la Feltrinelli adopts various formats to match its different sub-brands: la Feltrinelli Libri e Musica has a maxistore format in major cities (and smaller stores in minor cities), offering a vast assortment of books, music, home videos, video games, and areas for hosting events; la Feltrinelli Village includes medium-sized stores located in shopping centers; la Feltrinelli Express operates in travel retail with locations in train stations and airports.

In light of the digital revolution that has triggered a transformation of its traditional sectors (publishing, music, home video, and video games), la Feltrinelli decided to boost the experiential content in its assortment, opening cafes in its larger stores and launching a new format, RED. The first store opened in Milan in 2013, and the second in Florence in 2014.

RED stands for Read, Eat, and Dream, and conveys the experiential promise of the new format. To underscore its novelty and differentiate RED from other stores in the Feltrinelli portfolio, the branding strategy revolved around endorsement rather than sub-branding. In fact, RED is strongly associated with restaurant and café services, offering a unique combination of a more traditional book assortment and a range of selected food products.

This mix of restaurant plus bookstore makes it impossible to categorize RED exclusively as one or the other: tables are positioned in between the shelves, and books are placed right on the tables. Inside the store customers can spend time reading a newspaper or surfing the web on tablets provided free of charge. All in all, RED represents a cultural concept store where the concept of culture extends to encompass food.

9.3.4 Independent stores

Contact between the organization and its customers, and customer access to the organization's products can happen via touchpoints that are not owned by the organization, that is, either independent retailers or chain stores, both offline and online.[3] Stores come in every shape and size, but as far as value delivery, it's useful to classify them based on their chief product: the assortment.

Assortment refers to the set of products a store sells, broken down by category and brand or product variety in each category. Together the assortment plus the set of services the store offers its customers constitute the *format*: a traditional bookshop sells mostly books; a bookshop that also has a restaurant and a café, and hosts cultural events, art exhibits, and workshops, is more like a cultural concept store (Case History 9.2).

Assortment can be measured in terms of *breadth* and *depth*, like a product portfolio (Section 8.1.7). The first indicates the number and type of product categories sold; the second, the number and type of brands, or product variety in each category. By crossing these two dimensions, four kinds of stores emerge that can serve as consumer touchpoints, each with a different impact on the value delivery process depending on the assortment and services offered (Figure 9.4).

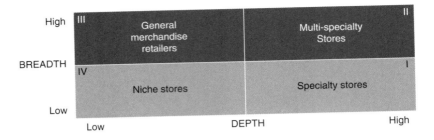

Figure 9.4 – Major retail distribution formats

9.3.4.1   Specialty stores

These retailers sell products and offer complementary services that fall exclusively into specific categories (Quadrant I). Waterstones in the UK, la Feltrinelli in Italy, and Thalia in Germany are all examples of European chains specialized in selling books, music, and other cultural products online and offline. Decathlon, Intersport, and SportDirect.com are chains specialized in sports; H&M, Promod, C&A, Peek & Cloppenburg, Yoox in fashion; IKEA in design; Expedia, eDreams, and LastMinute in tourism. These stores or chains offer consumers an assortment that revolves around precise categories, so their competence and image – specific to those categories – is what they convey to their customers in terms of specialized knowledge and services.

9.3.4.2   General merchandise retailers

This category is on the other end of the spectrum, with assortments encompassing numerous product categories (and a wide array of complementary services) but with little variety in each category (Quadrant III). Here there are supermarket or hypermarket chains, like the European giants Tesco, Sainsbury's, Migros, Carrefour, Auchan, Aldi, Ahold, Spar, Mercadona, Coop Norden, and Coop Italia, and at a global level Amazon. These retailers sell some creative products but again variety is very limited (with the exception of Amazon). In these cases, the service offered to consumers is convenience – easy access for purchasing products – rather than specialization.

9.3.4.3   Multi-specialty stores

Under this heading come department stores, offering both breadth and depth in their assortments (Quadrant II). Some of the most famous European chains include: Debenhams and Marks & Spencer in the UK, Galeries Lafayette in France, El Corte Inglés

in Spain, la Rinascente in Italy, and Breuninger in Germany. Every department is a specialized store of sorts, sharing many characteristics in terms of competence and image, but with a wide assortment that more closely resembles general merchandise retailers, and the convenience of a variety of product categories.

9.3.4.4   Niche stores

These are generally independent retailers whose assortment is neither broad nor deep (Quadrant IV), with formats that vary widely. Some are at the extreme end of specialization such as *boutiques*, which are very common in creative industries. Assortments focus on a single category (for instance, an art gallery, a shop specializing in books of photographs, a store offering a complete range of products for mountain climbers) with exceptional competence and image.

Although 'boutique' mainly refers to shops with a very high image, there are also less sophisticated formats that follow the same approach of extreme specialization. Common examples are newsstands or *automated stores* (from vending machines to electronic kiosks). Their strong suit is convenience, and they're most popular in creative industries such as publishing and home video, although some self-service stores even sell articles of clothing.

In some creative industries such as visual arts, fashion, design, and publishing, a particularly interesting retailing format is the *concept store*. Here customers find a very carefully selected, but extremely limited assortment of items that represent a lifestyle. Some examples are Colette in Paris, Clinic in Antwerp, Farenah in Sofia, xXx in Berlin, Hutspot in Amsterdam, Real in Lisbon, Clube Chocolate in Sao Paulo, and Q in Bangkok. In these stores, specialization centers on the search and selection of products, brands, or works of art that have a special association with a theme, a style, or an interest.

9.3.5   The indirect sales network

This network is made up of people who are contracted (but not directly employed) by the organization to handle its product sales. In some cases, this kind of network complements a direct one (Section 9.4.5).

Indirect salespeople can be freelancers or employees of a distribution company. Generally they have an agency or representation agreement, which may or may not be exclusive (selling only the organization's products as opposed to taking on other organizations and even competing products). Remuneration is usually based on a sales commissions, plus bonuses or incentives for hitting sales targets or for taking on additional responsibilities.

The main job for the indirect network is obviously to sell products. But having direct, constant contact with customers means these salespeople are key touchpoints for the organization, especially if (as is sometimes the case) it doesn't have a direct network, and so it has no other direct access to customers.

However, since the organization doesn't have complete control over an indirect network, it's particularly difficult to leverage in order to convey content and communications to customers. To ensure this happens, the organization has to negotiate with sales personnel and find an effective way to motivate them to take on these additional tasks.

9.4   OWNED TOUCHPOINTS

9.4.1   Digital tools

This category includes all the tools that make it possible for an organization to deliver digital content: websites; mini-sites for specific products, brands or events; accounts on social networks (like Facebook, Google+, Ren Ren, Twitter, Weibo); email; instant messaging; and smartphone content in general (which warrants a separate category: *mobile communication/marketing*).

These tools allow organizations to communicate interactively with a pre-identified audience. Normally this audience is indentified via registration, with individuals providing their personal data and agreeing to receive messages from the site/account owner.

Unlike traditional advertising, digital tools render communication more personalized, and establish a dialogue based on two-way communication. The advantages are obvious: the organization can select the target it wants to provide with content, and at the same time it can get invaluable feedback; by the same token customers can get content they're really interested in, as well as target the messages they send. In this sense, digital communication tools can be considered the evolution of more traditional direct marketing tools, sharing and actually augmenting their potential and effectiveness.

9.4.2   Direct marketing

Direct marketing is considered any *personalized means of contact with the target audience, aimed at delivering content solely for the purpose of communication or sales*. A vast range of tools fall into this category, but normally sales networks (direct or indirect) or the digital communication tools mentioned above wouldn't be included. The reason for this is that since they differ in terms of technology, effectiveness, and efficiency, they need to be managed separately.

The list of traditional tools covers direct response advertising (DRA), direct mail, and telemarketing. *DRA*, as its name suggests, consists in urging recipients to respond personally and directly to the advertiser, in a message delivered via mass media, be it print, television, or radio. For instance, in a television spot or radio ad, or in printed advertising material, there might be an invitation to contact a call center, or to send an email or text message, or to sign up to the organization's social account. With DRA, personalization happens after the initial invitation is sent, and only if the consumer responds by accepting it.

With *direct mail*, on the other hand, content and messages (in the form of letters, brochures, catalogues, and newsletters) are sent to specific recipients identified by the organization. Personalizing this type of communication requires personal data such as addresses. *Telemarketing* is a form of direct communication via telephone. This activity is generally handled by call centers (often outsourced to specialized companies) that receive *inbound calls*, solicited via other touchpoints, and make *outbound calls* promoting the organization's products, brands, and events.

The distinctive characteristics of direct marketing (and digital communication) render these tools extremely diversified, and as such complementary to traditional advertising.

● *The message is customizable and selective* because it can target specific recipients. In other words, it's not anonymous like traditional advertising. Direct marketing tools allow companies to build messages with special appeal for specific targets, making communication far more effective. For instance, a theater might do an emailing with different messages for long-term patrons, new season ticket holders, and people who are simply registered on the theater's website or social networks.

- *Tools are interactive*, enabling bi-directional communication between sender and recipients. This represents a radical change, because communication shifts from occasional to continual, establishing an ongoing dialogue between the two parties. In the theater mentioned above, before a show the call center could contact all the people who are members of the community (but not season ticket holders) to urge them to buy tickets, and then get feedback on their enjoyment and satisfaction after the show.
- *Responses are measurable*. Since communication can be personalized, direct marketing tools also make it possible to measure results more accurately. Returning to the theater, the call center can verify how many of the people contacted before the show actually bought tickets. Measuring response is a way to boost the efficiency of communication efforts because over time the organization can single out the more effective touchpoints for individual targets, and allocate resources more productively.

9.4.3 Events

Events can truly be considered *live communication* because contents are delivered to a target audience that is actually present. This is what makes events unique among touchpoints, and particularly well-suited to creating extremely rich communicative experiences. The variety of event formats is as infinite as the creativity of event designers, but there is one macro-categorization that can help in designing value delivery processes: the distinction between individual events and collective events (Rinallo, 2011).

Individual events are organized directly by a single organization for a specific audience. These can be one-time (an anniversary celebration or a flash mob to support fundraising) or recurring (fashion shows to present new collections); brief (a speech by a great artist to the patrons of a museum) or long (a temporary shop open for two months); spectacular (with show-business style special effects) or routine (a press conference);

online (a new product launch on Second Life or Facebook), or offline (a party to celebrate the same).

With *collective events*, on the other hand, any number of organizations can take part (often competitors); participants are allotted their own space and can stage their own initiatives.[4] Collective events are set up by specialized companies and designed to attract a vast audience, in some cases hundreds of thousands of people.

The most common of these in creative industries are *fairs*, which cover countless sectors: visual arts (from Art Basel for contemporary art to TEFAF in Maastricht for classical art); cinema (festivals where new films debut); television (NATPE); publishing (Frankfurter's *Buchmesse* and the London Book Fair); fashion (fashion weeks in Paris, London, Milan and New York); and design (from Milan's *Salone del Mobile* to London's Design Festival). As the confines between various creative industries blur (Section 1.3.4), many fairs have been repositioned, broadly targeting companies that do business in content, media, and entertainment industries (such as ShowBiZ Expo and the International Broadcasting Convention).

At these fairs, numerous exhibitors present their products and initiatives directly to their audience, with the triple aim of delivering content, setting up or shoring up commercial relationships, and (naturally) selling. The difference between individual and collective events is evident. With the first, the organization has total control and represents the sole focus of the event; with the second, hosting so many other participants (often competitors), the organization has to make an effort to take control and capture focus through initiatives (individual events) staged within the context of the collective event.

9.4.4 Owned stores and other physical touchpoints

One way for companies and non-profits to deliver content to their target audience is through physical touchpoints that they own. With sectors where organizations deal in physical products, *owned stores* are an option that offers advantages compared to independent stores (discussed in Section 9.3.4) both in terms of control and format.

Thanks to the direct control they afford, owned stores are more effective and productive touchpoints than independent ones. In fact, the company can take in all its revenues without having to pay a percentage to distributors in the form of margins (Section 8.3.5.4). What's more, store design can scrupulously reflect the positioning of the master brand and other brands in the portfolio, contributing to the company's overall image.

Speaking of image, a special kind of owned store is called the *flagship*. Since the store's primary objective is to build and reinforce image (Dolbec and Chebat, 2013), this dictates all related decisions. First and foremost, the location is normally in the city center or the main shopping district, where there's a regular flow of pedestrian traffic, often people who belong to a target representing a certain lifestyle. Next comes assortment, which mainly consists of products that are innovative, or that embody the history of the company, or that reflect a highly distinctive image. So the bottom line for flagship stores is communication, not commercialization. In fact, often they aren't even expected to generate high margins, but instead are seen as investments in communication.

Another special kind of store is a *factory outlet*, located directly in production facilities, or in metropolitan areas or shopping centers. Assortment is made up of goods that are either defective or outdated. Since prices are often rock bottom, outlets are clearly positioned to attract bargain hunters and are commonly found in creative industries like fashion and design where planned obsolescence is the order of the day (Section 8.1.5.1).

Midway between non-owned and owned stores (but much closer to the latter in terms of controlling and managing value delivery) are *franchised* stores and chains. This refers to a special type of contract between two independent organizations. The *franchisor* grants the right to sell its brands and products to the *franchisee* in exchange for a royalty on turnover and an entrance fee to become a member of the network.

Franchising is a fast and easy a way for firms that operate in creative industries to activate a broad distribution network, as compared to investing in owned stores. What's more, the franchisor can maintain rigorous control by setting down standards pertaining to sales methods and communication channels and require franchisees to respect them.

Moving beyond the stores, organizations that operate in creative industries, service providers in particular, can use their own *buildings* as touchpoints. Cultural institutions such as museums and theaters, organizations that run archeological sites and nature reserves, tourist destinations, amusement parks, and any service provider that offers hospitality as part of its value proposition (to include the ticket booth): the very places where all these organizations carry out their activities are invaluable touchpoints.

Exceptional examples are any number of European opera houses, or the Guggenheim in Bilbao, the Tate Modern in London, the Kiasma in Helsinki, or the Jewish Museum in Berlin. All these and countless others have become distinctive symbols of the organization they host (and the relative value propositions). Recognizing this potential, some companies invest in buildings that express architectural distinction, and often open them to the public to create a high value added touchpoint (Case History 9.3).

Case History 9.3

Salvatore Ferragamo: creating a company museum

Salvatore Ferragamo is arguably the company and the brand that epitomizes 'made in Italy' and the international luxury sector. Named after the man who founded the company in Florence in 1928, Ferragamo specializes in shoes and leather accessories, but also produces a clothing line and licenses eyewear and watches.

In 1995 the Salvatore Ferragamo Museum was established in Palazzo Spini Speroni, the corporate headquarters, with the primary aim of telling the story of the company and its founder. Today the museum also serves as a powerful vehicle for communicating the values and distinctive traits of the Ferragamo brand (Ostillio et al., 2013).

The museum is situated in the historical building where the company has been based since its foundation, a location that accentuates the strong ties between the brand and Florence, a city considered by many the world over as unique for its beauty, art history, artisan tradition, and product excellence. All these qualities have always been distinctive elements of the Ferragamo brand.

Moreover, the products on display and the explanation of production methods contribute to communicating the value of craftsmanship, attention to quality and manual skill that form the foundations of Ferragamo's competitive advantage with respect to many other 'made in Italy' luxury brands. Finally, the founder's passion for art, which is also represented in the museum, reinforces the association of Ferragamo products as unique objects, products of the expert hands of the skilled artisans who craft them.

Likewise, countless cultural institutions open info points in their host cities to provide easy access to their target audiences, especially those market segments that are unaccustomed to or uncomfortable with digital communication.

9.4.5   The direct sales network

Unlike the indirect network (Section 9.3.5), members of an organization's direct network are actually employees. This allows for greater control in assigning tasks, setting performance targets, and conveying content and information to and from the market.

There are myriad ways for the organization to structure its direct sales network, and as many roles within this network. The most traditional framework, commonly found in any kind of company, is the Sales or Commercial Department, whose staff answers to a Sales Director. Depending on its size and configuration, there may be several different roles in this unit, including *salespeople*. Their job is to contact customers directly, encourage them to purchase or repurchase the organization's products and brands, and invite them to participate in events and other initiatives.

The classic image of a salesperson is someone who works in the field, making calls to customers according to a set sales plan, typically covering a specific geographical area (province, region, or macro-territory). Another traditional role is the *shop assistant*.[5] Although both these roles are still familiar ones in many creative industries, the evolution of organizations and technologies has led to the emergence of new sales professionals.

Today direct sales are often done not by visiting customers in person, but via telephone (see *call centers* described in Section 9.4.2). And in the store itself, which is run by a Store Manager, there are both salespeople and *merchandisers*. These professionals don't work at a single store, but visit many or all the organization's retail outlets (owned and non-owned), dealing with everything from store layouts (window displays, shelves, stands) to checking prices, to collecting data on customers or competitors.

Naturally, for organizations that invest small amounts (or none at all) in advertising or other kinds of direct communication, the sales staff is the most critical touchpoint between them and their customers

(current and potential). This means that the sales network must include professionals who not only handle and finalize commercial transactions, but who transmit the positioning of the organization's value proposition, to ensure that it's transferred intact and free of distortions.

9.4.6   The package

The product itself (in case of a physical product) represents a formidable touchpoint with consumers. In fact, during the pre-consumption and purchase experiences, the consumer can interact with the product, and the package can be an exceptional means of delivering content and messages.

In many cases consumers interact with products in stores without any assistance from sales staff. It's here that the package (if there is one) serves to attract attention and prompt people to read the information on the label. A study by D'Astous et al. (2006) showed that in the publishing industry an attractive book cover increases the interest of potential consumers, whether the book be fiction or non-fiction. On the other hand, a cover that attempts to illustrate the content of a book has no effect on interest.

In many cases, the package becomes a communication medium once the consumer has purchased the product. For example, in fashion and design, products are displayed without packaging, which is only provided after the customer has decided to make a purchase. In this case, the package delivers content during the post-purchase experience, enhancing the product's communicative value.

Considering the key role that the package plays, it should be designed not only with aesthetics in mind, but also as a useful medium for delivering content. This is even more essential in today's digital world, where the package can contribute to creating viral communication, making the product itself go viral (Aral and Walker, 2011).

Putting a QR code on a label, or listing the social account, or adding an invitation to share ('likes' or 'shares', active or passive): if all these are properly designed (see Section 9.5.2) they can trigger the viral circulation of messages either during or after a purchase, exploiting the positive emotions associated with consumption and use.

9.5   EARNED TOUCHPOINTS

As we already know, earned touchpoints are generated by third parties. A blogger who writes a review on a show she's just seen, a consumer who comments on her social network about the last book she's read, a specialized magazine that publishes an article on a nature reserve, or simply a column in a newspaper on music that gives the setlist of a concert from the previous night: all these are examples of touchpoints between organizations (their products and brands) and customers, but none of them is initiated by the organizations themselves. This means they are beyond their control.

However, *beyond control doesn't mean outside the sphere of influence*. In fact, organizations can use various tools to shape these communications, actually providing content and information. The basic rule to keep in mind is that the people who do control these touchpoints pass the word on to others if they're convinced it's interesting. With these 'others' there may be formal relationships (a magazine or newspaper and its readers) or informal ones (a blogger with her contacts, a consumer with her friends). As a result, whether or not an organization succeeds in setting this information flow in motion depends largely on its *ability to create interesting messages and content*, prompting its dissemination via *word of mouth*. A number of tools are available to achieve this.

9.5.1   Public relations (PR)

The aim of PR is to create consensus and support: an environment that's favorable to the organization, its initiatives, its products, and its brands. But what must be emphasized is that not all public relations activities fall under the domain of marketing.

Lobbying, for instance, which is normally included in the category of PR activities, has to do with initiatives enacted by an organization (often in association with similar organizations) to defend or promote its interests among regulators and legislators. So although it isn't exactly about marketing, the effects of lobbying can impact marketing decisions. If, for example, the opera houses in a country lobby their government for more public subsidies to fund their productions, the success or failure of this activity may well impact the ticket prices for operas.

PR in marketing (sometimes called *marketing public relations*) involves a set of activities that aim to *build,* *reinforce, or defend the image* of an organization, its products, and its brands among select targets: communication media (in which case the term is *media relations*), special partners or customers (like sponsors, donors, loyal customers, celebrities), or generic partners or customers. Media relations are normally handled by an office, which, despite the media evolution, is still often called the *press office*. Its main job is to build and transfer news about the organization and its activities, ensuring that this news is considered interesting enough to pass on.

The umbrella term *publicity* includes press releases, press conferences, articles, or reports prepared ad hoc for specific media, and even events organized expressly for the media. Examples that come to mind here are previews of films for movie critics, guided 'after hours' tours of museums for journalists from national or local papers, complementary trips to new tourist destinations offered to travel writers from specialized magazines, and many more.

Activities targeting special partners and customers are often *exclusive events* as well as complementary products or free access to services, in particular for celebrities. The aim of these initiatives is to reward or reinforce 'preferred customer' status. With celebrities the idea is to leverage their endorsement to enhance the visibility of the products and services in question (Section 5.7). For generic partners and customers, events are the most-used advertising tool (see the Vodafone case in Chapter 5).

9.5.2   Viral marketing

The digital evolution of PR is all about *viral marketing*, also called *word-of-mouth* or *buzz marketing*. The aim here is to create content that consumers will voluntarily pass on via social networks (hence the term *word-of-mouse*), triggering a self-replicating viral process – creating a buzz.

The approach is identical to publicity: building interesting content (funny, curious, thought-provoking, emotional) that consumers appropriate as their own, sometimes adding their own comments and content and then passing it along through their preferred communication channels (like YouTube, MySpace, Facebook, and Ren Ren). These are all examples of platforms based on user-generated content, where viral marketing is most effective, although other digital tools also work such as instant messaging, email, and mobile marketing in general.

9.5.3 Guerrilla marketing

This refers to low-budget, unconventional advertising activities (graffiti, sticker bombing, flash mobs, micro-events, grassroots marketing, and so on). These initiatives are done in a clearly delineated time and place (which is where 'guerilla' comes from) and have a high impact on the public. Another unique feature that distinguishes guerilla marketing is the exceptional creativity involved in both staging these initiatives and in the media used to communicate them.

If once the underlying aims were typically communicative within the framework of paid touchpoints, today the main focus of guerilla marketing activities is buzz, generated through mobile communication and social networks. Thanks to the very low cost compared to traditional ad campaigns, it's easy to find these activities in any number of creative industries.

9.6 MANAGING COMMUNICATION PROCESSES: INTEGRATED MARKETING COMMUNICATION[6]

As we've just seen, an organization can exploit numerous touchpoints to deliver content and messages regarding its value propositions. Effective communication calls for the careful planning and integration of content and media, so that the messages that reach the target audiences are homogeneous and productive.

With respect to marketing communication decisions, these fall into two macro-areas: *what* content to deliver and *which* touchpoints to use as delivery vehicles. But prerequisites for these choices are identifying the target audience and setting communication objectives. Only after all these preliminaries are complete can the organization release the communication campaign and, when it's finished, measure the results. These stages taken together make up the communication process (Figure 9.5).

9.6.1 Identifying the target audience

Starting at the beginning, the first step in an effective communication process is to clearly identify the intended recipients of the messages and content the organization wants to deliver; in other words, the *target audience*. The more meticulous this stage is, the more appropriate the choice of tools and touchpoints will be, and the more efficient the subsequent resource allocation for communication.

As with the segmentation and targeting decisions outlined in Sections 7.7 and 7.8, choosing a target audience means first pinpointing and then profiling the groups of people who the organization hopes will receive its communication. Possible recipients might be current consumers, potential consumers, loyal consumers, corporate customers, distribution partners, opinion leaders, value agents in the production network, or others.

What's essential to remember, though, is that it isn't enough to simply identify these macro-groups; the organization needs to *profile its target audience*. Profiling is based on personal traits, consumption habits, typical product use, and above all habits and preferences with regard to communication media (so-called *media habits*).

This means that if an organization wants to communicate with seniors who are still fond of generalist television, or adolescents who spend hours every day on social networks they access via smartphones and tablets, the most appropriate messages and media for each target would be radically different. What's more, consumers indicate how they prefer to be contacted when they register on the organization's social account or website, so this provides valuable input as well.

The same holds true for instance with traditionalist distribution partners who would rather thumb through printed catalogues and brochures, as opposed to more innovative partners who'd rather get digital newsletters they can simply download onto their mobile devices. Likewise, a group of museum donors might prefer

Figure 9.5 – Stages in the communication process

exclusive events organized just for them, while that same museum might have club members who'd appreciate a monthly newsletter via email more.

What's essential to keep in mind is the fact that the target of the communication doesn't necessarily coincide with the target of the organization's value propositions. Classic examples are opinion leaders, or all those who serve as value agents in the value creation network: these are typical targets of PR activities or viral marketing, but are rarely the targets of consumption.

9.6.2   Setting communication objectives

The ultimate aim of all marketing communications is to guarantee an effective value delivery process. This said, for every individual campaign there may be a multiplicity of objectives (or 'products' of the communication process). There are various models for classifying these objectives,[7] but the common denominator is the reference to three spheres that are activated during the various stages in the consumer's experience or a corporate client's selection and use of a creative product:

- Cognitions.
- Affects.
- Behaviors.

The objectives related to *cognitions* have to do with *increasing the level of customer knowledge* regarding the elements of the organization's value propositions. So the point of this kind of campaign would be to provide information to the target audience that they then retain and use during their experience. An event created on social networks, a search engine optimization (SEO) initiative (boosting visibility of the organization's website, or the number of hits on a web page via major search engines), an ad on traditional media, or a press conference: all these can inform the public about a new product launch, for example. Email marketing or flyers in stores can let people know about product promotions.

Objectives pertaining to *affects* involve *creating and reinforcing favorable attitudes and preferences* for the organization's value propositions. When these attitudes center on emotional and value-based aspects, objectives are often labeled *consumer engagement*.

The point of this kind of campaign is to shape target consumers' beliefs and their image of the organization and its offerings, so that these perceptions become a part of their evoked set (Section 4.4.1.2)

that they tap into when making choices. For instance, an invitation-only event for potential sponsors to unveil future projects, or an ad campaign to support the repositioning of a brand, or a viral campaign based on attention-grabbing video footage posted on social platforms – all these initiatives typically aim at creating a favorable attitude toward the organization and its products/brands.

Last come *behaviors*. These objectives are meant to encourage in recipients the *intention to behave* in a certain way. In marketing jargon, this is referred to as a *call to action*, where the action in question might be: taking part in product creation, participating in an event, purchasing or repurchasing a product, gifting a product, word-of-mouth, signing up for an online promotion, and so forth. Various touchpoints can be used to elicit these behaviors.

9.6.3   Designing content: the creative decisions

This stage, by definition, represents the creative component of marketing communication. Once the organization has determined the target audience and relative objectives (both deriving from very rational analysis and assessment), the next step is to create contents and messages to deliver: it's all about what to communicate and how. The 'what' has to do with the *object* of the communication, what an organization wants to transmit to our audience. 'How' refers to the *mode* of communication, the combination of codes and techniques by which content takes form: text, images, formats, graphics, and so forth.

Now, though it's true that the 'what' should come before the 'how', both need to be considered, for obvious reasons. If marketing decides to use video footage, print media isn't appropriate; if the message is in the form of a long text, television isn't the right way to deliver it; transmitting an intensely emotional message would call for a dramatic stage event; if communication has to be highly professional and rational, a formal presentation is the best option. Again, although the usual sequence is first designing content and then selecting the vehicle for delivering it, in practice the two stages are closely interconnected, and influence one another intensely.

Creating communication content is an activity that often requires specialized competences. This explains why companies and non-profits usually commission *communication agencies* to handle everything from content design, creation, production, and 'airplay'.

With televised ad campaigns, the agency would come up with a message, turn it into a spot, handle production, coordinate all the people involved (the director, actors, technicians, and so forth), and then deal with broadcasting the spot, and selecting television channels that will air it and managing relationships with them. If instead the campaign is a price promotion communicated with flyers in stores, the agency would create a message to launch the initiative, design and print the flyers, and coordinate personnel for distributing them.

However, the organization needs to provide vital input upstream from content creation by compiling a *communication brief*. Like the research brief (Section 6.2), this document gives the agency the information it needs to create an effective campaign, including: the market context and position of the organization; the product, brand, or specific activity that will be the object of the campaign; the profile of the target audience; the communication objectives; previous and ongoing communication activities; benchmark and competitor communications; and the campaign budget (Table 9.1).

A brief is always a written document, one that is as concise as possible. The more constructive the input it contains for designing the campaign (and the less useless information that may create distortions and misunderstandings) the more productive the agency's efforts will be.

The diversity in designing communication campaigns comes from the specific touchpoints the organization opts to use. In the following sections, we'll explore three of these, one for each macro-category: advertising for paid touchpoints, websites for owned touchpoints, and viral marketing for earned touchpoints.

9.6.3.1 Designing an ad campaign

At the heart of any ad campaign is the content or message. A widely-used model for structuring an advertising message specifies the following:

- The *main benefit* or *promise*. This is what the organization, product or brand pledges to provide to the audience.
- The *reason why* is what makes the promise more credible, by offering arguments (rational or emotional) that give consumers an idea of the tangible and intangible attributes associated with the benefits in question.
- *Supporting evidence* includes proof that demonstrates the reliability of the reason why. This might be the brand itself (if it has a solid reputation and a positive image), expert opinions, consumer reviews, testimonials, and so on.
- The *mood* or *tone of voice* is conveyed through language, style, and the atmosphere the ad creates.

As an example, let's take a movie trailer for a dramatic film based on a bestseller, with an award-winning director famous for her work in this particular genre. The message might contain the promise 'a film that will move you like no other ever has', the reason why, 'based on the bestseller ...' and 'from the director of ...' and as for supporting evidence, 'nominated for six Academy Awards', with a tone of voice that's emotionally provocative thanks to the scenes and the background music chosen for the trailer.

Clearly the people who design the message decide whether to use all these elements, how to balance them, and what types of codes will work best, bringing to bear their creativity and keeping in mind the features and image of the product, brand, and the organization. Just think of a typical print ad by a luxury company, which is often simply a photo with the product in the center and the brand positioned like a signature in the corner, nothing more. That particular type of photography (the setting, color, models, and so on) is what gives the message its tone; the brand does the rest.

The combination of the elements described above gives rise to some generic advertising categories. *Cognitive ads* have a very rational appeal, with an overall tone that's

Table 9.1 – Contents of a communication brief

BRIEF
● Information on the market
● Information on the market position of the organization
● Information on the object of the campaign: the organization, product, brand or activity
● Profile of the target audience
● Communication objectives
● Previous campaigns
● Other ongoing campaigns
● Competitors' strategies and campaigns
● Campaign budget

based on reasoning and facts. (These ads can use a one-sided argument (obviously pro-organization/product/brand) or a two-sided argument that also addresses the sacrifices (such limited availability or a high price), but ultimately demonstrates that the benefits are far superior.

Comparative ads, which also fall into the cognitive category, serve to show how the product in question outperforms the competition and offers superior features.

Emotional ads elicit emotions in the target audience through any of the elements discussed above (the promise, the reason why, the supporting evidence, the tone, or a combination of the four). Ads that use an emotional tone often try to strike a humorous chord or use hyperbole (either through words or images) that transforms reality (the product or the purchase/consumption scenario) to trigger an emotional reaction that may be positive (joy, fun, and so on) or negative (fear, embarrassment, shame, and so forth).

Image ads convey messages almost exclusively through the aesthetic quality of images. These are common in the world of fashion, design, tourism, or advertising for monuments, archeological sites or nature areas, and exploit the beauty of the products themselves to capture attention and provoke an emotional reaction.

9.6.3.2 Web design

The website of a company or non-profit (like a mini-site dedicated to an individual product, brand or event) is completely different from any other kind of paid touchpoints or advertising. The two main reasons why are that customers access these sites because they want to (though organizations can make an effort to encourage them); and they can do so at any time on any day.[8]

Essentially, an organization leverages its website to deliver a continual flow of content to an audience that can't be pre-identified, made up of people who've learned about the site through other touchpoints. Access data mainly show how they behave (time of access, location, duration of visit, pages visited, and so forth), but not who they are. To find this out, the organization needs to either require registration to open certain web pages, or carry out ad hoc marketing research.

As a result, web design centers on *relevant and interesting information about the organization*. Beyond specific communication contents, there are certain things to keep in mind when designing a website that serve to encourage users to visit, to spend time browsing, and in the case of e-commerce, to make a purchase.

Taking off from the idea of a *servicescape* conceived for offline stores (Section 9.7.2), Harris and Goode (2010) propose the concept of an *e-servicescape*, effectively combining the findings of various studies on the elements of atmosphere that a website has to convey to its visitors to make their experience pleasurable and profitable (Hopkins et al., 2009; Srinivasan et al., 2002; Zeithaml et al., 2002).

There are three macro-components of the e-servicescape:

- *Aesthetic appeal* are all those aspects of web design that make a site enjoyable to navigate, and encourage users to spend time there: original, eye-catching graphics; video and audio features; colors, flashes, and pop-ups; entertainment (such as community interaction) – all these contribute to enhancing user enjoyment.
- *Layout and functionality* ensure effectiveness, and to be effective, a site has to be easy to use. Here the structure and mechanics are key, as well as the relevance of the information, easy-access help pages and FAQs, and so on. What's more, the set up of the site should reflect the purpose, that is, to satisfy the needs of a variety of users (for example, with separate sections for consumers and distribution partners, media, donors, and sponsors). All these elements contribute the perception of functionality.
- *Financial security* is a high priority if the site offers consumers the chance to purchase products and make financial transactions. Key aspects are security certification for payments, easy payment procedures (without too many steps), and the sense that privacy is respected and protected with regard to personal data.

9.6.3.3 Designing a viral campaign

When designing a viral campaign, an organization takes into account the mechanisms that circulate messages in social networks. A *social network* is made up of a set of actors and the ties among them, which can be direct (A and B are friends, or co-workers) or indirect (A is a friend of B, B is a friend of C, so A is tied to C through B). A sociogram is a handy tool for representing a social network, depicting actors as interconnecting nodes (Figure 9.6).

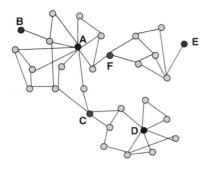

Figure 9.6 – A sociogram representing a social network

Within a network, the role and prominence of every actor differ based on the number and type of relationships she has. *Hubs* are actors who are highly interconnected, with numerous ties with other actors (A and D in the figure); *fringes* are actors who don't have many relationships (B and E); *bridges* connect different parts of the network (or different networks) that would otherwise be disconnected (C and F) (Van den Bulte, 2010). The number of ties is measured by an indicator termed *centrality*; hubs are the most central actors in their respective networks.

Digital social networks make it possible to measure the ties among actors and the centrality of each one; these measures lay the groundwork for designing viral campaigns. In fact, beyond interesting, appealing content (Chiu et al., 2007), what sets viral campaigns apart

is their use of various *seeding strategies*: singling out specific actors to send initial messages to, the ones who are most likely to share them with others (Case History 9.4).

At first glance, it would seem natural to focus seeding strategies on hub customers, assuming that since they have the most ties, they're the opinion leaders who can influence the largest number of fellow customers. Admittedly this is true in general terms, but it's essential to take a closer look at just how active these hubs are.

Second and equally important is to verify whether it would be more effective to make initial contact with bridges (Hinz et al., 2011). The rationale here is that although hubs tend to have an abundance of connections within a single social network (their group of friends, for instance), bridges have relatively fewer connections but with a variety of networks (different groups of friends, communities, and so on). So it all depends on the objective of the communication campaign: the best route might be to address initial messages to bridges if the organization wants to activate various networks, or to hubs when the aim is deeper penetration of a single network.

9.6.4   Selecting touchpoints

At this point it's time to select and schedule which touchpoints to include in the communication process. This means getting down to the specifics on the combination of touchpoints and the media to use for each

Case History 9.4

Automatic recommendation systems

Social networks lay the groundwork for a special kind of seeding strategy, automatic recommendation systems, which have proliferated in a wide range of creative industries. Amazon has pioneered these platforms, and made them a pillar of customer relations. Basically, a list of recommended products is sent to potential consumers who share characteristics with those who have purchased the same items in the past ('customers who bought this book also bought ...' 'travelers who went to this destination also visited ...').

Automatic systems are based on networks with nodes that are made up not only of actors, but also products, and function on the principle of *structural equivalence*. This reveals similarities in the ties between nodes: if two consumers have purchased several identical products (that is, they have similar ties) the system automatically tracks their transactions and messages both as to which ones are missing (items purchased by one and not the other). Likewise, if a consumer purchased certain products in the past, the system automatically informs her of new products with similar features.

The basic assumption with these platforms is that consumers with similar purchase patterns share the same preferences, which are relatively stable over time. Following this line of reasoning, if some people have made certain purchases but not others, it's because they're lacking the relevant information. So the system automatically fills this information gap.

one.[9] For instance: at the first level, the organization might opt to use radio ads, posters, a viral campaign on social media and events; next, it needs to select specific radio stations, types of posters and events, and ways to engage consumers on the web.

To make effective and efficient choices in this stage, the organization needs to leverage select indicators. As for *effectiveness*, the most common parameters are reach, frequency, and GRP (if possible), described in Chapter 5. *Efficiency* for traditional media is usually measured in *cost per mille* (CPM) calculated as follows:

$$CPM = \frac{cost\ of\ medium}{number\ of\ contacts} X\ 1000$$

Number of contacts (or exposures) refers to the maximum attainable by the medium. A similar indicator is *cost per rating point* (CPRP), obtained with the same formula but substituting rating points of the GRP formula (reach x frequency) for the number of contacts. With online advertising, however, the parameter is *cost per impression* (CPI), where *impression* refers to exposure to any form of advertising on a webpage (a banner, pop up, or other).

So the choice of touchpoints is *contingent on the objectives and budget of the single communication campaign*. If the aim is to reach the broadest possible audience, the best way to do so is with combinations that maximize overall GRP while respecting budget constraints. If instead the target is a limited audience, then direct touchpoints (the sales network, direct marketing) or media with less extensive reach are more appropriate.

With regard to *scheduling*, this also depends on the specific objectives of the organization. Is the campaign meant to support a new product launch? If so it should be done beforehand. Is the point to provide information on a promotion? This should take place at the same time. Generally speaking, scheduling is a function of the intensity of the impact the organization wants to make on the target audience.

And speaking of intensity, a distinction can be drawn based on timing. For example, *continuous* campaigns run over an extended period of time throughout the year (usually a certain number of weeks). This kind of scheduling serves to keep the communicative pressure intense and maintain high recall among the audience. *Occasional* campaigns, on the other hand, call for channeling investments within a shorter timeframe, following one of the following patterns:

- *Bursting,* concentrating communication in one specific period, timed to correspond to the launch of a new product or the debut of a film, the reopening of an archeological site, or the kickoff of a music tour.
- *Flighting,* focusing on a number of time periods, with gaps in between, an approach a theater might adopt for the launch of the new season, followed by communication on each individual show.
- *Pulsing,* a combination of continuous and flighting, typical of high-pressure sectors such as fashion, jewelry, and luxury goods in general.

9.6.5   Measuring the effects of communication

A vital stage in effective and efficient communication management is measuring its effects. This can only be done using pre-established objectives as the measuring stick. In other words, to ascertain effectiveness means to verify the extent to which objectives have been achieved; efficiency, on the other hand, equates to how productively resources have been used.

There are different perspectives that can be taken when measuring the effects of communication in terms of the timing (before or after the activation of touchpoints) and level of assessment (the touchpoints themselves, or the content, whether it's about the organization, product, or brand).

9.6.5.1   *Pre-activation measurements*

This is highly recommended for expensive touchpoints, to test creative choices before they are enacted to avoid mistakes that would be hard to correct. The marketing research methods used in these cases may be qualitative, typically focus groups (described in Section 6.4.4) or quantitative: surveys (Section 6.5.4) and experiments (Section 6.5.6).

The two most common assessments have to do with the concept and the content. The first is called a *concept test* (not to be confused with the product concept test described in Section 8.1.4.2.1). The aim here is to verify three factors: that the communication idea to be articulated via various touchpoints actually conveys the organization's messages; that this idea is understandable and enjoyable to the potential target audience; and that it's perceived as being consistent with the organization's image, products, and brands.

Obviously the concept pertains to the specific touchpoint in question. With owned stores, this would be format and atmosphere; for an event, the design; for an ad campaign, the creative idea. For instance, with a romantic movie that talks about love, betrayal, and family relationships, an organization could measure whether it's more effective to focus the ad campaign on only one of these themes or to try to communicate them all.

With touchpoints that deliver text (ads, promotions, emails, and so forth), the audience can be given the message directly. This is what's called a *copy test*, measuring comprehension, enjoyment, and the consistency of the message with the organization/product/brand, specifically in terms of linguistic, visual and graphic codes.

9.6.5.2   Post-activation measurements

The method for evaluating the after-effects of activation depends on the specific touchpoint and the relative objectives. Generally, a distinction can be drawn between measuring touchpoints directly and measuring the relationships between the touchpoint and the organization, its products, or its brands. The usual procedure involves quantitative research using a survey to verify the impact of touchpoints on cognitions, affects, or behaviors of the target audience (Section 9.6.2).

Measuring touchpoints directly means assessing *visibility/awareness* (cognitions), the *attitude* of the target audience, the *image* they have of the touchpoint in question (affects), and *how/how often* they use the touchpoint (behaviors). The focus of this assessment can be a specific advertising campaign, an event, a sponsored property, the network of owned stores, or the sales staff.

For example, with banners or pop ups on the web, analysts can measure *impressions* (how many times users see them based on how many hits the host webpage gets) or the *click-through rate* (how many people clicked on a banner, opened a video link, and so forth). As for advertising on traditional media, marketeers can measure visibility (readership for a newspaper; viewership for a TV series, and so forth); for stores the indicator might be awareness (the number of people who know about the store, and what exactly they know), store image, and visit frequency.

Measurements on the impact of touchpoints (both taken singly and jointly) have to do with their *contribution to reaching the organization's value delivery objectives*. The kind of measurement will therefore vary depending on whether these objectives take a more cognitive, affective, or behavioral slant.

For objectives relating to *cognition*, the two most important are awareness (Section 8.2) and inclusion of the organization and its products/brands in customers' evoked sets (Section 4.4.1.2). For awareness, the indicators are *recognition*, *recall*, and *top of mind*. The first of these refers to the ability of respondents to recognize the names of organizations/products/brands and their logos/distinguishing symbols; the second is the ability to remember them without being prompted. Top of mind, finally, equates to a list of the first names that respondents spontaneously mention: for example the top five European museums of contemporary art, or theaters in the city, or apparel brands, and so on.

With regard to level of awareness, from lowest to highest there's recognition, recall, and finally top of mind. By comparing prompted and unprompted responses (recognition and recall, respectively) an even clearer picture emerges of just how solid respondents' knowledge is.

Top of mind also indicates where the organization/product/brand fits into a consumer's evoked set. Since people often remember names of famous companies or brands without necessarily being customers of them or even having any prior experience with their touchpoints, when measuring top of mind analysts usually add direct questions like: 'What organizations/products/brands come to mind when you consider buying product X?' For example, 'Which destinations come to mind when you consider going on summer holiday?'

Regarding objectives relating to *affects*, here touchpoints help build, reinforce, or modify the image of the organization, its products, or its brands (Section 8.2). Once again, to verify this impact the organization needs to have a base measure of how its image is perceived in the minds of consumers before touchpoints come into play. So to find out if a store remodel has enhanced a company's image, if there are no before and after measurements to compare, it would be difficult to detect any change, much less ascribe this change to the store's new look alone.

As for objectives centering on *behaviors*, what to measure depends on what behaviors the company is trying to encourage in different stages:

- *Pre-consumption*: visits to the organization's website or mini-sites, information searches via major search engines, posts and recommendations about the organization on blogs or social platforms, store visits, requests made to call centers.

- *Purchase experience*: either online or offline, repurchases, upping purchase quantity or frequency.
- *Post-consumption*: posts and recommendations on social networks after having used or experienced the product, positive comments shared via social platforms, participation in a community.

9.7 MANAGING DISTRIBUTION PROCESSES: MULTI-CHANNEL INTEGRATION

Decisions regarding distribution processes are often labeled *go-to-market* because they relate to methods the organization uses to get its offerings to its customers. The three decisional macro-areas relating to these processes are: channel design, retail management, and trade marketing.

9.7.1 Channel design

A distribution channel is the *set of actors that participate in the distribution process*, that is, the activities they carry out to give final customers access to products and services offered by producers. These actors are generically called *distribution or commercial intermediaries*. Channel design simply refers to *decisions regarding the architecture of the distribution channel*.

There are two dimensions of channel design. The *vertical dimension* is the number of intermediation stages between producers and end users, and the nature of the agreements that regulate them. The *horizontal dimension* instead relates to distribution formats and the number of intermediaries in each one.

9.7.1.1 The number of intermediation stages

Depending on the number of stages, there are direct or indirect channels; the latter can be short or long (Figure 9.7).

With the *direct channel* there are no intermediaries between the organization and its customers. To guarantee access to value propositions, a company or non-profit would therefore sell its offerings in owned stores, in owned buildings, or through a direct sales network or a website. On the other hand, the *indirect channel* may count a variety of intermediaries: with the *short channel*, only the *retailer* comes between the producer and its customers; with a *long channel* there are one or more *wholesalers*.

It is worth noting that in many creative industries these terms aren't used; however, this doesn't mean these actors don't exist. An art gallery is typically a retailer, just like a television channel, where artworks are sold; an auction house plays the part of both retailer when its buyers are private collectors, or wholesaler when selling to galleries; in the movie industry, film distributors act as wholesalers who in turn sell their wares to cinema chains, which serve as retailers.

When choosing whether to use a direct or indirect channel, or a combination of the two, several variables come into play, but the bottom line is the *tradeoff between market control and investments and related risks*. The distribution process, in fact, calls for the carrying out of certain activities that serve to guarantee that value is delivered to the final customer.

First of all, there are *logistics*. With physical products this means moving goods from the producer to the market, and stocking them relatively close to stores. Take Amazon, for instance. This retailer, which is 'virtual' as far as Amazon customers are concerned,

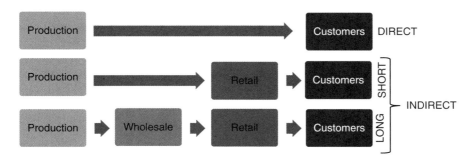

Figure 9.7 – Types of channels

actually has gigantic distribution warehouses located all over the globe. In other industries like movies or advertising, some logistics activities have disappeared because producers can deliver movies, sports, and the like straight to different links in the distribution chain in digital format.

Next come all the activities involved in creating and promoting the *assortment*, including selecting product categories and brands, and designing communication campaigns. As we saw above, the assortment is the 'product' offered by offline and online stores. To put together the proper assortment, organizations need to carefully identify the target they want to serve, and come up with strategies to stand out from the competition. As for designing communication, this we've already discussed in the previous sections.

Last of all are *additional services*, which include a vast range of activities from offering payment options such as installments, to providing logistical support for purchases (for instance, home delivery); from training on product use (guided tours for museum exhibits) to consulting on product purchases (personal shoppers in the fashion industry).

Taken together all these activities guarantee that value is delivered from producers to consumers. At this point, choosing among the different channels boils down to one question: Who does what? The answer depends on the tradeoff between control and investments.

What I mean by this is that these activities incur costs, which obviously call for investments (in warehouses, transportation, buildings, stock, interest charges, personnel, and others). Greater market control (over product and brand image, pricing, communication, and differentiation compared to alternative offerings) equates to bigger investments. Producers who can't or won't make these investments have no choice but to give up some degree of control and hand it over to intermediaries.[10]

So, for producers who want more control, the direct channel is more effective (albeit more expensive). However, if capital expenditures are an issue, a long indirect channel is more suitable. The short indirect channel is a way to mediate the tradeoff. To choose between these options, organizations have to decide the type and amount of investments they need to make, weighed against the level of control they want to secure.

Naturally, the first consideration is a *financial* evaluation based on breakeven analysis (Section 8.3.3).

Investments generate fixed costs; the higher these costs, the higher the BEP. This leads to the need to assess the potential market (Section 7.3.1) and the share of this market that the organization expects to win (Section 7.4). If the sales volumes from this share are above the BEP, the organization can afford the direct channel; if the opposite is true, the best option would be the indirect channel (short or long depending on relative investments).

An interesting example can be found in the motion picture industry. The major studios delivering their movies to the international market own their own distribution companies, which are tasked with serving both cinemas and the home video market. So they use a short indirect channel that they can afford because they churn out multi-million dollar movies every year. But independent filmmakers don't make blockbusters, so they have to rely on local distributors who in turn serve cinemas and the home video market. So they use a long indirect channel. As we already mentioned, digitalization is revolutionizing the industry, and in the future it's very likely that even small indies will be able to eliminate some intermediation stages.

When organizations compete in various markets (or segments) where they have different market shares, they'll probably adopt a mix of different channels. Direct or short channels make sense in bigger markets where market share is more substantial; long channels are the better option in smaller markets, or where penetration is low, or where direct channels are too expensive.

While financial evaluations take into account investments alone, *the degree of market control* must also be considered. There are undeniable advantages to having a direct presence on a market: producers can be certain that they're the ones to decide on retail price, product presentation, and communication. So essentially the positioning of the value proposition is conveyed to customers intact, as intended.

Moreover, in some circumstances, the producer might not be looking for exceptional financial results, or may even be willing to take a loss on certain products in exchange for total control over the market position. This is often the justification for setting up owned stores where offerings are presented, priced, and marketed as originally intended. Here flagship stores come into play (Section 9.4.4). But for producers who find physical owned stores beyond their budget, going virtual is always an option, and almost all organizations can afford a website.

9.7.1.2 The level of contractual integration

Two scenarios seem to emerge from the discussion above. Either producers guarantee access to their offerings via owned touchpoints, or they turn to independent intermediaries and set up distribution contracts. But there's also a third possibility that comes somewhere in between, where the tradeoff between control and investment risk is regulated with special contracts.

One such option is *franchising*, already outlined in Section 9.4.4. With this arrangement, the producer grants the exclusive to its distributors, who must follow its directives but without becoming subsidiaries. A very similar format is *exclusive distribution*, which is common in creative industries like fashion, design, music, publishing, and tourism. In this case (quite common when marketing products in international markets) the producer also draws up a contract with individual national distributors offering an exclusive (that is, promising to utilize no other distributors) on its products for a specific market. An exclusive distribution agreement usually involves wholesalers, so it's up to the distributor to choose which retailers will sell the products. Although contract clauses can vary considerably, producers have less control than with franchising.

9.7.1.3 Selecting distribution formats

The distribution format is the *combination of the assortment and additional services offered by an offline or online store*. (For a description of the main formats, see Sections 9.3.4 and 9.4.4.)

Depending on the type of channel (direct or indirect) the decision here is which format to distribute *with* or *in*. Clearly, for an organization that operates in a single creative industry and wants to open an owned store (online or offline), a specialized format is the logical choice because the assortment falls into the specific product categories of the sector. If, however, independent intermediaries will be part of the distribution network, decisions need to be made as to which formats are best suited for distributing specific products and brands.

However, as we've seen in Section 1.3.4, the boundaries between many creative industries are becoming blurred. As a result, many organizations are expanding the assortment they sell in owned stores to encompass related categories in addition to their own products, or to broaden the services they offer to complement

their assortment. Museums now have shops that offer a plethora of products from a variety of creative industries; theaters have restaurants and cafes; historical sites and nature reserves offer accommodation: all these are examples of organizations that are innovating their distribution formats to stand out from the competition and to provide their customers with a more satisfying experience.

In any case, to select the best distribution format, organizations need to make the same considerations as they did when choosing the channel. The place to start is with the financial aspects regarding investments and costs we discussed above, but not to be neglected are assessments of the positioning of the value proposition (Section 7.10).

The factors that most influence the choice of distribution format are the *target customers* the organization wants to serve and the *image* it wants to project to that target. As we can easily image, expert engaged customers who plan their purchases (Chapters 3 and 4) would prefer a specialized format, be it online or offline, where they can find an extremely deep assortment of the product categories they're looking for. On the opposite end of the spectrum, instead, customers who are less involved, less expert and who don't plan their purchases will probably prefer general merchandise formats because for them accessibility takes priority over more hedonic benefits. When they go to do their shopping, they buy the organization's products along with other product categories. Obviously these scenarios represent two endpoints on a continuum, and customer profiling of various market segments (Section 7.7.3) will guide the organization toward an effective choice of format.

The next consideration has to do with image. When we described how brand image is built (Section 8.2.2.2) we emphasized that this process consists of primary and secondary associations. Within the latter class there are also associations that tie into channels and distribution formats. Let's take an extreme example from the fashion industry. When apparel is sold in a high-class boutique, a concept store, or a corner in a department store, the impact on image is completely different from clothing offered for sale in a hypermarket or a local open-air market.

The associations that constitute the image of individual stores and brands of distributors are therefore transferred to all the products they sell. This can reinforce or damage the image of the organization, depending on whether the store image is in tune with the organization's products or not. On the other hand, an organization aspiring to enhance its image could seek out higher-end distributors, and convince them to carry its offering in their assortment as well.

9.7.1.4 *Selecting the number of intermediaries*

Another typical decision on the horizontal dimension of channel design pertains to the number of stores per type of distribution format, in other words, the *extensiveness* of distribution channels.

Broadly speaking, there are two distribution strategies at this level – *intensive* or *selective*. The first encompasses as many stores as possible, while the second, as the name suggests, involves only those intermediaries that meet specific criteria. Intensive distribution goes hand in hand with a mass marketing approach, while selective distribution is more consistent with a strategy focusing on a single segment or very few (Section 7.8.2).

The basic difference lies in the fact that with intensive distribution, the producer accepts all the distributors who want to sell its products and brands into the distribution network. (Clearly there are minimal entry requirements.) Instead, with selective distribution, distributors have to 'make the grade'. In other words, the producer would consider factors such as the store image and the typical clientele, store locations and assortments, financial solidity, and competence in offering certain services. In the movie industry, for instance, a major studio would distribute via multiplex cinemas, while independent filmmakers would normally resort to independent cinemas or small arthouse cinema chains.

9.7.1.5 *Channel architecture and lifecycles*

From the discussion above, what clearly emerges is that organizations far more often make decisions regarding the horizontal dimension than they do the vertical. In fact, the latter represents strategic channel decisions and calls for sizeable investments and risks. As for the horizontal dimension, relevant choices basically center on how to operationalize prior decisions. Choices about channel architecture are connected to the stages in the lifecycle of the organization, its products, and its brands. A new or recently founded company or non-profit wouldn't likely be big enough to invest in direct channels, so it would have to resort to vetted intermediaries or operate exclusively through its website. The same applies with an established business aiming to break into a new market.

By the same token, it's equally probable that once the organization has grown, it may decide to condense the length of its distribution channel, or even set up a direct offline channel (Case History 9.5). Another possible scenario is that the organization may be ready to multiply the variety of distribution formats or the number of intermediaries.

The same can be said for products and brands. In the initial lifecycle stage, only a few intermediaries would be willing to incorporate a 'new entry' into their assortment, because they see risk associated with innovation. As sales start to take off, the organization will gradually try to boost the number of intermediaries and formats (always with an eye to market image).

9.7.2 Retail management[11]

The management activities involved if an organization opts to open stores of its own are entirely different from production activities. So this strategy doesn't simply impact market control and investments; the scope of action changes as well. First, the organization

---

Case History 9.5

Zara: a store-centric company

Zara is one of the world's most popular fashion retailing brands. The chain, owned by a Spanish group called Inditex, has created a new category within the broader market of fashion: fast fashion. Products are inspired by high fashion and prêt-a-porter designs presented on the catwalks during major industry events, but they're are manufactured and distributed very rapidly and sold at prices that are accessible to the mass market.

Zara owns more than 1,800 stores the world over, each designed with an eye to aesthetic quality as well as customer comfort. Stores are located at hot spots in urban centers, for reasons of image and traffic. The main competitive advantage of Zara is its exceptional efficiency in managing the entire logistic chain. The heart of the logistic system is in Galicia, the region in

Spain where the company is headquartered. Here is the central warehouse through which all merchandise moves, whatever the production site and final destination (Ton et al., 2010).

The store plays a key role in this system. Direct control over the entire retail network translates into real time sales data that shows what's moving quickly and what's not. So Zara can recall items that aren't selling in a certain area, have them sent back to the central warehouse, and then reship them to other markets where rotation is higher. Stores are replenished twice a week, which means there's no need for a large stock. (Shipping takes 24 hours from Galicia to European stores, and 40 hours to the rest of the world.) Thanks to extensive data collection (from every store in every country) designers can also see which garments and styles are most popular in different markets, and create new collections and products that are guaranteed hits. In fact, Zara's failure rate on new products is 1 per cent, versus 10 per cent for the fashion industry in general (Ghemawat and Nueno, 2006).

Compared to the competition, Zara has extremely short production cycles, thanks to its ultra-efficient manufacturing-logistic system: four to five weeks from designer to customer for completely new styles; two for new versions of current products. This also means that Zara's creative team can start work on new collections much later than their competitors, exploiting information on the prêt-a-porter lines that received the most applause at the fashion shows. Last of all, garments are produced in relatively small lots, and the trendier pieces are manufactured internally. This allows Zara to realize an incredible number of items, creating the impression that there's always something new in the stores, which in turn keeps in-store traffic intense.

is now competing with other distributors, not producers; second, managing a store in a sustainable way, from a financial and productive standpoint, calls for entirely different methods compared to production.

Retail management involves making decisions about the product (assortment), price, and communication just like any other distributor would. In light of the aims of this chapter, here I'll focus only on some of these decisions relating to handling customer relations within the value delivery process.[12]

In Section 4.4.2 we saw that that the store represents an essential element in the consumer experience because it's the place where most of the shopping experience unfolds. The *servicescape* (Bitner, 1992) is made up of the set of stimuli triggered by the external and internal design of the store, the layout of the space and the displays, distinguishing symbols, in-store communication, and obviously the product assortment, complementary services, and the interaction with sales personnel. In other words, these are all the elements that, taken together, create the atmosphere that encourages the consumer to go in, to spend time, and to make purchases in the store (and even go back again).

Let's say an organization has picked the right products for its target, set prices aligned with value expectations, and designed effective communication outside the store. Shouldn't all this be enough to satisfy customer expectations? Or are there other decisions to be made? Well, now let's imagine a customer walking into the store, and ask ourselves: What would stop her from leaving without buying the products she was meaning to buy (beyond completely random circumstances)? What would stop her from buying other items that may have caught her eye while browsing in the store?

There are two possible answers: she's found the products she was shopping for, but when she took a closer look she realized they weren't really what she needed, or she didn't find them at all. So beyond decisions on assortment, prices, communication, and all things that create a pleasant in-store atmosphere, the remaining decisions have to do with drawing the consumer's attention to products and encouraging her to evaluate them.

Chandon et al. (2009) suggest a sequence of mechanisms that influence the attention and evaluation of the consumer in the store. Consumer *attention* basically refers to noticing products and looking them over. The *evaluation* process, on the other hand, is about remembering the product (if the consumer already has relevant information, as discussed in Section 4.3.3), and considering it when making a choice or a purchase.

There's no doubt that some variables impacting these processes are not within the power of the store owner, such as the consumer's characteristics (her involvement, past experience, and all the personal traits analyzed in Section 4.2.1) and competitors' actions. But other variables can be controlled, typically the management of exhibition space in terms of quality and quantity.

Although people are used to thinking about space in terms of size or quantity, a basic tenet in store management is the *quality* of the space, meaning its *capacity to foster customer interaction with products*. An example that readily comes to mind is that customers interact much more, both visually and physically, with items placed near the store entrance as compared to products in the back of the store. So the quality of an exhibition space is primarily determined by its position within the store. Depending on the path that the consumers would freely follow in the store, some areas are more prominent than others, capturing attention and prompting product evaluation by customers.

Yet beyond the horizontal dimension, which ties into how customers move around in the store, quality also has a vertical dimension. Products placed on the highest or lowest shelves or displays naturally attract less attention. In the world of grocery retail, this handy classification is used (Zaghi, 2013):

- *Ground level*, where consumers need to bend down to reach products.
- *Hand level*, where accessibility is optimal.
- *Eye level*, where customer attention is at a maximum.
- *Hat level*, where customers have to reach up, requiring the same effort as reaching products at ground level.

The *quantity* of this space also affects customer attention and evaluation. In fact, there's a minimum and maximum threshold of effectiveness. Below the minimum, the product display wouldn't enhance the visual impact of product spacing (for instance, a book placed on a shelf with dozens of others, as opposed to dozens of copies of the same book in a stack or lined up on a shelf). On the other hand, more space doesn't necessary translate into more attention, and excess space may actually divert attention from products.

The factors described above come into play when designing the allocation of space for the products in the assortment or for complementary services on offer. To draw attention to less prominent display areas, stores can use POP (Point of Purchase) materials: signage on products or displays, special displays, totems, even *corners* dedicated exclusively to a product/brand or line (often called *shop in shops*).

Our entire discussion so far has centered on producer-owned stores. But much of what we've said also applies to stores owned by other distributors. The difference is that in the first case, the producer has total control over the retail space and how it's managed;

in the second it has none. That means that relevant activities revolve around motivating and influencing distribution partners within the broader framework of trade marketing.

9.7.3 Trade marketing: managing relations with intermediaries

When an organization relies on a network of independent distributors to give target customers access to its offerings, managing the relationships with these partners becomes critically important to guaranteeing that the value delivery process is effective and efficient.

For a producer, distribution partners are customers in every sense of the word. As such the same considerations apply that we've discussed in the previous chapters. The organization needs to segment and select its distributors, identify their perceptions and expectations to ensure they're satisfied, and decide which value propositions to offer them. This in turn determines the marketing decisions and activities to carry out for these special kinds of customers. All this takes the name *trade marketing*.

It might seem pointless to build a specific strategy for intermediaries – after all, distributors should be interesting and willing to distribute products. But that isn't how it works. Distribution partners are companies like any others. They compete on the market, striving to stand out among the competition, and establish their own marketing strategies and activities. And their product is essentially their assortment.

So an organization can't assume that its products and brands are considered by definition consistent with the positioning that a potential distribution partner wants to establish for its value propositions. What often happens is that the distributor doesn't see this consistency in the positioning designed by the producer, but agrees to take on the products anyway. So after incorporating them into the assortment, the distributor modifies the positioning in the simplest possible way: by changing the price set by the producer.

What follows is that the producer, who can't control these intermediaries, has no other option but to try to influence them. In fact, the ultimate aim of trade marketing decisions is to reconcile the objectives of the producer and the distributor, in order to ensure that the value delivered to customers is what was originally intended when the value proposition was created.

An essential aspect to take into account is that a distributor has financial objectives ultimately related to the profitability of its assortment. The potential conflict with the producer, instead, lies in the fact that the latter adopts a portfolio approach, that is, the focus of its decisions is its products and brands, each of which has a role within the portfolio. On the other hand, the focus of distributors is their assortment (in other words, they use an assortment approach), in which those products and brands represent only a small (and often minimal) part.

So the producer must have thorough knowledge of *listing decisions* made by individual distributors, that is, the criteria and the methods they use for selecting products/brands to include in their assortments. Generally speaking, a distributor lists a product when its contribution to the general profitability of the assortment can be ascertained. This means that the producer has to anticipate any possible impacts that the product might have on revenues as well as costs for the distributor.

It would be a mistake to think that a product impacts revenues alone. In fact, when taking on a new product, a distributor faces *costs* that go beyond the purchase price. First there are *logistic* costs: the new product needs to be coded and priced, and inserted into the distributor's information system to make it trackable in stores and warehouses; there is product handling, which varies based on the product's size and weight, may require ad hoc procedures; and international shipping may also be a factor if the distributor handles delivery to foreign customers.

Then there are *product management* costs linked to product specificities: perishability (not only from a physical standpoint, but a market perspective as well, especially in creative industries where product lifecycles are often brief); security and insurance (for instance with artwork displayed in galleries); and promotion and communication (if the product doesn't live up to sales forecasts).

Last, there are *competitive* costs. These mainly refer to opportunity costs (Section 3.1.6.3), that is, lost revenues and margins when a new product substitutes or cannibalizes other products already present in the assortment. There are also potential costs inherent in the risk that customers don't see the product or brand as consistent with the store image or the distributor brand.

As for *revenues*, these too are initially only forecasts, seeing as there is no way to be certain how well the product will be accepted by customers. This uncertainty is seen by the distributor as a risk, and if it's considered excessive, the product won't get listed. As a rule, distributors insert a product/brand in their assortment only when they believe it can make a positive contribution to the overall profitability (greater than other product/brand options). But clearly financial assessments aren't the only ones distributors make. They also consider the contribution of products/brands to their image and to their stores. Yet even if this is positive, it's fairly unlikely that a distributor would keep a product/brand for very long if it didn't contribute to profit margins.

Turning back to the producer's perspective, the aim of trade marketing activities is to guarantee listing (that is, sell in), and to ensure that distributors support and promote its products/brands (sell out). So for a producer, the point of trade marketing activities is to convince distributors that its products have sales potential and can contribute to the profitability of the assortment.

Trade marketing activities include logistics to minimize the impact of products on relative costs for the distributor (scheduling deliveries as requested, designing easily transportable packaging and so forth), activities to support sales (such as promotional perks in cash or joint promotional initiatives), or even sales promotions directly targeting the distributor with various mechanisms, as outlined in Sections 8.3.6.3 and 9.3.3.

The intensity of trade marketing activities depends on several factors relating to the specificities of both the market and the organization. There are two that warrant special attention in light of their relevance for creative industries: power relationships and focus on marketing activities.

Power relationships in a distribution partnership refer to the capacity of one party to shape the decisions and activities of the other. If the relationship is balanced, there's reciprocal influence and continual give and take during negotiations. If there is an imbalance, the party with more power will obtain more favorable conditions.

Clearly in some situations power is skewed toward the producer. Examples that immediately come to mind are movie studios that produce blockbusters, or publishers of bestsellers, or producers of Broadway hits. Other items on this list might include luxury brands in fashion and design, or so-called 'starchitects'. In other circumstances, distributors have the upper hand, as is the case with Amazon in books and Apple/iTunes for music. Obviously the more power a producer has, the less it will need to invest in trade marketing and vice versa.

The *focus of marketing activities* consists of either push or pull strategies. *Push strategies* are actions that center on the distribution network, 'pushing' products along the channel to the final customer. *Pull strategies*, on the other hand, revolve around final customers who, thanks to marketing activities, are prompted to ask for products, 'pulling' them through the channel.

Normally, the more the organization leans toward push strategies, the more relevant trade marketing activities are; when pull strategies are preferred, consumer marketing activities move to center stage. Clearly, with the hyper-competition in today's markets, where retailers have taken on enormous power, producers infrequently make a clear choice of one approach over the other, and organizations that can afford an exclusively pull strategy are rare. A far more common practice is to adopt a mix, striking a balance between push and pull depending on the circumstances and the power relationships in play.

By the same token, it's also very likely that a number of small producers that populate many creative industries can't afford the investments needed to reach their final consumers. So they have no choice but to rely entirely on push strategies, with the medium- to long-term objective of achieving the scale that would make it possible to re-balance power relationships.

9.8   MULTI-MEDIA AND MULTI-CHANNEL INTEGRATION

As I've underscored in the introductory section of this chapter, the birth of a digital world has revolutionized both communication media and distribution channels, blurring the lines between the two. This has had a tremendous impact on how organizations manage communication and distribution processes. Proof can be easily found in the changes in the ways media are used (Section 9.1). These changes are triggered by the proliferation of touchpoints between organizations and customers, the loss of control of organizations over the way customers use media, and the growing number of opportunities for customers to create content themselves, to the point where this activity is becoming routine.

The consolidated model for managing (primarily paid) touchpoints, which has dominated market systems since the 1950s, is based on one simple rule: organizations pay to have control over communication and distribution flows. But as we've seen, this model is gradually losing its effectiveness and efficiency. The explanation is that earned touchpoints are relatively more effective than traditional advertising, and today digital channels make it possible to reach countless consumers at very little cost. So which model should an organization adopt?

The key to designing effective and efficient communication and distribution processes is *multi-media and multi-channel integration*. Chapters 3 and 4 investigated the cycle of consumer experience, outlining the different stages and possible touchpoints that allow access to the organization: advertising, products, sponsorships, personnel, website, stores, and so on.

Managing distribution and communication processes impacts all stages of the consumption experience. To ensure that value delivery happens effectively and efficiently, the relationship between the organization and its customers has to be seamless. In other words, there can be no variation in customers' perception of the quality and intensity of the experience, regardless of the stage of the experience or the touchpoint that provided access to the organization's products and brands. A company's website might be elegant, innovative, and interactive, but would it be seamless in combination with offline stores that are traditional, nondescript, and staffed with unprofessional shop assistants? Would it be seamless if call centers and stores provided contradictory product information, and worse still the product experience doesn't bear out either one?

Such a scenario would leave customers' expectations unfulfilled, diminishing their faith in the organization to keeps its promises, and ultimately creating dissatisfaction toward the relationship in general. In order to create a satisfying experience in all its stages, the key is to use communication and distribution channels that are integrated synchronically and diachronically. *Synchronic integration* means that in every stage of the consumer experience, the different touchpoints are used in a synergetic fashion to convey unequivocal messages that are self-reinforcing; *diachronic integration* means that these synergies are realized consistently during all stages in the experience. Figure 9.8 represents the two types of integration.

Let's look at an example. Imagine that an organization is planning a new product launch. The first objective of the communication process is to create awareness, so that the product is incorporated in the evoked set of the target customers. The organization plans an advertising campaign via traditional mass media (paid), designs a mini-site within its website dedicated to the new product (owned), and prepares an event to introduce the sales staff to the new product (owned) so they will be well-equipped to present it to distributors.

At the same time, the organization sets goals as far as behavioral goals. To facilitate acceptance on the market, in fact, it sets up a web couponing initiative (paid) and a viral campaign built on a series of videos that will circulate on social media (earned), to encourage consumers to access the mini-site to download coupons and 'share' these videos with their contacts.

So thanks to integrated management of a series of touchpoints, the organization intercepts customers during the pre-consumption stage of their experience. Additional touchpoints include POP material

for product displays (paid) reflected on the product label (owned) to capture consumers' attention and prompt them to include the product in their purchases. Integration of these touchpoints happens both within each stage of the purchase experience (synchronically) and with respect to the previous stage (diachronically).

To sum up, an organization that wants to achieve integrated management of its communication and distribution channels must first draw up an accurate map of the potential touchpoints that give its customers access to its value propositions during various stages of their experience. The next step is to design and transmit content, not only avoiding contradictory or conflicting messages, but ensuring that they are synergetic and reciprocally reinforcing to guarantee value delivery that is consistent with the organization's intentions.

9.9 CONCLUSIONS

In this chapter, we've explored the third process of managing value for the customer: value delivery. This process, as I've tried to demonstrate, is becoming more and more complex due to the evolution of distribution channels and communication media. As a result media are turning into tools not only for value delivery, but actual value generation,

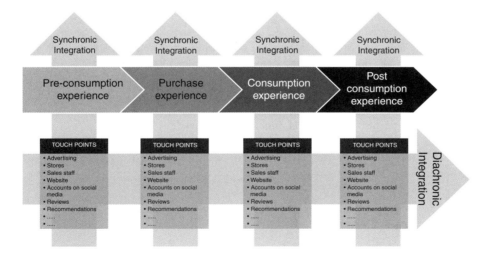

Figure 9.8 – Multi-channel and multi-media integration during the stages of customer experience

complementing the creation and positioning of value propositions.

Keeping this in mind, I've concentrated on the specificities of managing value from the viewpoint of producers of creative products. Today these organizations find themselves contending with a digital environment that offers myriad possible ways to secure customer access to their value propositions. But this new reality brings with it a higher risk that growing complexity translates into a loss of value in the delivery process, or, equally dangerous, into the appropriation of value by other actors in the production and distribution network.

The key word in this chapter is integration. The value delivery process, which involves what's normally called distribution and communication channels, requires synchronic and diachronic integration of all the touchpoints that a company or non-profit can have with its customers. This is the only way to guarantee the maximum process effectiveness and efficiency.

But the evolution of the system of channels and media, along with this need for integration, brings up once again the real issue in managing a multi-channel and multi-media environment: the search for a *balance between control and connectivity*. Clearly, the era of complete control is long gone. In fact, organizations now realize that they've lost some degree of control definitively, due to the increased power of other actors, customers above all.

But this loss is compensated by an opportunity that until recently didn't exist: the chance to leverage the enhanced connections among actors in the system to generate and transfer value in a whole new way. Taking advantage of connectivity also necessitates learning to manage the uncertainties that come with losing control. And this, within the context of communication and distribution, is becoming increasingly complex.

So the strategic considerations to make when setting up a system of touchpoints, designing channel architecture, and selecting communication media are contingent on how much control the organization is willing to give up to take advantage of potential connectivity. This evaluation calls for a change of culture, especially for managers and marketeers who grew up in a time when connectivity didn't exist, and control was fairly easy to attain.

This chapter is also the last one in which we adopt what we might consider a 'static' vision of the processes of managing value for the customer. In the next chapter we'll take on a dynamic perspective. In fact, most of what we've discussed in the previous chapters assumes that customers have no past relationship with the organization. Although we've addressed the influence of consumers' experience in the process of interacting with the companies and non-profits who supply the products they use, we haven't yet addressed how customer relations management should change over time. This is the topic of the next chapter.

REVIEW QUESTIONS

- What are the main environmental transformations that are shaping the media and channel environment?
- What are the differences between paid, owned, and earned touchpoints? How should they be selected by an organization?
- Which are the typical decisions to be taken when designing a communication campaign? How do they differ across paid, owned and earned media?
- How should an organization choose among the various channels of distribution? What are the main decisions related to designing and managing channel architecture?
- What are the complementarities between synchronic and diachronic integration? How should they be managed?

CASE STUDY

PICCOLO TEATRO DI MILANO: INTEGRATED MARKETING COMMUNICATION STRATEGIES FOR PRODUCT PROMOTION

This case was co-authored with Lanfranco Licauli, Director of Marketing and Communication of Piccolo Teatro

The Piccolo, as it's commonly called, was founded in 1947, making it the oldest permanent art theater in Italy – not to mention the most famous both nationally and internationally. The idea that inspired the theater's founders (director Giorgio Strehler and theatrical impresario Paolo Grassi, among others) was to create a municipal theater (financed primarily by city and state subsidies) that offered cultural excellence accessible to the widest possible audience. The Piccolo's slogan says it best: 'Art Theater for All.'

In 1998, the torch passed to Sergio Escobar and Luca Ronconi (serving as Director and Artistic Director respectively), underscoring the theater's international and interdisciplinary character, and spotlighting the Piccolo as the ideal cultural hub not only for Milan but for all of Europe.

Today the Piccolo has three venues: the original theater (488 seats), renamed *Piccolo Teatro Grassi*; an experimental space called *Piccolo Teatro Studio Melato* (368 seats), which also houses a theater school (opened in 1986 by Giorgio Strehler and currently under the direction of Luca Ronconi); and the main stage, the 968-seat *Piccolo Teatro Strehler*, which opened in January 1998. During its 65-year history, the Piccolo has staged more than 300 performances, which today include drama and dance, film events and festivals, round tables, and cultural forums and debates.

The Piccolo's distinctive positioning

From the very start, the Piccolo has always had a reputation for an international vocation and a focus on education. The Piccolo pursues its *international vocation* by organizing tours all over the world for its productions, and staging productions that are written and performed by foreign theater companies. In 1991 the Piccolo also became a Theater of Europe as a member of the UTE (Union of Theaters of Europe), an association founded by Giorgio Strehler and Jack Lang (former French Minister of Culture). The aim of the UTE is to promote cultural activities among European countries through a continual, collective exploration of European identity and the role of culture in forming this identity. With more than 10,000 performances and 3,000,000 spectators every year, the 20 theaters that make up the UTE offer a vast range of projects including festivals, co-productions, exhibits, workshops, symposiums, round tables, and publications.

To realize its mission to be an 'Art Theater for All' – contributing to people's well-being and growth through culture – the Piccolo's international vocation goes hand in hand with its commitment to *education*. In fact, the theater provides various educational paths to complement its theatrical offering through seminars and workshops in collaboration with (or conducted directly by) the world's leading universities and drama schools.

The theater's educational activities target a broad audience. For the general public, there are conferences and opportunities to meet artists. Through seminars and workshops, young people can get a taste of the theater, and researchers can delve more deeply into the language of the theater. Focusing on an even more specific target, both the Piccolo's theater school and masters programs co-organized with city universities are designed for people who aspire to become professional actors.

The Piccolo's communication strategy

There was a time when a theater could communicate its offering in the same way to its entire audience, but times have changed and demand for performing arts has become highly fragmented. Recognizing this new reality, the Piccolo's management team has come up with a communication strategy that is the cornerstone of a *multi-segment market strategy*.

Another major change, the digitalization of modern society, has made it very apparent that traditional touchpoints like advertising via mass media are losing their impact. This has prompted the decision to invest more persistently in touchpoints that create a direct relationship between the Piccolo and its targets (prioritizing digital media). In fact, direct participation and involvement translate into a higher number of contacts and ultimately bigger audiences.

The Piccolo's digital strategy consists of (Figure 9.9):

- A website offering a fully functional online ticketing system since 2010.
- Web TV with channels dedicated to the news, the season's shows, and interviews with the cast, as well as a YouTube channel.
- Accounts on various social media (Facebook, Twitter, and TripAdvisor).

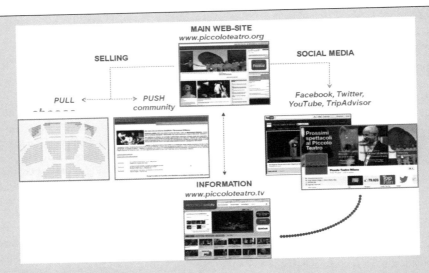

Figure 9.9 – Piccolo Teatro: The system of digital touchpoints

○ A smartphone app where users can find out what's playing, buy discounted tickets, and support the theater; this complements the already-activated digital library for iPads (*Edizioni Piccolo Teatro*).

The results to date are remarkable: 123,000 plus members of the Piccolo's community, more than 93,000 fans on Facebook, and 13,200 followers on Twitter. Tickets for individual shows are available online, but season tickets and group tickets have to be purchased through more traditional channels, by phone or from the promotions office. In the 2012–2013 season, the percentage of single tickets sold online hit a record 60 per cent of total tickets sales.

Touchpoints are combined and customized to fit the specific object of communication, whether it be the entire season, a specific event, or a single show. For the latter, the Piccolo's Marketing Department has come up with a classification system to make communication planning more efficient.

The ABCs of shows

The Piccolo categorizes each of its shows as A, B, or C, but not on the basis of aesthetic considerations or probability of success. Instead the theater's parameters are awareness, strengths, and critical areas relating to potential appeal for the public. The letter designation determines the most appropriate combination of communication channels.

A indicates what's called an *access show*, ideal for any kind of spectator, even first-time theatergoers. From this perspective, awareness of one or more elements of the show (the title, the playwright, the director, or the actors) is the essential draw for the target audience.

Normally, A shows are immediately understandable both in terms of the script and the production itself. An example from the 2012–2013 program is the *Odyssey*, based on Simon Armitage's adaptation of Homer's epic classic and staged by the American director Robert Wilson (Figure 9.10). This show was a co-production between the Piccolo and the National Theater of Athens, with the first responsible for designing the scenery, costumes, and sets, and the second providing the exceptional Greek cast who recited in the modern version of their native tongue.

The title, the original author of the epic poem, the director and the two co-producers were all elements that generated a high level of awareness and accessibility, making the *Odyssey* an exemplary A show. For this category, the communication strategy hinges on indirect communication tools (posters, ads in local papers, the theater's website) which deliver content that accentuates awareness, in this case leveraging the immediately-recognizable elements listed above.

B refers to shows that are *enriching*. With fewer elements of awareness, these productions' scripts and stages require a more discerning audience to be appreciated. An example of a B show from the 2012_2013 program is *Le retour* by Harold Pinter, directed by Luc Bondy and co-produced by the Piccolo with the Odéon-Théâtre de l'Europe of Paris, featuring an outstanding cast: Bruno Ganz, Louis Garrel, Pascal Greggory, and Emmanuelle Seigner.

Figure 9.10 – Piccolo Teatro: An example of advertising for *Odyssey*

The elements of awareness that this show could claim, such as the playwright, the title, the actors Bruno Ganz and Emmanuelle Seigner, and the co-producer Odéon-Théâtre, might be less relevant for people who are less familiar with the theater. In other words, with this and all B shows, spectators are expected to be more knowledgeable. As a result, in selecting tools for the communication campaign, the accent is on direct communication addressed to specific targets who are well-versed in performing arts, along with traditional impersonal touchpoints like advertising messages through various media. Coinciding with these actions are events offering opportunities for discussion and debate, education, and communication to identify and attract a new audience.

The final category, so-called '*research' shows*, are assigned a *C,* typically denoting even fewer elements of awareness. These are often either productions by young theater companies, or international shows in languages and theater genres that are not widely known. An example from 2012_2013 of a C show is *The Legend of White Snake* from Chinese opera theater, presented in the original language.

For a C show, communication is almost exclusively direct, with carefully identified targets, and content that highlights the characteristics that set it apart from more conventional shows. The tools used for similar campaigns include education and communication aimed at increasing knowledge and enhancing involvement of the most appropriate audience.

To highlight the differences in communications strategies for the three categories, the following sections provide a detailed comparison of two international shows: *Odyssey* and *The Legend of White Snake*. The description below also underscores how much complexity is involved in managing the international productions that the Piccolo is committed to offering.

The communication strategy for *Odyssey*

Odyssey debuted in Athens on 26 October 2012. After five months of sell-out crowds in the Greek Capital the play went on tour to Milan where it ran at the Piccolo Teatro Strehler from 3 to 24 April 2013 for a total of 21 performances. *Odyssey* was a huge hit among audiences and critics alike with 20,000 spectators and full houses nearly every night.

As with all A shows, the strengths of *Odyssey* revolved around awareness and the excellence of the title, the author, the director, and the production. Nevertheless, presenting a three-hour play in modern Greek, and filling nearly a thousand seats every night for a month is no mean feat. This explains the dual objectives of the marketing plan: to rise to the challenge of selling out all 21 performances, and to reinforce the Piccolo's image thanks to the audience success of the play.

In formulating the communication plan, the marketing team discussed strengths and weaknesses, as perceived by the potential targets of the show. The next step was to brainstorm creative ways to turn the weaknesses into points of interest and attraction.

The strengths were clearly the title, the director, and the value of the Piccolo brand. As for weaknesses, the two most obvious were the two things that were least familiar: the English poet responsible for retelling the Homeric classic, and the language of the play (modern Greek).

Marketing singled out three targets for the communication campaign, with the strengths and weaknesses above affecting each in differing degrees: regular patrons of the Piccolo, in particular season ticket holders; the 'educational' target, students of various ages with an interest in the distinctive characteristics of the show; and a 'new' audience, specifically the Greek community in Milan.

Piccolo's regulars, specifically season ticket holders, usually pay more attention to communication delivered by the theater through traditional channels (the season program magazine and presentation materials for individual shows) and the web (the site, Facebook page, and the app with the season program). The content addressed to this audience included all the elements of awareness and innovation, as well as the complementary activities designed for the other targets.

The initiative that best spotlighted the show's strengths was *Ulissi. Viaggio nelle odissee* (*Ulysseses: a voyage in odysseys*), a cycle of seven seminar-shows and 'itinerant' readings that took place from October to April 2013. The series, a veritable 'season within the season', was offered free of charge and presented in areas of Milan that had never before hosted similar events (such as the Justice Building, the Juvenile Detention Center, a pub, a local market, and others).

Some of the biggest names in contemporary theater took part in this project, accompanying the audience on a 'maiden voyage' of sorts through the city by way of readings spanning ancient and modern texts: from the *Odyssey* to Joyce; from the *Thousand and One Nights* to Plato and Aeschylus; from *Satyricon* to Karen Blixen; from the Epic of Gilgamesh to Cavafy and Seferis. The series represented a voyage within a voyage, and within the self, discovering in Homer's *Odyssey* the countless odysseys all around everyone. Some readings were also accompanied by reflections from prominent figures with a wide variety of backgrounds, all with a common commitment to civil and social activism.

The educational target was broken down into three segments: students from middle schools and high schools, students from universities and drama schools, and students from university language departments and language schools. For this target and for the Greek community, the Piccolo's marketing team designed specific communication to turn weaknesses into points of interest.

As for the first weakness, the author of the text, the aim was to transform the lack of notoriety of Simon Armitage into an opportunity to discover an outstanding English author and poet. The Piccolo's Press Office went to great lengths to generate interest in the work of Armitage among cultural commentators in the major newspapers; the outcome was an in-depth article published in a leading paper introducing the author, and reprinting an excerpt of his version of the *Odyssey*.

Likewise, the Marketing Department organized several symposiums and lessons in collaboration with various departments (Literature, Performing Arts, English Literature, and Languages) at the city's two main universities. The topic of these initiatives was the work of Armitage, in particular his retelling and subsequent translation of Homer's epic poem.

The fact that the text was written in modern Greek provided additional inspiration for special seminars for university students majoring in this language, as well as round tables held in Italian and Greek discussing current events in Greece. For high schoolers and drama school faculty and students, on the other hand, the novelty of retelling the Homeric classic represented the ideal topic of study.

The *Odyssey* also presented an opportunity to reinforce the already strong relationship between the Piccolo and the Greek community, again with the aim of transforming a limitation into an attraction. Specifically, promotional initiatives were the result of a collaboration between the theater and the Greek Consulate in Milan.

First, the Piccolo hosted the fifth annual festival of Greek culture entitled 'Milan meets Greece' from April 22 to 24, 2013. On the program were three theater-dance performances, with the participation of some cast members from the *Odyssey*. Second, a public panel discussion was organized with the actors in Greek with a simultaneous translation in Italian. This was a kind of 'immersion experience' for Italian students and residents who wanted to learn and practice Greek, as well as members of the Greek community interested in the Italian language. Beyond language learning, the event also served to promote the show.

The results of all these activities (above all the cycle *Ulissi. Viaggio nelle odissee*) could be accurately measured because all the initiatives were communicated through the website, where anyone interested in taking part in the supplementary activities was asked to make a reservation. The attendance data showed that the overall communication plan was a great success, generating around 20 per cent of the audience for the *Odyssey*.

The communication strategy for *The Legend of White Snake*

The Legend of White Snake was produced by the Jingju Theater Company of Peking; two evening shows were performed on the Piccolo's biggest stage during the 2012–2013 season. This particular theatrical genre is called 'Peking Opera', a mix of theater, music, song, and dance.

The relationship between the Piccolo and China is a longstanding one. After hosting several Peking Opera shows over the years, in 2002 the Piccolo went on tour to Peking. This initial success was followed by second tour in 2006, which in turn led to a partnership with the Shanghai Theatre Academy. The close ties with China are the driving force behind numerous fruitful relationships with Chinese institutions in Milan, which have become key contacts for the realization of initiatives offering

Figure 9.11 – Piccolo Teatro: An image from *The Legend of the White Snake*

in-depth exploration of the Chinese culture and language. The most prominent of these institutions are the General Consulate of China in Milan, the Italy–China Foundation, and the Confucius Institute of the University of Milan.

The criticalities of *The Legend of White Snake* were the theatrical genre (Peking Opera) and the language of the performance (Chinese). The Marketing Department at the Piccolo had no illusions about the challenge in communicating the exceptional value of the show, which in turn would lead to filling the Piccolo's largest venue for two performances.

As with *Odyssey*, the underlying aim of the communication plan was twofold: to highlight the show's strengths, and to turn its weaknesses into new communication opportunities. In this case, however, the weaknesses were far more substantial than the strengths.

Much like before, Marketing identified three main targets for communication: the Piccolo's regular audience, including season ticket holders; the educational target, broken down into students at university or drama schools, and language students at university or language schools (excluding high schools); and finally the Chinese community in Milan.

In analyzing its targets, Marketing began, as always, with the Piccolo's regular audience, in particular season ticket holders. Communication for them highlighted the specificities of the show, for instance excellence in the Peking Opera genre. Content was delivered via traditional media (newspapers) and digital channels. To more effectively convey the exceptional quality of the show, the title *The Legend of White Snake* was complemented with the genre *Peking Opera* (Figure 9.11).

The Piccolo also set up ad hoc activities for all the targets. An example was 'Awaiting the Peking Opera,' a seminar on Chinese theater offered in collaboration with the Confucius Institute. This initiative consisted of four sessions dedicated to an in-depth exploration of the ancient art of the Peking Opera: from the meaning of the makeup and the use of costumes, to the story of Mei Lanfang, the actor responsible for the Opera's worldwide fame. All these initiatives were held in Italian and Chinese (with two-way simultaneous interpretation), free of charge, although reservations were required.

Additional educational and language activities were organized as well, such as a workshop on Chinese theater-dance, designed with the Chinese community in mind along with anyone interested in Chinese culture. Here the communication focused on linguistic and cultural aspects.

The results of the communication plan showed that it generated around 44 per cent of the audience for *The Legend of White Snake*.

REVIEW QUESTIONS

1. The communication strategy of Piccolo Teatro mostly relies on the *ABC* classification of shows. What are the criteria used for the classification? How do shows positioned in the three classes differ?
2. What are the guidelines used to design the integrated marketing communication for shows in each class?
3. In the Piccolo's integrated marketing communication, educational activities play a very relevant role. What are the main reasons behind this choice? How is it deployed for the shows belonging to the ABC classes?

MANAGING CUSTOMER VALUE OVER TIME: CUSTOMER RELATIONSHIP MANAGEMENT

LEARNING OBJECTIVES

After reading this chapter you should be able to:

- Understand the value of organization–customer relations from the perspective of both parties.
- Distinguish the elements that denote the status of the relationship in its different stages.
- Design an effective customer relationship management process.
- Identify criteria to segment a customer base.
- Design relational activities consistent with the different stages of the relationship.

OVERVIEW

For many years the focus of Marketing centered exclusively on customer purchases. So marketeers thought their job was done when they had convinced customers to buy the organization's products or brands. It was as if underpinning the principles and recommendations of marketing was the assumption that both the customer and the organization suffered from long term memory loss. What I mean is, it was taken for granted that both sides approached each new potential contact opportunity – customers when they felt a certain need or desire again, the organization when it offered to satisfy that need or desire again – with no recollection of any previous encounters.

Of course, there was no denying that customers could leverage their prior experience in later purchase decisions, and the organization could leverage enhanced awareness due to previous contacts. But basically each new interaction was handled as a separate entity, so the prevailing perspective placed the single transaction at the heart of all decisions and activities. Marketing, on the whole, was *transactional*.

We spent most of Chapter 2 identifying the distinctive traits of contemporary marketing, with its central focus on managing customer value over time. Inherent to this view is an orientation that goes beyond the single purchase, with the focal point of decisions and activities being the relationship with the customer. So today marketing can essentially be called *relational*. This means that the work of marketeers doesn't stop with creating and delivering value propositions that satisfy customer expectations, but extends to managing customer relationships in the long run: not just a single magical encounter, but a series of satisfying encounters over time.

However, the discussions in the previous chapters give the impression that marketing still pays close attention to customers' purchase behaviors, and that the litmus test of value management processes is still the final purchase of the customers: this is proof that the organization's value propositions are aligned with their expectations. But it's also true that a purchase isn't the sum total of the possible interactions that customers can have with the organization.

Think back to the last chapter and the topics of multi-channel and multi-media environments we explored, and from there move back further to the very first chapters where I depicted an experience cycle in which the purchase is one of several stages. On reflection, what should clearly emerge is that when the focus of marketing encompasses the entire customer experience, the purchase is undeniably a key customer interaction, but certainly not the only one.

The customer-centric marketing model described in this book is a *relational* one that places customer value management processes within the broader framework of organization–customer relationships. The ultimate aim of marketing is to *establish, reinforce, grow, and maintain mutually satisfying relationships between the organization and its customers over time.*

This is the topic of the present chapter: customer relationship management (or CRM, as it's commonly called). My intention is to answer two main questions. First, what stages make up an organization's relationship with its customers? What will become clear in this chapter is that a relationship between a customer and a company or non-profit hinges on the concept of satisfaction. As highlighted in Chapters 3 and 4, it's satisfaction (how perceived value aligns with expected value) that generates the intention to repeat a purchase, and in so doing to create a flow of interactions with the organization.

As we'll see, although satisfaction is guaranteed to jumpstart a relationship, it won't necessarily provide enough energy to keep it going. In fact, the status of the relationship changes with time. A customer who feels like she has a special relationship with an organization wants to be treated in a special way, not just like any other run-of-the-mill customer. This feeling will also lead to different attitudes toward the organization, creating a particular kind of tie that might motivate her to adopt diverse behaviors, such as recommendations, support, and affiliation.

Basically, to ensure that customer relationships last, the organization has to implement specific analytical and decisional tools that help it distinguish between customers based on the status of their relationship. Then it can organize and conduct activities that demonstrate to these customers just what their status is.

This leads me to the second main question I'll try to answer: What types of analysis and decision making should be done during various stages of the customer relationship?

We'll see that CRM-related analysis and decision making don't *substitute for* – but rather *complement* – similar activities done within value creation and value delivery processes. At any point in its life (except when it's brand new), an organization has a wide range of customer relationships: some are stable and long-term, some are works in progress, some are new, and for some consumers there's no relationship at all. So at any given moment the decisions relating to value propositions have to be gauged to match the status of the organization's relationship with several different groups of customers.

Specifically, I'll focus on the more germane analysis and decisions for organizations that operate in creative industries. First off, I'll describe some useful indicators for identifying customers based on their relational status (current or prospective). This analysis is fundamental for organizations seeking to understand whether there are customers who are interested in embarking on a long-term relationship, and whether they are also interesting in light of organizational goals.

Then I'll give a detailed description of initiatives aimed at attaining specific relational objectives: to create and compensate customer loyalty (loyalty programs); to make sure customers remain loyal (retention programs); and last, to foster new relationships thanks to current customers who engage in positive word of mouth (referral programs).

Since all of these activities and decisions require investments and generate costs for the organization, before we begin to delve into these topics, it's important to highlight the motivations that prompt a company or non-profit to shift from a transactional approach to a relational one.

10.1   AT THE ROOT OF CRM: THE VIRTUOUS CIRCLE OF CUSTOMER SATISFACTION

The basic condition for the existence of a relationship is that the customer and the organization must first engage in a series of interactions. Let's imagine what it feels like for customers to make a first-time purchase from a company or a non-profit and compare that to buying from their regular source. What's the difference? For the latter, customers would probably respond by saying that they know the products well, they trust the organization, and they remember the communications it uses. But it's very likely they won't say the same for a new organization: in this case they don't 'feel' like they're in a relationship.

A relationship necessitates a certain level of mutual familiarity that grows over time. As the relationship continues, other ingredients are added, such as trust, loyalty, and engagement. So essentially, to transition from a pure transaction (a first-time purchase) to a connection that can be called a relationship, cognitive and emotional states must emerge in the two parties that make the tie special and unique compared to other less consistent connections.

But what elicits the customer's desire to establish a relationship with an organization? And conversely, what are the organization's motivations for doing the same with a customer?

10.1.1   The relationship from the customer's perspective

From the in-depth analysis of the cycle of customer experience in Chapters 3 and 4, the answer should be readily apparent. The impetus that sets in motion every relationship between a customer and an organization is satisfaction. When comparing the actual value obtained from consuming a product with the expected value, if the first exceeds the second, the customer will be motivated to make a repeat purchase and vice versa (no satisfaction, no repeat purchase).

As discussed in Section 3.2, satisfaction creates a cognitive predisposition and a positive emotional state that ties back into its source; this makes the customer want to replicate the interaction. But beyond the positive reinforcement that comes from a satisfying experience, are there any other reasons behind a customer's motivation to make a repeat purchase and establish a relationship with the producer of creative products?

Referring back to the analysis of the consumer experience, specifically the pre-consumption and purchase stages (Section 4.3.6 and 4.4), the answer should be clear. Establishing a relationship with the organization has two advantages for the customer: it simplifies the decision-making process and minimizes the risk associated with buying an experience product. In fact, satisfaction creates a positive attitude toward the product, the brand, and the organization that anchors them firmly in the customer's evoked set (Section 4.4.1.2). This in turn allows the customer to reduce the temporal and cognitive sacrifices related to searching and processing information before making a purchase (Figure 10.1).

What's more, a satisfying purchase makes the source of satisfaction (product, brand, organization) a quality clue for later purchases and uses: the customer expects to find the same quality and satisfaction when repurchasing the same product/brand as well as other products/brands from the same producer.

But it's also evident that staying in a relationship can also generate *sacrifices* for the customer. The most obvious in creative industries is the opportunity cost associated with not buying products or brands from other organizations. To illustrate, if a consumer buys a season ticket to the theater, she probably won't go to other shows in other theaters. And since variety seeking is a typical customer behavior in creative industries (Section 4.5.5), it's easy to see that customers might perceive a long-term relationship with a single organization as an obstacle preventing them from enjoying the variety of products available on the market.

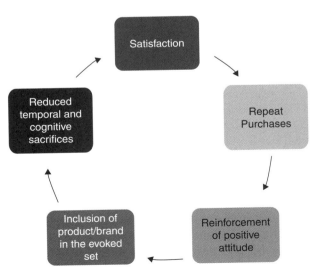

Figure 10.1 – The virtuous circle of satisfaction from the customer's viewpoint

This explains why a company or non-profit has to manage its relationships with its customers, constantly keeping the level of benefits higher than the sacrifices. This is what CRM is all about. And as we'll see, this means not only rewarding loyalty, but preventing customers from leaving the relationship entirely (Section 10.4.3.2).

10.1.2 The relationship from the organization's perspective

For the organization customer satisfaction also sets a virtuous circle in motion. This produces beneficial effects on the financial sustainability of its activities (and with for-profits, on profitability as well) because of the long-term impact of satisfaction on the two components of profit: revenues and costs.

As mentioned above, customer satisfaction triggers *repeat purchases*, which means that if an organization successfully satisfies most of its customers, it's more likely to see sales hold steady over time. This in turn makes it possible to plan activities more appropriately, allocate resources more efficiently, and ensure that these resources are more productive. For instance, a magazine that counts on a certain number of subscribers can plan the purchase of high quality (and high price) photo features well in advance, and negotiate more advantageous terms of payment as well.

As we know, satisfied customers engage in *positive word of mouth* (Section 4.5.1) and in doing so they activate a potential market (when they talk to people who aren't already customers). So satisfaction also creates potential additional revenues.

Lastly, satisfied customers *buy more products/brands from the same organization*, and have *less price elasticity* compared to new customers. As described in Chapter 8, an organization with satisfied customers becomes a quality clue in itself, generating advantages it can leverage when launching new products (Section 8.1.4) or brand extensions (Section 8.2.3.2.2).

In fact, customers who are satisfied with certain products/brands from the organization will be convinced they'll be equally satisfied with new ones. That also means they'll be less willing to accept offers from competitors, seeing that switching to a new supplier means risking dissatisfaction. As a result, customer satisfaction generates additional revenues that grow over time.

Beyond increased revenues, customer satisfaction also allows the organization to cut costs over time. In fact, as the relationship stabilizes and progresses, the organization will acquire deeper knowledge of its clientele that will make it possible to *allocate resources more efficiently* and avoid waste. For example, the magazine publisher mentioned above might design an email marketing campaign exclusively targeting loyal customers, which would have a better chance of a positive response compared to a campaign targeting a generic mailing list.

What's more, investing in getting to know customers at the outset of the relationship (to discover their preferences, perceptions, and behaviors) is a one-time effort that won't need to be repeated later on (at least not to the same extent). So the longer the relationship lasts, the more productive these investments will be over time, and *the lower the costs of the relationship* in each stage. Basically, satisfaction that generates repeat purchases also leads to lower relationship costs.

Combining the two effects (increased actual and potential revenues and decreased costs) provides an explanation for the positive effect of customer satisfaction on the profitability of a for-profit or the financial sustainability of a non-profit. Not only that, but better financial performance equates to additional resources that can be invested in improving and innovating products, touchpoints, or general promotional activities, which in turn leads to more satisfied customers.

But the benefits for the organization aren't simply financial. In fact, several studies demonstrate that customer satisfaction generates *employee satisfaction*, especially in highly professional organizations, as is the case with the vast majority of creative enterprises (Frey et al., 2013). If customers are satisfied, employees feel more appreciated for the work they do, and this motivates them to put more effort into generating ideas for new products and services, and to be more attentive to customer satisfaction. All this triggers an internal virtuous circle to complement the external one (Figure 10.2).

But for the organization, customer satisfaction can prove to be a double-edged sword. In fact, one of the criticisms most often leveled against companies that adopt a market orientation is that in the long run the rate of innovation flattens out (Christensen and Bower, 1996). On the basis of positive reinforcement that comes with satisfaction, customers tend to continually demand the same (or very similar) products.

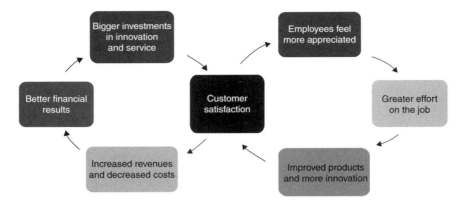

Figure 10.2 – The double virtuous circle of customer satisfaction from the organization's perspective

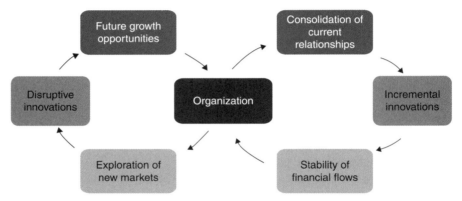

Figure 10.3 – The dual strategy of a creative organization

For example, if the founders of Cirque du Soleil had asked regular theater-goers or circus fans what new shows or acts they'd like to see, their suggestions would not have strayed far from traditional theater or circus formats. But the real innovation of Cirque du Soleil was actually to break the rules and blur the lines between one and the other.

So essentially the reinforcement mechanism would make satisfied customers more reluctant to accept *disruptive innovations* (changes that cause a discontinuity in an existing product category) and more open to *incremental innovations*, which are simply improvements on existing products. The takeaway here is that organizations that channel the bulk of their investments into consolidating relationships with current customers run the greatest risk of losing their innovative edge.

Now, with regard to creative industries, variety seeking causes a constant push for product innovation to the point at which it becomes a structural characteristic of these contexts (Chapter 1). So the warning from these findings should be taken particularly seriously in these industries.

That means the strategy of an organization that operates in a creative industry must always strike a balance between *consolidating relationships with current customers* to maintain financial stability and *exploring new markets and establishing new relationships in those markets* to activate a flow of disruptive innovations. Ideally, these innovations will open up growth opportunities for the future (Section 7.5.3) in a dual strategy of sorts, with each component fueling the other (Figure 10.3).

10.2 THE LIFECYCLE OF THE RELATIONSHIP WITH THE CUSTOMER

Customer relationship management involves calibrating value creation and delivery processes to suit the stage and the status of the relationship.[1] Like markets, products, and brands, customer relationships also evolve through an ideal lifecycle made up of several stages, each one corresponding to a set of elements that denotes the intensity, which in turn determines the relative status.

10.2.1 Introduction

As pointed out above, for a relationship to be born, the customer has to have a minimum number of interactions with an organization (or its products or brands) that elicits the feeling of having a special connection. What's more, satisfaction linked to the purchase and usage experience is a possible trigger for this relationship. So the tremendous effort the organization expends to satisfy its customers is the best guarantee that a potential relationship will transform into an actual one.

Repeated satisfaction from the first few product uses serves to demonstrate to the customer the reliability of the organization, which brings out an essential component: *trust*. Moorman et al. define trust as 'a willingness to rely on an exchange partner in whom one has confidence' (1993: 82).

Trust is essentially an *expectation of behavior* that one party in a relationship has toward the other (Castaldo, 2007), which leads them both to believe they can rely on one another. If a consumer goes on vacation to a Greek island and really enjoys herself, she'll probably want to go back to the same island as soon as she gets the chance. And if her second trip is just as satisfying, she'll expect the same whenever she goes in the future. This is a form of trust.

It's easy to imagine that the reverse is also true: an unsatisfied customer will grow to mistrust the supplier organization and in turn would not buy its products again (Research Focus 10.1).

Research on this topic (Garbarino and Johnson, 1999; Morgan and Hunt, 1994) shows that trust has several beneficial repercussions that go well beyond repurchasing. First, trust fosters a willingness to cooperate with the organization and to adopt certain behaviors: paying more attention to relevant communication, providing information when requested, giving positive feedback, participating in viral marketing initiatives, and so forth. The bottom line is that trust is one of the key

Research Focus 10.1

When the relationship with members of a museum 'stalls'

Do customers ever decide to stop purchasing from an organization even if they are satisfied? Reavey et al. (2013) tried to find an answer to this question by analyzing the motivations of people who failed to renew their membership with an art museum in the North Eastern United States.

The authors noted that many of these non-renewers weren't dissatisfied; instead they were motivated by changes in their lives or their lifestyles. Growing older or moving to another city meant more challenges involved in visiting the museum, and consequently enjoying the benefits of membership.

Unlike people driven by dissatisfaction, the non-renewers in the study continued to have a strong psychological tie to the museum and showed it: they would frequently mention the museum in conversation, they engaged in positive word of mouth, and they often remembered it; all this despite the fact they no longer visited it. Essentially the authors suggest that their relationship with the museum wasn't over, it was simply 'stalled'. In other words, since it hadn't progressed to the next stages, it hadn't been enriched with all the cognitive, emotional, and behavioral elements of a strong relationship, but manifested only a few non-behavioral aspects.

Based on their findings, Reavey et al. concluded that organizations should draw a distinction between *stalled* as opposed to *severed* relationships with members/customers. There are two valid reasons for their recommendation. First, some of the causes for the stall might pertain to factors the organization can control and possibly modify to persuade these members/customers to renew. Second, stalled customers can be encouraged to share via positive word of mouth (Section 10.4.3.3) as a way to leverage the resilient ties with the organization they still have.

ingredients for first establishing a relationship, and then growing and enriching it with additional benefits.

10.2.2   Growth

As the relationship grows, repeat purchases give rise to *loyalty* (to the product, brand, or organization as a whole). The traveler in the example above might extend her loyalty to all of Greece, and visit a different island every time she goes on vacation, making her a loyal customer to Greek tourist destinations in general.

In Section 4.5.4 we saw that merely making a repeat purchase isn't necessarily a sign of loyalty; instead it's often simply a habit. The essential difference lies in the underlying conviction that the value proposition in question better satisfies expected benefits compared to any other. Customer loyalty is the mark of a relationship enriched with trust that translates into regular repeat purchases.

At this stage in the relationship it's very likely that the customer interacts with the organization not only by buying its products, but also by taking part in various activities and events, interacting on social media, signing up for promotional initiatives, and so on. Raising the bar in the relationship in these ways is a sign of *engagement*. Vivek et al. (2012: 133) define customer engagement as 'the intensity of an individual's participation in and connection with an organization's offerings or organizational activities, which either the customer or the organization initiates.'

Engagement defines a psychological and emotional state of relational intensity between the customer and the organization. Customers who feel engaged with an organization spontaneously share their positive opinion with others, they're willing to take an active hand in co-producing value, and they're far more receptive to the organization's activities and initiatives.

As the relationship gradually evolves, its status changes, and along with greater intensity normally comes more openness to cooperate with the organization in various ways. Often this attitude leads to greater willingness to formalize the relationship through some form of *affiliation* or *membership*. Numerous cultural institutions use affiliation (Hayes and Slater, 2003; Slater, 2004), which allows customers to become partners or members. This gives them certain benefits, and in exchange they commit to cooperate in some way. Clubs are another kind of affiliation ('friends of' for example); these are smaller groups of customers that provide a variety of support

for organizational activities. Many companies use forms of affiliation that reward loyalty (as detailed in Section 10.4.3.1).

However, it would be a mistake to think that a positive relational attitude makes a customer acritical. In fact, quite the opposite is true. A consolidated relationship is based on the customer's perception of *fairness*, and every customer knows perfectly well that interaction instigated by an organization is motivated by its desire for some gain, either in revenues, or knowledge, or image. Benefits always come with sacrifices, as reiterated from the start.

But customers who feel they have a special, stable connection with an organization don't simply have a positive attitude and a willingness to cooperate; they'll also expect their comments and preferences to be recognized, respected, and appreciated. This is what the concept of fairness is all about (Oliver and Swan, 1989): the perception that there is a balance between benefits/sacrifices for the customer and costs/revenues for the organization.

If customers perceive that their positive view of the relationship (which translates into repurchases and recommendations, for instance) corresponds to an opportunistic attitude of the organization (which wants to take a lot and give a little), a feeling of unfairness will emerge, with negative repercussions on the relationship and ultimately the organization itself.

Essentially, a customer who has a consolidated relationship with an organization expects a win-win game. Both parties, in their own ways, have a share in the value generated by this relationship. For the customer, that means value propositions that meet her expectations; for the organization, financial, information, and image flows. The perception of a fair value distribution reinforces the relationship and makes it evolve.

10.2.3   Maturity

When the relationship between the customer and the organization is based on trust and the perception of fairness, and turns into loyalty and engagement, the intensity peaks and the relationship is mature and consolidated.

At this stage, the relationship is enriched with other elements. First, there's *commitment*, which Moorman et al. (1993: 316) describe as 'an enduring desire to maintain a valued relationship.' The customer commits (first to herself and then to the other party) to continue to invest in the relationship, and not to substitute it with something else.

Commitment is a strong driver of willingness to cooperate and to accept various requests from the other party in the relationship, in the conviction that doing so will benefit the relationship itself. Both theoretical and empirical studies on long-term relationships (Gruen et al., 2000; Gustafsson et al., 2005; Morgan and Hunt, 1994) show that the emergence of commitment is a powerful mechanism that pushes customers to keep up their relationship with the organization and to take part in value co-creation processes.

Beyond commitment, another key ingredient in a mature relationship for organizations that operate in creative industries is *identification* (which I already touched on in Section 4.5.6). It is defined by Bhattacharya and Sen as 'an active, selective, and volitional act motivated by the satisfaction of one or more self-definitional (i.e., "Who am I?") needs' (2003: 77).

From this the conclusion can be drawn that identification is the product of a choice made by consumers pertaining to their ties with a specific organization that they believe can contribute to their self-definition, their identify. Identification is a sign of attachment to the organization (its products and brands) that is so strong it makes the emotional and cognitive aspects of the relationship take precedence over solely commercial considerations (post-purchase satisfaction) (Case History 10.1).

When consumers identify with an organization, they tend to dedicate a great deal of time to it, above and beyond purchasing and consuming its products. Among other things they pay careful attention to communications, generating content themselves; they act as spokespeople for the organization in social conversations; and they disseminate pertinent information.

Figure 10.4 sums up the various elements that determine relationship status in various stages, highlighting the fact that all these factors are strongly related: an increase in one element triggers increases in the others as well.

Case History 10.1

Teatro Regio of Turin: a story of commitment to a city, and more

Turin's Teatro Regio opened its doors in 1740, and immediately became a protagonist on the international cultural scene of the times, in light of its size (2,500 seating capacity), its splendid décor, the quality of its technical equipment, and above all, the performances staged there.

But the illustrious history of this theater was tragically interrupted in 1936, when it was destroyed by a terrible fire. After being closed for nearly four decades, it was finally reopened in 1973. Today the Regio hosts a variety of programs: opera, ballet, symphonic and choral concerts, and chamber music, with the participation of the theater's own orchestra and chorus, in addition to a series of collateral activities targeting an array of audiences, with a special focus on schools.

The Regio is known for its amazing capacity to maintain and consolidate relationships with its audiences, as the statistics clearly show. In fact, it counts more season-ticket holders than any other opera house in Italy, a number that has remained constant over time. The Regio also takes in the largest number of donations from income tax contributions.[2] What's more, the average occupancy rate for its shows is 98 per cent (2013 data), which equates to 250,000 spectators per year, in addition to season ticket holders.

Underpinning the close ties that the Regio has built with its audience is undoubtedly the exceptional quality of the programs it offers, which translates into highly satisfied spectators. In addition to this, the theater has demonstrated a strong commitment toward the city of Turin, the region of Piedmont, and the surrounding regions as well.

In fact, the Regio is a hub of the city's cultural life. Its vast spaces host all the major official cultural events (the inauguration of the annual book fair, public ceremonies, meetings with municipal authorities, among others). What's more, for the past 20 years the Regio has spearheaded a project aimed at introducing opera to students of all ages from the city and the region.

This project consists of educational pathways targeting not only students (around 50,000 per year from nursery school to high school) but also teachers and families. Various didactic options are available covering the history of opera as well as current trends in this art form; students can even get first-hand experience by actually performing in an opera.

Also, to make it easier for fans living in surrounding regions to come to the Regio performances, the theater schedules a number of afternoon shows, so people who live far away won't find themselves traveling home late at night.

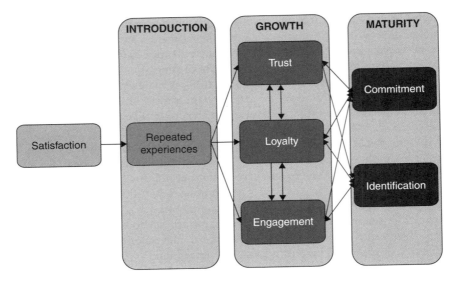

Figure 10.4 – The elements of relationship status

10.3 FACTORS IMPACTING THE RELATIONSHIP LIFECYCLE

From our discussion so far, it might seem like any kind of a relationship between a customer and an organization is destined to progress through the different stages in the cycle, constantly increasing in intensity and mutual collaboration, as long as it's grounded from the start in customer satisfaction. If this were true, the initial point of contact would be the only determinant of the entire cycle, and it would be easy for all organizations to build solid relationships. But that's not the way things work.

In the real world, competitors are constantly trying to persuade customers to abandon their current supplier and switch to their organizations because they offer a better value proposition. But more than this, there are certain individual traits that can shape the progress of the relationship in any one of the different lifecycle stages

First comes *variety seeking*, a very common behavior among consumers in creative industries. With so many options to choose from, and the hedonic and communicative value that countless creative products offer, customers come to prize variety for variety's sake. Many are motivated primarily by a desire for exactly this when they're looking to buy and consume a creative product. What's more, they may see a special relationship with a single organization as a limitation,

hindering them from satisfying their desire for variety. This said, variety seeking doesn't create an obstacle to the customer-organization relationship if the latter has a portfolio of products (Section 8.1.7) or brands (Section 8.2.4) that's sufficiently deep and broad to satisfy customers' need for variety (at least in part).

Second, customers differ in terms of their *relational orientation*, that is, their inclination to embark on a long-term relationship. Since a consolidated relationship creates reciprocal expectations, people may perceive the components of sacrifice of any relationship as exceeding the benefits.

For example, some customers might adopt a more cautious relational profile if they suspect that a long-term relationship with an organization would expose them to a flood of communications, asking them to collaborate, share data, take part in surveys, and so forth. Customers with a limited relational orientation, although they're satisfied, might not want to invest in a relationship with the organization, so they keep the relational intensity low and limit themselves simply to repurchasing products.

Garbarino and Johnson (1999) studied the customers of a non-profit theater on Broadway. They demonstrated that for consumers with a high relational orientation, the intentions regarding future activities linked to that relationship (buying tickets for individual shows, renewing season tickets, making donations to support the theater) were determined not by satisfaction but by trust and commitment. On the other hand, for consumers with limited relational orientation, their future behavioral intentions depended exclusively on their satisfaction.

The implication of these findings is that customers with high relational orientation can also accept a healthy dose of dissatisfaction without rejecting the relationship out of hand (since it's based on trust and commitment). But customers who have low relational orientation have no motivation to continue investing in the relationship if they're not satisfied.

A third significant individual characteristic pertains to *skepticism*, or *a negative attitude toward the information provided by the potential partner in the relationship.* This skepticism can apply across the board to the information sourced from any organization, or from certain ones (only the ones with a negative image in the mind of the customer); toward any information tool or channel or only some (for example, only advertising messages or promotions); toward information on any object of communication or only some (such as information on a sweepstake).

Customers who are highly skeptical won't believe that the organization seeking contact truly wants to establish a long-term relationship; they'll have a negative bias toward the relationship, believing that it can't possibly be fair because the organization has everything to gain. Customers with this outlook tend to avoid establishing relationships and instead adopt opportunistic behaviors toward all their suppliers to exploit every interaction for the greatest possible gain.

10.4 MANAGING CUSTOMER RELATIONSHIPS THROUGHOUT THE LIFECYCLE

CRM consists in a series of activities designed and realized in relation to the lifecycle of the customer relationship. So depending on the status and the stage of this relationship, each customer is targeted with specific value propositions and activities.

Obviously the degree of personalization of the organization's proposals follows the same rationale as behind defining overall market strategies: proposals can be highly personalized with a one-to-one marketing approach, or the complete opposite, very standardized as with mass marketing. Wherever an organization chooses its

positioning, anywhere between these two endpoints on the marketing continuum, market segmentation once again proves useful in managing relationships with customers (Section 7.6).

In fact, the first step in CRM is to *classify customers with regard to the status and stage of their relationship.* So the process used for market segmentation is exactly this, a classification that can be used for CRM as well. After segmentation of customers comes profiling and finally designing specific activities dedicated to each group.

10.4.1 Identifying segmentation criteria for the customer base

With segmentation relating to CRM, the organization is dealing with its current customers, not generic market customers (as with segmentation in general). This is why the segmentation bases in the CRM process consist of parameters that highlight the status and stage of every customer's relationship with the organization.

To run a segmentation of the customer base, the organization needs certain data on these customers, in other words a *customer database*. The richer it is, the more detailed the segmentation; without it, CRM simply can't be done. A customer database on final consumers normally provides the following information:

- *Contact information*: name; address; telephone: email address; social accounts; permission to use data.
- *Demographics*: age and birth date; gender; marital status; members of immediate family.
- *Socio-economic characteristics*: profession; disposable income; ownership of specific goods that indicate financial means (house, car, household appliances).
- *Lifestyle*: how consumers spend their free time (sports, vacations, community service); whether or not they use cultural products and services and if so which ones; product and brand preferences.
- *Media habits*: how/how often consumers use TV, radio, newspapers, magazines, the web, and specific types of all these media.
- *Behaviors associated with the organization*: duration of the relationship; purchase frequency; average quantity and total quantity purchased; type of products/brands purchased; method/channel of purchase; payment method; purchase of competing products/brands; word of mouth.

- *Reaction to solicitation by the organization*: participation in events, promotional initiatives, viral marketing campaigns.
- *Contact with the organization*: information requests/complaints on various touchpoints.
- *Value for the organization*: overall value of purchases; word of mouth generated; number of contacts on social media; role in social media (hub, bridge or fringe: Section 9.6.3.3).

On the basis of these data, the organization can identify the most appropriate parameters for whatever analysis it wants to run on its customers, and construct different segments accordingly. For instance, if the editor of a glamour magazine wants to promote an invitation-only evening gala for its long-standing customers, it could use data on the start date of customer relationships; if on the other hand it wants to put together an initiative for recently-acquired customers with a specific lifestyle, other data would be more useful.

Every customer interaction that the organization tracks will feed into the database, but ad hoc marketing research can provide valuable input as well. Here the data is potentially far richer, covering customer expectations, their relational orientation, degree of trust, commitment and identification, their loyalty, and more. Obviously before inserting these data in the database they need to be codified (in quantitative or qualitative terms), which often calls for reprocessing research findings (for instance: 'strong' 'moderate' 'weak' trust; or 'high' 'medium' 'low' relational orientation).

The map of parameters to use for segmentation criteria is potentially enormous; its size depends on the technology and skills available to the organization, as well as its analytical competences in marketing. In any case, a set of common indicators is used to classify customers based on the status and the stage of their relationship. This is detailed in the following sections.

10.4.1.1   RFM indicators

RFM stands for recency, frequency, and monetary value in reference to the customer's purchase history. It's quite a simple set of parameters first established to identify targets for direct marketing campaigns. The underlying assumption is that customers who've made purchases most recently or most frequently or for the most money will be most likely to repurchase from the same supplier. (In other words, they're the most loyal.)

Recency measures the time since the latest purchase; *frequency* is the interval between purchase and repurchase within a unit of time; *monetary value* is the total amount of all the purchases the customer has made from the organization, again within a unit of time.

RFM indicators provide information based on the vitality of the relationship (if purchases are recent and frequent) and the value for the organization. Combining these data with the duration of the relationship gives an indication of customer loyalty. These parameters are easy to build if the organization can track customer purchases; if not, specific research is required.

10.4.1.2   Behavioral indicators

These have to do with customers' past and future behaviors (that is to say, behavioral intentions). Both can reveal the degree of customer satisfaction, loyalty, and trust in different ways. With regard to *past behaviors*, some indicators focus on purchases, so they're useful for measuring the degree of loyalty.

Purchase quotas measure the amount customers dedicate to the organization's product/brand as a percentage of what they spend on a specific product category over a pre-set unit of time. Seeing as exclusivity (100%) is quite rare, except in very particular circumstances, benchmark values are usually used. These are subjectively set, but should reflect the typical customer purchase habits (for instance, the market average).

The *purchase sequence* measures the succession of purchases of products/brands in a given category over a unit of time; the aim here is to ascertain whether there's a pattern of repeat purchases of the organization's products/brands. In this case, too, the sequence that reflects loyalty is subjectively set, but again it should be reasonable in light of customer habits on the market.

Sharing information and judgments on social media by customers is another indication of their trust (the number of shares, retweets, and likes, for instance). But these parameters should be used with caution. First, sharing is something that might happen with people who've simply enjoyed the content of message of an organization without having any other interaction. Since sharing can also be the result of a viral marketing campaign, or a solicitation by the organization itself, it's more a measure of enjoyment than trust. So the organization should try to discern which shares are made by customers who are satisfied or committed to the organization, and which are simply reactions to a stimulus.

With regard to *future behaviors*, indicators that measure *willingness to buy* (WTB) and *willingness to pay* a certain price (WTP) are often used to assess loyalty. But it's vital to remember that people's claims with regard to their future behavior aren't very reliable because there's no way to know what situations customers could find themselves in when facing decisions, or what actions competitors might undertake that could influence those decisions.

A very common indicator used to reveal customer trust in an organization (which goes beyond satisfaction) is *willingness to recommend* (WTR). This reflects the reliability perceived by customers, which creates reassurance, which then leads them to recommend the organization and its products/brands to other people.

10.4.1.3 Cognitive and affective indicators

Some of the qualifiers of the status of a relationship (trust, commitment, identification) relate to both the cognitive and affective sphere, aspects that are not fully captured by the behavior indicators outlined above. So to make accurate measurements in this case, the organization needs to run specific research by means of a questionnaire with items formulated for this specific purpose. Normally the interviewee's answers are expressed on a quantitative scale so the organization can come up with an average number to assign to each customer.

Trust is a typically cognitive construct (that generates positive and negative affective states), which can be defined as recognition by the customer that the organization is capable of keeping its promises. So to ascertain the level of trust, customers would be asked about their perceptions of competency, honesty, integrity, and reliability (Chaudhuri and Holbrook, 2001; Garbarino and Johnson, 1999; Morgan and Hunt, 1994).[3]

Engagement, a construct with both a cognitive and an affective component, is reflected in certain participation behaviors by customers toward an organization. Examples are participation in an activity or campaign run by the organization, commitment expressed through positive word of mouth, and activity on social media relative to the organization. Beyond asking customers directly, information on engagement can be gleaned by observing things like word of mouth activated in referral programs (Section 10.4.3.3), responses

to email campaigns or social media marketing, or conversations on the organization's blogs or other digital channels.

Attachment also has cognitive and affective components, and is a sign of a powerful role that the organization (its products and brands) plays for customers in terms of self-definition. So questions that reveal the level of attachment would seek to clarify how important the organization is for the customers, how intensely they feel it to be part of their self-identify, and how strong their affective ties are with the organization (Malär et al., 2011; Thomson, 2006; Whan Park et al., 2010).

Identification can be considered an expression of attachment. Customers identify with an organization when they use it (its products, brands, activities, distinctive signs in their self-categorization processes), and feel that the characteristics of the organization coincide with their self-definition (Bhattacharya and Sen, 2003). So beyond verifying attachment, further questions can delve into whether consumers use any of the organization's distinctive signs (badges, gadgets, ornaments) as expressions of self-identity, the extent to which they identify with the values and activities of the organization, and how often they mention the organization in conversation.

Lastly, *commitment* is also a construct with cognitive and affective content reflecting a desire for a long-term, mutually satisfying relationship. The organization can ascertain the level of commitment with questions that center on whether customers want to keep up the relationship, their expectations for reciprocal satisfaction, the pride they feel in being part of the relationship, and their willingness to cooperate to make the relationship a mutual success (Garbarino and Johnson, 1999; Morgan and Hunt, 1994).

10.4.2 Building segments and profiling customers

Once segmentation criteria for the customer base are identified, the next two stages are identical to the ones described for segmentation in Section 7.6. In concrete terms, the organization selects the criteria that best fit the goals underlying the segmentation, and on the basis of those criteria it creates groups of customers that are internally homogenous, but differ from other groups.[4] After building the segments, the organization profiles the customers that belong to each one on the basis of other characteristics that are relevant to the purposes of the analysis in question.

10.4.3   Designing relational activities

The effectiveness of CRM is contingent on the availability of clear information that enables the organization to design and execute ad hoc activities to match the stage and status of the relationship. Each of these activities has specific relational objectives to reach, within the framework of the more general goal of moving forward toward a mature relationship connected with all the elements described above (trust, loyalty, engagement, commitment, and identification).

10.4.3.1   Loyalty programs

Loyalty programs are *initiatives aimed at fostering and rewarding customer loyalty*. Though these initiatives can take a wide variety of forms, they share certain key characteristics (Dorotic et al., 2012):

- The aim is to foster loyalty in *behaviors* (measured by repeat purchases, increased purchase frequency, increased average quantities, cross purchases), and on a *cognitive and affective* level (generating more positive attitudes toward the organization, in turn enhancing its image).
- Loyalty programs have to be *structured*; in other words, customers can enjoy benefits only through formal participation (enrollment or membership, often with tangible proof such as a card or customer code), with different membership levels associated with clearly defined mechanisms.
- Programs must be *long term*, instead of just lasting a few weeks or months like other promotions; rewarding customer loyalty involves activities and mechanisms that are diluted over time (typically years), with investments in the relationship by both parties.
- There must be a *clear rewards system*, requiring members to collect points of some sort in order to earn specific rewards that correspond to their 'level' of loyalty (discounts, gifts, or access to the next membership tier).
- They're based on *personalized marketing actions*. Thanks to its in-depth knowledge of loyalty program members and their personal characteristics, the organization can provide real value through its actions and rewards.

Designing an effective loyalty program equates to successfully balancing the benefits with the sacrifices customers have to make, to encourage them to become members and to maintain this status. Obviously, a customer who sees relatively few advantages and too many costs associated with membership wouldn't be very motivated to join.

Keep in mind, though, that *benefits* can relate to all the categories of value discussed in Section 3.1:

- *Utilitarian*: for instance, getting discounts on products, complimentary services, or free products/services from other organizations.
- *Hedonic*: invitations to exclusive events, personalized treatment, access to specially designed shows or attractions.
- *Communicative*: belonging to a group of customers with distinctive characteristics and social status.
- *Ethical*: contributing to growing the organization and realizing its mission, donating to a non-profit by becoming a member.

Sacrifices can also be classified by different types, both monetary and non-monetary: the expense of accessing benefits; the time and cognitive effort needed to participate in a program and earn rewards; the opportunity cost of joining one organization, precluding others; the fear of having to sacrifice privacy.

There are two typical *structures* for loyalty programs, based on either purchase frequency or customer tiers. With the first, customers reach point levels to get specific benefits; there are no access restrictions, so all members have the chance to earn related benefits. With the second, customers who meet certain requirements are assigned to pre-established groups, and each group gets access to specific benefits. The first structure focuses on utilitarian and hedonic benefits, the second on communicative and ethical benefits.

There's also a distinction between *stand-alone* and *multiple-vendor* programs, which respectively involve either a single organization or several partner organizations. For instance, some exhibit spaces in a city might set up partnerships with theaters, retailers, gas stations, or other organizations to create a joint loyalty program that lets customers collect points and cash in rewards from any partner.

10.4.3.2   Retention programs

The fact that customers keep up a relationship is a sign of their loyalty toward an organization. So it's no coincidence that the aim of all loyalty programs is customer retention. But that doesn't mean the only way to retain customers is to reward loyalty.

A retention program consists of a series of activities specifically designed by an organization to prevent customers from leaving the relationship, a phenomenon that marketeers refer to as *churn* (or for members who fail to renew, *attrition*). For instance, a lifestyle magazine publisher with a subscriber base might set up a program to encourage current customers to renew their subscriptions. The same could apply to a theater, a foundation that manages an archeological site or an open space, or a company that runs an amusement park. Before setting up a retention program, though, the organization must run in-depth analysis with two aims in mind relating to churn: understanding possible reasons and identifying a set of predictors (Research Focus 10.2).

The most likely *reason* is customer *dissatisfaction*. Seeing that this depends on a negative disconfirmation of expectations (Section 3.2), the organization needs to find out which components of its value proposition failed to meet customer expectations, and then plan actions to make improvements as needed. But often these actions take time, so it's crucial to come up with a quick response, a contingency program to activate the moment dissatisfaction surfaces, especially in the case of a customer complaint (Section 4.5.3).

These are called *recovery programs*, which are immediate, structured, and planned activities aimed at preventing dissatisfaction leading to churn out. Dissatisfaction can be interpreted as the result of an unbalanced relationship, in the sense that the customer perceives a discontinuity in mutual fairness (Section 10.2.2). In this case the organization has to rebalance the relationship as soon as possible (Ringberg et al., 2007; Smith et al., 1999), which is the underlying aim of recovery programs.

The relative activities might have a more *utilitarian* focus, or a more *relational* one. Examples of the first type might be giving cash back, replacing the product (or providing the service again) free of charge, or offering reimbursement for the defective product or the disservice. The second type would include apologizing, taking responsibility, assuring the customer that whatever the reason for the dissatisfaction it won't happen again, demonstrating empathy, explaining the possible causes, responding rapidly, and taking the initiative.

For example, if a customer is buying a book that has a torn cover, the bookseller could spontaneously offer her a discount; an exhibit center that has temporarily closed some of its spaces might proactively offer its apologies (and a discount on admission!) before customers complain. The first activities emphasize

Research Focus 10.2

Predicting attrition for museum membership

Bhattacharya (1998) studied the members of a museum in a city in the northeastern US over a six-year period, focusing on people who failed to renew their membership. The aim of the study was to identify the variables that systematically distinguished these people from others who did renew, to then utilize these data as member behavior predictors.

The author only analyzed the museum's member database for data that were quantifiable because they referred to members' behavior (rather than their perceptions). The potential determinants of attrition fell into three categories:

○ *Reasons for joining*: whether people bought their membership or received it as a gift, and if their interest in the museum was professional (that is, if they were artists).

○ *Type of membership*: the tier (ordinary members or patrons), the transition from one tier to another over time, participation in special interest groups, the duration of the relationship, how quickly they renewed their membership once it expired.

○ *Support behaviors for the museum*: donations and volunteer work.

Results showed that the chances of non-renewal were greater among members who were gifted their membership, those who dropped to lower tiers over time, those with a shorter relationship, those who renewed long after the yearly expiration, and those who donated less frequently.

For all the other variables no statistically significant relationships emerged, showing that the probability of attrition was not impacted by whether or not members were artists, or belonged to a specific membership tier, or moved up to a higher tier, or supported the museum through volunteer work.

To sum up, this study showed that members of a museum aren't equally likely to fail to renew membership. Further, by accurately analyzing specific variables the organization can predict this negative behavior.

fairness in terms of striking a benefit/sacrifice balance; the second underscore the close affective ties and reciprocal commitment.

But customers can also leave a relationship with an organization because of the *actions of competitors*, who do all they can to show that they can offer value propositions that are better suited to customer needs. Constant surveillance is therefore needed so the organization can anticipate possible competitor offers that would be particularly attractive to its target, and propose alternatives.

Actions intended to obstruct the attractiveness of competitor offerings focus on reinforcing the customer's commitment by demonstrating the organization's commitment, which in turn underscores reciprocity. These actions can be more utilitarian or more symbolic, focusing on different aspects of the relationship.

The first offer the customer *tangible advantages* but one time only (unlike loyalty programs). Here are some examples: a promotion that offers current customers special product discounts (a fashion company can organize an invitation-only evening for its customers where they can get a deep discount); another that offers product giveaways (a museum schedules free visits for loyal customers).

Initiatives that underscore symbolic aspects play up the *affective ties* underpinning the relationship. Examples include sending birthday greetings (by mail, text, or email); thanking customers through an email marketing campaign for their contribution to the organization; or setting up invitation-only events where the organization's top executives can meet customers to thank them personally and shore up their relationships.

When considering indicators that anticipate dissatisfaction or the attractiveness of competing offerings, this brings up a critical aspect of customer retention: defining a set of parameters that can predict possible churn to enable the organization to plan corrective measures that can prevent it from happening. Let's try to imagine a customer who ends her relationship with a former supplier, and assume that this decision wasn't simply a spur of the moment impulse (which is possible, but practically impossible to predict). Now let's ask ourselves: What will that customer do before taking this step?

Some typical customer behaviors leading up to churn out include *complaining*, *requesting information on alternative offerings*, or *increasing purchases from other organizations*. So basically, when customers aren't satisfied with an organization's product, they'll often complain. If, however, they've received a competitor's proposal, they'll probably activate the organization's touchpoints to see if it has comparable offerings. And they might increase their purchases from other organizations. If the organization has a system of touchpoints that's truly integrated and a customer database that's properly managed, these customer interactions can trigger a red flag and activate a retention response. But without these triggers in place, it's hard to anticipate customer churn out.

10.4.3.3   Referral programs

The organization can set up referral programs *to encourage its satisfied customers to engage in positive word of mouth*. The ultimate goal here is *customer acquisition*, but as explained below, research shows that referral programs also increase retention of current customers.

There are a variety of referral programs, but they all share a core mechanism: rewarding current customers when they use positive word of mouth to bring new customers into the organization. The reward could be cash for customers who make recommendations to friends who in turn make purchases. For example, a pay TV platform might offer cash to subscribers for any contacts they provide who actually become new subscribers. The prize might only be for the recommender, or it might be for the receiver too (who might get a discount on the subscription, for instance).

Referral programs are very common thanks to digital channels that make them highly affordable and efficient. What's more, research shows that new customers activated with referrals tend to have a higher-than-average retention rate and generate substantial economic value for the organization (Schmitt et al., 2011). So the bottom line is that referral programs offer a greater return on investments than other customer acquisition initiatives.

To guarantee effectiveness, recommenders have to feel that the benefits associated with making a referral outweigh the sacrifices, since their word is what's being 'acquired' (Ryu and Feick, 2007). These *sacrifices* aren't simply time and effort spent on making the referral. There's also the social risk that the receivers might be dissatisfied with the offering in question, as well as the psychological risk of putting satisfaction 'up for sale'. In fact, many customers consider this a physiological consequence of a positive relationship with an organization that should spontaneously trigger a referral, so some would feel uncomfortable getting paid for making positive comments to friends about a product they're satisfied with.

Research shows that referral programs also *enhance the loyalty of the recommenders* (Garnefeld et al., 2012). In fact, disseminating positive word of mouth and recommending an organization are perceived as forms of commitment that need to be followed up by action. Customers who recommend a product or brand and then go out and buy a different one would see their self-esteem suffer and would risk disapproval from the very people on the receiving end of their referrals.

This is even more relevant when we consider that customers normally make referrals to the people they're closest to (Ryu and Feick, 2007), especially because strong ties minimize the sacrifices associated with passing on information. With close friends people can neglect to mention or take for granted certain information because they know each other so well; if they had to make a recommendation to someone who's only an acquaintance, they'd have to spend more time and effort to come to the same understanding.

10.5   EVALUATING THE QUALITY OF CUSTOMER RELATIONSHIPS

For an organization to effectively manage customer relationships, it must systematically monitor their quality. This is the only way to verify whether programs are producing expected results, and in turn whether the entire CRM process is effective and efficient. Assessing relationship quality doesn't center on the individual customer, but on the stage and status of all relationships with all customers.

Seeing that the foundation of any long-term relationship is always *customer satisfaction*, systematically tracking satisfaction is fundamental. To come up with a measure of satisfaction, quantitative marketing research is used (typically a survey) with a structured questionnaire.

But first, the organization has to discover customer expectations relative to each individual component of the value proposition (products, brands, touchpoints), the organization as a whole, and their relationship with the organization. Digging deeper, the organization also needs to gather information on customers' judgments with regard to each component by which it measures their expectations.

In general, expectations are measured by having customers rate the importance of various factors on a quantitative scale; judgments, on the other hand, are measured by using the same scale to rate the organization's performance on each of these factors. The results serve to build an importance-performance matrix (outlined in Section 8.1.5.2.1) on product assessments; this matrix highlights areas of satisfaction where relationships can be consolidated and dissatisfaction where there's room for improvement.

Measuring image, trust, loyalty, engagement, attachment, commitment, and identification are the next analytical steps to get an indication of the quality of the organization's relationships with its customers. All the parameters described in Section 10.4.1 pertaining to individuals can be used together (with regard to all customers) for this purpose. As for image, the same rationale applies that's outlined in Section 8.2.2.2 relative to the brand, which can be extended here to encompass the entire organization.

Beyond these indicators are others that are used especially for assessing relationship quality. One that measures customer satisfaction and trust in the organization is called the *Net Promoter Score* (NPS) (Reichheld, 2003). To compile this score, the organization asks one simple question: 'How likely is that you would recommend product/brand/organization to a friend or colleague?' and answers run from 0 to 10, with 0 meaning 'no chance' and 10 'extremely likely'.

To come up with the NPS, analysts subtract all the 9s and 10s (responses from people who are considered promoters of the organization) from those who answered anywhere from 0 to 6 (detractors).[5] The result is a net rating of satisfaction, and above all of the level of trust of the customer base. And since trust leads to loyalty, often the NPS is used as an indirect indicator of the latter as well.

Customer loyalty toward the organization can be measured with the *Customer Retention Rate* (CRR). The formula for calculating this index is:

$$CRR = \frac{C_{t_1} - NC_{t_1}}{C_{t_0}}$$

where C_{t_1} stands for the total number of customers at the end of period t_1 (typically a year), NC_{t_1} is the number of new customers acquired during the period t_1 (during the year), and C_{t_0} is the number of customers at the end of the previous period (the previous year). For example, if a magazine counted 234,789 subscribers at the end of 2013, and in 2014 it acquired 12,345 new subscribers, but at year-end 2014 it had 233,668 subscribers, its CRR equals 94.2 per cent: (233.668 – 12.345)/234.789.

The *Churn Rate* (CR), similar to the CRR, indicates the average defection rate, and is calculated as the reciprocal of the CRR. In the example above, the CR is 5.8 per cent (1–94.2 per cent). The CR can also be used to find the *average customer lifetime* (ACL), calculated with this formula:

$$ACL = \frac{1}{CR}$$

So again in the example above, the average customer lifetime is around 17 years (1/0.058). In fact, the index measures the average percentage of customers who churn out on an annual basis, and how many years it will take for the entire customer based to be renewed if the same number of customers leave every year.

Of course, this interpretation assumes that the organization loses customers at a constant rate, not a very realistic assumption when taking on a static perspective of organization–customer relationships. But keeping this premise in mind, the ACL can simply give an idea of how long on average customer relationships would last if no action were taken by the organization or its competitors.

One final indicator can be used to summarize the financial value of the relationships that the organization has with its customers: the *Customer Life Time Value (CLTV)*, also known as *Customer Equity*. This represents the monetary value of the individual customer during the entire lifecycle, and in aggregate form, the monetary value of the entire customer base.

The CLTV is the value of the revenues that the organization can obtain from a customer during the entire lifecycle of the relationship, less the costs incurred in acquiring, serving, and retaining that customer, generating a cash flow. To take into account the value of time, cash flows have to be discounted by a rate equivalent to the cost of capital, which results in the *net present value of cash flows deriving from a single customer*.

There are several formulas for calculating this number but most of them are variations on the original proposed by Wayland and Cole (1997):

$$CLTV = \sum_{t=1}^{n}\left(Q_t \times M_t\right) \times d^t - \sum_{t=1}^{n}\left(D_t + R_t\right) \times d^t - A_1$$

where Q_t represents the quantities purchased by the customer in each unit of time t; M_t is the potential margin on each purchase; d^t the discount rate, representing the cost of capital; D_t costs incurred in growing the relationship; R_t costs of retention; A_1 costs incurred in time period 1 to acquire the customer; and n the lifespan of the relationship in years, so the estimate can be taken for the ACL.

What becomes apparent from this formula is that the current value of the customer base increases with the number of customer purchases and the margin on each one; conversely, the value of the customer base decreases as the cost of acquiring and retaining customers increases. It's also natural to assume that the longer the organization can extend the average lifespan of customer relationships, the higher the CLTV will be.

10.6   CONCLUSIONS

The topic of managing relationships with customers over time is one of the most critical in contemporary marketing. In fact, the ability to maintain and grow these relationships is the most tangible proof of success for a company or non-profit with regard to satisfying customer expectations.

The previous chapters of this book have investigated the processes that constitute customer value management from a static perspective, as if the interaction between organization and customer happened in a single moment in time. In this chapter, these processes have been placed in their proper temporal framework, highlighting the fact that they must be modulated according to the stage and the status of the customer–organization relationship. Marketing is about satisfying customer expectations, and expectations also emerge in relation to the duration and intensity of the relationship with the organization. It stands to reason that a long-term customer expects to be treated differently than a new customer.

It's expectations, therefore, that shape relationships. These can vary in intensity, and be enriched with certain characteristics that emerge only through systematic and satisfying interaction. As we've learned, every relationship goes through a lifecycle, with every stage marked by special relational aspects that strengthen ties, making them more beneficial for both parties.

When customers are satisfied time and time again, they'll experience trust, engagement, loyalty, commitment, and attachment, and may even come to identify with the organization. This happens when the organization plays such a vital role in the lives of customers that they incorporate its characteristics into their self-identity. In light of these considerations, relationships with customers call for an ad hoc management approach, which in turn involves specific programs encompassing activities structured with clear objectives in mind.

What is now clear is that the steps leading up to effective customer relationship management revolve around identifying different groups of customers in relation to their status. This means the organization needs to build and feed a database and a series of indicators that allow it to monitor customer relationships, both at an individual and comprehensive level. What's more, by providing the right fuel for its database, both in terms of quantity and quality, the organization can manage relational activities efficiently and effectively.

This description of customer value management over time concludes the analysis of the four processes that are the primary responsibility of the Marketing department in an organization that produces creative products. In the previous chapters, I've referred to the decision maker as the organization or individual managers. But how analysis is conducted and how decisions are made (and how effective and efficient they prove to be) are factors that are highly contingent on how the company or non-profit

is organized: What units are tasked with which activities? Who does what? What procedures are in place?

Specifically, much of this depends on what role Marketing plays in the organization and how this department interfaces with the units that are more directly responsible for creative processes that produce the organization's value propositions. Given the importance of this topic, I've decided to address it in the final chapter of this book.

REVIEW QUESTIONS

1. Why do customers value long-lasting relationships with an organization producing creative products? And why does the organization do the same?
2. What elements influence the intensity of the relationship along the stages of its lifecycle? How do these elements exert their influence?
3. What are the different stages of a customer relationship management process? What are the outcomes of each stage?
4. What are the typical indicators that can be used to segment a customer base?
5. What are the main characteristics of loyalty programs? What about retention programs? And what are the specificities of referral programs?
6. What are the major indicators for evaluating the quality of the relationship between an organization and its customers?

CASE STUDY

THE NATIONAL TRUST: A MEMBER-CENTRIC ORGANIZATION

The *National Trust for Places of Historic Interest or Natural Beauty*, or, as it's more commonly known, simply the *National Trust*, is a non-profit organization dedicated to the preservation of Britain's historic and natural heritage. In 1895 the National Trust was founded by four people concerned with the conservation of certain historical places, and promptly made its first property acquisition: five acres of land at Dinas Oleu, in Wales.

Official recognition came in 1907 with the National Trust Act. Since then, the organization has grown in size, importance, and popularity, to become the biggest conservation non-profit in Europe. In fact, the National Trust has more than 300 holdings (including 59 villages, 49 churches, and 742 miles of British coast) and counts nearly four million members. Every year, Trust pay-for-entry properties attract more than 19 million visitors (tens of millions more visit Trust countryside places), and the organization's annual revenues total 435.6 million pounds (2012 data).

The mission

The mission of the National Trust is to preserve places of historical or natural importance (buildings and open spaces) that are at risk of decay or destruction, guaranteeing access 'forever, for everyone'. This ambitious goal is achieved through three main activities: acquiring new properties; maintaining, leasing, or selling current properties; and organizing visits.

New properties can be acquired in two ways: either through direct purchases of lands or buildings, or donations from private individuals. But the process isn't an automatic one: new acquisitions must be of national importance and have a financial endowment in place that can cover maintenance costs of the property for the next 50 years. If the acquisition is successfully concluded, the National Trust restores the property in an effort to bring it back to its original condition; in the case of buildings, this includes decorations and furnishings. The organization's constitution also allows for selling some – but not all – properties. Certain estates can be deemed 'inalienable', so they cannot by law be sold, in keeping with the Trust's mission.

Property maintenance, one of the organization's core activities, is often directly related to managing visits. In fact, too many visitors could result in irreparable damage, but by the same token restricting access to a property or open space would run counter to the organization's very mission.

Financing the activities of the National Trust

Since the National Trust is independent of the government, fundraising strategies and programs are critical to enable the organization to pursue its mission and offer consistently high quality visitor services.

The Trust's principal fundraising activities include memberships, rents, entrance tickets, donations, and other related visitor services (restaurants, shops, accommodation and so forth). The first of these is the biggest source of revenue by far. In fact, thanks to its nearly four million members, subscription fees account for almost half of the funds in the Trust's coffers every year. Also vital to the running of the organization is the support of more than 70,000 volunteers. Although their efforts can't be considered financing, their contribution is one of the reasons for the success of the National Trust.

Membership

In 2012 the National Trust counted 3.93 million registered members, with a renewal rate of 84.2 per cent and 757,000 new signups. All it takes to become a member is simply to pay a fee; the amount varies depending on a number of criteria: annual or lifetime membership, single or group membership (such as families), and personal or gift membership.

Members have the right to free and unlimited access (and parking) to all National Trust properties. What's more, they also receive a subscription to the organization's magazine, a guide to all the places on the registry, and a vote in elections for half of the seats on the Council of the National Trust.

Tenants have a special form of membership. They lease certain properties (normally farm land or cottages), paying rent and handling maintenance in exchange for the right of use. Beyond this, they also enjoy free access to other National Trust holdings (for themselves, an additional guest, and a child), but they don't vote or participate in the Annual General Meeting. The National Trust has also set up reciprocity agreements with similar organizations in other countries of the world, so UK members enjoy free access to other sites when travelling abroad.

With regard to the number of members, in the early years of the National Trust there were far fewer, but the past 30 years has seen a real boom in membership. In 1970, during the Trust's 75th anniversary celebrations, members numbered just over 220,000, a figure that rose to a million in 1981, doubling in 1990 and again in the following decade. There are three reasons for growth in the last decade, two of which represent socio-cultural trends: the increase in domestic tourism in the UK, and the emergence of new ways to connect with the national culture. The third reason ties directly into decisions made by the National Trust, specifically the new marketing strategies adopted by the organization.

Marketing strategies for attracting new members

As for macro-areas of intervention in marketing strategies, two had the most impact on increasing membership: changing product management (as far as owned properties were concerned) and redefining communication strategies.

With regard to the first point, the National Trust concentrated its attention on enhancing the member experience with two aims: to transmit the value of the building or space in question (in keeping with the mission) and more importantly to make visits enjoyable, not boring. To do this, the organization invested in three key areas:

- *Better experience for visitors*. With this aim in mind, in the mid-2000s the organization launched the program *Bringing Properties to Life* to make visits as interactive as possible. This initiative contrasts with the philosophy that guided the National Trust for decades – conservation above all, at all costs – conveying the message to the public that visits should leave little or no 'footprint'. Today, instead, visitors can literally 'live' the properties, touching and using objects, eating and lodging on great estates, and getting a full understanding of what life was like when these properties were still in use. All this creates the perception that they are special places.

- In changing the underlying philosophy, the *role of property managers* had to change as well. If once they were 'conservers' today they've become 'organizers' of events and activities that bring to life the special qualities of each place. To support this role change, a *training program* was run for all property managers to give them in-depth knowledge of the uniqueness and importance of the property in their care, and to teach them how to transmit the 'spirit of the place'.
- *Service leadership*. This means managing the entire experience as a set of services to offer visitors. Every stage of the visit (from reception to accommodation, from restaurants to educational tours) is seen as a service opportunity, and personnel are prepared to satisfy visitors' different needs, answering their questions and responding to their requests, all with an eye to enhancing the overall visit experience.
- *Programming*. This involves event planning both on a daily and annual basis, to improve overall efficiency in running the properties and to ensure an effective use of resources. An essential element of programming activity is *measuring results*. During the year, visitors are asked to express their satisfaction regarding a series of aspects and the experience as a whole. The basic unit of measurement is *enjoyment*, measured on a scale from one to five. When the program to improve visitor experience was launched, around 90 per cent of respondents said they found their visit 'enjoyable'. National Trust management set a program goal: to have 70 per cent of visitors describe their experience as 'very enjoyable'; in 2013, the final results were close, with 66 per cent.

The National Trust also changed tack on its *communication strategies*. Traditionally, the membership campaign was linked exclusively to visits: anyone who came to a Trust property and was not yet a member was invited to join when they finished their visit. Today, the National Trust leverages a wider range of media and direct marketing to reach a broader target audience. Current communication therefore includes two additional channels:

- *Paper-based*: brochures inserted in newspapers and magazines, and door-drops.
- *Online*: mainly through the National Trust website and social media.

The online channel has represented an enormous opportunity for the organization in recent years, becoming its main communication tool and the cornerstone of the entire communication strategy. Advantages in terms of flexibility, measurement, and direct communication are ideally suited to the National Trust's aims. One of these is to measure behavioral responses of various market segments depending on the communication channels used, an objective that presents a real challenge today, in particular with regard to traditional channels.

Member segmentation

The Trust's new marketing strategies are based on segmentation established in the mid-2000s and systematically updated thanks to visitor surveys. The potential market, according to the organization, is the so-called 'UK days out market' made up of British adults who spend at least one day a year away from home on holiday. The National Trust commissioned Opinion Leader, a research institute, to conduct a study, which estimated this market at 42 million individuals and identified seven different segments based on attitudes and motivations regarding spending 'days out'. These segments are the following:

- *Young experience seekers* love spending holidays outdoors, normally with friends; they are open to new experiences and discoveries.
- *Live life to the full*; independent and refined, these visitors prefer to avoid crowds and follow their own preferences and opinions.
- *Curious minds* are always open to new stimuli and searching for new things to learn.
- *Out & about* are people who love to socialize and to share the experiences they have, in particular when they visit very unusual places.
- *Home & family* are people who prefer to use days out to get together with family and friends for special occasions; here too their main interest is sharing with the group.
- *Kids first families* want to find experiences that place a priority on their children's needs.
- *Explorer families* with children are interested in days out as learning opportunities that everyone, young and old, can share.

By means of an annual visitor survey, the National Trust verifies whether it has successfully reached its various targets, measuring the penetration in different segments. For instance, the most recent surveys show that the majority of regular visitors (80%) are part of the following segments: 'Curious minds,' 'Out and about,' and 'Explorer families'.

At a central level the organization can therefore set up strategies for attracting new members, focusing on the target markets where there is less penetration, and at the same time organizing activities, events, and services that could make the offering more attractive for these targets. To do so, the National Trust has identified the main motivations and benefits sought by each segment, as well as typical behaviors and preferences with regard to specific ways to spend time away from home.

This overview also enables the National Trust to effectively run its operations at a local level. In fact, thanks to the descriptions of each segment, the Trust has created a guide for the staff of each individual property. By asking visitors a series of short questions, they can quickly be assigned to one of the seven segments, and their expectations and preferences can be decoded. All this makes it possible for the National Trust to offer more customized services.

Membership management

Seeing as members account for approximately 85 per cent of visits to National Trust properties, we can readily assume that management dedicates as much effort to fostering loyalty among current members as it does to recruiting new ones. In fact, the organization's success as far as member loyalty is remarkable. Proof of this is the fact that the renewal rate among members is 85 per cent. This figure shouldn't be surprising considering that survey data show stable member satisfaction, with an average score of 9 out of 10. If we also consider a 55 per cent NPS (Net Promoter Score), the organization unquestionably enjoys a very strong relationship with its members, which is particularly impressive in a period of economic recession.

In addition, data show that the longer the relationship with the organization, the more likely membership will be renewed. In fact, the retention rate for long-term members is around 90 per cent. It follows that the churn rate is higher among newer members, which has prompted management to analyze this specific target more closely.

Research investigated the differential motivations that prompted new members and long-term members to join, as well as the reasons for deciding not to renew membership. The results show that while new members joined for the chance to visit National Trust properties, the long-term members wanted to contribute to the conservation of these properties. This datum is apparently corroborated by the geographical distribution of members, which is more concentrated in areas where there are more Trust-owned properties.

Moreover, by far the most common reason people cited for not renewing their membership was the fact that they hadn't used their member card; in other words, they hadn't visited any National Trust buildings or spaces in the previous year. From a joint analysis of this datum and the different motivations of recent and long-term members, management realized they needed to encourage new members to visit and to encourage an altruistic motivation for contributing to conservation to emerge, accentuating this, rather than simply the chance to visit properties for free, among new members.

REVIEW QUESTIONS

1. The National Trust has shown astonishing growth in membership in the last 20 years. What are the main reasons behind that growth? What are the major decisions implemented by the management team?

2. National Trust customer relationship strategies have mostly focused on member acquisition rather than strengthening relationships with actual members. What risks would the organization face in the long term if the focus remains the same?

3. In the last few years the Trust has developed a thorough segmentation process of its membership base so as to come up with services specifically addressed to the different targets. How did they build this process and what are the segmentation criteria they used?

ORGANIZATIONAL ISSUES

INTEGRATING MARKETING AND CREATIVITY

LEARNING OBJECTIVES

After reading this chapter you should be able to:

- Identify the typical barriers to integration between Marketing and Creativity.
- Distinguish the various mechanisms that can foster integration.
- Choose the most appropriate mechanisms consistent with the specific barriers identified.
- Design an effective marketing planning process.
- Make an effective marketing plan.
- Carry out SWOT analysis.

OVERVIEW

As I see it, the best way to end this book is to go back to the beginning and bring it full circle. In the previous chapters we've taken an in-depth look at the main analytical and decision-making models linked to the stages in the value creation process. Managing this process is the primary responsibility of Marketing in organizations that operate in creative industries.

But by focusing on typical decisions and activities, we've left aside the role of Marketing somewhat. When it did come up in Chapter 2, I underscored the fact that in an organization offering creative products, whatever part Marketing plays is shaped principally by the organizational culture. In other words, this culture is what determines whether or not marketeers have much leeway in decision making, and so forth.

Although in extreme situations, there may not even be specifically assigned marketing roles, throughout this book the general assumption is there's an optimal situation. In other words, the discussion has been based on an organization with a specialized unit, made up of clearly defined and formalized roles, tasked with making marketing decisions and granted a certain degree

of autonomy. But even when this isn't the case, the role and responsibilities of marketing are both cultural and managerial: to represent the viewpoint of the customer and guarantee that it's taken into consideration in *all* organizational decisions (Chapter 2).

So Marketing's top priority is to keep the organization aligned with the market. But what exactly does this mean as far as day-to-day operations are concerned? It means systematic coordination, collaboration, contamination, and compromise between Marketing and other departments, especially those responsible for creative production.

This leads us to the topic I'll address in this final chapter: integration between Marketing and organizational units that handle production of creative offerings. These would encompass the Editorial Board in publishing; Programming or Product Management in radio and television; A&R (Artists and Repertoire) in music; the Artistic Director in art; the Style Office in fashion; curators in museums; and so on. Since these units have different names depending on the organization or industry, I'll simply use 'Creativity' as an umbrella term to refer to them all.

Here are the two questions I try to answer: What are the barriers that impede the integration of Marketing and Creativity? What tools are available to the organization (and to Marketing in particular) to encourage and achieve an effective level of integration?

Integration is a mandatory condition for aligning the organization with the market in terms of the decisions, activities, and objectives of Marketing and Creativity, to ultimately include their vision of the market and the organization's primary goals. *But integration alone isn't enough.* As I've often reiterated throughout this book, sometimes an outside observer might take certain things for granted that unfortunately don't happen in the actual running of an organization. So while it might seem reasonable to assume that Marketing and

Creativity would work together in harmony to achieve artistic, market, and financial success, in real life the relationship between these two units is frequently anything but harmonious, rooted as it often is in mutual misunderstanding and mistrust.

That's why the first topic I'll address is *typical barriers to integration*, which are both cultural and organizational. The first can be ascribed to diverse 'thought worlds', in other words, the different approaches, mental models, and habits the two units adopt to analyze reality, and to decode, interpret, and interact with it. Mutual incomprehension and suspicion that habitually permeate relationships are often entrenched in these divergent thought worlds. Although similar barriers are often considered insurmountable, once they're recognized they can be modified with effort, perseverance, and the right set of tools.

Organizational barriers, on the other hand, depend on how the company or non-profit is structured and how it functions. Since these barriers are not innate to the organization but instead are the product of past choices, they too can be disassembled to pave the way for more productive inter-functional relationships and ultimately a true alignment between the organization and the market.

Next, we'll turn our attention to analyzing *typical tools* that give organizations the power to break down these barriers, which in turn foster integration. There are many different kinds, but here I'll focus on the tools that research and experience have proven most effective in creative industries. Seeing that the most common levers relate to how an organization is set up and run, I'll detail specific tools relating to organizational structure and managerial systems that are most effective in achieving integration.

Within the framework of analyzing integration tools, one question I'll specifically explore is *marketing planning*. The outcome of this planning system is a marketing plan, which is not only vital for organizing internal Marketing activities; it also represents a potent instrument for coordinating and collaborating with all the other organizational units. Although not all organizations use a marketing plan, those that do usually have highly structured marketing activities. The entire department lends a hand in compiling the marketing plan. In fact, this process takes up much of the time and effort of marketing personnel, and encompasses all the decision-making areas we've addressed and explored in this book (which makes it a perfect conclusion!).

11.1 BARRIERS TO INTEGRATION

Many obstacles in an organization can make Marketing–Creativity integration more challenging or less effective. Properly identifying and managing these barriers is a precondition for gaining the benefits of integration. A wealth of literature on cross-functional collaboration has investigated what can hinder a productive relationship between Marketing and other divisions in an organization, especially those responsible for creativity and innovation in companies (Fisher et al., 1997; Griffin and Hauser, 1996; Maltz, 1997).

As mentioned above, the main barriers to integration between Marketing and Creativity fall into two main categories: cultural and organizational.

11.1.1 Cultural barriers

Cultural barriers between the two units arise out of the *different backgrounds and competences of personnel*. Creative teams usually have artistic or humanistic backgrounds whereas the education and experience of marketing people is normally business-centric. This means the two groups tend to have different priorities, access different information environments, perceive and interpret environmental stimuli in different ways, and even use different jargon. Because of all this, it's not uncommon to find that mutual understanding is very complicated and operations are highly inefficient.

Creative people focus much more on the aesthetic and technical qualities of a product and on the evaluations of experts in the field; their reward mostly comes from the recognition of their peers. On the contrary, marketeers are generally more attentive to the perceptions and judgments of customers on product quality, and more sensitive to the market and financial performances of products and brands; the success of value propositions in the market is their reward. In short, generally speaking the former group rely on aesthetic judgment and intuition whereas the latter use analytical thinking to support their decisions.

All these factors may lead to the creation of an in-group identity of one unit built on its contraposition to the other. This feeds into stereotypes, which often affect inter-group relations. ('Marketing people have one-track minds; for them it's all about business results.' 'Marketing people are clueless about the quality of our products.' 'Creative people have no sense of the market because all they see is the artistic value of products.' 'Creative people are only satisfied when a happy few appreciate a product and the majority of consumers reject it.') What's more, each unit develops its own idiosyncratic language that is seldom clearly comprehensible to anyone else. Worse still, it's not rare for a functional identity to develop to the detriment of organizational identity; in other words, people feel a stronger sense of belonging to their unit than to the company as a whole.

All these factors lead to the creation of two separate communities whose members find it difficult or costly (psychologically or operationally) to invest time and energy in increasing interdepartmental collaboration. What seriously suffers as a result is the quality and frequency of communications, and the willingness to share resources, to understand each other and to strive toward the same goals and objectives.

11.1.2   Organizational barriers

Organizational barriers are the result of *organizational structure and managerial systems* that are not properly designed or implemented to favor cross-functional collaboration. Organizational structure pertains to the allocation of tasks and responsibilities within the organization: establishing units, their roles, and the procedures they'll use to accomplish whatever they're assigned to do. Managerial systems consist in the set of processes that makes the structure work: communication systems, planning and control, training, compensation, and so forth.

The most common barrier can be traced to *incompatibility or lack of complementarity of typical departmental objectives* (or in the worst case, no objectives at all). In fact, Creativity's priorities are usually linked to innovation, new product launches, and the discovery of new talents, whereas Marketing is driven by results in terms of market share growth, brand development, and market creation. These divergent objectives lead to different timelines, which in turn dictate how the two units make decisions and perform tasks, further reinforcing the conviction that allocating time and effort

to interact and collaborate with the other unit adds no value to their own activities.

Another organizational barrier can emerge if there's an *ambiguous definition of decisional domains* of the two functions, which may lead to interdepartmental conflict. Since most product- and market-related decisions require the joint contribution of the two units, if both aren't perfectly clear on where their responsibilities end and others begin, this may lead to inefficient and ineffective implementation.

Here are some typical scenarios. With a new product launch, if job descriptions aren't clear, this could lead to confusion as to who's responsible for designing relevant activities. Or with a communication campaign, if one unit gets in the habit of taking over on the other's responsibilities, a veteran Artistic Director might feel justified in advancing her proposals, even though communication should be handled by Marketing instead. These examples show how the two units risk overlapping, encroaching on one another's territory, acting more on the basis of their perceived decisional domain than their formal one.

The last major organizational barrier is a *disparity in status* of the two departments. If one of the two units traditionally has a higher standing within the organization, if top managers are regularly recruited from one unit and not the other, or if compensation levels are appreciably skewed, it's very likely that instead of encouraging integration, the organizational climate between the two departments will lead to divergence, mutual distrust, and conflict.

11.2   INTEGRATION MECHANISMS

The negative effects of cultural and organizational barriers to Marketing–Creativity integration can be overcome by implementing a set of mechanisms that differ in substance and the potential to foster collaboration.

There are two main categories of integration mechanisms:[1] organizational structure and managerial systems (Figure 11.1).

11.2.1   Organizational structure

There are several structural levers that can be used to favor Marketing–Creativity integration. The first is

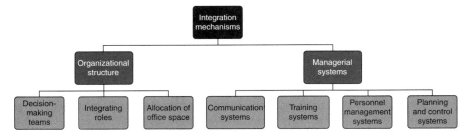

Figure 11.1 – Integration mechanisms

the creation of *decision-making teams* made up of members of both units. These teams can be tasked with market performance objectives, product- and market-related decisions and marketing activities. Another option is to set up temporary cross-functional teams responsible for specific projects, for example developing new products, designing consumer-participative processes, or putting together promotional materials. Both permanent and temporary cross-functional teams are suitable for establishing integrated goals for the two units and develop a sense of ownership over team decisions.

The second structural mechanism is setting up specific *integrating roles*. These combine creative and business competences in order to increase the efficiency and effectiveness of product- and market-related decisions. In various creative industries we find product managers, brand managers, and category managers whose job it is to integrate the decisions and activities of Marketing and Creativity (Research Focus 11.1).

The last structural mechanism pertains to *allocating office space* to the two units. Close physical proximity facilitates informal communication, unplanned meetings, and quicker exchange of information. So it stands to reason that placing two organizational units close together enhances interaction by overcoming infrastructural barriers which curb information flow, and cultural barriers that are grounded in unfamiliarity with each department's people, practices, and work routines.

11.2.2 Managerial systems

Communication systems are essential. Designing formal procedures that govern information flows between the two units is a way to increase interaction and in turn enhance activity integration. For example, when Marketing shares its research findings with Creativity, together they can come up with a common sense of how well the market accepts different products and brands; or if the two units schedule regular meetings, by working collectively personnel can plan promotional activities that are timed to coincide with new product development. Communication systems can also affect the level of interdepartmental collaboration by enhancing mutual understanding and reciprocal trust. Another example: if marketing people participate in some creative meetings (and vice versa), the staff of the two divisions can get an insider's view of each other's work routines, tasks, and decision-making procedures, and develop a more comprehensive understanding of the thought worlds of their colleagues.

Training systems are another valuable tool an organization can use to favor Marketing–Creativity integration. Joint training programs can be set up for Marketing and Creativity; personnel from one unit can sit in on the other's training; sessions can focus on team building and team working. These are some examples of ways in which the two departments can share a knowledge repository made up of cognitive schemes for interpreting market phenomena and guiding market actions (Troilo, 2006). In other words, training systems can help personnel of the two units overcome cultural barriers anchored in limited access to the cognitive schemes and knowledge repositories of colleagues in the other unit.

Other essential managerial systems have to do with personnel, specifically *evaluation, compensation, career paths, incentives, and rewards*. All these can guide individual and group behaviors towards specific short-term and long-term objectives, and encourage people to

Research Focus 11.1

Integrating roles in the fashion industry

The players in this global competitive arena, who range from major international groups to local SMEs, all strive to build their own distinctive style, one that their customers will recognize and appreciate. The key to success is the ability to take stylistic creativity and turn it into symbolic value for consumers, but this makes integration more and more critical. In fact, stylists and creative people have to work side by side with the departments that handle market relations, typically Marketing and Sales. All this has led many companies to spend considerable effort on discovering the most effective mechanisms that would secure this integration, in keeping with the organization's culture and the markets it seeks to serve.

The research of Cappetta and Cillo (2008) focuses on one such mechanism: the creation of specialist organizational roles. These authors analyze case studies to explore the choices made by four European fashion houses in different markets or segments: Salvatore Ferragamo, maker of luxury leather shoes, bags, and accessories; Furla, offering leather bags and accessories for a mid-range market segment; Diesel, a global leader in casual wear; Escada, positioned in upscale women's apparel.

All these companies share the same aim: to foster integration between Marketing (and Sales) and organizational units responsible for product design. Each enterprise invests in creating or reinforcing integration roles, albeit assigning them different labels and slightly different tasks.

At Ferragamo integration is the responsibility of *Merchandisers*, who serve as liaisons between Design, Operations, Marketing, and Sales. A vital part of their job is gathering information from the distribution network pertaining to sales performance for the different collections and products. They then interpret this information to discern customer preferences and trends, and convey their insight to other units who in turn factor in this feedback when designing future collections and planning production.

At Furla, on the other hand, it's the *Product Manager* who plays the role of integrator, supervising the creation of new collections from start to finish, acting as the nexus in the network of connections among various organizational units that have a hand in the process. Basically, during product development the Product Manager ensures that the creative intuitions of the designers are respected, as long as they're not so eclectic as to risk straying too far from market preferences or costing too much to realize.

Diesel has *Brand Managers* with both technical product competences and marketing expertise who are assigned two primary tasks. First, they systematically monitor changes in customer tastes, new segments and benefits that may emerge, and price trends; they then supply all this input to the creative teams who use it when developing new collections. Second, Brand Managers uphold the brand philosophy, ensuring that it guides stylistic choices in the pursuit of innovation and distinction.

Finally, Escada has opted to create the position of *Knowledge Integrator*. The key responsibility for this role is to manage the bi-directional information flow (from the market to the company, and from the designers to the commercial divisions), ensuring that all the organizational units act on the basis of a homogeneous, shared knowledge repository.

Here's how the authors summarize their findings (p. 3): 'The crucial part of the integrator's job is maintaining a dynamic alignment of the company's different divisions over time. On one hand, the integrators transform market knowledge into a language which is comprehensible and useful for the designers in developing the new collections, guiding the stylistic area towards perceived market preferences. On the other hand, these integrators are in charge of transferring the distinctive style of the collection first to operations – working on the technical feasibility of the collection – and then to the sales force – working on the communication codes.'

---

commit to achieving them. Organizations can use these systems to focus attention and commitment on attaining enhanced interaction and collaboration between the two departments.

An example might be designing joint incentives for the two units, such as establishing compensation levels and mapping out career paths that are comparable across units to avoid any perception of inequality in terms of salary, or giving access to top organizational positions and career opportunities. These initiatives can overcome cultural barriers perpetrated by the perception of differential departmental status that may prevent a collaborative environment from emerging between units.

Planning and control systems are also critical managerial mechanisms that allow the organization to coordinate, assess, and improve the decision-making processes of different units. These systems enable

Marketing and Creativity to align their own objectives and plans, to leverage the competences and knowledge of the other unit in order to make their own actions more incisive, and to gain a deeper understanding of each other's processes and activities.

In short, planning and control systems can enhance collaboration by overcoming organizational and cultural barriers, the first arising from divergent functional objectives and the second from limited knowledge of one another's domain of action. These systems are vital not only for integrating Marketing and Creativity but also for guaranteeing effective and efficient marketing decisions and actions. In light of this, I'll devote the next sections to marketing planning and the marketing plan, the main tool at Marketing's disposal for integrating with other organizational units.

11.3   THE EVOLUTION OF PLANNING SYSTEMS

Marketing planning fits into the broader framework of organizational planning, the process that includes setting objectives, deciding on activities to carry out to achieve them, and determining the quantity and quality of resources required and how to secure them. The formal document that results from this process is the *marketing plan*.

Companies and non-profits that use a formal planning process structure it in such a way that every organizational unit programs its activities in light of its own objectives and those of the organization as a whole. For example, a publishing company would have a publishing plan with timing on new launches and updates of the catalogue; a marketing plan that outlines communication, promotion, and distribution activities to support the products; an organizational plan that details policies on hiring, career advancement, and incentives; a financial plan that describes how to raise the resources needed for investments; and so on.

The temptation here would be to assume that all companies and non-profits in creative industries plan their future activities, but sadly this couldn't be farther from the truth. The chief prerequisite for planning – one rarely found among these organizations – is an organizational culture with an ingrained understanding of the need to set clear objectives at every level, and to measure the effective and efficient use of resources.

Moreover, several studies reveal that in many cases effective planning processes are the outcome of a series of transitions and adaptations that take years to be assimilated by the organization. In fact, numerous authors suggest that organizational planning systems gradually evolve through a number of stages toward increasingly sophisticated models (for example see Kotler and Dubois, 1986).

The first stage can be called ground zero, when there is *no planning* at all. This would refer to newly-founded organizations, or those with deep-seated cultural resistance toward any type of planning for organizational activities (not to mention a lack of adequate competences). In these scenarios activities are handled on a day-to-day basis, which means raising resources is an ongoing undertaking. Planning is often considered a luxury 'we can't afford' or a relatively low priority investment.

The next stage is when the realization begins to dawn that some planning is needed, at least for raising and utilizing financial resources. The tool used here is the *budget*. This is nothing more than a forecast of the costs and revenues that organizational activities will generate in the following year. Generally, the budget is accompanied by a calculation of prospective cash flows to make the information gleaned from the planning process more meaningful.

Admittedly, drawing up a budget shifts the attention from daily operations to future activities. But this tool focuses exclusively on the financial aspects of organizational activities, without clarifying the connections between activities and results. So basically the usefulness of the budget is limited to monitoring financial equilibrium.

When an organization goes from simply drawing up a budget to planning all activities to carry out in the following year, it's truly raising the bar. At this point the *annual plan* comes into play. In a market-oriented organization, the takeoff point for this plan is usually forecast market performance, which provides a baseline for estimates on production volumes, financing needs, human resources, and so forth.

Now the budget becomes a financial summary of the annual plan, which in turn serves as a formal tool for integrating activities assigned to various organizational units. Integration makes it possible to coordinate timing, allocate resources more efficiently, and exploit synergies. In other words, it's integration that maximizes effectiveness and efficiency.

Organizations that have a more sophisticated planning process in place also adopt an even longer timeframe in what is normally referred to as a *strategic plan* (generally covering a three-year period). The motivation behind a long-term perspective is that strategic decisions (including marketing decisions, see Chapter 7) don't have immediate effects, but instead produce results in the medium term; to implement such decisions a series of activities must be carried out over time. This explains why some organizational activities only make sense within the context of a broader system that spans a number of years.

This represents the final evolutionary stage in planning systems. In market-oriented organizations, it goes without saying that the focal point of a strategic plan is the market and the phenomena impacting demand and competition in that market. Beginning with a rundown of the threats and opportunities in the environment (the market environment in particular), the plan provides an overall picture of the competitive scenario in question. With this in hand, the organization is able to recognize the actions it needs to take to modify or maintain its position in the individual areas of the market where it competes.

11.4   THE MARKETING PLAN

So, the marketing plan is a formal document, compiled by the organizational unit tasked with marketing decisions and activities (typically the Marketing Department). This plan sets down the *market objectives* to achieve in the upcoming year, the *marketing activities* that must be carried out in order to do so, and the relative *investments and costs*.

When the Marketing Department is adequately sized and structured, responsibilities are allocated among various roles (product managers, brand managers, communication managers, trade marketing managers, and others), and each one prepares a plan pertaining to his or her activities. So the marketing plan can include several constituent plans: a plan for each product or brand, a communication plan, a promotional plan, a marketing research plan, and so on and so forth for each category of activity.

The process of compiling a marketing plan takes place in a series of stages; the outcome of each is a section of the plan:

- Providing market analysis and diagnosis.
- Setting market objectives and formulating marketing strategies.

- Designing marketing programs.
- Action planning.
- Budgeting.
- Auditing.

Auditing comes after the plan has been executed (Section 11.4.6), so this stage doesn't produce a section of the plan, but a separate document (the marketing audit report). At the end of the year covered by the plan, this report ascertains whether or not pre-set objectives have been achieved, and if not, offers possible reasons why.

To be an effective tool for integrating Marketing and other organizational units, including Creativity, the marketing plan has to be conceived as a *communication tool* that serves to coordinate the units and to negotiate the resources needed to carry out activities. Basically, Marketing's aim is to persuade the other units that the activities it proposes will be effective, to provide input that can be used for facilitating coordination, and to solicit the necessary resources.

The last point doesn't refer solely to money, but rather any type of tangible or intangible resource that serves to conduct marketing activities: human resources to handle the biggest workload, consensus and commitment on projects on the agenda, and relationships without obstacles to hinder their effectiveness, to name a few.

An effective marketing plan is one that can demonstrate the quality of the activities it proposes. But how do we determine this quality? The answer is simple: *The quality of marketing activities is contingent on their effectiveness in reaching pre-set objectives, and in keeping pace with market evolution.*

So the more effective a plan is in revealing the opportunities generated by market evolution and the threats to the organization's institutional and competitive positions, the more valid its proposals will be in terms of relative activities and resources. As a result, the first stage in drawing up a marketing plan – analyzing and diagnosing market evolution – is essential to ensuring the plan serves its purposes in terms of communication, coordination, and negotiation.

This explains why the marketing plan should be seen as an internal communication project, and as such the messages it transmits should be chosen in light of the target audience. To enhance its communicative capacity, the plan generally begins with an *executive summary* that briefly outlines the contents, allowing readers to get a preliminary picture of what will be detailed in the sections to follow.

11.4.1 Providing market analysis and diagnosis

The aim of this stage is two-fold. The first is *analysis*: tracking noteworthy market phenomena that can potentially impact the organization and its market health. The second is *diagnosis*: interpreting phenomena in terms of type and intensity of their relative impact.

When drawing up a marketing plan, this stage produces a single section that serves as useful input for formulating objectives and strategies. But from a conceptual standpoint, analysis and diagnosis are separate, and managers and teams who compile the plan must keep them that way. For the first, objectivity is the priority, so the idea is to simply report the phenomena that are most influential in shaping market evolution; for the second, on the other hand, interpretation calls for subjectivity, which doesn't mean having a free rein, but rather competently and responsibly making sense of the various market phenomena and how they all interrelate.

So we can sum up the analysis and diagnosis stage with these questions:

a. How is the market changing?
b. What is the organization's current market position and how is that changing?

The organization needs to consider market evolution in both quantitative and qualitative terms. It's crucial to identify the variations in the size of the overall market and in individual components (segments, geographical areas, distribution channels, and so forth) to discern possible growth opportunities. Equally essential is detecting changes in the configuration of the market with regard to organizations that operate there (new competitors breaking into the market as opposed to veterans who are leaving it; customer segments that are gaining ground and others that are dwindling) and strategies and actions that these players undertake.

Qualitative and quantitative changes are clearly correlated, since it's the supply and demand dynamic that informs the lifecycle of the market itself (Section 7.2). In the analysis and diagnosis stage, discovering the underlying causes of change (or non-change) is vital. Awareness of these factors gives the organization an edge, a greater chance of intervening to exploit the resulting opportunities or defend itself from relative threats.

This is why it's useful to adopt a broader perspective when doing analysis, which means capturing all market factors – both internal and external – that can impact its quantitative and qualitative evolution. This stage in the marketing plan therefore goes beyond describing the organization's current market position to encompass a view of the macro-environment and the market environment.

11.4.1.1 *Macro-environmental analysis*
Several types of factor constitute the macro-environment surrounding any market:[2]

- Demographic.
- Macro-economic.
- Technological.
- Regulatory.
- Socio-cultural.
- Natural.

The marketing plan has to take into account any of the above that can potentially impact market evolution (Table 11.1).

Table 11.1 – Factors that constitute the macro-environment

Macro-environmental factors	Possible evaluation factors (for corporate clients in parenthesis)
Demographic	Population size and breakdown by: - age range (enterprise size class) - gender (industry) - place of residence (business area)
Macro-economic	GNP Level of consumption (investments) Unemployment rate Inflation rate Interest rate Exchange rate

(continued)

Table 11.1 – Continued

Macro-environmental factors	Possible evaluation factors (for corporate clients in parenthesis)
Technological	ICT Development index IDI Technological Infrastructure Level of technological competence in the general population (organizations) Technological standards on the market
Regulatory	Public subsidies Tax regmine applicable to the industry Law and regulations pertainting to products Anti-trust laws Consumer protection laws Environmental protection laws
Socio-cultural	Dominant and marginal values (organizational values) Dominant culture and sub-cultures (organizational values) Lifestyles (management style, decision-making styles) Level of education (competences) Sensitivity towards specific matter of public debate
Natural	Climate change Impact on population Exploitation of natural resources Seasonal weather Difference among regions/geographical area

Demographic factors have to do with variations in the population living in the geographical areas covered by the market; the idea is to highlight the causes behind changes, say, in the benefits customers seek or the size of market segments. Keep in mind that 'population' can refer to both consumer markets (the people who live in a given area) and business markets (organizations, companies, or institutions).

Let's consider a consumer market with an aging population, and take an example in the publishing industry. New needs may emerge in this scenario due to the declining physical abilities of consumers (who might want books with larger typeface or home delivery for their purchases). Or, these same consumers may start looking for hedonic benefits linked to nostalgia or identity (a penchant for books set in the past, or dedicated to the memory of certain places).

Macro-economic factors are the general characteristics of the economy that impact the behaviors of market players. Unemployment rates, interest rates, inflation, and exchange rates can all have considerable influence on the evolution of supply and demand.

For instance, a high unemployment rate leads to a general decline in people's spendable income, normally penalizing creative products, which aren't seen as essential compared to other product categories. On the other hand, a low rate of inflation would produce stable prices or even price declines, prompting people to consume more creative products. Likewise, when interest rates are low, new markets open up, and organizations are prone to invest in new products and processes.

Technological factors refer to the evolution of the technological infrastructure of the market in question; the development of technologies available to market players (in terms of production, distribution and communication); and general proficiency in utilizing these technologies. Technological change is perhaps the most powerful force as far as its potential for modifying the production and consumption scenario is concerned. In fact, thanks to upgrades in technology, organizations are better equipped to satisfy customer expectations more effectively (adding new benefits) and efficiently (reducing sacrifices).

An example that has come up repeatedly in the previous chapters is the evolution of digital technologies, which are revolutionizing countless creative industries, both on the production and consumption side. At the same time, more and more people are becoming tech-savvy, and have ready access to more powerful technological infrastructures. All this is causing an exponential explosion of certain markets (see digital music) while shrinking others (recorded music).

Regulatory factors, relating to laws that govern the behaviors of market players, can foster or hinder their actions or decisions, shaping the size and configuration of the market. For instance, many European countries offer tax breaks on investments in the movie industry to promote filmmaking, encouraging the launch of new films and activating demand. On the other hand, other regulations such as viewer restrictions (R, PG-13, and the like) exclude younger consumers and curb demand.

Socio-cultural factors play a major role in the evolution of creative product markets. These tie into the dominant values in a society, lifestyles, consumption cultures and sub-cultures, the general knowledge of consumers, and any other aspect relating to the deep-seated convictions of the market population (consumer or business). As often mentioned in Chapters 2 and 3, these factors are the main determinants of value expectations in creative sectors, in light of their positioning value (communicative and identity).

Factors related to the *natural environment* are last on this list, but they're becoming increasingly critical. This includes macro-factors linked to climate change and the exploitation of natural resources, which have tremendous impact on markets such as tourist destinations, to cite just one example. But there are also micro-factors to consider, for instance the weather during a given season or time period in a specific part of the world. Naturally, an especially wet and rainy summer will be detrimental to the market for live open-air events, but by the same token will drive demand for indoor theater performances.

11.4.1.2   Market environment analysis

This refers to the evolution of the supply–demand dynamic that emerges in any given market. With the help of the tool described in Chapter 7, the manager or team in charge of the marketing plan should describe the present stage in the market's lifecycle, its current size and the size of market potential gaps, as well as their underlying causes. In addition, the plan should break down the market into segments, accurately identifying the characteristics and attractive aspects of each one. This serves to highlight which market

opportunities are emerging, and which ones are shrinking or disappearing altogether.

Last of all, the marketing plan should clearly show the positions of current and possible future market competitors. For the former, the plan should detail their results (in terms of sales, market share, growth rate, and so on); the positioning of their value propositions (via perceptual and preference maps); and the key marketing decisions that have produced these results. The point of all this is to bring to light the strengths and weaknesses of every organization on market. For possible new entrants, however, the plan should speculate on the value propositions they might offer and market segments they could target, to assess the potential impact on the positions of incumbents.

11.4.1.3   Market position analysis

During the analysis stage, the marketing plan mustn't neglect to represent the organization's current position and its evolution in recent years. Clearly, the organization's present position is the outcome of prior decisions and actions on one hand,[3] and serves as input for the future on the other.

Analyzing the current position means, once again, taking a quantitative and qualitative perspective, with the first based on performance indicators detailed in Chapter 7 (breakdown of sales results and market share), and the second on choices as to product, brand, price, distribution, and communication pertaining to different value propositions. The aim of this analysis is to reconstruct a detailed map of cause–effect relationships between actions and results, a map that serves to verify the effectiveness and efficiency of organizational decisions.

Other analytical tools that a manager or team can use when drawing up the marketing plan, specifically regarding the organization's current position, are described in Chapters 7, 8, and 9. These relate to the creation of value propositions, product management, brand management, price management and management in a multi-channel and multi-media environment.

11.4.1.4   Diagnosis: the SWOT model

But simply identifying the phenomena impacting the evolution of the market and the organization's position in that market isn't enough to stake out a clear path on market objectives and activities to undertake in the following year. What's still missing is an interpretation of those phenomena that allows the organization to move from 'what' and 'why' to 'therefore.' The most common model used to do this is called *SWOT analysis*, which stands for strengths, weaknesses, opportunities, and threats.

Basically, as we now know, market phenomena are associated with a vast range of factors (both macro- and micro-environmental) relating to supply and demand, single entities or groups of organizations, current market players or potential entrants, and so forth. This being the case, the organization needs a model that represents these different phenomena with a system of unequivocal codes, a model that makes it possible to compare and contrast them all.

The interpretative codes used in SWOT analysis are very simple. Every event external to the organization (either in the macro- or the market environment) is interpreted as an *opportunity to capture* or a *threat to the organization's positions*. All internal elements that determine the organization's current position (quantitative and qualitative) are either *strengths* or *weaknesses*, if the organization wants to pursue those opportunities or defend itself from those threats, both in absolute terms and relative to other organizations.

The interpretative power of SWOT analysis derives from its simplicity. In fact, assuming that all firms and non-profits want to survive today and prosper tomorrow, it's easy to see that they need to take advantage of opportunities and defend themselves from threats, and to do so they need to leverage their strengths and neutralize their weaknesses.

To reinforce its communicative power even further, SWOT analysis is usually translated into a matrix depicting events that represent opportunities or threats (Figure 11.2). For opportunities, the matrix shows where the organization has strengths it can exploit to take full advantage of them or weaknesses that might prevent it from doing so. For threats, instead, strengths emerge that can serve as the foundation for defensive barriers, as well as weaknesses that may represent real hazards.

The matrix serves as a representation of general strategic implications based on a diagnosis of various phenomena. When the organization's strengths correspond to market opportunities, this is where marketing will concentrate its efforts in order to capture them and turn them into positive results (Quadrant I). However, for opportunities where the organization shows weaknesses (Quadrant II), marketing managers need to reflect on the causes underpinning these weaknesses and whether or not to develop resources and competences to compensate for them in order to capitalize on these opportunities in the future. The threats that arise where the organization has more strengths would be motivation for setting up contingency plans for defending the current position (Quadrant III). And finally, and most critical of all, are threats where the organization shows weaknesses (Quadrant IV). Depending on how serious these threats are, the organization may need to come up with defensive actions for the medium- to long-term, so as to avoid jeopardizing the financial and market stability of the organization.

Here's an example. Let's take a publishing house that puts out hobby magazines (cooking, gardening, model building and collecting among others), and say that the Marketing Director is working on the marketing plan for next year. On average, of the magazines in the portfolio, 10 per cent of sales come from subscriptions, and in-store sales account for the remaining 90 per cent. As for the company's revenues, 40 per cent are generated from magazine sales and 60 per cent from advertising. The company sells both offline and online versions of every title, with the latter available by subscription only.

Figure 11.2 – SWOT matrices

All the publisher's titles are market leaders in their respective topics, and enjoy impressive brand awareness and image, as does the corporate brand. This is thanks to the fact that company has always implemented a brand endorsement strategy (Section 8.2.4.2), and earmarked sizeable investments for the master brand.

Recent phenomena characterizing the macro-environment include: a recession, expected to last a few more years, which brings with it a drop in consumer purchases and advertising investments; less free time for the average person, which means less time spent on hobbies; a decrease in the birth rate, which ultimately leads to a smaller population; and a rise in immigration, resulting in more people who don't speak the native language.

Noteworthy market phenomena are: the exit of two medium-sized competitors, due to the recession; more free websites and blogs dedicated to the same topics covered in the publisher's magazines; the emergence of an online publisher of hobby magazines, with subscriptions and single issues that cost around 50 per cent less than our publisher; and fewer stores that sell magazines and newspapers.

So the market outlook is quite bleak, with almost all of the macro-environmental and market phenomena described above representing a threat to the publisher's market positions. As cases in point, the shrinking population and the economic recession, as well as the fact that people have less and less free time, all point to a contraction in future sales. Add to this free websites and blogs, and new online competitors, and the publisher's market position is even more tenuous. But opportunities are out there, such as the potential emergence of a new segment: readers who speak different languages other than the native tongue. Taking advantage of this opportunity may be the access route to new markets abroad. Another opportunity comes from market share that's now left open by the exit of the two competitors mentioned above.

The strengths the publisher can leverage to defend its position are brand awareness and image of the various products in the portfolio. With the right marketing activities, these could ensure a pool of loyal readers and may also lead to line extensions (Section 8.2.3.2.2), launching new titles in foreign languages. In any case, the first thing to do is to formulate plans for online development, countering the competition in that channel, and to set up strategies for recovering

efficiency, responding to the price attack by these competitors.

So back to our Marketing Director. She can assume that two phenomena – the recession and less time spent on hobbies – are only temporary, and that the publisher has what it takes to defend itself successfully from both. The new online competitors are a different story, because these are threats where the publisher has weaknesses due to a more traditional business model with a much higher cost structure. To respond the publisher will have to rethink its strategy almost entirely. Instead, the emerging segment and the market space that was once occupied by the two former competitors are both opportunities to take advantage of by leveraging brand strength, which may attract the readers who no longer find their magazines on the shelves.

The example above also reveals *the major limitation of traditional SWOT analysis: it makes no distinction between the different kinds of threats and opportunities.* For an organization, in fact, not all opportunities are equally attractive, just as not all the threats are equally dangerous. For our publisher, the rising popularity garnered by online competitors might be a much more serious threat than the decrease in the amount of free time people spend on their hobbies. By the same token, the emergence of a segment of resident foreigners might be a less attractive opportunity than the market left open by two former competitors.

There is a way to capture these differences and to make SWOT analysis more relevant, for the purposes of formulating marketing strategies. That is to introduce parameters for comparing and contrasting the various opportunities and threats, as well as strengths and weaknesses.

Here are some very effective criteria, in the form of questions. How attractive is a given opportunity? What are the chances that the organization can capture it successfully? As for a threat, how much damage could it cause? How likely is it to actually occur? To implement these parameters, the manager or the team drawing up the plan have to give their opinion on relevant market events, and on each of the significant elements inside the organization. These opinions make the diagnostic value of the SWOT analysis even more powerful by revealing how solid the organization's strengths are and how severe its weaknesses.

Once analysis and diagnosis is complete, the organization will recognize the potential of its offerings.

Having highlighted the relationships between recent changes in the market and the organization's current position, it can formulate hypotheses on growth opportunities that will be explored more fully in the next stage of the plan.

11.4.2 Setting market objectives and formulating marketing strategies

A number of factors combine to determine market objectives: on the one hand, opportunities and threats that arise from market evolution that were diagnosed in the previous stage; on the other, the organization's general aims and the mission it intends to pursue. Achieving market objectives isn't an end in itself, but instead serves to reach broader goals that are typically financial for companies, and institutional for non-profits.

The mission is *the ultimate aim of the organization, why it exists and functions*, and ideally why it stands

apart from other organizations (Case History 11.1). So the mission serves as a guideline for the strategic choices and actions, including marketing. Going back to our publisher in the example above, if market analysis shows growth in the market for gossip tabloids, the company may well decide to ignore this opportunity in light of its mission, which is to 'disseminate the culture of active free time based on learning and developing competences.'

Market objectives are expressed in terms of quantitative indicators, typically sales (value and volume) and market share (likewise). To make auditing more effective, it's useful to break these data down on various levels of the market: sales and share per segment, geographical area, distribution channel, and so forth. This helps more clearly discern possible discrepancies between actual results and forecasts.

For a description of how to set objectives and formulate the right marketing strategies to achieve

Case History 11.1

The mission of New York's Museum of Modern Art (www.moma.org)

Founded in 1929 as an educational institution, the Museum of Modern Art is dedicated to being the foremost museum of modern art in the world. Through the leadership of its trustees and staff, the Museum of Modern Art manifests this commitment by establishing, preserving, and documenting a permanent collection of the highest order that reflects the vitality, complexity, and unfolding patterns of modern and contemporary art; by presenting exhibitions and educational programs of unparalleled significance; by sustaining a library, archives, and a conservation laboratory that are recognized as international centers of research; and by supporting scholarship and publications of preeminent intellectual merit.

Central to the Museum of Modern Art's mission is the encouragement of an ever-deeper understanding and enjoyment of modern and contemporary art by the diverse local, national, and international audiences that it serves. To achieve its goals the Museum of Modern Art recognizes the following:

º Modern and contemporary art originated in the exploration of the ideals and interests generated in the new artistic traditions that began in the late nineteenth century and continue today.
º Modern and contemporary art transcend national boundaries and encompass all forms of visual expression, including painting and sculpture, drawings, prints and illustrated books, photography, architecture and design, and film and video, as well as new forms yet to be developed or understood, that reflect and explore the artistic issues of the era.
º These forms of visual expression are an open-ended series of arguments and counter-arguments that can be explored through exhibitions and installations and are reflected in the Museum's multi-faceted collection.
º It is essential to affirm the importance of contemporary art and artists if the Museum is to honor the ideals on which it was founded and remain vital and engaged with the present.
º This commitment to contemporary art enlivens and informs our evolving understanding of the traditions of modern art.
º To remain at the forefront of its field, the Museum needs an outstanding professional staff and must periodically reevaluate itself, responding to new ideas and initiatives with insight, imagination, and intelligence. The process of reevaluation is mandated by the Museum's tradition, which encourages openness and a willingness to evolve and change.

In sum, the Museum of Modern Art seeks to create a dialogue between the established and the experimental, the past and the present, in an environment that is responsive to the issues of modern and contemporary art, while remaining accessible to a public that ranges from experts and scholars to young children.

them, refer back to Section 7.5. But here it's worthwhile to emphasize that even though many marketing strategies are anchored on the implicit assumption of growth (in sales or share), in some situations organizations might have different aims: for instance, consolidating or reducing the market position, or even retreating from a certain market altogether.

Consolidating the market position is usually what organizations do at the end of a growth phase, after having expanded market share. The reasoning behind this objective is to obtain returns on investments (returns that may be financial, image, institutional, among others), while gearing up for a new period of growth in keeping with the flow of the market lifecycle (Sections 7.2 and 7.12).

In operational terms, organizations can pursue this objective by:

- Shoring up their strengths.
- Minimizing/neutralizing their weaknesses.

As we've seen in the previous stage, analysis and diagnosis reveal strengths and weaknesses. Once these are identified, if any modifications to the value propositions are needed, these are outlined in the marketing plan along with relative investments and resources, a timeline for implementation, and possible barriers to overcome. All this ensures that the strengths are leveraged for future development plans, and weaknesses are minimized so as not to thwart those plans.

Reducing the market position is often called *harvesting*. Generally speaking, this would be a viable option when an organization realizes that market conditions will no longer generate results that serve to achieve its more general goals and/or its mission. So the logical move would be to focus solely on a profitable portion of the market. Harvesting can be done by paring down either:

- The number of segments/customers served.
- The number of value propositions.

In the first case, management needs to analyze the attractiveness of each segment/customer, in both financial and strategic terms. To calculate the margin that would be lost, the organization considers the drop in revenues – and reduction in costs – that would follow an exit from less attractive segments. But beyond 'number crunching,' non-financial repercussions mustn't be ignored, such as loss of image and competences. Likewise, in the second case, after evaluating the attractiveness of individual value propositions, and the pros and cons of eliminating each one (Section 8.1.5.3),

the organization can decide whether or not to go ahead with harvesting.

Retreating from the market is a strategic choice that generally comes into play when the market is in decline (Section 7.2), or when the organization's weaknesses make it impossible to operate in that market profitably, either from a financial or institutional perspective. Clearly, the organization needs other markets to move into, either ones that are growing or that offer the opportunity to pursue organizational objectives. If no such options exist, deciding to exit a market means going out of business entirely. Leaving a market may involve selling owned brands or product competences, or simply closing the organization down.

11.4.3   Designing marketing programs

This is when specific marketing activities are decided on that serve to reach market objectives, within the framework of the strategies set down in the previous section of the marketing plan. Basically, designing marketing programs consists of constructing a map of prospective cause–effect relationships, the same map that is compiled retrospectively when analyzing the organization's current position (Section 11.4.1.3). The question to answer is: Which activities are expected to contribute to which objectives? The more meticulous the manager/team is in breaking down objectives, the more accurately will they draw connections between activities and objectives.

Activities are the outcome of typical decisions relating to value proposition creation, product management, brand management, price management, and management of a multi-channel and multi-media environment, for each of the target segments the organization aims to serve. (For individual decision-making models, see Chapters 7, 8, and 9.)

11.4.4   Action planning

The actions referred to here are the implementation of activities decided on in the previous stage. In concrete terms, the manager/team has to establish:

- When the activities will be carried out.
- Who will be responsible for each one.

As for the first point, timing relates to when a given activity will begin and end. Although for some activities exact dates can't be set while the plan is being drafted, it's still important to try to establish as accurate a timeline as possible.

Assigning responsibilities obviously means deciding who does what. In the Marketing Department, depending on their organizational roles, individuals will be assigned tasks, offered incentives to perform them, and evaluated on their performance. Accountability is crucial so that later, during the auditing stage, if the organization falls short in any way it can discover why.

11.4.5   Budgeting

Last of all, the budget is a document that sums up forecasts of revenues and costs associated with the marketing plan, which represent the determinants of profits or losses. The budget serves not only to demonstrate the financial result of the set of marketing activities, but also to pinpoint the costs of each one, so that any discrepancies can be scrutinized in the auditing stage.

11.4.6   Auditing

The final stage consists of verifying whether or not the pre-set objectives have been achieved. As we've already said, this stage comes after all the others are concluded, when all the decisions in the plan have actually been made and the activities carried out. That said, in some cases organizations may run audits first at intermediate intervals to monitor progress and then at year's end for final confirmation.

But auditing isn't only about corroborating success or failure in reaching objectives. Instead, this stage serves to reveal the reasons for missing or exceeding targets. So auditing entails analyzing variances in results and deciding how they can be rectified, if need be.

Variances refer to market and budget objectives. In the first case, the idea is to determine where the organization succeeded in hitting its targets, and how far off it was when it failed to do so. Backtracking on the analysis-decision-action-result path leads to the causes for these variances. In some cases, objectives are achieved but budget estimates aren't respected. For instance, an organization may have successfully reached its goal of growing market share by 10 per cent, but it costed 20 per cent more than anticipated. The aim of examining budget variances is to evaluate how efficiently resources are utilized.

Both for market and budget objectives, analyzing variances reveals the underlying causes and suggests *possible corrections* in terms of decisions, actions, timing, and responsibilities that will provide input for the planning process for the following period or year.

11.5   CONCLUSIONS

And so we come to the end; our long journey through the world of marketing in creative industries is about to conclude. In this last chapter I've tried to tie together all the strings running through the previous chapters, where I've presented a marketing management model that's appropriate for creative industries, and then provided an analytical description of it. My intention was essentially to underscore the fact that in an organization, it's not enough to have the competences to make all the typical marketing decisions detailed here. Analytical and decisional competences can only be effective in a climate of collaboration, mutual understanding, and trust in the organization. This ensures that every person and each organizational unit has faith in the ability of all the others to do their job effectively.

People need motivation, incentives, and rewards (when they've earned them). This is the only way they'll be willing to dedicate their competences and energy to the organization. But this is an issue that goes beyond the scope of this book. In this final chapter, I wanted to focus on tools that can be implemented to foster integration between Marketing and Creativity, so that at least some of the relational challenges can be avoided or minimized, and the organization can move in the direction of productive collaboration.

In any case, the long path that we've taken in this book should demonstrate beyond a doubt that marketing can do great things for creativity. Marketing management, when it's done correctly, effectively, and appropriately, is one of the keys to success for companies and non-profits that operate in creative industries.

REVIEW QUESTIONS

1. What are the main cultural and organizational barriers to Marketing–Creativity integration? Why and how are they different? How are they interconnected?
2. What are the effects of integration mechanisms related to organizational structure? And what are the effects of those related to managerial systems?
3. What are the different stages of a marketing plan? What are the outcomes of each stage?
4. What are the main components of macro-environmental analysis?
5. How can opportunities and threats, strengths and weaknesses be assessed?

NOTES

1 CREATIVE INDUSTRIES

1. It is interesting to note that in the US the term *copyright industries* is used. The EU groups together both traditional cultural industries and more modern ones such as fashion, design, and video games in the cultural economy. France presented the first study aimed at quantifying the economic value of creative ventures in 2006, but adopted a very conservative approach which took into account only traditional cultural industries.
2. Interested readers can find exhaustive descriptions in Hesmondhalgh (2002); Hartley (2005); Hesmondhalgh (2007); UNCTAD (2008); and Santagata (2008).
3. Interesting research on motivation to re-consume creative products was carried out by Russell and Levy (2012).
4. For readers who are interested in further reading on this topic, I recommend two seminal works: Baudrillard (1983) and Lyotard (1984).

2 A CUSTOMER-CENTRIC MARKETING MODEL FOR CREATIVE INDUSTRIES

1. In these first two chapters I always refer to 'product' or 'service' simply to introduce the topic of the specificities of creative industries. As we gradually turn our attention to marketing, we'll move the product back into place as one of the components of an organization's offering and of the value provided to consumers.
2. Case in point: when referring to creative 'industries', interdisciplinary literature more commonly uses terms such as 'fields' (for example, *cultural fields*: Bourdieu, 1984), 'worlds' (*art worlds*: Becker, 1982), or more often 'systems' (the tourism system – Mill and Morrison, 2009; the fashion system – Barthes, 1990).
3. Ryan et al. (2010) give a detailed interpretation of one of the Gob Squad's performances in terms of consumption experience.
4. The most consolidated research tradition centers on the movie industry, where researchers have proven that reviews by critics are capable of impacting both box office sales when a film is first released and in the weeks immediately following (Basuroy et al., 2003; Eliashberg and Shugan, 1997; Lampel and Shamsie, 2000; Moon et al., 2010; Reinstein and Snyder, 2005). In other creative

industries too research has shown that reviews can influence the choices made both by consumers as well as producers, such as with live performances, (Reddy et al., 1998), publishing (Sedo, 2008), and fashion (Cillo and Prandelli, 2012).
5. The first year, one book was presented every week for the eight weeks leading up to the British Book Award. Later the program adopted the format that continued until it ended in 2009.
6. Other examples that have been the subject of extensive analysis in the world of visual art include Abstract Expressionism, which emerged in the 1940s and 1950s (Caves, 2000: 216–18), and more recently modern Indian art, which won internationally recognition from the mid-1990s to the 2000s (Khaire and Wadhwani, 2010).
7. Chris Cornell, singer and guitarist for the group.

3 THE CONSUMER SIDE OF THE MARKET: THE CONSUMPTION EXPERIENCE

1. This classification builds on one proposed by Holbrook (1999). This author's model includes a third dimension: the consumer's level of activity in attaining product value, which gives rise to a distinction between *active value* and *reactive value*. The first refers to 'physical or mental manipulation' that the customer does on or with the product to extract its value. The second, instead, is the value the customer obtains from a practically passive relationship with the product, which may be appreciation, contemplation, admiration, and so forth. In my opinion, this distinction is far too subtle, and in some cases difficult to apply, so I prefer to use only the other two dimensions Holbrook suggests.
2. In researching collectors of contemporary art and visitors to contemporary art exhibits, Chen (2009) showed that both types of consumers have a powerful spiritual motivation. They express this as the desire to find stimuli for their most intimate reflections and existential doubts, shelter for the soul from suffering, and space for a sense of the profound that is lacking in daily life.
3. We can also add *physiological resources* to this list, referring to the physical conditions, the energy, and the effort expended in the various stages of the consumption experience. Although undoubtedly these resources are significant (a consumer who is hard of hearing may have a less

satisfying experience listening to music, for example), I believe that they are relatively less relevant than the others. The reason is that creative products, compared to other product categories, require fewer physiological resources. What's more, the stock of these resources that every consumer has can be considered one of the personal characteristics that gives rise to specific expectations, so we'll deal with these resources as they relate to said characteristics. Basically, as far as physiological resources go, I'll assume that they are a given and that their impact on the purchase and consumption experience is homogeneous in each individual consumer with regard to various categories of creative products.

4. The most detailed typology of consumption practices, which I refer to and adopt here, was proposed by Holt (1995), who studied spectators at US baseball games.

5. Holt (1995) uses the term *accounting* instead of *associating* and *categorizing*.

6. Holt (1995) uses a slightly different label for these activities, and for the practice described later on. I think that some of the distinctions and denominations Holt proposes do not clearly delineate the activities in question, so I prefer a different classification.

7. This case study, co-authored with Marilia Sciulli, is an adaptation of her graduate dissertation. Data were collected via in-depth interviews with teachers and dancers, and through netnographic analysis of a number of forums dedicated to tango.

4 THE CONSUMER SIDE OF THE MARKET: THE OTHER STAGES OF THE EXPERIENCE

1. My aim here is not to detail all the research on the topic of aesthetic taste. For an overview of various research streams, interested readers can refer to Hoyer and Stockburger-Sauer (2012) and Wagner (1999).

2. The compensatory model that represents a product's expected value as the weighted average of the assessment of its attributes was developed in studies on beliefs and attitudes conducted by Ajzen and Fishbein (Ajzen and Fishbein, 1980; Fishbein, 1963; Fishbein and Ajzen, 1975).

3. The original model proposed by Mehrabian and Russell (1974) advanced the hypothesis that one of the emotional responses of the individual is *dominance*, which refers to the feeling of control over the surrounding environment and the freedom to act. As a result, this model became known by the acronym PAD (pleasure, arousal, dominance). However, later empirical studies (Donovan and Rossiter, 1982; Russell and Pratt, 1980) demonstrated that the impact of dominance on individual behavior is minimal, which is why I decided not to include it here.

4. To distinguish between these last two types, we need data that the author doesn't report, that is, how many people

bought a book in a bookstore (in which case we can hypothesize an unplanned purchase) or in a store with a generic assortment of merchandise, which also happens to include books (in which case we can more easily imagine an impulse purchase).

5. This case study, co-authored with Davide Neri, is an adaptation of his graduate dissertation. Data were collected via in-depth interviews with players and shop owners, through participant observation of a number of Magic gaming events, and through interviews with managers of Wizards of the Coast, a Hasbro company.

5 THE BUSINESS SIDE OF THE MARKET

1. According to a recent report by IEG/Performance Research (2013) on decisions relating to sponsorships by a hundred or so companies worldwide, the most important objectives are: increasing brand loyalty (for 80% of respondents); creating awareness/visibility (77%); changing or reinforcing image (65%); demonstrating social responsibility (51%).

2. In practice, product placement can either be *paid placement* when there is monetary compensation, or *non-paid placement* when the commercial transaction involves an exchange that has economic (but not monetary) value, for example, providing free advertising space or merchandise. In both cases, placement is the outcome of a commercial transaction, and not a purely creative choice, and it's this type of placement that I'll discuss in the remainder of this chapter.

7 IDENTIFYING TARGET MARKETS AND CREATING VALUE PROPOSITIONS

1. By innovation I'm not referring exclusively to technology (like 3D in the movie industry or e-books in publishing), but any innovation in the typology of production factors and/or how they are combined. For example, free daily newspapers such as *Metro* have given rise to an innovation in the newspaper industry because production and distribution requires a new combination of factors, as compared to traditional newspaper publishing.

2. In the pharmaceutical industry, for example, the total eradication of a disease would eliminate the need for the drugs that cure it.

3. All the different market metrics (potential, actual, and for single organizations) can be measured in terms of volume (number of units sold) or value, the latter equaling quantity multiplied by the corresponding benchmark price (average retail price or product price set by individual organizations).

4. The market potential gap can also be calculated as the difference with respect to the entire current market, in which case the formula is as follows:

$$PotGap_t = MktPot_t - Mkt_t$$

where Mkt_t represents the current market at time t.

5. These data are hypothetical, used simply to illustrate how to make an estimate.

6. In many creative industries, there are marketing research companies that run panels (Section 6.5.5) made up of consumers or distributors; these panels provide data on sales and market share for various competitors.

7. To calculate these indicators of market share algebraically, multiply the ratio representing market share ($S_{i\,t}/S_{tot\,t}$) by the ratio $P_{sc\,it}/P_{sc\,it}$ which, being equal to 1, doesn't modify the value of market share; then invert the denominators of the two ratios.

8. Multiply $P_{sc\,i\,t}/S_{tot\,t}$ by the quantities n/n_j and N_t/N_t (which equal 1, so they don't change the value) and invert the denominators of the three ratios.

9. Clearly, this doesn't hold true for a market with only a small number of customers. An example would be the Old Masters in visual arts. There being so few art galleries that offer relevant services (appraisal, consulting, and so on), at such exorbitant prices, they do so in an extremely personalized fashion. In the business market, instead, an interesting example is provided by sponsorships of world sporting events (the Olympics, the World Cup, Formula 1), where once again the package offered to sponsors tends to be highly personalized.

10. Actually, the authors don't claim that comfort and customer care constitute basic factors; instead they simply underscore the fact that these benefits don't impact satisfaction. Having measured only linear relationships between benefits and satisfaction, the type of analysis they conducted didn't allow them to detect any impact on one single extreme of the variable 'satisfaction', without affecting the other. This is also probably the reason why they didn't identify excitement factors. In any case, the label 'basic factors' is my personal interpretation.

11. There are a number of data analysis methods that can provide a picture of positioning. The most common and effective are multivariate analysis methods, which allow the organization to take into account several variables simultaneously. The two main classes are *attribute-based* and *non-attribute-based*. The first (which include models such as factor analysis, discriminant analysis, and correspondence analysis) are based on capturing respondents' judgments regarding the individual components of the positioning by rating them via numerical scaling or ranking. The second (including multi-dimensional scaling) reveals perceptions of similarity/dissimilarity among all the pairs of value propositions to investigate (via numerical scaling). For further reading on these methods, I recommend Aaker et al. (1998).

12. The invention of the e-reader is generally credited to NuvoMedia with its Rocket eBook and Gemstage with the SoftBook Reader, which both debuted in 1998. However, Amazon created the actual market for electronic books, thanks to its joint launch of the Kindle in 2009 along with a vast catalogue of digital books.

8   CREATING VALUE WITH THE PRODUCT, THE BRAND, AND THE PRICE

1. The proliferation of digital content makes it possible to accentuate the number of levels, and the multiplication of individual products, by *unbundling* (Section 8.1.5.2.3). This refers to selling products separately that were previously only offered as a set. For instance, now consumers can buy a single instead of an entire CD, or one newspaper article instead of an entire issue, or one chapter of a book.

2. For simplicity's sake, I'll refer mainly to the consumer market for creative products. That said, the considerations I make here can be applied to the business market, while acknowledging the differences between the two. What's more, the two lifecycles are closely interrelated because demand for creative products in business markets derives from demand in the consumer market (Chapter 5). For example, if sales of contemporary Chinese paintings are on the rise, it's very likely that corporate support linked to this art form will grow as a result, because the benefits of enhanced awareness and image transfer underpinning corporate support may be more easily acquired by investing in a product category that's enjoying enhanced visibility and increased sales on the market (all other conditions being equal).

3. Clearly this is true in general terms. Take the length of hiking trails, for instance. This characteristic impacts functional benefits such as easy accessibility, and requirements of no particular athletic prowess. But that doesn't mean that hiking trails can't generate other kinds of benefits (or sacrifices). For example, very long trails could generate a hedonic benefit linked to self-concept for certain market segments (the self-image of an expert hiker) or exclusivity, which would be a communicative benefit.

4. In many creative industries, particularly for products where a blockbuster strategy applies, sales during and immediately following the product launch are considered critical. In fact, these sales are proof of market appreciation, and as well as the possibility to recover pre-launch investments. Another factor to consider is the word-of-mouth effect.

5. What's become very popular today are online STMs. Consumers are invited to interact with a computer program that presents a series of products, different advertising messages, and other informational material, and then they're allowed to make their purchase choices.

6. Data on importance and performance is collected via quantitative marketing research so they can be generalized for the entire market. The two indicators can be built

by gathering data with a numerical scale, and then measuring averages from the sample. In light of the discussion in Chapters 3 and 4, it's clear that the importance of attributes for customers is an indicator of the value they expect, while relative performance is an indicator of the value they perceive. This explains why the importance-performance matrix can also be used to improve the overall value proposition, inserting product attributes not only in the evaluation, but also in all components of the proposition.

7. The two motivations are often interrelated. In fact, the drop in sales due to market decline can be so extreme as to make it impossible to cover product costs, triggering systematic losses. But in some cases there is no connection at all. Even with solid sales there may be inefficiencies in management that generate costs that are too high to be recovered.

8. Managers mustn't forget that since image is the fruit of judgment, it can be positive or negative. In the latter case it creates negative value that obviously leads to opposite reactions from customers. Since organizations seek positive brand image, in the rest of the book I'll talk about image with positive connotations.

9. The *Nation Brand Index*, invented by Simon Anholt and published annually by GfK Roper, is a yearly assessment of most OECD countries on the basis of economic, cultural, social, and technological criteria (Anholt, 2009). Data are collected through interviews with a variety of categories of stakeholders: citizens, tourists, investors, and others.

10. For simplicity's sake, I refer to consumers, but for corporate clients the same considerations are also valid (acknowledging the differences between the two markets).

11. The 'demand curve' comes from classic Economics jargon. But in marketing it's much more common to use 'revenue curve'. However, to be consistent with the mathematical formulas presented in this section, which are derived from Economics, I'll use the term 'demand curve'.

12. So it corresponds to the first derivative of total revenues.

13. 'Profit equals zero' can be considered representative of the financial sustainability of all non-profit institutions.

14. Consider the effects of lower production and distribution costs in numerous creative industries thanks to digital technologies.

15. Another possible solution is to rely on public subsidies. This is the case for all state-owned or public organizations. As mentioned in Chapter 1, public funding is also available in nearly all creative industries because they are considered vital to the advancement of society and the identity of the host community.

16. 'Fixed' shouldn't be confused with 'independent'. Remember, one of the benefits corporate clients look for when purchasing property rights for creative products is achieving awareness and reach. So most likely as these increase, the potential revenues of the sponsee grow because property rights have greater value for corporate

clients. In this sense, revenues aren't independent of volumes; instead the total is fixed. Here's an example: sponsoring a sports team might cost one million euro or three, depending on the fan base that team has, but that amount isn't set as a variable, like 15 euro per fan, for instance. That said, sometimes a variable component does come into play, and is often paid ex-post as a performance bonus.

17. In Economics this level is traditionally referred to as the *reservation price*.

18. *Conjoint analysis* is a commonly used technique for determining the maximum price level by means of simulating customers' choice processes. With this technique, respondents aren't given a single product but a series of fictional product profiles with different prices. These profiles are created by combining various product attributes (price included); respondents are then asked for their judgments on each one. Based on this feedback conjoint analysis allows researchers to establish the different price thresholds. For further reading on this technique, I recommend Green and Srinivasan (1978, 1990).

19. For this reason this method is also called *segmentation pricing*.

20. This is why it's associated with an additional category of pricing methods known as *profit-based*.

9 DELIVERING VALUE TO THE CUSTOMER: MANAGING A MULTI-MEDIA, MULTI-CHANNEL ENVIRONMENT

1. The POE model was created to distinguish between various communication media in relation to the ownership/control by the organization that uses them. In light of the transformations in today's media, I believe this model can be extended to apply to any type of touchpoint.

2. *Circulation* in publishing means the difference between the number of printed copies less the number of unsold copies, which leaves the number of copies that are actually sold.

3. In some creative industries, the concept of a 'store' is a broad one. In the television industry, for instance, pay TV platforms (cable or satellite) represent for owners of television stations the equivalent of independent 'stores'. The same applies to museums and exhibition centers for visual artists, and theaters for performing artists. On the other hand, DTTV or broadcast network channels can be compared to owned stores (Section 9.4.4), just like permanent repertory companies or orchestras.

4. In this sense, collective events are borderline paid and owned touchpoints.

5. In terms of their contact with the target audience, shop assistants are comparable to people who work in the ticket booth of a non-profit, or a company that sells tickets for access to its products or services. More examples

include the staff of organizations responsible for public open spaces like national parks, such as security guards, receptionists, and guides.

6. Marketing communication isn't the only communication activity undertaken by companies and non-profits, which in fact systematically communicate with various stakeholders in a number of ways. *Financial communication*, obviously, is addressed to investors, government, and donors, who want updates on financial forecasts and results, and spending reports. *Institutional communication* instead is sent to third parties that interact with the organization to realize its mission; these would include local communities to garner consensus and support; government agencies to obtain authorization and support; and others who are involved in projects and initiatives. *Internal communication* is between the organization and its employees and collaborators, to ensure a positive organizational climate to support the organization's projects and activities. Finally, *marketing communication* is designed specifically for market players (customers, distributors, and competitors) for the purpose of creating a strong image for the organization and its activities, promoting the sale of its products and brands.

7. Some of the most popular, especially in the world of advertising, are the AIDA model (Attention, Interest, Desire, Action), and the hierarchy of effects framework, which classes objectives as Awareness, Knowledge, Liking, Preference, Conviction, or Purchase.

8. This is why this kind of communication is usually called *pull* (as is 'pulled' or initiated by the customer). However, advertising and other more traditional forms of contact are *push*, because they're initiatives taken by organizations, not solicited by customers. One effect of the ubiquity of the digital channels described in Section 9.1.1 is a shift in weight of the two forms of communication, with *pull* predominating more than ever before.

9. In the jargon of traditional advertising, these decisions are part of *media planning*.

10. Clearly, producers can maintain control over certain activities while outsourcing them. For instance, an organization that wants to control logistics doesn't necessarily have to own trucks or warehouses; it can simply buy related services from specialized companies. The difference is between design and execution. With direct control, producers choose how to design activities, but leave the actual execution up to external service providers. With indirect channels, both design and execution are taken over by intermediaries, but producers can try to motivate and influence them through trade marketing activities (Section 9.7.3).

11. In this section I'll focus on decisions regarding offline stores; go to Section 9.6.3.2 for a discussion of online stores.

12. For further reading on retail management, I recommend Castaldo et al. (2013) and Levy and Weitz (2012).

10   MANAGING CUSTOMER VALUE OVER TIME: CUSTOMER RELATIONSHIP MANAGEMENT

1. Here and in the following sections, for simplicity's sake I'll refer to relationships with customers. But the same concepts apply (with appropriate adaptations) apply for all the actors the organization has relationships with. In creative industries these ideas are especially pertinent for donors and corporate clients; the organization can design ad hoc relational activities for them following the guidelines described in the following sections (after having identified the stage and the status of the relationship).

2. The Italian law allows taxpayers to devolve five per thousand of the amount due on their income tax to non-profits that undertake artistic, cultural, and social activities or international cooperation.

3. For a review of the scales used to measure trust, I recommend Castaldo (2007).

4. To be more precise, the organization 'extracts' customers from the database using a variety of techniques, from simple cross tabulation to reveal associations among variables, to more sophisticated *data mining*. The first relate to an a priori approach to market segmentation; the second to an a posteriori one (Section 7.7.2).

5. The customers who respond with a 7 or 8 are called *passives*, who are satisfied but wouldn't go so far as to recommend the organization to others.

11   INTEGRATING MARKETING AND CREATIVITY

1. Again, the literature on cross-functional cooperation is quite rich in recommendations on various integrating mechanisms. I suggest Leenders and Wierenga (2002) and Dawes and Massey (2005) for further reading on this topic.

2. The basic analytical model for the macro-environment is called PEST, which stands for politics, economics, society, and technology. The evolution of societies and markets has gradually led to the inclusion of other types of factors, expanding the model with respect to the basic version.

3. The timeframe to use depends on the specific actions undertaken by the organization in the years prior to the plan. As a rule, the previous year is a standard benchmark, because the current position is undoubtedly contingent on the activities included in the relative marketing plan. But if the annual marketing plan is part of a three-year strategic plan, as described above, the key decisions in this longer time horizon should also be taken into consideration.

BIBLIOGRAPHY

Aaker, D.A. and Keller, K.L. (1990) "Consumer Evaluations of Brand Extensions," *Journal of Marketing*, 54, 1, 27–41.

Aaker, D.A., Kumar, V., and Day, G.S. (1998) *Marketing Research* (New York: Wiley).

Addis, M. and Holbrook, M.B. (2010) "Consumers' Identification and Beyond: Attraction, Reverence, and Escapism in the Evaluation of Films," *Psychology & Marketing*, 27, 9, 821–45.

Ahuvia, A.C. (2005) "Beyond the Extended Self: Loved Objects and Consumers' Identity Narratives," *Journal of Consumer Research*, 32, 1, 171–84.

Ainslie, A., Dreze, X. and Zufryden, F. (2005) "Modeling Movie Lifecycles and Market Share," *Marketing Science*, 24, 508–17.

Ajzen, I. and Fishbein, M. (1980) *Understanding Attitudes and Predicting Social Behaviour* (Englewood-Cliffs, NJ: Prentice-Hall).

Albrecht, CM, Backhaus, C., Gurzki, H., and Woisetschläger, D.M. (2013) "Drivers of Brand Extension Success: What Really Matters for Luxury Brands," *Psychology & Marketing*, 30, 8, 647–59.

Allee, V. (2008) "Value Network Analysis and Value Conversion of Tangible and Intangible Assets," *Journal of Intellectual Capital*, 9, 1, 5–24.

Als, H. (2011) "Shadow and act. Shakespeare without words," *The New Yorker*, May 2.

Anand, N. and Peterson, R.A. (2000) "When Market Information Constitutes Fields: Sensemaking of Markets in the Commercial Music Industry," *Organization Science*, 11, 3, 270–84.

Anderson, E.W. (1988) "Customer Satisfaction and Word of Mouth," *Journal of Service Research*, 1, 1, 5–17.

Andrade, E.B. and Cohen J.B. (2007) "On the Consumption of Negative Feelings," *Journal of Consumer Research*, 34, October, 283–300.

Anholt, S. (2009), The Anholt-GfK Roper Nation Brands Index Methodology and Quality Control for the 2009 NBI Study, GfK Roper Public Affairs & Media.

Aral, S. and Walker, D. (2011) "Forget Viral Marketing: Make the Product Itself Viral," *Harvard Business Review*, 89, 6, 34–5.

Arbore, A. and Busacca, B. (2011) "Rejuvenating Importance-Performance Analysis," *Journal of Service Management*, 22, 3, 409–30.

Arnett, J. (1993) "Three Profiles of Heavy Metal Fans: A Taste for Sensation and a Subculture of Alienation," *Qualitative Sociology*, 16, 4, 423–43.

Arnould, E. and Wallendorf, M. (1994) "Market-Oriented Ethnography: Interpretation Building and Marketing Strategy Formulation," *Journal of Marketing Research*, 31, November, 484–504.

Arnould, E.J. and Price, L.L. (1993) "River Magic: Extraordinary Experience and the Extended Service Encounter," *Journal of Consumer Research*, 20, 1, 24–45.

Arnould, E.J., Price, L., and Zinkhan, G. (2002) *Consumers* (New York: McGraw-Hill).

Arthur, D. and Sherman, C. (2010) "Status within a Consumption-Oriented Counterculture: An Ethnographic Investigation of the Australian Hip Hop Culture," *Advances in Consumer Research*, 37, 386–92.

Bae, Y. and Lee, H. (2012) "Sentiment Analysis of Twitter Audiences: Measuring the Positive or Negative Influence of Popular Twitterers," *Journal of the American Society for Information Sicence and Technology*, 63, 12, 2521–35.

Balasubramanian, S.K., Kaarh, J.A., and Patwardhan, H. (1996) "Audience Response to Product Placements. An Integrative Framework and Future Research Agenda," *Journal of Advertising*, 35, 3, 115–41.

Barnes, M. (2011) "Music to Our Ears: Understanding Why Canadians Donate to Arts and Cultural Organizations," *International Journal of Nonprofit and Voluntary Sector Marketing*, 16, 115–26.

Barney, J. (1986) "Strategic Factor Markets: Expectations, Luck, and Business Strategy," *Management Science*, 32, 10, 297–326.

Barthes, R. (1977) *Image-Music-Text* (London: Fontana).

Barthes, R. (1990) *The Fashion System* (Berkeley and Los Angeles: University of California Press)

Bass, F.M. (1969) "A New Product Growth for Model Consumer Durables," *Management Science*, 15, 5, 215–27.

Basuroy, S., Chatterjee, S., and Ravid, S.A. (2003) "How Critical Are Critical Reviews? The Box Office Effects of Film Critics, Star Power, and Budgets," *Journal of Marketing*, 67, 4, 103–17.

Baudrillard, J. (1983) *Simulations* (New York: Semiotext(e)).

Baumol, W.J. (1967) "Performing Arts: The Permanent Crisis," *Business Horizons*, Autumn, 47–50.

Becker, H.S. (1982) *Art Worlds* (Berkeley and Los Angeles: University of California Press).

Belk, R. (1988) "Possessions and the Extended Self," *Journal of Consumer Research*, 15, September, 139–68.

Belk, R. (2009) "Sharing," *Journal of Consumer Research*, 36, 5, 715–34.

Belk, R., Ger, G., and Askegaard, S. (2003) "The Fire of Desire: A Multisited Inquiry into Consumer Passion," *Journal of Consumer Research*, 30, December, 326–51.

Belk, R., Wallendorf, M., and Sherry, J.J. (1989) "The Sacred and the Profane in Consumer Behaviour: Theodicy on the Odyssey," *Journal of Consumer Research*, 16, 1, 1–38.

Bhattacharya, C.B. (1998) "When Customers Are Members: Customer Retention in Paid Membership Contexts," *Journal of the Academy of Marketing Science*, 26, 1, 31–44.

Bhattacharya, C.B., Hayagreeva, R., and Glynn, M.A. (1995) "Understanding the Bond of Identification: An Investigation of its Correlates Among Art Museum Members," *Journal of Marketing*, 59, 4, 46–57.

Bhattacharya, C.B. and Sen, S. (2003) "Consumer-Company Identification: A Framework for Understanding Consumers' Relationships with Companies," *Journal of Marketing*, 67, 2, 76–88.

Bilton, C. (2007) *Management and Creativity: From Creative Industries to Creative Management* (Oxford: Blackwell Publishing).

Bitner, M.J. (1992) "Servicescapes: the Impact of Physical Surroundings on Customers and Employees," *Journal of Marketing*, 56, April, 57–71.

Boorsma, M. (2006) "A Strategic Logic for Arts Marketing. Integrating Customer Value and Artistic Objectives," *International Journal of Cultural Policy*, 12, 1, 73–92.

Botti, S. (2000) "What Role for Marketing in the Arts? An Analysis of Arts Consumption and Artistic Value," *International Journal of Arts Management*, 2, 3, 14–27.

Bourdieu, P. (1984) *Distinction: A Social Critique of the Judgement of Taste* (London: Routledge).

Bowker (2012) *Annual Report on US print book publishing for 2012*. Available at: http://www.bowker.com/assets/downloads/products/isbn_output_2002–2011.pdf.

Boyd, D. (2011) "Social Networks Sites as Networked Publics. Affordances, Dynamics, and Implications," in P. Papacharissi (ed.), *A Networked Self: Identity, Community, and Culture on Social Networks Sites* (Routledge: New York).

Brandt, R.D. (1988) "How Service Marketers Can Identify Value-Enhancing Service Elements," *Journal of Services Marketing*, 2, 3, 35–41.

Brennan, I. (2008) "Brand Placement in Novels. A Test of the Generation Effect," *International Journal of Advertising*, 27, 4, 495–509.

Bright, J. (2013) "Africa's Music Industry Grows to its Own Beat," *This Is Africa*, June 26.

Busacca, B. and Arbore, A. (2011) "Rejuvenating Importance-Performance Analysis," *Journal of Service Management*, 22, 3, 409–30.

Calcagno, M. (2012) "Trend emergenti nelle produzioni artistiche. Logiche partecipate e creazione del valore," *Il Capitale Culturale: Studies on the Value of Cultural Heritage*, IV, 15–29.

Cappetta, R. and Cillo, P. (2008) "Managing Integrators where Integration Matters: Insights from Symbolic Industries," *International Journal of Human Resource Management*, 19, 12, 2235–51.

Cappetta, R., Cillo, P., and Ponti, A. (2006) "Convergent Designs in Fine Fashion: An Evolutionary Model for Stylistic Innovation," *Research Policy*, 35, November, 1276–90.

Carù A. and Cova B. (2011) *Marketing e Competenze del Consumatore* (Milano: Egea).

Castaldo, S. (2007) *Trust in Marketing Relationships* (Cheltenham, UK: Edward Elgar).

Castaldo, S., Grosso, M., and Premazzi, K. (2013) *Retail and Channel Marketing* (Cheltenham, UK: Edward Elgar).

Castells, M. (1996) *The Rise of the Network Society* (Oxford: Blackwell).

Castells, M. (1997) *The Power of Identity* (Oxford: Blackwell).

Castells, M. (1998) *End of Millennium* (Oxford: Blackwell).

Caves, R.E. (2000) *Creative Industries: Contracts between Art and Commerce* (Cambridge: Harvard University Press).

Celsi, R.L., Randall, L.R., and Leigh, T.W. (1993) "An Exploration of High-Risk Leisure Consumption through Skydiving," *Journal of Consumer Research*, 20, 1, 1-23.

Center for Cultural policy Research (CCPR) *Baseline Study on Hong Kong's Creative Industries for the Central Policy Unit, HK Special Administration Region Government*, University of Hong Kong.

Chandon, P., Hutchinson, J.W., Bradlow, E.T., and Young, S.H. (2009) "Does In-Store Marketing Work? Effects of the Number and Position of Shelf Facings on Brand Attention and Evaluation at the Point of Purchase," *Journal of Marketing*, 73, 6, 1–17.

Chandrasekaran, D. and Tellis, G.J. (2011) "Getting a Grip on the Saddle: Cycles or Chasms," *Journal of Marketing*, 75, 4, 21–34.

Charters, S. (2006), "Aesthetic Products and Aesthetic Consumption: A Review," *Consumption, Markets & Culture*, 9, 3, 235–55.

Chaudhuri, A. and Holbrook, M.B. (2001) "The Chain of Effects from Brand Trust and Brand Affect to Brand Performance: The Role of Brand Loyalty," *Journal of Marketing*, 65, April, 81–93.

Chavarrìa, M. (2012) "Joan Francesc Marco: 'El Liceu debe reducir su número de funciones'," *La Vanguardia*, November 29.

Chen, Y. (2009) "Possession and Access: Consumer Desires and Value Perceptions Regarding Contemporary Art Collection and Exhibit Visits," *Journal of Consumer Research*, 35, 6, 925–40.

Chen, Y., Liu, Y., and Zhang, J. (2012) "When Do Third-Party Product Reviews Affect Firm Value and What Can Firms Do? The Case of Media Critics and Professional Movie Reviews," *Journal of Marketing*, 75, September, 116–34.

Chevalier, J.A. and Mayzlin, D. (2006) "The Effect of Word of Mouth on Sales: Online Book Reviews," *Journal of Marketing Research*, 48, August, 345–54.

Childress, C.C., and Friedkin, N.E. (2012) "Cultural Reception and Production: The Social Construction of Meaning in Book Clubs," *American Sociological Review*, 77, 1, 45–68.

Chiu, H.C., Lee, M., and Chen, J.R. (2007) "Viral Marketing: A Study of E-Mail Spreading Behavior across Gender," *Journal of Website Promotion*, 2, 3/4, 17–30.

Choi, J.A., Stotlar, D.K., and Park, S.R. (2006) "Visual Ethnography of On-Site Sport Sponsorship Activation: LG Action Sports Championship," *Sport Marketing Quarterly*, 15, 2, 71–9.

Christensen, C.M. and Bower, J.L. (1996) "Customer Power, Strategic Investment, and the Failure of Leading Firms," *Strategic Management Journal*, 17, 3, 197–218.

Cillo, P. and Prandelli, E. (2012) "Come la critica influenza le scelte di cambiamento delle imprese: un'analisi longitudinale sull'innovazione stilistica nel settore della moda," *Finanza Marketing e Produzione*, 1, 69–92.

Cito, M.C. and Troilo, G. (2013) "Configuring Theatre Experience: A Metaphor-based Research," *Proceedings of the 12th AIMAC Conference*, Bogotà.

Collett, P. (2009) "Selecting agency support: Best practice in brokering positive relationships," *Journal of Sponsorship*, 2, 3, 257–66.

Corna, V. and Troilo, G. (2005) "Interpreting the Reading Experience: An Introspective Analysis," *8th AIMAC Conference Proceedings*, Montreal.

Cornwell, T.B. and Maignan, I. (1998) "An International Review of Sponsorship Research," *Journal of Advertising*, 27, 1, 2–21.

Costabile, M. (1992) *Prezzo e Consumatore* (Milano: Egea).

Csikszentmihalyi, M. (1997) *Finding the Flow: The Psychology of Engagement with Everyday Life* (New York: Basic Books).

Cupchik, G.C., Leonard, G., Axelrad, E., and Kalin, J.D. (1998) "The Landscape of Emotion in Literary Encounters," *Cognition and Emotion*, 12, 6, 825–47.

d'Astous, A., Legoux, R., and Colbert, F. (2004) "Consumer Perceptions of Promotional Offers in the Performing Arts: An Experimental Approach," *Canadian Journal of Administrative Science*, 21, 3, 242–54.

d'Astous, A., Colbert, F., and Mbarek, I. (2006) "Factors Influencing Readers' Interest in New Book Releases: An Experimental Study," *Poetics*, 34, 134–47.

Daellenbach, K. (2012) "Understanding the Decision-Making Processes for Arts Sponsorship," *International Journal of Nonprofit and Voluntary Sector Marketing*, 17, November, 363–74.

Dahl, D.W. and Moreau, P.C. (2007) "Thinking Inside the Box: Why Consumers Enjoy Constrained Creative Experience," *Journal of Marketing Research*, 44, 3, 357–69.

Dawes, P.L and Massey, G.R. (2005) "Antecedents of Conflict in Marketing's Cross-Functional Relationship with Sales," *European Journal of Marketing*, 39, 11/12, 1327–1344.

Day, G.S. (1999) *The Market Driven Organization: Understanding, Attracting, and Keeping Valuable Customers* (Free Press).

Daymon, C. and Holloway, I. (2002) *Qualitative Research Methods in Public Relations and Marketing Communications* (London: Routledge).

Dean, D.H. (2003) "Consumer Perception of Corporate Donation. Effects of Company Reputation for Social Responsibility and Type of Donation," *Journal of Advertising*, 32, 4, 91–102.

Deeter-Schmelz, D.R. and Sojka, J.Z. (2004) "Wrestling with American values: An Exploratory Investigation of World Wrestling Entertainment as a Product-Based Subculture," *Journal of Consumer Behaviour*, 4, 2, 132–43.

Delattre, E. and Colovic, A. (2009) "Memory and Perception of Brand Mentions and Placement of Brands in Songs," *International Journal of Advertising*, 28, 5, 807–42.

Deloitte (2014) *Football Money League Report*, Sports Business Group (Manchester, UK).

Denniston, C. (2003) "The dark age of tango," www.history-of-tango.com/dark-age.html (accessed February 23, 2013).

Department of Arts, Culture, Science and Technology (DACST) South Africa (1988) *Creative South Africa: A Strategy for Realising the Potential of the Cultural Industries*.

Department of Communications, Information Technology and the Arts (DCITA) Australia (2004). *Creative Industries Cluster Study,* 3 vols., Canberra, Department of Communications, Information Technology and the Arts.

Department of Culture Media and Sport (DCMS) (1998) *Creative Industries Mapping Document* (London: DCMS).

Deshpande, R. and Webster, F.E. (1989) "Organizational Culture and Marketing: Defining the Research Agenda," *Journal of Marketing,* 53, 1, 3–15.

de Gregorio, F. and Sung, Y. (2009) "Giving a Shout out to Seagram' s Gin: Extent of and Attitudes towards Brands in Popular Songs," *Brand Management*, 17, 3, 218–35.

DiMaggio, P. (1987) "Classification in Art," *American Sociological Review*, 52, 4, 440–55.

Dijkstra, K., Zwaan, R.A., Graesser, A.C., and Magliano, J.P. (1994) "Character and Reader Emotions in Literary Texts," *Poetics*, 23, 139–57.

Dolbec, P.Y. and Chebat, J.C. (2013) "The Impact of a Flagship vs a Brand Store on Brand Attitude, Brand Attachment and Brand Equity," *Journal of Retailing*, 89, 4, 460–66.

Domb Krauskopf, A. (2010) *Tacky and Proud. Exploring Tecnobrega's Value Network*, Convergence Cultural Consortium Report.

Donovan, R.J. and Rossiter, J.R. (1982) "Store Atmosphere: An Environmental Psychology Approach," *Journal of Retailing*, 58, 1, 34–57.

Dorotic, M., Bijmolt, T.H.A., and Verhoef, P.C. (2012) "Loyalty Programmes: Current Knowledge and Research Directions," *International Journal of Management Reviews*, 14, 217–37.

Douglas, M. and Isherwood, B. (1979) *The World of Goods* (New York: Basic Books).

Duffy G. (2009) "Tecnobrega beat rocks Brazil," *BBC >Click*, February 13.

Elberse, A. (2007) "The Power of Stars: Do Star Actors Drive the Success of Movies?," *Journal of Marketing*, 71, 4, 102–120.

Elberse, A. (2011) "Marvel Enterprises, Inc.," *Harvard Business School Case*, N9-511-097.

Elberse, A. and Golod, M. (2011) "Maria Sharapova: Marketing a Champion (B)," *Harvard Business School Case*, 9-507-066.

Eliashberg, J. and Shugan, S.M. (1997) "Film Critics: Influencers or Predictors?," *Journal of Marketing*, 61, April, 68–78.

Featherstone, M. (1991) *Consumer Culture & Postmodernism* (London and Newbury Park: Sage).

Fishbein, M. (1963) "An Investigation of the Relationships between Beliefs about an Object and the Attitude toward that Object," *Human Relations*, 16, 233–40.

Fishbein, M. and Ajzen, I. (1975) *Belief, Attitude, Intention and Behavior: An Introduction to Theory and Research* (Reading, MA: Addison-Wesley).

Fisher, R.J., Maltz. E., and Jaworski, G.J. (1997) "Enhancing Communication between Marketing and Engineering: The Moderating Role of Relative Functional Identification," *Journal of Marketing*, 61, July, 54–70.

Florida, R. (2002) *The Rise of the Creative Class. And How It's Transforming Work, Leisure, Community and Everyday Life* (New York: Basic Books).

Fox, K.J. (1987) "Real Punks and Pretenders," *Journal of Contemporary Ethnography*, 16, 3, 344–70.

Frey, RV., Bayón, T., and Totzek, D. (2013) "How Customer Satisfaction Affects Employee Satisfaction and Retention in a Professional Services Context," *Journal of Service Research*, 16, 4, 503–17.

Friedman, M. (1985) "The Changing Language of a Consumer Society: Brand Name Usage in Popular American Novels in the Postwar Era," *Journal of Consumer Research*, 11, March, 927–38.

Füller, J. and Matzler, K. (2007) "Virtual Product Experience and Customer Participation – A Chance for Customer-Centred, really New Product," *Technovation*, 27, 378–87.

Füller, J., Hutter, K., and Faullant, R. (2011) "Why Co-Creation Experience Matters? Creative Experience and its Impact on the Quantity and Quality of Creative Contributions," *R&D Management*, 41, 3, 259–73.

Garbarino, E. and Johnson, M.S. (1999) "The Different Roles of Satisfaction, Trust, and Commitment in Customer Relationships," *Journal of Marketing*, 63, 70–87.

García, R. (2013), Teatro de le resistencia, *El Pais*, July 27.

Garnefeld, I., Iseke, A., and Krebs, A. (2012) "Explicit Incentives in Online Communities: Boon or Bane?," *International Journal of Electronic Commerce*, 17, 1, 11–38.

Ghemawat, P. and Nueno, J.L. (2006) "Zara: Fast Fashion," *Harvard Business School Case*, 9-703-497.

Giving USA (2012) *The Annual Report on Philanthropy for the Year 2011* (Indianapolis: Center on Philanthropy at Indiana University).

Glynn, M.A. (2000) "When Cymbals Become Symbols: Conflict Over Organizational Identity Within a Symphony Orchestra," *Organization Science*, 11, 3, 285–98.

Glynn, M.A. and Lounsbury, M. (2005) "From the Critics' Corner: Logic Blending, Discursive Change and Authenticity in a Cultural Production System," *Journal of Management Studies*, 42, 5, 1031–55.

Golder, P.N., Mitra, D., and Moorman, C. (2012) "What Is Quality? An Integrative Framework of Processes and States," *Journal of Marketing*, 76, 1, 1–23.

Goulding, C. (2000) "The Museum Environment and the Visitor Experience," *European Journal of Marketing*, 34, 3/4, 261–78.

Goulding, C, Shankar, A., and Elliott, E. (2002) "Working Weeks, Rave Weekends: Identity Fragmentation and the Emergence of Mew Communities," *Consumption, Markets and Culture*, 5, 4, 261–84.

Green, P.E. and Srinivasan, V. (1978) "Conjoint Analysis in Consumer Researach: Issues and Outlook," *Journal of Consumer Research*, 5, 2, 103–23.

Green, P.E. and Srinivasan, V. (1990) "Conjoint Analysis in Marketing: New Developments with Implications for Research and Practice," *Journal of Marketing*, 54, 4, 3–19.

Griffin, A. and Hauser, H.R. (1996) "Integrating R&D and Marketing: A Review and Analysis of the Literature," *Journal of Product Innovation Management*, 13, 3, 191–215.

Griswold, W. (1987) "The Fabrication of Meaning: Literary Interpretation in the United States, Great Britain, and the West Indies," *American Journal of Sociology*, 92, 5, 1077–117.

Gruen, T.W., Summers, J.O., and Acito, F. (2000) "Relationship Marketing Activities, Commitment, and Membership

Behaviors in Professional Associations," *Journal of Marketing*, 64, July, 34–49.

Guenzi, P., Santini, S., Penna, D., and Boni, D. (2013) "Caso Unicredit: La valutazione della sponsorizzazione della UEFA Champions League," *Economia & Management*, 1, 11–26.

Guerzoni, G. and Troilo, G. (1998) "Silk purses out of sows' ears: mass rarefaction of consumption and the emerging consumer-collector," in M. Bianchi (ed.), *The Active Consumer* (London: Routledge).

Gustafsson, A., Johnson, M., and Roos, I. (2005) "The Effects of Customer Satisfaction, Relationship Commitment Dimensions, and Triggers on Customer Retention," *Journal of Marketing*, 69, 4, 210–18.

Gwinner, K. (1997) "A Model of Image Creation and Image Transfer in Event Sponsorship," *International Marketing Review*, 14, 3, 145–58.

Gyory, M. and Glas, G. (1992) *Statistics of Film Industry in Europe* (Bruxelles).

Harris, L.C. and Goode, M.M.H. (2010) "Online Servicescapes, Trust, and Purchase Intentions," *Journal of Services Marketing*, 24, 3, 230–43.

Hartley, J. (2005) (ed.) *Creative Industries* (Malden and Oxford: Blackwell Publishing).

Hawkins, E.R. (1954) "Price Policies and Theories," *Journal of Marketing*, 18, January, 233–40.

Hayes, D. and Slater, A. (2003) "From 'Social Club' to 'Integrated Membership Scheme': Developing Membership Schemes Strategically," *International Journal of Nonprofit and Voluntary Sector Marketing*, 8, 1, 59–75.

Hennig-Thurau, T., Henning, V., and Sattler, H. (2007) "Consumer File Sharing of Motion Picture," *Journal of Marketing*, 71, October, 1–18.

Hennig-Thurau, T., Henning, V., Sattler, H., Eggers, F., and Houston, M.B. (2007) "The Last Picture Show? Timing and Order of Movie Distribution Channels," *Journal of Marketing*, 71, 63–83.

Hesmondhalgh, D. (2007) *The Cultural Industries* (London and Thousand Oaks: Sage) (1st edn, 2002)

Hinz, O., Skiera, B., Barrot, C., and Becker, J.U. (2011) "Seeding Strategies for Viral Marketing: An Empirical Comparison," *Journal of Marketing*, 75, 6, 55–71.

Hirsch, P.M. (1972) "Processing Fads and Fashions: An Organization-Set Analysis of Cultural Industry Systems," *The American Journal of Sociology*, 77, 4, 639–59.

Hirschman, E.C. (1983) "Aesthetics, Ideologies and the Limits of the Marketing Concept," *Journal of Marketing*, 47, 3, 45–55.

Hirschman, E.C. and Holbrook, M.B. (1982) "Hedonic Consumption: Emerging Concepts, Methods and Prepositions," *Journal of Marketing*, 46, 3, 92–101.

Hoffman, D.L. and Novak, T.P. (1996) "Marketing in Hypermedia Computer-Mediated Environments: Conceptual Foundations," *Journal of Marketing*, 60, 50–68.

Hoffman, D.L. and Novak, T.P. (2009) "Flow Online: Lessons Learned and Future Prospects," *Journal of Interactive Marketing*, 23, 1, 23–34.

Holbrook, M. B. (2005) "Art versus Commerce as a Macromarketing Theme in Three Films from the Young-Man-with-a-Horn Genre," *Journal of Macromarketing*, 25, 1, 22–31.

Holbrook, M.B. (1999) *Consumer Value: A Framework for Analysis and Research* (New York: Routledge).

Holbrook, M.B. and Hirschman, E.C. (1982) "The Experiential Aspects of Consumption: Consumer Fantasies, Feelings, and Fun," *Journal of Consumer Research*, 9, September, 132–40.

Holbrook, M.B. and Addis, M. (2007) "Taste versus Market: An Extension of Research on the Consumption of Popular Culture," *Journal of Consumer Research*, 34, 3, 415–24.

Holt, D.B. (2004) *How Brands Become Icons. The Principles of Cultural Branding* (Cambridge: Harvard Business Press).

Holt, D.B. (1995) "How Consumers Consume: A Typology of Consumption Practices," *Journal of Consumer Research*, 22, June, 1–16.

Hopkins, C.D., Grove, S.J., Raymond, M.A., LaForge, M.C. (2009), "Designing the e-Servicescape: Implications for Online Retailers", *Journal of Internet Commerce*, 8, 23–43.

Horyn, C. (2012) "When You Want to Say that's How to Dress," *International Herald Tribune*, September 12.

Howard, J.A. and Sheth, J.N. (1969) *The Theory of Buyer Behavior* (New York: John Wiley & Sons).

Hoyer, W.D. and Stokburger-Sauer, N. (2012) "The Role of Aesthetic Taste in Consumer Behavior," *Journal of the Academy of Marketing Science*, 40, 1, 167–80.

Huang, C. (2005) "File Sharing as a Form of Music Consumption," *International Journal of Electronic Commerce*, 9, 4, 37–55.

Huang, P., Lurie, N.H., and Mitra, S. (2009) "Searching for Experience on the Web: An Empirical Examination of Consumer Behavior for Search and Experience Goods," *Journal of Marketing*, 73, 55–69.

Hume, M. (2008) "Developing a Conceptual Model for Repurchase Intention in the Performing Arts: The Roles of Emotion, Core Service and Service Delivery," *International Journal of Arts Management*, 10, 40–55.

Hume, M., Sullivan Mort, G., and Winzar, H. (2007) "Exploring Repurchase Intention in a Performing Arts Context: Who Comes? And Why Do They Come Back?," *International Journal of Nonprofit and Voluntary Sector Marketing*, 12, 135–48.

IEG (2013) *Sponsorship Decision-Makers Survey Report* (Chicago).

International Federation of the Phonographic Industry (IFPI) (2012) *Digital Music Report 2012. Expanding Choice, Going Global.*

International Intellectual Property Alliance (IIPA) (2006) *Copyright Industries in the US Economy: The 2006 Report*. Available at http://www.iipa.com/pdf/2006_siwek_full.pdf.

Ipsos MediaCT (2012) "Breakfast Radio: The Most Important Media of the Day?," *Bite Sized Thought Piece Report*.

Ipsos MediaCT (2013a) *Tech Tracker Report*, 2nd Quarter.

Ipsos MediaCT (2013b) "The Pulse of the Affluent Market," *The Mendelsohn Affluent Barometer*, February.

Isherwood, C. (2012) "Visit to Warhol's World, In All Its Goofy Glory," *The New York Times*, January 23.

Jeffcutt, P. and Pratt, A.C. (2002) "Managing Creativity in the Cultural Industries," *Creativity and Innovation Management*, 11, 4, 225–33.

Jeppesen, L.B. and Frederiksen, L. (2006) "Why Do Users Contribute to Firm-Hosted User Communities? The Case of Computer-Controlled Music Instruments," *Organization Science*, 17, 1, 45–64.

Jobst, J. and Boerner, S. (2011) "Understanding Customer Satisfaction in Opera. First Steps toward a Model," *International Journal of Nonprofit and Voluntary Sector Marketing*, 16, 1, 50–69.

Johnson, J.W. and Ellis, B. (2011) "The Influence of Messages and Benefits on Donors' Attributed Motivations: Findings of a Study With 14 American Performing Arts Presenters," *International Journal of Arts Management*, 13, 2, 4–15.

Johnston, R. (1995) "The Determinants of Service Quality: Satisfiers and Dissatisfiers," *International Journal of Service Industry Management*, 6, 5, 53–71.

Joy, A. (2001) "Gift Giving in Hong Kong and the Continuum of Social Ties," *Journal of Consumer Research*, 28, 2, 239–56.

Joy, A. and Sherry, J.R. (2003) "Speaking of Art as Embodied Imagination: A Multi-Sensory Approach to Understanding Aesthetic Experience," *Journal of Consumer Research*, 30, 2, 259–82.

Kano, N. (1984) "Attractive Quality and Must Be Quality," *Hinshitsu. The Journal of the Japanese Society for Quality Control*, 14, 2, 147–56.

Karniouchina, E.V., Uslay, C., and Erenburg, G. (2011) "Do Marketing Media Have Life Cycles? The Case of Product Placement in Movies," *Journal of Marketing*, 75, May, 27–48.

KEA (2006), *The Economy of Culture in Europe* (Brussels: KEA European Affairs).

Keller, K.L. (2012) *Strategic Brand Management: Building, Measuring, and Managing Brand Equity*, 4/e Englewood Cliffs, NJ: Prentice-Hall).

Keller, K.L. and Aaker, D.A. (1992) "The Effects of Sequential Introduction of Brand Extensions," *Journal of Marketing Research*, 24, February, 35–50.

Kelly, G.A. (1955) *The Psychology of Personal Constructs* (Norton, New York).

Kerrigan, F. (2010) *Film Marketing* (Oxford: Butterworth).

Ketcham, C. (2012) "Monopoly Is Theft: The Antimonopolist History of the World's Most Popular Board Game," *Harper's Magazine*, October 19.

Khaire, M. and Wadhwani, R.D. (2010) "Changing Landscapes: The Construction of Meaning and Value in a New Market Category – Modern Indian Art," *Academy of Management Journal*, 53, 6, 1281–304.

Kleinschafer, J., Dowell, D., and Morrison, M. (2011) "Doing more with less. Understanding the Contributions of Regional Art Gallery Members through Marketing Segmentation," *Arts Marketing: An International Journal*, 1, 1, 39–55.

Klenosky, D.B, Gengler, C. and Mulvey, M. (1993) "Understanding the Factors Influencing Ski Destination Choice: A Means-End Analytic Approach," *Journal Of Leisure Research*, 25, 4, 302–79.

Kneepkens, E.W.E.M. and Zwaan, R.A. (1994) "Emotions and Literary Text Comprehension," *Poetics*, 23, 125–38.

Ko, Y.J., Gibson, H., and Kim, M. (2011) "Understanding Donors: A Case of University Performing Arts Programs in the USA," *International Journal of Nonprofit and Voluntary Sector Marketing*, 16, 166–82.

Kotler, P. and Dubois, B. (1986) *Marketing Management* (Paris: Publi-Union).

Kotler, P. and Keller K.L. (2011) *Marketing Management*, 14/e (Englewood Cliffs, NJ: Prentice Hall).

Kozinets, R.V. (2001) "Utopian Enterprise: Articulating the Meanings of Star Trek's Culture of Consumption," *Journal of Consumer Research*, 28, 1, 67–88.

Kozinets, R.V. (2002) "The Field Behind the Screen: Using Netnography for Marketing Research in Online Communities," *Journal of Marketing Research*, 39, February, 61–72.

Kwortnik, R.J. and Ross W.T. (2007) "The Role of Positive Emotions in Experiential Decisions," *International Journal of Research in Marketing*, 24, 324–35.

Lagier, J. and Godey, B. (2007) "A Scale for Measuring Aesthetic Style in the Field of Luxury and Art Products," *International Journal of Arts Management*, 9, 2, 39–50.

Lakhani, K.R. and Kanji, Z. (2008) "Threadless: The Business of Community," *Harvard Business School Case*, 608–707.

Lampel, J. and Shamsie, J. (2000) "Critical Push: Strategies for Creating Momentum in the Motion Picture Industry," *Journal of Management*, 26, 2, 233–57.

Larsen, G., Lawson, R., and Todd, S. (2010) "The Symbolic Consumption of Music," *Journal of Marketing Management*, 26, 7–8, 671–85.

Leder, H., Belke, B., Oeberst, A., and Augustin, D. (2004) "A Model of Aesthetic Appreciation and Aesthetic Judgments," *British Journal of Psychology*, 95, 489–508.

Lee, H.K. (2010) "Between Fan Culture and Copyright Infringement: Manga Scanlation", in D. O'Reilly and F. Kerrigan (eds) *Marketing The Arts: A Fresh Approach* (London and New York: Routledge), pp. 153–70.

Lee, M. and Faber, R.J. (2007) "Effects of Product Placement in On-Line Games on Brand Memory: A Perspective of the Limited-Capacity Model of Attention," *Journal of Advertising*, 36, 4, 75–90.

Leenders, M.A.A.M. and Wierenga, B. (2002) "The Effectiveness of Different Mechanisms for Integrating Marketing and R&D," *Journal of Product Innovation Management*, 19, 4, 305–17.

Leibenstein, H. (1950) "Bandwagon, Snob and Veblen Effects in the Theory of Consumer's Demand," *Quarterly Journal of Economics*, 64, 2, 183–207.

Lemos, R. and Castro, O. (2006) *The Paraense Tecnobrega Open Business Model*, IDRC Report.

Lester, P. (2012) "Gaby Amaranto," *The Guardian*, February 16.

Levy, M. and Weitz, B.A. (2012) *Retailing Management*, 8/e (New York: McGraw-Hill).

Leyshon, A. (2001) "Time-Space (and Digital) Compression: Software Formats and the Geographical Reorganisation of the Music Industry," *Environment and Planning A*, 33, 1, 49–77.

Liu, Y. (2006) "Word of Mouth for Movies: Its Dynamics and Impact on Box Office Revenue," *Journal of Marketing*, 70, July, 74–89.

Lusch, R.F., Vargo, S.L., and Tanniru, M. (2010) "Service, Value Networks and Learning," *Journal of the Academy of Marketing Science*, 38, 19–31.

Lyotard, J.F. (1984) *The Postmodern Condition: A Report on Knowledge* (Manchester: Manchester University Press).

Maggi, F. (2012) *La sponsorizzazione nel motor sport: il ruolo di organizzatori, team e sponsor*, Unpublished DBA (Milano: Università L. Bocconi).

Malär, L., Krohmer, H., Hoyer, W.D., and Nyffenegger, B. (2011) "Emotional Brand Attachment and Brand Personality: The Relative Importance of the Actual and the Ideal Self," *Journal of Marketing*, 75, July, 35–52.

Malhotra, N. (2005) *Marketing Research. An Applied Orientation* (Englewood Cliffs, NJ: Prentice Hall).

Maltz, E. (1997) "An Enhanced Framework for Improving Cooperation Between Marketing and Other Functions: The Differential Role of Integrating Mechanisms," *Journal of Market Focused Management*, 2, 83–98.

Mandelli, A. and Accoto, C. (2012) *Social Mobile Marketing* (Milano: Egea).

Manetti, A. (2013) *Facciamo Tango!* (Firenze: Edizioni Clichy).

Marinelli, N. and Palomba, G. (2011) "A Model for Pricing Italian Contemporary Art Paintings at Auction," *The Quarterly Review of Economics and Finance*, 51, 212–24.

McCracken, G. (1989) "Who Is the Celebrity Endorser? Cultural Foundations of the Endorsement Process," *Journal of Consumer Research*, 16, December, 310–21.

MEDIA Salles (2012), *European Cinema Yearbook* (Milano).

Mehrabian. A. and Russell, J. A. (1974) *An Approach to Environmental Psychology* (Cambridge, MA: MIT Press).

MercoPress (2007) "Buenos Aires Tango Industry Attracts 3.5 million People Annually," June 14.

Miles, M.B. and Huberman, A.M. (1994) *Qualitative Data Analysis* (Sage, Thousand Oaks).

Mill, R.C. and Morrison, A.M. (2009) *The Tourism System* (Dubuque: Kendall Hunt Publishing).

Moon, S., Bergey, P.K., and Iacobucci, D. (2010) "Dynamic Effects Among Movie Ratings, Movie Revenues, and Viewer Satisfaction," *Journal of Marketing*, 74, January, 108–21.

Moorman, C., Deshpandé, R., and Zaltman, G. (1993) "Factors Affecting Trust in Market Research Relationships," *Journal of Marketing*, 57, 1, 81–101.

Morgan, R.M. and Hunt, S.H. (1994) "The Commitment-Trust Theory of Relationship Marketing," *Journal of Marketing*, 58, 3, 20–38.

National Readership Survey – NewsWorks (2014) *Newsbrand Readership Report* (London).

Naughton, J. (2007) "Radiohead Find There's Gold at the End of In Rainbows," *The Observer*, November 18.

Nelson, M.R. (2002) "Recall of Brand Placements in Computer/Video Games," *Journal of Advertising Research*, March–April, 80–92.

Nelson, R.A. (2004) "The Bulgari Connection: A Novel Form of Product Placement," *Journal of Promotion Management*, 10, 1/2, 203–12.

Nelson, M.R. and Devanathan, D. (2006) "Brand Placements Bollywood Style," *Journal of Consumer Behaviour*, 5, 211–21.

Nielsen, R.K. and Linnebank, G. (2011) *Public Support for the Media: A Six-Country Overview of Direct and Indirect Subsidies* (Oxford: Reuters Institute for the Study of Journalism)

Oatley, K. (1994) "A Taxonomy of the Emotions of Literary Response and a Theory of Identification in Fictional Narrative," *Poetics*, 23, 53–74.

Oberholzer-Gee, F. and Strumpf, K. (2007) "The Effect of File Sharing on Record Sales: An Empirical Analysis," *Journal of Political Economy*, 115, 1, 1–42.

Oliver, R. and Swan, J.E. (1989) "Consumer Perceptions of Interpersonal Equity and Satisfaction in Transactions: A Field Survey Approach," *Journal of Marketing*, 53, April, 21–35.

Oliver, R.L. (1997) *Satisfaction: A Behavioural Perspective on the Consumer* (New York: McGraw Hill).

Ostillio, M.C., Carù, A., and Leone, G. (2013) "Corporate Museum as a Pillar for Brand Authenticity in Luxury Companies: The Case of Salvatore Ferragamo," *Proceedings of the 12th AIMAC Conference*, Bogotà.

Parasuraman, A., Zeithaml, V., and Berry, L. (1985) "A Conceptual Model of Service Quality and its Implications for Future Research," *Journal of Marketing*, 49, Fall, 41–50.

Penna, D. and Guenzi, P. (2014) "How to use a sponsorship platform to support an international master brand strategy: The UniCredit UEFA champions league sponsorship," *Journal of Brand Management*, 21, 133–49.

Peteraf, M.A. (1993) "The Cornerstones of Competitive Advantage: A Resource-Based View," *Strategic Management Journal*, 14, 3, 179–91.

Peterson, R.A. (1982) "Understanding audience segmentation: From elite and mass to omnivore and univore," *Poetics*, 21, 4 243-58.

Peterson, R.A. and Anand, N. (2000) "The Production of Culture Perspective," *Annual Review of Sociology*, 30, 311–34

Peterson, R.A. and Kern, R.M. (1996) "Changing Highbrow Taste: From Snob to Omnivore," *American Sociological Review*, 61, 5, 900–7.

Picard, R.G. (2005) "The Nature of Media Product Portfolios," in R.G. Picard (ed.), *Media Product Portfolios: Issues in Management Multiple Products and Services* (Mahwah, NJ: Lawrence Erlbaum).

Pine, B.J. and Gilmore, J.H. (1999) *The Experience Economy: Work is Theatre and Every Business a Stage* (Cambridge: Harvard Business School Press).

Plummer, J. (1974) "The Concept and Application of Lifestyle Segmentation," *Journal of Marketing*, 38, January, 33–7.

Porter, M. (1980) *Competitive Strategy* (New York: Free Press).

Porter, M. (1985) *Competitive Advantage: Creating and Sustaining Superior Performance* (New York: Free Press).

Powell, W.W. and Snellman, K. (2004) "The Knowledge Economy," *Annual Review of Sociology*, 30, 199–220.

PQ Media (2010) *Global Branded Entertainment Marketing Forecast 2010–2014* (Stamford, USA).

Prahalad, C.K. and Hamel, G. (1990) "The Core Competence of the Corporation," *Harvard Business Review*, May–June.

Prahalad, C.K. and Ramaswamy, V. (2003) "The New Frontier of Experience Innovation," *Sloan Management Review*, Summer, 12–18.

Reavey, B., Howley Jr., M.J., and Korschun, D. (2013) "An Exploratory Study of Stalled Relationships among Art Museum Members," *International Journal of Nonprofit and Voluntary Sector Marketing*, 18, 2, 90–100.

Reddy, S.K., Swaminathan, V., and Motley, C.M. (1998) "Exploring the Determinants of Broadway Show Success," *Journal of Marketing Research*, 35, August, 370–83.

Reichheld, F.F (2003) "The One Number You Need to Grow," *Harvard Business Review*, December, 46–54.

Reinstein, D.A. and Snyder, C.M. (2005) "The Influence of Expert Reviews on Consumer Demand for Experience Goods: A Case Study of Movie Critics," *Journal of Industrial Economics*, 53, 1, 27–51.

Richins, M.L. (1994) "Valuing Things: The Public and Private Meanings of Possessions," *Journal of Consumer Research*, 21, 3, 504–21.

Richins, M.L. (1997) "Measuring Emotions in the Consumption Experience," *Journal of Consumer Research*, 24, 2, 127–46.

Rifkin, J. (2000) *The Age Of Access: The New Culture of Hypercapitalism, Where All of Life is a Paid-For Experience* (New York: Putnam).

Rinallo, D. (2011) *Event Marketing* (Milano: Egea).

Ringberg, T., Odekerken-Schröder, G., and Christensen, G.L. (2007) "A Cultural Models Approach to Service Recovery," *Journal of Marketing*, 71, 194–214.

Rogers, E.M. (1962) *Diffusion of Innovations* (Glencoe: Free Press).

Rokeach, M. (1973) *The Nature of Human Values* (New York: Free Press).

Rook, D.W. (1985) "The Ritual Dimension of Consumer Behavior," *Journal of Consumer Research*, 12, 251–64.

Rook, D.W. (1987) "The Buying Impulse," *Journal of Consumer Research*, 14, September, 189–99.

Russell, C.A. (2002) "Investigating the Effectiveness of Product Placements in Television Shows: the Role of Modality and Plot Connection Congruence on Brand Memory and Attitude," *Journal of Consumer Research*, 29, 3, 306–18.

Russell, C.A. and Belch, M. (2005) "A Managerial Investigation into the Product Placement Industry," *Journal of Advertising Research*, March, 73–92.

Russell, C.A. and Levy, S.J. (2012), "The Temporal and Focal Dynamics of Volitional Reconsumption: A Phenomenological Investigation of Repeated Hedonic Experiences", *Journal of Consmer Research*, 39, 2, 341–359.

Russell, J.A. and Pratt, G. (1980) "A Description of the Affective Quality Attributed to Environments," *Journal of Personality and Social Psychology*, 38, August, 311–22.

Ryan, A., Fenton, M., and Sangiorgi D. (2010) "A Night at the Theatre: Moving Arts Marketing from the Office to the Kitchen and Beyond," in D. O'Reilly and F. Kerrigan (eds) *Marketing The Arts: A Fresh Approach* (London and New York: Routledge), pp. 214–30.

Ryu, G. and Feick, L. (2007) "A Penny for Your Thoughts: Referral Reward Programs and Referral Likelihood," *Journal of Marketing*, 71, 1, 84–94.

Santagata W. (2008) *Libro bianco sulla creatività* (Roma: Commissione sulla Creatività e Produzione di Cultura in Italia, Ministero per i Beni e le Attività Culturali).

Sawhney, M.S. and Eliashberg, J. (1996) "A Parsimonious Model for Forecasting Gross Box-Office Revenues of Motion Pictures," *Marketing Science*, 15, 113–31.

Sayre, S. (2001) *Qualitative Methods for Marketplace Research* (Thousand Oaks and London: Sage).

Schau, H.J., Muñiz, A.M., and Arnould E.J. (2009) "How Brand Community Practices Create Value," *Journal of Marketing*, 73, 5, 30–51.

Schmitt, B.H. (1999) *Experiential Marketing: How to Get Customers to Sense, Feel, Think, Act, Relate to Your Company and Brands* (New York: The Free Press).

Schmitt, P., Skiera, B., and Van den Bulte, C. (2011) "Referral Programs and Customer Value," *Journal of Marketing*, 75, January, 46–59.

Schouten, J.W. and McAlexander, J.H. (1995) "Subcultures of Consumption: An Ethnography of the New Bikers," *Journal of Consumer Research*, 22, 1, 43–61.

Seabrook, J. (2012) "The Song Machine: The Hitmakers behind Rihanna," *The New Yorker*, March 26.

Sedo, D.R. (2008) "Richard & Judy's Book Club and 'Canada Reads': Readers, Books and Cultural Programming in a Digital Era," *Information, Community and Society*, 11, 2, 188–206.

SGAE (2012) *Anuario Sgae de las artes escénicas, musicales y audiovisuales* (Madrid).

Shrum, W. (1991) "Critics and Publics: Cultural Mediation in Highbrow and Popular Performing Arts," *American Journal of Sociology*, 97, 2, 347–75.

SIAE (2012) *Annuario statistico dello spettacolo* (Roma).

Simpson D. (2012) "Soundgarden: King Animal," *The Guardian*, November 8.

Slater, A. (2004) "Revisiting Membership Scheme Typologies in Museums and Galleries," *International Journal of Nonprofit and Voluntary Sector Marketing*, 9, 3, 238–60.

Slater, A. (2007) "Escaping to the Gallery: Understanding the Motivations of Visitors to Galleries," *International Journal of Nonprofit and Voluntary Sector Marketing*, 12, 2, 149–62.

Smith, A.K., Bolton, R.N., and Wagner, J. (1999) "A Model of Customer Satisfaction with Service Encounters Involving Failure and Recovery," *Journal of Marketing Research*, 36, 3, 356–73.

Smith, W.R. (1956) "Product Differentiation and Market Segmentation as Alternative Marketing Strategies," *Journal of Marketing*, 21, 1, 3–8.

Sparrow, J. (1998) *Knowledge in Organizations: Access to Thinking at Work* (Sage, London).

Spradley, J.P. (1979) *The Ethnographic Interview* (New York: Holt, Rinehart & Winston).

Spradley, J.P. (1980) *Participant Observation* (New York: Holt, Rinehart & Winston).

Srinivasan, S.S, Anderson, R., and Ponnavolu, K. (2002) "Customer Loyalty in E-Commerce: An Exploration of its Antecedents and Consequences," *Journal of Retailing*, 78, 41–50.

Stone, P. (2008) "That Easy Second Book," *The Bookseller*, September 3.

Sung, Y., Choi, J., and De Gregorio, F. (2008) "Brand Placements in Korean Films, 1995–2003: A Content Analysis," *Journal of International Consumer Marketing*, 20, 3–4, 39–53.

Tabor, M.B.W. (1995) "A Lesson on Selling a Book by its Cover," *The New York Times*, September 4.

Tapscott, D. and Williams, A.D. (2006) *Wikinomics: How Mass Collaboration Changes Everything* (New York: Penguin).

Thompson, J.B. (2010) *Merchants of Culture: The Publishing Business in the Twenty-First Century* (Cambridge: Polity) (2nd edn, 2012).

Thomson, M. (2006) "Human Brands: Investigating Antecedents to Consumers' Strong Attachments to Celebrities," *Journal of Marketing*, 70, July, 104–19.

Thyne, M. (2001) "The Importance of Values Research for Nonprofit Organizations: The Motivation-Based Values of MUSEUM VISITORS," *International Journal of Nonprofit and Voluntary Sector Marketing*, 6, 2, 116–30.

Ton, Z., Corsi, E., and Dessain, V. (2010), "Zara: Managing Stores for fast Fashion," *Harvard Business School Case*, 9-610-042.

Trimble, C.S. and Rifon, N.J. (2006) "Consumer Perceptions of Compatibility in Cause-Related Marketing Messages," *International Journal of Nonprofit & Voluntary Sector Marketing*, February, 29–47.

Troilo, G. (2002) "Postmodernità, consumo e marketing dei beni artistici e culturali," *Micro & Macro Marketing*, 11, 9–32.

Troilo, G. (2006), Marketing Knowledge Management. Managing Knowledge in Market Oriented Companies (Cheltenham and Northampton: Edward Elgar)

UNCTAD (2008) *Creative Economy Report*. Available at http://unctad.org/en/Docs/ditc20082cer_en.pdf.

UNCTAD (2010) *Creative Economy Report*. Available at http://unctad.org/en/docs/ditctab20103_en.pdf.

UNESCO (2012a) "From International Blockbusters To National Hits: Analysis of the 2010 UIS Survey On Feature Film Statistics," *UIS Information Bulletin*, n. 8.

UNESCO (2012b) *The Media Landscape in 28 Countries: Results From a UIS Pilot Survey* (Montreal: UNESCO Institute for Statistics)

Van den Bulte, C. (2010) "Opportunities and Challenges in Studying Customer Networks", in S. Wuyts, M.G. Dekimpe, E. Gijsbrechts, and R. Pieters (eds), *The Connected Customer: The Changing Nature of Consumer and Business Markets* (New York and Howe: Routledge), pp. 7–35.

Van Noort, G., Voorveld H.A.M., and van Reijmersdal, E.A. (2012) "Interactivity in Brand Web Sites: Cognitive, Affective, and Behavioral Responses Explained by Consumers' Online Flow Experience," *Journal of Interactive Marketing*, 26, 4, 223–34.

Vargo, S.L. and Lusch, R.F. (2004) "Evolving To A New Dominant Logic For Marketing," *Journal of Marketing*, 68, 1–17.

Vavra, T.G. (1997) *Improving Your Measurement of Customer Satisfaction: A Guide to Creating, Conducting, Analyzing, and Reporting Customer Satisfaction Measurement Programs* (Milwaukee, WI: ASQ Quality Press).

Vivek, S.D., Beatty, S.E., and Morgan, R.M. (2012) "Customer Engagement: Exploring Customer Relationships beyond Purchase," *Journal of Marketing Theory and Practice*, 20, 2, 127–45.

Völckner, F. and Sattler, H. (2006) "Drivers of Brand Extension Success," *Journal of Marketing*, 70, April, 18–34.

Wagner, J. (1999) "Aesthetic Value: Beauty in Art and Fashion," in M.B. Holbrook (ed.) *Consumer Value: A Framework for Analysis and Research* (New York: Routledge).

Walmsley, B. (2011) "Why People Go to the Theatre: A Qualitative Study of Audience Motivation," *Journal of Customer Behaviour*, 10, 4, 335–51.

Ward, J.C. and Ostrom, A.L. (2006) "Complaining to the Masses: The Role of Protest Framing in Customer-Created Complaint Websites," *Journal of Consumer Research*, 33, September, 220–30.

Wayland, R.E. and Cole, P.M. (1997) *Customer Connections: New Strategies for Growth* (Boston, MA: Harvard Business School Press).

Webster, F.E. (2002) "Marketing Management in Changing Times," *Marketing Management*, 11, January/February, 1–17.

Webster, F.E. and Wind, Y. (1972) *Organizational Buying Behavior* (Englewood Cliffs, NJ: Prentice Hall).

Weiser, M. (1991) "The Computer for the 21st Century," *Scientific American*, 265, 3, 94–104.

Whan Park, C., Jaworski, B., and MacInnis, D. (1986) "Strategic Brand Concept Management," *Journal of Marketing*, October, 135–45.

Whan Park, C., MacInnis, D., Priester, J., Eisingerich, A., and Iacobucci, D. (2010) "Brand Attachment and Brand Attitude Strength: Conceptual and Empirical Differentiation of Two Critical Brand Equity Drivers," *Journal of Marketing*, 74, 6, 1–17.

Wijnberg, N.M. and Gemser, G. (2000) "Adding Value to Innovation: Impressionism and the Transformation of the Selection System in Visual Arts," *Organization Science*, 11, 323–29.

Wikström, P. (2009) *The Music Industry: Music in the Cloud* (Cambridge, UK: Polity Press).

Zaghi, K. (2008) *Atmosfera e visual merchandising: ambienti, relazioni ed esperienze. Il punto vendita come luogo e strumento di comunicazione* (Milano: Franco Angeli).

Zaghi, K. (2013) *Visual merchandising e relazioni di canale. Valore, comunicazione, produttività* (Milano: Franco Angeli).

Zaichkowsky, J.L. (1985) "Measuring the Involvement Construct," *Journal Of Consumer Research*, 12, 3, 341–52.

Zaltman, G. (1997) "Rethinking Market Research: Putting People Back In," *Journal of Marketing Research*, 34, 424–37.

Zaltman, G. and Coulter, R.H. (1995) "Seeing the Voice of the Customer: Metaphor-Based Advertising Research," *Journal of Advertising Research*, 35, 35–51.

Zeithaml, V.A., Parasuraman, A., and Berry, L.L. (1990) *Delivering Quality Service – Balancing Customer Perceptions and Expectations* (New York: The Free Press).

Zeithaml, V.A., Parasuraman, A., and Malhotra, A. (2002) "Service Quality Delivery through Web Sites: A Critical Review of Extant Knowledge," *Journal of the Academy of Marketing Science*, 30, 4, 358–71.

ZenithOptimedia (2013) *Advertising Expenditure Forecasts* (London).

Zolfagharian, M.A. and Cortes, A. (2011) "Motives For Purchasing Artwork; Collectibles And Antiques," *Journal of Business & Economic's Research*, 9, 4, 27–42.

INDEX